Echoes from the
Poisoned Well

Echoes from the Poisoned Well

Global Memories of Environmental Injustice

Edited by
Sylvia Hood Washington, Paul C. Rosier,
and Heather Goodall

LEXINGTON BOOKS

A division of
ROWMAN & LITTLEFIELD PUBLISHERS, INC.
Lanham • Boulder • New York • Toronto • Oxford

LEXINGTON BOOKS

A division of Rowman & Littlefield Publishers, Inc.
A wholly owned subsidiary of The Rowman & Littlefield Publishing Group, Inc.
4501 Forbes Boulevard, Suite 200
Lanham, MD 20706

PO Box 317
Oxford
OX2 9RU, UK

British Library Cataloguing in Publication Information Available

Library of Congress Cataloging-in-Publication Data

Echoes from the poisoned well global memories of environmental injustice /
edited by Sylvia Hood Washington, Heather Goodall, and Paul Rosier.
    p.   cm.
Includes bibliographical references and index.
ISBN-13: 978-0-7391-0912-0 (hardcover : alk. paper)
ISBN-13: 978-0-7391-1432-2 (pbk. : alk. paper)
    1. Environmental justice—Historiography.   I. Washington, Sylvia Hood,
1959–   II. Goodall, Heather.   III. Rosier, Paul C.   IV. Title.
GE220.E24   2006
363.7—dc22   2006000381

Printed in the United States of America

∞ ™ The paper used in this publication meets the minimum requirements of
American National Standard for Information Sciences—Permanence of Paper
for Printed Library Materials, ANSI/NISO Z39.48–1992.

To my daughters,
Sarah Allyson and Lauren Alicia Washington
and my husband Gary Seldon Washington

SYLVIA HOOD WASHINGTON

To my boys, Maxwell and Casey

PAUL C. ROSIER

To Joe Flick, a Gamilaraay man who was passionate
in his commitment to justice for indigenous people
and their land, all over the world

HEATHER GOODALL

Contents

Foreword   xi
  Martin V. Melosi

Introduction   xiii
  Sylvia Hood Washington, Paul C. Rosier, and Heather Goodall

Part One: Foundations and Origins of Environmental Injustice

1   Citizen Activism for Environmental Health: The Growth of a
    Powerful New Grassroots Health Movement   3
    Lois Gibbs

2   Gendered Approaches to Environmental Justice: An Historical
    Sampling   17
    Nancy C. Unger

3   Fond Memories and Bitter Struggles: Concerted Resistance to
    Environmental Injustices in Postwar Native America   35
    Paul C. Rosier

4   "My Soul Looked Back": Environmental Memories of the
    African in America, 1600–2000   55
    Sylvia Hood Washington

5   Indigenous Peoples, Colonialism, and Memories of
    Environmental Injustice   73
    Heather Goodall

6   Racist Property Holdings and Environmental Coalitions:
    Addressing Memories of Environmental Injustice   97
    Bill E. Lawson

7   Racialized Spaces and the Emergence of Environmental
    Injustice   109
       K. Animashaun Ducre

Part Two: North American Memories of Environmental Injustice

8   Wadin' in the Water: African American Migrant Struggles for
    Environmental Equality in Cleveland, Ohio, 1928–1970   127
       Sylvia Hood Washington

9   Memories of (No)Place: Homelessness and Environmental
    Justice   143
       Cynthia J. Miller

10 Citizens against Wilderness: Environmentalism and the Politics
    of Marginalization in the Great Smoky Mountains   157
       Stephen Wallace Taylor

11 Environmental Justice, Urban Planning, and Community
    Memory in New York City   171
       Julie Sze

12 Ferrell Parkway: Conflicting Views of Nature in a Mixed Use
    Community   183
       Jane Bloodworth Rowe

13 "We Come This Far by Faith": Memories of Race, Religion,
    and Environmental Disparity   195
       Sylvia Hood Washington

Part Three: Indigenous Memories of Environmental Injustice

14 Suttesája: From a Sacred Sami Site and Natural Spring to a
    Water Bottling Plant? The Effects of Colonization in Northern
    Europe   209
       Rauna Kuokkanen with Marja K. Bulmer

15 What Lies Beneath? Cultural Excavation in Neocolonial
    Martinique   225
       Renée Gosson

16 Plight of the Rara'muri: Crises in Our Backyard   245
       Four Arrows (aka Don Trent Jacobs)

17 Main Streets and Riverbanks: The Politics of Place in an
    Australian River Town   255
       Heather Goodall

18   "Taking Us for Village Idiots": Two Stories of Ethnicity, Class,
     and Toxic Waste from Sydney, Australia   271
       Peggy James

19   The Mirrar Fight for Jabiluka: Uranium Mining and
     Indigenous Australians to 2004   285
       Jacqui Katona

20   Guardians of the Land: A Maori Community's Environmental
     Battles   299
       Rachael Selby and Pataka Moore

21   Parameters of Legitimation and the Environmental Future of a
     Taipei Neighborhood   311
       Anya Bernstein

22   Remembering the Mother River: The Impact of Environmental
     Injustice on National Identity in Contemporary China   331
       Jane Sayers

23   Environmental Justice and Popular Protest in Thailand   345
       John Walsh

24   "Aiee, Our Fields Will Be Destroyed": Dubious Science and
     Peasant Environmental Practices in Madziwa, Zimbabwe   355
       Guy Thompson

25   Shell International, the Ogoni People, and Environmental
     Injustice in the Niger Delta, Nigeria: The Challenge of
     Securing Environmental Justice in an Oil-based Economy   371
       Phia Steyn

26   The Community, Industry, and the Quest for a Clean Vaal
     River 1997–2004   389
       Elise and Johann Tempelhoff

Epilogue   409
     Jeffrey K. Stine

Maps   411

Index   415

About the Contributors   425

Foreword

The environmental justice movement has had a profound effect on how we think about environmentalism and environmental history in the United States. Beginning in the 1980s, environmental justice advocates reinvigorated the demand for civil rights in a new political arena. They focused on the disproportionate exposure to health and pollution risks faced by people of color at home and in the workplace. These risks, they argued, could result from unintentional or intentional efforts to site polluting industries and waste disposal facilities almost exclusively in minority neighborhoods or to place minority workers in harm's way on the job. The goal of the environmental justice movement was urban-focused and essentially political, directed at the government, private industry, and what they believed to be a white-middle-class-dominated environmental movement more interested in nature preservation than human health and well-being. The earliest literature on environmental justice topics also reflected these goals and was clearly polemical in form. Such incendiary terms as "environmental racism" and more clinical academic definitions such as "environmental equity," were set aside and replaced by the concept of "environmental justice." The latter term offered a more positive, more inclusive concept to interject into the political discourse and suggested a broader objective—justice—than simply the eradication of racist actions.

The efforts of environmental justice advocates met with skepticism and resistance, but once the issue was on the table it could not be removed. While changes in environmental regulations and the practice of siting landfills and incinerators did not occur overnight and remain uneven, the connection of race to environmental concerns cannot be ignored in any debate over problems of pollution and health risks.

While the convergence of civil rights protest and environmentalism opened a new phase in the environmental history of the nation, the political

objectives of the environmental justice movement quickly exposed limitations in addressing broader issues than race. What about the significance of
class—and gender—in affecting environmental equity? Could class status or
gender considerations be equally important or more important in placing
people at risk? Environmental justice advocates did not dismiss class and
gender as variables in environmental risk, but many—initially at least—gave
them a lesser status. Some, however, broadened the definition of environmental justice to be more inclusive. From a political perspective, a broadened
definition offered an opportunity to gain new supporters, but it also threatened to water down the powerful claims that had put environmental justice
within the political arena in the first place. Thus the balancing act among
race, class, and gender goes on.

Despite controversy surrounding the environmental justice movement,
there is little doubt that it has forced a reconsideration of environmental
goals and objectives in the United States. Also, by making clear that environmental risks affect different groups of people in disproportionate ways, it
also stresses the need for us to understand that environmental values and
perceptions are culturally constructed. There is no single perspective that can
guide our thinking about making the world a better place to live.

Environmental historians have an important role to play as well. While the
environmental justice movement began as a political movement and while
much of the early literature in the field set out to support objectives imbed-
ded in the concept of environmental justice, it is important for historians to
contribute their expertise in several ways. First, documenting the rise of the
environmental justice movement will help—and has helped—to place it
within the context of an evolving environmental movement in the United
States. Second, questioning and evaluating the claims made by environmental
justice advocates as well as detractors—especially the relative importance of
race, class, and gender in exposure to risk—through well-researched case
studies can inform the issues in a positive fashion. And third, by looking
back in history—before the 1980s—for examples of environmental racism or
environmental injustices—historians can help demonstrate that these actions
are not necessarily bound by time and not exclusively or distinctively American in origin and practice. This volume should go a long way in helping to
address all three of these points, and even open up some new issues to pon-
der and study further. The following chapters represent a diversity of
approaches and topics and make for valuable reading.

Martin V. Melosi
University of Houston
Houston, Texas

Introduction

Sylvia Hood Washington, Paul C. Rosier, and Heather Goodall

This compendium of chapters arose from a call for papers which would reflect on the memories of environmental justice from the perspective of communities and groups that had been environmentally marginalized as a result of racism, technological development, and globalization. An influential stimulus for this CFP had been Sylvia Hood Washington's experience of directing an Environmental Justice and Literacy project, which sought to capture the environmental memories of black Catholics in the United States as a foundation for creating a large-scale environmental education project. Washington had found an overwhelming interest among blacks to "speak to" their memories of environmental inequalities which they had claimed had existed since the turn of the twentieth century. Their accounts of how and why they came to exist in environmentally marginalized spaces overwhelmingly contradicted the longstanding notion that racial and social minorities either tolerated or ignored environmental assaults to their communities because "pollution" represented work.[1]

The emerging environmental justice movement has created greater awareness among scholars that communities from all over the world suffer from similar environmental inequalities. This volume takes up the challenge of linking the focused campaigns and insights from African American campaigns for environmental justice with the perspectives of the broader global range of environmentally marginalized groups. The editorial team has drawn on Washington's work, on Paul C. Rosier's study of Native American environmentalism, and on Heather Goodall's work with Indigenous Australians to seek out insights into the relationships between memories of injustice and demands for environmental justice in the global arena. The collection contributes to environmental historiography by providing "bottom up" environmental histories in a field which so far has mostly emphasized a "top down" perspective, in which the voices of those most heavily burdened by environmental degradation are often ignored. It serves as a modest step in filling the lacuna in environmental history by providing the viewpoints of peoples and of indigenous communities which traditionally have been neglected while linking them to a global context of environmental education.

Scholars of environmental justice, as much as the activists in their respective struggle, face challenges in working comparatively, in trying to locate the differences between local struggles as well as to celebrate their common ground. In this sense, the chapters in this book represent the opening up of spaces for future conversations rather than any simple ending to the discussion. The contributions, however, reflect growing awareness of that common ground and a rising need to employ linked experiences and strategies in combating environmental injustice on a global scale, in part by mimicking the technology and tools employed by global corporations that endanger the environmental integrity of a diverse set of homelands.

The modern environmental justice movement has been inspired and animated by African Americans. It developed initially from the historical pattern of inequitable distribution of environmental waste and the placement of locally unwanted land uses (LULUs) in minority, ethnic, and poor communities, especially those of African American, Hispanic, and Native American communities.[2] This movement represents a unification of formerly disparate responses to industrial modernity, with its production of chemical wastes and other dangerous by-products, linked to the patterns of racial, ethnic, and class discrimination that have historically defined American power relations. African Americans, for example, were from the very beginning of their forced immigration and slavery subjected to hostile natural and built environments that characterized the slave plantations and slave industries of the New World. They also systematically tried to respond and ameliorate these conditions with varying success as a direct relation to their evolving political influence.[3] Environmental sociologist Robert J. Bullard has argued that the historical patterns of environmental inequities in the United States became particularly insidious and more deadly after the birth of the modern environmental movement in the early 1970s. It was then that "[b]oth government and industry responded to white neighbourhood associations with their NIMBY (Not In My Backyard) organizations by siting LULUs according to the PIBBY (place in blacks' backyard) strategy."[4]

Contemporary environmental justice cases like Warren County in 1982 and the ongoing struggles over environmental injustice are examples of the wider phenomenon of raced-based spatial power, that is the exercise of power through the use of space. This links the present day exposure of impoverished and powerless communities to industrial waste, pollution, and danger to the earlier histories of racial marginalization and concomitant environmental disenfranchisement that took place in the Jim Crow and earlier slave geographies of the emerging United States. Most broadly, these are all expressions of the histories of colonialism, colonial expansion, and imperialism across the globe of Europeans from the sixteenth century, resulting in the social construction of marginalized "others" within conquered and colonized geographical spaces.

The history of Native–white relations is also a history of environmental inequalities. As Native American activists and writers like Jace Weaver and Winona LaDuke have argued, Native American environmental justice campaigns originated at the moment of contact in the late fifteenth century. The efforts of indigenous groups to retain title to their homelands, and to sustain their ecological relationships once that land was taken at gunpoint or abandoned in one of the mini-diasporas that marked North American spatial reorganization during the colonial era, occurred throughout the spaces of the Americas and through the centuries since initial contact. But their experiences are those of other colonized peoples discussed in this volume—the Zimbabwean, Ogoni, Maori, Sami, and others.

As white settlement expanded rapidly in the second half of the nineteenth century, Native Americans countered environmental depredation and degradation in various ways. They protested allotment policies that stripped them of the best reservation farmland and compelled them to adopt European land-use practices that divided clan networks and limited community-oriented production.

Colonized and displaced groups were not only socially and politically disenfranchised but environmentally disenfranchised since they were perceived as a direct environmental threat to the individual, personal bodies of the colonizers and to the larger "body politic" of the colonizing society. These "othered" groups had to be constrained and constricted from the geographical spaces of the colonizing race or ethnic groups.[5] Access to environmentally fit geographic spaces was initially predicated on an entitlement based on the racial and ethnic identity of the embodied colonizer who, in most cases from the sixteenth century onward, were white (and male) or who were defined to be more "white" than a predetermined "other" in an ever-changing spectrum of "whiteness" in colonized societies. Tracing the exercise of spatial power through colonialism means that we can compare the ways these processes have worked in different continents which were subject to the practices and policies by a male-dominated Eurocentric or Western power elite.

This volume takes up the issues of environmental injustice, in this wide sense of the exercise of racialized spatial power, across the globe. The emergence and construction of racialized space is elucidated in the chapters in Part 1, Foundations and Origins of Environmental Injustice, where authors offer overviews and conceptual frameworks that link the detailed case studies in Parts 2 and 3. The foundation chapters in Part 1 are opened by Lois Gibbs's account of the role of class in the grass roots movement at Love Canal, one of the defining examples of an environmental justice struggle. Bill E. Lawson in "Racist Property Holdings and Environmental Coalitions" and Kishi Animashaun's "Racialized Spaces and the Emergence of Environmental Injustice," each interrogate more broadly the construction of racialized space within the United States. Lawson's chapter points out how the history of land use and property rights in the United States is the basis for past and present memories of environmental inequalities by marginalized groups. Sylvia Hood Washington provides a long duree of the environmental injustices which Americans of African descent have encountered from the time of their initial captivity in Africa, the middle passage, chattel slavery, and legalized racial segregation in the United States. The sociological, philosophical, and gendered basis for this environmental marginalization is elucidated more fully by the chapters of K. Animashaun Ducre, Nancy C. Unger, and Bill E. Lawson.

Animashaun Ducre's analysis of the formation of racialized spaces in particular forms a key theoretical link between the examples of contemporary injustice and the studies of conflicts which have emerged from the colonial processes of exercising spatial power. The impact of colonialism and of modernity on colonized indigenous peoples is discussed in relation to the Americas by Paul C. Rosier in "Fond Memories and Bitter Struggles," in which he argues that while Native American demands for environmental justice have accelerated since World War II, they have been animated by memories of environmental injustices that are written into the histories of virtually all Indian nations in the United States; given these histories and the contemporary economic struggle that Indian nations face, these campaigns have been driven by the recognition that "almost every environmental issue in Indian country is an environmental justice," as Cherokee attorney Dean Suagee put it. Nancy C. Unger brings her analysis of gendered histories to the discussion in a series of key environmental injustice case studies in which she links her analysis of African American and Native American women's experiences. Heather Goodall, in "Indigenous Peoples, Colonialism and Memories of Environmental Injustice," takes up the discussion in a chapter with a global scope, ranging from Australia to northern and southern Africa and across Asia, which suggests both parallels and differences between the calls for environmental justice which are based on indigeneity, on race, and on class.

The memories of environmental injustice arising from the histories of the United States are explored in the six chapters in Part 2, North American Memories of Environmental Injustice. Sylvia Hood Washington's "Wadin' in the Water" provides specific and historically documented recollections of environmental injustices which derived from the creation of "racist property holdings" and racially constructed spaces as defined earlier by Lawson and Animashaun Ducre. "Wadin' in the Water" elucidates how legal discrimination in housing and inequitable responses to municipal services for racially segregated spaces created a marginalized environment for middleclass African Americans prior to the emergence of the modern environmental justice movement. This community found itself enmeshed in a public debate, mistakenly portrayed by previous historians as a class-based struggle, with an African American mayor to have a sustainable community. Washington's chapter "We Come This Far by Faith" provides a history of how intraracial divisions along religious affiliation can work to perpetuate and/or exacerbate environmental inequities in ethnic subgroups living in the same geographical space. The memories of African American Catholics documented in Washington's work clearly reveal an environmental illiteracy not based on race but upon religious affiliation and faith geographies. Julie Sze's chapter, "Environmental Justice, Urban Planning, and Community Memory in New York City," emerges from her own work as an environmental justice activist in the city and illustrates how urban planning and zoning is remembered as being a primary force in creating environmentally inequitable spaces for minority and ethnic groups today. Cynthia J. Miller's chapter, "Memories of (No)Place," cogently demonstrates the environmental plight of the homeless and their memories of how they were socially constructed as the ultimate environmental "others" and the spatial marginalization which accompanied this marginalization. Taylor's chapter, "Citizens against Wilderness" and Rowe's chapter, "Ferrell Parkway," reveal how memories of environmental inequality and "nature" are class and economically based. Both chapters provide the readers with memories of people who found themselves in opposition to environmental activists, considered outsiders who were struggling to preserve what they remembered as a pristine environment, a memory which the locals contested based upon their interpretation of a land's particular value.

In Part 3, Global Memories of Environmental Injustice, thirteen chapters explore diverse locally initiated struggles from around the world in which local histories and global forces have each contributed to the specific nature of memory and conflict. The authors take up the difficult task of engaging concepts developed in the United States with local perspectives on the key themes of environmental injustice. One way to consider these chapters is by looking at the clusters of perspectives within geographic regions. In Africa, three chapters investigate very different examples of environmental injustice which are nevertheless linked by histories of colonialism as well as contemporary issues of class power and globalization. Phia Steyn examines environmental devastation in Ogoniland (Nigeria), the product of what M. J. Watts calls "petro-violence," highlighting the extent to which African environ-

mental justice movements have to contend with both the powerful forces of
economic globalization and postcolonial ethnic social divisions that have fur-
thered political marginalization of minority groups like the Ogoni. Guy
Thompson draws on his extensive fieldwork in the Madziwa region of Zimbabwe in exploring peasants' memories of British colonial agricultural policies in Rhodesia from 1940 to 1965. The memories of community elders,
Thompson found, were strengthened and animated by the contemporary
context of Zimbabwe's state agricultural regime, which has maintained continuities with colonial practices by retaining an interventionist extension service that delocalizes political authority and environmental stewardship. Elise
and Johann Tempelhoff discuss a post-Apartheid conflict in South Africa's
industrial heartland, where a marginalized agricultural community is challenging industrial pollution from the giant ISCOR corporation.

The chapter by Rauna Kuokkanen with Marja Bulmer moves the focus to
Europe, when they examine the intersection of global water commodification and indigenous people's cultural rights through a study of the Sami people's fight to maintain control of a sacred site, Suttesaja, in northern Finland.
Kuokkanen was one of four Sami women involved in the defense of Suttesaja. The chapter considers the long-term impact of colonialism on the Sami's
ability to maintain cultural integrity and to prevent the commercialization of
the sieidi, their sacred spaces, which underwrite an environmental ethic that
produces memories of environmental relationships which define Sami identity today.

In the Americas, Four Arrows, a Native American educator and author,
charts the urgent needs of the Rara'muri of Central Mexico, whose ability to
preserve their culture and land base now faces two sets of pressures that have
fueled deforestation. Drug cartels clearing land for illegal plantations and
State agents undertaking government-approved logging are each undermining Rara'muri independence and cultural integrity. On Martinique in the
Carribean, Renée Gosson describes how postcolonial "departmentalization"
of the island has both cemented an already oppressive relationship between
this former colony and France and has initiated a whole new set of assimilationist practices on environmental and cultural levels. In this French West
Indian island, where the majority of the population is of African descent,
resisting the disinheritance of slavery and colonialism has demanded a focus
on reestablishing a "psychic rootedness in the land." Gosson argues that
"Martinican writers and songwriters alike challenge their audiences to dig
beneath the pleasant façade of a colonial past, and present."

From Asia three chapters offer insights into environmental justice
demands at differing levels. John Walsh explores the extent to which memory
and identity have shaped the Isaan people's popular movement, as a Lao ethnic minority embedded within northern Thailand, in their struggle against
the Pak Moon dam, one of the many massive engineering works constructed

on the Mekong River. Jane Sayers has analyzed the turmoil produced as high numbers of rural people from the Yellow River heartland are forced or drawn into migration seeking urban work while riverine environments suffer deterioration and neglect. Her chapter traces the mobilization by the Chinese State of peasant memories of the Yellow River as dragon to seek to intervene in such processes. Anya Bernstein undertakes a complex and nuanced investigation of how a local, long-established Chinese community in Taipei, Taiwan, has mobilized memories of actual and imagined relations with past land use in order to authorize its opposition to the expansion of industrial development into a residential and rural area.

In Australia, indigeneity, class, migrancy, and dislocation are all factors in diverse conflicts over justice which can be seen to exemplify the environmental and cultural dimensions of spatial power. Indigenous author Jacqui Katona explains how both memories of past struggles and the sustained significance of Mirrar traditional knowledge of "country" have shaped the community's largely successful battle against the Jabiluka uranium mine in Arnhem Land in tropical and remote northern Australia. In rural, grazing and cotton-farming western New South Wales, Heather Goodall has traced the way English settlers over two centuries tried to use the natural environment of Australia's huge Darling River to build an unchallengable structure of racialized segregation to shore up their civic and economic power. Aboriginal people's rising cultural and political reassertion since the 1970s has combined with the erratic nature of the river itself to challenge and ultimately undermine this racialized landscape. In Aotearoa/New Zealand, Maori authors Rachael Selby and Pataka Moore have written movingly about another rural struggle, that of the Ngati Raukawa community to reclaim its ownership and control over the Hokio Stream, beside which they had been forced for decades to watch helplessly as it was diverted and polluted. The chapter charts their painstaking and ultimately successful campaign to regain recognition of their ownership and, just as importantly, to regain custodial control over the river so they could restore its health and cultural significance. Finally, in highly urbanized Sydney, Peggy James charts the frustrations of recently immigrant workers, faced with living and working on land which had been industrially polluted in the past and which now faced further pollution from a high temperature waste incinerator. In a struggle which mirrors that described by Washington and others in American cities, this disempowered community in Sydney found itself ignored not only by government but by the big environmental NGOs as well. James argues persuasively that the environmental movement needs to reflect deeply on its practice to identify those areas where it is simply reinforcing the inequities of state power.

Yet while Parts 2 and 3 can be considered separately, Peggy James' chapter points out that an important way to explore the conversations initiated in this volume is to follow the key themes which link the case studies of the United States in Part 2 with the global examples in Part 3. Water is one theme which is central to many communities in their understanding of justice. Washington, in "Wadin' in the Water," reflects on the meaning and memory of water for the Lee-Saville community in Cleveland, Ohio; Walsh documents the Isaan struggle against the Pak Moon Dam in northern Thailand; Goodall in "Main Streets and Riverbanks" charts the way racial politics have been conducted through battles over the waters of the Darling River in rural Australia; Sayers writes about the state's mobilization of traditions and memories of the Yellow River in China; the Tempelhoffs describe a working class community's campaign against the pollution of the Vaal River and its subterranean waters in South Africa; Selby and Moore describe the way a Maori community is reclaiming and revitalizing the Hokio Stream in Aotearoa/New Zealand; Kuokkanen and Bulmer discuss the deeply contested meanings of the Sami people's spring waters of Suttesaja in Finland; while Rosier documents Native American challenges to contamination of the waters, fish and, above all, cultural significance of their rivers.

Another key theme is the contested creation and management of national parks. Rowe and Taylor in the United States and Katona in Australia are each opening up questions around the problem that the conceptions of such parks are seldom shared across all sections of their users and residents. In each chapter, the authors explore the ways in which the implementation of national park regulations has been manipulated to serve limited and sectional interests. Rural land justice issues are a focus for Thompson [Zimbabwe], Sayers [China], Goodall [Australia], and Bernstein [Taiwan]. The particular dimensions of urban environmental justice issues are taken up by Sze [New York], Washington ["We Come This Far by Faith"], and Miller [Boston] in the United States, and by Bernstein [Taipei/Taiwan] and James [Sydney] in Asia and Australia. And in a volume where all authors consider history in engagement with environment, Miller [Boston], Sze [New York], Bernstein [Taiwan], and Gosson [Martinique] specifically take up the question of how memories are mobilized around and through place.

Industrial pollution and the campaigns of people of color, working class, and immigrant communities to challenge it are documented by Gibbs, Sze, and Washington in the United States and by James in Australia and the Tempelhoffs in South Africa. Yet another theme is the engagement of small communities mobilizing, despite a failure of large lobby group or environmental NGO support, to take on the globalized economic power of big industry and transnational corporations. The urban examples of Gibbs, James, and Bernstein can be compared with the accounts of rural contamination and conflict by Katona, the Tempelhoffs, Selby and Moore, Steyn, Rosier, Kuokkanen, and Four Arrows. Whether in urban or rural environments, all trace courageous attempts to challenge the intimidating weight of the transnational companies which seek to commodify community cultures and health.

The chapters in the book are all looking at the ways in which such injustices and the conflicts which arose from them can be understood, compared, and learned from across often quite different situations of colonialism and modernity. The volume has been developed to include as much as possible the voices of those "others" who have been marginalized as a direct consequence of colonialism, imperialism, and globalization. Indigenous people have in many ways led the attempts to work out radical alternatives to the corporate and military nationalism and more recently globalized assault on environmental justice. Indigenous authors Kuokkanen, Katona, Four Arrows, and Selby and Moore each analyse such struggles and engage with the foundation chapters of Rosier and Goodall to chart the emerging strength of indigenous voices demanding environmental recognition. With little investment in the nation state, indigenous people are offering transnational and globalized models for networking, activism, and identity which may allow new patterns of effective mobilization for groups seeking environmental justice.

Another parallel theme in the response to modernity and its industrial and technological impact has been environmentalists' critique of western technological development. This critique has identified the deep polarization in western philosophy [and probably that of all the three major monotheisms, Judaism, Christianity, and Islam] between human culture and "nature," which, however revered and respected it might be as "God's work," is nevertheless to be subjected to human control and domination. At the extreme, such environmental approaches as Deep Ecology have been deeply antihumanist, while some have been unable to identify the social injustice which has characterized colonial expansion and spatial power, preferring instead to focus on the general human impact on the earth. These extreme positions have earned the criticism of the environmental justice movement for their failure to understand the patterns of domination over humans which are fundamental to spatial power. Some environmental justice activists and scholars have suggested that the class and race (affluent and white) of leaders of twentieth-century conservation and wilderness movements has hampered them from recognizing the impact of modern industrial society on minority and ethnic communities, which some may have perceived to be part of the threatening environment rather than its victims.[6]

However, such extremes are not the only position within the environmental movement, which is complex and multifaceted. Not a polarized opposition between "mainstream" environmentalism and environmental justice positions, the reality is most often a continuum with the many positions and many ambivalences of the stands and strategies that both individuals and movements take. The consequences are continual tensions within the movement between the priorities of social justice and ecological goals. The ways in which these tensions are expressed, negotiated, fought over, and, sometimes, resolved have also worked out differently in different countries around the globe. This collection reflects this important theme across broad historical and geographical axes.

Finally, the authors emphasize that how people have conceived of and striven for justice is shaped by the ways in which place and environment are understood, the ways in which places carry meaning for the people who live within and across them. This social and intellectual dynamic forces us to consider memory and the ways in which it acts to embody both the past and the present. Understanding and appreciating the knowledge embedded in the memories of communities that have been environmentally disenfranchised is critical to knowing more fully the social ecology of the world at large and the environmental costs of technological developments. The decision to advance is usually contingent on the benefits outweighing the costs. All of the costs, however, will never be fully understood until we include the human costs of environmental inequalities. It is often said that "history is written by the conquerors." This collection contributes to the ongoing effort to create an alternative narrative that links the past to the present by demonstrating the continuing ways in which historically marginalized communities suffer the costs of environmental degradation and the consequences for a world that has shrunk in space and time since the beginning of the colonial era. There is only one world ecosystem and it is environmentally "colorblind." The environmental assault on any geographical space will have global impact and result in an environmental assault on all humanity. Culling the environmental memories of a diverse set of people and peoples will hopefully help guide scholars, activists, and citizens grappling with a challenge to build a sustainable society not only to construct a more just world but also a more peaceful world. For where there is no justice there is no peace.

NOTES

1. A history of this project is more thoroughly discussed in Washington's chapter, "My Soul Looked Back."

2. A precursive environmental justice movement led by African Americans began in the Depression and accelerated in the post–World War II period to address the environmental degradation and concomitant public health problems which their population faced because of legal racialized zoning and restrictive covenants. Read "The Urban Conservation Movement" chapter in Sylvia Hood Washington, *Packing Them In: An Archaeology of Environmental Racism in Chicago, 1865–1954 (Lanham: Lexington Books, 2004)*.

3. Colin Palmer, "The First Passage, 1502–1619" in Robin D.G. Kelley and Earl

Lewis, eds. *To Make Our World Anew, A History of African Americans, eds.* (Oxford: Oxford University Press, 2000).

4. Laura Westra and Bill Lawson, eds. *Faces of Environmental Racism, Confronting Issues of Global Justice, 2nd Edition* (Lanham: Rowman & Littlefield Publishers, Inc., 2001) p. 19.

5. Mary Poovey, *Making of a Social Body.*

6. Sylvia Hood Washington, *Packing Them In: An Archaeology of Environmental Racism in Chicago, 1865–1954 (Lanham: Lexington Books, 2005).*

I

FOUNDATIONS AND ORIGINS OF ENVIRONMENTAL INJUSTICE

1

Citizen Activism for Environmental Health
The Growth of a Powerful New Grassroots Health Movement

Lois Gibbs

The year 2003 marked the twenty-fifth anniversary of the Love Canal crisis. The Love Canal community's efforts successfully won the relocation of 900 working-class families away from a leaking toxic waste dump and awoke a nation to the hazards of toxic chemicals in our environment. Overcoming powerful resistance from government and a multi-billion-dollar company, Occidental Petroleum, this grassroots effort demonstrated how ordinary citizens can gain power through organizing to win their struggle. Love Canal sparked a new social justice movement nationwide around concerns about environmentally linked health problems and the right of corporations to increase their profits through calculated decisions to sacrifice innocent families.

This new grassroots movement, fighting for the rights to clean air, water, food, and soil, continues to grow today. While traditional American environmentalism focused on protecting the natural environment, the new movement is as much about protecting public health as it is about protecting the environment. Traditional environmentalism used legislative strategies to win change, but the grassroots leadership of the new movement believes that systemic change comes from the bottom up. Grassroots leaders believe that people plus organization equals power—more power than the money and influence that corporations bring to bear on elected representatives. As a

3

result, the grassroots strategy is to build power at the local and state levels in a sufficient number of states influence federal-level representatives and policies.

There is another fundamental difference between the two movements. Because traditional environmentalism focused on regulations and regulatory controls, it inevitably wound up debating how much pollution can be released into the air or the water. The new movement, however, is focused on prevention. Grassroots leaders are asking, "Why do we have to burn our trash? Why do we allow dioxin-laced wastewater from a pulp mill's bleaching process to be discharged into our rivers when a nontoxic alternative exists?"

Neither approach is right or wrong or superior to the other. The overarching goal of protecting the environment and all living things is the same for both segments of the movement. When operating on a parallel path, the two approaches together can make significant progress in protecting the environment and public health.

The grassroots environmental movement has a long history of success. Its most important achievement has been building a diversified base of support. The movement is broad and deep and includes workers, people of color, indigenous peoples, faith-based organizations, and rural and urban families; parent-teacher organizations concerned about pesticides and schools built near pollution sources; doctors, nurses, and other health professionals working to transform the health care industry; and those who make their living fishing or depend on fish as a primary food in their diets.

Even arguments about whether society must choose between jobs or protecting the environment have begun to take a positive turn. Both grassroots leaders and workers are demanding that industries follow practices that do not threaten the health or environment of surrounding neighborhoods. Where industries cannot operate without polluting the environment, "just transition" programs are being developed to prepare the workforce for alternative jobs.

THE CHOSEN ONES

At the base of the grassroots and environmental justice movement are the chosen ones—communities targeted by polluting industries and sacrificed in the name of economic growth and profits. Communities with environmental health impacts tend to be working-class communities, low-income communities, and/or communities of color. People in grassroots environmental organizations do not believe that environmental and public health threats they face are coincidental or due to the random placement of industrial complexes or waste disposal facilities. Communities at risk believe their neighborhoods were deliberately targeted because of their economic and political weakness. As a result, this is a movement that is as much about justice and human rights as it is about public health and the environment.

Two written documents provide compelling evidence that communities are in fact chosen for waste disposal or industrial plants based on demographic criteria and the assumption that the communities lack political clout. One is a report by Cerrell Associates completed for the State of California Solid Waste Division in 1984. The other was a memo written in 1989 by Eply Associates for Chem-Nuclear Systems, Inc., which was hired by the North Carolina Low-Level Radioactive Waste Management Authority to assist in the site selection and operation of a regional low-level radioactive waste disposal facility.

When the Cerrell report was first exposed, government officials and corporate public relations people said it was a unique example and that it did not represent the industry's normal approach to siting. Then, in 1993, the Eply memo was exposed in a report prepared by attorneys for the Chatham County (North Carolina) Board of Commissioners called the *Report on the Site Selection Process for the North Carolina "Low-Level" Radioactive Waste Disposal Facility* (Farren 1992). As in the Cerrell report, the most important criteria for siting were demographic. Both reports identify "communities least likely to resist." Communities easiest to target are Southern, Midwestern, and rural: are open to promises of economic benefits; contain residents on average older than middle age and with a high school education or less; are low income; and are not involved in social issues.

The Chatham County report (Farren 1992) reviewed internal documents obtained during litigation and concluded that there is ample evidence that the site selection process involved a concerted effort to locate potentially receptive and politically palatable potential site areas rather than seek the most technically suitable sites, as the rules require. This plan was backed by a public relations effort to monitor local reactions and convince people in the site areas to accept the site (p. 28).

This report (Farren 1992) described the site-selection process implemented by Chem-Nuclear following the advice of the Eply memo. At what was described as "perhaps the most critical site selection meeting," a small group of people discussed what had been learned regarding each of the possible twenty-one sites for the disposal of low-level nuclear wastes. The following is an excerpt from a description of that meeting.

There were numerous discussions of nontechnical matters such as: degree of economic distress, past activity as to environmental issues, likely degree of opposition, race, influence and attitudes of local officials, troublesome land use characteristics (for example, chicken farmers were thought to be strongly opposed to the siting of such facilities) and potential resistance from corporations with nearby operations (p. 17).

The chart in table 1.1 was generated at this meeting where many sites were eliminated from consideration. The listed factors were "at least a partial basis" for the decisions made that day.

The Cerrell and Eply reports provide clear evidence that the siting system works against certain communities. Those who control the decision making are making economic that violate human rights—not scientifically based environmental decisions—when permitting a facility that poses human health risks. Decision makers are determining who will take the health and environmental risks and who receives the benefits. Not surprisingly, it turns out that people of color and low-income communities are being forced to take the risks.

Recently, New York City's new mayor Mike Bloomberg spoke bluntly

Table 1.1.   Summary of Factors Considered in Eliminating or Including Communities as Candidates for the Siting of a Low-Level Radioactive Waste Site in North Carolina

Site	Factors Considered	Disposition
Wake/Chatman	Owned by CP&L Paper Co.	In
Coleridge	Houses fairly wealthy	Out
Snow Camp	Fairly Affluent	Out
Cherry Grove	Residences of site—minority owned	In
Farmington 1	Fairly affluent	Out
Gold Hill 1	Dynamite Company—explosives/munitions not compatible with site	Out
Gold Hill 3	Very depressed area	In
Watson	Poultry operations—impressive—Holly Farms, some new homes—affluent; agriculture Poultry, population—problems	Out
Bakers	Poultry—everywhere—surrounded	Out
Waxhaw	Lots of poultry houses	Out
Hornsboro	Distressed environment	In
Ghio	Trailers everywhere; foreclosures then resells, distressed county	In
Silver Hill	Poultry houses; large Campbell Soup plant	Out
Marston	Distressed area, buffer would have to be in game land (violates criteria)	Out
Hoffman	Distressed area, major wetlands	In
Millstone Lake	Sheriff Goodman . . . concerned about job loss	In
West End	Very near Pinehurst; Fox Fire Village	Out
Slocumb	Affluent	Out
Williams	Marshy areas/standing water (but considered potential volunteer—see below)	In
Berea	Distressed county	In
Moriah	Roxboro economic development—active	In

Source: Farren (1992)

about building new incinerators in poorer areas of the city. *"If you were to put an incinerator on Park Avenue,"* the mayor explained, *"you would drive away the revenue base that supports this city."* The fact of the matter is that where you tend to site things, unfortunately, tends to be in areas that are also in proximity to people who are just starting their ways up the economic ladder.

FIGHTING BACK

What many elected representatives, corporate decision makers, and corporate foot soldiers within government agencies all failed to anticipate is that although targeted communities may have little formal education and lack financial resources, they are willing to put everything, including their lives, on the line to stop the poisoning. The families in "chosen communities" are unwilling to accept or tolerate that some communities are worthy of a safe environment for their families while others are not.

Families in these communities have everything at stake; their homes represent a lifetime of investments, and their children are their lives. For these reasons, community groups have waged determined, persistent, public battles and have won far more than they have lost. Families in the mostly low-income African American community of Warren County, North Carolina, lay down in the middle of the street to stop trucks from dumping PCBs in their neighborhood. The community lost that phase of the fight, and the PCBs were buried in 1984. Unwilling and unable to give up, because doing so meant the destruction of their families and their community, neighbors continued to oppose the dump. Years of pressure paid off, and in 2001, the state began cleanup of the site using nonincineration technology.

Community after community has carried signs, held marches, distributed leaflets at candidates' fundraisers, and undertaken civil disobedience when necessary to protect their children, their homes, and their neighborhoods. If someone wee to ask the protesters if they could have pictured themselves carrying signs before the issue surfaced, they would likely answer, "Absolutely not." Law-abiding, taxpaying citizens are forced to move from the anonymity of their homes out into the streets, a difficult step for anyone and a big leap for most.

Although many grassroots leaders have not likely read much about Frederick Douglass ([1857] 1985), they would agree with his description of how change happens: "He who wants change without struggle is like the farmer who wants crops without plowing" (p. 204). History has shown us that to win justice, average people cannot work only within the system but must work outside the system as well.

CONTROL, CONFUSION, AND CONFLICT

Groups trying to work within the system to influence the siting process face enormous obstacles, beginning with a public participation process that is designed to inhibit—not promote—public involvement. Communities often want to believe that the system of public participation is open and honest. Leaders and citizens want to fully participate in public hearings or meetings to discuss a proposal that local families believe will harm their health and environment. Community leaders begin with the belief that when the truth is exposed, the right thing will happen. It is this belief that motivates grassroots leaders to work for days, weeks, or months doing research, identifying experts to testify on their behalf, and preparing for the hearing.

In fact, public participation hearings to determine the soundness of a proposed new facility or a proposal to clean up a site are primarily a means to control the public, defend the predetermined decisions, and present a false sense of public involvement and open decision making. It generally takes only one hearing experience for community leaders to understand that the information they so desperately wanted to share—wanted to be heard—was not taken seriously.

The entire public participation process is designed to exclude the people who are most directly affected by siting decisions. The hearings are generally scheduled at inconvenient times for working people—either during the day or late into the evenings, creating child care difficulties. Usually, the corporation or government experts speaking in favor of the proposal speak first. Often, these individuals are allowed more time to present their comments than the local community representatives. Men and women whose lives and community are at risk are given three to five minutes to speak, usually only after the proponents of the proposal have finished. Experts from both sides of the proposal control the discussion for the first two hours, while the local residents and their families sit in the audience, confused, bored, and angry. The anger builds as they wait with overtired children while paid professionals speak. When they are finally allowed to speak, their lay testimony is dismissed as unsupported or unscientific.

Community leaders know that their community was not chosen based on science or because it had great soil structure, isolated aquifers, or the right wind patterns. Intellectually, they know that the proposal has more to do with demographics than science—yet they are forced to address the scientific flaws of the proposal.

THE DEMAND FOR ABSOLUTE
PROOF OF HARM

Another obstacle that is next to impossible for grassroots groups to overcome is proving that they are sick from chemical exposures in terms of absolutes, not just beyond a reasonable doubt. When it comes to corporate polluters, the operating principle is that toxic chemicals are presumed innocent of harming human health unless proven guilty. Yet even in our criminal system, juries are asked to convict when there is enough evidence to convince them beyond a reasonable doubt. Juries are not asked to be absolutely certain. Placing the burden of proof on communities instead of the polluters is unjust and serves corporate interests at the expense of protecting public health.

Although having to prove that exposure to chemicals has harmed people is an unfair burden, grassroots groups have become sophisticated health investigators who use common sense as their guide. Grassroots group's most valuable assets are people and common sense. Since resources are limited, they often cannot hire scientists and legal experts. But they do understand what they see around them. They know when something is wrong. They can see odors, taste the foulness of their drinking water, and observe an increase in disease.

In almost every instance, professionals have later confirmed the hypotheses or conclusions made by local lay people. If this lay science reaches the public at all, it does so through the media. The public demands a level of proof only beyond a reasonable doubt. It is public opinion that forces government scientists to undertake further studies. It was mothers in Woburn, Massachusetts, who in 1979 discovered a cluster of leukemia cases among neighborhood children who were drinking from the same well water. When health authorities from the state and federal agencies investigated, they concluded that there was no connection between the drinking water and the clustering of disease. The Woburn parents persevered, making maps that showed the clustering of leukemia cases along pipelines from a particular contaminated drinking water well. Local parents took these maps to health officials, politicians, and journalists who they thought would help them. It was not until years later that the Massachusetts Department of Health confirmed the connection of disease to the water supply and closed the drinking water well. These efforts, like those at Love Canal, opened the eyes of the public, educating people and helping the movement grow.

In San Jose, California, mothers sharing conversation at a local playground discovered that many children in their neighborhood were born with identical heart birth defects. They too believed it was connected to the water supply. As was the case at Woburn, it took years of pushing and fighting with the health department and presenting maps of disease patterns to the media to confirm their finding and finally shut down the contaminated well.

In Brownsville, Texas, it was again parents who discovered the cluster of children in their community who were born with their brains outside instead of inside their skulls. And in Tucson, Arizona, and Elmira, New York, it was the citizens who uncovered a large number of young boys in the same school with testicular cancers.

In each of these situations, parents brought the issues to the attention of the proper authorities only to be dismissed. When this happened, they were often described as hysterical women or housewives in an attempt to belittle those who drew the links between exposure to chemicals and adverse health effects. Despite being dismissed, being belittled, and facing accusations that somehow parents rather than toxic chemicals were responsible, community leaders stand their ground and continue to push for action. Angela Days, a mother from Fairhaven, Massachusetts, who has a son with leukemia, said it well in one of her speeches: "*We are like mother bears protecting our cubs. We are standing on our hind legs our claws exposed and prepared to fight to the finish.*"

MOVEMENT ON THE RISE

As more and more communities began to connect and share stories, the pattern became very familiar. Certain communities were being deliberately chosen to be placed at risk from environmental chemicals in their air, water, or land. They began to understand the way the system controlled them and how to fight back. Taking the battle to the streets was outside their normal behavior, but they recognized that it was the only way to get the government to respond to their concerns and to obtain help.

The movement continued to grow as more and more communities began connecting with each other, sharing lessons learned, and offering support. Workshops and meetings were held to discuss how to do a health survey or what type of environmental testing was needed to define links between contamination and adverse health effects. The media began covering stories about Woburn, Tucson, and other places where children were suffering from environmental chemical exposures. This new attention by the mass media helped to educate the public and helped to strengthen the movement.

This new movement has established itself as a serious organized network, with the local leadership being mostly women. The network has designed itself differently from most national movements. It has no single office in Washington D.C. that sets the agenda and is central to the movement. Nor does it have a single national leader. Instead, the groups in the movement are connected to each other through a loose network. The traditional pyramid corporate structure has been replaced by more of a spider web. The strength in this structure is that it builds a strong base and encourages the development of new leaders, independence, and autonomy. This model also is more difficult for opponents to disrupt because there are thousands of groups instead of a single group and small number of leaders. In addition, if you believe the grassroots perspective on how systemic change happens, this is the model that builds that base to create lasting change—all politics are local.

ACCOMPLISHMENTS

Armed with a willingness to do whatever it takes to win, the grassroots environmental movement has achieved a great deal during the past two decades. Significant laws have been passed, such as Superfund, which provides a pool of money to clean up hazardous waste sites. A community grants program now exists that provides up to $50,000 per Superfund site for community groups to hire technical experts. Recycling has become a household norm. Prior to the grassroots movement's activities, recycling was thought to be something hippies did on campus. Now people look at you strangely if you throw a can in the trash.

More than 1,000 landfills have been closed either because they could not meet new stronger regulations, which the movement helped pass, or because citizens blocked their construction.

In 1982, grassroots leaders came together at a roundtable discussion meeting to develop a strategy to stop the land filling of hazardous waste. The strategy was to force corporations to abandon land filling by making it more expensive to bury waste than to reduce and reuse materials or substitute less hazardous chemicals. To accomplish this, leaders realized that they must close existing landfills, stop new landfills from being built, and increase transportation costs of shipping wastes. Grassroots leaders joined together wherever proposals for new commercial facilities sprang up.

From the beginning of the campaign, every new proposal, except one in Colorado, has been beaten. Most of the existing commercial landfills were closed, which left only a few commercial disposal facilities open nationwide. This means that most companies have to ship their waste long distances if they want to use this disposal alternative, causing transportation costs and the associated accident insurance costs to skyrocket. Today, the construction of new commercial toxic/hazardous waste landfills has been virtually stopped, and waste reduction and reuse and chemical substitution are now commonplace in the industry. There is no federal law that prohibits the burial of toxic/hazardous waste. It is the people who will not allow it to happen.

Another major accomplishment has been the passage of right-to-know legislation, which has reduced waste and toxic chemical usage. The strategy for passing this legislation was locally based but nationally effective. Right-to-know legislation began as a worker issue. Workers in industrial plants wanted to know what they were working with and what was stored and transported to and from the plant. Labor organized to get this information.

Later, they formed a coalition with nonlabor organizations and passed city-specific right-to-know laws. Soon, more cities were being organized around this issue, and corporations began to worry not only about releasing the information to the public but also about having to fill out a different form for each city for each of their facilities. Eventually, the corporations lobbyists in Washington D.C. began applying pressure to standardize the paperwork and minimize the information they had to reveal. In 1986, the federal Community Right-to-Know law was passed as part of the Superfund legislation to clean up toxic dumpsites.

The grassroots movement has used this same strategy on other issues. For example, in 1987, a campaign was designed to stop the use of Styrofoam packaging. McDonalds Corporation was targeted because it is a high-profile company vulnerable to public opinion. Grassroots leaders believed that if they could get enough consumers to push McDonalds to stop using foam sandwich boxes, other fast food restaurants would follow their lead, decreasing the demand for Styrofoam. The campaign, launched in Vermont, involved children, schools, religious institutions, county governments, and those faced with the potential siting of an incinerator or landfill. This was a broad-based effort that greatly expanded the movement. Soon, schoolchildren everywhere joined the campaign, and in restaurants across the country people were saying no to Styrofoam. On 1 November 1990, McDonalds announced that it would no longer use Styrofoam sandwich packaging. McDonalds's decision was not the only victory: entire counties, churches, and statehouses banned the use of Styrofoam. Elementary and high school groups, who came together around this issue, continue to work on environmental issues within their schools and communities.

Environmental justice and human rights have been a constant theme at each level of growth of the movement. In October 1991, a powerful event took place that propelled the issues of justice and human rights onto the doorsteps of the president and congressional leaders. The First National People of Color Environmental Leadership Summit brought together many diverse cultures and communities for political and spiritual growth. A set of principles was agreed on, and newly formed coalitions began their collective work. Over the years, these webs of connection have grown and become stronger. So has the movement.

In February 1994, President Bill Clinton signed an executive order on environmental justice issues. The president was responding to the powerful organized efforts of groups such as the Indigenous Environmental Network, Southern Organizing Committee, Southwest Network for Economic and Environmental Justice, Asian Pacific Environmental Network, United Church of Christ, and others. The environmental justice executive order begins to acknowledge the obvious: that communities of color and low-income communities receive more than their fair share of polluting waste sites.

The order provides guidance for federal and state agencies to examine whether communities of color or low-income areas are being deliberately targeted by polluting industries over alternative sites. It also suggests reviewing whether the cleanup process is different in communities of color or low-income communities than it is in other communities. Although there are few legal and financial handles behind the order, organizations have used the executive order to stop many potentially dangerous facilities from being built in communities across the country.

MOVING THE MOVEMENT
BEYOND SINGLE ISSUES

At one time, people believed that Love Canal was an isolated event. But in 1980, when the U.S. Environmental Protection Agency took a closer look, they found 30,000 other potential Love Canals. Then the public heard that communities of color and low-income communities were being specifically targeted by polluting industries. However, most people still felt safe—so long as they did not live near a Love Canal or were not in a targeted community.

This presumption of safety ended in September 1994, when the U.S. Environmental Protection Agency released a draft report on the health effects of dioxin. Dioxin comes primarily from the combustion of chlorine. According to many scientific research papers, dioxin causes cancer, depresses the immune system, and causes developmental problems, infertility, skin disorders, and more. Dioxin also crosses the placenta and has been linked to adverse effects on the developing fetus such as learning disabilities, attention deficit disorder, developmental problems, and birth defects.

The U.S. Environmental Protection Agency acknowledged that on average, Americans had accumulated enough dioxin in their bodies so that any additional exposure could cause adverse health effects in some people. The general public receives continual, low-level exposure to dioxin through our food supply, so no one is safe. Every time parents give their children milk, cheese, beef, or fish, they are feeding them dioxin. As mothers breast–feed their infants, they transfer their body's accumulation of dioxin to their children.

The exposure of the entire U.S. population to dioxin offered the grassroots movement an opportunity to reach a broader public, providing common ground with all Americans, not just those living near toxic discharge sites. A new effort, the Stop Dioxin Exposure campaign, was launched in April 1995. The campaign's main goal is a sustainable society in which there is no dioxin in our food or breast milk because there is no dioxin formation, discharge, or exposure.

The campaign is working with diverse array of people, including nurses, parent-teacher organizations, organized workers, physicians, religious groups, organic farmers, and organization of people living near toxic discharge sites. In March of 1996, more than 500 people came together at the Third Citizens Conference on Dioxin to define and refine strategies for the campaign. Working groups were established, and coalitions were built. This campaign has broadened and deepened the movement.

On 21 April 1997, in response to this growing public concern about involuntary exposure of children to pesticides, dioxin, and other toxic chemicals, President Bill Clinton issued another executive order. This order, titled "Protection of Children from Environmental Health Risks and Safety Risks," (U.S. President 1997) states, "A growing body of scientific knowledge demonstrates that children may suffer disproportionately from environmental health risks and safety risks" (p. 1). The order asks federal agencies to make it a high priority to identify and assess environmental health risks and safety risks that may disproportionately affect children. Again, while there are few teeth in this executive order, it provides a tool to educate and mobilize the public around issues of human health and environmental chemical exposures.

FORMING COALITIONS

Several very powerful coalition efforts have proven to be a good model for both broadening the movement and deepening its impact. Health Care Without Harm is one such model. This coalition works together with local, statewide, national, and international organizations to transform the health care industry's practices and purchases to eliminate pollution without compromising safety or care. Each organization, at each of the various levels of work, plays a critical role in the strategy to accomplish the overarching goal.

For example, the coalition sought to have the health care industry replace its toxic products with safe alternatives that either pose no public health and environmental chemical risks or are less damaging through their life cycles. The coalition identified the largest purchaser of health care production in the United States—Kaiser Permanente—and pressured it to commit to change its purchasing practices. The coalition believed that if you can change the largest purchaser, as was done with McDonald's, the small purchaser will find safer products at reasonable prices.

While one segment of the coalition worked to secure a meeting with high-level corporate executives, other segments worked to identify nasty products and alternatives and to build a base of pressure. At the base, local grassroots groups worked to close down medical waste incinerators and to pass local ordinances and laws around dioxin. Hospitals across the country began to see groups carrying signs that urged the closure of the incinerators and demanded that doctors fulfill their oath to "first do no harm."

Dioxin resolutions were introduced in towns, cities, and counties across the country. Berkeley, California (home of Kaiser's corporate offices), passed a strong ordinance after an extensive public debate. When Kaiser finally met with representatives of the Health Care Without Harm coalition, the company agreed to phase out the use of plastics with chlorine due to the strong public opinion generated by the public debate and the city ordinance. This decision by Kaiser will by itself significantly change health care purchases, and these will change the waste stream. Health Care Without Harm is working with groups all across the globe to stop the use and disposal of chlorinated products.

BROADEN THE REACH, DEEPEN THE IMPACT

The movement for environmental justice has grown as different segments of our population recognized the health risks from exposure to chemicals in the environment. Workers knew they were being placed at risk in their workplaces. They fought for years for protective health and safety programs. Vietnam veterans spoke out for years about how they had been harmed by the dioxin in Agent Orange during the Vietnam War. Then Love Canal brought the issue of hazardous waste to the attention of the American public. Soon afterward, the public learned how low-income communities and communities of color were being targeted by polluting industries. The public sympathetically supported each of these groups, but there was no massive outcry for justice, for change.

During the past five years, with the realization that dioxin and other toxic chemicals are posing serious health risks to children, a choir of voices has finally begun to surface, sounding the call for change. Every man, woman, and child is at risk without his or her consent or knowledge. And it will likely take every man, woman, and child to move society away from corporate domination, in which industry's rights to pollute, profit, and damage health and the environment supersede the public's rights to live, work, and play in a safe environment. Society needs the grassroots movement to grow and broaden to be able to win this crucial political fight.

REFERENCES

Cerrell Associates, Inc. 1984. *Waste to energy, political difficulties facing waste-to-energy conversion plant siting.* Sacramento: California Waste Management Board Technical Information Series.

Douglass, Frederick. [1857] 1985. The significance of emancipation in the West Indies. Speech, Canandaigua, New York, 3 August 1857, collected in pamphlet by author. In *The Frederick Douglass papers.* Series 1, *Speeches, debates, and interviews,* Vol. 3, edited by John W. Blassingame, 1855–63. New Haven, CT: Yale University Press.

Farren, D. J. 1992. *Report on the site selection process for the North Carolina "Low-Level" Radioactive Waste Disposal Facility.* Raleigh, NC: Chatham County Board of Commissioners and the Chatham County Site Designation Review Committee.

U.S. President. 1997. *Protection of children from environmental health risks and safety risks.* Executive Order 1997–21–04.

2

Gendered Approaches to Environmental Justice
An Historical Sampling

Nancy C. Unger

While race and class are regularly addressed in environmental justice studies, scant attention has been paid to gender. The environmental justice movement formally recognized in the 1980s in no way, however, marks the beginning of the central role played by women in the long history of its concerns.[1] Abuses based in gender as well as race and class have subjected women to a variety of environmental injustices. However, women's responses to the ever-shifting responsibilities prescribed to their gender, as well as to their particular race and class, have consistently shaped their abilities to affect the environment in positive ways. Especially they have used their unique strengths and experiences based on their gendered identities (frequently but not always maternal) to the benefit of themselves and oppressed others. Through a sampling of women's contributions, the relationships among gender, race, class, and environmental justice activism prove to be not just occasionally and peripherally a part of recent American history, but rather a varied yet pervasive force from the pre-Columbian period to the present.

PRE-COLUMBIAN NATIVE AMERICAN WOMEN: AGRICULTURAL PRACTICES AND POPULATION CONTROL

To generalize about the role of gender in pre-Columbian America is a dangerous business, as gender relations were highly variable. For example, the

17

hierarchy of tribes in many places was determined less by gender and more by age and lineage. Some tribes were matrilineal. In others, women served as advisers and sometimes as leaders, as shamans, and as warriors. Gendered divisions of labor were also rarely rigid.[2] Men, however, frequently manipulated the environment by burning, hunting, and fishing. In areas where tribes practiced agriculture, women were usually the primary distributors of the corn, beans, squash, and pumpkins they planted, weeded, and harvested.[3] In Southeastern New England, for example, from about 1000 A.D. to the time of European settlement, the corn alone produced by women provided about 65% of their tribes' caloric input.[4] Native American women, unlike the Europeans to come, were not planting their corn in neatly plowed rows bereft of all other vegetation. In New England they instead planted each hill with four grains of maize (corn) and two of pole beans that would twine around them. Between the hills they grew squash and pumpkins so that as their vines grew and spread, they would smother the soil from late growing weeds. By not leaving the soil totally exposed, they shielded it from excessive sun and rain and cut down drastically on the amount of weeding that subsequent European farming methods would necessitate.[5]

Even those soils cultivated under Native women's methods ultimately tired and crop yields lessened. Indian peoples then moved onto new, untilled soils. Early European colonists, stunned at this flagrant "waste," urged the fertilization of the land already under cultivation, especially since it could be done with relative ease due to the abundance of local fish. Indians, in view of the small numbers of their people combined with the seemingly endless amount of easily accessible untilled land, rejected this solution as absurdly labor intensive. These contrasting approaches to the problem of soil depletion highlight the two cultures' dramatically different land values, ultimately based on issues of population.[6]

Indians did not live in total harmony with nature. Like all living beings, they were by no means exempt from changing, in permanent and meaningful ways, the environment in which they lived.[7] An important, gender-based factor, however, distinguishes the Indians' treatment of resources from the patterns subsequently established by Europeans. What allowed Indians to live in North America in sustainable ways for centuries was not that they were careful to conserve and use wisely every resource: plant, animal, soil, or water. If Indians did, in the occasional extreme case, hunt one species into local extinction, plenty of others remained. Their lifestyle continued to be sustainable, even as its individual elements changed over time. The key to their ability to carry out what William Cronon calls "living richly by wanting little," was that they controlled their numbers, so that this "rich" lifestyle remained sustainable and could be enjoyed equally by all, the ultimate goal of the modern environmental justice movement. Native American women's greatest environmental impact came not through their gathering, irrigation projects, horticulture, fishing, herding, or preservation of foods. Instead, their greatest single impact came through their nearly universal practice of prolonged lactation.

Breastfeeding was very common for a child's first three years, but among some tribes the practice lasted for four years and sometimes even longer. Certainly breast feeding in the first two years had enormous practical benefits, primarily convenience and mobility. It was also valued because it brought decreased fertility. Because Native Americans actively sought to control their populations, breastfeeding was routinely extended past the period where children could easily thrive on solid foods, and frequently more than twice as long as in Europe.[8] Along with prolonged lactation, Native American women, like their European counterparts, also practiced infanticide and abortion.[9] To guarantee population control, breastfeeding was sometimes combined, as in the case of the Huron and California's Ohlones, with sexual abstinence, a practice also utilized by many indigenous peoples worldwide, including those who lived along the Amazon and within Africa's Congo basin.[10] By carefully controlling their populations, keeping them below their "carrying capacity," Indian women made a crucial contribution to their peoples' ability to live easily sustainable lifestyles. Their populations were also periodically checked by factors including wars, droughts, and floods. In addition they endured "lean" winters, during which the sometimes intentionally limited stores of food ensured that the weakest were winnowed out.[11] But these latter factors alone cannot account for the remarkably stable (although larger than previously believed) numbers of Indians estimated to have populated what is now the United States.[12]

If prevailing gender relations had prohibited Indian women from employing measures of population control, some populations would have grown unchecked, compromising Indians' ability to move on to fresh lands for farming or hunting when the old ones had been depleted. The area where a "controlled" burn had flamed out of control could not have simply been abandoned in the confidence that fresh and fertile lands were readily available nearby. The species hunted into local extinction would not have been a provincial problem, but a widespread catastrophe. Native American women's active and welcome role in limiting their people's population reflects Indian perceptions of partnership with, rather than stewardship over, the land. It also reflects Indian gender relations, in that women shared more of a sense of control and partnership with their men than did their European counterparts. In addition, the role of Native American women in controlling their reproduction highlights the crucial and far too frequently overlooked role that population density plays in environmental justice issues.

ENSLAVED WOMEN: LIMITING POPULATION, FORCING EXPANSION OF LAND CULTIVATION

Europeans brought dramatic changes to the relationship between Native Americans and the environment, changes frequently facilitated by the people they brought with them as forced labor. The enslaved used their environmental knowledge to subtly undermine the institution that bound them. Plantation books kept by slave owners note the different field work expectations and/or performances based on sex. Because most slave owners shared the gendered perception that all men were smarter, more easily trained, and better workers than women, enslaved men were granted the majority of available skilled work.[13] Like the more elite enslaved men, enslaved women also served as house servants, but an additional variety of jobs remained almost exclusively within the male domain: stable worker, blacksmith, driver, horse breaker, cooper, carpenter, etc. In the nineteenth century a disproportionate number of women (almost 90 percent) worked in the field, regularly outnumbering the men.

Women's reproductive cycles proved a particular challenge as owners balanced their demands for strenuous labor from female slaves with the recognition that such labors could prohibit crucial human reproduction. Slave miscarriages "should never be the case on a well organized plantation," wrote Haller Nutt, of Araby Plantation in Louisiana, and were a sign that "there is something wrong—[the female slave] has been badly managed and worked improperly." To avoid miscarriage, "women in the family way should avoid ploughing—and such heavy work as fit only for men."[14] In his "Rules for the Plantation," published in a South Carolina newspaper, John Billiller noted that "Sucking and pregnant women must be indulged as circumstances will allow."[15] While women who successfully birthed babies on Nutt's plantation were rewarded with exemption from field work for a month, women who miscarried received an even longer dispensation and were to be "nursed more carefully" to ensure successful subsequent pregnancies.

Slaves manipulated plantation policies concerning reproduction for their own purposes. Methods used previously to control local homeland populations to their own benefit were adapted in their new situations as forms of resistance to slavery. The demands of forced field labor precluded most enslaved women's ability to breastfeed with sufficient frequency to suppress ovulation. Instead, they limited reproduction by using the environmental knowledge brought from Africa and the Caribbean concerning the abortifacient qualities of a number of medicinal plants also available in North America (especially cotton root).[16] Such practices not only reduced their masters' supplies of new generations of forced laborers, but also served as a kind of strike, since reproduction was considered an important enslaved women's role, contributing to higher prices for women considered to be promising "breeders."[17] Enslaved women risked great harm when they intentionally terminated their own pregnancies. One owner advised, if "the woman is to blame herself [she] should be severely punished for it when she gets well."[18]

In the words of historian Judith Carney, "subordinated peoples used their own knowledge systems of the environments they settled to reshape the terms of their domination."[19] While slave owners may have considered the fieldwork carried out by women to be unskilled labor left to them by default, they nevertheless benefited from the gendered expertise of female field hands. Women's agricultural expertise in rice, indigo, corn, and cotton production stemmed back to specialized knowledge and hand tool experience garnered in their native lands.[20] All field workers were, of course, subject to the will of the master. Within the cabins of the enslaved, however, women were highly valued and generally enjoyed greater gender equity than did white women.[21] Agricultural experience and wisdom combined with this sense of themselves as valued persons empowered enslaved women. Limiting their masters' supplies of new slaves was only one of the many forms of passive resistance to white tyranny. Of particular interest is the passive refusal of field workers to fertilize increasingly depleted cotton fields or to terrace untilled hillsides. While field workers, disproportionately women, did not refuse outright to increase their masters' crop yields, the expensive tools required were ill used, forever breaking or disappearing mysteriously. Costly fertilizers were applied improperly. So widespread were these actions that slave owners preferred to view them as further proof of their slaves' laziness and stupidity rather than as calculated forms of resistance, and quickly abandoned terracing and fertilizing efforts.[22] As the soils became exhausted and cotton yields shrank, expansion onto fresh lands became imperative if King Cotton was to thrive, or even to survive.

Prior to the Civil War, many northerners, including Abraham Lincoln, professed not to oppose slavery where it existed, but wished "only" to prevent its spread. To cotton-growing southern whites, the crucial issue of soil depletion meant that to prevent the spread of slavery *was* to ultimately bring about its demise. The actions of field workers, disproportionately female, hastened the necessity for the geographic expansion of slavery. A series of political compromises opened some new territories to the institution, delaying but ultimately not preventing the day of reckoning: the Civil War. In other words, enslaved women's environmental knowledge empowered them to indirectly play a role in facilitating their own freedom.

MIDDLE CLASS WOMEN: NINETEENTH-CENTURY FOUNDATIONS FOR ENVIRONMENTAL JUSTICE

By the 1850s nearly a fifth of the national population was living in towns and cities. As the ranks of this more urban group swelled during the early industrialization prior to the Civil War, their lifestyles, particularly their gender relationships, came to influence the way virtually all Americans defined "true womanhood," or woman's proper sphere. Although the pre-scribed woman's sphere in many ways circumscribed their involvement to activities inside the home, it nonetheless ultimately encouraged the notion of free white women as uniquely qualified and obligated to seek environmental justice.

The concept of woman's proper sphere refers to an idealized domestic environment of home, upheld by four pillars: piety, purity, submissiveness, and domesticity. Within this home, women were described as innately dependent, affectionate, gentle, nurturing, benevolent, and sacrificing. Mor-ally and spiritually superior to men, women (mothers, ideally) within this sphere maintained a high level of purity in all things, and bore the complete responsibility for inspiring and cultivating purity within all of the home's inhabitants. According to the prescriptive literature of the day, true happi-ness for these ideal women was found not in selfish pursuits, but in renounc-ing themselves in favor of total dedication to the service of others.[23]

Although this concept of true womanhood tied women more closely to their pre-industrial daily routines, it delivered to them a greater, more pow-erful, and often autonomous role within their own homes, as middle-class men were increasingly tied to the more public world of politics, power, busi-ness, professions, and money. This change for women was limited primarily to the urban middle class, yet its impact ultimately spread across geographic, class, and even racial lines. Countless books, magazines, pamphlets, speeches, and sermons held up the middle-class home as an example for fam-ilies of virtually all classes, ethnicities, and income levels: a soothing retreat from the fast-paced, secular, cold, and crass commercialism of modern life, a haven in a heartless world made possible by the endless domestic and cul-tural pursuits of the woman at its center.[24]

The women who internalized the values of the "sphere" found themselves on the horns of a dilemma. Ideally, their pure, domestic feminine world was wholly divorced from the tainted masculine public world. In reality, how-ever, the two worlds intertwined. Women discovered that to protect their sole basis of power, they often had to immerse themselves in the world of men. The course from domestic to public life was long and often convoluted, but it was a journey many women felt they had no choice but to undertake. By 1915 a progressive noted in a university bulletin, "The woman's place is in the home. But today, would she serve the home, she must go beyond the home. No longer is the home encompassed by four walls. Many of its impor-tant activities lie now involved in the bigger family of the city and the state."[25]

During the Progressive era (circa 1890–1917), many middle-class female reformers, primarily but not exclusively white, claimed that male domination of business and technology had resulted in a skewed value system. Profit had replaced morality, they charged, as men focused on financial gain as the sole measurement of success, progress, and right. Men profited, for example, by selling impure food and drugs to an unsuspecting public. In the factories whose profits turned a few individuals into millionaires, workers toiled long hours for low wages in unsafe conditions, only to go home to urban ghettos rife with poverty, crime, and disease. Precious, nonrenewable resources were ripped from the earth with no thought to their conservation, let alone preservation.[26] In the face of so much gross injustice, environmental and otherwise, women, long prescribed to be the civilizers of men, staged protests and organized reform efforts. The nature of their proposed solutions, including resource conservation and wilderness preservation, reveal new insights into the power of gender in early industrialized society. An appreciation of that power will enrich examinations of other reform movements as well, as one women's resource preservation program, and its contributions to environmental justice, illustrates.

GENDER AND ENVIRONMENTAL JUSTICE IN THE EARLY TWENTIETH CENTURY

Mrs. Robert Burdette of Pasadena served as the first president of the women's California Club, established in 1900 in the wake of the state's first and abortive women's suffrage campaign. Burdette spoke plainly of the gendered divide across the nation on issues of natural resource conservation: "While the women of New Jersey are saving the Palisades of the Hudson from utter destruction by men to whose greedy souls Mount Sinai is only a stone quarry . . . the word comes to women of California that men whose souls are gang-saws are mediating the turning of our world-famous Sequoias into planks and fencing worth so many dollars."[27]

By 1910 there were hundreds of women's conservation clubs with a combined national membership, according to activist Lydia Adams-Williams, of one million.[28] Most male conservationists were happy to exploit to the fullest the prescribed notion that women were, unlike greedy materialist men, motivated purely by good, by the desire to uplift and improve society. In particular, women were presented as the guardians of natural resources that needed to be protected for the enjoyment of all rather be sacrificed for the enrichment of the powerful few. In 1910, Congressman Joseph Ransdell, chair of the National Rivers and Harbors Committee, identified himself as "a representative of the men who need and wish the help of women," declaring, "We know that nothing great or good in this world ever existed without the women."[29]

Women, however, especially the very class of women who were joining reform groups and clubs, appeared in some cases to be contributing more to resource depletion than preservation. After the lull in high fashion during the Civil War, new and elaborate styles in clothing and accessories erupted on the fashion scene. Women's hats featured lavish displays of feathers. "The extremely softening effect," proclaimed one fashion magazine, "is ever desirable, especially for ladies no longer young."[30] Sometimes the entire bird was reconstructed, making it appear as if the wearer had a living bird, often roosting in an artificial nest, perched on her head. Other times only select feathers were plucked, sparing the life of the bird, but only temporarily. Frequently these harvests rendered the birds flightless, guaranteeing a quick kill for the nearest predator.

By 1910, the activities of the Audubon Society (begun by Boston socialite Harriet Lawrence Hemenway in 1896 in response to the slaughter of the Florida heron) were augmented by those of the two hundred and fifty women's clubs active nationwide specifically in bird and plant protection. Marion Crocker, who strove to alert club women to the dangers of soil erosion, took up the campaign to dissuade women from wearing feathers in their hats.[31] With strip mining destroying the landscape and children dying in the mines of black lung disease, ladies focusing their conservation efforts on birds' feathers seems trivial at first glance, and appears related only to bird protection rather than human-centered environmental justice. The significance of the save-the-birds campaign is revealed when placed in historical context: there had been an estimated nine *billion* passenger pigeons in the United States prior to European colonization—more than twice the number of *all* birds in the country in the modern day. Passenger pigeons were hunted for sport as well as for pig feed. The last of the species died in captivity in 1914, within weeks of the Carolina parakeet, which had been hunted into extinction for its striking plumage.[32] It has been conservatively estimated that in the late nineteenth century, five million birds a year were killed throughout the world for their feathers.[33] Resistance to further extermination of birds, Crocker insisted, was vital to the preservation of the human race. During this period before the widespread use of insecticides, birds provided virtually the only check on the insect population that threatened crops prior to harvest.[34] Warned Crocker, "If we do not follow the most scientific approved methods, the most modern discoveries of how to conserve and propagate and renew wherever possible those resources which Nature in her providence has given to man for his use but not abuse, the time will come when the world will not be able to support life and then we shall have no need of conservation of health, strength, or vital force, because we must have the things to support life or else everything else is useless."[35]

Men could not be trusted to carry out the crucial task of saving the birds, and, ultimately, humanity, asserted Lydia Adams-Williams, who promoted herself in 1908 as the first woman lecturer and writer on conservation.

According to Adams-Williams, "Man has been too busy building railroads, constructing ships, engineering great projects, and exploiting vast commercial enterprises" to consider the future.[36] Speeches on the floor of the U.S. Senate gave fuel to such charges, including Missouri's James A. Reed's response to a 1913 bill introduced to protect migratory birds: "Why should there be any sympathy or sentiment about a long-legged, long-beaked, long-necked bird that lives in swamps and eats tadpoles. . . . Let humanity utilize this bird for the only purpose that the Lord made it for . . . so we could get aigrettes for the bonnet[s] of our beautiful ladies."[37] To the horror of those who saw clearly the crucial role that the pest control provided by wild birds played in national and international economies and ecosystems, Reed dismissed the protection of birds as trivial, born out of "an overstrained, not to say maudlin sympathy for birds born and reared thousands of miles from our coast."[38] Such widespread anthropocentric and nationalistic views left many women believing that, in the words of environmental historian Carolyn Merchant, "Man the moneymaker had left it to woman the moneysaver to preserve resources."[39] According to Adams-Williams, it fell to "woman in her power to educate public sentiment to save from rapacious waste and complete exhaustion the resources upon which depend the welfare of the home, the children, and the children's children."[40]

Crocker and her fellow reformers sought legislation protecting the birds, but took more immediate action as well. When the powerful millinery industry deflected their criticisms, proclaiming itself merely acceding to the demands of women, Crocker and her colleagues focused on educating the female hat-buying public. Some of their pleas were designed to appeal to maternalism. Aigrettes, for example, were "harvested" during the breeding season, when the feathers were at the height of their beauty, leaving the parents dead and the young to die of starvation. "Remember, ladies," urged a California Federation of Women's Clubs newsletter, "that every aigrette in your hat costs the life of a tender mother."[41] Crocker herself chose not to play the maternal card directly. She stressed the necessity of birds in interrelated plant and animal kingdoms, reminding her listeners of the crucial roles birds played in agriculture and pest control. "This is not sentiment," she stated flatly, "It is pure economics."[42]

The response to Crocker's pleas for women specifically to take action, combined with the campaigns of other various women conservationists, ultimately resulted in a variety of successes, indicated by the plea from a Colorado legislator to the president of the General Federation of Women's Clubs: "Call off your women. I'll vote for your bill."[43] In October of 1913, a new Tariff Act outlawed the import of wild bird feathers into the United States, and in 1916 Supreme Court Justice Oliver Wendell Holmes ruled that wild birds "are not in the possession of anyone and possession is the beginning of ownership."[44] Women continued to wear hats, but milliners throughout the United States and Europe bowed to the legal and societal pressures to dramatically reduce their dependence on feathers as primary decoration, the exception being peacock feathers, which are shed naturally. Thus, prior to achieving suffrage, by basing their arguments primarily within their sphere of home and family, women were able to wield legislative influence, and, by preserving millions of birds, protect complex and vital environmental relationships from ruin by a powerful American industry.

ECOFEMINISM CHALLENGES THE POSTWAR PATRIARCHAL RESURGENCE

Following the triumph of women's suffrage, patriarchal traditions did not disappear from the American scene. Nonetheless, the upheavals caused by two world wars and the intervening depression forced perpetual challenges to the traditional gender stereotypes and prescribed spheres. With the Cold War, however, came new, stricter and more rigid prescriptions. The perception of communism as a powerful threat to American freedoms and ways of life produced a pervasive fear. Patriarchy, Christianity, and especially the heterosexual nuclear family were prescribed as not only socially desirable, but politically necessary if the nation was to survive—and to triumph over—the communist menace.[45] The ideal American family, glorified as the greatest bulwark against communism, featured a husband and father who produced the family's single income, leaving a wife whose sole occupation was caring for her family, especially serving her husband and raising good patriotic Americans.

With her publication of *Silent Spring* in 1962, pioneer ecofeminist Rachel Carson challenged male notions of power and progress, specifically the governmental fathers' attitudes toward industrial waste as well as their vast reliance upon pesticides, especially DDT. One woman's praise for Carson denounced the highly touted postwar notion that "Father Knows Best" (the title of one of the era's many popular TV shows in which a happy, nuclear family is shepherded through life's little hazards by a wise and benevolent patriarch): " 'Papa' does not always know best. In this instance it seems that 'papa' is taking an arbitrary stand, and we, the people are just supposed to take it, and count the dead animals and birds"[46] Despite her many male critics in the scientific community who dismissed her as overly sentimental, if not hysterical, Carson's radical critique of the country's dependence on chemical pesticides has come to be widely recognized as one of the most influential books of the twentieth century. Through her rejection of prevailing gender stereotypes of female subservience to male wisdom, Carson has been credited with making the public aware of attempts by the scientific-industrial complex to manipulate and control nature to the ultimate detriment of all, thereby inspiring the environmental justice and ecofeminist movements of subsequent decades.[47]

What is ecofeminism? The answer depends on which ecofeminist is asked.[48] Some argue that women are better qualified to understand and therefore right environmental wrongs. In most parts of the world, because of gender relations, women are the ones who are "closest to the earth," the ones who gather the food and prepare it, who haul the water and search for the fuel with which to heat it. Everywhere they are the ones who bear the children, or in highly toxic areas, suffer the miscarriages and stillbirths or raise damaged children. Because, as one Brazilian woman puts it (echoing the sentiments of American Lydia Adams-Williams expressed nearly a century earlier), by dedicating themselves to the pursuit of immediate profit, "Men have separated themselves from the ecosystem," it falls to women to fight for environmental justice and to save the earth.[49] Within the United States, a variety of mutually exclusive forms of ecofeminism rival for dominance. One branch emphasizes the power of goddess mythology and argues that women, especially as mothers, are the natural guardians of "Mother Earth." Their horrified rivals counter that these kinds of claims perpetuate old gendered stereotypes. They argue that women and nature are mutually associated and devalued in western culture and that it is because of this tradition of oppression that women are better qualified than men to understand and empathize with the earth's plight, and to more fairly distribute its resources. These ecofeminists see the anthropocentrism that is so damaging to the earth as just one strand in a web of unjust "isms" including ageism, sexism, and racism, that must be destroyed in order to achieve a truly just world.

"POWERLESS" HOMEMAKERS IN THE MIDWEST ATTACK WAR AND THE GLOBAL ENVIRONMENTAL DEGRADATION CAUSED BY RAMPANT MATERIALISM

In the autumn of 1971 about a dozen Wisconsin homemakers began a unique effort to remake American culture: "Women for a Peaceful Christmas" (WPC). The founders had previously worked in various political campaigns, but they found that altruistic letters by women who were perceived as "just housewives" yielded no results. They were inspired by the nationwide Women's Boycott for Peace held in June of that year, organized by women in Ann Arbor, Michigan.[50] Citing Gallup poll figures reflecting that 78 percent of American women wanted the United States out of Vietnam by the end of the year, these women decided to "speak in a language all men can understand: refuse to support a wartime economy."[51] "Money talks," noted one of the WPC founders. "This is our non-violent form of pressure." Added another,

"We do not want to support the economy which is killing our sons."[52] Members of WPC wanted more than "just" peace. They sought a "reordering of national and personal priorities," beginning with a turning away from the waste and conspicuous consumption that had come to characterize the United States, especially during Christmas and Hanukkah.[53] Their goal was not a holiday boycott, but rather they offered alternatives designed to make celebrations "more meaningful, less commercial, less wasteful, and more peaceful," with suggestions ranging from gift ideas (including handcrafts, environmentally friendly canvas shopping bags, and organic cleaning products), to alternatives to energy-consuming Christmas lights. "If you don't want your Christmas celebrations to be controlled by the monoliths that corrupt governments and pollute environments," WPC urged women, the sex that did the vast bulk of holiday shopping, "take matters into your own hands. Don't buy the pre-packaged, disposable Christmas! Make your own."[54]

Under the slogan "No More Shopping Days Til Peace," WPC organized ostensibly powerless homemakers into a "quiet revolt against 'an economy which thrives on war and the destruction of our earth's resources.'" Its members entertained "no illusions of making much of a dent in an economy that encourages over consumption," and yet their message rapidly spread nationwide (aided by press coverage ranging from church bulletins to national publications including the *Christian Science Monitor* and *Newsday*, as well as support from the National Association for the Advancement of Colored People). They celebrated women's ability to "however infinitesimally, slow down the breakneck speed of American consumerism" and preserve precious natural resources for all.[55]

As the war in Vietnam came to a close, the focus of WPC shifted increasingly to environmental issues. Mindful of worldwide food and energy shortages and of pollution and economic uncertainty, its members campaigned especially against waste.[56] When asked by a disapproving reporter during the group's fourth year of operation if their goal was to undermine "The American Way of Life," founder Jan Cheney responded, "I hope so. We have to rethink the way we live. I can't believe we're so dependent on [useless, manufactured] 'things' that we can't learn to make useful things, instead of what Madison Avenue tells us what we want."[57] WPC denounced traditionally commercial Christmas celebrations as "wasteful of the earth's energy and resources, and encourag[ing of] a thing centered, rather than a people-centered way of life."[58] Simplified, environmentally friendly alternatives allowed individuals "to decide what's really important in life and what just gets in the way."[59]

Gendered aspects of WPC's crusade have been carried into the new millennium. *Bitch Magazine: Feminist Response to Pop Culture* regularly urges its readers to recognize and resist the oppression of women, including media insistence that women find power, joy, and fulfillment while bonding with each other in an endless round of spending sprees on non-essential goods. In the 2003 "Bitch Holiday Gift Guide," *Bitch* cofounder Lisa Jervis alerted readers to Buy Nothing Day, a project of Adbusters Media Foundation, and urged consideration of the global ecologic and economic repercussions of women's consumption that is "most fevered" during the winter holiday season, including the perpetuation of sweatshop labor and waste of natural resources. Noting that the wealthiest 20 percent consume 80 percent of the world's resources, the Buy Nothing Day campaign offers a variety of alternatives to rampant materialism, promoting a "shopping-frenzy-free" holiday season.[60]

Women For a Peaceful Christmas was just one of many organizations of women during the 1970s that was refusing to allow gender-based stereotypes of their powerlessness to thwart environmental justice, especially at the local level. As women dominated the leadership and ranks of a variety of community efforts designed to protect the environment, successful environmental grassroots organizations included LAND (League Against Nuclear Dangers), originated by homemakers in 1973 who, without previous activist experience, opposed a proposed nuclear power plant in Rudolph, Wisconsin.[61] These women were white and middle class, in their thirties or forties; most were raising young children and were not employed outside the home.[62] They were, claims one scholar, "naturals" for activist work because their role as the primary caregivers to their children had previously involved them in broad humanistic/nurturing issues, their interactions with other activists were minimally contentious, and their lack of conventional power left them with little to lose.[63] Ridiculed for their lack of scientific credentials, LAND members educated themselves about nuclear hazards. Most significantly, they worked to educate and gain the support of the entire community, not just appeal to those perceived to be in power.[64] Accordingly, they did not restrict their activities to producing the tools of traditional male dominated efforts: petitions, reports, graphs, and charts. LAND utilized innovative consciousness-raising techniques that required no specialized knowledge to appreciate, including placing Burma Shave–style protest signs along roadways, writing anti-nuclear lyrics to popular songs, and staging a highly publicized release of red balloons tagged with postcards describing the various radioactive substances they represented.[65] The balloons' finders, spread across several states, returned the postcards to LAND, vividly demonstrating the traveling range of airborne contaminants. Of the written materials LAND did circulate, many were based on information provided by prize-winning scientist and biostatisician Rosalie Bertell, the Roman Catholic "Rebel Nun" who preferred "not to tackle government and industry herself but 'to work directly with people [all over the world] and support them with scientific information'" written in clear, layperson's terms.[66] In 1980, the Wisconsin Public Service Commission bowed to widespread opposition, much of it generated by LAND, and canceled plans for all eight proposed nuclear power plants. When LAND disbanded in 1983, many of its members became active in groups concerned with nuclear issues on the state, national, and international level.[67]

MODERN CAMPAIGNS FOR ENVIRONMENTAL JUSTICE BY WOMEN OF COLOR

Members of WPC and LAND suffered the effects of lingering gendered stereotypes but, by virtue of their class and color, enjoyed many privileges not shared by women activists of color, especially those in economically depressed communities. Beginning in the 1950s, mining companies, in a series of actions later denounced as "Plundering the Powerless," aggressively gutted lands held by Chicanos and especially by Native Americans for nuclear fuel.[68] Native American women established the national organization Women of All Red Nations (WARN) in 1978 to strengthen themselves and their families in the face of ongoing attacks on Indian culture, health, and lands. In 1980, WARN drew attention to the fantastically high increase in miscarriages, birth defects, and deaths due to cancer on Indian reservations in areas of ongoing intense energy development (especially uranium mining) including Nebraska, the Southwest, and western South Dakota.[69] WARN's emphasis on the drastic increase in childhood cancers of the reproductive organs (at least fifteen times the national average) made the demands for action by mothers particularly compelling. Sister Rosalie Bertell's observations on genetic defects and environmental health hazards on the extensively mined areas were quoted throughout this campaign.[70] But the involvement of many WARN members was motivated by a variety of factors in addition to maternal concerns, including property rights and values based in gendered traditions. Among the Navajo, for example, land often belonged to the women, since it could be passed down from father to daughter, uncle to niece.[71] In addition, many men had died as a result of their work as miners (the risk of lung cancer increased by a factor of at least eighty-five), leaving their widows to band together seeking compensation.[72] WARN also worked to inform Native American women of their rights to resist an aggressive government-funded mass sterilization program WARN termed genocidal.[73] At a WARN sovereignty workshop Indian women were told they "must lead." Activists urged them, "Control your own reproduction: not only just the control of the reproduction of yourselves . . . but control of the reproduction of your own food supplies, your own food systems" to rebuild traditional native cultures and ways of living with the earth.[74]

Women of color perpetually bring unique perspectives to ongoing issues concerning their environments. Toxic waste facilities, chemical emissions, and health risks from air pollution disparately affect communities of color. In the modern environmental justice movement African American women in particular, frequently the heads of single-parent households, bring a legacy of assertiveness, leadership, and maternal concerns. They play a prominent role in a number of community organizations, waging campaigns against environmental dangers in the workplace and the home, especially in areas known as "brown fields" because of their toxicity.[75] Latinas too emphasize their dual role as mothers and workers in combating environmental hazards. In California, for example, they continue to build on a long legacy of struggle led by the United Farm Workers against various pesticides, particularly those affecting reproduction. Aided by activist organization Communities for a Better Environment, Latinas also played a significant role in forcing the government to remove La Montana, the mountain of concrete rubble created by the freeway collapses during 1994 Northridge earthquake, that was dumped in their community.[76]

CONCLUSION

Women's perspectives on their environments, and their contributions to environmental protection, have changed dramatically across time and space, especially as affected by class, race, and responses to prescribed gender roles. As a result, American history presents innumerable examples of women's activism—in a myriad of forms—and its contributions to environmental justice.

NOTES

Early versions of portions of the material in this essay concerning sexuality appear in "Women, Sexuality, and Environmental Justice in American History," *New Perspectives in Environmental Justice: Gender, Sexuality, and Activism*, Rachel Stein, ed., (New York: Rutgers University Press, 2004), 45–60. A Mary Lily Grant funded research at the Sallie Bingham Center for Women's History and Culture at Duke University. Additional research support was provided by an Arthur Vining Davis Grant from Santa Clara University. Mary Whisner generously provided editing expertise.

1. See Elizabeth Blum, "Linking American Women's History and Environmental History," *H-Environment* 28 May 2001, <http://www.h-net.org/~environ/his toriography/uswomen.htm> (28 May 2001), Bibliographies.

2. See Nancy C. Unger, "Women, Sexuality, and Environmental Justice in American History, "*New Perspectives in Environmental Justice: Gender, Sexuality, and Activism*, Rachel Stein, ed., (New York: Rutgers University Press, 2004), 46–49.

3. See Morrill Marsten to Jedediah Morse, November 1820, Thomas Forsyth

Papers, Volume 1T, p. 65, Lyman Draper Manuscripts, Wisconsin Historical Society, Madison (WHS).

4. Carolyn Merchant, *Earthcare* (New York: Routledge, 1995), 92–95.

5. See Ibid., 91–108.

6. See William Cronon, *Changes in the Land* (New York: Hill and Wang, 1983), 45, 151–52.

7. See Ibid., Carolyn Merchant, *Ecological Revolutions* (Chapel Hill: University of North Carolina Press, 1989), Richard White, *The Roots of Dependency* (Lincoln: University of Nebraska Press, 1983), and William Tydeman, "No Passive Relationship," *Idaho Yesterdays* 39, no. 2 (1995): 23–28.

8. Thomas Forsyth, "Manners and Customs of the Sauk and Fox Nations of Indians," 1827, Forsyth Papers, Lyman Draper Manuscripts, Volume 9T, p. 20, WHS.

9. Russell Thornton, *American Indian Holocaust and Survival* (Norman: University of Oklahoma Press, 1987), 31. See also Walter O'Meara, *Daughters of the Country* (New York: Harcourt, Brace and World, 1968), 84, John Demos, *The Tried and the True* (New York: Oxford University Press, 1995), 77.

10. Thornton, *American Indian Holocaust and Survival*, 31, Adam Hochschild, *King Leopold's Ghost* (New York: First Mariner Books, 1999), 73. See also Liese M. Perrin, "Resisting Reproduction," *Journal of American Studies* 35, no. 2 (2001): 258–59, 263, 266.

11. See Forsyth, "Manners and Customs," 15.

12. Ibid., 15–42. See also Wilbur Jacobs, "The Tip of an Iceberg," in *The Fatal Confrontation* (Albuquerque: University of New Mexico Press, 1996): 77–89.

13. Roger Ransom and Richard Such, *One Kind of Freedom* (Cambridge: Cambridge University Press, 1977), 104–105. See also Eugene V. Genovese, *Roll, Jordan, Roll* (New York: Vintage Books, 1972, 1974), 495.

14. Haller Nutt, "Directions in the Treatment of the Sick," *Journal of the Araby Plantation, 1843–1850*, 194–95. Haller Nutt Papers, Special Collections Library, Duke University.

15. A.B. [John Billiller], "Rules for the Plantation," Sumterville, South Carolina news clipping, 3 Nov. 1847, McDonald Furman Papers, Special Collections Library, Duke University.

16. For historiography see Perrin, "Resisting Reproduction," 255–74. See also Sharla M. Fett, *Healing, Health, and Power on Southern Slave Plantations* (Chapel Hill: University of North Carolina Press, 2002), 65, 176–77.

17. Perrin, "Resisting Reproduction," 256.

18. Nutt, "Directions in Treatment of Sick," 194.

19. Judith Carney, *Black Rice* (Cambridge: Harvard University Press, 2001), 162.

20. See Ibid, 108–122.

21. See Christie Farnham, "Sapphire? The Issue of Dominance in the Slave Family, 1830–1865," in Carol Groneman and Mary Beth Norton, eds., *To Toil the Livelong Day* (Cornell University Press, 1987).

22. See Eugene Genovese, "Soils Abused," in Carolyn Merchant, ed., *Major Problems in American Environmental History,* (Lexington MA: D.C. Heath and Company, 1993): 236–41.

23. See Lydia H. Sigourney, "Home," *Whisper to a Bride* 1850, in Mary Beth Nor-

ton, ed., *Major Problems in American Women's History* 2nd ed., (Lexington, MA: D.C. Heath and Company, 1996), 109–110, and n.a., *The New Female Instructor*, (London, Thomas Kelly, 1834; reprint London: Rosters Ltd, 1988).

24. See Nancy C. Unger, "The Two Worlds of Belle La Follette," *Wisconsin Magazine of History*, 83, no. 2 (Winter 1999–2000): 82–110.

25. In Nancy Woloch, *Women in the American Experience* (New York: Alfred A. Knopf, 1984), 299.

26. Nancy C. Unger, *Fighting Bob La Follette* (Chapel Hill: University of North Carolina Press, 2000), 86–87.

27. Carolyn Merchant, "Women of the Progressive Conservation Movement: 1900–1916," *Environmental Review* 8 (1984): 59.

28. Lydia Adams-Williams, "A Million Women for Conservation," *Conservation: Official Organ of the American Forestry Association*, 15 (1909): 346–47.

29. Merchant, "Women of Progressive Conservation Movement," 63.

30. Joseph Kastner, "Long Before Furs, It was Feathers That Stirred Reformist Ire," *Smithsonian* 25, no. 4 (July 1994): 100.

31. See Priscilla G. Massmann, "A Neglected Partnership," Ph.D. diss., University of Connecticut, 1997.

32. Bill Bryson, *A Walk in the Woods* (New York: Broadway Books, 1998), 204–205.

33. Kastner, "Long Before Furs," 97.

34. Massmann, "Neglected Partnership," 168.

35. Merchant, "Women of the Progressive Conservation Movement," 64–65.

36. Ibid., 65.

37. Kastner, "Long Before Feathers,"103.

38. "Ill Advised Sarcasm," *La Follette's Magazine* 5, no. 35 (30 Aug 1913): 3.

39. Merchant, "Women of the Progressive Conservation Movement," 65.

40. Ibid.

41. Ibid., 72.

42. "Mrs. Marion Crocker on the Conservation Imperative, 1912," in Merchant, ed., *Major Problems*, 355.

43. Ibid., 68.

44. Ibid.

45. See Elaine Tyler May, *Homeward Bound*. (New York: Basic Books, 1988).

46. Vera Norwood, "Rachel Carson," in Mary Jo Buhle, ed., *The American Radical* (New York: Routledge, 1994), 313–19.

47. See Stewart Udall, "How Wilderness was Won," *American Heritage* (February–March 2000): 98–105, and Norwood, "Carson," 313–15.

48. See Noel Sturgeon, *Ecofeminist Natures* (New York and London: Routledge, 1997), Karen Warren, ed., *Ecofeminism* (Bloomington: Indiana University Press, 1997), Mary Heather MacKinnon and Moni McIntyre, eds., *Readings in Ecology and Feminist Theology* (Kansas City: Sheed and Ward, 1995).

49. Carolyn Merchant, *Radical Ecology*, (New York: Routledge, 1992), 205.

50. See "Women Plan Boycott for Peace on June 21," *Des Moines Register* 3 June 1971, p. 11, folder 8, Women for a Peaceful Christmas (WPC), WHS.

51. William S. Becker, "Women Push for Peaceful Christmas," Clipping from unidentified Canton, Illinois newspaper, folder 8, WPC, WHS.

52. William Becker, "'Money Talks,' Women Say; Boycott Shopping in War, Waste Production," unidentified clipping, file 8, WPC, WHS.

53. Dorothy Link, "Christmas Can Be Saved for Future Generations," *The Catholic Herald Citizen*, 21 Nov., 1971, file 8, WPC, WHS.

54. Press Release, Nov., 1973, folder 8, WPC, WHS.

55. Whitney Gould, "Women for Peaceful Christmas Shun Opulence," *The Capital Times* (Madison, WI), 14 Nov. 1971, p. 7, file 8, WPC, WHS. Nancy Lambrecht, "Women Promote Peaceful Presents," 4 Dec. 1974, *The Daily Cardinal* (Madison, WI), folder 8, WPC, WHS.

56. Lambrecht; 1974 Press Release, folder 8, WPC, WHS.

57. "Fair Displays Ideas for Non-Commercial Holiday," *The Capital Times*, 27 Nov. 1974, file 8, WPC, WHS.

58. 1974 Press Release, WPC, WHS.

59. "Fair Displays Ideas."

60. Lisa Jervis, "The Bitch Holiday Gift Guide," *Bitch* (Fall 2003):94.

61. See Virginia Kemp Fish, "We Stopped the Monster: LAND in Retrospect," 1994, in LAND, Box 1-folder 1, WHS.

62. Ibid., 8.

63. Ibid., 5. Virginia Kemp Fish, "Widening the Spectrum," *Sociological Imagination*, 31 no. 2, (1994): 106.

64. Gertrude Dixon, "How We Have Organized and Acted," in Jack Miller, *A Primer on Nuclear Power* (Melville, MN: Anvil Press, 1981), 44.

65. Lyrics in LAND 3–17, postcards LAND 1–2, WHS.

66. Elaine Carey, "Honors Piling up for the Rebel Nun," 25 Jan. 1987, *Toronto Star* in LAND, 1–4, WHS. See also Phil Mader and Judi Cumming, "Environmental Activism: The Case of Rosalie Bertell," *Archivist: Magazine of the National Archives of Canada* 116 (1998): 20–29.

67. Fish, "We Stopped the Monster," 2.

68. Gail Robinson, "Plundering the Powerless," *Environmental Action* (June 1979): 3.

69. Eda Gordon, "Health Study Exposes Water Contamination on Pine Ridge Reservation," *Black Hills Report* March 1980 (1) 5:1.

70. Rosalie Bertell, "Uranium: Employment, Use and Health," *Prairie Messenger* 1 March 1981, in LAND 4–9, WHS.

71. Loretta Schwartz, "Uranium Deaths at Crown Point," *Ms.* (Oct. 1979): 81.

72. Tom Barry, "Bury My Lungs at Red Rock," *The Progressive* (Feb. 1979): 25–28.

73. "The Women's Health and the Future Generations Workshop," WARN Report (June–Dec. 1979): 33–42. See Nancy C. Unger, "Women, Sexuality, and Environmental Justice in American History."

74. WARN Report II. 1979. "The Sovereignty Workshop." June–Dec. LAND Papers, Box 7-file 14, WHS.

75. See Marie Bolton and Nancy C. Unger, "Pollution, Refineries, and People," *The Modern Demon* (France: University of Clermont Press, 2002), 425–37.

76. Manuel Pastor and Rachel Morello-Frosch, "Assumption Is Wrong—Latinos Care Deeply About the Environment," *San Jose Mercury News*, 8 July 2002, 6B.

3

Fond Memories and Bitter Struggles
Concerted Resistance to Environmental Injustices in Postwar Native America

Paul C. Rosier

We are a part of everything that is beneath us, above us, and around us. Our past is our present, our present is our future, and our future is seven generations past and present.

—Haudenosaunee precept

The immense landscape of the continental interior lay like memory in her blood.

—N. Scott Momaday, *The Way to Rainy Mountain*

> The river cod [Burbot]
>   so excellent in taste
> This rich fish is my fondest memory
>   of my tradition . . .
> It's full of mercury
>   they said
> I try not to cry.

—Margaret Sam-Cromarty (Cree)

Are we disposable to the government? These are some of our thoughts this uranium brings out to the front.

—Floyd Frank, Navajo uranium miner

"Downwinders," according to oncology nurse Rebecca Barlow, have memories of "watching the clouds, playing in the 'snow' in the summer, sweeping the ash from their cars and the ash burning their skin as it fell on them. They talk . . . of being so poor they didn't have a choice to throw away goods that had been grown on ground covered with nuclear ash." Barlow testified to federal officials meeting on the Navajo Nation that "downwinders" also "tell of a government that told them that these tests were 'safe' and wouldn't hurt them, when there is now evidence that shows that the government knew of the potential devastating effects and 'sacrificed' those people anyway." Many of the cancer patients Barlow treated came from families devastated by radiation-related cancers. One such family was left with just three members of an original twenty-seven.[1] Of 150 Navajo who worked in the Shiprock, New Mexico uranium mine "133 had either died of radiation-induced lung cancer or had contracted cancer and severe respiratory ailments such as fibrosis by 1980."[2] Such mortality rates trigger memories of a different era when Native American death rates approached 90 percent, the result of a biological holocaust that spread through their communities.

Environmental injustice has also occurred in white communities, but, as in Latin America and Africa, Native Americans have 500 plus years of memories of it. As Jace Weaver argues in *Defending Mother Earth*, "Natives view the environmental depredations being visited upon them as merely one more manifestation of the colonialism that has attacked their lives for over five hundred years. Ecojustice, therefore, cannot be discussed apart from that racism and colonialism."[3] The stories of these environmental depredations, called "war stories" by some, memories and myths by others, are poignant, disturbing, affirming. Lance Hughes, a Northern Cheyenne invested in preserving his reservation from the ravages of strip-mining, tells of how his ancestors died defending the right to retain a homeland. "Our reservation," he writes, "thus represents the blood and tears of our grandparents, who willingly gave their lives so that we might live here." Facing organized and persistent pressure from multinational energy companies for the right to mine (and undermine) reservation ecologies, Hughes argues that "[by] necessity, then, Indian tribes are major players in the environmental justice movement."[4] Native American environmental justice issues are broad-based. As Cherokee attorney Dean Suagee contends, "If environmental justice problems are characterized by disproportionate impacts on communities of color or low-income, then almost every environmental issue in Indian country is an environmental justice issue."[5] This essay offers a modest survey of environmental justice issues in postwar Indian country and of the ways in which Native Americans' struggles for environmental health and sovereignty intersect with those of other people of color presented in this volume.

Environmental memories begin with creation stories. Grace Thorpe, founder of the National Environmental Coalition of Native Americans, writes that the Navajo "emerged from the third world into the fourth and present world and were . . . told to choose between two yellow powders. One was yellow dust from the rocks, and the other was corn pollen. The people chose corn pollen, and the gods nodded in assent. They also issued a warning. Having chosen the corn pollen, the Navajos were to leave the yellow dust in the ground. If it was ever removed, it would bring evil."[6] The Navajo, Pueblo, and other tribes have experienced this particular evil. Corbin Harney, a Shoshone Elder, spoke about the traumatic impact of uranium mining in Nevada. "In my part of the country, we saw that nuclear radiation was making our lives shorter. I've seen children born without legs. I've seen cats born with just two legs. I've seen a lot of humans die of diseases caused by radiation."[7] Many Native Americans, the Navajo for example, believe that when a person becomes ill it reflects an imbalance between the earth and its inhabitants; the physical illnesses and death that Navajo miners have suffered from uranium mining thus indicate the extent to which mining has damaged Native Americans' harmony with the earth. Oneida activist Kla Kindness believes that drug and alcohol use "is due to the nature of the [mining] work: digging up mother earth is what it is, and there is some kind of mentality that develops from working in a destructive way."[8]

Native Americans' sense of this toxic history and their environmental and spiritual traditions compel activists like Hughes, Kindness, and Thorpe to revisit a suite of historical memories and restore a theology of interaction with the natural world. George Tinker, Professor of American Indian Cultures and Religious Traditions at the Iliff School of Theology, emphasizes the spatiality of Native environmental relations, in contrast with temporality of non-Natives. "The land and spatiality are the basic metaphor for existence and determine much of a community's life. In my own tribe, for instance, every detail of social structure—even the geographic orientation of the old villages—reflected a reciprocal duality of all that is necessary for sustaining life."[9] "Traditional" Native American ethnic identity derives from a particular geography, which provides opportunities to maintain customs as well as to procure the subsistence that allows them to be practiced. Teresa Leal argues that environment should be defined as "where we live, work and play but also where we worship."[10] The loss of territory or the ecological destruction of territory means the loss of opportunity to practice ceremonies that provide meaning to all dimensions of life. Thus environmental relations form the foundation for the spiritual health of a community in addition to the physical health of the individual. Writing in 1978, Bobby Lake displayed this link between culture and space in an angry letter to government officials protesting indiscriminate spraying of the defoliant 2,4,5,T on residential areas and the Yurok-Karak sacred religious grounds (California): "By what right and authority does the dominant society have to commit genocide against the Indian people and the entities of Nature? By what legal right and authority does the dominant system have to pollute the Indian ancient village sites, ceremonial grounds, burial sites, religious prayer sites, and native residences in general? That is the question or questions to be answered."[11]

These questions and "place-based identities," to use Devon Pena's term, drive the Native American environmental justice movement. Pena describes the efforts of acequia farmers of Colorado and New Mexico to preserve traditional space as resulting in their "weav[ing] these cognitive maps into the tapestry of a "resistance identity."[12] He writes that "concerted resistance to displacement and environmental degradation is one of these examples of the profound collection and rearticulation of a sense of place by local cultures that see themselves to be unjustly endangered by globalization and its discontents."[13] His argument applies to Native Americans' struggle for environmental justice in all its various forms in the twentieth century, all linked to maintaining a cultural space deemed "homeland," a process that Pena calls *"re-emplacement* of local culture."[14] Efforts to reclaim expropriated, stolen, or ceded land, which intensified after World War II, can be tied to environmental justice, especially since much of the land—the Black Hills and Blue Lake, for example—was considered sacred. Similarly, Native American efforts to secure fishing and hunting rights guaranteed in nineteenth-century treaties are environmental justice issues. As Pena argues, "The reinhabitation of violated places is a fundamental objective of the environmental justice movement."[15] Without the place there can be no process, whether spiritual or cultural. The violation of spaces Native Americans depended upon for subsistence and custom weakened Native identities and thus spurred political action. Memories of eating fish and of the centrality of fish in cultural maintenance practices galvanized, for example, a new generation of tribal activists intent on protecting their Indianness, which in turn provided models for "concerted resistance."

Efforts by various Native American groups to secure federal intervention in treaty disputes began in earnest in the 1940s, especially in the Pacific Northwest, where a number of Indian nations depended on salmon for food and for rituals. In March 1942 the U.S. Supreme Court ruled in *Tulee v. Washington* that Indians in Washington State could fish off-reservation without a state fishing license because of 1854 and 1855 treaties. But it allowed the state to define allowable fishing practices on the basis of "conservation," thus giving state officials legal tools for denying Native Americans unrestricted fishing access. As the state passed stringent conservation measures to limit Indian fishing rights, Native Americans mounted legal and political challenges to them.

Just as the sit-ins staged by young African American activists in the early 1960s helped publicize and energize the civil rights movement, so too did fish-ins by Native Americans publicize and energize the nascent treaty rights movement; activists associated with the National Indian Youth Council formed in 1961 had participated in "freedom rides" and other civil rights demonstrations on behalf of African Americans, learning the art of civil disobedience in that similar struggle against racial discrimination. In the early 1960s and beyond, Native Americans in the Pacific Northwest began to protest the denial of treaty rights by defying state law and fishing Washington's and Oregon's waters. Marlon Brando, Jane Fonda, Dick Gregory, and other celebrities traveled to Frank's Landing and other sites of protest in Washington State to support these acts of civil disobedience.[16] Men and women were jailed and fined for engaging in acts of peaceful civil disobedience, usually in the face of intimidation and violence. Politicized by the beating of women and children during such protests, Sid Mills of the Yakima community renounced his obligation to the United States after serving in Vietnam by proclaiming, "My first obligation now lies with the Indian people fighting for the lawful Treaty Right to fish in the usual and accustomed waters of [the Pacific Northwest]."[17] The Native American version of what African Americans faced in Birmingham and other southern cities elicited support from President Lyndon Johnson, who pledged to back the Puyallup tribe in its lawsuit with Washington state officials.

This pressure culminated in the famous Boldt Decision of 1974. After several years of studying the issues involved—the treaties, the history of state regulation, the migratory patterns of the fish—Judge George Boldt decided in *United States v. Washington* (known as the Boldt Decision) to uphold the rights of Native Americans in Washington state as well as Oregon to fish off-reservation sites using whatever method they chose, regardless of state laws, and to share equally the commercial catch of fish, or 50 percent of the "harvestable fish." Boldt developed two themes in his decision: One, that despite the evolution of industrial society "the mere passage of time has not eroded, and cannot erode, the rights guaranteed by solemn treaties that both sides pledged on their honor to uphold"; and two, Indians of the region depended on fish (salmon and steelhead) for sustenance and for cultural traditions, noting that salmon fishing "constituted both the means of economic livelihood and the foundation of native culture."[18] In a sense, Boldt viewed the treaty in two traditional contexts: one, in a classic white conception of property rights, a treaty is a contract and thus must be respected; and two, in an Indian world, fishing was cultural.

Boldt's decision provided a legal precedent and inspiration for other tribes facing similar battles. The Chippewa of Wisconsin and Minnesota also resisted state fishing and hunting regulations that they believed ignored treaties of 1837 and 1842, which established the Chippewa's usufruct rights in off-reservation waters and land. Chippewa were especially angry that Wisconsin officials applied their regulations to traditional Chippewa practices like spearfishing both *on reservations* as well as off reservations. As the state cracked down on Chippewa fishing, tribal elders began to fish at night to avoid prosecution. Such acts of resistance ultimately led to a showdown over Chippewa treaty rights. After a series of legal challenges that lasted until 1991, Judge Barbara Crabb upheld the usufruct rights of the six bands of Wisconsin Chippewa, enabling the Chippewa to establish their own regulations for off-reservation hunting, wild rice harvesting, and fishing of walleyes and muskies.[19]

Court decisions affirming Native treaty rights had great impact. Besides providing food and a livelihood for Native Americans of the Pacific Northwest, the salmon keeps their culture alive. The Columbia River Inter-tribal Fisheries Commission (CRITFC), which coordinates tribal conservation programs in the Pacific Northwest, puts it in stark terms. "Salmon are part of our spiritual and cultural identity. . . . The annual return of the salmon allows the transfer of traditional values from generation to generation. Without salmon returning to our rivers and streams, we would cease to be Indian people."[20] The rebirth of Native fishing has also brought about economic opportunity, which in turn has engendered social change. Tribal salmon fishing operations have created a reason for younger Indians to return to their reservations. Andy Fernando of the Upper Skagit Community called the Boldt Decision "a catalyst" to reverse the flow of talented tribal members from the reservation to Pacific Northwest cities. After Boldt, "many Indian people returned to their [nations] at first only to fish. But now they stay on because they see renewed activity in their tribal communities. Those people bringing skills have found welcoming tribal councils and communities eager to tap their knowledge and experience."[21] The Chippewa have a similar relationship with the walleye, which has provided their nutritional needs for centuries; over half of Chippewa families today consume the fish, while some tribal members earn cash income from fish sales. Those Chippewa who risked imprisonment, intimidation and violence to fish walleye using the traditional methods of gillnetting or spearfishing by torchlight did so because they were continuing a practice that was older than the treaties of the 1800s. As with Washington State Native Americans, the right to fish transcended issues of subsistence and politics for the Chippewa and other Indians of the Great Lakes. Reconnecting with old ways such as spearfishing helped to restore a community's spiritual and cultural integrity. Nick Hockings of the Chippewa Wa-Swa-Gon Treaty Association sees culture as an important way to attack the roots of social dysfunction, including alcoholism. "I think [a solution] lies in going back to traditional ways, to start acting more like our ancestors—very proud, honest, trustworthy. The Indian people don't want to be totally separate, but we need to have a sense of identity. Each person needs to feel complete and a spiritual connection with the earth and the environment. When people feel good about who they are . . . they don't need the crutch of alcohol."[22] The fight for treaty rights has also facilitated resistance to other environmental crises. Chippewa Elder Frances Van

Zile has helped lead the opposition to Exxon's proposal to build the Crandon zinc-copper sulfide mine in Wisconsin, arguing that Exxon officials "don't care if we live or die. All they want is that copper and zinc."[23] The Chippewa have succeeded in both resisting Exxon's overtures and in securing support from formerly hostile white communities in the process.

The fish-ins of the 1960s linked Native American issues to the larger context of civil rights. These acts of civil disobedience, practiced years before the 1982 Warren County, North Carolina protests that generated the term environmental justice, found expression in various reservation battles, in particular the defense of Black Mesa, a rich coal region straddling the Hopi and Navajo nations. In 1966 the Bureau of Indian Affairs had negotiated lease rates well below those given non-Indian owners. As the "rip-off" became public and as the devastation from strip-mining became visible, Hopi and Navajo came to the defense of their lands. The Black Mesa crisis also became a *cause celebre* for white environmentalists and supporters of Indian rights; CBS, ABC, *The Washington Post*, and *The New York Times* covered the story and turned Black Mesa into a symbol for the exploitation of Indians and the devastation of the environment at a time when many Americans were coming to grips with national environmental problems.

Numerous groups—Central Clearinghouse, the Committee for Traditional Indian Life, the Committee to Save Black Mesa, and Black Mesa Defense—organized to pursue both environmental and economic justice for the exploited Hopi and Navajo. In Black Mesa Defense's 1970 publication "Myths and Techno-Fantasies," Jack Loeffler, a non-Native, noted that it examined "the role of the mythic process within an environmental context" to determine the ways in which Native Americans' belief systems mediated a technological imperative of domination, citing the Hopi's and other tribes' environmental philosophy of stewardship "wherein Man was responsible, within his capabilities, for the maintaining of the balance of Nature."[24] Loeffler defined Native American ecological relationships by exploring Hopi environmental perspectives across generations. "[T]here are still some Indians who remember how it once was—Indians who somehow have remained convinced that the march of progress is doomed to a tragic dead end. Others of these Indians are young, and their eyes reflect the fire of dissent against a system that threatens not only the remaining cultures, but the life of Mother Earth herself."[25] One Hopi elder told Loeffler, "In those days, the air was clear and everyone could see far. We always look to the Earth Mother for food and nourishment. We never take more than we need. . . . When the white men came, everything started to get out of balance. The white brother has no spiritual knowledge, only technical. . . . Now there is a big stripmine. . . . They cut across our sacred shines and destroy prayers to the six directions. Our prayers go in all directions for everything so that there will be balance. We are not to use the earth in a way that is destructive."[26]

Anger turned into action. Navajo sheepherders gathered to talk about Peabody Coal Company's strip mining operation and the invasion of their homes. Ted Yazzi had confronted bulldozers to prevent a construction crew from building a road "wide as the Hollywood Freeway" in front of his house. This particular road was moved as a result. "I still wonder what would have happened if I did not say anything," he said. Other Navajo protested the destruction of a gravesite, a sweathouse, and other structures without their "consent." Traditional Navajo also staged a "sit-down strike" as well as formed a picket line. "Imagine," a young Navajo said, "seeing long-hair Navajos carrying picket signs." Politicized by such action, one young Navajo confronted a non-Navajo (a supporter of Black Mesa defense as it turned out) after seeing truck after track barrel through his homeland. "I am a full-blood f . . . ing [sic] Navajo," he announced. "And you better watch it on this road. . . . This is our road."[27]

Black Mesa politicized Native Americans around the country just as Earth Day politicized environmental citizens around the world. The assertion of traditional ecological relations dovetailed with and fueled a new commitment to reservation environments on the part of young Native Americans. In July 1970 the Boy Scouts of America (BSA) organized the first annual "Environmental Encampment for American Indian Youth," which involved some 300 Native American youth taking part in discussions of soil and water conservation, wildlife management, and environmental ecology. The director of the BSA's "American Indian relationships" program noted: "We hope to help build a strong cadre of young Indian conservationists and sustain a bold program in every Indian community throughout the oncoming years. We believe that we can learn much from the Indian people in regards to conserving the land." The BSA's Project SOAR (Save Our American Resources) offered workshops on "how [Native Americans] can take action back in their communities."[28]

Native Americans took action in their communities in the early 1970s by supporting conservation programs and by protesting strip-mining and other destructive processes. In the late 1970s and into the 1980s, the problem of radiation poisoning from mining and storage of nuclear materials became salient and has since dominated the Native American environmental justice movement. Uranium mining began on the Navajo and Laguna Pueblo reservations in the 1940s and 1950s as the Cold War evolved. By the time the first wave of mining leases ended in the 1970s the damage to miners and the environment was clear. As noted above, rates of cancer and respiratory ailments among former Navajo were found to be very high. But non-miners also suffered health problems that continue to this day because uranium tailings, byproducts of the mining operation, found their way into community water supplies and even materials used for building reservation homes. On the Laguna Pueblo reservation in New Mexico, the Anaconda Copper Company earned roughly $600 million over the life of its lease, which led to development of the world's largest uranium mine. While the company provided employment to hundreds of Pueblo miners, it too left the reservation with contaminated water supplies and land.[29] The health problems of Navajo and Pueblo miners alarmed Native Americans, as did two notable cases of radioactive poisoning. On July 16, 1978, an accident near Churchrock, New Mexico, released nearly 100 million gallons of radioactive water into both Navajo and non-Navajo environments, a more serious environmental threat than that of Three Mile Island. And in the late 1970s, Sioux officials discovered an illegal cache of 3.5 million pounds of radioactive tailings on the Lakota Reservation.[30]

Native Americans responded to these crises in several ways. Local groups like the Navajo Uranium Radiation Victims Committee and Navajo Nations Dependents of Uranium Workers Committee waged a long (and partly successful) campaign to secure justice for Native American uranium workers.[31] Prominent Native American advocacy groups like the National Congress of American Indians (NCAI) and the Association on American Indian Affairs began to publish newsletters and guides on environmental issues, tracking a growing health crisis.[32] The NCAI also formed working groups like the National Indian Nuclear Waste Policy Committee to "promote environmental protection" in Indian country. In 1987 the NCAI signed a five-year cooperative agreement with the Office of Radioactive Waste Management of the Department of Energy to facilitate the sharing of information on "the siting and transportation of high-level radioactive nuclear waste."[33] However, some activists found the NCAI too accommodating with federal officials. In July 1990 Native Americans from twenty-three tribal communities gathered on the Navajo reservation for the first "toxics powwow," a conference called Protecting Mother Earth—The Toxic Threat to Indian Land; the conference was organized by the Indigenous Environmental Network (IEN) and the Navajo group Diné Citizens Against Ruining Our Environment (Diné CARE), assisted by Greenpeace. Regular meetings have since been held by groups like the National Tribal Environmental Council (NTEC), which formed in 1991 to assist tribal communities in protecting their environment. To help Native Americans fight against proposed nuclear storage or mining projects, other Native groups like the IEN have set up information networks providing environmental information, current regulations, and profiles of companies doing business with tribal officials.

The vicious pattern of environmental racism that unfolded during the 1960s and beyond impelled these Native American activists to participate in the 1991 First People of Color Environmental Leadership Summit. The Summit brought together over 300 Native, African, Latino, and Asian American delegates and a number of delegates from Canada, Central and South America and Puerto Rico, solidifying what one delegate called a "multiracial movement for change." Delegates identified the ways in which people of color suffered from environmental racism and articulated the need to fight that racism by championing respect for the natural world and politicizing organizations on a grassroots level.[34] In the end, they fashioned the "Principles of Environmental Justice," which has served as the ideational and spiritual foundation of the national environmental justice movement. The seventeen principles reflect the demands and philosophies of both urban and rural constituencies. Only one principle—number 11—explicitly focused on Native American issues, calling for the U.S. government to respect the treaties it signed with Indian nations and to "affirm the sovereignty and self-determination of the indigenous peoples whose land it occupies." But the first and last principles reflect the spiritual foundation that underlies Native activism. Number 1 emphasizes that "Environmental justice affirms the sacredness of Mother Earth, ecological unity and the interdependence of all species." Number 17 closes the statement by reinforcing a commitment to "Mother Earth" to "ensure the health of the natural world for present and future generations." The Preamble placed the general struggle in the context of "over 500 years of colonization and oppression resulting in the poisoning of our communities and land and the genocide of our peoples."[35]

Winona LaDuke emphasized this theme and an increasingly global perspective in her response to events marking the 500th anniversary of Columbus's "discovery" of America. In "We Are Still Here: The 500 Years Celebration," she contended that "the ecological agenda is what many indigenous people believe can, and must, unite all peoples in 1992. That agenda calls for everyone to take aggressive action to stop the destruction of the Earth, essentially to end the biological, technological, and ecological invasion/conquest that began with Columbus' ill-fated voyage 500 years ago.... It is this legacy of resistance that, perhaps more than any other single activity, denotes the essence of 1992."[36] Native Americans' increasingly pan-tribal perspective and concern about "radioactive colonialism"[37] also found expression at the World Uranium Hearing held in Salzburg, Austria in September 1992, at which men and women from around the world testified to the damage created by nuclear energy development. Native American activists offered several statements. Laguna Pueblo activist Gloria Lewis, who lived near one of the world's largest open-pit uranium mines, testified that the "Laguna people and tribal officials were never warned about the hazards and consequences of uranium mining on Indian lands. . . . This type of industrial genocide must stop, and as parents we have a responsibility to our children to make sure that this historic error of uranium development be taught in their schools." Laurie Goodman of the Diné (Navajo Nation) testified on behalf of Diné CARE, also focusing on the need for education to politicize tribal members to seek environmental justice. "Our lands are chosen, because our people are isolated and lack access to technical information.

Most have only a basic level of formal education and have little organized political opposition. . . . [E]ducation is needed for affected people to make informed decisions that determine their destiny."[38] This education would draw upon a new suite of painful environmental memories that revealed the intersection of racial prejudice, poverty, and what Carolyn Merchant called "the malignant side effects" of industrial capitalism.

Charles Lee has argued that "[p]eople of color [who] live in communities are not only targeted for the disposal of environmental toxins and hazardous waste but in fact live in fully disposable communities to be thrown away when the population they hold have outlived their usefulness."[39] Courts have sanctioned what activists call "spatial racism." For example, the Ninth Circuit Court of Appeals argued in 1985 that "Indian reservations may be considered as potential locations for hazardous waste disposal sites . . . because they are often remote from heavily populated areas."[40] This logic made Indian reservations a target of federal negotiators desperate to find a solution for a burgeoning quantity of nuclear and hazardous wastes. Their assiduous efforts to get Native communities to participate in the Monitored Retrievable Storage (MRS) program fueled concerted resistance by a new generation of Native activists who argued that mining and waste storage proposals constituted "environmental racism," a charge applied in particular by Native critics of the MRS program. These critics consider the efforts of Corporate America to dump waste on or mine toxic materials from their reservations as a form of ecocide that threatens human life. For example, Darelynn Lehto, vice president of the Prairie Island Mdewantkanton, opposed a MRS proposal, telling Minnesota state senators that "[i]t is the worst kind of environmental racism to force our tribe to live with the dangers of nuclear waste simply because no one else is willing to do so."[41]

In the 1990s Native American communities have considered but ultimately rejected proposals to place solid, hazardous, and nuclear waste landfills on their reservations; opponents have been aided by groups like the National Tribal Environmental Council (NTEC) and Indigenous Environmental Network. Grace Thorpe's lobbying effort through the National Environmental Coalition of Native Americans helped persuade New Mexico's congressional delegation to cut off funding for the MRS program. Thorpe, the daughter of the great Sac and Fox athlete Jim Thorpe, has become a leading opponent of economic development that threatens environmental damage. Like Lehto, she contested the argument made by advocates of waste storage projects who contend that Native Americans are best equipped to deal with industrial wastes because of their philosophy of stewardship. "The nuclear waste issue is causing American Indians to make serious environmental and possibly genocidal decisions regarding the future of our people. It is wrong to say that it is natural that we, as Native Americans, should accept radioactive waste on our lands, as the U.S. Department of Energy has said. It is a perversion of our beliefs and an insult to our intelligence to say that we are 'natural stewards' of these wastes."[42]

As in African American communities struggling for environmental justice, women have been leaders in this crusade for environmental justice, beginning with the women who risked beatings and jail defending treaty rights in the Pacific Northwest. Women of All Red Nations (WARN) grew out of the American Indian Movement in 1975 to focus on women's issues, linking the survival of Indianness to the protection of women's health in the face of the devastation caused by uranium mining and other assaults on Native environments.[43] In *The Death of Nature*, published in 1980, Carolyn Merchant acknowledged Native American women's activism against uranium mining, fitting it in a larger framework of women activists around the world from Love Canal "housewives" to women's participation in the Chipco movement in India.[44] And Jace Weaver noted that the majority of participants at the 1995 North American Native Workshop on Environmental Justice (which yielded the volume *Defending Mother Earth*) were women. Native women have been particularly active in leading opposition against nuclear waste dumps in the American West. Mescelaro Apache Rufina Marie Laws, aware of the Navajos' health problems, started Humans Against Nuclear Waste Dumps to oppose her tribal council's proposal to accept nuclear waste storage. Navajo Jane Yazzi voiced concern for future generations in protesting a proposed incinerator and dump on her reservation. "It's not just temporary, my children and grandchildren will have to live on this land forever."[45] Margene Bullcreek of the Goshute tribe has organized several protests against nuclear waste proposals, arguing, "We don't know what will happen years from now. As a traditionalist, we respect Mother Earth. We are doing this for future generations and our children."[46]

Campaigns for environmental justice in Native communities have had political and economic repercussions, dividing tribes and electorates between anti-dumping and anti-mining activists and those who believe that economic development trumps environmental protection because of endemic poverty. Even as groups like the Navajo Uranium Radiation Victims Committee and Navajo Nations Dependents of Uranium Workers Committee fought to secure justice for Native American uranium workers, energy companies once again sought to mine Navajo land for uranium. In the mid 1990s, the Texas-based company Hydro-Resources Incorporated proposed a new mining project near the Navajo community of Crownpoint. The legacy of the Navajos' experience with uranium mining has led to firm resistance from the Eastern Navajo Dine Against Uranium Mining, yet other Navajo supported the project's creation of jobs, thus dividing the community and even families.[47] Environmental justice, when it is achieved, can come with significant costs. For example, the Navajo Nation voted on July 25, 2003, to prohibit Peabody Western Coal Co. from accessing the Navajo Aquifer for its mining operations, but the decision could cost the Hopi Nation $7.7 million and the Navajo Nation $30 million in operating expenses, roughly one-third of each nation's tribal budget. And each tribal government would have to fire over one hundred employees, adding to the 228 Indian employees laid off from the mine, provided that Peabody could not locate a different water source.[48] Thus economic justice proposals will continue to compete with environmental justice agendas for the votes of politicians and citizens alike.

In addition to fighting environmental racism and protecting reservation environments for future generations, Native American activists have offered a timely critique of industrial society. They have called on their tribal councils to limit corporate control of reservation resources and to consider sustainable nonextractive energy production through solar and wind power projects. Laurie Goodman, a member of the Navajo group Citizens Against Ruining Our Environment, testified at the 1992 World Uranium Hearing in favor of spiritually sound and environmentally safe economic development. "Our people are being sacrificed to satisfy America's need for ever more energy. . . . Why should we sacrifice our land, culture and future generations so that the dominant society can continue to live a lifestyle that demands and depletes our resources? Viable alternatives which are cleaner, safer and cheaper are available."[49] Various tribes have pushed the development of wind and solar energy, which is cleaner and considerably less invasive than coal or uranium mining. For example, as Peter Asmus relates, "some traditional Hopi . . . revere the spiritual power of the earth so greatly that they refuse to allow infrastructure such as power lines to scar the land. Photovoltaic [solar] panels offer a solution that satisfies both ancient cultural practices and future needs."[50] A number of other Native communities have started to fund wind power projects, including several tribes that had rejected waste dumping proposals in the early 1990s. Native communities like the Hopi have other reasons to oppose invasive mining operations—those tribes that have contributed significant energy resources to fuel the expansion of industrial America have not only borne the brunt of industrial pollution but have been neglected in terms of access to electricity. As a young Hopi put it during the 1970s, "Don't tell me about an energy crisis. I don't even have electricity in my village."[51] A. David Lester, the executive director of the Council of Energy Resource Tribes, the principal Native American organization focused on energy development, noted that in the year 2000 "Indian Tribes own significant energy and water resources that produce electric power for millions of other Americans. Tribes have borne a disproportionate share of the burden from energy development, yet are among those who benefit least from it."[52] Wind and solar projects have the potential of both preserving the integrity of reservation land and improving Native Americans' access to electricity.

Native activists and thinkers, while rejecting the argument that Native

Americans are "natural stewards" of industrial wastes, do embrace the notion that their traditions have meaning for America and the world. As Grace Thorpe asserted, "We cannot shirk our responsibilities for protecting the land, for protecting the waters and for protecting the air. . . . We, the Indian people, must set an example for the rest of the nation."[53] Environmental stories are not "some romanticized falsification of Native memory," George Tinker writes, but components of a theology of survival. "What I have suggested implicitly is that American Indian peoples may have something of value—something corrective to Western values and the modern world system—to offer to the world. . . . What I am most passionately arguing is that we must commit to the struggle for the just and moral survival of Indian peoples as peoples of the earth, and that this struggle is for the sake of the earth and for the sustaining of all of life."[54] Europeans first and Americans after them have developed and commodified romantic notions of Native Americans—the Noble Savage, the tearful environmentalist, the "natural steward." Native Americans ask non-Indians to take seriously the message of limits that is at the core of their environmental philosophies. When Hopi traditionalists were forced to fight for environmental justice in the U.S. court system by filing suit against the Peabody Coal Company, they issued a statement amounting to a clarion call for concerted resistance to all forms of environmental devastation. "We should not have had to go this far [working in "the white man's courts"]. Our words have not been heeded. This might be the last chance. We can no longer watch as our sacred lands are wrested from our control, as our spiritual center disintegrates. We cannot allow our control over our spiritual homelands to be taken from us. The hour is already very late."[55]

ACKNOWLEDGEMENTS

I want to thank my ever patient and supportive family—my wife Debra and my two most excellent boys, Maxwell and Casey. In addition, many thanks to the Villanova University Department of History for its 2004 Summer Research Grant, which supported archival research in Native American environmental activism.

NOTES

1. Kathy Helms, "Victims of Nuclear Fallout Tell Their Stories," *Gallup Independent*, May 21, 2004. http://www.gallupindependent.com/052004victims.html
2. Jace Weaver, ed., *Defending Mother Earth: Native American perspectives on environmental justice* (Maryknoll, N.Y.: Orbis Books, 1996), pp. 47–48. For inter-

views of Navajo miners, see "Memories Come To Us in the Rain and the Wind," http://www.inmotionmagazine.com/brugge.html. See also Peter Eichstaedt, *If You Poison Us: Uranium and Native Americans* (Sante Fe: Red Crane Books, 1994).

3. Weaver, p. 107.

4. Gail Small and Lance Hughes, "War Stories," *The Amicus Journal*, Spring 1994 v. 16 n. 1: 38. See also Winona LaDuke, *All Our Relations: Native Struggles for Land and Life* (Cambridge, Mass.: South End Press, 1999), Ch. 4: "Northern Cheyenne: A Fire in the Coal Fields."

5. Dean B. Suagee, "Environmental Justice and Indian Country, *Human Rights*, Fall 2003, v30, n. 4: 16. See also Tom B.K. Goldtooth, "Indigenous Nations: Summary of Sovereignty and Its Implications for Environmental Protection." In Bunyan Bryant, *Environmental Justice: Issues, Policies, and Solutions* (Washington, DC: Island Press, 1995).

6. Quoted in LaDuke, *All Our Relations*, p. 97.

7. Ulla Lehtinen, "Environmental Racism: The US Nuclear Industry and Native Americans," *The Ecologist*, March–April 1997 v. 27 n. 2: 44.

8. Amanda Siestreem and Paul Rowley, "An Interview with Sayo': Kla Kindness: An Oneida Woman Talks About Mining," *Cultural Survival Quarterly*, v. 25 no. 1, 2001: 2.

9. George Tinker, "An American Indian Theological Response to Ecojustice," in Weaver, *Defending Mother Earth*, p. 164.

10. Joni Adamson et al., eds., *The Environmental Justice Reader: Politics, Poetics, and Pedagogy* (Tucson, AZ: The University of Arizona Press, 2002), p. 20.

11. Bobby Lake to Supervisor, Humboldt County, Agricultural Commission, April 5, 1978. National Congress of American Indians papers. National Anthropological Archives, Suitland, MD. Box 231. Folder: NCAI Special Issues, Natural Resources, Environmental Issues.

12. Devon G. Pena, "Endangered Landscapes and Disappearing Peoples?: Identity, Place, and Community in Ecological Politics," p. 65. In Adamson et al., eds. Also see Pena's book *Tierra y vida: Mexican Americans and the Environment.* (Tucson: University of Arizona Press, 2002).

13. Pena, p. 72

14. Pena, p. 73.

15. Pena, p. 75.

16. For coverage see Fay G. Cohen, *Treaties on Trial: The Continuing Controversy over Northwest Fighting Rights* (Seattle: University of Washington Press, 1986); and Charles Wilkinson, *Messages from Frank's Landing: A Story of Salmon, Treaties, and the Indian Way* (Seattle: University of Washington Press, 2003).

17. "Statement by Sid Mills," *The Renegade*, May 1969, p. 10. Princeton University Western Americana Collection, Firestone Library.

18. Francis Paul Prucha, ed. *Documents of United States Indian Policy* (Lincoln: University of Nebraska Press, 2000), p. 269.

19. On March 8, 1974, Fred and Mike Tribble of the Lac Courte Oreilles Chippewa band were arrested by officials of Wisconsin's Department of Natural Resources for spearfishing on Chief Lake in violation of state conservation laws. Their arrest was just one of dozens of cases where Chippewa had been detained. But

this arrest triggered a lawsuit by the Lac Court Oreilles band, which claimed that treaties permitted off-reservation spearfishing. The suit named as a defendant Lester Voight, the director of Wisconsin's DNR. In what is called the Voight Decision, Judge James Doyle of the U.S. District Court ruled in 1978 against the Chippewa. But in January 1983 a U.S. Court of Appeals overturned the decision, determining, as Judge Boldt had, that nineteenth century treaties were still valid legal documents. For coverage of these events, see Larry Nesper, *The Walleye War: The Struggle for Ojibwe Spearfishing and Treaty* Rights (Lincoln: University of Nebraska Press, 2002); and Rick Whaley with Walter Bressette, *Walleye Warriors: An Effective Alliance Against Racism and for the Earth* (Philadelphia: New Society Publishers, 1994).

20. "The Importance of Salmon to the Tribes," Columbia River Inter-tribal Fisheries Commission, http://www.critfc.org/main.html. See also Donald Sampson, "Message from the Executive Director," Columbia River Inter-tribal Fisheries Commission, http://www.critfc.org/main.html

21. Andy Fernando, "Introduction," p. xxv. In Fay G. Cohen. *Treaties on Trial: The Continuing Controversy over Northwest Fishing Rights.*

22. (Lucia Mouat, "Leader Pushes for Indian Sense of Identity,") *The Christian Science Monitor*, July 9, 1990. French explorers named one band of Chippewa the Lac du Flambeau, or Torch Lake, because they noticed its members fishing for walleye at night with torches.

23. Zoltan Grossman and Al Gedicks, "Native Resistance to Multinational Mining Corporations in Wisconsin," *Cultural Survival Quarterly* 25, no. 1 (Spring 2001): 4. On the Crandon Mine controversy, see Al Gedicks, *The New Resource Wars: Native and Environmental Struggles against Multinational Corporations* (Boston: South End Press, 1993).

24. *Myths and Techno-Fantasies* ("The first publication of the Black Mesa Defense Fund."), p. 6. Princeton University Western Americana Collection, Firestone Library.

25. "The Time of the Great Purification: As Spoken by Hopi Elders to Jack Loeffler," *Myths and Techno-Fantasies*, p. 6.

26. Ibid., p. 11. Loeffler closes: "And so it would seem that the Hopis know intuitively what our culture learns only in retrospect—that man is a part of Nature and must live within the limits of necessity."

27. "The Black Mesa Navajo Speak," *Black Mesa Fact Sheet*, February 14, 1970, pp. 8–9. In *Rainbow People*, no date, no volume. Princeton University Western Americana Collection, Firestone Library. See also "Navajo Way Threatened: Economic Development or Colonialism," p. 8. Kathy Hall examines Black Mesa in "Impacts of the Energy Industry on the Navajo and Hopi" in Robert D. Bullard, ed., *Unequal Protection: Environmental Justice and Communities of Color* (San Francisco: Sierra Club Books, 1994).

28. *Birney Arrow*, July 26, 1970. The *Birney Arrow* was published on the Northern Cheyenne reservation, one of a growing number of reservation newspapers. Princeton University Western Americana Collection, Firestone Library.

29. In negotiating the Navajo and Pueblo leases the Bureau of Indian Affairs failed to secure provisions for company cleanup of the sites after the mining operations ceased. And federal inspectors found numerous violations in the mines themselves

that added to Indian miners' health risks. For coverage of these issues see Ward Churchill, *Struggle for the Land: Indigenous Resistance to Genocide, Ecocide, and Expropriation in Contemporary America* (Monroe, Maine: Common Courage Press, 1993). Leslie Marmon Silko places uranium mining at the center of "the witchery" in *Ceremony*, the product of her memories of the radioactive Laguna Pueblo reservation.

30. See Donald Grinde and Bruce Johansen, *Ecocide of Native America: Environmental Destruction of Indian Lands and Peoples* (Santa Fe, N.M.: Clear Light Publishers, 1995), pp. 211–13.

31. Navajo and Pueblo efforts to secure compensation for their miners culminated in July 2000, when President William Clinton signed into law the Radiation Exposure Compensation Act (RECA) Amendment Act of 2000. In announcing the program, Energy Secretary Bill Richardson said, "Justice for our nuclear workers is finally happening. The government for a change is on their side and not against them." http://www.navajoboy.com/ARTUS.HTM

32. For example, the Association on American Indian Affairs began publishing the bulletin "Indian Natural Resources" in the mid 1970s. Its February 1979 issue covered the efforts of Navajo miners to secure compensation for illness and death. See "Uranium Miners Seek Compensation," pp. 1–2. Princeton University Western Americana Collection, Firestone Library. NCAI records are found in the Smithsonian's National Anthropological Archives, Suitland, Maryland. See in particular Box 231 and Box 240.

33. See *NCAI News*, December 1987. In "NCAI Bulletin," Princeton University Western Americana Collection, Firestone Library.

34. For coverage of the summit see Karl Grossman, "The People of Color Environmental Summit," in Robert D. Bullard, ed., *Unequal Protection: Environmenal Justice and Communities of Color* (San Francisco, Sierra Club Books, 1994). A 1987 report entitled "Toxic Wastes and Race in the United States" concluded that nearly half of Native Americans and Pacific Islanders lived in a community with a toxic waste site. See Benjamin F. Chavis, Jr., and Charles Lee, eds., "Toxic Wastes and Race in the United States: A National Report on the Racial and Socio-Economic Characteristics of Communities with Hazardous Waste Sites" (New York: Commission for Racial Justice, United Church of Christ, 1987); see also Benjamin A. Goldman and Laura Fitton, "Toxic Wastes and Race Revisited: An Update of the 1987 Report on the Racial and Socio-Economic Characteristics of Communities with Hazardous Waste Sites" (Washington, D.C.: Center for Policy Alternatives, 1994). For coverage of multiracial environmental coalitions, see Dorceta Taylor, "Environmentalism and the Politics of Inclusion," in Robert Bullard, ed., *Confronting Environmental Racism: Voices from the Grassroots* (Boston: South End Press, 1993). See also "In Defense of Mother Earth: The Indigenous Environmental Network" in Luke Cole and Sheila Foster, *"From the Ground Up": Environmental Racism and the Rise of the Environmental Justice Movement* (New York: New York University Press, 2001).

35. Printed in Giovanna Di Chiro, "Nature as Community: The Convergence of Environmental Social Justice," In William Cronon, ed., *Uncommon Ground: Rethinking the Human Place in Nature* (New York: Norton, 1996), pp. 307–309. See http://www.ejrc.cau.edu/summit2/IndianCountry.pdf for data on the Second National People of Color Environmental Leadership Summit.

36. Winona LaDuke, "We Are Still Here: The 500 Years Celebration," *Sojourners*, October 1991. Available at http://www.ratical.org/ratville/AoS/500yrsNukes.html LaDuke listed various organizations actively resisting industrial activity on indigenous lands, such as CONAIE (Confederation of Indigenous Nationalities of Ecuador), SAIIC (South and Central American Indian Information Center), the Indigenous Women's Network, Seventh Generation Fund, and the International Indian Treaty Council.

37. See Ward Churchill and Winona LaDuke, "Native North America: The Political Economy of Radioactive Colonialism," in M. Annette Jaimes, ed., *The State of Native America: Genocide, Colonization, and Resistance* (Boston: South End Press, 1992).

38. No author. "Testimonies, Lectures, Conclusions. The World Uranium Hearing, Salzburg 1992." See http://www.ratical.com/radiation/WorldUraniumHearing/GloriaLewis.txt; and http://www.ratical.org/radiation/WorldUraniumHearing/LaurieGoodman.txt

39. Charles Lee, "Urban Environmental Justice," *Earth Island Journal*, Spring 1993: 41.

40. Weaver, p. 109.

41. Quoted in Grace Thorpe, "Our Homes Are Not Dumps: Creating Nuclear-Free Zones," in Weaver, p. 51.

42. No author. "Pauite-Shoshone Overwhelming [sic] Oppose Nuclear Storage at Ft. McDermitt." *The Circle*, October 31, 1994: 36.

43. See in this volume Nancy Unger's excellent essay, "Gendered Approaches to Environmental Justice: An Historical Sampling," which includes coverage of WARN. Celene Krauss examines the role of women in environmental justice campaigns in "Women of Color on the Front Line," in *Unequal Protection: Environmental Justice and Communities of Color.*

44. Carolyn Merchant, *The Death of Nature: Women, Ecology and the Scientific Revolution* (NY: Harper Collins, 1980), p. xv.

45. Quoted in Grace Thorpe, "No Nuclear Waste on Indian Land," in Alvin Josephy, et al., *Red Power: The American Indians' Fight for Freedom*, 2nd edition (Lincoln: University of Nebraska Press, 1999), p. 163.

46. "Leavitt Reiterates Opposition to Nuclear Waste Storage," *Ojibwe News*, June 6, 1997.

47. For data and documents on this controversy visit: http://www.sric.org/endaum/index.html

48. Sean Patrick Reily, "Gathering Clouds: Arizona's Navajo and Hopi Tribes Have Won a Water-Rights Battle Against the Coal Company That Has Sustained Their Fragile Economies." The Los Angeles Times, June 6, 2004 (accessed at http://www.angelfire.com/ca6/senaawest/bmwater/gathering.html. For other examples of this conflict between economic development and environmental protection see Paul C. Rosier, *Native American Issues* (Westport, Conn.: Greenwood Press, 2003), ch. 6.

49. http://www.ratical.org/radiation/WorldUraniumHearing/LaurieGoodman.txt

50. Peter Asmus. "Landscapes of Power: Can Renewable Energy Help Native Americans Reclaim Their Resources." *The Amicus Journal*, Winter 1998: 13.

51. Quoted in Donald Fixico, *The Invasion of Indian Country in the Twentieth Century* (Niwot: University Press of Colorado, 1998), p. 145.

52. Council or Energy Resource Tribes. "Indian Energy 2001: Energy Solutions." http://www.certredearth.com/fall01/energy.shtml. The Department of Energy supported Lester's claim. "Household energy availability and use on Indian lands are significantly below that of non-Indian households. In fact sizable Indian populations have no access to electricity at all. This perpetuates a low standard of living, as energy supply and economic well-being are closely linked." See Department of Energy, "Energy Consumption and Renewable Energy Development Potential on Indian Lands, April 2000." http://www.eia.doe.gov/cneaf/solar.renewables/ilands/introduction.html

53. Grace Thorpe, "No Nuclear Waste on Indian Land," p. 163.

54. Tinker, p. 172.

55. No author. "Hopis Sue U.S." *Warpath*, v. 4. n. 6 (circa 1970). Princeton University Western Americana Collection, Firestone Library. In the same issue see also Ed McGaa (Eagle Man), "Rediscover Mother Earth: The Dilemma of the Non-Indian World."

4

"My Soul Looked Back"

Environmental Memories of the African in America, 1600–2000

Sylvia Hood Washington

> *Lord, I've been 'buked and I've been scorned*
> *And I've been talked 'bout as sure as you're born*
> *And my soul looked back and wondered*
> *How I got over, my Lord*
>
> —Negro Spiritual

Looking back through the memories of my childhood in the 1960s in Cleveland, Ohio my mind is filled with images of the mountainous piles of trash that lined the main roads which brought you into my racially segregated quasi suburban African American community. These piles of trash did not belong to the members of my community's but rather it was the trash of "others," both black and white, who felt that this part of Cleveland and this neighborhood was the right place to dispose of their trash. As Norm Krumholz, a senior urban planning professor at Cleveland State University, recently reminded me, my childhood community has always had (since the 1960s) the highest income level in the city of Cleveland, Ohio. Despite their economic prosperity, the continuous complaints of this community to city hall about this environmental nightmare was virtually ignored for decades. This non-response however did not halt or hamper the demands of their political and civic leaders for an environmentally salient geographical space. The majority of residents in this area were considered "middle class" African

Americans and they had voluntarily fled the polluted environment of the city.

With manicured lawns and massive flower gardens residents struggled mentally and physically with externally induced environmental inequities that they tried to control and manage on their own until the city finally took action. Their problem with the inequitable policy of garbage disposal in their community as well as with other environmental problems was tied to the fact that they existed in what Kishi Animashaun describes in her essay as a "racialized space" despite their economic prosperity. Their fight for environmental equality, elucidated in greater detail in this collection's essay, "Wadin in the Water" was typical of other environmental justice struggles faced by African American communities across the country that emerged in the latter of the twentieth century.

From the Middle Passage to the new millennium, the environmental memories of the African in America are ones that elucidate a continuous struggle against a persistent pattern of severe environmental inequalities with morbid or mortal consequences in "racialized spaces." For four hundred years, these memories of and about Africans in America inform us that they were continuously packed into dense and many times deadly geographical spaces which they had little or no control over for generations . Over the course of several generations African American communities would be used as the "ultimate sink" for America's waste in every sense, both social and physical. Across the country their geographical spaces would act as society's catch basin for vice, garbage and finally toxic substances.[1] Their environmental memories are also filled with recollections of marginalized "built" environments which contributed to or exacerbated their public health problems such as inadequate sewers, lead contaminated homes, sick buildings, and massive transportation highways which constantly spewed combustion products into their air space. The direct consequence of environmental inequalities then and now has manifested itself in the form of disproportionate public health and environmental health problems among African Americans like typhoid fever, cholera, the "White Plague," asthma, high cancer rates, miscarriages, genetic deformities and learning disabilities.

The claim of morbid marginalized living environments by African Americans or their supporters, as a direct consequence of their socially constructed race, started in at least the seventeenth century. The condition of environmental inequality in American communities of African descent is a lasting legacy that began with the inhuman conditions of the Middle Passage.[2] They would again encounter environmental inequalities on New World slave plantations which they were forcibly constrained to occupy for more than two hundred years. This history of being forcibly confined to degraded environmental spaces for the vast majority of African Americans in America continued after their liberation from slavery and throughout the Reconstruction period. This historical pattern of environmental inequality and disproportionate environmental health problems among African Americans also continued into the twentieth century even after millions fled their former plantations and sharecropping communities of the South. Fleeing from a socially and racially oppressive agrarian South, African American migrants flocked into America's Northern and Midwestern urban industrialized cities in search of a better life both economically and socially.

In the two "Great Migrations" to these regions, which occurred in the first half of the twentieth century, migrating African Americans found themselves literally packed into environmentally marginalized spaces that had devastating impacts on their health.[3] African American migrants entering these urban spaces during this time period would experience inordinately high mortality and morbidity rates from typhoid fever and tuberculosis as a direct consequence of environmental inequalities produced by legal, race-based zoning and restrictive covenants.[4] Unable to escape the ghettos produced by raced based policies until almost the last quarter of the twentieth century, African Americans in cities like Chicago, Cleveland, and New York fought to overcome or minimize the environmental threats that existed in these communities. African Americans seeking environmental relief had to wait until the real enforcement of the country's 1968 Fair Housing Act which allowed them to escape to "whiter" and "cleaner" environmental spaces.

The primary objective of this essay is to provide an overview of the long-term cognition and memory of environmental degradation and environmental inequalities of African Americans, their observers, and their supporters. This environmental cognition has been reflected in the speeches or writings of renowned African American leaders like Booker T. Washington, W.E.B. Dubois, the Reverend Dr. Martin Luther King, and Reverend Jesse Jackson; as well as in the memoirs of escaped slaves and enslaved Africans.[5] This essay although admittedly not exhaustive will provide a glimpse into how the environmental inequalities that African Americans faced were perceived by themselves or interested observers for more than four hundred years.[6]

The environmental memories of and about Africans in Americas for this essay have been drawn from a mélange of first person narratives, biographies, autobiographies, and literature beginning with the Middle Passage and concluding with contemporary memories of environmental racism. Although the vast majority of these documents are primarily focused on their socio-economic and/or political condition of the African in America, they also contain small windows into their environmental conditions. These environmental conditions are sometimes explicitly described but in some instances they are implied since there seems to be an explicit assumption in some of these documents that Africans in America were completely and totally disenfranchised in all facets of life. History shows that the environmental experiences and memories of the African in America were not uniform, however, the overwhelming environmental experience for most of them were in no way equal to the first European colonists and subsequent European immigrants in America.

This historical pattern of environmental marginalization began with brutal conditions of the slave ships that existed in the West African holding pens and in the Middle Passage's slave ships. Unlike indigenous and First World people the majority of Africans who originally came to America in the seventeenth century came by force and were viciously torn from their own indigenous and natural environment by fellow countrymen. A large percentage of the captured Africans bound for slavery perished on the inland trek to the Slave Coast, since they were forced to walk hundreds of miles by their captors in the most inhuman fashion. Historians have now concluded that "Half of the more than 20 million Africans captured and sold into slavery never even made it to the ship."[7] The brutal conditions were described in 1738, by the English slave trader Francis Moore who stated, "Their way of bringing them is, tying them by the neck with leather tongs, at about a yard distance from each other, thirty or forty in a string, having generally a bundle of corn, or an elephants tooth upon each of their heads."[8]

The Middle Passage was the second part of the three legged route of the Atlantic Slave Trade that began with a route from Europe to Africa, a route from Africa to the Americas, and terminated with a route from the Americas to Europe.[9] Spanish slave traders during the beginning of the formalized Atlantic Slave Trade estimated that up to forty percent of the slave cargo would perish on route to the New World primarily because of the unsanitary conditions that the slaves were subjected to during the Middle Passage and because of rampant communicable diseases which went unchecked and untreated during their transport.[10] Scholars now estimate that 1 million to 2.2 million slaves perished during the Middle Passage.[11]

Most of the recalled environmental memories of the Middle Passage by enslaved Africans, their captors, or observers depict absolutely cruel conditions that were unfit even for most beasts of burden. These environmental conditions are described in detail in the classic and often cited first-person description of the Middle Passage by the formerly enslaved Olaudah Equiano, a citizen of the Ibo country near Benin in what is today's Nigeria. Olaudah's autobiography, *The Interesting Narrative of the Life of Olaudah Equiano or Gustavas Vasa, The African,* published in 1791 informs the reader that the enslaved Africans bound to the New World were packed into the bowels of the slave ships so that that the "the whole ship's cargo were confined together . . . [becoming] absolutely pestilential. . . . The closeness of the place and the heat of the climate added to the number of the ship which

was so crowded that each had scarcely room to turn himself almost suffo-
cated us. This produced copious perspirations so that the air became unfit
for respiration . . . and brought on a sickness amongst the slaves, of which
many died."[12]

These same deadly environmental conditions are also described by the
European surgeon, Alexander Falconbridge, who was forced to work on the
slave ships. Falconbridge's narrative points out that "the exclusion of the
fresh air is among the most intolerable. For the purpose of admitting this
needful refreshment, most of the ships in the slave trade are provided,
between the decks, with five or six airports on each side of the ship, of about
six inches in length, and four in breadth; in addition to which, some few
ships, but not one in twenty, have what they denominate wind-sails. But
whenever the sea is rough and the rain heavy, it becomes necessary to shut
these, and every other conveyance by which the air is admitted. The fresh air
being thus excluded, the Negroes' rooms very soon grow intolerably hot.
The confined air, rendered noxious by the effluvia exhaled from their bodies,
and by being repeatedly breathed, soon produces fevers and fluxes, which
generally carries off great numbers of them."[13] Falconbridge also points out
in his description that the lack of air wasn't the only environmental problem
that Africans faced on the Middle Passages that was beyond the "human
imagination." The deck area "that is the floor of their rooms, was so covered
with the blood and mucus which had proceeded from them in consequence
of the flux, that it resembled a slaughter-house."[14] These environmental conditions according to Falconbridge contributed to epidemics and high mortality rates among the African cargo.

Africans surviving these horrific conditions of the slave march and the
Middle Passage ended up living and working in marginalized and deadly
environmental conditions in a New World.[15] Their environment in the
United States would again be one that they had and still have very little "ultimate" control over because of who they were or how they were classified:
chattel property, subhuman and social undesirables. More than likely they
found themselves on a slave plantation or working in industries that in many
cases exposed them to another set of marginalized environmental conditions
that could prove just as deadly as the Middle Passage.

The brutal and hostile environmental conditions that enslaved Africans
encountered both in the Middle Passage and on the continent for several
hundred years was directly tied to several European philosophies that articulated them as either non-humans or sub-human heathens who more expend-
able than either the European or the Native American (or Indian).[16] Carolyn
Merchant points out her in essay on environmental justice that "African
Americans presented more difficult problems for European colonizers than
did Indians. Although both Indians and blacks were regarded as savage, Africans and Indians were constructed differently and treated differently.

Although Indians were of a different color than whites, white-black differences seemed more pronounced than those between Indians and whites."[17]

An example of this racialized environmental distinction was the efforts of the Mexican Viceroy, Marques de Villamanrique in 1586 to protect the Indians from the dangerous work of the copper and gold mines. The Viceroy asked the Spanish government for the additional importation of three to four thousand African slaves, even though both groups suffered from high mortality rates caused by lung cancer diseases and industrial accidents tied to hostile environmental conditions of the mining industry. Within three years of the viceroy's request he "recommended that all free blacks and mulattoes (children of Spaniards and blacks) in the colony be forced to labor in the mines . . . as a substitute for Indian workers."[18] African slaves working on the Spanish and Portuguese sugar plantations in the Americas had mortality rates as high if not higher than those who had been forced to work in the gold and copper mines. They too replaced Indian workers because "The Crown did not take kindly to the use of Indians on the sugar plantations."[19] Scholar Winthrop D. Jordan in his seminal work, *White over Black, American Attitudes Toward the Negro, 1550–1812* points out that the English colonies (in America) embrace of permanent slavery for Africans by the end of the seventeenth was undoubtedly influenced by their frequent exposure to the practices in Hispaniola.[20]

The environmental conditions of the rice plantations in the United States were the most lethal for African American slaves. Slaves working the rice plantations in America were exposed to numerous environmental hazards that included but were not limited to snakes, alligators, extreme heat, and constant moisture. According to the contemporary observer of these conditions, Captain Basil Hall "[Rice] is the most unhealthy work in which the slaves were employed, and they sank under it in great numbers. The causes of this dreadful mortality are the constant moisture and heat of the atmosphere, together with the alternate floodings and dryings of the fields, on which the negroes are perpetually at work, often ankle deep in mud, with their bare heads exposed to the fierce rays of the sun."[21]

Africans were generally described as being more apelike and as heathens by Europeans both before and during the Atlantic Slave Trade and their environmental degradation was indisputably impacted by these stereotypes. Third-party observers of African slaves in America at this time frequently described them as "being treated as if [they] had no soul."[22] This prevalent and longstanding attitude toward people of African descent hung over American society for centuries and explains the descriptions of the marginalized environmental conditions on many of the plantations by former slaves during the antebellum and postbellum periods. In 1841 nineteen-year-old Francis Henderson, an escaped slave from a plantation outside of Washington D.C., gave the following description of living conditions on his former plantation: "Our houses were but log huts—the tops [were] partly open—

and rain would come through. My aunt was quite an old woman, and had been sick several years. In rains I have seen her moving from one part of the house to the other, and rolling her bedclothes about to try to keep dry—everything would be dirty and muddy. I lived in the house with my aunt. My bed and bedstead consisted of a board wide enough to sleep on—one end on a stool, the other placed near the fire. My pillow consisted of my jacket—my covering was whatever I could get. My bedtick was the board itself."[23]

Several decades later Jacob Stroyer (a former slave who was born in 1849 on a plantation twenty-eight miles from Columbia, South Carolina) stated in an oral history interview that on his plantation the housing for slaves were built for two families. This housing however was not sufficient to protect the slaves from the natural elements, forcing many to seek shelter or relief outside of the structure. According to Stroyer the slaves could not "sleep in their cabins in summer, when it was so very warm. When it was too warm for them to sleep comfortably, they all slept under trees until it grew too cool, that is along in the month of October. Then they took up their beds and walked."[24]

Josiah Henson, the escaped slave whose memories provided author Harriet Beecher Stowe with the model of Uncle Tom, also provides a description of marginalized environmental living conditions for slaves. Henson spent thirty years on a plantation in Montgomery County, Maryland before becoming a Methodist preacher, abolitionist, lecturer, and founder of a cooperative colony of former slaves in Canada. According to Henson's memoirs the slaves were

"lodged in log huts, and on the bare ground. Wooden floors were an unknown luxury. In a single room were huddled, like cattle, ten or a dozen persons, men, women, and children. All ideas of refinement and decency were, of course, out of the question. We had neither bedsteads, nor furniture of any description. Our beds were collections of straw and old rags, thrown down in the corners and boxed in with boards; a single blanket the only covering. Our favourite way of sleeping, however, was on a plank, our heads raised on an old jacket and our feet toasting before the smouldering fire. The wind whistled and the rain and snow blew in through the cracks, and the damp earth soaked in the moisture till the floor was miry as a pig sty. Such were our houses. In these wretched hovels were we penned at night, and fed by day; here were the children born and the sick—neglected."[25]

The environmental conditions of slave quarters given in the testimony of the former slave Theodore Dwight Weld to the American Anti-Slavery Society was more detailed but consistent with that of Henson's and Stroyer's. Weld stated in his testimony that:[26]

The huts of the slaves are mostly of the poorest kind. They are not as good as those temporary shanties which are thrown up beside railroads. They are erected with posts and crotches, with but little or no frame-work about them. They have no stoves or chimneys; some of them have something like a fireplace at one end, and a board or two off at that side, or on the roof, to let off the smoke. Others have nothing like a fireplace in them; in these the fire is sometimes made in the middle of the hut. These buildings have but one apartment in them; the places where they pass in and out, serve both for doors and windows; the sides and roofs are covered with coarse, and in many instances with refuse boards. In warm weather, especially in the spring, the slaves keep up a smoke, or fire and smoke, all night, to drive away the gnats and musketoes, which are very troublesome in all the low country of the south; so much so that the whites sleep under frames with nets over them, knit so fine that the musketoes cannot fly through them.

Some of the slaves have rugs to cover them in the coldest weather, but I should think *more have not.* During driving storms they frequently have to run from one hut to another for shelter. In the coldest weather, where they can get wood or stumps, they keep up fires all night in their huts, and lay around them, with their feet towards the blaze. Men, women and children all lie down together, in most instances.

Weld pointed out in his testimony that there could have been exceptions to his encounters and experiences with the environmental conditions faced by slaves but his observations were based on his own experience and personal observations of plantations in Georgia and South Carolina. According to Weld, slaves were packed into housing structures that provided them little protection from the natural elements and disease vectors like mosquitoes. Weld stated that:[27]

> [slave] huts are generally built compactly on the plantations, forming villages of huts, their size proportioned to the number of slaves on them. In these miserable huts the poor blacks are herded at night like swine, *without any conveniences of bedsteads, tables or chairs.* O misery to the full! to see the aged sire beating off the swarms of gnats and musketoes in the warm weather, and shivering in the straw, or bending over a few coals in the winter, clothed in rags. . . . God alone knows how much the poor slaves suffer for the want of convenient houses to secure them from the piercing winds and howling storms of winter, especially the aged, sick and dying. Although it is much warmer there than here . . . I suffered for a number of weeks in the winter, almost as much in Georgia as I do in Massachusetts.

This recollection of severe and life-threatening living environments was again echoed in the testimony of the one-hundred-year-old former slave Richard Carruthers during the Depression era WPA Oral History Project.[28] According to Carruthers "the boss men had good homes but the niggers had log cabins and they burned down oftentimes. The chimney would catch fire 'cause it was made of sticks and clay and moss. Many the time we have to get up at midnight and push the chimney away from the house to keep the house from burnin'up."[29]

The recollection of the environmental conditions which characterized American slavery by the British actress, Fanny Kemble, are consistent with those of the former slaves. Kimble's memories were based on her experiences as a slave mistress on one of the largest rice plantations in the United States. Kemble was married to Pierce Butler, a member of the elite, in 1836 and her observations came from her first-hand encounters with slaves on Butler Island. In 1838 she would make the following observations about the plantation's slave infirmary:[30]

> Buried in tattered and filth blankets . . . here, in their hour of sickness, lay those whose health and strength are spent in unrequited labor for us . . . here lay some burning with fever, others aching with rheumatism, upon the hard, cold ground—here they lay like brute beasts. . . . Now pray take notice that this is supposed to be the hospital of an estate where the owners are supposed to be humane and the negroes remarkably cared for.
>
> Such of these dwellings as I visited today were filthy and wretched in the extreme. . . . Instead of the order, neatness and ingenuity which might convert even these miserable hovels into tolerable residences, there was the reckless, filthy indolence which even the brutes do not exhibit in their lairs and nests.

The marginalized environmental conditions for African Americans persisted after slavery ended and some of the former slaves who participated in the WPA oral history project asserted that their housing and overall living conditions were actually worse after they were freed than before the Civil War. George Simon a seventy-four-year-old former slave who was a child during slavery told his WPA interviewers that he thought that "the Negro was better off during slavery than now. Then someone always look after them, plenty to eat, enough clothes and a sleeping place, with a doctor around when he needed one."[31] A similar conclusion was articulated to the interviewers by the ninety-one-year-old former slave Liza Smith who was eighteen years old when the Civil War ended. According to Liza the slaves on her plantation were much better off before the Civil War ended because they "was kept clean and always wid plenty to eat and good clothes to wear. . . ." After freedom the former slaves according to Liza were marginalized because "den times was so hard nobody wanted us many Negroes around, and de work was scarce, too. Hard times!"[32]

A similar and more detailed assertion that environmental conditions for former slaves had worsened after the Civil War came from James Lucas. Lucas had been a former slave of the Confederate president, Jefferson Davis. before he took the presidential office of the Confederacy. Lucas, who admitted that he admired Davis, claimed "After de War was over de slaves was worse off den when dey had marsters. Some of 'em was put in stockades at

Angola, Louisiana and some in de terrible corral at Natchez. Dey weren't used to de stuff de Yankees fed 'em. . . . Dey caught diseases and died by de hundreds, just like flies. Dey had been fooled into thinkin' it would be good times, but it was de worst times dey ever seen."[33]

These assessments are consistent with those articulated, by the most prominent African American political leader at the turn of the twentieth century, Booker T. Washington. Washington in his autobiography, *Up From Slavery*, made a similar observation regarding the decline of environmental conditions for African Americans in the Reconstruction period. Remembering his visits to Washington, D.C. as a student during the Reconstruction period, Washington recalled the fate of blacks who had left their agrarian communities for the cities in search of a better life: "I saw many [black] men who but a few months previous were members of Congress, then without employment [and] in poverty. . . . How many times I wished then, and have often wished since that by some power of magic I might remove the great bulk of these people into the country districts and plant them upon the soil, upon the solid and never deceptive nature of Mother Nature . . . that may be slow and toilsome but . . . nevertheless is real."[34]

W. E. B. Dubois, a contemporary and political rival of Booker T. Washington, was one of the first academics to systematically study African Americans and their environmental conditions in the north (Philadelphia) and the south (Atlanta). Dubois's *Philadelphia Study* clearly describes the inadequacy of sanitary infrastructures and marginalized housing for African Americans in the urban environment at the end of the nineteenth century.[35] In *Souls of Black Folks*, his study of southern blacks in Atlanta, Dubois characterizes rural southern blacks as poor and ignorant and compares their living conditions to Philadelphia blacks. Dubois observed that, like their northern city cousins, southern African Americans were packed into substandard housing that was almost always old, bare, and unplastered, with a black and smoky fireplace in need of repair. Unlike the north, though, Dubois believed that the conditions in the rural south did offer an environmental advantage for African Americans: "Of course, one small, close room in a city without a yard, is in many respects worse than a larger single country room. . . . The single great advantage of the Negro peasant is that he may spend most of his life outside his hovel, in the open fields."[36] Even though Dubois felt that city life provided greater socioeconomic opportunities for blacks, he also realized that blacks were making a trade-off in terms of their environment and health by leaving the rural agrarian workforce of the South: "The toil, like all farm toil, is monotonous, and there are little machinery and few tools to relieve its burdensome drudgery. . . . But with all this, it is work in the pure open air, and this is something in a day when fresh air is scare."[37]

In his earlier autobiography, *Dusk of Dawn, An Essay Toward an Autobiography of a Race Concept*, Dubois described in greater detail the environmental dilemmas of urban blacks (especially those he considered to be more cultured and socially accomplished) produced by voluntary and forced racial segregation. Dubois observed that "negroes living in segregated environments found themselves living among diseased people in a crime-ridden geography where city services of water, sewerage, garbage-removal, street cleaning, lighting, noise and traffic regulation, schools and hospitalization are usually neglected or withheld."[38] Dubois felt that any attempt by "negroes" to move away from these segregated and environmentally disenfranchised areas was being thwarted by racist legislation and city ordinances that tried to legalize racial segregation.

History has shown that Dubois's concerns were justified since the last decades of the nineteenth century and more than half of the twentieth century in America was fiercely segregated because of Jim Crow laws and or rampant implementation of race-based restrictive covenants, racialized zoning, and defacto planning practices. Most of these practices and policies were validated by the Supreme Court decision of *Plessy vs. Ferguson* in 1896 which supported a public policy of separate but equal facilities.[39] These laws and this decision literally and figuratively kept African Americans confined and segregated to environmentally marginalized geographical spaces until the last quarter of the twentieth century even after the 1954 Supreme Court decision of *Brown vs. Board of Education* which overturned the *Plessy vs. Ferguson* decision.[40] "More than 400 state laws, constitutional amendments, and city ordinances legalizing segregation and discrimination were passed in the United States between 1865 and 1967. These laws governed nearly every aspect of daily life, from education to public transportation, from health care and housing to the use of public facilities."[41] Although 79 percent of the Jim Crow laws were legislated by the South they were also created and enforced in the Western, Midwestern, and Northeastern states.[42] African Americans were barred from numerous environmental and recreational spaces that included parks, pools, fishing, boating as well as the classically known spaces of housing, buses, schools, lunch counters, and theaters.[43] During this period, in the state of Mississippi, individuals who tried to promote equality between the races could be imprisoned for up to 6 months and or fined up to 500 dollars.[44]

Oral history narratives of individuals who grew up in the Jim Crow era also provide evidence of the continuing environmental marginalization of African American communities. Ann Pointer, an African American woman who grew up in Macon County, Alabama during the Depression gave the following description of her living environment during this era:[45]

The house we were living in only had two rooms. One room and a kitchen. Mama had six children, and her and papa made eight. There was no walls in this house. It was just the boards on the outside. . . . There was no ceiling. You could look up and see the [tin] roof because it was just the joist and the tin through there. When it rained, it leaked. We didn't have a refrigerator or nothing like that. We didn't have a well in the yard. We had to go to a spring for water. [The landlord] would not dig a well. He did not make it pleasant for his tenants. You lived in that house, and mama would take cardboard and put [it] up where the wind was blowing in, because when you [were] laying in the bed in the winter-time, the air would be blowing up the sheets on the bed.

And the floor, there were cracks in the boards. Mama stop[ped] up them cracks as best she could with what she had to keep [out] anything that wanted to come in there, any small animal, a possum or anything else. . . .

And in the wintertime, you couldn't open the windows. You'd be sitting to an open fireplace like this, and they'd have the door wide open. Everybody would be sitting near the fireplace here, and you sit as close as you could, and your legs in front would be [blistered] from being burnt from sitting too close to that fire.

George Kenneth Butterfield Jr., an African American who grew up in Wilson Carolina described in his Jim Crow oral history narrative how railroad tracks were routinely used as the separating "racial junction" which kept white and black communities apart. The disproportionate number of unpaved dirt roads and blight were also strong signifiers that you had entered the black side of town. Butterfield asserts in his narrative that:[46]

Southern towns are laid out in the same fashion, basically, and you could use your senses and sense where you are and where you're not. And if you keep driving, your can see the quality of the housing decreasing and blight setting in—abandoned cars and people hanging on the streets and then you begin to see blacks. You know you're getting closer to the black community, and you can just go right in and find it.

Still living in the shadows of Jim Crow and racial segregation, civil rights leader Dr. Reverend Dr. Martin Luther King's last major agenda for the civil rights struggle in the late 1960s, the Poor People's Campaign, was aimed at addressing the horrific environmental conditions of urban blacks and the poor as a direct consequence of their social and economic disenfranchise-ment.[47] In 1970, two years after King's assassination, civil rights leaders and African American politicians would decry the nation's attention toward the new environmental movement because it failed in their opinion to recognize the historically persistent environmental marginalization of African Americans in the country. The Reverend Jesse Jackson Jr., African American mayors like Gary Hatcher and Carl B. Stokes and many African American leaders asserted in 1970 (the first year of the national celebration of Earth Day) that blacks in America were not inclined to join the new movement because they had historically been and still were environmentally disenfran-chised because of their race.[48] These African American leaders pointed to the still marginal sewer infrastructures, rat infestations and uncontrolled waste dumping which plagued African American communities and which were creating environmentally based public health problems that had been virtually eliminated in most white American communities twenty-five to seventy years earlier.[49] They publicly lamented that African Americans environmental conditions were potentially lethal and particularly insidious since they were not allowed at that time to escape from these conditions because of racist real estate practices. The rigidity of their spatial and environmental confinement continued to take place even though President Lyndon Baines Johnson had signed the 1968 Fair Housing Act which was designed to give African Americans equal access to better housing and communities.[50] The November 1970 *Business Week* article, "To Blacks Ecology is Irrelevant" quoted African American James Spain, urban affairs director of Allied Chemical Corporation and President of the Association for the Integration of Management as saying that "Blacks are double victims. We suffer from pollution as much as anyone, but we're not the beneficiaries of the affluence that produced the pollution."[51]

The echoes of King's assessment would reverberate ten years later in the discourse of environmental justice activists and scholars like Robert L. Bullard. Bullard, the most renowned environmental justice scholar and activist in the world, asserts that the contemporary environmental justice movement took place because of the incompleteness of the civil rights struggle in securing full political and social equality for African Americans. Bullard points out in his seminal environmental justice monograph, *Dumping in Dixie,* that even though "Blacks have made tremendous economic and political gains in the past three decades with the passage of equal opportunity initiatives at the federal level. Despite legislation, court orders, and federal mandates, institutional racism and discrimination continue to influence the quality of life in many of the nation's black communities."

The failure of the mainstream environmental movement to address the environmental concerns of African American communities and the emergence of the environmental justice movement is best articulated by Peggy Shepard. Shepard, the African American founder of the West Harlem Environmental Action Team (WEACT) and one of the leading environmental justice activists in the United States, pointed out in a 2004 public radio interview:[52]

> that the mainstream environmental movement was founded back in the 70's primarily to begin a series of legislation and regulation . . . and resulted in the Clean Air Act, Clean Water Act and some wonderful environmental protections. But it has been the people of color in the environmental justice movement that has focused on healthy, sustainable communities, which focuses on community-level impacts of the environment, and that's where the mainstream envi-

ronmental movement has fallen short, . . . the environmental justice movement
has been very strong in ensuring and working to change policies so that environmental impacts are lessened and so that there is actual decision making being
made about our communities by the folks who live there.

The major premise of today's environmental justice movement in America
echoes James Spain's commentary of 1970. In essence this movement argues
that today's defacto racially segregated communities of African Americans
are victims of contemporary inequitable environmental policies. The environmental history of African Americans however clearly shows that environmental inequities among this population are a historical legacy that has
always existed and is fact the norm. To say today that the American society
has had no role in creating environmental inequitable communities for African Americans because they have voluntarily chosen to live in these environmentally marginalized spaces is an ahistorical and false claim. The
overwhelming historical evidence shows that who they were and how they
were perceived and remembered (in the most negative sense) by the larger
white body politic and social body over time strongly determined the environmental quality of their living spaces for over four hundred years. This
pattern and practice of environmental inequity according to senior environmental philosopher Bill Lawson is an illustration of the "colonial model of
urban planning" rooted in the belief that only 'whites' deserve environmental justice because they are the only ones who appreciate and therefore
deserve environmentally salient spaces like homes and parks; as opposed to
blacks who 'will only destroy them.' "[53] African Americans whose communities have been subjected to this paradigm are clearly aware in many cases
that contemporary planning decisions have led to toxic incinerators, failed
levees, and illegal waste practices in their areas. Many have cried out "We
know they aren't building these things in rich white neighborhoods. They
wouldn't stand for it. This is genocide against poor people and all people of
color."[54] This is why current environmental justice activists like Hazel and
Cheryl Johnson from Chicago's Altgeld Gardens feel that the path to this
dilemma is a long and unforeseeable one. Their environment continues to be
polluted on a daily basis. Environmental injustice is not a bad memory but
an insidious reality that they still continue to struggle against like many
other African American communities in the United States in the new millennium.[55]

NOTES

1. Joel Tarr, *Search for the Ultimate Sink: Urban Pollution in Historical Perspectives* (University of Akron Press: 1996).

2. The term "African Americans" is used in this essay to denote the multi-ethnic

background of African American people in America (i.e., West Indian, Caribbean, African, and African American).

3. The term "environment" for this discussion is broad in scope and refers to both the natural and built environment.

4. Sylvia Hood Washington, *Packing Them In: An Archaeology of Environmental Racism in Chicago, 1865–1954.* (Lanham, MD: Lexington Books, 2004).

5. For a more complete environmental justice history of African Americans read Sylvia Hood Washington's chapter, "An Archaeology of Environmental Justice" in *Packing Them In: An Archaeology of Environmental Racism in Chicago, 1865–1954* (Lanham, MD: Lexington Books, 2004).

6. For this essay the term "America" will be used to refer to the country, "United States of America" and not the North American continent although slavery did exist in other countries in the continent.

7. Charles Johnson, Patricia Smith, and the WGBH Research Team, *Africans in America, America's Journey through Slavery* (New York: Harcourt Brace and Company, 1998), p. 70.

8. Johnson, Smith and the WGBH Research Team, 67.

9. Colin A. Palmer, "The First Passage, 1502–1619." In *To Make Our World Anew, A History of African Americans,* (Oxford: Oxford University Press, 2000), pp. 11–14.

10. Palmer, p. 15.

11. Johnson, Smith, and the WGBH Series, p. 70.

12. Olaudah Equiano "The Horrors of the Middle Passage, The Interesting Narrative of the Life of Olaudah Equiano." In *Readings in African-American History,* third edition (Belmont, CA: Wadsworth & Thomson Learning, 2001),13.

13. Alexander Falconbridge in *Excerpts from Slave Narratives,* Chapter 7 (June 21, 2004) http://www.vgskole.net/prosjekt/slavrute/y.htm

14. Ibid.

15. For detailed studies on the slave trade please read Hugh Thomas, *The Slave Trade* and Elizabeth Donnan (ed.), *Documents Illustrative of the History of the Slave Trade to America,* 4 vols. (1930–1935).

16. Winthrop D. Jordan, "The Souls of Men" and "The Bodies of Men." In *White over Black, American Attitudes Toward the Negro, 1550–1812* (University of North Carolina Press, 1968) provides an excellent historical overview of this struggle in American colonies.

17. Carolyn Merchant," Shades of Darkness: Race and Environmental History," Environmental History Journal, Vol. 8, No. 3. http://www.historycooperative.org/journals/eh/8.3/merchant.html July 2003.

18. Palmer, p. 19.

19. Ibid, p. 21.

20. Winthrop D. Jordan, *White over Black, American Attitudes Toward the Negro, 1550–1812* (University of North Carolina Press, 1968), pp. 60–61.

21. Johnson, Smith and WGBH Series, p. 83.

22. Jordan, pp. 231–232.

23. Francis Henderson, *Excerpts from Slave Narratives,* Chapter 13 (June 21, 2004) http://www.vgskole.net/prosjekt/slavrute/13.htm

24. Jacob Stroyer, "My Life in the South." In *Excerpts from Slave Narratives*, Chapter 14, (June 21, 2004) http://www.vgskole.net/prosjekt/slavrute/14.htm

25. "Uncle Tom's Story of His Life": An Autobiography of the Rev. Josiah Henson. In *Excerpts from Slave Narratives* Chapter 12, (June 21, 2004) http://www.vgskole.net/prosjekt/slavrute/12.htm

26. Theodore Dwight Weld, *American Slavery As It Is: Testimony of a Thousand Witnesses*. New York: American Anti-Slavery Society (June 21, 2004) http://docsouth.unc.edu/neh/weld/weld.html

27. Ibid.

28. WPA refers to the Works Progress Administration which sponsored and produced the Federal Writers' Project Slave Collection in the 1930s.

29. Norman R. Yetman, ed. *Voices from Slavery, 100 Authentic Slave Narratives*, p. 52.

30. Johnson and Smith, p. 359.

31. T. Lindsay Baker and Julie P. Baker, *The WPA Oklahoma Slave Narratives* (Norman and London: University of Oklahoma Press), p. 385.

32. Ibid, p. 388.

33. Norman R. Yetman, *Voices from Slavery* (Mineola, New York: Dover Publications, 2000), pp. 219–20.

34. Booker T. Washington, *Up From Slavery* (New York: Dover Publications, 1995), p. 43.

35. W.E.B. Dubois, *The Philadelphia Negro, A Social Study* (Philadelphia: University of Pennsylvania Press, 1996).

36. W.E.B. Dubois, *Souls of Black Folks* (New York: Gramercy Books, 1994), p. 108.

37. Dubois, *Souls of Black Folks*, p. 111.

38. W.E.B. Dubois, *Dusk of Dawn, An Essay Toward an Autobiography of a Race Concept* (Piscataway, NJ: Transaction Publishers, 2992), p. 182–83.

39. This decision supported the right of states to physically segregate the races and provide separate accommodations (supposedly equal) in all facets of life.

40. For a more in-depth discussion about race and planning read "Planning and Environmental Inequality," in *Packing Them In: An Archaeology of Environmental Racism in Chicago, 1865–1954* (Lanham, MD: Lexington Books, 2004) and David Delaney, *Race, Place and the Law, 1836–1948* (Austin: University of Texas Press, 1998).

41. Susan Falck. "Jim Crow Legislation Overview," http://www.jimcrowhistory.org/resources/lessonplans/hs_es_jim_crow_laws.htm (June 28, 2004)

42. Ibid.

43. Colin Fisher, "African Americans and the Frontier of Leisure: The 1919 Chicago Race Riot and Access to Nature," (paper presented to the annual meeting of the American Historical Association, San Francisco, January 3–6, 2002).

44. Martin Luther King, Jr., NHS Jim Crow Laws, (June 23, 2004) www.nps.pov/malu/documents/jim_crow_laws.htm

45. William H. Chafe, Raymond Gaines, Robert Korstad, eds., *Remembering Jim Crow: African Americans Tell About Life in the Segregated South* (New York: The New Press, 2001), p. 44.

46. Chafe, Gaines and Korstad, pp. 131–32. Wilson's narrative includes a claim that there were "23 miles of unpaved dirt roads [in black communities] compared with less than one mile in white communities."

47. For a detailed description of King's role read Sylvia Hood Washington's essay "Environmental Justice" in the *Encyclopedia of Leadership* (Thousand Oaks, Calif.: Sage Publications, 2004).

48. Sylvia Hood Washington, Dissertation, *Packing Them In, A 20th Century Working Class Environmental History*, (Case Western Reserve University), 2000.

49. Andrew Hurley, *Environmental Inequalities: Class, Race, and Industrial Pollution in Gary, Indiana, 1945–1980*, (Chapel Hill: University of North Carolina Press, 1995); Martin Melosi, "Equity, Eco-Racism, and Environmental History," *Environmental History Review* 19 (Fall 1995): 1–16; Dorceta Taylor, "American Environmentalism: The Role of Race, Class, and Gender in Shaping Activism 1820–1995," *Race, Gender and Class*, p. 5 (1997).

50. Douglass S. Massey and Nancy A. Denton, *American Apartheid, Segregation and the Making of the Underclass* (Cambridge: Harvard University Press, 1993).

51. "To Blacks Ecology Is Irrelevant." In *Business Week*, November 14, 1970, p. 48.

52. Tavis Smiley Interviews Dr. Beverly Wright, Peggy Shepard, and Senator John Kerry about environmental issues in minority communities. Excerpts taken from the National Public Radio transcript, April 22, 2003. http://www.xula.edu/dscej/news%20and%20events/TavisSmileyInterview.html July 5, 2004.

53. Bill Lawson, "Living in the City," in *Faces of Environmental Racism*, 2nd ed. (Lanham, MD: Rowman and Littlefield, 2001), 49.

54. David Pellow, *Garbage Wars, The Struggle for Environmental Justice in Chicago* (Cambridge: MIT Press, 2002), p. 138.

55. See their essay, *"There Are No Flowers Here" Altgeld Gardens and the Birth of the Environmental Justice Movement in Chicago, 1979–2003* in this collection for a more detailed description of ongoing environmental justice struggles.

5

Indigenous Peoples, Colonialism, and Memories of Environmental Injustice

Heather Goodall

> Nothing that memory cannot
> Reach or touch or call back.
>
> —*Don Mattera, District Six Museum,*
> *Cape Town, South Africa*

A photograph circulates proudly among environmental activists and Aboriginal people in Australia who were involved in the attempt in 1980 to prevent the Ranger uranium mine proceeding on Aboriginal land in Australia's tropical northern wetlands. You can almost hear the chants of "Keep Uranium in the ground!" and "Hands off Aboriginal Land" as you look at the image of the tall Aboriginal seaman, striding across the street in the exclusive business district of Sydney in 1980, the weight of a large bucket of dirt shared precariously with a young white environment activist. They are surrounded by Aboriginal campaigners for land rights from across Australia, by leaders of the peace movement and by unionists, both black and white, protesting about dangers to workers.[1] As they pause at the glass doors of the mining company office, and the camera flashes, those of us in that mixed bunch of activists who were there can still see the next movement: the seaman swings the bucket up to his shoulder and hurls the dirt across the foyer's gleaming tiles, leaving a graphic symbol of the distress that the Ranger mine was causing to the traditional owners at Oenpelli.[2]

The memories of struggle for environmental justice in this volume are diverse, each as unique as this Australian demonstration against uranium mining on Aboriginal land. Many involve people like the seaman and the

Aboriginal unionists, indigenous[3] to the lands they are seeking to defend. They might act alone or in coalitions like this campaign where indigenous and non-indigenous activists from a broad range of movements joined together. Other chapters of this book take us to conflicts which do not involve Indigenous people, like the early landmark campaign in the United States in Warren County in 1978, where the term environmental justice was coined. These were mounted by African Americans and communities of color who identified racism and class but not indigeneity as the key issues in their struggles to win justice.[4]

The unity in this Australian photograph was riddled with simmering tensions. Within weeks there were mutterings by unions that their workers' jobs in the mines were in jeopardy, while there was hurt outrage from the environmentalists when Indigenous traditional owners began negotiating with the mining company. The anti-uranium campaign in Australia was painfully divided along and across lines of class, color, and principle, and has struggled through shifting alliances to maintain united fronts over many years. The continuing desire to work together despite and throughout such strains suggests the recognition of the importance of environmental crisis across all sectors of contemporary society although many unresolved issues remain around what constitutes environmental justice and for whom.

This chapter sketches out a framework for identifying the sources of tension as well as some of the common ground between indigenous and non-indigenous communities in their experiences of environmental injustice and their campaigns to bring about change. A theoretical and political link can be seen if indigenous perceptions of environmental injustice are located within the wider framework of colonialism[5], which shapes many of the continuing themes in indigenous activism. Not all colonized peoples were indigenous to the area of the colony. In some colonies, like India, Burma, and Indochina, there had been layers of migration and settlement before the Europeans. Yet in most areas there was a known group of peoples whose identity and economy was most directly related to their origins on that land.

History is central to questions of how those indigenous people have understood environmental injustice because the exercise of colonial power has had a spatial expression: it can be mapped onto the ground. Power in colonies has been exercised through control over space and environment.[6] What are the places that the colonizers could go freely but the colonized could not? Where could colonized people build or rent a house and where were only colonizers comfortable and welcomed? This spatial expression of power can be seen in the architecture and fabric of the buildings of the colonisers, and in the ways land has been appropriated and landscapes reconstructed. Fences, gates, and doors was designed to allow some to enter and some to remain uncomfortably waiting. Living spaces, cooking, and bathing areas were all set up to foster some types of lifestyles and invalidate others.

Contemporary conditions of injustice are impossible to understand or change without an understanding of how they arose and of what people remember as they look at today's landscapes.

As reflections of the past, memories are one of the few ways to explore indigenous experience. Memories are recomposed over time and in each retelling, and so can never be transparent windows on to the past. But then neither are the official archives which present only the colonizer's perceptions. It is often only in memory—that is, in the oral record of life stories and in the informal collections and performances of community traditions— that indigenous people's perceptions can be glimpsed and explored. As people talk about their memories of simple, everyday movements around their town, they reveal the colonial geographies of exclusion which have otherwise left few landmarks. There may have been "Whites Only" signs, but just as often the barriers were invisible, recalled only in casual jokes like those that Australian Aboriginal people tell today in a town along the Darling River about "Crow's Corner," beyond which they could not venture into the segregated main street, so they hovered there "like a mob of black crows."[7] Memories about such ordinary things, as much as the memories of trauma and conflicts, are crucial for understanding the ways people's movement around and use of their own country became distorted under colonial conditions.

There are five themes in the community narratives and in the public campaigns of indigenous peoples around the globe which suggest the ways in which colonialism has generated environmental injustice. They are dispossession, displacement, entrapment [and control], invisibility [arising from settler environmental nationalism], and globalization [along the patterns set by colonialism]. Each of these processes had an environmental impact: by depriving the colonized of their land for their cultural, social, and economic needs; by forcing them into severely disadvantaged and precarious environmental living and working conditions; by marginalizing sustainable indigenous land and water management practices and imposing far more damaging and destructive exploitative regimes which have consequences for all of contemporary society.

The impacts of these colonial processes sometimes overlap and at others are quite distinct. All are gendered: forcing different impacts and outcomes for men and women and altering gender relations dramatically and continuously. Many of my examples relate to settler colonies, like Australia (where my work has been focused), the United States, South Africa, and Israel-Palestine. But the themes addressed here are common also to indigenous peoples in previously colonized but not European-settled colonies, in cases like India where the dams on the Narmada have caused immense impacts on indigenous peoples and like Burma which has shut the Karen people out of their homelands altogether with its colonial-established borders.

DISPOSSESSION

Dispossession from their land is the experience which has been central to most indigenous people[8] and it has shaped their approaches to environmental questions. The trauma of the violence, death and terror which has so often been the means of invasion has become embedded into knowledge about land and environment. The overwhelming proportion of the victims were Indigenous people.[9] There continue to be heated debates over the exact death toll[10] but the unquestionable outcome of the violence, whatever the exact body count, was widespread horror which crossed into intergenerational memory.[11] This was compounded by the impact of disease, with the mere presence of settlers bringing new viral and bacterial infections to which the indigenous populations of Australia had no immunity. Spread at times deliberately [for some bacterial infections] but more often inadvertently [for all the viral illnesses and many others], the epidemic nature of these new diseases caused havoc in the most densely populated indigenous communities.

Such experiences are never forgotten. They are instead held in the memories of the colonized people, shaped into narratives which might be direct recountings or the more elaborate allegorical genres of oral tradition. Whatever the form, they became in Australia an integral part of the knowledge embedded in the landscape by Indigenous peoples, then taught to children as they were shown around the country over coming generations.[12]

Such experience is widespread among colonized indigenous peoples. It is familiar to those who faced the early European expansion in the Americas, for whom the equivalent names might be Sand Creek, where over 200 Cheyenne were killed and mutilated in 1864. It is just as familiar for those most recently colonized, the Palestinians in the Middle East, for whom place names like Dir Yassin, Balad al-Shaykh, Dawayima, and Tantura[13] evoke memories of massacre and violence arising from the ethnic cleansing of 1948 during which Israeli settlers "swept" over three quarters of a million Palestinians from their houses, fields, and groves.[14] Embedding history into the landscape in this way irrevocably changes relationships to these places, and it means that memories work to keep the pain of past generations' dispossession very clearly before the eyes of those in the present.

A second direct impact on indigenous people and on their environment was their loss of custodial control over their lands. As the survivors regrouped after the impact of violence and disease, they found they had lost any management role. They had not previously lived in some romantic harmony with their environment. In Australia, Aborigines had managed and shaped the landscape over centuries through frequent mosaic burning, fish-traps and eel-farming canals, targeted harvesting and replanting, with their greatest effect being to create and nurture the extensive eucalypt and grassland plains. Their acquired ecological knowledge can be found in ceremonial songs which show these centuries of learning how to work with the country.[15] But indigenous owners' maintenance of low populations and low-impact methods had a far slower impact on the fragile environments than the intensive stocking and mono-cropping which was introduced with such devastating impact by the British in the 1840s. This colonizer damage was so severe that the western plains of NSW were in collapse from deforestation and erosion by the 1890s.[16] Despite crisis management over the next 50 years, the slow deterioration of the inland riverine grasslands in the eastern states, the foodbowl of Australia, has continued, to the grief and frustration of the remaining indigenous owners. Their knowledge of valuable native crops and productive harvesting regimes was not only ignored but denigrated as "waste" and "disorder." A Ngiyampaa man, Brad Steadman, still living on his country at Brewarrina in 1996,[17] argued the senselessness of this destructive land management in both the grazing and industrialized cotton farming he was witnessing around him:

> There's no understanding of the country there, you might as well try and nail a fence into the sky . . . it doesn't work . . . you've got to *know* the country.

One outcome of dispossession has been that indigenous owners were denied the economic product of their land. They were invariably forced into poverty and into the cash economy as "landless" laborers on immensely disadvantaged terms. The "divide and rule" cultures of colonialism have often driven wedges of prejudice between indigenous peoples and working class settlers, so that labour unions have often been of little help. The economic dimension of dispossession is seldom recognized by today's "first world" campaigners for wilderness preservation who continue to view the landscape as a site for passive aesthetic consumption, often denying or obscuring the complexity of the human past of places they would prefer to characterize as "pristine wilderness." Such ecological activists seek alliances with indigenous owners at times, hoping to gain the valuable symbolic endorsement of pre-industrial cultures for their campaigns against commercial exploitation. In the process, they essentialize and homogenize Indigenous people in their need for exotic, readily narratable "traditional wisdom."[18] They have often then been shocked when these indigenous owners negotiated with the would-be developers or miners for some economic return, as was the case in the uranium mine campaigns of the 1980s.[19]

The third major effect of dispossession is the deep disturbance which it has caused to social, political, cultural, and spiritual processes within indigenous societies. Traditionally, social and cultural life was mediated through relations with land: political status derived from fulfilment of custodial obligations to land, which then allowed a whole range of consequent social negotiations. Social interactions, marriages, and education all took place along lines of land relations, and cultural knowledge, including that about historical change, was inscribed within knowledge about places and environment.[20] Denial of access to traditional land severely disrupted, although it did not end, such relationships. Complex strategies have developed to sustain links to land both in practice and in imagination, and rich, adaptive indigenous cultures based on tradition have emerged in Australia. However the sense of severe disruption, in all aspects of life, was well expressed by Joe Flick, a Gamilaraay elder from the northern Darling floodplain in New South Wales, when he was asked in 1998[21] how he felt the environment of his country had changed:

I can see my lifeline all washed away by greed. See, I look at the Earth's life cycle in a different that the white fellas do, I think.

Years ago this place was like a big puzzle all the animals were put in place, all the trees were put in place, all the Aboriginal people were put in place. . . . We had all our camps along that river. We only used fire when we wanted to burn off and make the feed nice and green for our animals to come back in so we could get a feed . . . everything was in there . . . in place.

So one day a big cyclone came—that's the invasion of the whites . . . blew everything to pieces. . . . Knocked all the trees down, tore big holes into the hills, scattered the Aboriginal people, scattered the animals, all the birds, and scattered our fish. And after a cyclone we always think of the after effect, what's going to happen—there's going to be a heartbreak, there's going to be an epidemic, and we've got nowhere to run.

Well, that happened and it broke out in this country, a worse disease than heart failure, worse than AIDS. That disease was *force*. It came with that cyclone the white man put on it. The Aboriginal people were forced off their hunting ground, they were forced off their camping grounds. The Aboriginal women were forced to have sex with the white man. The Aboriginal men were forced to slave labour. The Aboriginal children were forced into institutions. And see, this force is still going on. So she's a bad disease this force.

This is the way I look at the Aboriginal people's lifetime. They were contented, because they were all in that puzzle where they all had their little part to play. And then this epidemic broke out . . . she's still killing our rivers. Still ripping our trees out. Still tearing big holes in the ground. So the cyclone never ended for the Aboriginal people.

Despite these severe effects on their relationship to their country, there has been resistance to dispossession by indigenous peoples in all colonized countries. It has taken many forms, from armed conflict, sabotage, and guerrilla warfare to the longer term strategies of secret visits to their country and oral traditions to sustain intergenerational land knowledge; political and legal cases to gain recognition of land rights; mobilising international pressure to regain access; and mounting culturally re-assertive strategies like joint management of parks and wilderness areas.[22] The greatest success has been by those peoples who have been able to remain close to their traditional lands, and who have therefore been able to sustain or reactivate both their economic links and their spiritual and cultural relations with their country. An example is drawn in this volume from Aotearoa/New Zealand, where Selby and Moore describe the long process by which the Ngati Raukawa of Ngatokowaru have regained control over the place and the meaning of their traditional country.

DISPLACEMENT

Restoration of access to and sustainable management over traditional lands has been far harder for peoples who have been displaced by long distances from their own country. Displacement was a frequent strategy of colonialists: to utilise the labour of the colonised; to claim their land or to break up the links between the people themselves or the people and their land. The euphemisms for these policies differ from colony to colony: "Indian Removal" in 1830 in the United States; "Concentration" in the 1930s in Australia; "Transfer" in Israel in 1948. The effects were the same. The journeys of displacement, traversing their own or other colonised people's country into exile, have often become burned into memory even if they have never reached the archives. Those which have been recorded include the horror of the Middle Passage for enslaved Africans, the unspeakable conditions on countless European slave trading ships, causing many deaths and leaving scars which no doubt passed far beyond the generations who survived its terrors to the Americas and the East Indies. For the Cherokee in the United States, it was the Trail of Tears, 1838–39, as they were forced off their land and made to march through a bitter winter far to the west to unsafe and transitory reservations. For indigenous Australians, the stories are about the cattle truck journeys in the 1930s from Tibooburra and Angledool to Brewarrina, from Carowra Tank to Menindee, each of them termed "concentration" sites by the "Protection Board" which was overseeing the rationalisation of dispossession in the 1930s.[23] An example of parallel experiences can be seen in the repeated displacements suffered by African American populations in "urban renewals" in United States cities, known colloquially as "negro removal"[24] in an acknowledgement of its racialized goals.

Forced migrations of indigenous peoples left memories of the places and communities which had disappeared. These imagined homelands continue not only to haunt the yearnings of exiles, but to act as rallying calls for demands for restoration of access and for compensation for lost lands. An example of such a powerful "disappeared" place is District Six, in Cape Town, South Africa, on Khoi-San land, which had become a thriving community of Khoi-San and Xhosa peoples under early colonial conditions. The

Group Areas Act of 1960 built on British colonial legislation to declare this land "Whites Only," and the forced migration began, bitterly resisted every inch of the way. First dispossessed then displaced were the indigenous Africans who had been declared "illegal" on their own land, then the other peoples who had joined the community, the "Coloreds" and the Indian South Africans descended from the indentured workforce of the early twentieth century. The last families were forced out in 1982 as bulldozers lined up to raze the site. This vibrant and tenacious community and its place were memorialized in continuing protests against Apartheid, first in the powerful installation by Sue Williamson called "The Last Supper," documenting both the vitality of the community and the process of demolition.[25] Then the campaign was taken up in the Hands Off District Six campaign from 1987 to stop any development of the site without involvement of the original inhabitants.[26] In post-Apartheid South Africa, the memory of District Six is celebrated in order to shape the new society emerging from that most environmentally unjust of colonialisms. Similarly, in Palestine, the disappeared places include a myriad of Palestinian villages which were bulldozed or left in ruins in the *Nakba* or Catastrophe of 1948: Majdal Sadek, Kakoun, Lubia are just some of the names.[27] Others have been claimed by Israelis and renamed in Hebrew, the fate of Ayn Hawd which has now become an Israeli artists colony renamed Ein Hod, widely advertised on the Internet. But, like District Six, Ayn Hawd is not forgotten but instead its memory is sustained in stories which not only reclaim the place but insist that the community be acknowledged as well.[28] So environmental injustice in relation to community displacement, forced migration or exile, has been the injustice of loss and separation, but it contains within it the power of memory to mobilize people to regain their lost places.

The displacements of individuals have been just as painful but perhaps harder to overcome. The governments of the United States, Canada, and Australia each developed policies to separate young indigenous people from their land and communities. This was another exercise of power through control over space which has had environmental consequences: the removal of adolescents from their own homelands and communities has meant that fundamental knowledge about place and environment was not passed on to these young people in the crucial teaching which traditionally occured as they grew to maturity, which meant in turn that they have been less able to sustain cultural practices in relation to land nor have they been able to pass on traditional knowledge of environmental conditions and cultures to their children. Each of these settler colonies adapted various educational and labour management antecedents to create an assimilatory tool. Some were gendered in their operation, like that in NSW, Australia, where child removal practices were aimed specifically at young, prepubertal girls in an openly eugenicist attempt to lower the birth rate of their rural Aboriginal communities. [29] In the United States it was Indian Boarding Schools[30] and in Canada Native Residential Schools.[31] In Finland a similar effect was created in the mandatory attendance at remote boarding schools which were not assimilatory, being attended by all ethnic groups, Sami and Finns, but which were still effective in separating young people at the critical periods of their childhood and adolescence from their country and the community who could teach them about it.[32] This loss of country and community for some was irrevocable: in NSW 25 percent of the stolen children in the early twentieth century were never able to return home. But for many courageous young people who fought their way back to their community, such policies failed to destroy their identification as indigenous people, although they did undoubtedly undermine their knowledge of their land.

The final form of displacement which has direct environmental implications is that of the borders imposed as "nations" are created in response to the ideology and policies of colonialism and then decolonization. The "nation state" is a concept generated and refined in the crucible of colonialism. Anderson has identified four archetypal forms of nationalism and three, including the earliest, are directly related to colonial power conflicts.[33] Certainly the cultural and political conflicts over colonial domination ensured that anticolonial movements took the form of nationalism to express their identity and directions for the future. The resulting nation states adhered to the illusions of "nationhood" that citizens would share fundamental characteristics, including cultural values and ethnicity. While some nations represented themselves as an [often illusory] melting pot of mixed identities, in fact the pressures for uniformity and conformity have been notorious in causing the repression of ethnic minorities and indigenous peoples. The borders of these new states themselves were created out of the expediencies of the coloniser's rivalries with neighbouring colonizers, and then by opportunistic negotiating in the final stages of decolonization. The deep tragedy of the partition of India and Pakistan is a case in point.[34] Indigenous peoples under colonial rule, particularly in Asia where there had been a series of incoming migrations prior to the imposition of colonial power, had already found themselves marginalized as "tribals" [British India] or "hill people" [French Indochina]. Border creation took no regard at all for the interests in land of those indigenous colonized peoples. The Karen of Burma tried to seize their chance and declared their own independent state in 1949 between Burma and Thailand. But with no precedent in British colonial rule in Burma, the indigenous Karen were ignored by international authorities, and ever since their lands and their people have been prey to a series of Burmese military state governments.[35] Another example is the Isaan people, an ethnic Lao people caught on the Thai side of the border and stripped of their rights over language, education, and land even before the Pak Moon dam was built on their country.[36] An unfolding contemporary example is the "Wall" which is being built across Palestinian land in the Occupied West Bank by Israel, an extension of an effective border and a dominating physical presence which has disrupted land use, devastating Palestinian access to and management of their lands and intensifying the pressure for "transfer" or forced migration. Displacement in these situations has occurred without the indigenous peoples themselves moving away. Instead the existence of internationally endorsed borders shape the relationship between them and the land which they regard as the source of their identity.

ENTRAPMENT AND CONTROL

The theme within indigenous memories which is most readily identifiable as environmental injustice is entrapment, relating to the incarcerated situations into which indigenous peoples have been forced by dispossession and displacement. The reserves, government stations and church missions in Australia have direct similarities with the reservations in the United States, the Bantustans in South Africa, the "Arab Quarter" in the *Qesbah* in French Algiers, and the refugee camps in Palestine. Historically, there are strong resonances with the strategies for containment and control of the previously displaced Jewish populations suffering persecution in Europe over centuries of diaspora, even before the murderous ghetto period of the Nazi dominance. And there are parallels with the urban slums of the northern cities of the United States in which African Americans were trapped after escaping the South during Reconstruction; the impoverished immigrant suburbs set in the midst of industrial dumping grounds in Sydney; or again the squatter camps on the outskirts of Port Moresby or Manilla to which rural people have drifted after being forced off subsistence farming land by colonial plantation mono-cropping or the "modern" cash economy.

While indigenous communities in confinement were subject to appalling social, economic, and environmental conditions, the hardships also generated an intense sense of solidarity. This may not always have been fulfilled in the stress of every day life: there are many stories of betrayal and collaboration. But where underground cultures of resistance flourished, it made difficult situations bearable. So memories of such entrapment sites are often not entirely negative: recalling instead the closeness of mutual support to sustain a secret culture. But even the most positive memories are permeated with deep ambivalence, depicting as well the humiliating compromises before the overbearing pettiness of institutional power.

Some confinement sites were created directly as an outcome of colonial strategies, others were an almost negligent by-product of dispossession or displacement. Most deliberate were Bantustans and reserves created as means of containment and justified on the basis of the "traditionalism" of the colonized. But this label was never intended to reflect the dynamic of any real pre-colonial cultures, but instead was conceived as a static "primitivism," unable to cope with change, and usually said to be the cause of indigenous people's disadvantage. The communities forced into such sites had been disempowered because of their colonized status: their rights and interests were not recognized and they themselves not regarded as "real" citizens because of their "primitive" and "traditional" lifestyles. In British colonies like Australia, where indigenous people as subjects of the Crown were said to be entitled to full protection under the law, they were denied full civil rights or equal pay as workers because they were labelled "not yet ready," forever "in the waiting room" of colonialism.[37] In a circular argument, residence on a reserve could be used to prove this status. Reserve, reservation, and Bantustan populations were not serviced with the regular infrastructure of public health or municipal services because they were "not citizens." Settler colonial states went to great lengths to ensure this was so in reality: in the 1930s for example, a major NSW rural town altered its municipal boundaries to ensure the Aboriginal camp on its edges could not vote.[38] The label of "primitive" in Australia conveyed the specific "traditionalism" of being nomadic, which allowed an easy dismissal of Aboriginal populations as by definition transients, no matter how many generations of any one family had lived in the same camp nor the fact that they were living on their own country. So the camps were never connected to the civic infrastructure like water piping or sewage collection, because this would legitimize their presence and offer a sense of entitlement to stay.

Other entrapment sites were dumping grounds for exhausted people after the gruelling journeys of displacement. The reservations of "Indian Territory" beyond the Mississippi River to which the Cherokee and others trudged at the end of the "Trail of Tears" in 1839 were such sites, although they were soon to be dismembered and their populations displaced again as settler expansion demanded more land. The concentration stations in Australia have names like Menindee and Brewarrina in NSW in the 1930s and Warrabri in Central Australia in the 1950s, where an initially resident community of local indigenous people was massively inflated by displaced peoples from distant areas to achieve "rational" management of the colonized populations.[39] Other sites again have been less officially established. They have been simply the first available place of refuge for exiled displaced peoples, victims of colonizing ethnic cleansing and expulsion, the most recent being the Palestinian camps throughout Lebanon and the occupied West Bank in towns like Jenin after 1948.

However differently created, each of these concentration sites have experienced similar results because they were the overcrowded and under-resourced dumping grounds for disempowered populations. Invariably they have been situated on poor quality land in commercial terms, often inade-

quately watered and shaded, and always ecologically stressed by overpopula-
tion as well as by geographic disadvantages like flooding. These sites have
characteristically suffered the massive health costs of environmental discrimination: the preventable diseases arising from lack of environmental infrastructure (lack of sanitation, poor drainage, contaminated water,
overcrowding) and from poverty: rapid spread of epidemic diseases because
of poor nutrition, no access to necessary but expensive medical treatments,
no immunizations, poor nutrition leading to malnutrition or morbid obesity,
heart disease and diabetes, and the stress-related high rates of trauma, substance abuse, and intercommunity violence.[40] The siting of polluting, high-
risk facilities, from garbage tips to toxic waste storages, close to such confinement areas is a frequent occurrence as these communities, being already
disempowered and by definition "transitory," can be made to carry the burden of modernity's industrial development with little danger of successful
protest. The black population of South Africa, whether in "Bantustans" or
in the massive urban squatter settlements, were invariably living "downwind
and downstream" of polluting industries,[41] just as were Indigenous Australians in reserves and African Americans in inner city urban slums.

Yet without barbed wire and constant security, which few such confinement sites had, they have seldom functioned strictly to imprison their residents. This demands the question: Was complete confinement ever the major
goal? In many cases it was not. An underlying purpose is most clear in the
South African example of fully blown Apartheid, which was built directly
with the scaffolding supplied by British colonial regulations, which had
themselves been crafted in other British colonies like Australia. This purpose
was to ensure maximum compliance of colonized peoples, who far outnum-
bered the British and Afrikaner settlers, in the industrial, mining, and
domestic industries throughout the rest of the country. The labor of the colonized was necessary but it could best be controlled if workers knew they
could always be deported back to where they "really" belonged, their "traditional homelands" in the Bantustans. So the Bantustans were set aside, on
the poorest 13 percent of the land for over 70 percent of the population.[42]
Additionally, dependent African families would need to be left in the impoverished Bantustans as no residential accommodation could be legally found
for them in "white" areas. Only the minimal wages of individual family
members working in industry or mining and living miles away in "single
men's" barracks or as "live-in" domestics in white residential areas could
produce enough cash to keep the family alive. The colonial state was effectively holding African families as hostages to guarantee the working family
member's compliance, or he or she too would be sent back to starve in the
"homeland." The "homelands," based on spurious claims of "tradition" as
the basis for allocating living space, effectively declared Africans "illegal"
across the whole of the rest of their own country.[43] Many Africans, as did

others affected by colonialism like the South African descendants of the large numbers of Indian coerced and indentured laborers, risked deportation by living in the massive squatter camps like Soweto outside Johannesburg. They daily ran the gauntlet of checkpoints to review their "Passes," which designated not only their "race" but their rights to move or live outside their allocated homeland. The pass laws were the tools of an elaborate labor control system, fundamentally based on settler land appropriation, the force of armed police and army, and the ideological power to define the colonized as forever "illegal." While more elaborate than in other colonies, the South African case was based on the same strategies and often the same sets of laws which had circulated throughout the British empire with its migratory officials, and indeed across the whole settler world.[44]

Indigenous peoples in confinement sites are intensely vulnerable: those settler authorities who were charged with protecting them have often had the most interest in seeing them further harmed or displaced yet again. One example of their vulnerability is Wounded Knee, the site of the massacre of despairing Lakota Sioux in 1890 who had survived the "Indian Wars" only to die at the hands of the soldiers in their "safe" home on Pine Ridge Reservation. A more recent example is that of the hundreds of Palestinian dead in the refugee camps of Sabra and Shatila in 1982, dispossessed and displaced into these southern Lebanese confinement camps, then abandoned by the occupying army charged with their protection but composed of the settlers who had dispossessed them in the first place.

INVISIBILITY: SETTLER
ENVIRONMENTAL NATIONALISM

Colonizers have not only been military or commercial exploiters but have often been seeking roots for themselves as well. Despite accusing colonized indigenous peoples of being "nomadic," it was European colonists who were invariably the most distant from home and the most mobile. At times settlers were themselves escaping from repression and exploitation, like the religious dissenters who settled in America in the eighteenth century, the political radicals and displaced Irish who came to Australia in the nineteenth, and the European Jews urgently seeking refuge in Israel in the twentieth. Nevertheless, while such experiences sometimes generated empathy, settlers' attempts to secure their own futures were directly spatial, quite literally being about embedding their structures and claims into the soil. This has in most cases led to callous and brutal destruction of colonized peoples themselves and erasure of the evidence of their occupation in fact and in ideas.

In Australia there have been examples of these two processes, embedding and symbolically erasing, taking place side by side. Nineteenth-century collectors and amateur ethnographers gathered up Aboriginal people's tools and weapons, taking them away to museums and trophy rooms, at the same time as they organized local history groups to build memorial stone cairns on main roads to mark the routes of early pioneering white "explorers."[45] In Israel the process is more recent: the remains of villages "cleansed" of inhabitants in 1948 and the memories of Palestinian presence in them has been widely erased. A recent film made by an Israeli and a Palestinian filmmaker traces a journey along the United Nations partition line of 1947, now well within claimed Israeli borders. In village after village, the physical remains of Palestinian houses have been pulled down or built over. Village names have been changed or translated from Arabic to Hebrew. The recently immigrant settlers seem unaware, or at least deny any knowledge, of former Palestinian owners and certainly of how they were forced to leave, and instead offer a largely mythical ancient past when asked to tell the story of the country.[46]

Such an "invention of tradition" which ignores indigenous owners is common in settler societies like South Africa and Australia. An alternative form of "invisibility" is to trivialize indigenous culture and draw on the old social Darwinian justifications of colonialism as the inevitable march of higher civilisations. This was widely used in most European settler colonies, but such can also be seen in the racialized hierarchy of politics in Malaysia, for example, or in contemporary Indian national disregard of Adivasi, the indigenous "tribals." Perhaps its most recent articulation was early in 2004, by Benny Morris, Professor of History at Ben Gurion University in Israel, who explicitly drew the links between colonial expansion in North America and in Palestine:

> The great American democracy could not have been achieved without the extermination of the Indians. There are cases in which the general and final good justifies difficult and cruel deeds that are carried out in the course of history. . . . Without the uprooting of the Palestinians, a Jewish state would not have arisen here.[47]

Even where indigenous people are recognized as citizens, it is assumed that their interests derive only from—and are identical with—those of the settler/nationalist state. National elites, even at their most anti-colonial, have frequently embraced modernity, identifying their goals to be the establishment of a nation state, which although independent of the colonizers, continues to share the conception of a "modern" nation as having coherent citizenry who shared histories, values, and loyalties.[48] Gandhi was a notable exception in his rejection of many of the values of western modernity, yet his Indian nationalist protégés, like Jawaharlal Nehru, who actually took up the reins of government in the newly independent nation, remained deeply imbued with a desire to "build a nation."

In the case of India, this has been carried out along the same lines of disadvantage to indigenous peoples, the Adivasi, as was the case under the British Raj. A major example is the widespread commitment to large dam building in India, which Nehru himself supported most famously in 1955 when he stated that "Dams are the temples of modern India." While he came to regret this statement, the national commitment to dam building has been sustained. India is the third largest dam builder in the world, having built 3,300 dams in the 50 years after independence. Arundhati Roy has argued that: "Dam-building grew to be equated with Nation-building" The main losers in these projects have been the people displaced by the massive dams, and the vast majority of them are Adivasi, or tribal people. The Sardar Sardovar dam in Gujerat, on the Narmada River, for example, has affected large numbers of people on the dam area upriver into Madhya Pradesh state. Over 57 percent of the immediately displaced peoples have been Adivasi whose hill lands were to be flooded, with the rest being Dalits [untouchable castes who are also deeply discriminated against] or Adivasi who had been displaced once already from other forest areas turned into nature reserves. Roy has explained:

> The ethnic "otherness" of their victims takes some of the pressure off the Nation Builders . . . it's much easier to justify. . . . In India, the fact is that there are no sort of vertical social bolts that connect Adivasis and Dalits to, let's say, the communities that will be deciding to make or design projects like this. So, there's no social connection. They just slough off into the sea. It doesn't really matter. You don't really know them. They don't have names or faces or anything.[49]

To date, the government has failed to offer any land to relocate the displaced: it claims to have none available. This story, and indeed India's disregard of its "invisible" indigenous peoples, is not uncommon in Asia. In this volume, Walsh describes the conflicts of Isaan people [ethnically Laotian] who are trapped by "modern" borders in northeastern Thailand and who now face massive dam building on their traditional lands on the upper Mekong River.

The implications of invisibility are that the lands which continue to be inhabited by indigenous peoples are regarded as being "empty." This is just how they appeared on the official maps used to plan the British nuclear tests in Australia in the 1950s. The words "Vacant Land" were marked right across the center of South Australia, where Yankunytjatjara people continued to hunt, camp, and have ceremonies. Yet no survey was carried out into these areas before the first mainland detonations in 1953, and only a single patrol officer, with no motor vehicle, just a train ticket, was employed to research the movements of the indigenous owners known to be based there. Both the Australian and the British governments were contemptuous of Aboriginal safety, indicated by Alan Butement, Australian Chief Scientist, when he criticized the worried patrol officer in 1956 for "placing the affairs of a handful of natives above those of the British Commonwealth of Nations."[50] A parallel example would be the Columbia River in the north western corner of the United States, where indigenous people have suffered the massive engineering distortion of extensive dams, choking off their salmon, and have continued to have the invading impact of industrial and nuclear waste sites imposed on the upper reaches of their river.[51]

While endorsement by indigenous peoples is often sought by environmental campaigners, some wilderness protection campaigns exhibit settler environmental nationalism. In European settler societies in particular, the myths of national origin which settlers have woven for themselves often depict settlers to have battled an awesome wilderness, struggling against environments which have not ever been touched by humans. In the case of Australia, the harsh and unpredictable environment is usually depicted as overcoming the brave, battling farmers. In the United States, the settlers are more often the triumphal winners, turning the forests into productive farmlands, but at the cost of the sublime wilderness itself. The untouched and untamed qualities of these imagined wildernesses are important in settler narratives which justify the colonizers' authority to be sole claimant to the land, as well as to celebrate their heroism. Those members of settler societies who have mounted campaigns to try to save the remnants of the wilderness may not necessarily reject this mythology. Instead of recognizing the role of indigenous peoples in creating, knowing, managing, and owning the pre-European landscape, they may be seeking, on the contrary, to preserve the archetypal wilderness because of its mythic "pristine" and prehuman qualities. An example is the National Parks Society in NSW, a large group of citizens who campaign tirelessly for the creation of new national parks. They were bitterly opposed to Aboriginal campaigns to jointly manage any such new parks because they insisted that indigenous people would not know how to look after the native environment. Another sustained example is the common practice of many mainstream environmental organizations in South Africa under the Apartheid regime of endorsing the racially discriminatory laws which obstructed access to "wilderness" areas for Africans and which limited African involvement in such organizations, despite their pressing need for environmental justice.[52]

There have been some political and legal victories in forcing settler colonies to "see" indigenous peoples, that is to recognize not only their existence and presence but their rights. In Australia, as in Canada, political action has produced land rights legislation in many states as well as the federal territories. Such victories reflect successful recruitment of allies from among the settler societies, from the ranks of left-wing activists, environmentalists, and even nationalist sympathizers. Too often, however, such victories have been eroded by adversarial legal challenges. The nation states which have emerged from colonial eras have so far not demonstrated much ability to respond to indigenous demands to render them visible again by restoring justice to them and their lands.

GLOBALIZATION: "IN THE NATIONAL INTEREST"

Economic globalization might have offered a way out by opening up avenues for indigenous peoples to negotiate directly with transnational corporations rather than through the national government. Instead such impact has invariably occurred along lines of powerlessness established initially by colonization then consolidated by post-colonial nation states. Transnational corporations utilize national legal and social structures wherever they are available to them, even at the same time as their penetration is destabilizing such structures. So the patterns of communication and control in the national structure, the "social bolts" to which Arundhati Roy refers, are seldom disrupted. Where Indigenous people are left in control of any land, it is invariably of commercially inhospitable areas which are occasionally found to be resource rich. They are perceived by the nation to be "empty" and therefore can be readily claimed and exploited as national property, to the further detriment of remaining indigenous owners. The self-interest of settler states or post-colonial national elites is usually best served by ignoring and further marginalizing indigenous colonized minorities where the interests of the latter might jeopardize the nation's claim over such profits.

Globalizing economies of course have deeply ambivalent relations with nation states. Where there are conflicts, transnational corporations seek to undermine the nation's authority. Yet they often find they can further their campaigns for access to natural resources most effectively if they draw on the rhetoric of nationalism and the celebration of the local. In Australia, transnational mining corporations have effectively used the rhetoric of "national interest" to further dispossess the indigenous land owners. In the Northern Territory and Western Australia, campaigns against Land Rights and Native Title legislation have been heavily funded by transnational mining companies, but their rhetoric has been entirely conducted in terms of "the national interest." The slogans stress the claim that indigenous minorities has no right to "hijack" or "lock up" such national resources which should be used "to benefit all Australians." Such campaigns have unquestionably heightened the hostility of the settler population in Australia toward indigenous peoples, exacerbating tensions and undermining Aboriginal civil and social rights still further.[53] In this volume there are two diverse but parallel examples of colonized indigenous people, the Sami in Finland[54] and the Mirrar people in northern Australia,[55] who are battling not only transnational corporations but their national populations as well as they try to protect their culturally significant resources.

The effects of the increasing penetration of global networks have not always weakened the position of indigenous peoples. Awareness and political contacts have been growing over the last 50 years as indigenous peoples have broken into the international forums of negotiation associated with the United Nations. Such emerging international networks found strong support among the confederations which were developing within nation states between indigenous communities, demonstrated in the meeting in September 2004 of the Indigenous Environmental Network (IEN), held in the Black Hills of South Dakota, when a wide range of Native American non-government organizations shared their experiences in mobilizing against environmental injustices.[56] Such networks across continents were greatly expanded as the internet has become more accessible, leading to more effective, because better informed, support from non-indigenous allies around the globe. At times, such support is disturbingly romanticized and naïve, and has become a limitation where allies expect indigenous peoples to fulfill static caricatures of "noble savages" or "primitive ecologists" in their search for exotic, pristine "wilderness." More information flowing more rapidly however is the most effective tool for overcoming such romanticized paternalism, and as direct communication and joint planning of support campaigns becomes increasingly possible over the Internet, the voices of indigenous peoples are being heard ever more directly, speaking for themselves. More than ever before, such channels of communication may allow indigenous colonized peoples to reach beyond the invisibility imposed on them by the nation state borders in which they or their land is held.

CONCLUSION

Colonialism offers a valuable lens for considering environmental injustice because it operates spatially. Colonial governments carve up space into zones designated as belonging to the colonizer or to the colonized, then controls who enters, who leaves, and what their behavior must be in each zone. In practice, colonizers have free movement, while the disempowered colonized peoples may exist "legally" only in some areas and are by definition "illegal" in all others. Sometimes this is done to exclude them, to deny their legitimate rights, and to make them invisible. Sometimes the purpose is to contain them, which then forces them into situations of extreme vulnerability to harm and to the effects of the most toxic and exploitative environmental health conditions. But the purpose might also be to control their movements across the wider "illegal" zones of their colonised country, that is not to keep them out but to keep them compliant and controllable when in the "colonizer's" zones.

It is not only indigenous people who have been colonized, and the experiences of indigenous colonized groups may often intersect with those of other colonized minorities, or majorities. Yet indigenous people are in a most disempowered position, as so much of their economy, cultural, social, and political life is directly derived from relations to their land. Where there have been waves of settlement prior to colonization, as in India and Malaysia, the indigenous "tribal" peoples had been marginalized already and found themselves marginalized still further by colonizers. The "new nations" which arose in circumstances of decolonization were stimulated by the anti-colonial struggle, but have also been conceptually and physically shaped by modernizing colonialism to endorse the idea of a coherent "nation" state and to agree to colonizer-defined borders. These new nations continue to marginalize and often to further repress indigenous people, as "primitives" who are not full citizens and, potentially, perhaps even traitors to the idea of the nation.

Indigenous expressions of concern about the environment are therefore made up of three components. Indigenous demands, firstly, are often made in terms of their loss. They demand recognition of their ownership of their country and specifically call for the reopening of access to their lost places, for restoration of their rights and status and for compensation for the loss of their economic base. Secondly, indigenous peoples frequently mount a critique of the exploitative economies and destructively inappropriate technologies of colonizers and their successors, based not only in inequality of access but, more fundamentally, on their specific indigenous knowledges of place which have social, economic, scientific, cultural, and spiritual dimensions. Finally, indigenous peoples' demands may also be protests in response to acute and specific damage to land and people based on an immediate threat: a dam, a mine, a toxic waste dump, a nuclear test site and radiation damage or further invasion, dispossession and displacement. Although the last component is the closest to those of working class and minority group demands for recognizing environmental injustice, the previous two set a wider agenda. There are many areas of common ground between all these groups and relationships are far more complex today than they were even two decades ago. Yet there remains a need for informed recognition and genuine negotiation to generate alliances for change. This is important because, as Howitt has argued in his analysis of indigenous people's conflicts with both nation states and resource companies in the Asia Pacific:

> Recognition of indigenous rights threatens the prerogatives of Capital and the State to make decisions for whole societies regardless of their treatment of their

citizens. . . . In challenging these unquestioned prerogatives, indigenous peoples are providing a foundation for envisioning alternative futures—genuinely new world orders—in which justice, equity, diversity and sustainability are achievable goals.[57]

NOTES

1. Terminology: language is fluid and always politically deployed. The use of capital letters in this essay follows current Indigenous usage in Australia. This may not be the same as that elsewhere. The terms adopted by Indigenous peoples to name themselves, when used as proper nouns, are capitalized here, such as Aboriginal, Indigenous and, less consistently, Black. Where these terms are used as adjectives in this essay they are not capitalized.

2. See Katona in this volume on the long term campaign by traditional owners, the Mirrar people, to stop the second mine in the area, at nearby Jabiluka.

3. "Indigenous" is a problematic term, often questioned after centuries of colonial domination and cross-cultural sexual relationships, but in most places there is a generally accepted popular concept of indigeneity. It is not uncontested: some newer settlers claim indigeneity, in opposition to even more recent colonization [see Bernstein on Taiwan, this volume]. Colonizers often claim indigeneity through cultural as well as political means. In some southeast Asian states like Laos, indigenous peoples are severely disadvantaged if they advertise their identity as indigenous and therefore use terms like ethnic minority in order to engage with state authorities and international NGOs. For all these reasons, the term indigenous is used flexibly in this chapter, on the understanding that despite such claims and counterclaims, there is a common body of experiences shared by all those people whose origin is understood to arise most directly from the land.

4. Foreman, C.H. and Melosi, M.V.: "Environmental Justice: Policy Challenges and Public History" in Melosi, M.V. and Scarpino, P. (eds.) *Public History and the Environment*, (Malabar, Fl.: Kreiger Publishing Co, 2004).

5. An approach with much in common with Animashaun, this volume.

6. A rich and complex analysis of colonial power exercised through the environment is Nancy J. Jacobs: *Environment, Power and Injustice: A South African History*, (Cambride: Cambridge University Press, 2003).

7. Isabel Flick and Heather Goodall: *Isabel Flick: The Many Lives of an Extraordinary Aboriginal Woman*, (Sydney: Allen and Unwin, 2004).

8. A few in harsh climates, like the Sami of far northern Europe or the Pitjantjatjara of Central Australia, have not faced invasion, but still have irrevocable alterations to their lives.

9. Boyce, J., "Fantasy Island" in Manne, R. (ed.) *Whitewash: On Keith Windschuttle's Fabrication of Aboriginal History*, (Melbourne: Black Inc. Agenda, 2003) pp. 17–80.

10. Moses, A.D, "Revisionism and Denial," in Manne: *Whitewash*, pp. 337–70.

11. Morris, B., *Domesticating Resistance : The Dhan-Gadi Aborigines and the Australian State*, (Oxford : Berg, 1989).

12. Wilpi, recounting childhood teaching in Goodall, H: *Invasion to Embassy: Land in Aboriginal Politics*, (Sydney: Allen and Unwin, 1996) pp. 34, 61.

13. Morris, B., "The causes and character of the Arab exodus from Palestine: the Israeli defense forces intelligence service analysis of June 1948" in Pappé, I. (ed.): *The Israel/Palestine Question*, (London: Routledge 1999); Pappé, I., "Were They Expelled? The History, Historiography and Relevance of the Palestinian Refugee Problem," in Karmi, Ghad and Cortran, E. (eds.), *The Palestinian Exodus, 1948–1988*, (London: Ithaca, 1999); Palestine Remembered: http://www.palestinerememb-ered.com/Haifa/Balad-al-Shaykh/index.html.

14. A chilling description of the "sweeping" campaign of violence is given by a participating member of the local Israeli armed force, known colloquially as *matate* or "brooms," which perpetrated the massacres and expulsions in northern Palestine, recorded at Farud Kibutz, in Sivan E., and Khleifi, M., *Route 181: Fragments of a Journey in Palestine-Israel*, a film directed by Sivan and Khleifi, co-produced by Momento! [France], Sourat Films [Belgium], Sindibad Films [UK] and WDR [Germany], 2003.

15. An example being the work of A. E. Newsome on red kangaroo habitat data embedded in *Red Kangaroo Dreaming Stories in the MacDonnell Ranges*, Alice Springs, cited in Knudtson, P. and Suzuki, D., *The Wisdom of the Elders* (Sydney: Allen and Unwin,1992) p. 134.

16. "Report of the Royal Commissioners of Inquiry into the Condition of the Crown Tenants in the Western Division of New South Wales," NSW Legislative Assembly, *Votes and Proceedings*, Vol. 4, 1901.

17. Brad Steadman, b. 1965, interview with author, Barwon River, Brewarrina, 1996.

18. Brosius, J. Peter, "Endangered Forest, Endangered People: Environmentalist Representations of Indigenous Knowledge," *Human Ecology*, 25(1):47–69, 1997.

19. Bradbury, D., (dir.) *Jabiluka*, (Sydney: Frontline Film Foundation, 1997), Morrison, J., "Protected Areas, Conservationists and Aboriginal Interests in Canada," in Ghimire, K.B. and M.P. Pimbert (Eds.), *Social Change and Conservation: Environmental Politics and Impacts of National Parks and Protected Areas.* (London: Earthscan. 1997), Suchet, S., *Indigenous People's Rights and Wildlife Management: Experiences from Canada and Southern Africa, Lessons for Australia.* Phd, Macquarie University. 1998

20. Williams, N. *The Yolngu and Their Land: A System of Land Tenure and the Fight for Its Recognition*, (Canberra: AIAS, 1986); Myers, F., *Pintupi Country, Pintupi Self,* (Washington and Canberra: Smithsonian and AIAS, 1986).

21. Joe Flick, b. 1923, interview with author, Dubbo, NSW, 1998.

22. For examples of survival strategies and land campaigns in NSW, Australia, see Goodall: *Invasion to Embassy*, passim.

23. Ibid, pp. 201–18.

24. Sylvia Hood-Washington, personal communication, December 2004.

25. Now permanently on display in the Smithsonian Institute's Museum of African Art, Washington D.C. See brief description and glimpses at: http://africa.si.edu/exhibits/insights/williamson2002–3-1.html

26. District Six Museum: http://www.districtsix.co.za/frames.htm, Coombes,

Annie E., *History after Apartheid : Visual Culture and Public Memory in a Demo-cratic South Africa*, (Durham : Duke University Press, 2003).

27. Sivan E., and Khleifi M., *Route 181: Fragments of a Journey in Palestine-Israel*, 2003.

28. Shalbak, I., "Palestine/Israel: History, Negation and Aspirations," paper delivered Building on Sand: Nation, Borders, Myth and History, Symposium, University of Technology, Sydney, August 2004.

29. Victoria Haskins and Margaret D. Jacobs, "Stolen Children and Vanishing Indians: The Removal of Indigenous Children as a Weapon of War in the United States and Australia, 1870–1940," in James Marten, (ed.) *Children and War: An Historical Anthology*, (New York and London: New York University Press) 2002; Haebich, A., *Broken Circles: Fragmenting Indigenous Families 1800–2000*, (Fremantle: Fremantle Arts Centre Press, 2000).

30. Basil H. Johnston, *Indian School Days* (Norman: University of Oklahoma Press, 1988).

31. *Breaking the Silence : An Interpretive Study of Residential School Impact and Healing as Illustrated by the Stories of First Nations Individuals.* Ottawa : Assembly of First Nations, 1994.

32. See Rauna Kuokkanen this volume.

33. Anderson B., *Imagined Communities: Reflections on the Origin and Spread of Nationalism*, (London: Verso, 1983).

34. Hasan, M., "India's Partition Revisited" in his (ed.) 2000: *Inventing Boundaries : Gender, Politics and the Partition of India*, (New Delhi, Oxford : Oxford University Press, 2000) pp. 1–25 ; Buthalia, U., *The Other Side of Silence: Voices from the Partition of India*, (London: Hurst and Co, 2000).

35. Howitt, R., Connell, J., and Hirsch, P. (eds.) *Resources, Nations and Indigenous Peoples: Case Studies from Australasia, Melanesia and Southeast Asia*, (Melbourne: Oxford University Press, 1996).

36. See Walsh this volume.

37. Dipesh Chakrabarty *Provincialising Europe: Post-Colonial Thought and Historical Difference,* (Princeton : Princeton University Press, 2000) p. 8.

38. Goodall: *Invasion to Embassy*, pp. 173–78.

39. Ibid, pp. 193–218.

40. Mager, A.K., *Gender and the Making of a South African Bantustan: A Social History of the Ciskei, 1945–1959*, (Portsmouth: Heinemann, 1999); Durning, A.B., *Apartheid's Environmental Toll*, (Washington, D.C.: Worldwatch Institute, 1990).

41. Durning, A.B., "Apartheid's Environmental Toll," p. 17 (Washington D.C.: WorldWatch Institute, World Watch paper 95, 1990) cited in Hallowes, David and Butler, Mark: "Power, Poverty and Marginalised Environments: A Conceptual Framework," in McDonald, David A., ed. *Environmental Justice in South Africa* (Athens, USA & Cape Town: Ohio University Press & University of Cape Town Press, 2002), pp. 51–77.

42. Lemon, A., *Apartheid: A Geography of Separation*, (Farnborough, Hants. : Saxon House, 1976).

43. Cohen, R., Muthien, Y.G., and Zegeye, A., eds *Repression and Resistance: Insider Accounts of Apartheid*, (London; New York: Hans Zell Publishers, 1990);

Harvey, Robert, *The Fall of Apartheid: The Inside Story from Smuts to Mbeki,* (New York: Palgrave Macmillan, 2003); Dovers, S., Edgecombe R., and Guest, B. (eds.) *South Africa's Environmental History: Cases and Comparisons.* Ecology and History Series. (Copublished with David Philip, Cape Town OAF. Athens: Ohio University Press, 2003).

44. See similar strategies in early colonial America, O'Brien, J. "They are so frequently shifting their place of residence": land and the construction of social place of Indians in colonial Massachusetts" in Daunton, M. and Halpern, R. (eds.), *Empire and Others: British Encounters with Indigenous People, 1600–1850,* UCL Press, 1999; and in Queensland, Australia, Evans R., Saunders, K., Cronin, K., *Exclusion, Exploitation and Extermination: Race Relations in Colonial Queensland* (Sydney: Australia and New Zealand Book Co., 1975).

45. Tom Griffiths, *Hunters and Collectors: The Antiquarian Imagination in Australia,* (Cambridge: Cambridge University Press, 1996).

46. Sivan and Khleifi, *Route 181: Fragments of a Journey in Palestine-Israel,* 2003.

47. Benny Morris, Professor of History at Ben Gurion University, Israel (quoted in "Survival of the Fittest" by Ari Shavit, *Haaretz Magazine,* January 9, 2004).

48. Dipesh Chakrabarty, *Provincialising Europe;* Ilan Pappé, *A History of Modern Palestine: One Land Two Peoples,* (Cambridge: Cambridge University Press, 2004) pp. 1–13.

49. Arundhati Roy, "The Greater Common Good," http://www.narmada.org/gcg/gcg.html; Roy, "Dammed" Transcript of interview for "Wideangle," PBS, 18th Sept 2003, http://www.pbs.org/wnet/wideangle/shows/dammed/transcript.html

50. Royal Commission into British Nuclear Tests in Australia: *The Report of the Royal Commission into British Nuclear Tests in Australia* (Canberra: Australian Government Publishing Service, 1985).

51. White, Richard, *The Organic Machine: The Remaking of the Columbia River,* (New York: Hill and Wang, 1995).

52. Khan, Farieda "The Roots of Environmental Racism and the Rise of Environmental Justice," in McDonald: *Environmental Justice in South Africa* (2002), pp. 15–48.

53. Richard Howitt, John Connell, and Philip Hirsch, "Resources, Nation and Indigenous Peoples," in their co-edited volume: *Resources, Nation and Indigenous Peoples: Case Studies from Australasia, Melanesia and Southeast Asia,* (Oxford and New York: Oxford University Press, 1996) p. 21.

54. See Ruokkanen this volume.

55. See Katona this volume.

56. Talli Nauman: "Indigenous Environmental Justice Issues Enter the Global Ring," *Citizen Action in the Americas,* No. 14, September 2004, http://www.americaspolicy.org/citizen-action/series/14-ien_body.html#development. See Rosier this volume for a detailed discussion of Native Americans and environmental justice campaigns.

57. Richard Howitt, et al.: "Resources, Nation and Indigenous Peoples," p. 21.

6

Racist Property Holdings and Environmental Coalitions
Addressing Memories of Environmental Injustice

Bill E. Lawson

A clear conscience is usually the sign of a bad memory

—Anonymous

Memory is the diary that we all carry about with us

—Oscar Wilde

There is often distrust when persons of color and whites have to work together to resolve environmental problems. Often the distrust has been generated by a history of racist actions and racial insensitivity to the concerns of persons of color. While there are numerous examples of these types of interactions, my focus herein will be the African American experience in the United States, particularly their attempts to find affordable and suitable housing. Since housing along with food and healthcare are often considered "primary goods," it is essential to examine how this good is distributed in a given society.[1] This is especially important in a society that is found on liberal tenets that require respect for the life plans of individuals.

According to John Rawls, one of the leading political philosophers of the twentieth century, primary goods are things that every rational person is presumed to want (1). These goods have value to a rational person no matter what his or her plan of life might be. In his important books *A Theory of*

Justice (2) and *Political Liberalism* (3) Rawls argues that the allocation of these goods is subject to the constraints of justice and that processing these goods has a bearing on a rational person's self-concept. The cornerstone of Rawls's account of social justice is his belief that the least-advantaged members of society, as measured by their possession of the primary goods, should be the gauge by which we judge the justness of the basic structure of society (4).[2]

In the case of housing how should we evaluate the justness of a society that has put legal and social restrictions on the ability of a segment of its population to get housing that it can afford? My interest here is the attempts to prevent African Americans, living in urban areas, from being able to purchase housing and live in neighborhoods that are consistent with their life plans. Here my concern is the ability of African Americans to buy homes in areas that they could afford to live but were often prevented from doing so. There are, of course, other housing issues. These include but are not limited to conditions of housing stock, affordable housing, and safe neighborhoods. Nonetheless I want to focus on the use of racist legal and non-legal means to keep blacks out of white neighborhoods. These practices will be the central focus of this chapter. It is from these attempts I get the phrase "racist property holding." Racist property holdings are those properties owned through practices that were done and are done to prevent African Americans from buying homes in white neighborhoods. These are African Americans that could afford housing in white neighborhoods and were prevented from doing so.

While my focus is on the African American experience with housing, I believe however that my conclusions are applicable to the experiences of other non-white groups that must join with whites to resolve environmental problems. I will return to this point later in the chapter. For the moment let's note that there are feelings of distrust when there has been a history of what persons of color see or feel as unjust interactions around the use and ownership of property. Ownership of property in the United States is connected to our understanding of property rights.

Closely connected to the right to property are two related issues that very rarely come into play in daily discussions of the formation of environmental coalitions. Very rarely considered are the issues of racist property acquisitions and racist property holdings. By this I mean the manner in which property was acquired and the manner in which it has been held. While the right to privately own property and to have its value protected is seen as a basic right, it is often a forgotten fact that much of the property owned currently is connected to the country's racist history. That is, whites came to own property when the government enforced laws that prevented persons of color from owning or acquiring property or enacted policies that took lands from persons with a historical claim to the land. The land taken becomes the property of whites. With land ownership the notion of property rights "kicks" in. Whites then view their defense of property as the expression of a right. Persons of color, on the other hand, see the private property right defense as a continuation of the racism that has prevented them from having a say in the basic decisions about land use and ownership.

THE VALUE OF PROPERTY

One of the basic beliefs that govern social and political life in the United States is that citizens have a right to own private property. Not only is the right to own property sacred, but it is thought that the government has a duty to protect the individual's right to own property. This property right gives property owners domain over their property. The right to own private property and to have a say over its use is to be respected and protected by the government. People are rightly self-interested when it comes to protecting their property. Is this conception of property rights helpful when it comes to resolving environmental problems through multiracial coalitions? Is the issue of "racist property holdings" a problem for environmental justice?

These are important questions and must at least be considered in the push for environmental justice. My aim in this chapter is to raise for consideration the manner in which answers to these questions impact on our understanding of environmental justice and racism. In order to do so, I want to explore the way the desire to protect the property rights and property value for white citizens has worked against the interest of persons of color in general and African Americans in particular. It is my contention that federal, state, and local government officials have always worked to protect the interests of propertied whites. This does not mean that no African Americans benefited from practices and policies to protect property. Two points should be remembered, first, it does not follow that because some African Americans benefited that the practices and policies were not racist. Second, the fact that some blacks benefited does not mean that the primary beneficiaries were not whites. This is clearly the case when it comes to the protection of property.

In the United States, protection of property is one of the main focuses of economic concern. Property values must be protected. When the property interests of landowners need protection, it is the role of the government to ensure that their interests are protected. When the government fails to protect the property and property rights it is the duty of property owners to protect their property. In the current context, I contend that property interests are accorded a certain amount of serious regard. Does the notion of property interest present a serious problem for environmental justice? I think it does. Consider those on the political right who contend that the right to property is essential to what it means to be an American. Any attempt by the government to "tell" or "force" persons to sell or rent their property to someone they do not want to, is a violation of the essential principles upon which this country was founded. Once the government uses its power to force you to use your property for aims that are not your own liberty and freedom are undermined. Governmental regulations that force homeowners to sell their homes to persons not of their choosing violate another sacred right, the right of free association. Persons should be allow to sell their or not sell their property as they see fit. Persons should be able to live in neighborhoods with persons of their choosing. Closely connected to the right to sell your property to whomever you choose is the right to choose their neighbors, the schools their children attend, and the social organization to which they belong and who can become a member of these arrangements. When the government forces persons to live with persons not of their choosing and it seems that these "others" do not share the same values, the economic value of their property diminishes. The government then is not protecting their property. It is also hurting their children because it reduces the value of the property they would inherit from their parents if the government had not forced them to live with persons not of their choosing. Person on the political right might argue that since the right to property is so essential to any restriction on land use can not be justified. This view would call into question the legitimacy of the Fair Housing Act. Nonetheless, we should remember that a sale of property by private sellers is not covered by the act. Still, it raises the provocative question: are fair *housing laws* a form of property taking. Taking here means unjustified infringement on the property rights of citizens to use their property as they see fit. This is a complex issue and one that needs examination. Nonetheless, let us assume for the moment that fair housing laws are not unjustified. We would still have the problem of people trying to protect their property value from being lower by persons they do not want to associate with. Do we have a clash of interest at this point? It would seem that some whites wanting to keep African Americans out of their neighborhood and African Americans wanting to have the right to live where they want to and can afford is a clash of interests.

From the perspective of protecting property, attempts by whites to keep African Americans out of their neighborhood was nothing more than standing up for their basic right to protect their property. However, when we connect the protection of property rights with a history of racist ideology and actions, we have a serious problem for intergroup relations. Let's look briefly at some of the practices used to keep property values up and African Americans out.

KEEPING PROPERTY VALUES
UP AND NEGROES OUT

While there are many practices and policies that had as the goal of keeping white neighborhood free of African Americans, I want to highlight four well known practices: Zoning restrictions, restrictive covenants, redlining, and intimidation. For a detailed exploration of these practices, I recommend Sylvia Washington's forthcoming book *Packing Them In: An Archeology of Environmental Racism in Chicago, 1865–1954*.[3] Her book is an excellent history and analysis of the manner in which racism his impacted on both housing and healthcare for African Americans. Washington gives us the disturbing history of environmental racism in Chicago. She notes that:

> African Americans who migrated to northern cities in the late nineteenth and early twentieth century were not welcomed with open arms by the larger body politic and social body. They were regarded and treated by the larger white social body as undesired and unwanted environmental and public health "nuisances" and forced to live and work in unhealthy and (physically and socially) degraded urban environments.[4]

In her work, Washington documents how the development of racially segregated neighborhoods was not the chance happening of voluntary association by African Americans. Many scholars have tried to explain urban segregation by pointing out that people like to live with their own kind, i.e., race. Even if this claim were true, the best way to ensure African Americans the right to freely associate with other African Americans would have been to let them make their own choice about where they wanted to live. This was not done. Regardless of topography (north or south) or locality (urban, rural, or suburban), African Americans in the United States were subjected to disciplinary actions that enforced their physical separation by law, social custom, or physical force.[5] The first of these practices was exclusionary zoning.

EXCLUSIONARY ZONING

When we examine housing patterns in the major American cities we find that areas zone for the worse environmental exploitation are generally those areas with high proportions of persons of colors. This can be explained by the use of zoning regulations to designate areas of the city for the housing of nonwhites, particularly African Americans. This means that African Americans were not allowed to live in certain neighborhoods. Excluding African Americans from certain neighborhoods by using zoning laws was the norm from the late 1880s until 1917. In 1917, the United States Supreme Court unanimously struck down a Louisville Kentucky racial zoning ordinance ruling that denial of full use of property "from a feeling of racial hostility" was unconstitutional (*Buchanan v. Warley*).[6] This type of zoning it was thought prevented whites from having the right to sell their land. Again, we have the protection of property rights for whites. It was unclear that this ruling benefited African Americans. This ruling had a least two ramifications: It forced whites to find another legal method to bar African Americans from whites neighborhoods, and second, the ruling did not bar using zoning regulations the purpose of placing unwanted hazards and vices in African American neighborhoods.

The history of many urban areas shows that neighborhoods with African Americans were most often marked out for the stationing of the cities vice area. In these areas prostitution, drugs, gambling, and other vices were relegated. The goal was to keep these vices out of white neighborhoods. The same zoning attitudes seem to exist when it came to decisions regarding environmentally hazardous waste and manufacturing.[7] But the problem remained as how to legally keeping African Americans out of white neighborhoods. When the United States Supreme Court ruled that zoning regulation could not bar African Americans from living in a particular area, the concept of restrictive covenants came to the fore.

RESTRICTIVE COVENANTS

Restrictive covenants are deed restrictions that apply to a group of homes or lots, property that's part of a specific development or subdivision. They are normally put in place by the original developer, and are different for every area of homes.[8] One aspect of the use of restrictive covenant became a part of a national trend. Deeds were drawn barring the sale of property to non-whites. The impetus behind the creation of restrictive covenants was the idea that racial separation of residences was necessary to maintain property values, real estate profits, and neighborhood stability.[9]

So widespread was the notion of restrictive covenants that the 1939 FHA Underwriting Manual contains instruction on the writing of Racial Restrictive Covenants:

> The Valuator should realize that the need for protection from adverse influences is greater in an undeveloped or partially developed area than in any other type of neighborhood. Generally, a high rating should be given only where adequate and enforced zoning regulations exist or where effective restrictive covenants are recorded against the entire tract, since these provide the surest protection against undesirable encroachment and inharmonious use. To be most effective,

deed restrictions should be imposed upon all land in the immediate environment of the subject location. . . . Recommended restrictions should include provisions for the following. . . . Prohibition of the occupancy of properties except
by the race for which they are intended. [10]

Like zoning restriction, restrictive covenants were challenge by African
Americans in the courts. It is interesting to note that Lorraine Hansberry's
novel *A Raisin in the Sun* draws on the experience of her father, Carl Hansberry, who brought a suit against restrictive covenants to the United States
Supreme Court. While the initial suit was not successful, in 1948 the United
States Supreme Court in *Shelley v. Kraemer* ruled racial restrictive covenants
unconstitutional. Not satisfied with just keeping African Americans out of
white neighborhoods, white real estate agents and insurance companies
developed the practice of insurance redlining.

INSURANCE REDLINING

Redlining: Unfair discrimination based not on the risk's characteristics but
on its location. The term is commonly associated with an insurer's refusal to
consider insuring any home or business within a specific area marked by a
line drawn on a map. [11]

Sociologist Gregory Squires notes:

Racial minorities and neighborhoods containing large numbers of minority residents are discriminated against in the provision of property insurance. This is
a systematic reality, not an anecdotal occurrence. In studies by fair housing
councils, insurance commissioners, academics, and others throughout the
United States, residents of minority communities have been discouraged while
residents of predominantly white neighborhoods have been encouraged to do
business with insurance agents. Whether or not this discrimination is intentional, traditional industry practices adversely affect racial minorities and
undermine the redevelopment of urban communities. [12]

The failure to provide insurance or adequate insurance has a negative impact
of the stability of a community. Home repairs are connected with closely
with the quality of the homeowners insurance. Home buying decisions are
based on the availability of homeowners insurance. African Americans
remember when they find out that their homes are under insured or cannot
be insured.

INTIMIDATION

When all of the legal means fails, whites have turned to physical intimidation
as a way to discourage Africans Americans from moving into white neigh-

borhoods. While there are numerous examples of racial intimidation, the views of Lorraine Hansberry on this issue are quit revealing. In her unpublished letter to the *New York Times* in 1964, which will be cited at length, she writes:

April 23, 1964

To the Editor,
The New York Times:
With reference to civil disobedience and the Congress of Racial Equality stall-in:

My father was typical of a generation of Negroes who believed that the "American way" could successfully be made to work to democratize the United States. Thus, twenty-five years ago, he spent a small personal fortune, his considerable talents, and many years of his life fighting, in association with NAACP attorneys, Chicago's "restrictive covenants" in one of this nation's ugliest ghettoes.

That fight also required that our family occupy the disputed property in a hellishly hostile "white neighborhood" in which, literally, howling mobs surrounded our house. One of their missiles almost took the life of the then eight-year-old signer of this letter. My memories of this "correct" way of fighting white supremacy in America include being spat at, cursed and pummeled in the daily trek to and from school. And I also remember my desperate and courageous mother, patrolling our house all night with a loaded German luger, doggedly guarding her four children, while my father fought the respectable part of the battle in the Washington court.

The fact that my father and the NAACP "won" a Supreme Court decision, in a now famous case which bears his name in the lawbooks, is—ironically—the sort of "progress" our satisfied friends allude to when they presume to deride the more radical means of struggle. The cost, in emotional turmoil, time and money, which led to my father's early death as a permanently embittered exile in a foreign country when he saw that after such sacrificial efforts the Negroes of Chicago were as ghetto-locked as ever, does not seem to figure in their calculations.[13]

At least two points should be drawn from Hansberry's letter. First, African Americans were embittered by both the racist attitudes and actions of whites. Secondly, whites often seem to forget the racist actions of the past and point to the progress that has been made towards what they think is racial progress.

While to some these tactics may be seen as wrong or ill advised, these actions should be seen as nothing more than persons trying to protect their property. Nevertheless, these act of intimidation left feeling of resentment in the mind of many blacks who were blocked from achieving their dreams. These tactics also impacted on the beliefs of other blacks who saw the behavior of whites as a clear sign of how little whites care for the welfare of their fellow citizens.

DISTRUST AND COALITIONS

It may be raised as an objection here that in the past 20 to 30 years the situation of persons of color in general and blacks in particular has improved to the point that it no longer makes sense to speak of race as a factor in housing policy. It is clear that there is a difference of opinion regarding the current role of race in housing policy. There have been numerous studies that indicate that whites and blacks in the United States see their respective positions in the state quite differently. To the degree that survey data accurately depict people's views, blacks live in a different world from whites. To whites, racial discrimination has declined almost to the vanishing point and the future of racial equality is promising. To blacks, on the other hand, racial discrimination is extensive and (at most) grudgingly yielding; the situation of blacks may be worsening; and black suffering result from structural biases and white indifference or hostility. Thus, whites and Blacks in the United States disagree about how much social progress has been made in race relations. It seems clear that many blacks feel that social and economic policies have been and remain geared towards the interests of whites over the interests of people of color. Yet through all of this, blacks and other racial minorities are asked to be race transcending. This means forgetting the racist history of property holdings and act as if we are starting from ground zero. Whites often cannot understand why persons of color just cannot forgive and forget. The racist actions are in the past it is claimed.

For black citizens race transcending mean not putting the interest of one's own race above the legitimate interest of members of other races. We live in a society that has constantly put the interests of whites over the interests of blacks. In part, the interests of whites are given more weight because we live in a society that has always valued the interests of whites over persons of color. Many in the environmental justice movement claim that they are concerned to remove any barriers that prevent African Americans from living in environmentally degraded areas and for them to have a voice in environmental policies. Nevertheless, as philosopher Howard McGary notes: It is one thing to say that there should not be any racial barriers that prevent African American advancement and quite another thing to say that African American interests should be promoted. Today most African American leaders are trying to find ways to promote legitimate African American interests in a society that has demonstrated too little regard for these interests.[15]

Many in the environmental justice movement have faith that liberal democracy can work to resolve both social and environmental problems.

They think that black and white interests converge around environmental issues. They may believe as Bernard Boxill writes that self-interest will override racist attitudes. "Even when people have racist attitudes, most will resist indulging them when doing so will be seriously detrimental to their interests." [16] A review of public policies regarding blacks causes this belief to be of questionable worth.

It is this racial history and current claims that race no longer matters that impacts on interactions between persons of color and most often—white property owners. It is this history that often makes members of racial and ethnic groups feel uneasy about the working of a society that puts emphasis on the individual effort while lumping all members of a racial group together. This history has bred distrust between the racially defined groups. Without trust workable environmental coalitions will fail.

Given the history of racist practices meant to keep blacks out of white neighborhoods, it should not be surprising that there is distrust of whites by blacks when it comes to issues of land use. Howard McGary discusses the issue of distrust in the area of health care. It should be clear to any knowledgeable person that in the case of health care there have been past policies and practices that have certainly played a role in engendering distrust.[17] Deplorable medical services, involuntary sterilization, the use of blacks as human guinea pigs, as was the case in the Tuskegee study have engendered feeling of distrust of both the health care system in particular and whites in general. The same issues regarding trust arise in the area of housing. McGary notes, and I agree, that past denial of rights have not always flowed from malevolent motives. As our discussion on the sanctity of private property shows, persons can be concerned with the values of their property and not intending to harm blacks. But when there is a hurtful history the persons affected are quick to see the attitudes of current land owners as having the same motives as the ardent racist.

A review of black American history does not provide much hope for blacks putting trust in many whites to do the right thing. Because of this history many blacks are reluctant to trust whites. They feel that most whites cannot be trusted not to act with racist motivation, or to act without racist intent. Part of the problem here is that many whites often seem to have no memories of the bad things that have been done to African Americans. The failure to remember the wrongs done to persons of color are documented in this volume. All over the planet persons of color have negative memories about their interactions with whites around the issue of land use and ownership. This lack of remembering is not limited to land use issues.

DIFFERENT MEMORIES

Few whites seem to remember the attempts to keep blacks out of white neighborhoods. Often there is very selective memory of the part of whites about the acts of intimidation as a means to prevent blacks from moving into formerly all white neighborhood. In a clear example of wanting to be on the right side of history, it is often very difficult to find whites who will admit to being a part of a mob or quickly moving out of the neighborhood when black families start to move in.

This turns out to be the same phenomenon that makes it difficult to find whites who protested integration in the south in the 1950s and 1960s. Nonetheless, African Americans remember the racist history. The same phenomenon takes places in discussions of environmental wrongs. What this means is that there must be open and frank discussion about the racial history of the particular community and the United States. While the social interest of whites and blacks often converge, the checkered history of protecting property has a negative effect on social interaction between the races. In the end, property owners can have any interest they want in keeping mass transit or any environmental disruption out of their neighborhoods. However, in the final analysis persons of color often come to the table with memories of the racist history. Part of the goal for environmental policy makers is to convince racial and ethnic stakeholders, as much as possible, that the rationales given by whites do not represent a continuation of the racist history. It will be uncomfortable for all stakeholders, both whites and persons of color. Whites cannot become defensive and claim that they are not responsible for the past situation. Regardless of how whites feel, racial and ethnic persons see whites as gaining from a legacy of racist property acquisition and attempting to maintain the status quo. Persons of color, on the other hand, cannot be on the attack. The goal is to compromise and work out a plan that will solve the common issues of environmental concern. Hopefully, it will engender trust. This must be the trend of future environmental policies and practices.

In conclusion, my goal when I started writing this chapter was to articulate why there was sometime distrust between the races when it came to forming environmental coalitions. I suggested that persons of color, blacks in particular, bring to the table memories of past injustices involving the use of land. I concluded that the history of property use must be put on the table at the outset to prevent misunderstanding about persons motives for trying to protect the value of their property or controversial land use proposals. Whites cannot be defensive and persons of color cannot be on the attack. The goal is to get the history on the table so the mistakes of the past will not be repeated. In this regard, the issue of trust becomes very important. What does it mean to trust members of a group that has used property ownership laws to your group's disadvantage? This question must be answered. One of the first steps to answering it is to realize that there are these concerns over the history of land use and ownership. This is also often the first step to successful coalitions. Of course, none of this guarantees that the coalition will be successful; it is often difficult to overcome bad memories.

NOTES

1. McGary, H., *Distrust, Social Justice, and Health Care. The Mount Sinai Journal of Medicine*, Volume 66, Number 4, September 1999, p. 236.

2. Ibid.

3. Washington, S., *Packing Them In: An Archeology of Environmental Racism in Chicago, 1865–1954* (Lanham, Md.: Rowman and Littlefield, 2004).

4. Washington, ibid., chapter 5.

5. Washington, ibid., chapter 5.

6. Gotham, K. F., *Race, Real Estate, and Uneven Development: The Kansas City Experience, 1900–2000* (Albany: State University of New York Press, 2000), p. 38.

7. See this book.

8. Jane Wickell, *Your Guide to Home Buying/Selling*, http://homebuying.about.com/

9. Gotham, K. F., *Race, Real Estate, and Uneven Development: The Kansas City Experience, 1900–2000* (Albany: State University of New York Press, 2002), 37.

10. Sources: Robert Weaver, *The Negro Ghetto* (New York: Harcourt, Brace and Company, 1948), p. 72. Originally in Federal Housing Administration, Underwriting Manual, 1939, sections 932 and 935.

11. http://glossary.reference-guides.com/Insurance/Redlining/

12. http://www.nhi.org/online/issues/79/isurred.html

13. Nemiroff, R. and L. Hansberry, *To Be Young, Gifted, and Black: Lorraine Hansberry in Her Own Words* (Englewood Cliffs, N.J.: Prentice-Hall, 1969).

14. Minorities and Majorities

15. Howard McGary, *Race and Social Justice*, (Malden, Mass.: Blackwell Publishers, 1999), p. 192.

16. Bernard Boxill, "The Underclass and the Race/Class Debate," in Bill E. Lawson, ed., *The Underclass Question* (Philadelphia, Penn.: Temple University Press, 1992), p. 24.

17. McGary, p. 239.

REFERENCES

Gotham, K. F. (2002). *Race, Real Estate, and Uneven Development: The Kansas City Experience, 1900–2000*. Albany, State University of New York Press.

McGary, H. (1999). *Distrust, Social Justice, and Health Care*.

Nemiroff, R. and L. Hansberry (1969). *To Be Young, Gifted, and Black; Lorraine Hansberry in Her Own Words*. (Englewood Cliffs, N.J.: Prentice-Hall).

Washington, S. (2004). *Packing Them In: An Archeology of Environmental Racism in Chicago, 1865–1954*. (Lanham, Md.: Rowman and Littlefield).

7

Racialized Spaces and the Emergence of Environmental Injustice

K. Animashaun Ducre

Environmental racism constitutes any action that differentially affects persons based on their race or class. This action can be a deliberate one, or an unintended consequence. Previous scholarship has focused on the disproportionate outcomes and discriminatory policies resulting from environmental inequality. Today, attention has turned toward the social and political climate that gives rise to environmental inequality. *What are the antecedents of environmental racism and injustice?* The standing arguments in the research have stemmed from the notion of *causality* and *temporality*. The introduction of *racialized spaces* as a theoretical framework is important for investigating causality and temporality as it relates to the emergence of environmental unjust situations. This framework informs current discourse and expands upon the notions of justice put forth by community leaders and scholars, and circumvents the limitations posed by earlier work. The purpose of this chapter is to present scholarly contributions to the theory on racialized spaces and to build a bridge between this theoretical framework and the experiences shared by environmental justice communities.

ENVIRONMENTAL JUSTICE RESEARCH AND ITS LIMITATIONS

"While we have contributed greatly to policymakers' understanding of exposure and environmental hazards we have by now largely exhausted the answers that current methods offer. We need to rethink the environmental justice project and to be more intellectually open and methodologically creative."[1] One of the most consistent criticisms in regards to environmental justice research is its preoccupation with investigating disproportionate outcome, rather than processes that enable environmentally unjust situations and policies to occur. Related to this, there is very little theorizing on the societal patterns that reproduce inequality in the form of environmental inequality.

In previous research, environmental justice scholars have articulated three explanations of environmental injustice: 1) economic, 2) sociopolitical, and 3) racial.[2] Many critics who reject the notion of intentional environmental discrimination rely on market determinism of the economic explanation.[3] These authors suggest that lower property values attract poor residents *and* industrial chemical complexes simultaneously, emphasizing that there is no intent to place the poor and people of color in vulnerable positions. Sociopolitical explanations of environmental injustice describe inequality of power differentials within siting processes within local, state, and federal environmental policies that lead to disproportionate impact. This explanation is referred to as *procedural justice*[4] or *procedural equity*.[5] In addition, these explanations describe restricted access to governmental resources that leave poor neighborhoods and communities of color vulnerable to the promises of hazardous industry.[6] Finally, the racial discrimination explanation emphasizes the institutional, as well as the individual acts of discrimination born out of prejudice.

These explanations have two major weaknesses. First, it is difficult to neatly categorize the complex processes that go into discriminatory outcomes. Many of these processes occur simultaneously. Furthermore, these processes influence one another. For example, economic explanations are embedded, both directly and indirectly, within racial explanations. Examples later in this chapter will highlight communities that are constrained by both economic decline, racial discrimination in housing, as well as the lack of political influence. The multiple oppressions experienced by marginalized folks in the United States make it very difficult to tease out the "isms." While empiricists can statistically control for the impacts of space, time, race, and other variables in an empirical analysis, theorists are often forced to ignore confounding variables in creating a concise framework. This framework produces an ideal type of environmental justice community, for which there are numerous exceptions.

Secondly, assumptions that rely on the economic, sociopolitical, and racial explanations articulated above, inevitably lead to remedies limited to distributive justice. Therefore, increasing access to financial markets, expanding civic participation, and/or affirmative action-oriented policies to address minority participation are the key means of achieving environmental justice.

These remedies are based on an *integrationist-centered* ideology, an ideological foundation rooted in the American civil rights movement. Some call into question the political success of a movement based on an integrationist-centered approach in both the civil rights and environmental justice movements. One scholar notes, "a narrow focus on issues of distributive justice neglects the search for social structures and agents that cause the environmental problems." Likewise, some scholars stress that the aims of the civil rights movement failed to confront structural racism and oppression.[7] Harvey also critiques the way in which the principles of environmental justice fall short:

> But it is exactly here that some of the empowering rhetoric of environmental justice itself becomes a liability. . . . The abstractions cannot rest solely upon a moral politics dedicated to protecting Mother Earth. It has to deal in the material and institutional issues on how to organize production and distribution in general, how to confront the realities of global power politics and how to displace the hegemonic powers of capitalism not simply with dispersed, autonomous, localized, and essentially communitarian solutions . . . but with a rather more complex politics that recognizes how environmental and social justice must be sought by a rational ordering of activities at different scales.[8]

The environmental justice movement presents a critical perspective on the social structure of accumulation, mass production, and consumption, human rights and globalization. Activists have an opportunity to critique capitalism via environmental degradation and exploitation. Critically evaluating the ideology behind distributive justice and expanding the notion of justice may serve to build a discourse that goes beyond mere legislative and legal tactics.

THEORY OF RACIALIZED SPACES: A WORKING DEFINITION AND RATIONALE

Theoretical starting points that describe the emergence of environmental racism and injustice are lacking. Likewise, the application of a theory on racialized spaces has been limited up until this point. Few sources put forth a comprehensive theory on racialized spaces. For some, racialized spaces constitute the dominant group's affirmation of Otherness.[9] Thus, their articulation of racialized space encompasses the idea of racist thought as praxis. Others limit their conceptualization to the political economy of space from a neo-Marxian perspective.[10] Meanwhile, Massey and Denton[11] articulate how private actions and institutional policies worked together to create urban ghettoes. The early work of the Chicago School also spent a significant portion of their scholarship on human ecology and the race relations cycle linking it spatially within zones of the center city.[12] The working definition provided in this chapter presents a framework that combines space, social

relations, and power, and how these elements inform one another. My definition of racialized spaces is:

> *Historic practice and spatial designation of a particular area for racial and ethnic*
> *minorities as a means of containment and social control. This practice serves to*
> *reinforce preconceived notions of Otherness or, result in the creation of culturally*
> *inferior Other.*

The key themes in this definition for racialized space are history, containment, and social control. History acknowledges the genealogy of patterns
that push and pull the poor and people of color under racial and/or class
segregation. Examples include violence, deed restrictions, restrictive covenants, blockbusting, redlining, slum clearance, and the creation of public
housing. Containment emphasizes the geographic isolation of Others within
racialized spaces from, and by, those with power. Social control refers to the
methods that maintain racialized spaces like surveillance and institutional-
ization.

HISTORICALLY SITUATING THE FORMATION
OF RACIALIZED SPACES

"The segregation of American blacks was no historical accident; it was
brought about by actions and practices that had the passive acceptance, if
not the active support, of most whites in the United States"[13]. According to
authors, there are three ways in which African-Americans in particular have
been spatially isolated deliberately from white Americans: violence, restrictive covenants, and blockbusting. The first collective actions against black
encroachment into white space resulted in violent eruptions. Examples
include the race riots in major cities between 1900 and 1920. The riots were
reactions to the steady stream of black migrants into New York in 1900, East
St. Louis in 1917, and Chicago in 1919. Violence arose in the form of angry
mobs, cross burnings, and bombings to illustrate white resistance to black
encroachment. More organized efforts came in the form of neighborhood
improvement organizations and homeowner associations. Homeowners
worked formally to bar the sale and rental of homes to blacks and other ethnic minorities, in the form of restrictive covenants, restrictive deeds, incorporation, and zoning.[14] Restrictive covenants were enforceable agreements
made between property owners that prohibited the sale or rental of their
property to nonwhites for a specified period of time, typically 20 years.
These covenants began to appear around the turn of the century and persisted until the Supreme Court declared them unconstitutional in 1948. Prior
to the use of restrictive covenants, individual landowners created deed

restrictions for similar purpose until the Supreme Court also struck it down in 1917. However, it was not until the formal creation of restrictive covenants that entire neighborhoods were organized against the entry of nonwhites. Davis referred to these acts as a form of privatized Jim Crow, which succeeded in erecting exclusive white walls in Los Angeles during the 1930s and 1940s. After the legal defeat of restrictive covenants, some affluent suburban communities in the 1950s favored a new form of white separatism by flexing their political power and lobbying for incorporation and rezoning. In regards to the *Lakewood Plan*:

> The Los Angeles County Supervisors agreed to let Lakewood contract its vital services (fire, police, library, and so on) at cut-rate prices determined by the county's economy of scale (i.e. indirectly subsidized by all county taxpayers. This allowed suburban communities to reclaim control over zoning and land use without the burden of public expenditures proportionate to those of older cities. . . . Residents of minimal cities could zone out service-demanding low-income and renting populations.[15]

While Davis text is a case study of Los Angeles and may not be generalizable, there are similarities among neighborhood incorporation movements nationwide. By 1930, 981 cities, towns, and villages had adopted some form of zoning ordinance, impacting more than 46 million people.[16] Today, over 32 million Americans live within a residential community association that typically represent new communities where membership is mandatory.[17] One of the more important facts to note is that during this time period in which zoning ordinances emerged, many of the Southern blacks were not fully enfranchised. Therefore, their living spaces remain unincorporated and their backyards were subsequently slated as the de facto dumping grounds that other neighborhoods refused to host. In the case in Texarkana, Texas in 1964, an all-white zoning board permitted the construction of African American subdivision built on top of highly contaminated wood treatment plant site.[18] A process called *expulsive zoning* has been documented and it has severe implications for environmental justice. This process involves the rezoning of predominantly black residential areas to industrial areas by all-white planning boards.[19]

As white fear mounted, the space for nonwhite residences became smaller and thus, more costly. As result, real estate agents and their boards profited through a strategy called blockbusting. Here, agents targeted an area for racial/residential transition and steered nonwhite residents in that direction. Meanwhile, agents played upon white fears by advancing the idea of an invasion, spurring white flight. Those same agents would amass property, convert them into rental units and sell to African American or other non-white families. They were able to meet non-white residents' demand for property at the highest bidder. This practice persists, today. Over the years, the government played a greater role in fostering racialized spaces. The private actions of landowners and home associations set the stage for institutional policies that continued the pattern of spatial isolation of minorities. Meanwhile, the suburbanization of white America increased dramatically. Federal programs, such as the Home Owners Loan Corporation (HOLC) and urban renewal projects emerged out of the racist ideologies of the defunct restrictive covenants.

HOLC was a New Deal program whose purpose was to make home financing easier through low-interest home loans and uniform mortgage payments. The home finance system for urban residents was founded upon a ratings system based on risk. Riskier areas became synonymous with blacker areas within the central cities. This ratings system influenced subsequent housing initiatives under the Federal Housing Administration and the Veteran's Administration and evolved into what is referred to as redlining. According to Wright, "explicit endorsement of segregation—by class and race—was not only an outcome of federal housing policies; it was a stated principle in every government housing program."[20] Blacks were targeted in the selection and location of public housing. In addition, slum clearance and highway programs had a disparate impact on people of color and the poor.

CONTAINMENT

One scholar writes, "Segregation by law is the clearest manifestation of the physical control of the space of an inferior group, a group excluded from full membership in the polity, a group that must be morally, politically, and physically *contained*."[21] The previous section outlined the historical progression in the politics of containment: People of color and their mobility were at times individually sanctioned and/or constrained through institutional discrimination.

Why have racialized spaces become a form of containment? Philosophers Lawson and Mills contend that blackness has been equated with evil in a dichotomy against white as good and pure. For Lawson, "racializiation is the manner in which conceptions of racial standing enter into our understanding of social contexts and experiences."[22] Hence, attitudes regarding urban (black) versus suburban (white) socio-spatial relations also become racialized: "For many persons, their understanding of the patterns of behavior associated with a racial group is connected with space, giving meaning to the differences in lifestyles and standards of living based on a racial criterion."[23] Mills goes further by introducing the dichotomy between black and white within the body politic as one culturally superior and inferior, organic and inorganic, essential and non-essential. He contends that space is constructed by relations of power and it is constructed discursively. Thus, if the Other is somehow demonized, containment as a strategy becomes critical. The racist attitudes behind the politics of containment are seen as protection strategy against the scourge of evil. The most extreme form of containment are concentration camps, as witnessed in Nazi Germany with Jews and the American practice of internment to Japanese Americans during World War II. In fact, Bauman speaks of the inhumanity as a function of social distance: "With the growth of distance, responsibility for the other shrivels, moral dimensions of the object blur, till both reach the vanishing point and disappear from view."[24] The distance can be physical, such as the separation of whites suburban residents from inner city ghetto residents, or this distance can be mental, viewing housing project residents as lazy, criminal, menacing, and intellectually inferior. In regards to the African American experience, Massey and Denton conclude that these deliberate containment practices have resulted in the *hypersegregation* of blacks, which set their experiences apart from other racial and ethnic minorities. Accordingly, they contend that blacks are isolated on all of the five dimensions of geographic segregation: uneven, isolation, clustered, concentrated, and centralized. Unevenness is characterized by a population distribution of over- and underrepresentation of racial minorities. Isolation refers to the low probability of sharing interracial neighborhoods. A clustered geographic space is a dense area predominated by one racial minority, while concentrated space is not only dense, but small. Centralized refers to the creation of geographic space so distinct that it becomes identified as the urban core.

While many acknowledge race as a social construction, I contend that race is also spatially constructed. The result, Barton[25] says, is the creation of distinct *cultural landscapes* for whites and blacks in America. Furthermore, these landscapes are separate and unequal. These spatial arrangements reflect and reinforce social relations. It reinforces the differences in gender (women's private space versus men's public space), race (the black urban core or the Latino Barrio versus the luxury high rise or suburban gated community). For Harvey[26] and Lefebvre,[27] the production of social space is primarily coded by a class system. Each group has knowledge of the spatial segregation, for it is coded in our language. Metaphors like, "this side of the tracks" and "Uptown" abound, and they are infused with meaning beyond simply location. They evoke racial and class subtexts. In addition to reinforcing class distinction, the production of space is also involved in social and cultural reproduction. People begin to "know their place" in society and adapt their behavior according to its dictates.[28] Space is relational in a sense that it pits these dichotomies against one another. However, space is also hierarchical.[29]

SOCIAL CONTROL

The utilization of social control in the maintenance of racialized spaces is best illustrated in the writings of Michel Foucault. His presentation of the *panopticon*—an omnipotent gaze—reflects the degree of social control of the dominant over Others.[30] Social control from periphery involves *surveillance*: the guarding of white and/or affluent spaces from invasion. Pat Hill-Collins contends that one of the critical elements in the new politics of containment is surveillance. In regards to black women's oppression, she writes: "Where segregation used to keep Black women out of the classroom and boardroom, surveillance now becomes an important mechanism of control."[31]

Davis has a chapter dedicated to the militarization of space in his case study of Los Angeles.[32] There is a trend among prosperous residents and architecture designers for high-tech gates, alarm systems, and security around both private residents and public spaces. It is evident that the emergence of cameras and electronic fences are meant to keep out undesirables. Surveillance is an inevitable byproduct of containment. To erect physical and mental boundaries around particular spaces, one must maintain constant guard to ensure privacy and control.

Another Foucauldian element that is useful for a framework on racialized space is his articulation of a *carceral archipelago*, a reconstruction of social institutions based on the model of the prison. Illustrations of this archipelago typically present each institution in the form of a distinct sphere, complete with rules and regulations to guide conformity around its subjects/prisoners. Along with the prison, other examples of distinct spheres would be schools, mental institutions, churches, etc. Racialized spaces expand upon this notion of an archipelago with spheres representing distinct race and ethnic identities, class, or gender. These spheres/spaces are socially ordered, and its citizens/prisoners contained and guarded to maintain control. The creation of an urban core is an example of a carceral archipelago. As suburbs grew, the commercial and business interests followed suit. Now, residents of the urban core are characterized by extreme poverty and unemployment.[33] Mobility and access to resources found in the suburbs are further blocked by poor public transportation systems between those within the urban core and the resource-rich periphery.

RACIALIZED SPACES AND
ENVIRONMENTAL JUSTICE

So, how does racialized spaces relate to the emergence of environmental justice communities? The idea is that communities of color and poor neighborhoods are spatially designated as inferior. Through both de jure and de facto acts of segregation, vulnerable pockets are formed to house the undesired population. In many cases, the undesirables are the poor and people of color. The result is that the spaces and its inhabitants are viewed in either two extremes: invisible or hypervisible. In certain instances, racialized spaces are perceived to be invisible and the policies and policymakers fail to take into account the needs of its inhabitants. For example, these communities may lack adequate municipal services such as parks and recreation, sanitation, police, and medical facilities. These spaces are often marked by substandard infrastructures like hospitals and schools. While policymakers respond to appeals from corporate and other affluent interests, the voice of the occupants within racialized spaces seems absent.

In the other extreme, the density of racial and ethnic minorities and/or those with low socioeconomic status serve to make their communities highly visible to outsiders, thereby reinforcing stereotypes. This results in an ideological binary between black (and brown) and white space. Those that occupy space outside of the racialized space tend to have monolithic images of those that live within those spaces. All of these perceptions make it possible for the development of environmental racism and injustice. The following offers examples of community campaigns that I was involved in as an organizer for Greenpeace in its environmental justice campaign from 1994–1999.

GEOGRAPHIC ISOLATION OF INDIAN COUNTRY AND ENVIRONMENTAL RACISM

A Native American reservation is most likely the most extreme contemporary example of racialized spaces. Territories for Indian occupation were carved out and designated by treaties over a century ago. The isolation is not only geographic, but it is political, since certain tribes are recognized as sovereign nations. This isolation makes them particularly appealing to hazardous industry, especially the nuclear industry. In the late 1980s, the nuclear industry began a campaign to site nuclear storage facilities on Indian land, from proposed low-level waste storage sites among the Mescalero Apache, in Ward Valley among the lands occupied by the Colorado River Indian tribes, and a high level site at Yucca Mountain.

Small tribal governments were ill equipped to handle the technicalities involved in complex industrial processes and representatives from the mining, nuclear, and chemical, and pulp and paper processing corporations were well aware of this fact. The number of projects slated for Indian country prompted the formation of the national Indigenous Environmental Network (IEN) in 1988.[34]

THE *INVISIBILITY* OF FOREST GROVE AND
CENTER SPRINGS, LOUISIANA

Black and white members of the community group, Citizens Against
Nuclear Trash (CANT) waged a nine-year battle to defeat a proposed uranium enrichment facility in their town of Homer, Louisiana. The proposed
nuclear facility site was to be situated within the predominantly African
American neighborhoods of Forest Grove and Center Springs that were
established by black freedmen over a hundred years ago. The CANT case is
an example of racialized space and invisibility. Despite the significant history
and permanence of Forest Grove and Center Springs, the environmental
impact assessment and license application for the enrichment facility failed
to mention the existence of the historic black towns. In fact, the site plans
proposed to close the road that connected the two invisible towns.

BAYVIEW HUNTERS POINT AND ECONOMIC
CONTAINMENT IN SAN FRANCISCO

Despite being home to the largest concentration of homeowners in the city
of San Francisco, the predominantly African American community of Bay-
view-Hunters Point on the southern edge of San Francisco is host to the
city's two power plants, the professional sports stadium, the city's wastewater treatment facility, the defunct and highly contaminated Naval base, and
a large chemical warehouse corridor. In a fight to defeat a proposal for a
third power plant in the neighborhood, residents rallied together and
claimed that adverse health impacts existed from current industry. Soon after
our campaign, the San Francisco Health Department revealed that Bayview
children had the highest reports of asthma and respiratory-related cases in
the entire city. Eventually, the new power plant project was defeated, but
Bayview is faced with an almost insurmountable task of neighborhood
cleanup and economic revitalization. Residents have the highest level of
unemployment and this fact makes it very difficult to reject projects with the
promise of jobs. Rising costs for housing in San Francisco makes it virtually
impossible for families to move out of the area making Bayview Hunters
Point a prime example of racialized spaces and economic containment.

FEDERAL HOUSING INITIATIVE PUTS
NEW ORLEANIANS ON LANDFILL

The community around Agricultural Street in New Orleans was established
during the 1970's pursuit of urban renewal and revitalization efforts of cities
all across the United States. The Agricultural Street community was mar-

keted specifically to African Americans as part of the federal initiative to increase minority homeownership. However, new homeowners were not told that their new homes were built upon a former unregulated municipal landfill.

After successful mobilization on the part of the community, the Environmental Protection Agency designated a part of the area as a Superfund site, making federal funds available for environmental remediation. However, residents were chagrined to learn that the EPA had no plans for relocating the residents. Rather, the agency's recommendation for cleanup was to remove a few feet of contaminated soil and replace with new soil over a liner.

FROM SUGARCANE TO CANCER ALLEY

Cancer Alley is used to describe the industrial-residential corridor from New Orleans to Baton Rouge along the Mississippi River. This 85-mile stretch is host to over a hundred chemical complexes, including oil refineries, fertilizer plants, electrical stations, grain elevators, etc. While there are both black and white residents along Cancer Alley, the US Commission on Civil Rights confirmed that black residents bear a disproportionate impact from polluting industry. Black residents are more likely to live closer to these complexes. The connection between racialized spaces and Cancer Alley is based upon the historic spatial location of minorities in the area. Before the advent of industry, the land along the Mississippi was comprised of large sugarcane plantations. After the abolition of slavery, freedmen and their families remained on the grounds of these plantations as sharecroppers. With the slow growth and subsequent demise of the sugar cane industry, these large agricultural tracts were attractive to offers of immense chemical complexes. Thus, poor, black tenants found themselves boxed in between large chemical giants.

CAUSALITY AND TEMPORALITY: STANDING ARGUMENTS IN THE ENVIRONMENTAL JUSTICE DEBATE

The issues of causality and temporality arise in previous theorizing on environmental injustice. Early explanations tried to pinpoint a particular actor or action as agents in the emergence of environmentally unjust situations. With temporality, these explanations assume that certain events precede others. Underlying both is the debate on whether environmental racism is solely a deliberate act, or an unintended consequence of unrelated acts that result in discriminatory outcomes. A conceptual framework built around racialized spaces is a more complex model than previous explanations. Unlike the others, it does not highlight one actor or one process. In fact, it acknowledges the fact that there are multiple actors and simultaneous actions that give rise to environmental inequality. It rises above micro theoretical products that emphasize various state and corporate actors. Instead, it is a macro-perspective that encompasses not only spatial relations, but also social and temporal dynamics that make it possible for environmental racism and injustice to emerge. It speaks to process, rather than outcomes. It offers a novel approach: space is an independent and influencing variable, when combined with race and socioeconomic status in the location of environmental hazards and the greatest adverse impacts. The underlying assumption dictates that spaces where people of color and the poor inhabit are not randomly assigned. Instead, they have been designated through a history of white separatism. In addition, these racialized spaces have been vigorously maintained, constraining the physical mobility on the part of marginalized Others.

There are three major assumptions made in the articulation of racialized spaces. First, space is power and it is rooted in conflict.[35] The process of dividing people into distinct zones by race and class constitutes an exercise in power. Moreover, resistance on the part of marginalized Others can be seen as a contestation of power against the construction of racialized spaces. The second assumption is that space has a dialectical relationship with social relations. In other words, it informs and, is reinforced by the social order. Harvey notes that once a spatial arrangement has been established, it tends to institutionalize all other aspects of social behavior.[36] On the other hand, the social order dictates spatial arrangements.

Finally, contemporary forms of racialized spaces need not be intentional, given their historical construction. Decisions made today on spaces that were created as a part of segregationist strategy are in effect, racialized. These three assumptions behind the theory on racialized spaces allude to the dynamics between power, space, and race relations, both past and present.

How can this theory help overcome the limitations of environmental justice research and support social action geared toward alleviating environmental burdens among the poor and people of color? First, the racialized space perspective allows activists to move beyond the Environmental Protection Agency as the leading agency for policy changes. In fact, racialized spaces also address inequality within federal housing, transportation, and urban development programs. Subsequently, solutions must also be sought through the cooperation of Federal Departments of Housing and Urban Development (HUD), Transportation (DOT), as well as Health and Human Services (HHS).

It allows activists to move beyond the distributive justice paradigm, and put forth a discourse on power relations. In what many call the post-segrega-

tion era, racialized spaces emphasizes the persistence in the geographic isolation of the poor and people of color.

Pulido's work represents a positive departure from previous environmental justice research. In her article, "Rethinking Environmental Racism"[37] she
links elements of historical geography, white privilege, and its influence on
environmental racism in Los Angeles. She concludes, "this process highlights not only the spatiality of racism, but also the fact that space is a
resource in the production of white privilege . . . although whites must go to
ever greater lengths to achieve them, relatively homogeneous white spaces
are necessary for the full exploitation of whiteness.[38]

I have attempted to provide a new theoretical framework as an explanation
for disproportionate impacts of environmental hazards on communities of
color and the poor. This is clearly a starting point for a broader discussion
on race, space, and toxics. Its adoption dictates that future research focus on
applying this theoretical construction to case studies of environmental justice communities and the replication of previous research using space as an
independent variable. Evidence of environmental injustice is mounting.
Now, we must uncover the structural mechanisms that operate in the creation of these vulnerable communities.

NOTES

1. A. S. Weinberg, "The Environmental Justice Debate: A Commentary on Methodological Issues and Practical Concerns," *Sociological Forum* 13, no. 1 (1998): p. 31.

2. Robin Saha and P. Mohai, "Explaining Racial and Socioeconomic Disparities
in the Location of Unwanted Land Uses: A Conceptual Framework" (paper presented at the Annual Meeting of the Rural Sociological Association, Toronto,
Ontario, 1997).

3. Anderton et al., "Environmental Equity in Superfund: Demographics of the
Discovery and Prioritization of Abandoned Toxic Sites," *Evaluation Review* 21, no.
1 (1997), B. M. Baden and D. L. Coursey, "The Locality of Waste Sites within the
City of Chicago: A Demographic, Social, and Economic Analysis," *Resource and
Energy Economics* 24, no. 1–2 (2002), V. Been, "Locally Undesirable Land Uses in
Minority Neighborhoods—Disproportionate Siting or Market Dynamics," *Yale Law
Journal* 103, no. 6 (1994).

4. Robert Kuehn, "A Taxonomy of Environmental Justice," *The Environmental
Law Reporter* 30 (2000).

5. Robert D. Bullard, *Unequal Protection: Environmental Justice and Communities of Color* (San Francisco: Sierra Club Books, 1994).

6. Luke W. Cole and Sheila R. Foster, *From the Ground Up: Environmental Racism and the Rise of the Environmental Justice Movement, Critical America* (New
York: New York University Press, 2001).

7. Manning Marable, *Beyond Black and White: Transforming African-American
Politics* (London; New York: Verso, 1995).

8. David Harvey, *Justice, Nature and the Geography of Difference* (Cambridge, MA: Blackwell Publishers, 1996), 400.

9. Bill Lawson, "Living for the City: Urban United States and Environmental Justice," in *Faces of Environmental Racism*, ed. L. Westra and B. E. Lawson (Lanham, MD: Rowman & Littlefield, 2001), Charles Mills, "Black Trash," in *Faces of Environmental Racism*, ed. L. Westra and B. E. Lawson (Lanham, MD: Rowman & Littlefield, 2001).

10. David Harvey, *Social Justice and the City* (London: Edward Arnold, 1973).

11. Douglas S. Massey and Nancy A. Denton, *American Apartheid: Segregation and the Making of the Underclass* (Cambridge, MA; London: Harvard University Press, 1993).

12. Robert Ezra Park, Ernest Watson Burgess, and Roderick Duncan McKenzie, *The City* (Chicago: University of Chicago Press, 1967).

13. Massey and Denton, *American Apartheid: Segregation and the Making of the Underclass*, 15.

14. Mike Davis, *City of Quartz: Excavating the Future in Los Angeles*, 1st Vintage Books ed. (New York: Vintage Books, 1992), Massey and Denton, *American Apartheid: Segregation and the Making of the Underclass*, Gwendolyn Wright, *Building the Dream: A Social History of Housing in America*, 1st ed. (New York: Pantheon Books, 1981).

15. Davis, *City of Quartz: Excavating the Future in Los Angeles*, 165–66.

16. Wright, *Building the Dream: A Social History of Housing in America*.

17. Harvey, *Justice, Nature and the Geography of Difference*.

18. Bullard, *Unequal Protection: Environmental Justice and Communities of Color*.

19. Cole and Foster, *From the Ground Up: Environmental Racism and the Rise of the Environmental Justice Movement*.

20. Wright, *Building the Dream: A Social History of Housing in America*, 219.

21. Mills, "Black Trash," 85.

22. Lawson, "Living for the City: Urban United States and Environmental Justice," 46.

23. Ibid., 48.

24. Zygmunt Bauman, *Modernity and the Holocaust* (Ithaca, NY: Cornell University Press, 1989), 192.

25. Craig E. Barton, ed., *Duality and Invisibility: Race and Memory in the Urbanism of the American South, Sites of Memory: Perspectives on Architecture and Race* (New York: Princeton Architectural Press, 2001).

26. Harvey, *Social Justice and the City*.

27. Henri Lefebvre, *The Production of Space* (Oxford, UK; Cambridge, MA: Blackwell, 1991).

28. Rob Shields, "Spatial Stress and Resistance: Social Meanings of Spatialization," in *Space and Social Theory*, ed. Georges Benko and Ulf Strohmayer (Cambridge, MA: Blackwell Publishers, 1997).

29. Sharon Zukin, "What's Space Got to Do with It?: Reply to Gans," *City & Community* 1, no. 4 (2002).

30. Michel Foucault, *Discipline and Punish: The Birth of the Prison*, 2nd Vintage Books ed. (New York: Vintage Books, 1995).

31. Patricia Hill Collins, *Fighting Words: Black Women and the Search for Justice, Contradictions of Modernity; V. 7* (Minneapolis, MN: University of Minnesota Press, 1998), 39.

32. Davis, *City of Quartz: Excavating the Future in Los Angeles.*

33. William Julius Wilson, *The Declining Significance of Race: Blacks and Changing American Institutions* (Chicago: University of Chicago Press, 1978).

34. Cole and Foster, *From the Ground Up: Environmental Racism and the Rise of the Environmental Justice Movement.*

35. Susan Fainstein, "Justice, Politics, and the Creation of Urban Space," in *The Urbanization of Justice*, ed. E. Swyngedouw (New York: New York University Press, 1997).

36. Harvey, *Justice, Nature and the Geography of Difference.*

37. Laura Pulido, "Rethinking Environmental Racism: White Privilege and Urban Development in Southern California," *Association of American Geographers. Annals of the Association of American Geographers* 90, no. 1 (2000).

38. Ibid.: 30.

BIBLIOGRAPHY

Anderton et al. "Environmental Equity in Superfund: Demographics of the Discovery and Prioritization of Abandoned Toxic Sites." *Evaluation Review* 21, no. 1 (1997): 3.

Baden, B. M., and D. L. Coursey. "The Locality of Waste Sites within the City of Chicago: A Demographic, Social, and Economic Analysis." *Resource and Energy Economics* 24, no. 1–2 (2002): 53–93.

Barton, Craig E., ed. *Duality and Invisibility: Race and Memory in the Urbanism of the American South.* Edited by Craig E. Barton, *Sites of Memory: Perspectives on Architecture and Race.* New York: Princeton Architectural Press, 2001.

Bauman, Zygmunt. *Modernity and the Holocaust.* Ithaca, NY: Cornell University Press, 1989.

Been, V. "Locally Undesirable Land Uses in Minority Neighborhoods— Disproportionate Siting or Market Dynamics." *Yale Law Journal* 103, no. 6 (1994): 1383–422.

Bullard, Robert D. *Unequal Protection: Environmental Justice and Communities of Color.* San Francisco: Sierra Club Books, 1994.

Cole, Luke W., and Sheila R. Foster. *From the Ground Up: Environmental Racism and the Rise of the Environmental Justice Movement, Critical America.* New York: New York University Press, 2001.

Collins, Patricia Hill. *Fighting Words: Black Women and the Search for Justice, Contradictions of Modernity; V. 7.* Minneapolis, MN: University of Minnesota Press, 1998.

Davis, Mike. *City of Quartz: Excavating the Future in Los Angeles.* 1st Vintage Books ed. New York: Vintage Books, 1992.

Fainstein, Susan. "Justice, Politics, and the Creation of Urban Space." In *The Urbanization of Justice*, edited by E. Swyngedouw. New York: New York University Press, 1997.

Foucault, Michel. *Discipline and Punish: The Birth of the Prison*. 2nd Vintage Books ed. New York: Vintage Books, 1995.

Harvey, David. *Justice, Nature and the Geography of Difference*. Cambridge, MA: Blackwell Publishers, 1996.

———. *Social Justice and the City*. London: Edward Arnold, 1973.

Kuehn, Robert. "A Taxonomy of Environmental Justice." *The Environmental Law Reporter* 30 (2000): 10681–703.

Lawson, Bill. "Living for the City: Urban United States and Environmental Justice." In *Faces of Environmental Racism*, edited by L. Westra and B. E. Lawson. Lanham, MD: Rowman & Littlefield, 2001.

Lefebvre, Henri. *The Production of Space*. Oxford, UK; Cambridge, MA: Blackwell, 1991.

Marable, Manning. *Beyond Black and White: Transforming African-American Politics*. London; New York: Verso, 1995.

Massey, Douglas S., and Nancy A. Denton. *American Apartheid: Segregation and the Making of the Underclass*. Cambridge, MA; London: Harvard University Press, 1993.

Mills, Charles. "Black Trash." In *Faces of Environmental Racism*, edited by L. Westra and B. E. Lawson. Lanham, MD: Rowman & Littlefield, 2001.

Park, Robert Ezra, Ernest Watson Burgess, and Roderick Duncan McKenzie. *The City*. Chicago: University of Chicago Press, 1967.

Pulido, Laura. "Rethinking Environmental Racism: White Privilege and Urban Development in Southern California." *Association of American Geographers. Annals of the Association of American Geographers* 90, no. 1 (2000): 12.

Saha, Robin, and P. Mohai. "Explaining Racial and Socioeconomic Disparities in the Location of Unwanted Land Uses: A Conceptual Framework." Paper presented at the Annual Meeting of the Rural Sociological Association, Toronto, Ontario 1997.

Shields, Rob. "Spatial Stress and Resistance: Social Meanings of Spatialization." In *Space and Social Theory*, edited by Georges Benko and Ulf Strohmayer, 186–202. Cambridge, MA: Blackwell Publishers, 1997.

Weinberg, A. S. "The Environmental Justice Debate: A Commentary on Methodological Issues and Practical Concerns." *Sociological Forum* 13, no. 1 (1998): 25–32.

Wilson, William Julius. *The Declining Significance of Race: Blacks and Changing American Institutions*. Chicago: University of Chicago Press, 1978.

Wright, Gwendolyn. *Building the Dream: A Social History of Housing in America*. 1st ed. New York: Pantheon Books, 1981.

Zukin, Sharon. "What's Space Got to Do with It?: Reply to Gans." *City & Community* 1, no. 4 (2002): 345–48.

II

NORTH AMERICAN MEMORIES OF ENVIRONMENTAL INJUSTICE

8

Wadin' in the Water

African American Migrant Struggles for Environmental Equality in Cleveland, Ohio, 1928–1970

Sylvia Hood Washington

Water is a strong metaphor in the memories of African Americans. It has been perceived and remembered as a means of liberation for the enslaved such as biblical reference to God's parting of the Red Sea for the Israelites, which the title of this essay refers to. Water is also employed by African Americans as a metaphor and a memory of relief typified by the negro spiritual invocation "I'm gonna lay down my burden, down by the river side." Finally water conceptualized and remembered as a form of purification, was not only held by African Americans but also by sanitarians in Western societies until the early quarter of the twentieth century. Unfortunately the concept and image of "water" was negatively transformed for many African American communities after slavery and especially for those who had migrated to industrialized Northern and Southern urban cities. Water for many of them came to be perceived as potentially deadly with its poisoning and toxic degradation first by the unmitigated disposal of raw sewage; and eventually by untreated or minimally industrial effluents that poured into the sources of water flowing through and around African American communities. This chapter examines a precursive environmental struggle by African Americans, living in Cleveland, Ohio's Lee-Seville community, who sought to protect themselves from the environmental hazards which were posed by water; in this case sewage contaminated water, due to environmental racism.

This was the community that I grew up in and where I first experienced and witnessed a fight for what is now called environmental justice. For almost fifteen years I walked as a child through wild fields of rolling hills and small creeks that were dotted with fruit trees. I can still see them in my minds' eye the large wild beehive shaped blackberries or the dew misted ruby red strawberries growing in the fields at the end of my street. The berry vines were nestled under the emerald leaves of tall shade trees and overgrown rose bushes which had been planted but abandoned by earlier residents who had lived in temporary war housing. Large creeks of water could be found sprinkled through what contemporary scholars and past political adversaries called vacant "open" land. Young boys of the neighborhood ritually captured frogs and small fish in this vacant space, built massive tree houses and camped out because they were miles away from recreation and camping facilities which during the 1960s were not truly open to African Americans. Adult residents in the area frequently went into these fields to hunt pheasant, possum and even trap rabbits. This childhood vision of a warm summer morning in June, 1967 on the outskirts of Cleveland in an all-black working-class and middle-class neighborhood is really of "The Village" (formerly Miles Heights) that was part of the larger Lee-Seville community. My parents and the majority of their fellow black neighbors had come to this neighborhood in the late 1950s and early 1960s seeking a place that would feel like home and home for them had been rural farms in Alabama embedded or cleared from the massive pine forests of the Deep South. I remember the adults in this community telling the children that they came to this place because they wanted a clean and natural place filled with trees, flowers, and gardens to raise their families. I was always told while growing up by my own family that they had intentionally fled the city as soon as they could after migrating north. They wanted their families to be able to breath clean air and to be away from the smoke, stench-filled air, and urban violence which they felt were characteristic of the city. They also felt that the prospects of living and owning a home in the suburbs were slim if not impossible for blacks. My parents like many of their black neighbors were determined not to stay in the segregated and unnatural urban spaces where the vast majority of blacks living in the Cleveland Metropolitan area during this time were concentrated.[1]

This desire for building and maintaining a sustainable living space drove them into a bitter battle with the first African American mayor of a major city in the United States, Carl B. Stokes. Although recent scholarship has couched this struggle in terms of a political debacle, I and those who lived there still remember this fight as part of an ongoing environmental struggle for a sustainable community that had begun during the early decades of the twentieth century and became exponentially, unexpectedly, and ironically exacerbated by an African American mayor who they had just elected into office.

This essay is an elucidation of this African American migrant community's more than forty-year attempt to obtain and maintain an optimal environment by demanding water treatment systems (especially sewage systems) that were equivalent to white communities in Cleveland, Ohio. Proposed development plans for public housing in the former Miles Heights area in 1966 became the superficial basis of a heated intra-racial environmental battle between the middle-class and working-class African American residents and their African American mayor. The reality of the struggle was the frustrated and longstanding demand for equal environmental infrastructures which had been denied to them for forty years. More than thirty years after the battle had ended Drew Chillious, the eighty-four-year-old former president of the Lee-Seville Citizens' Council and opponent of the public housing project would still angrily question "Why not put it [public housing] in the affluent white neighborhoods like Bay Village. They [the city] really didn't accept the will of this black community. We were a large emerging lower middle class black community . . . and I still don't understand why they wanted projects in a black middle class community." According to Chillious the city attempted to hold entitled city services ransom in exchange for unwanted public housing.

Miles Heights, the proposed development site, had been a former suburb of Cleveland. It was also the first place in the metropolitan area where African Americans could own their homes outright instead of being subjected to tenuous "land contracts." Wilbur H. Watson points out in *The Village, An Oral Historical Ethnographic Study of a African American Community* that " Miles Heights (The Village) was incorporated in August, 1927, by the Cuyahoga County commissioners upon petition of the required number of property owners. The Village then had a population of less than 1500 people. The assessed valuation on real and personal property totaled only $5,663,600.[2] The Village during the first quarter of this century had settlements of German and Italian immigrants but quickly became integrated and eventually predominantly African American because of the population increases to stemming from the Great Migrations from the South. This turnover in the racial demographic was also due to the voluntary relocation of African Americans from the city's inner ring ghettos.

The suburb of Miles Heights elected an African American mayor, Arthur R. Johnson, a little over two years after its incorporation. Johnson decided not to seek re-election for a third term as mayor in 1930 because of rampant corruption taking place in his administration. Embroiled by the corruption scandal, the Village administration failed to address the community's environmental infrastructural problems. The small community was plagued by poor health services and with the lack of other critical public health amenities. The failure of the Miles Heights government to provide a sanitary environment for its residents led to its decision to vote for its annexation to the City of Cleveland. The results of a health survey of the village published in 1932 revealed that less than 50 percent of the households and streets had sanitary convenience and this lack of requisite sanitary infrastructures was viewed as a major health threat to the Cleveland Metropolitan area. The village report concluded that "This means that a typhoid hazard exists and in some respects it will be an advantage to have the suburb annexed. For if typhoid breaks out, it knows no political boundaries.' " This vote for annexation was therefore based upon a sincere belief on the part of municipal officials and politicos that residents would gain an improvement in procedures for sewage disposal would have been mutually beneficial to Miles Heights and Cleveland residents. Their objective was to secure preventive health care and a higher quality of life by tapping into the more advance sewer infrastructures of the Cleveland sewage system. The residents successful vote for the annexation of the village in the fall of 1931 was due in large part to its African American residents, the village majority, who favored annexation. They believed that the annexation would provide them with the needed environmental infrastructures that would make their community more livable after the standard and perfunctory political maneuvering.[3]

A contemporary report by the City of Cleveland's Health Division which compared deaths due to typhoid fever from 1878–1928 supported the concerns of the Miles Heights community. The 1928 report stated that although there were no deaths due to typhoid in the city as a result of "the 100% filtration of Cleveland's water supply [just as in 1919] a decided decrease in the cases of typhoid fever prevailing occurred following the filtration of a major portion of the city water supply by the opening of the Division Avenue filtration plant." The report also emphasized that there was concern about potential future outbreaks stemming from inadequate water treatment in the outlying and suburban areas. "It cannot be too emphatically stated that the only satisfactory and permanent safeguard against a recurrence of typhoid fever is the ultimate provision for the complete treatment of all sewage entering the lake through the sewage disposal plants of municipalities of this vicinity, so that the effluent from city plants is completely innocuous as regards the presence of the bacteria causing typhoid fever and other waterborne disease."[4]

Even though the African American residents of the former Miles Heights suburb voted for annexation to Cleveland to obtain improved environmental structures in their community their political decision would be virtually fruitless for over a decade. The Watson study points out that "By the end of [World War II], some 14 years after annexation of old Miles Heights to the City of Cleveland, little had changed with respect to the living conditions in the Village. Unpaved roads, open sewage ditches, outhouses for the elimination of human waste, homes without running water and open mosquito infested swamps were still present."[5]

Some relief from these dismal environmental conditions came about through the construction of wartime housing in the area for migrant war workers and returning war veterans beginning in 1944. "In 1944 the Cleveland metropolitan war-housing development completed a project in the Seville area, just East of 153rd street (eastern border of the village) and South of Seville and. . . . In 1946, the Cleveland Metropolitan Housing Authority also opened several new temporary housing projects for 'in-migrant war workers,' including the 'Seville Homes Extension' project." The Seville Homes development included physical plants for supportive services, an elementary school and a shopping mall that included a grocery store, a drug store, and a separate building for a recreation center. [6] The development of this housing also brought about the development of additional sewage and environmental infrastructures that were mandated by law.

A 1950 seven-page letter from the CMHA director, Ernest J. Bohn to Cleveland mayor, Thomas A. Burke stated that the housing in this area was created by Congress and was predicated upon the development of requisite infrastructures as a result of the "Lanham Act (war housing) that was amended by the enactment of a new Title V. This bill provided that Army barracks and other temporary structures, and unused surplus war materials, could be converted into emergency living quarters for veterans. The Federal Public Housing Authority could act only in those communities who cooperated by making land available and installing at its own cost the necessary utilities, roads and streets." nine hundred six housing units were developed in the Cleveland metropolitan area and 56 of these were the Seville Homes Extension.[7]

According to Bohns' letter the City of Cleveland along with the city administration enacted Ordinance No.302–46 to make arrangements with the CMHA and the federal government to develop the temporary housing. The Federal Public Housing Authority letter to the CMHA at this time made it clear that the following infrastructures had to be in place or corrected for the establishment of "maximum" temporary housing developments: "grading, water distribution system (including fire hydrants and water meters), gas distribution system, roads, circulation walks and the cleaning of existing ditches."[8] $250,000 was made available to construct the temporary war/veteran housing by several subsequent appropriation ordinances. This money along with $37,100.00 from the Federal Public Housing Authority was used to develop and construct the following infrastructures with their associated costs: underground utilities ($73,385.81) electrical distribution systems ($37,179.80) municipal utilities connections ($2,894.91) and community facilities ($6,123.00). Overall $285,193.57 was expended in developing the temporary war housing and supporting infrastructures.[9]

The Seville Homes housing units were eventually demolished in 1958 and the families were ordered to vacate the premises since housing for them became available with the passage of the G.I Bill. A 1957 Annual Report for CMHA stated that the need for temporary housing for returning veterans was alleviated as a result of the G.I. Bill of Rights because "the Veterans Administration could guarantee private loans for those who could afford to build or purchase a home. For those who could not, public housing built for war workers (both permanent and temporary) was converted into veterans housing."[10]

Many of the African Americans who came to the Lee Seville neighborhood between the 1940s and early 1960s were either war industry workers or war veterans who were seeking a place that was similar to the homes that they had left in the South. The vast majority of these residents were migrants who had came from the unspoiled environs typical of farms and rural communities in Alabama, Georgia, and Mississippi; and they were unaccustomed to the smell and grime of an industrialized city. Many of the African Americans in this community articulated that they wanted a clean and natural place filled with trees, flowers, and gardens to raise their families. They wanted their families to be able to breathe clean air, and to be away from the smoke, stench-filled air, and urban violence which they felt were characteristic of the urban city. They also felt that the prospects of living and owning a home in the suburbs were slim if not impossible for African Americans: and today's urban historians have proven that they were right.[11] Many of the African American residents were determined not to live in the segregated and unnatural urban spaces where the vast majority of African Americans found themselves concentrated in Cleveland area during this timeframe.

The vast majority of African Americans who came to Cleveland starting around 1910 tended to settle on the east side of the city.[12] Between 1940 and 1959 the Lee-Seville–Miles community would increase its African American population from 9.4 percent to 19 percent whereas other east side communities closer to Cleveland's downtown area would have African American populations as high as 95.4 percent.[13] The reasons cited by African American Lee-Seville homeowners, in the heat of the public housing controversy, for settlement in this particular area was consistent with a 1959 observation made by the Cleveland Community Relations Board in a report on non-white settlement patterns. The report asserted that an increase settlement by African Americans in "areas of single and two-family residences . . . were concomitant with the economic and social ability of an increasing number of the non-white population to afford and desire home ownership in better neighborhoods."[14] The housing stock available to African Americans moving into the Lee-Seville–Miles according to report was comparable at least in age to those of the surrounding suburbs; less than 25 percent of housing was more than 40 years old.[15] The report, however, also made it clear that there were "informal and formal pressures within the City to contain non-whites within specified areas" resulting in a pattern which has a "heavy concentration of those areas in which non-whites live."[16]

By the mid 1960s the Lee-Seville area was recognized as one of the most physically and socially desirable African American enclaves in the city of Cleveland. Prior to the passage of the United States Fair Housing Act in 1968, the community was as close as most African Americans could get to living in the suburbs. It was far removed from the city's urban core and physically atypical of most African American ghettos in the city. Lee-Seville's physical environs resembled more of its contemporary surrounding white suburban communities like Maple Heights or Warrenville Heights with green lawns, bungalows, and large amounts of green space. However, unlike their white suburbanites and equivalent white middle-class communities in the city, Lee-Seville residents still had deficient sewage infrastructures when they voted their first African American mayor, Carl B. Stokes into office in 1967. The infrastructures which they needed were never built by the city even with the contemporary construction of war housing. The residents of this community out of sheer necessity became environmental activists whose persistent demands were eventually recognized by the larger "white" community but unfortunately not acted upon because of race, class, and politics. Residents of this community hoped in 1966 that their environmental fight for an equal living space would finally be ameliorated with a African American mayor in office. Their hopes however would be shattered by an intra-racial fight between themselves and the African American mayor for their failure to accept his proposal to build low-income housing in the neighborhood.

INTRA-RACIAL ENVIRONMENTAL RACISM

Current and past scholarship has typically couched this struggle in terms of a class debacle between poor and middle-class African Americans without seriously taking into account the prevailing evidence that supports the argument that this fight was part of an ongoing environmental struggle for a sustainable community by African Americans in the area that had begun during the early decades of the twentieth century. African Americans living in this area were torn over proposed construction of low-income housing for inner-city African Americans by the Cleveland Metropolitan Housing Authority (CMHA) especially since they felt that their longstanding demands for poor city infrastructures had not been met or addressed. Propositions about developing this particular area by the city of Cleveland began in 1966. An article which ran in the early summer of 1966 in the *Cleveland Plain Dealer* indicated that Cleveland's Mayor Locher and Council President Stanton had gone into the community to tour a 70 acre site in Lee-Seville to see if "private housing should be built on developer Alvin Krenzler's Leewood Industrial Park Site." According to the article Council President Stanton felt that there was "a need for private housing and that the site seemed logical." The article also indicated that Director Bohn of the CMHA predicted that "a $4.5 million single-family project will start next spring."[17] Prior to Mayor Stokes coming into office the efforts of the city administration in the development of the area had been directed toward the construction of private housing. An article appearing in the *Cleveland Press* in March 1967 stated that the outgoing "white" Mayor Locher wanted "the city to buy the 67 acre site soon to sell to private developers to build 570 single family, two family and row house units."[18] As stated earlier in this essay this proposed site was not vacant land; the vast majority of this land could be characterized as a vibrant green space filled with trees and wildlife indigenous to Ohio.

On June 27, 1966 an emergency resolution was adopted by the Cleveland City Council "on the second and third reading" with a vote of 32 to 0 "declaring the necessity and intention to appropriate the 67 acre Lee-Wood parcel." In less than a year the Cleveland City Council would issue ordinances to appropriate the land for $915,000 and approve engineering services for the site. By July of 1968 the council would approve "employment of a firm to prepare design, marketing and cost information services for Lee-Seville plans for low and moderate-rental housing."[19]

Efforts to realize the proposed development continued along with the controversy well into 1970. By the first Earth Day, April 22, 1970, the major political and social issue in Cleveland would still revolve around the public housing battle between the newly elected African American Mayor Carl B. Stokes and the African American community of Lee-Seville. On April 22, 1970, the first national recognition of Earth Day, large segments of the country poured onto college campuses and into the streets to usher in a "new consciousness intent on preserving the environment."

The persistent environmental issue which was of paramount importance to many of the African American residents of Lee-Seville at this time continued to be the proper and fair development of "open space" and needed infrastructures. Many feared that this open space was on the verge of becoming transformed into another marginalized city ghetto. This was something that they had worked hard to escape from by moving into at least a quasi-suburban space. The sentiments of African Americans living in the area and who were opposed to the proposed CHMA low-income housing mirrored those expressed in the Earth Day editorial, "Slums and Pollution" which appeared in Cleveland's African American newspaper, *The Call and Post*. The editorial concluded with the assessment that "The choice isn't between the physical environment and the human. Both go hand in hand, and the widespread concern with pollution must be joined by a similar concern for wiping out the pollutants of racism and poverty."[20]

In an affidavit taken in a legal action to stop the proposed CMHA low-income housing construction, the African American councilman of the area, Clarence Thompson asserted that the proposed low income housing would "eventually create another slum in what is now a beautiful area" and that "environmental facilities should be developed for the 600 homes." Thompson made it very clear in his affidavit that "the present Negro ghetto" had "been created by the choice of the persons residing therein" but that the proposed low-income housing was being forced upon the African American community by racist public policies. Thompson stated that "The segregated low income housing to be owned and operated by CMHA is in violation of constitutional guaranties of equal protection of the laws and due process of the law since CMHA is deliberately forcing said project on this community without due regard for the health , safety and morals of the present residents or the proposed tenants of the housing project."[21]

Two other affidavits taken from African American residents, Henry Simon and Brunson Ballard, living in the area during this period echoed the same complaints and concerns expressed by Thompson. Henry Simon would state in his affidavit that his health was endangered and would continue to be as well as that of "other residents in the Lee Seville area" as long as the open sewers on the CMHA tract were not properly serviced. Simon claimed that the area "is now a Negro residential ghetto, by choice of about one thousand (1,000) families now residing therein" and that the CMHA's proposed development violated state and federal laws "since the safety, health, sanitary and storm sewer, school and recreational facilities are grossly inadequate to meet the needs of the families presently residing therein; and bringing any additional families of any size will only compound these problems."[22]

Mayor Carl B. Stokes, himself a product of Cleveland's urban ghetto, sincerely felt that the opposition of Lee-Seville residents was the same in nature as "white" bigotry which he said prevented low-income housing from being built earlier in the area in 1950.[23] In a town hall meeting in Lee-Seville, Stokes informed the residents that "around 1950 [that] this same general area and the adjacent areas became the subject of great zoning disputes—industrial versus residential zoning disputes . . . [and that] it is a matter of Cleveland History that opposition to more Negroes moving into Ward 30 motivated some of the parties." According to Stokes' when the Cleveland Metropolitan Housing Authority in June of 1952 proposed a 900 suite development in Miles Heights they were met with opposition to the project "from people who didn't want more Negroes moving into the ward."[24] Stokes pointed out in his presentation that the proposed CMHA housing project eventually failed because the proposed public housing at that time became "a city wide issue" and petitions were quickly circulated by the city's white residents "to kill any new public housing in the entire city of Cleveland. . . . The project

was dropped despite the great need for low-income families that need relocation for housing."[25]

Mayor Stokes and those who supported him made it clear in this controversy that they felt that the only opportunity for low-income African
Americans to have quality living environments was the development of public housing in a middle-class African American area like the Lee-Seville area.
During this controversy Mayor Stokes would complain in an address to Yale
students that "If I can't build housing for the poor African American people
in a African American neighborhood, how am I going to build housing for
people anywhere?"[26] The African American residents of Lee-Seville, however, claimed that they had moved out of the city because they felt that they
and their families were not receiving equal access to adequate housing,
municipal services, and school systems because they were living in a highly
segregated and racialized ghetto. They expressed fear that the proposed
housing for low-income families would recreate and exacerbate the same
conditions which they had fled and were fighting in their new (and still segregated) environment. Many historians, sociologists, and other intellectuals
concur both now and then with their expressed concerns that inner-city
neighborhoods, especially racially segregated ghettos, did not and still do
not receive the same quality of municipal services and education as those
obtained in "white" suburbs. The Supreme Court eventually decided in
favor of the Lee-Seville residents argument in the late 1970s.[27]

Lee-Seville residents felt that they could and should demand the type of
environmental and civil infrastructure changes for their community which
they felt they were entitled to as taxpayers. They wanted the same municipal
benefits and services which they felt "white" neighborhoods had already
possessed: adequate sewers, lighted streets, proper waste management and
disposal, and paved and safe streets.

A 1970 newspaper article "New Housing Project Flayed by Thompson"
quoted Stokes' primary adversary, Clarence Thompson, an African American city councilman for the Lee-Seville area (Ward 30) as saying that "he was
not against low-income housing. 'I'm for the taxpayers,' he said. 'I want to
see them get what they have not gotten for their tax dollars in past years.'"
A contemporary fact sheet released by the CMHA would acknowledge the
environmental problems of the area by stating that the "Construction of [the
low-income housing] development will allow elimination of serious flooding, drainage and traffic and congestion problems in adjacent neighborhoods."[28] The continuing battles between Mayor Carl B. Stokes and Lee
Seville community leaders ultimately lead to lawsuits between this African
American neighborhood and the city; and played a critical role in the mayors' decision not to seek re-election.[29]

African Americans living in the community were divided about the proposed Cleveland Metropolitan Housing Authority public housing develop-

ment. A neighborhood periodical, the *Lee-Seville View*, that was developed during the controversy contained articles that stated that "Two thirds of Lee-Seville and Ward 30 approve CMHA's plans for new housing—just as the Mayor said." This particular periodical also made it clear that the existing community did not have at that time adequate environmental infrastructures (water, sewer, paved streets, and fire protection). Even though the periodical was written by supporters of the proposed CMHA project they made it very clear in their reports that the development was predicated upon the implementation of these needed understructures. The newsletter pointed out that the development of these needed infrastructures in the Lee-Seville had been proposed by the Mayor's office through legislation which had been brought before the City Council. According to the above article "the legislation was now blocked in Council" and if approved would begin immediately. The enumerated environmental improvements identified in the report would "Alleviate flooding, with storm and sanitary sewer outlets. . . . Run a new sanitary trunk sewer outlet through the whole area, especially relieving drainage problems in Miles Heights and Clearview. . . . Run a culvert . . . to replace the open ditch on city-owned land and. . . . Put a water main in Seville Road . . . with cross connections. It would increase water supply and pressure and would mean better fire protection."[30] The open ditch was contained in the area of the proposed site of the public housing development.

The proposed environmental improvements identified in the above report, however, represented only a fraction of those that had been identified and proposed by the Mayor's office. The Mayor's office had proposed ten emergency ordinances and four emergency resolutions for infrastructure improvements which they felt were needed if the housing project was to be implemented. Over 80 percent of these infrastructure improvements was directly aimed at improving existing environmental conditions in this community.[31] This assessment of environmental problems was stated in more explicit form in the 1968 report, *Statement of Problems and Objectives for Action in the Lee-Seville Community* which was prepared by the Lee-Seville/Lee-Harvard Central Planning Committee.[32] The historical concerns of the African American residents of Lee-Seville over inadequate infrastructures for the community were validated by the Mayor's office. The problem however was that the needed improvements were conditioned on the community's acceptance of the politically controversial low-income CMHA housing.

A contemporary response letter written from the Director of CMHA, Irving Kriegsfield, to Mrs. Richard Taylor, president of the League of Women Voters of Cleveland, in response to the organizations concerns over the proposed City legislation which was tied to the CMHA project also indicated that the existing Lee-Seville community was in dire need of adequate environmental infrastructures. According to this letter "the total cost of all the sewer and water improvements in the package of legislation pending before City Council calls for expenditure of $2,060,000. This figure includes only $110,000 for paving of East 153rd Street and Seville Road. An additional $1,000,000 in street paving authorization is to be introduced . . . later. The City of Cleveland has a 50% water and sewer project grant application of approximately $958,000. pending before the Federal Government. Total water and sewer estimate—1,916,000." The letter goes on to point out explicitly as objectives some of the improvements already identified in the previous paragraphs for "all existing homes in the entire area" but also notes that efforts will be made for the "Elimination of 100 acres of vacant dumping grounds" and "New Street Lighting."[33]

An article which ran in the Cleveland Plain Dealer during this controversy stated that "Angry homeowners from the Lee-Seville area appeared at City Hall yesterday to complain about inadequate sewers that have resulted in flooded basements during two recent storms, and to file damages against the city."[34] The article stated that the continued environmental problems and public housing controversy in the area was being exacerbated by retaliation from Mayor Stokes and his administration. The article quoted Councilman Thomas of the ward as lamenting that "For months I have asked that the sewers in the area be cleaned out and have had no response from the Service Department." Councilman Thompson also charged in the articled that "Legislation for improvements in the sewers is tied to the Lee-Seville project which the people do not want" and that legislation that he had introduced for a study of the sewer situation in the area was "being held up—as is most legislation—by Stokes."[35] The article also quoted several women from the area who said that they had to clean raw sewage out of their basements. One attacked the city for trying to bargain with her, promising sewers if the Lee-Seville development is approved. "We deserve sewers now. This is what brings about the opposition," she said.[36]

Flooding in Miles Heights was a continuing and devastating problem for many of its residents that had existed since the 1920s. Every spring or summer when there was a heavy rainfall, basements would fill with water which sometimes would exceed over 7 feet in depth. There was widespread concern among the residents over the sewage which entered their homes and its associated health impacts that came with the annual floods. Sanitarians in both Europe and the United States knew that fecal contaminated water was the cause of typhoid fever by the late 1880s.[37] Parents feared that their small children who were fascinated with the ceiling high waters would encounter disease carrying rats that came in with the flood waters as well as the entry of raw and untreated human excrement and basic sewage that would also be circulating in the waters. The streets like those in the immigrant neighborhood, the Back of the Yards, described in Upton Sinclair's *Jungle* would also turn into channels and children were also kept indoors because of the overflow of sewage waste that could have been potentially inside the waters.[38] Residents interviewed during this controversy like "Henry Simon, 15002 Ohio Avenue S.E. . . . said water was three feet deep in his basement Sunday. Clothing and other property was damaged" or "Mrs. Thomas Scott, 16313 Bryce Avenue, S.E., [who] said her bathroom and a recently installed $5,000 kitchen were damaged. 'Sunday, I had Niagara Falls in my basement. I can't stand it any longer.'"[39]

"On February 13, 1969, a taxpayers suit was filed in the Court of Common Pleas with Mr. And Mrs. Zerubbabel Evans . . . for the benefit of all taxpayers in the Lee Seville area. The city of Cleveland, City Council, CMHA and others were made defendants in the action."[40] The legal action brought by the Evans was critical in determining the final outcome of the battle between the community, the mayor, and CMHA. The Evans filed a legal injunction "enjoining defendants U.S. Department of Housing and Urban Development, and the Cleveland Metropolitan Housing Authority . . . from maintaining a custom, policy or practice of racial discrimination in the selection of sites for low income housing projects within the territorial jurisdiction of defendant CMHA, which discrimination is a badge and incident of slavery, unlawful under the 13th Amendment to the United States Constitution; 42 USCA, Section 1983 and the Fair Housing Act of 1968; and the segregation attendant thereto is a deprivation of due process and the equal protection of the laws as set forth in the United States Constitution, Amendment XIV."[41]

Their specific charges and supporting affidavits made it very clear that the fight was for a safe, healthy and equitable living environment which they felt could not take place with the development of intentionally racially segregated housing. The complaint filed by the Evans identified at least four environmentally hazardous conditions and or areas in the Lee-Seville community which they felt had not been addressed by the city in over twenty years. The first two environmental issues stated that "Because of a totally inadequate sewer system to handle the flow of sewage and other waste materials, plaintiffs' basement is flooded following a heavy rain or a constant rain that lasts for two (2) days or more. Said basement and those of persons similarly situated, remains damp, wet and odorous until fully dried and aired out." and that "In the southeasterly section of defendant CMHA Parcel No. 1, and within about one hundred (100) yards of the Clara Tagg Brewer Elementary School, there is an open sewer running through said section of said tract, which condition has existed prior to, and since, the ownership of said tract by defendant CMHA, endangering, daily the lives of the residents of the Lee-Seville Area and the lives of those residents in the surrounding and adjoining areas; that said condition does not provide for a decent, healthy and sanitary environment and is violative of the privilege to which these plaintiffs are entitled."[42]

The third area identified as an environmental problem in the Evans' com-

plaint was "the Miles Island area [where] there is another open sewer whose
waste materials flow from industrial plants located immediately on the north
side of Seville Road and west of Lee Road. This sewer dumps its waste into
a vacant lot at the southerly end of East 158th Street, flows through what
would ordinarily be the lawn between the sidewalk and the curb under a
make shift bridge in front of two (2) homes, openly, to the easterly boundary
line of the last house on Alonzo Avenue; the sewage then goes underground
for the length of said property line, then flows, openly, along the rear property boundary line of the residents . . . Plaintiffs, and all others similarly
situated, because of said unsanitary conditions, are being deprived of the full
and equal benefit of laws for the security of their lives and property and are
being deprived of the equal protection of the laws and of certain privileges
and immunities as set forth in Amendment XIV of the Constitution."[43] The
Evans won the case against the defendants.

The proposed CMHA housing development in the late 1960s was eventually defeated but there were no winners. Mayor Stokes did not seek re-election and the African American middle-class community never received all of
their demands in terms of urgently needed infrastructure changes. On rainy
days Lee-Seville residents literally and figuratively found themselves "wadin'
in the water" which flooded their basements and streets. A completely
upgraded sewage system for the entire area did not arrive until years after
the housing debacle ended and many other public services continued to
evade the residents thus making the possibility of a quality residential "green
space" an elusive concept. The site was eventually developed into an industrial park around the mid to late 1980s and an interstate highway (I-480/271)
was completed around the outer perimeters of the community. Most of the
middle-class and working African Americans and or their adult children
eventually left the areas as housing opened up to them in what had been traditionally white suburbs (Shaker Heights, Cleveland Heights, Garfield
Heights, Warrenville Heights, Solon and Bedford Heights).

African Americans who moved into the Lee-Seville area were pursuing
and demanding what we now call today a "sustainable environment" and
they were not consumed by just earning a living and merely existing. They
were concerned and fought hard battles to have a community environment
which was livable in all facets (water resources, solid waste management, and
civic resources). They also recognized that they were at risk in being trapped
into environmentally inequitable spaces because of their race. Finally they
came to understand that public policies which ultimately determined the
environmental integrity of those spaces could not be determined by the race
of the politicians. In their case their worst opponent was a fellow African
American who held tremendous power because of his historical and social
position. Struggles like theirs are now recognized as being endemic to global

struggles for environmental justice by marginalized people around the world.

NOTES

1. Cuyahoga Plan: A Report on Population and Race, 1970–1979. (March, 1979).

2. Wilbur H. Watson, *The Village, An Oral Historical Ethnographic Study of a African American Community* (Atlanta: Village Vanguard, Inc., 1989), 49.

3. Ibid., 61–62.

4. Division of Health, *1928 Annual Report*, City of Cleveland, Ohio. 14–15.

5. Watson, op.cit. 24.

6. Ibid., 128–29.

7. Letter from Bohn (CMHA director) to Burke (Cleveland mayor), Cleveland, Ohio, January 5, 1950. Mayoral Papers, Western Reserve Historical Society (WRHS), p.1.

8. Orendorff (assistant director) to Bohn, Cleveland, Ohio, Aug. 5, 1946. Mayoral Papers, WRHS.

9. Bohn, op.cit., 4.

10. *Annual Report*, 1957. Cleveland Metropolitan Housing Authority, Cleveland, Ohio.

11. Kenneth Jackson, *Crabgrass Frontier, The Suburbanization of the United States* (New York: Oxford University Press, 1985) and Thomas Sugrue, *The Origins of the Urban Crisis, Race and Inequality in Postwar Detroit* (Princeton: Princeton University Press, 1996).

12. Community Relations Board. *Non-White Residential Patterns*, City of Cleveland, Cleveland, Ohio,1959, 6.

13. Community Relations Board. op.cit., 19.

14. Community Relations Board, op.cit., 6.

15. Ibid., 17.

16. Ibid., 12.

17. Cleveland Plain Dealer, June 2, 1966. Chronology of Events, Carl Stokes Papers, Western Reserve Historical Society (WRHS).

18. Ibid.

19. Mr. Pilch, Res.1506–66. Chronology of Events, Carl Stokes Papers, WRHS.

20. Whitney M. Young, "Slums and Pollution," *The (Cleveland) Call and Post*, Editorial Page, August 25, 1970.

21. Clarence Thompson, Affidavit no. 2, 2. *Zerubbabel Evans and Shirley Evans v U.S. Housing Authority, Secretary, Department of Housing and Urban Development and Cleveland Metropolitan Housing Authority and Carl B. Stokes, Mayor of Cleveland*, C69.324 (1969).

22. Henry Simon, Affidavit no. 1, 2. *Zerubbabel Evans and Shirley Evans v U.S. Housing Authority, Secretary, Department of Housing and Urban Development and Cleveland Metropolitan Housing Authority and Carl B. Stokes, Mayor of Cleveland*, C69.324 (1969).

23. Leonard N. Moore. *Carl B. Stokes and the Rise of Black Political Power*, (Urbana: University of Illinois Press, 2002).

24. Carl B. Stokes. Town Hall Meeting Statement, Clara Tagg Brewer School, June 12, 1969, pp. 3–4. Carl B. Stokes Papers. WRHS.

25. Stokes, loc.cit.

26. "Stokes Rips Council for Deadlock on Housing in Lecture at Yale Bud Weidenthal," *Cleveland Press*, April 1, 1969. Carl Stokes Papers, WRHS.

27. Devereux Bowly, Jr. *The Poorhouse: Subsidized Housing in Chicago, 1895–1976*, (Carbondale, IL: Southern Illinois University Press, 1978), 189–94. The Supreme Court decision was based on its 1976 decision in Gautreaux v. Chicago Housing Authority.

28. Cleveland Metropolitan Housing Authority. *Fact Sheet: Miles Heights Housing Development*. Carl Stokes Papers. Western Reserve Historical Society.

29. Cleveland Encyclopedia.

30. Reverend Claude W. Cummings. "The Future? What Are the Facts in Lee-Seville? What Is the Future?," *Lee-Seville View*. Vol. 1 No. 1, Spring 1969. It is important to note that this paper was sponsored by the Lee-Seville Ministerial Alliance. Ministers in the area were strong advocates of Mayor Stokes and were in conflict with the neighborhood organization leadership which filed legal action to stop the proposed CMHA low-income housing development.

31. *Legislation Pertaining to Lee-Seville* and *Information Sheet: Cleveland City Council Action (Before Adjournment) on 14 Pieces of Legislation for the Development of Lee-Seville*. Carl Stokes Papers, WRHS.

32. Lee-Seville/Lee-Harvard Central Planning Committee and William A. Gould & Associates, Architects and Planners. *Statement of Problems and Objectives for Action in the Lee-Seville Community*, September 6, 1968, Carl Stokes Papers, WRHS pp. 6–8.

33. Kriegsfeld to Taylor, Cleveland, Ohio, April 16, 1969. Carl Stokes Papers, WRHS.

34. Robert G. McGruder, "Lee-Seville Blames City for Flooding," *The Plain Dealer* (Cleveland), July 23, 1969, 6D.

35. Ibid.

36. Ibid.

37. Martin v. Melosi, *The Sanitary City: Urban Infrastructure in America from Colonial Times to the Present*, (Baltimore: Johns Hopkins University Press, 2000), 137–39.

38. Ibid.

39. Ibid.

40. Ibid.

41. *Zerubbabel Evans and Shirley Evans v U.S.Housing Authority, Secretary, Department of Housing and Urban Development and Cleveland Metropolitan Housing Authority and Carl B. Stokes, Mayor of Cleveland*, C69.324 (1969).

42. *Zerubbabel Evans and Shirley Evans v U.S.Housing Authority, Secretary, Department of Housing and Urban Development and Cleveland Metropolitan Housing Authority and Carl B. Stokes, Mayor of Cleveland*, C69.324 (1969), pp. 6–7.

43. Evans, loc. cit.

9

Memories of (No)Place
Homelessnessss and Environmental Justice

Cynthia J. Miller

and the way i see it this place is mine and these streets belong to me
because i live here i'm not just passing by this is where i spend my day
and my night this is where i hang my hat or lack thereof this is where i
sleep and drink and work and dine and YOU are just passing by, coming
into my home and passing me by with downcast eyes one part sympathy
two parts hate as you turn your face away. i don't barge through your
front door and disrespect you like this i don't do any of that.

—Rachel

INTRODUCTION[1]

We often think of homeless individuals as somehow "placeless." They are
more mobile—their geography of identification appears to be fluid, rather
than fixed. They seem to lack the most common terrain of identity laid claim
to by the domiciled population—a stable location from which they can draw
(and onto which they can project) their preferences, values, and idiosyncra-
cies. The key descriptor of their identities is not an individual one of personal attributes, but a collective one of social condition. They are "the
homeless." And invisibility is a valuable life skill more often than it is an
obstacle. Understanding the role of "place," then, in the lives of the homeless—and the role of the homeless in the life and history of a "place"—can
be difficult. This is especially true in the case of the unsheltered homeless—
those individuals and families who do not spend their nights in shelters, but

143

in cars, in ATM kiosks, in alleys, and beneath overpasses. Investigating the links between environmental justice and the homeless sets the stage for them to be recognized as a visible and significant part of the life of a community, and at the same time asks that they reflect on their environments in ways which construct them as subjects in relation to their surroundings, rather than as objects in the surroundings of others.

This essay presents an examination of what one homeless individual referred to as "memories of no place"—narratives of lives lived on the streets, where personal history becomes public, and public history becomes personal. In an effort to help build a more inclusive environmental history of Boston's downtown area and begin calling attention to issues of environmental justice among the homelessness, this work explores links between self and surroundings among the city's unsheltered homeless, focusing in particular on a community-based life-writing project, in which all individuals who participate are homeless. These writings, or in some cases, dictations, are narrated, illustrated and often enacted by their writers, to build a complex picture of how their identities have been formed and influenced by where and how they have lived—"re-placing" the writers' lives within the community. The environmental life-writings produced as part of the group's efforts offer their writers opportunities to engage with their environments in a range of ways which drawn on memory, experience, and perception, in order to illustrate the intricate interweaving of place with the identities of the homeless. The result is not only the elaboration of "ecological identity" among the contributors, but also the construction of a different sort of environmental history—one which calls attention to the various environmental inequalities faced by the homeless population. *why*

A COMMUNITY OF INJUSTICE

As an embedded community, homeless individuals reside in sites of multiple injustices. They are generally the most disadvantaged of the extremely poor.[2] Whether living on the streets by choice, or due to soaring housing costs, low wages, inadequate healthcare, or ever-tightening limits on public assistance programs, homeless people are generally bracketed apart from the wider community's concerns for social and environmental justice. In fact, many relate feelings of being an integral part of the general population's perceived injustices: "Hell, guys like me? I'm their pollution." Anthropologist, Joanne Passaro, explains that Americans have a cultural tendency to place blame on the homeless (in particular, men), and to see them as shouldering the sole responsibility for their circumstances—as having failed in the performance of their designated social roles.[3] This perception of "unworthiness" eases the complicated feelings and difficult questions which confront the general population about homelessness, and allows homeless individuals, and the injustices they face, to be dismissed—either falling well outside the realm of consideration on environmental issues such as dumping, toxic run-off, and affordable housing, or being added to the bottom of that list of ills plaguing the community.

A constellation of factors, chiefly, poverty and the lack of affordable housing, are seen as key elements in the rising number of homeless in American cities. While housing is not considered affordable if its cost exceeds more than 30 percent of a renter's income, the average cost of a one-bedroom apartment in Boston is currently $1,135/month, which would require hourly earnings of $23.60 to meet the "affordable" criteria.[4] According to the National Low Income Housing Coalition, the annual income required to rent a one-bedroom apartment in Boston is $45,400, while the average annual income of Boston's renters is $41,148.[5] Dollars and cents alone, then, place affordable housing at the top of the list for causes of homelessness.

That image of extreme poverty becomes linked with Passaro's notion of "unworthiness" in the generalized image of homelessness within a community. Commonly reported stereotypes of homelessness are most often of people loitering outside shelters, panhandling on corners and in bus stations, and sleeping on park benches; and since the people who live on the streets— the unsheltered homeless—are the most visible, they tend to be the most closely associated with homelessness. As writer and activist Steve Vanderstaay explains:

> Homeless people on the street are also the most feared and least identified with: people who die ignominious deaths in trash compactors, who freeze outside the doors of hospitals, and who have been burned alive while sleeping on park benches. They are the most hated of homeless people; loathed for their destitution, their apparent inability to provide for themselves, and for the conflicting array of emotions they evoke in passersby.[6]

Many individuals, however, remain unsheltered, facing these severe social and environmental conditions, as a result of one of the most significant injustices facing the homeless community: the shelter system. There is an ever-growing shortage of beds in city shelters, and while Boston's annual shelter census showed a twenty-nine-person decrease in shelter population for the winter of 2002–2003,[7] the U.S. Conference of Mayors reported an average 13 percent increase in demand for emergency shelter in all major cities for the winter of 2003, with 84 percent of cities surveyed, including Boston, turning away 30 percent of requests for shelter from individuals, and a full one-third of requests from homeless families.[8]

Additionally, many homeless individuals find remaining on the streets preferable to conditions in city shelters. As one homeless man, Warren, relates:

> I was sick of being a second-class citizen and a pariah. I was sick of being herded from shelter to shelter among a throng of human cattle. And I was sick of watching people slowly dying, trapped in a morbid cycle of shelters, day labors, and liquor stores.

Warren's comments mirror the sentiments and stories of many people describing their reasons for choosing life on the streets. For some, it is a marker of pride and autonomy; for others, it represents another aspect of their individuality—connection and attachment to place. As Joe, a man in his thirties who had been living in the alley next to a downtown church for much of the past three years, explained during a writing session,

> I don't have much that's mine. Just this crap here I keep with me. And this alley I'm writin' about. This is mine. Ain't nobody sleeps here but me. Ain't nobody pisses here but me. Nobody filthyin' up the place, either, 'cept those damn drunk kids who got no respect for nobody or nothin'. And the church, of course, when they trot out their trash once a week to keep me company. And there's been some stuff worth sharin' my alley with in there, too. Not so bad.

REBUILDING HISTORIES

Joe's explanation begins to illustrate how the status of being homeless—undomiciled—brings greater complexity to Wendell Berry's notion that in order to know who we are, we must know where we are.[9] Our identity, he writes, is defined to a large degree by our sense of place, our sense of home, and by the traits of our environment. The writers I discuss here see themselves, and are seen, almost solely through the lens of place—the guy under the bench near the "T," the woman on the heating grate, the old man in the alley. . . . The challenge in their writings is to draw out the stories which animate those relationships with place in ways that retrieve the individual, and his or her thoughts, feelings, and actions, from invisibility.

This exploration of the intersection of personal and public history among Boston's homeless is, in a very real sense, a work-in-progress—an ongoing, multi-year project on environmental oral histories and life-writing among individuals whose voices are often at the margins of the history of place and community. The project began somewhat organically, the result of two informal writing groups held at day programs—one in an outreach facility, the other, in the basement of a downtown church with a meal program. The writers' groups have met weekly for just over two years—sometimes with only one or two writers, other times with seven or eight, and additional facilitators. Writing sessions might last for most of the morning, or for only half an hour, as the writers' needs, abilities, and patience dictated.

Over time, other facets have been added to the research, such as image-based work and more formalized place biographies, in order to add depth and detail to the writers' narratives and experiences. The project has also been consolidated into a more systematic framework, which includes demographic information, and structured interviews but is still opportunistic in nature, relying on the contacts of those already contributing, individuals taking advantage of an existing day program service, or those more deeply "hidden" who receive clothing and blankets from an outreach van. While the 32 individuals who have contributed to this project thus far represent only one half of 1 percent of Boston's documented homeless, their narratives represent roughly 10 percent (in winter) of those homeless who choose or are forced to find accommodations outside the shelter system. Demographically, they roughly mirror the city's larger demographics of homelessness, with four times as many men as women, and in terms of race, slightly under 50 percent Caucasian, about 36 percent African American, and 12 percent Hispanic. Although at city, state, and national levels, children are the fastest increasing homeless population, there is no "under-18" representation in this project.

As will be discussed later, the writings and images produced through this work have moved through and beyond the community of homeless people living downtown, and been brought into the public realm through Web pages, photo exhibits, informal publications, and advocacy efforts, in continuing efforts to integrate their lives and experiences into the wider communities considerations of social and environmental justice.

HOMELESSNESS AND TIES TO PLACE

One significant aspect of exploring the role of "place" with homeless individuals is the absence of a common cultural illusion that human beings are all somehow autonomous souls or minds, floating free of the environment. Anthropologist Louis Dumont observed that:

> . . . each person is conceived of as "a particular incarnation of abstract humanity." . . . A kind of sacred personalized self is developed and the 'individual as individual' is seen as inviolate, a supreme value in and of itself.[10]

In contrast, individuals living on the street tend not to detach, but to firmly situate their lives within particular times and places. Forty-year-old Dragon, for example, who has been living on the streets for the fifteen years since his discharge from military service, took me on his own version of a "walking tour" of downtown Boston to illustrate a writing he had just fin-

ished, linking environmental and personal degradation, as he connected
alleys and corners to specific seasons and years and events of his life on the
street, tying many of them to life lessons learned, or the rise and fall of his
personal characteristics and beliefs. In talking about his winter at the Ruggles
T-stop he related that

> Now that place there . . . turns you as black as shit. Not that I ain't already
> black . . . but I mean, on the inside . . . dark . . . hard as that wall over there, and
> just as pissed on . . . and you turn into the place . . . or it turns into you . . . I
> ain't too sure how that shit goes, but it's still in me . . . winter . . . back in '97
> . . . the trains screechin' on the rails . . . the stench of piss and cigarettes . . .
> pigeon shit . . . it's all hangin' there in me . . . black . . .

While individuals on the streets may live without the formal claim to place
that inheres in the domiciled population, many of those with whom I work,
like Dragon, use their environments, no matter how temporary, as tools to
ground their identities. As one woman suggested "maybe we pay closer
attention to where we are, 'cause that's now, and that's all we are." That
"closer attention" made itself apparent time after time in the writing groups'
narratives, whether written, oral, or in a few cases, even visual. After a while,
it became clear that whether one wanted to understand life histories or map
death sites; find a soup kitchen or hide from outreach; nearly all knowledge
derived from being "place-less" was, in fact, based in place. Chronicling that
knowledge—formalizing thoughts and experiences long-forgotten or
deemed insignificant—can play an important role in recognizing assets, valo-
rizing abilities, and helping to rebuild a strong sense of identity among
homeless individuals, as well as documenting the ways in which development
and regeneration for one segment of the community can result in degradation and further marginalization for another.

Billy, who lives on the edge of Boston Common, has been hospitalized
twice as a result of toxic substances poured over the contents of dumpsters
by local restaurant staff, in an effort to discourage homeless individuals from
looking there for food. In an essay about his decreasing sense of safety on
the streets, Billy wrote:

> Diving. You think it's my recreation, but it's my livelihood. You think it's my
> hobby, but it's my survival. You. You throw out enough food everyday to feed
> me and all my boys and not even miss it. Isn't it enough that I demean myself,
> take myself down to your dumpster and dive in? I don't do spare changin'. I
> don't beg. I just eat your food when you're done with it. But no, that ain't
> enough for you, is it? You go and pour out bleach over all that God given food,
> just to make sure I can't eat. Just to make sure that Billy don't scare away your
> fancy customers. Just to make sure they don't have to eat in the same place as
> me. Or maybe you just want me to die.

Revitalization efforts in the neighborhoods around Boston Common continue to push individuals living on the streets farther away from developing areas, and expanding surveillance and control around exclusive hotels, restaurants, offices, and condominiums, rising up in sharp contrast to homeless life on the streets. As a result, homeless people are increasingly moved away from the safety of areas in close proximity to the Common, and further into locations where their physical safety is at greater risk, and their senses of being "in place" are significantly diminished:

> Okay, so it probably didn't do much for business when I'd sneak under those little heat lamps out front for a couple minutes. But it was the dead of winter, and oh, were they warm! Now I don't even stop before getting moved along, further down into Chinatown, where I know I don't belong. I get lost in there. There are too many streets I don't know, people I don't know, screaming at me things I don't understand. I hate to admit this, especially at my age but I get confused, and a little scared.

> —Bettey, age 57

ENVIRONMENTAL LIFE-WRITING

In order to better understand those things that contributed to the writers' feelings of being "in place" and the impact of events which diminish that sense, we initially approached several broad questions about their relationship to place: How did memories and experiences of earlier "places"—their environment, in its broadest sense—affect or shape writers' present day attitudes, values, fears, and relationships with place? In what places did they feel most "at home," most like "themselves," in contrast to Bettey's Chinatown experiences? How had these places changed during the course of their homelessness? How had changes in the environment around them changed the quality of their lives?

The value of these initial questions in environmental life-writing and in examining the linkages between social and environmental injustice is that they continue to illustrate some of the ways in which homeless identities are firmly rooted in place—or in many places; how critical "place" is to homeless identity, and how damaging when that sense of being "in place" is weakened or taken away. There is, in fact, a landscape of homelessness. In *Grand Central Winter*, Lee Stringer writes of the homeless terrain: "Like Ellison's *Invisible Man*, we had receded into that part of the landscape that refused to support the American Dream."[11] Over and over, narratives found in the group's environmental life-writings point to the significance of the environment in the lives of the unsheltered homeless. Not simply in terms of exposure to the elements, but in terms of the creation and maintenance of a sense of self, illustrating that marginalization of the homeless can occur on levels other than economic or social. Members of the writing group indicated that they often experience their environments more intimately, draw different levels of knowledge from them, and have more pronounced feelings of environmental alienation—at least from that part of the environment to which the domiciled population has laid claim:

> some say it's the daffodil that marks the spring, others claim it's a rodent but the only problem is they've got the wrong rodent pinned. they all wait around for this groundhog to tell them when things are going to be warming up but in reality it's the rat. when the rat shows its face after a cold winter it means spring is here. spring isn't pretty flowers and april showers, spring is rats and heaps of trash, and right after spring comes summer and a sizzling heap of new problems and big shots telling you where to go.

> —Rachel

As Rachel's essay illustrates, experiences of place include not only perceptions and valuations of particular sites or environments, but also feelings about places and what happens in them. Significant environments may change over the life-course as needs, interests, and concerns change, but positive or negative affective associations with place often remain, shaping attitudes and interactions with one's surroundings. With that in mind, environmental autobiography asks writers to think back and describe how the environment of their past, including the physical, as well as the cultural landscape, has helped make them the unique individuals they have become. In this case, members of the writing group were are asked to think back to an earlier event that was to them, significant, and in as much detail as possible, describe the setting. They were then asked to move forward to a moment in their lives which they felt had been influenced by that earlier moment somehow, describe it, and write about how the two are interrelated—thus creating an environmental thread through the events of their lives. Tommy, a man in his early fifties, wrote about the changes in his childhood neighborhood, a neighborhood becoming increasingly degraded and marginalized by nearby gentrification:

> as soon as no one was looking, we bolted out through the gate [of the playground] and down the sidewalk so fast that all you could hear was the slamming of sneakers on the concrete—and then the sounds of us yelling and shrieking because we'd got away with it again. I played something like Army, crawling on my belly on the pavement around the tenement buildings, ripping my elbows and the knees of my pants . . . gravel ground in everywhere. . .dodging cars . . . always forgetting to watch where my shadow was . . . gave me away every time. About a year ago, I was living in a construction site near the old neighborhood, and I fell one day and got hurt kinda bad . . . bloody . . . but I laid there feeling

that same old sting . . . smelling the dust of the concrete and it felt like not much had changed . . . Even though they'd turned the place into a shit-hole full of rats junkies and broken glass, it still seemed the same somehow.

Can these memories be relied on to paint a true picture of the past in the lives of people whose present is complex and often troubled, or do past environments become idealized by comparison, leaving us simply to wonder about the degradation of lives and places? As environmental writer, Luke Wallin, points out, reaching back into the past is always susceptible to idealized or false memory.[12] Thus, environmental autobiography is a particularly subjective writing tool, and, in the spirit of anthropologist Karl Heider's "Rashomon Effect," the hardest from which to glean a particular level of cultural "truth."[13] However, if we accept as our end goal, the construction of a picture of "ecological identity" among these homeless writers—an illustration of how the self is construed in relation to the environment—then absolute truth of memory becomes unnecessary, and the internalization of cultural values which lead to idealized memory is of equal or greater significance. As Norm, a writer who had cycled in and out of homelessness for nearly a decade due to an injury, explained: "Society is always telling us how we *should* be, and never seeing the value in what we are. Maybe my memories of how things used to be give me a little of that back."

THE LANDSCAPE HISTORY

In order to expand on the experiences and knowledge derived from life on the streets, and learn more about the trajectory of social and environmental injustice in the lives of the homeless, participants were introduced to the idea of "place biographies" or landscape histories, and asked to think and describe a significant place over time, from their first experience to the present. This approach not only served to document the continuing marginalization and degradation of the areas frequented by the homeless, but also served to create an environmental thread through the places and events of the participants' lives, rooting them "in place" in very observable ways.

The focus of this approach is to choose a particular site—a building, waterfront, woods, alley—and follow it through time, paying attention to the ways in which its appearance, uses, and what was expected of it, as well as the people and activities which animated it, changed over time, loosely following a model such as is offered by John Brinckerhoff Jackson in "The Westward Moving House," in which he traces several generations of a family through the houses in which they lived—looking at the ways the house serves as an artifact which both reflects and shapes the culture and psychology of the family.[14] This sort of historical study, when used *as* an historical study, can lend itself to a relatively impersonal perspective on "place." However, when modified so as to encompass not all of the history of a site, but only an individual's experiences of it (and their handed-down knowledge of any informal lore), landscape history becomes a powerful tool for situating knowledge and experience in specific locations. When narratives are controlled for variables such as gender or age, landscape histories can also give clues to how such variables impact the experience of particular sites, for example, in terms of safety or accessibility. Members of the writers' group have provided landscape history narratives which have proven useful and interesting, not only for their "subaltern" qualities, but for their indication of sites significant to the lives and experiences of the homeless.

When asked to choose a location and write this sort of personal landscape history or place biography, nearly one third of the writers or contributors chose the alley behind the Boston Public Library as their focus. An essay by Joanna, a forty-one-year-old woman who has been on and off the streets for four years illustrates:

> Four years ago, the street right behind the BPL didn't see much traffic. Not from us, and not from anyone else. It was quiet . . . peaceful . . . a cut-through, I think, more than anything, and maybe a place to park without a resident sticker and not get caught. But with all that quiet, and those big heating grates from the library, it was a good place for some of us to sleep, you know? And not a lot of people knew about it. But then the condos came to the block alongside the library—big, bright, tall and expensive. The whole neighborhood changed. They didn't want us homeless people ruining their view of the architecture, you know . . .

Rory's narrative continues the history:

> . . . about a year ago, they banned the boys with the Outreach Van from bringing blankets and socks there on their rounds—thinking that would move us along. Now the place is crowded at night—so crowded you don't feel safe anymore. Nobody wants the vans pestering and checking up. Vehicles on the street where we're tryin' to sleep . . . headlights . . . not knowin' who they are until they're right on top of us. . . . We don't want their "outreach"—we want to be left alone and be safe. And everybody's fighting for the grates. . . . After this winter, I'm movin' on—outta the high-rent district.

Joanna's and Rory's writings along with several others, speak to not only the history of the site as they've lived it, but to power, fear, economic development, mainstream attitudes toward homelessness, and obstacles to the services which try to address it.

Often, the writers' historical narratives served to highlight significant environmental issues in the homeless community, such as demolition, gentrification, the many lives of squatter space, and exposure to the elements. One of the group members, Rodney, wrote in elegant detail of winter days spent sledding down the mountainous-seeming hill of the Common, mounding it up into bumps for an extra thrill, and then burying friends in the snow until they shook themselves free. As he wrote further, this memory became intricately interwoven with a recent adult memory of finding a homeless friend buried in snow, frozen to death after a night spent without shelter. "I used to love winter. Tore outside with the very first flake. Now, winter is the enemy. It kills. One dead here, another there, little bits of death marking places I sleep and eat and sit . . . that's a little bit of my own death, right there."

As Rodney read his essay aloud for the group, each member echoed his sadness and related similar experiences—or realized they had known some of the same people—not through the identification of name, but by death site. When talk wore down, they decided that in the following session, they would all write narratives of a place where someone they knew had died. Soon, most were morbidly joking about "the dead zone session"—black humor that linked them to each other in a way they hadn't been before.

FROM ENVIRONMENTAL
WRITING TO ACTIVISM

That early unanticipated teamwork was only the beginning of the collaboration and community fostered by the act of life-writing. While the environmental life-writings created by the group have been deeply empowering on an individual basis, they have taken on far more active lives and lessons for the writers and a much wider community. Our weekly sessions have evolved from simply quiet time to sit and write with an available facilitator, to time when writings—and struggles with writing—are shared, creating a community of shared stories and experiences. It all began one day when Walter, a man in his late fifties, read a piece he had just completed about his season under the highway overpass, getting sicker weekly from the exhaust fumes of cars passing overhead. The others listened to Walter's words quietly, at first, and then some began to interject questions, reminiscences, similarities. Another writer quickly sketched Walter's scene as it was evoked for him, and at the end of half an hour, we were planning the creation of an anthology—a collection of stories, themes, and pictures that would express the shared and yet unique histories, angers, hopes, and visions of the writers.

These collaborations have taken other paths, as well, and significantly altered the stage on which the struggles of homelessness are acted out. In the fall of 2003, writers were all given disposable cameras and asked to take pictures of their environments—significant people and places in their lives.

Those images have been formed into a traveling photo exhibit, "Images from the Streets," which includes the photographer-writers narrations of the images, as a community awareness-raising event. Several of the photographer-writers have been asked to speak to community groups and classes about their works, and lives and landscape of the homeless community, adding faces and humanity to the wider community's concept of homelessness. Additionally, Doris, a homeless woman with community theater background, has turned her environmental history writings into several one-act plays, which she and other homeless actors have performed on Boston Common, illustrating for the community-at-large, in an environment where *she* is the one "in place," the challenges faced by those living on the streets: "As the Heat Rises," about a night spent on a heating grate; "Don't Let Them Take My Cart Away," on the fear of robbery and assault; and "Understanding the Territorial Imperative," or how to find a place to sleep that isn't already taken.

But perhaps even more significantly with respect to social justice activism, the recently formed HEAT (Homeless Emergency Action Taskforce), composed of homeless individuals and other homeless advocates, has complied a number of groups' writings as testimony to the environmental conditions facing Boston's homeless population, and utilized them in lobby efforts to highlight pressing environmental justice issues using the voices of the homeless themselves. First-hand experiences with the ways in which toxic environments, dumping, unsafe sites, violence, and overcrowding all disproportionately affect the city's homeless underclass are finding their way into mainstream politics of place, through mailings, leaflets, and readings in increasingly public forums. And while still existing very much on the margins of the life of the city, each story validates experience, reanimates the past, helps to create relationships and communities in the midst of isolation and degradation, and retrieves a bit of a life from the landscape of invisibility.

NOTES

1. All uncited quotations are taken from the homeless writers' group. The authors prefer to remain anonymous, but I would like to extend to them my sincere thanks for their generosity of time and spirit, as well as the use of their writings.

2. Peter Rossi, *Down and Out in America* (Chicago: University of Chicago Press, 1989).

3. Joanne Passaro, *The Unequal Homeless* (New York: Routledge, 1996).

4. Robert Shea, "Variations in Causes of Homelessness: U.S. Perspective," paper presented at the Annual Meetings of the Gerontological Society of America, November, 2003, San Diego, CA.

5. Winton Pitkoff, et al., "Out of Reach 2003: America's Housing Wage Climbs," National Low Income Housing Coalition. http://www.nlihc.org/oor2003.

6. Steven Vanderstaay, *Street Lives* (Philadelphia: New Society Publishers, 1992), 4.

7. "Homeless in the City of Boston, 2003," *Annual Census Report*. http://www .cityofboston.gov/shelter/pdfs/report/pdf.

8. Mary Leonard "Homelessness, Hunger Worse, Mayors' Report Finds," *The Boston Globe* [online]. http://www.boston.com/news/nation/washington/articles/ 2003/12/19/homelessness_hunger_worsen_mayors_report_finds/.

9. Wendell Berry, *What Are People For?* (San Francisco: North Point Press, 1990), 14.

10. Louis Dumont, *Homo Hierarchicus: The Caste System and Its Implications* (Chicago: University of Chicago Press), 5.

11. Lee Stringer, *Grand Central Winter* (New York: Washington Square Press, 1998), 57.

12. Luke Wallin, "Environmental Writing and Minority Education" [online], *Voices in English Classrooms, Honoring Diversity and Change,* ed. Helen C. Lodge. http://www.lukewallin.com/wemined.htm.

13. Karl Heider, "The Rashomon Effect: When Ethnographers Disagree," *American Anthropologist 90: 73–81.*

14. John Brinkerhoff Jackson, "The Westward Moving House," *Landscapes*, ed. Ervin H. Zube, 2: 8–21.

10

Citizens against Wilderness
Environmentalism and the Politics of Marginalization in the Great Smoky Mountains

Stephen Wallace Taylor

The phrase "environmental justice" carries certain connotations in common usage. Those concerned with environmental justice have habitually concerned themselves with the depredations wrought by corporations and municipalities, taking advantage of politically and economically disenfranchised populations in choosing sites for the construction of polluting factories and the disposal of toxic wastes. But what happens when the desire to preserve certain environmentally sensitive areas collides with the interests of the local population? Can the concept of environmental justice be used to understand the dynamics of such a situation? To put it another way, is it possible for environmentalists to be guilty of environmental injustice?

The best-known advocate of the formation of the Great Smoky Mountains National Park was nature writer Horace Kephart, who left a cozy librarian's job in St. Louis in 1900, going in search of a mythical pioneer lifestyle. Kephart believed he had found it in the woods of Swain County, North Carolina, in a solitary place he called "the Back of Beyond" in the headwaters of the Little Tennessee River. Kephart's meticulous description of the physical environment hearkens back to the naturalist writings of Lewis and Clark, but his signature work, *Our Southern Highlanders,* contains many misleading stereotypes of the region's people. Just as Margaret Mitchell's romance of the plantation South and Thomas Dixon's violent white supremacist novels helped shape popular views of the typical "southern experience," Kephart's backwoods adventures helped mislead readers into seeing the upper Little

157

Tennessee River valley as an isolated and virginal wilderness. Though he was frequently identified with the preservationist mentality of the early twentieth century, Kephart's style and influence place him among the ranks of Mary Noailles Murfree and the other local colorists of the southern mountains. Despite Kephart's romanticism, at the first meeting of a committee formed to choose a site for a national park in the southern mountains, developer Harlan P. Kelsey distributed copies of *Our Southern Highlanders* to the other members, claiming that it contained "the truest description of this area available," thus helping to convince the committee that despite more than forty years of logging, mining, and railroad activity funded by outsiders, the population and environment of the Smokies were unique and worthy of preservation.[1]

Unlike national parks created from public lands in the West, the Great Smoky Mountains National Park was culled from lands already in private hands. There was no federal money available for purchasing such large blocks of land, so park advocates had to raise funds for land acquisition from private sources. Local fundraising campaigns were never more successful than in diminutive Bryson City, the seat of Swain County, North Carolina. In the first day of the campaign alone, Bryson City's boosters raised over $25,000 from over 200 citizens—in a town with a total population of less than 1600 inhabitants. It would later raise another $22,500. Though the city of Asheville, widely regarded as a leader in the park movement, had twenty-five times as many people, it raised only five times as much money in three weeks as Bryson City did in a single day. Because of their role in its creation and because the proposed park boundary was less than three miles from the city limits, residents of Bryson City maintained a proprietary interest in the park and considered it their own.[2]

Having acquired the core of the land for the park, the park service sought to determine the best way of using it. Some boosters envisioned a sort of living forest preserve in which residents would continue to live in their own homes within the park, and both boosters and park service officials made promises to that effect. Park service officials hoped the "quaint mountain ways" of these residents would attract visitors, but the residents became an embarrassment to the park when they insisted on continuing to fish, hunt, and grow crops on what they still saw as their land. In 1938 the park service commissioned a team of consultants to report on ways to present the park service's vision of mountain culture. The committee disapproved of the relatively modern reality of life in the Smokies and insisted on the removal of all structures and artifacts constructed after 1890. They emphasized live demonstrations of the "pioneer lifestyle" and even recommended that former residents be invited to remain in the park area and "live as their ancestors did." According to this plan, the park service would be placed in the dubious position of removing contemporary frame dwellings and replacing them with log cabins, disposing of all farm tractors, and dismantling any structures deemed "inappropriate" for the intended audience.[3]

When wartime necessity gave the Tennessee Valley Authority the impetus to construct Fontana Dam along the Little Tennessee River, the North Shore land omitted from the park boundary eventually came into the hands of the federal government, though not immediately those of the national park service. Despite the tremendous upheaval the construction of Fontana Dam produced, most residents accepted the TVA presence in the area. But TVA lost much of this support over its handling of land acquisition issues, especially the acquisition of 44,400 acres on the north side of the reservoir area. This area was located above the high water mark of the reservoir and thus would not be flooded. But the project would destroy state highway 288, the twisting gravel road which ran along the northern shore of the river. This would leave the residents of the small towns of Proctor and Bushnell, as well as those of the more isolated coves along Hazel Creek and Noland Creek completely without road access.

In previous TVA projects, the agency had offered to replace any roads inundated or rendered useless, but because labor and other resources were so scarce during the war, the War Production Board refused to allocate the necessary workers and materials for the construction of a road which was not directly necessary for the war effort. TVA General Manager Gordon Clapp then proposed settling claims for the loss of access directly with the individuals affected, and making no attempt to provide a replacement road. Instead, the agency opted to compensate the county and the state—the legal owners of the road.[4]

TVA officials negotiated a settlement involving Swain County, the state of North Carolina, and the National Park Service. The settlement called for TVA to purchase the North Shore land and turn it over to the park service for inclusion in the Great Smoky Mountains National Park. The acquisition of this land would absolve both TVA and the state of any responsibility for replacing the outdated road, because there would be no residents needing road access. Upon receiving the needed funding from Congress, the park service would assume responsibility for replacing the old road with a new parkway as part of its master access plan for the Smokies, giving Swain County a means of attracting tourists to compensate for the lack of property tax revenue. TVA would pay $400,000 to a trust fund for the retirement of Swain County's debts, and a new road, built by the state of North Carolina, would link U.S. highway 19 to the park boundary, where the park service road would begin. TVA had in effect transferred most of its roadbuilding obligation to the park service along with the land, but the park service considered its obligations to the nation—and in particular its environmental stewardship mission—more important than local considerations, making the construction of the road extremely unlikely.[5]

Ironically, a state initiative aimed at improving road access further under-mined plans for the north shore road. In the early 1950s, the state highway commission embarked on a massive roadbuilding program under Governor William Kerr Scott. So-called "county roads," actually state-maintained sec-ondary routes, received much of the commission's attention. The most expe-dient means of obtaining a road from Bryson City to Fontana in this political climate was to straighten and pave existing county roads. But any such route through Swain County would cross park service lands, and just as the park service could not build roads outside the park, the state could not build any roads inside it. The logical alternative was to improve existing routes through Graham County, outside the park boundary along the south shore. The new route, designated North Carolina 28, explicitly replaced the remnants of old highway 288, which was removed from the state mainte-nance system. By the mid-1950s, the two points—Bryson City and Fon-tana—were thus already connected by a decent two-lane paved road, as TVA and the park service had intended when planning the replacement of the old highway. State highway location engineer R. Getty Browning proposed that the state and the park service could both benefit from reconsidering the 1943 agreement, and that perhaps the park service might offer to contribute some money toward the improvement of other roads and tourist facilities outside the park in lieu of building the north shore road, an idea which park service director Conrad Wirth liked as well. Environmentalists petitioned Congress to authorize a transfer of funds for that purpose, to no avail.[6]

In the early years of the park, Tennessee community leaders had worked to ensure that their side of the park was easily accessible and heavily pro-moted, and it naturally followed that the Tennessee side would have more substantial accommodations for tourists. The North Carolina side of the park did not benefit from the same sort of unified development strategy. While the Western North Carolina Associated Communities (WNCAC), formed in 1946, helped promote "specific projects of general value to the entire area, economically, socially, educationally, and aesthetically," that organization resisted efforts to make the park the primary tourist destina-tion in western North Carolina. The communities that had once fought over which one could be the park's gateway now strove to prove they had other things to offer in addition to the park. Bryson City's boosters would find few allies in their attempts to turn the park into a moneymaking enterprise. Bryson City, unlike Cherokee (the only other town in North Carolina directly bordering the park), had little that was genuinely unique to attract tourists visiting either the park or other attractions in the Smokies, and its pleas for WNCAC attention went largely ignored.[7]

Just as it lacked distinctiveness, Bryson City lacked the advantages of loca-tion. The federal highway through the park, U.S. 441, connected Gatlinburg to Cherokee and proceeded south through Dillsboro to Franklin, bypassing

Bryson City. Attempts to have N.C. 28 redesignated as U.S. 441-W, thus attracting a share of the Knoxville and Atlanta traffic, failed. Moreover, while N.C. 28 provided excellent access from Bryson City to Fontana Dam, most of its length was in neighboring Graham County. While this detail may at first seem meaningless, it gains significance in light of the extremely small tax base in Swain County, which withered largely because of the formation of the park. A new road within the park would itself be immune to development, but would funnel traffic around the western half of the park directly into Bryson City, where tourist development could proceed and provide a needed injection of revenue. But the state road could host plenty of taxable development along the way, and as long as it remained the only way around Fontana Lake, Graham County would get the tax dollars generated by tourist traffic. From the national perspective, the two roads were interchangeable, except that one was inside the park and not yet built, while the other was outside the park and already built. But the state highway did not satisfy the needs of Swain County's politicians and entrepreneurs, many of whom had contributed money to create the park in the first place. Swain County's Board of Commissioners and its Chamber of Commerce jealously sought to hoard what little tourist traffic came through, but were thwarted. Moreover, the disputes over access had placed Bryson City's plans to attract tourist dollars on hold.[8]

Under intense pressure from North Carolina Governor Luther Hodges, the park service did begin constructing the north shore road at the eastern end, where the state connector had been completed in the late 1950s. Park service officials initially envisioned building the road only as far as Goldmine Branch, approximately three miles into the park boundary. Their aim was to demonstrate to Swain County that it would be better to use Bryson City as a jumping-off point for activities within the park than to construct a through road within the park boundary. So certain were park officials that their vision of the north shore would work that they even spent scarce park service funding to survey an alternate route for the road which would make construction beyond Goldmine Branch impossible.[9]

Problems quickly appeared with the north shore development plan. The lack of electric power and the limited supply of drinking water would have made the recreation sites unattractive to many tourists. Remedying those conditions, on the other hand, would cost the park service a lot of money, and might well compromise the area's appeal to preservation-oriented visitors. Moreover, the access road—the north shore road—proved to be far more difficult and expensive to construct than originally anticipated. The road was cut through unstable rock which decomposed upon exposure to air. The roadbed crumbled almost as soon as it was cut, necessitating many additional hours of cut-and-fill activity for what park service personnel saw as dubious improvements in the stability and quality of the road. Furthermore, cutting deeper into the Anakeesta rock formation underlying the roadbed would likely result in unacceptable damage to the park's now-clean streams, releasing toxic heavy metals and lowering the pH of the water to dangerous levels for wildlife.[10]

The park service temporarily halted construction of the north shore road several times because of these stability problems in the underlying rock. In January of 1964, after about seven and a half miles had been completed, a series of massive and nearly fatal landslides caused a public panic. Despite the panic, a five mile section at the eastern end of the north shore route was opened for public use in October of 1965. The construction of this road, as far as it went, visibly scarred the landscape, upsetting environmentalists. After 1966, the park service placed all future development of the north shore—recreational facilities such as the Monteith Branch campground, as well as roads—on indefinite hold. Tourists, predictably, stayed away, preferring the conveniences they found on the Tennessee side of the park. Local people, frustrated by the park service's moratorium on construction and the resulting economic stagnation, came to refer to the unfinished park road as the "Road to Nowhere."[11]

Even before the north shore road debacle, many North Carolina leaders blamed their Tennessee counterparts for "hijacking" the development of the park for the benefit of Tennessee. But by the 1960s, local strategies for the development of the North Carolina side of the park were sidetracked by efforts to maintain the "rustic" or "backcountry" atmosphere—an atmosphere to which the North Carolina side originally had little claim, thanks to the lumber companies—and by the high cost of any major changes in the park's infrastructure. The Wilderness Society, the Isaak Walton League, and the National Wildlife Federation influenced both park policy and congressional action despite the fact that one survey indicated that only 5.7 percent of visitors to the park intended to use day hiking facilities, 0.4 percent intended to fish, 0.3 percent participated in horseback riding, and 0.6 percent went tubing.[12]

Ironically, much of the territory celebrated by environmentalists as "primeval wilderness" was the same territory nearly destroyed by the logging and mining companies one or two generations earlier, before the formation of the park. In the intervening years, nature had reclaimed the area to the point that many of those protesting against the road seemingly believed it would cut through virgin forest. The north shore road became a symbol for the struggle between developers and environmentalists. Developers saw the road as the one chance for Swain County and especially Bryson City to get its "fair share" of the tourist dollars attracted by the park, while environmentalists, deploring the commercialization of the Tennessee entrances to the park, sought to prevent the same fate from befalling the quieter, more remote North Carolina side by having large areas legally designated as permanent wilderness. One wilderness advocate wrote: "Those of us who have hiked and camped there remember the frothy streams, the unrestrained vegetation and abundant wildlife, we remember the ridges and valleys, the blueberry-hung meadows, the vistas, and the primeval solitude. . . To us, and to many others, the Smokies are one of the few nearby places offering uninhabited miles of the nature which greeted white men in America centuries ago, and which is rapidly being chiseled away." Another preservationist, perhaps unaware of the early history of the park movement in western North Carolina, expressed frustration with the revenue-oriented rhetoric of the Bryson City boosters: "Will these people ever understand that the [park] exists preeminently to be held in trust as a wilderness museum for all citizens . . . and that *a fortori* [sic] the park . . .was not established to provide a source of revenue for Swain County citizens or for any others?"[13]

Swain County Democratic Party chairman Henry Truett, who had long operated tourist-oriented businesses in the area, responded by accusing the environmentalists of trying to put the county under a "dictatorship." Kelly Bennett, the longtime booster, wrote the editor of *Wildlife in North Carolina,* a publication of the state Wildlife Resources Commission, calling an article describing the "wilderness character" of the area a "truly grotesque . . . product of reprehensible . . . ignorance." The county board of commissioners demanded that the editor retract the article and apologize to the county.[14]

The sense of grievance nursed by many residents of Swain County found its voice in two groups, differing in their methods and emphasis but united by a firm belief that the federal government and the national environmentalist lobby had victimized them and their region. The earlier impulse to build the north shore road as a means to economic prosperity gave rise in the 1980s to a group calling itself Citizens Against Wilderness (CAW), while the sense of a lost way of life fueled the activities of the North Shore Cemetery Association.

Taking its militant-sounding name from members' opposition to the persistent efforts of environmentalists to designate the entire north shore as a wilderness permanently protected from further development, Citizens Against Wilderness called repeatedly for the full development of the North Carolina side of the park along the lines of the existing Tennessee development. Like their ancestors who called for the full development of hydroelectric power, mining and timber resources in the area, they sought outside investment to restore their "rightful share" of the prosperity the rest of the nation enjoyed. Borrowing loosely from dependency theory, they bemoaned the fact that Tennessee received most of the economic benefits of the park, and they saw environmentalists' attempts to preserve the rest of the Smokies intact as a ploy to keep their region poor and unhappy. The group attacked on a number of fronts, accusing the park service of faulty geology, the Democratic Party of indolence, and the state of Tennessee of elitism. While the group professed to be non-partisan, several self-proclaimed "concerned Democrats" publicly vowed to support ultra-right-wing Senator Jesse Helms because of his anti-environmentalist and anti-wilderness rhetoric. Helms courted these voters by appealing to their sense of outrage at the government's "broken promises." When Tennessee's Senator James Sasser, the co-sponsor of a wilderness preservation bill, attempted to visit the area in 1987, he was confronted by angry protesters waving signs. Two of the protesters leaped in front of the senator's van, and one assaulted a park ranger who attempted to convince the group to stand aside to allow Sasser to pass. The group's leader, Linda Hogue, demanded that Sasser take the time to listen to her complaints. North Carolina reporters quoted Sasser as saying, "I don't want to listen to Swain County," while Tennessee reporters recorded the statement as "I'm not going to listen to every person in Swain County." Among the accusations leveled at Sasser was that he and fellow Tennesseean Howard Baker were introducing the bill in order to protect Tennessee's tourist industry.[15]

While Citizens Against Wilderness promoted a vision of a prosperous future, the North Shore Cemetery Association promoted the reenactment of the rituals first begun in the aftermath of the departure of Ritter Lumber Company from Proctor in 1927. Members of the association gathered frequently to decorate the cemeteries on the north shore, principally in and around Proctor. As access to water had defined communities for those who came to Hazel Creek, Goldmine Branch, or Epps Springs, access prevented by water now defined a community for those forced to leave and their descendants. The association served as a surrogate community for all those whose ancestors were buried in the north shore area. Their members, notably president Helen Cable Vance, seized opportunities to gain attention for their causes: preserving the area's cemeteries, obtaining road access to those cemeteries, and publicizing a version of the area's history which focuses on lost opportunities and economic development while minimizing the inherent instability and temporariness of that development. The North Shore Cemetery Association later became the North Shore Historical Association, seeking to play much the same role in promoting the history of the north shore as the Cherokee Historical Association played in promoting the history of the Eastern Band.[16]

The National Park Service provided this group with water and jeep transportation to the north shore cemeteries so that participants could decorate the graves of ancestors buried there. Their decoration ceremonies, to which the media were invited, frequently included speeches denouncing their victimization by the "federal government," by which they seem to have meant primarily the National Park Service and the TVA. This sense of victimization and displacement tied the members together, and the annual decoration ceremonies at each cemetery cemented their historical identity as the people who gave up their land for an ungrateful nation, just as rituals of school and church attendance helped cement their identity as members of a geographically defined community fifty or sixty years earlier, and in much the same way that gatherings of the United Daughters of the Confederacy and the Sons of Confederate Veterans tend to unite other white southerners with a sense of grievance at the "injustices" perpetrated against the South during and since the War Between the States.[17]

This graveyard political action committee worked closely with every candidate for the area's House seat since the 1960s, and found a warm audience in both Democratic and Republican candidates. Every few years, their representative in the House introduced legislation calling for a road to the North Shore cemeteries, based upon the 1943 agreement. No longer was the road supposed to be for economic development, nor even for access to the park as a whole. It was merely a means of visiting the dead more conveniently.

In a television interview with reporter Bill Landry, North Shore Cemetery Association president Helen Cable Vance visited several cemeteries near her childhood home. She broke down with emotion as she pleaded, "It's not too much to ask, to be able to go back home, is it?" This image became the dominant image of the displaced residents of Fontana in the eyes of many. But the unedited videotape reveals that Landry prompted Vance as follows: Landry: "Would you say that it's not too much to ask to go back home?" Vance: "Yes." Landry: "Go ahead, say it." Vance, more emotionally: "It's not too much to ask, to go back home, is it?" In the edited version of the interview which was aired on Knoxville's WBIR-TV, the prompting disappears and Vance's comment is falsely presented as a spontaneous emotional reaction to her return to the north shore cemeteries. It is clear from the unedited videotape that Vance and her interviewer were working together to present a sentimentalized vision of the region's past in order to influence current policies.[18]

Indeed, the cemetery association's approach to influencing government policies regarding the north shore land was quite creative. Several members of the cemetery association sued TVA, the Department of the Interior, Swain County, and the State of North Carolina in 1983 for specific performance, claiming breach of the 1943 agreement to build the north shore road. Among other charges, the suit claimed that the government had violated the group's First Amendment freedom of religion by preventing them from visiting and decorating the graves of their ancestors. While this was an innovative tactic, the federal district court dismissed the case, declaring that the plaintiffs were only "incidental beneficiaries" of the agreement among TVA, the park service, the state, and Swain County, and thus they had no standing to sue. The Fourth Circuit Court of Appeals affirmed the decision of the district court, on the grounds that the agreement clearly stated that any action by the park service would be contingent upon congressional funding. Understandably, no member of either court dared publicly address the question of freedom of religion. Only Chief Judge Harrison L. Winter dissented in the breach of contract issue, arguing that the park service's decision not to *seek* further congressional funding constituted a breach of the agreement. The court's majority opinion only fueled the group's smoldering sense of grievance against the federal government.[19]

Their anger might just as reasonably be directed at Horace Kephart and other writers like him, and at a public whose perceptions of the area were nourished by what such writers wrote. Because of the formation of the national park and the construction of Fontana Dam, both of which were planned by people whose understanding of the region was limited largely to the romanticized tales promulgated by Kephart, a region characterized by rapid economic oscillation became an economically depressed "nature museum," a monument to a past lifestyle which is also often overly romanticized by the reminiscences of those who remember it as their own childhood. The environmental and economic depredations of mining and timber companies created a region which needed to be "reformed," and the failed reform attempts of the federal government informed by the stereotypes Kephart helped popularize, gradually turned Kephart's "Back of Beyond" from a misperception into a reality. Vance's desire to "be able to go back home" indicts (even if it does not convict) not only those who believed in the myth of the Back of Beyond, but also those who have turned her home into an embodiment of that myth. Ironically, it also confirms the inherently temporary nature of the prosperity brought by the lumber and mining companies before "the government" took over, a prosperity which Vance's generation had expected to inherit and which they continued to believe was unjustly stolen from them.[20]

NOTES

1. Horace Kephart, *Our Southern Highlanders: A Narrative of Adventure in the Southern Appalachians and a Study of Life among the Mountaineers* (Knoxville: University of Tennessee Press, 1976), xi–xlvi, 28–74, 265–349; Carlos C. Campbell, *Birth of a National Park in the Great Smoky Mountains: An Unprecedented Crusade which Created, as a Gift of the People, the Nation's Most Popular Park* (Knoxville: University of Tennessee Press, 1960), 30, 36, 140, 141; Henry D. Shapiro, *Appalachia on Our Mind: The Southern Mountains and Mountaineers in the American Consciousness, 1870–1920* (Chapel Hill: University of North Carolina Press, 1978), 189; Daniel Smith Pierce, "Boosters, Bureaucrats, Politicians, and Philanthropists: Coalition Building in the Establishment of the Great Smoky Mountains National Park" (Ph.D. diss., University of Tennessee, 1995), 35–37, 48; see also Allen Batteau, *The Invention of Appalachia* (Tucson: University of Arizona Press, 1990) 89–92; Christopher Bren-

den Martin, "Selling the Southern Highlands: Tourism and Community Development in the Mountain South" (Ph. D. diss., University of Tennessee, 1997), 195–98; Jack Temple Kirby, *Rural Worlds Lost: The American South, 1920–1960* (Baton Rouge: Louisiana State University Press, 1987), 80–87; Jack Temple Kirby, *Media-Made Dixie: The South in the American Imagination* (Baton Rouge: Louisiana State University Press, 1978), especially 1–22 and 64–77; and J. W. Williamson, *Hillbilly-land: What the Movies Did to the Mountains and What the Mountains Did to the Movies* (Chapel Hill: University of North Carolina Press, 1995).

2. Pierce, "Boosters," 90–91, 95–97, 161–71; Interview with Granville Calhoun by John Parris, in "Only the Dead Remain at Medlin," *Asheville* (N.C.) *Citizen*, March 8, 1968; Margaret Lynn Brown, "Smoky Mountains Story: Human Values and Environmental Transformation in a Southern Bioregion" (Ph.D. diss., University of Kentucky, 1995), 142–51, 160–62, 216–34; Carlos C. Campbell, *Birth of a National Park*, 80, 130–33.

3. Pierce, "Boosters," 179–203, 216–18; Brown, "Smoky Mountains Story," 142–45, 167–71.

4. Michael J. McDonald and John Muldowny, *TVA and the Dispossessed: The Resettlement of Population in the Norris Dam Area* (Knoxville: University of Tennessee Press, 1982), passim; Bruce J. Schulman, *From Cotton Belt to Sunbelt: Federal Policy, Economic Development, and the Transformation of the South, 1938–1980* (New York: Oxford University Press, 1991), 206.

5. William C. Fitts to Gordon R. Clapp, February 22, 1944, TVA Office of the General Manager, Administrative Files, Box 386; F. W. Cron to H. J. Spelman, June 11, 1946, Management Records, Box VII, Folder 1; F. W. Cron to H. J. Spelman, June 11, 1946, Management Records, Box VII, Folder 1, and H. J. Spelman to B. P. McWhorter, June 10, 1952, Management Records, Box VII, Folder 2, Great Smoky Mountains National Park (hereafter GSMNP) Archives; *Asheville Citizen-Times*, February 24, 1952;. On the origins and development of the old township system for highway maintenance, see Cecil Kenneth Brown, *The State Highway System of North Carolina* (Chapel Hill: University of North Carolina Press, 1930). On fire control as a problem in the earliest days of the park, see Pierce, "Boosters," 207–209.

6. *Greensboro Daily News* July 5, 1951; *Smoky Mountain Times*, July 5, 1951, July 12, 1951; *Winston-Salem Journal* August 13, 1950; Minutes of the North Carolina State Highway Commission, December 10, 1943, February 1, 1944, July 19, 1944, March 23, 1945, June 20, 1945, November 28, 1945, April 24, 1946, June 27, 1946, November 27, 1946, July 29, 1948, September 30, 1948, December 2, 1948, February 24, 1949, July 28, 1949, February 1, 1951, March 1, 1951, July 7, 1951, December 20, 1951, March 26, 1953, July 30, 1953, October 30, 1953, April 1, 1954, September 9, 1954, August 2, 1956, microfilm reel S.55.4p, North Carolina State Department of Archives and History; Edward S. Zimmer to Regional Director, Region One, November 21, 1952; Conrad Wirth to Edgar L. McDaniel, Jr., March 9, 1953; Dan Hale to Senator Styles Bridges, January 19, 1953; Management Records, Box VI, Folder 1, GSMNP Archives; *Smoky Mountain Times* July 5, 1951, July 12, 1951.

7. Campbell, *Birth of a National Park*, 12–24; see also John Thomas Whaley, "A Timely Idea at an Ideal Time: Knoxville's Role in Establishing the Great Smoky Mountains National Park" (M.A. thesis, University of Tennessee, 1984); L. Alex Too-

man, "The Evolving Economic Impact of Tourism on the Greater Smoky Mountain Region of East Tennessee and Western North Carolina" (Ph.D. diss., University of Tennessee, 1995), 210–12, 239–59.

8. Conrad Wirth to George Shuford, January 24, 1957; Hillory A. Tolson to W. H. Rogers, May 21, 1957; Hillory Tolson to George Shuford, May 21, 1957; George Shuford to Conrad Wirth, May 8, 1957; Management Records, Box VII, Folder 3; Elmer F. Bennett to Luther L. Hodges, April 26, 1960, Management Records, Box XIII, Folder 6; Henry Wilson to Stewart Udall, May 9, 1962, Management Records, Box VI, Folder 5, GSMNP Archives; *Asheville Citizen*, September 3, 1960.

9. Perry Abbott to J. L. Obenschain, February 4, 1960, J. L. Obenschain to F. W. Cron, February 5, 1960, Management Records, Box VII, Folder 5; Elbert Cox to Conrad Wirth, June 8, 1962, Management Records, Box VII, Folder 7; GSMNP Archives.

10. Fred Overly to [Elbert Cox], August, 19, 1960, Fred Overly to Elbert Cox, March 2, 1962; Management Records, Box XIII, Folder 10; Fred Overly to Elbert Cox, January 20, 1961, Elbert Cox to [Conrad Wirth], February 6, 1961, Thomas Vint to Elbert Cox, April 20, 1961, Management Records, Box VII, Folder 6; George W. Fry to [Elbert Cox], January 6, 1964, Management Records, Box VI, Folder 10; *Report of the Technical Committee for the Inspection of the Bryson-Fontana Road Construction, Great Smoky Mountains*, April 25, 1962; Eric Erhart, "Inspection of Great Smoky National Park Project 9A1"; Eugene R. DeSilets to Robert G. Hall, April 12, 1962; Management Records, Box VII, Folder 7, GSMNP Archives; see also R. R. Seal, "Geochemistry of Acidic Drainage in the Great Smoky Mountains National Park: Implications for the Southern Appalachians" (abstract), *Proceedings of the Eighth Annual Southern Appalachians Man and the Biosphere Conference*, 55.

11. *Smoky Mountain Times*, April 26, 1962; April 18, 1963; Alfred H. Barker, Jr., to J. A. Todd, January 28, 1964, Management Records, Box VII, Folder 10; George W. Fry to Regional Director, October 1, 1965; Management Records, Box VII, Folder 11, GSMNP Archives.

12. "Transportation Concepts: Great Smoky Mountains National Park," (anonymous internal report) 1–48; The Wilderness Society, "A Special Memorandum to Members and Cooperators," May 20, 1966, Vertical File, Great Smoky Mountains National Park Library; miscellaneous correspondence, Management Records, Boxes VI and VII, GSMNP Archives; John D. Peine and James R. Renfro, *Visitor Use Patterns at Great Smoky Mountains National Park* (Resource Management Report SER-90, U.S. Department of the Interior, National Park Service Records, National Archives Southeast Region), 41.

13. Henry Wilson to Roger Ernst, October 28, 1957; Harvey Broome to Henry Wilson, November 2, 1957; Harvey Broome to Roger Ernst, October 30, 1957; Joel Dimmette to Dwight D. Eisenhour [sic], September 15, 1957; Dan Hale to Fred A. Seaton, October 26, 1957; George A. Shuford to Conrad L. Wirth, May 8, 1957; Secretary of the Interior to Henry Wilson, November 4, 1957; Henry Wilson to Secretary of the Interior, September 6, 1957; Henry Wilson to Dwight D. Eisenhower, October 24 (?), 1957; Roger Ernst to Henry Wilson, December 30, 1957; Harvey Broome to Roger Ernst, December 11, 1957; E. T. Scoyen to Harvey Broome, December 19, 1957; Jeanne Shearer to The Governor, February 11, 1958 (quoted);

C. H. Wharton to Herman E. Talmadge, May 25, 1959; Management Files VI-2; Hallett S. Ward to Conrad Wirth, February 9, 1960; Dan Hale to Conrad L. Wirth, February 10, 1960 (quoted); A. L. Edney to Conrad L. Wirth, February 11, 1960 (quoted); Management Files XIII-4; GSMNP Archives, Gatlinburg, Tennessee; *Smoky Mountain Times*, December 19, 1957, December 26, 1957, May 19, 1960, May 26, 1960, ; *Asheville Citizen*, February 3, 1960, February 4, 1960, February 5, 1960; Henry Wilson, "Trout Stream Wilderness or Road," *The Living Wilderness*, Autumn 1958, 1–4.

14. *Asheville Citizen-Times*, May 29, 1960; Kelly Bennett to [Rod] Amundson, August 15, 1960, Management Files XIII-10, GSMNP Archives, Gatlinburg, Tennessee; *Asheville Citizen* August 17, 1960.

15. *Asheville Citizen-Times*, January 3, 1992, January 14, 1989, January 15, 1989; *Smoky Mountain Times* July 27, 1989, August 31, 1989, September 21, 1989, January 5, 1989, January 12, 1989; *Asheville Citizen-Times*, August 27, 1987; Knoxville News-Sentinel, August 27, 1987; *Knoxville Journal*, August 27, 1987; on support for Helms, see also Charles S. Bullock, III, and Mark J. Rozell, "Southern Politics at Century's End" and Thomas A. Kazee, "North Carolina, Traditionalism, and the GOP," in Charles S. Bullock, III, and Mark J. Rozell, eds., *The New Politics of the Old South: An Introduction to Southern Politics* (Lanham, Md.: Rowman and Littlefield, 1998), 3–21 and 141–65.

16. *Waynesville Mountaineer*, February 22, 1984; *Smoky Mountain Times*, March 29, 1984; *Asheville Citizen*, December 18, 1985, July 29, 1986, September 3, 1986; *Asheville Citizen-Times*, May 3, 1987; *Asheville Citizen*, May 14, 1987.

17. *Asheville Citizen*, July 29, 1986, May 3, 1987, August 27, 1987; *Knoxville News-Sentinel* August 27, 1987, September 20, 1987.

18. *Asheville Citizen-Times*, October 3, 1987, February 26, 1988; *Asheville Citizen*, June 26, 1988, March 10, 1987, March 12, 1987; *Maryville-Alcoa Daily Times*, March 28, 1984; Helen Cable Vance, interview by Bill Landry (unedited videotape at GSMNP Archives).

19. *Vance et al v. TVA et al* (738 Fed. 2d. 1418).

20. For more information on the rapid economic isolations of the economy of western North Carolina, see Stephen Wallace Taylor, *The New South's New Frontier: A Social History of Economic Development in Southwestern North Carolina* (Gainesville: University Press of Florida, 2001).

11

Environmental Justice, Urban Planning, and Community Memory in New York City

Julie Sze

INTRODUCTION

Environmental justice activism has been a central feature of New York City's recent political history. For over two decades, communities of color in New York City have protested noxious facilities in their neighborhoods, with varying degrees of success. From the North River Sewage Treatment Plant in West Harlem, the Brooklyn Navy Yard Incinerator in Williamburg, the Bronx-Lebanon Medical Waste Incinerator in the South Bronx, and the Sunset Park Sludge Treatment Plant, to campaigns against waste transfer stations and power plants, low-income communities of color have used the language of environmental racism to protest the siting of polluting facilities.

This chapter focuses on the role of history and memory in how local New York City activists of color constructed particular issues as examples of environmental racism and their activism against these as environmental justice campaigns. In particular, I examine the polarizing legacy of mid-twentieth-century development and urban renewal policy.[1] In New York City, the main architect of urban renewal was Robert Moses, who transformed the physical and social geography of the city through the construction of public housing, parks, and highways where stable working-class communities once stood.[2] The history and memory of urban renewal and redevelopment policies, the personification of these trends through Robert Moses, and the infrastructure he built are actively cited by contemporary environmental justice activists to tell a particular tale about the destructive effect of urban planning policy and practice in their neighborhoods.

Environmental justice leaders invoke the figure of Robert Moses, because he directly shaped the physical landscape of their communities through both what he built (public housing and highways) and what he didn't (parks). Moses' overt and covert racism in planning New York City have been well-documented.[3] But what is less well-recognized is how his legacy continues to resonate. To environmental justice activists, it represents a cautionary tale of top-down planning, and the worst excesses of urban renewal and development policy. These memories, along with the role of state intervention in the destruction of the industrial waterfront, are used by environmental justice activists to reject current attempts by private actors and public agencies to functionally designate their neighborhoods as dumping grounds for the City's noxious uses. The historical legacy of race-inflected highway, housing, and open space policies is important to understanding the visceral community response to the city's contemporary planning, environmental, and land-use policies. History and memory ensure that race and racism form the primary framework through which to understand the community anger that drives environmental justice campaigns. Environmental justice leaders perform what urban anthropologist Steven Gregory calls "purposeful acts of memory" to construct their racial, collective, and political identities in the present.

This chapter focuses on West Harlem, Red Hook, and the South Bronx to show how environmental justice activists utilize specific narratives and memories of their neighborhoods to counter government and corporate views of their communities. I begin with a brief overview of local environmental justice campaigns. In each, activists describe their neighborhood as historically vibrant, recalling the waterfront as bustling sites of working-class employment and leisure. In part, environmental justice activism represents an affirmation of these areas as racialized spaces and viable communities, in contrast to state and corporate interpretations of these as mere geographic spaces and sites for noxious uses. Community memory of what "was" shapes the bottom-up vision of regeneration. These narratives are invoked in order to press for a locally driven, community-centered planning process.

LOCAL NARRATIVES OF RACE, SPACE AND BLIGHT: SPECTRES OF URBAN RENEWAL AND REDEVELOPMENT

There is perhaps no more important topic in twentieth-century urban history than the role of race and the decline of the central city.[4] New York City, like others in the mid-century, undertook an aggressive urban renewal and economic development policy that left a mixed legacy.[5] Contemporary critics argue that this history contributed to the decline of New York City's manufacturing base that hit working-class residents and people of color particularly hard.[6] In contrast to state policy discourses of urban renewal and redevelopment, contemporary activists of color promote their own narratives that emphasize local and community activism in the face of urban change affecting a wide range of issues, from education, housing, land use, and environmental policy.[7] The relationship between history, memory, and environmental justice is most clear in those neighborhoods scarred by mid-century urban renewal projects, in particular, by highway-building. These neighborhoods share racial and economic characteristics, a physical landscape shaped by zoning, and social and political histories as centers for working-class waterfront employment.[8]

What follows is a description of three communities—West Harlem, Red Hook, and the South Bronx—where environmental justice activism and community memory are intertwined, and where environmental justice campaigns have emerged in response to siting proposals.

West Harlem

The recent history of environmental justice activism in West Harlem began in 1986, when community outrage erupted in response to the beginning of operations of a $1.3 billion North River Sewage Treatment Plant located at 137th Street along the Hudson River. West Harlem Environmental Action (WEACT) was founded in March 1988 by local residents to address ongoing community struggles around the poor management of the plant. WEACT spearheaded the organizing and legal campaign, as well as acting as a community watchdog to monitor the operations of the plant, which had numerous design flaws from its outset.[9]

Residents who lived next to facility complained about the foul odors, from the sewage emanating from it, and about suffering from respiratory problems from the air pollution. These rancid odors included a strong smell of rotten eggs and of unprocessed sewage. Activists linked poor air quality to high asthma rates in Upper Manhattan, which are among the highest in the nation. Using mobilization tactics and a public civil disobedience strategy, activists who called themselves "The Sewage Seven" (West Harlem District Leaders Peggy Shepard and Chuck Sutton, State Senator David Paterson, former Councilmember Hilton Clark, and three others) were arrested for holding up traffic during rush hour on the West Side Highway in front of the plant on Martin Luther King Day in 1988. They were wearing gas masks and carrying signs to dramatize the indignity of their community functioning as the "toilet bowl" for Manhattan. Peggy Shepard, who went on to become executive director of WEACT, uses this description of the plant as the "toilet bowl" at many community meetings and public hearings on the North River Sewage Treatment Plant. This description of the neighborhood as a toilet bowl is meant to show official disregard of community, as the literal "dumping ground" for noxious facilities. Disrespect as a result of racism explains, to WEACT and local residents, why there is a profusion of polluting infrastructure (such as six of the seven diesel bus depots in Manhattan), alongside a lack of environmental amenities (like parks and open space) in Harlem.

Although the plant did not open until well after the end of Robert Moses' reign in the 1960s, he is still the pivotal figure in its history. The plant was first proposed in 1914, but laid dormant until the 1960s when design studies and the siting process reemerged. One of WEACT's founders, Vernice Miller, documents that the siting history and poor planning process of the North River Facility was replete with class and race discrimination.[10] For example, the plant was moved from a proposed site in the white and affluent Upper West Side to Harlem in part because the facility was deemed "incompatible" with development plans for the West Side (but was acceptable for Harlem). Implicit in this decision was the political weight given to the development and recreation plans for the Upper West Side over the interests of the African American and working-class residents in West Harlem. Moses' investments in the Upper West Side were directly related to his underinvestment in parks in Harlem, and lack of recreation for racial minorities more generally. Thus, when it was obvious that the facility was going to be built regardless of local protest, the community reluctantly accepted an offer in the late 1960s to build a state park atop the facility, which finally opened in 1993.

When plans for the facility reemerged in the 1960s, local residents and prominent black politicans from Harlem immediately registered their displeasure. For example, Manhattan Borough President (and Harlem resident) Percy Sutton testified at a public hearing that the facility would "stigmatize" West Harlem. He called the facility an "indignity" and that "these are the indignities that make people feel they are not equal . . . I am hurt, deeply hurt, that you do not understand what you are doing to Harlem."[11] This social and racial stigmatization is a theme that remained constant over three decades of community opposition to the facility. For example, Shepard describes the complex relationship between people of color, places, and community development: "the spaces in which we live affect our spirit and our actions. Oppressive physical surroundings perpetuate and reinforce their resident's oppression. The processes by which our habitat is planned and built keep people isolated, disempowered and depressed."[12] Elsewhere, she builds on these themes, describing the air quality and childhood asthma epidemic in West Harlem as not just a crucial issue of public health, but also contributing to a community-wide sense of depression. This depresssion is a result of vast numbers of youth of color, who should be in their prime, but are in fact stricken from chronic asthma, and who in fact, die from asthma attacks. To combat this sense of despair, WEACT politicizes these symbols of air pollution and poor health. For example, WEACT members often wear gas masks and bring asthma pumps to public demonstrations as a way to dramatize how the air itself has become their enemy in Upper Manhattan.

WEACT's focus on community participation is a direct result of their alienation from the planning and political process durings Moses' reign. As Miller notes: "local communities suffer when they are not informed or included in land use planning and development for their own communities. The residents of West Harlem paid a huge price learning this lesson." The lesson from the last thirty years of the facility's history is that political participation, education, and community monitoring matter. Thus, she believes, through the formation of activist groups like WEACT, that "the community will never again be taken advantage of in such a blatant manner."[13]

This continued vigilance is evident in contemporary community planning efforts on the West Harlem riverfront. WEACT became involved with waterfront planning because of its activism around the North River facility and its concern over the historical and continued inequity in open space and parks development and funding. WEACT's program director, Cecil Corbin-Mark, describes, "the waterfront used to be a beautiful center for commerce and recreation, and of business." [14] He recalls that it was home to ferry services to New Jersey, Brooklyn, and upstate New York and was filled with meatpackers and doll manufacturers. The area fell into disrepair over the last half century, into a litter-strewn stretch of asphalt, largely devoid of people and populated by storage facilities, auto repair shops, gas stations, and parking lots. In 1998, WEACT initiated a community-driven planning process on the waterfront through their "Harlem on the River Plan" to address this history of state intervention in their community.[15] Their plan re-envisions their waterfront, not as a "toilet bowl" for the rest of the city, but as a site for West Harlem residents to live, work, and play. It seeks to redress decades of city neglect of its needs. With this long and complex history of neglect, this process is only at the beginning of a complex, expensive, and highly politicized multi-year quest to return the waterfront to local Harlemites.

Red Hook

Red Hook on the Brooklyn waterfront, like West Harlem, was scarred by urban renewal and development policy. The Red Hook Houses, built in the 1930s for dock workers, houses 80 percent of its residents, mostly poor people of color. The area was devastated by Robert Moses' highway-building. The highway cut off their neighborhood from the rest of Brooklyn, thereby isolating it.

The problems of top-down planning in New York were not restricted temporally to mid-century urban renewal. The fiscal crisis of the 1970s also was a factor in the creation of de facto environmental sacrifice zones in New York City. Eddie Bautista, a longtime community organizer describes the role of municipal neglect on his neighborhood. Bautista grew up in Red Hook in the 1960s, when 8,000 longshoremen still toiled on the docks, and Erie Basin was one of the busiest shipping centers in the country. It was also shaped by the condemnation of housing to clear room for a container port that was never built, solid waste transfer stations, hazardous waste, and other toxic facilities. Red Hook has been a hotbed of twenty years of activism over waste facilities. These include waste transfer stations and a proposed sludge treatment plant. One of the first environmental justice campaigns that Bautista worked on was the 1992 fight against the city's proposal to build a sludge plant in Red Hook, which was effectively turned back by protest.

Bautista's youthful route to environmental activism is rooted in the culture and history of Red Hook and fiscal crisis New York City. His consciousness of the role of the city on his life became clear in the 1970s. According to Bautista: "1977 was a turning point, not only for myself, but for our whole community. Hip-hop began to emerge as a street culture, and the Yankees won the World Series. That same year, the City began a sewer reconstruction project that stretched along one block, and abandoned it when the fiscal crisis hit. We were exposed to the sewer, which we called 'the trench,' for over a year. Me and my friends would take garbage bags, and build rafts. Like urban Huck Finns, we swam in the trench alongside giant sewer rats."[16]

Bautista describes another critical moment in Red Hook that same year, when a building collapsed across the street where he lived, killing a young neighbor and her father. The collapse of the buildings was precipitated by the sewer project. City surveyors did not adequately examine the housing stock before commencing the project. He remembered the community anger at Mayor Beame who came to the neighborhood after the collapse hit the front page of the *Daily News*.[17] The city responded to the collapse by condemning dozens of buildings, promising to build replacement housing for the community, but ultimately it reneged on that promise. He recalls: "Entire families never recovered from this trauma, and the community was destroyed." For Bautista, the city is either a force of neglect or active destruction that must be counterbalanced by community activism. This experience shaped the contours that his environmental justice activism evolved into. As he explains, "the nexus of environmental justice and community memory continues to drive me, professionally and personally."[18]

South Bronx

Lastly, we turn to the South Bronx. In many ways, it is the community facing the most complex challenges, heavily burdened by a punishing transportation and polluting infrastructure as a result of its unique geography. As the only borough in New York linked to the mainland of the United States, it is bounded by the city's most concentrated highway and bridge infrastructure, translating into thousands of vehicles crossing through the community daily. Moses built the major transportation infrastructures that went through the South Bronx from the 1930s to the 1960s, including the Triborough Bridge (connecting the Bronx, Manhattan, and Queens); the Bronx-Whitestone Bridge, the Bruckner, Sheridan, Major-Deegan and the Cross-Bronx Expressways. Add to its unique geographic position, the decline of manufacturing and destructive urban planning that scarred West Harlem and Red Hook, and the result is a community in social and political crisis, suffering from a public health catastrophe in terms of asthma and public health.[19]

For Carlos Padilla, past chairman of the South Bronx Clean Air Coalition and longtime resident, many of the problems in the South Bronx stem from economic and land use development and policy that comes from the outside with little community consultation. The coalition formed in 1991 in response to the building of the Bronx Lebanon Medical Waste Incinerator, which was going to add medical waste incineration to the heavy burden of already existing polluting facilities.[20] The incinerator stacks were torn down in 1999 in part due to community organizing. Padilla personalizes the air pollution problem, because his daughter has asthma. According to Padilla, "what angers me is that some want to get the better of life at the expense of others, including their health. Profit at my children's expense makes me angry. These people from the incinerator are not from the community. They don't employ the community. But they take the resources and health of the community."[21]

Padilla draws attention to the inequity in siting polluting facilities in poor neighborhoods and communities of color: "The issue is the selection process. . . . When something's good, it's theirs, and when it's bad, it's ours." In sharp contrast to external top-down economic and land-use development is community-based planning that foregrounds local capital and leadership. Padilla dreams of a waterfront that is managed by a South Bronx-based development company, shares of which are owned by community members. For Padilla, the South Bronx waterfront is key to this vision of community-led revitalization that keeps money in the area. Padilla remembers the South

Bronx waterfront as a vibrant place of leisure and work, rather than a place cut off from the community, where garbage goes to be sorted, sludge processed and medical waste burned. Say Padilla: "I remember fishing for eels in the East River, the potatoes, produce, stuff from Coca-Cola, Alexander's and Tiffany Street, coming from the South, going out by rail. When rail died, industry died. We need a blue collar base back. Yes, we need trees and gardens, but we need to build good jobs so we can choose where we want to go, and afford to go there, instead of keeping us in a prison up here. Don't promise us a park that smells like a shithole. We need to bring in new products—not garbage."[22] Like Shepard in West Harlem, he reviles the disrespect implicit in a local park being next to a waste facility, or as he describes, "a shithole." In addition to the coalition, there are many community groups involved in grassroots planning in the Bronx that are trying to implement a community-based vision for the waterfront that returns it to vibrancy, and away from garbage, pollution, and waste.[23]

CONCLUSION

West Harlem, Red Hook, and South Bronx residents use their community history of negative intervention and municipal neglect in the community in their environmental justice organizing around polluting facilities. History and memory, specifically of urban renewal and land-use planning, shape the response of activists in these communities to contemporary land use and environmental policy decisions. Environmental justice activists respond to these facilities with anger and suspicion, interpreting them within a historical context of community dissolution and neglect. In each, the community suffered from blight initiated in the name of urban renewal policy, particularly from highways. Local activists remember when their areas where sacrificed in the name of the urban development. They also know that residents still suffer from the fallout of highways, sewage treatment plants, and waste facilities, especially in terms of high rates of pollution exposure, and asthma rates.

Thus, the siting of new facilities is interpreted by environmental justice activists as an attempt by the city to frustrate the further renaissance of neighborhoods that the city itself had set into decline through destructive public planning. In contrast to top-down planning that ignored the needs of local communities of color, environmental justice activists focus on community-based planning of their waterfront for recreation and local, non-polluting economic development as a corrective to the history of urban renewal and the worst excesses of urban redevelopment policy. It is a difficult task, with a complicated past, and an uncertain future. Despite this difficulty, environmental justice activists continue to press forward, often against the plans of the city and of private polluters and developers. Driven by memories of their neighborhoods as better places that once were, environmental justice activists are fully engaged in local land use, economic and environmental politics, to simultaneously return the communities to their former status within New York City as sites of work and leisure, and to improve them beyond this history.

NOTES

1. Intimately linked to housing, through the removal of "slums," the Urban Renewal Act of 1949 ushered in an era of urban redevelopment that included major spatial re-alignments. Historians have documented that how these policies were enacted particularly damaged low-income neighborhoods and racial minorities. The well-known phrase "Urban renewal is Negro removal" captures the racially disproportionate effect of urban renewal. The housing built under urban renewal did not require private developers to build affordable housing. Developers built housing, often racially exclusionary, with higher rental rates than the housing destroyed. African Americans were displaced at up to six times their rate of the population in some cities. Constrained by cost factors and housing segregation, the displacement forced onto African Americans and other racial minorities in the cities as a result of urban renewal efforts functioned to increasingly concentrate those displaced into remaining poor and minority areas, leading to increasing ghettoization. Redevelopment policy and urban renewal thus facilitated "blight" and decline in certain neighborhoods, at the same time it was aimed, in theory, at destroying it in others. Thomas Sugrue, *The Origins of the Urban Crisis: Race and Inequality in Post-War Detroit* (Princeton University Press: Princeton, 1996); June Manning Thomas, *Redevelopment and Race: Planning a Finer City in Post-War Detroit* (Baltimore: Johns Hopkins University Press, 1997).

2. Robert Caro's monumental biography of Moses provides an in-depth look at how he sought federal urban renewal and highway funds to amass power with little public accountability. Robert Caro, *The Power Broker: Robert Moses and the Fall of New York* (New York: Vintage, 1975).

3. In his capacity as Commissioner of the New York City Department of Parks and Recreation, Moses built 255 parks, only one of which was in Harlem. He spent millions to build, enlarge, and improve Riverside Park on the Upper West Side, but neglected the area between 125th and 155th Street in West Harlem. Ibid, 509–510. Also, he purposely built the freeways out to the beaches and recreation areas in Long Island with bridges too low for buses to pass through, essentially denying access to these facilities to those who were dependent on public transportation. For other recreation areas with bus access, blacks who were able to charter buses were often denied parking permits. Ibid., 318.

4. Urban historians have documented how white flight was initiated and accelerated by complex economic, political, and cultural factors. These included white fear of African Americans, block-busting by real estate agents, and federal transportation and housing policy that subsidized racialized suburbanization. Historians have examined theories of pathology and the relationship between the discursive realm and

public policy, especially around housing. For example, "infiltration theory" became a self-fulfilling prophecy. The language of infiltration depends on ideas of naturalized contagion, degeneration and blight. Proponents of this view argued that residential transformation necessarily deteriorated neighborhoods, and this deterioration was racially coded. In other words, neighborhoods change, but rarely for the better. Raymond Mohl, "The Second Ghetto and the 'Infiltration Theory' in Urban Real Estate, 1940–1960" in *Urban Planning and the African American Community: In the Shadows,* ed. June Manning Thomas and Marsha Ritzdorf, eds. (Thousand Oaks: Sage Publications, 1997), 58–74.

5. The city, through its Committee on Slum Clearance actively "moved against" industrial districts in the mid-twentieth century. Joel Schwartz, *The New York Approach: Robert Moses, Urban Liberals and the Redevelopment of the Inner City* (Columbus: Ohio State University Press, 1993).

6. For a discussion of the role of zoning and the decline of manufacturing, see Robert Fitch, *The Assassination of New York* (New York: Verso, 1993); Tom Angotti and Eva Handhardt, "Problems and Prospects for Healthy Mixed-Use Communities in New York City," *Planning Practice and Research* 16, no. 2 (2001): 145–154. Urban renewal also displaced and dispersed thousands of primarily black and Puerto Rican working-class residents throughout the city. For example, the primarily minority Columbus Hill neighborhood is now Lincoln Center, a site of high culture, its minority and working-class past virtually obliterated from memory. The neighborhood fabric in the South Bronx, home to stable white ethnic neighborhoods, was destroyed for decades as a result of highway building and other macro-policy and demographic forces. Marshall Berman, *All That Is Solid Melts into Air: The Experience of Modernity* (New York: Penguin, 1982).

7. Steven Gregory, *Black Corona: Race and the Politics of Place in an Urban Community* (Princeton: Princeton University Press, 1998).

8. Each of these neighborhoods share racial and poverty demographics, housing stock, zoning designations. According to the 2000 Census, these neighborhoods have higher than the city-wide averages in population of African American or Latinos, and percentage of populations receiving government assistance. New York Department of City Planning, Based on U.S. Census Bureau 2000 Census PL File and SF 1, retrievable at http://nyc.gov/. The neighborhoods where environmental justice activism takes place in New York City are mixed-use industrial waterfront communities, particularly vulnerable to the city's zoning and land-use policy. Residential zones have the most protection from noxious uses, and industrial, the least. Mixed-use areas often have close concentrations of housing and industrial uses, with potentially negative health effects in terms of pollution exposures. Zoning and race are connected in New York City in terms of neighborhood demographics, and transition of zoning uses. Juliana Maantay, *Industrial Zoning Changes and Environmental Justice in New York City: A Historical, Geographical and Cultural Analysis* (Ph.D. diss., Rutgers University, 2000).

9. Peggy Shepard, "Issues of Community Empowerment," *Fordham Urban Law Journal* 21, no. 3 (1994): 739–755. In 1992, WEACT, along with the Natural Resources Defense Council (NRDC), a major national environmental group, sued the City of New York and the Department of Environmental Protection in state

court in response to numerous water quality and air pollution violations. The lawsuit was the first in the city's history where it had been sued for creating a nuisance from smells. It charged that the smells were a result of "intentional, unreasonable, negligent, reckless and abnormally dangerous siting, design, construction and operation of the plant." In 1993, the parties reached a settlement agreement that called for strict enforcement of corrective actions by the state and the city at the facility, required monitoring, and $1.1 million dollars to be given to WEACT and NRDC toward the establishment of the "North River Fund" to address a range of community, environmental, and public health issues. The settlement agreement forced the city to carry a $55 million program to reduce odors from the plant. This lawsuit was significant because it decreed that local government may not always have the "last word" on citizens' interests; it showed how external action can be taken to improve the operations of a facility; and it may create new legal obligations for cities for "community targeted resources." Nancy Anderson, "The Visible Spectrum," *Fordham Urban Law Journal* 21, no. 3 (1994): 723–38.

10. Vernice Miller, "Planning, Power and Politics: A Case Study of the Land Use and Siting History of the North River Water Pollution Control Plant," *Fordham Urban Law Journal* 21, no. 3 (1994): 707–722.

11. Ibid., p. 718.

12. Shepard, 745.

13. Miller, 733.

14. Cecil Corbin-Mark, interview by author, tape recording, New York City, 15 December 2001.

15. WEACT made specific recommendations to the city and state in the areas of economic development, parks and open space, transportation, arts/culture/entertainment, urban design, environmental restoration, and history. Their plan featured a landscaped park area along the riverfront, a walkway, a bikeway, and a pier for water dependent uses (for recreational and fishing uses), including an aquatic learning center. The plan also included connections to Riverside Park, and restored piers for ferry service and riverfront uses. It featured wholesale and retail marketplace development with entertainment, art and cultural uses, and emphasized improved safety and traffic design to reduce vehicular accidents.

16. Eddie Bautista, "Garbage Wars: The Struggle for Waterfront Justice," *Journal of Community Advocacy and Activism* 3, no. 1 (1998): 17–28.

17. Eddie Bautista, interview by author, tape recording, New York City, 22 May 2002.

18. Bautista, "Environmental Justice and Memory," 23 August 2004, personal email (27 August, 2004).

19. Jill Jonnes, *We're Still Here* (Boston: Atlantic Monthly Press, 1986). Marshall Berman, *All That Is Solid Melts into Air: The Experience of Modernity* (New York: Penguin, 1982). E.L. Birch, "From Flames to Flowers: The Role of Planning in Re-Imaging the South Bronx," in *Imaging the City: Continuing Struggles and New Directions,* ed. L. Vale, & S.B. Warner (New Brunswick: Center for Urban Policy Research, 2001): 57–93.

20. The incinerator, which cost almost $20 million dollars to build, was built to burn 48 tons of medical waste per day from fifteen hospitals throughout the region.

By the time that the incinerator closed, the facility had been cited for over five hundred violations of toxic releases.The incinerator was sited just blocks away from 2300 units of public housing, three public schools, and several parochial schools in one of the poorest Congressional Districts in the nation.

21. Carlos Padilla, interview by author, tape recording, New York City, 15, April 1999.

22. Ibid.

23. For example, the Hunts Point 197A Plan, which addressed land use and development strategies in the Hunts Point area of the South Bronx, was organized first by The Point Community Development Corporation, and coordinated by Sustainable South Bronx/the Point Community Development Corporation.197A refers to the communiyt planing provision in the 1989 New York City Charter Revision. Recommendations of the 197A plan were: to develop cleaner transportation in the area in the Fish Market; to promote public transportation by renovating the Hunts Point Station; the creation of a South Bronx bike/pedestrian greenway, and the creation of environmentally sustainable economic development on the waterfront through the creation of Rivermarket (a retail as opposed to a commercial food market), and the Factory Boathouse/ Ecology Center. The plan was submitted formally in 2000 but the city has not acted on it thus far.

12

Ferrell Parkway
Conflicting Views of Nature in a Mixed Use Community

Jane Bloodworth Rowe

Environmental disputes sometimes result from conflicting definitions of nature. The construction of nature as that non-human world that exists apart from human culture has prevailed in this country for the last century although some rural residents still define nature as a force that envelops everything, including human life and culture.[1] These rural residents are sometimes the victims of environmental injustice because mainstream groups, arguing for preservation of tracts of uninhabited land, advocate procedures that threaten to destroy communities and desecrate the environment in inhabited areas adjacent to wilderness tracts. These residents must struggle to gain a voice in environmental disputes because their construction of nature conflicts with those of the opposition, which often includes government or industry officials and mainstream environmental groups. Scholars have noted that conflicts in environmental public hearings often boil down to the question of who has the right to speak on behalf of nature.[2] As Foucault noted, the "procedures of exclusion in discourse"[3] which encourage hegemony and discourage minority opinion, are well known.

The discourse of government officials, organized environmentalists, and rural residents who spoke at public hearings surrounding a controversial road construction project in Virginia Beach, VA was the subject of this research. The language used by groups and individuals who spoke at these public hearings or who wrote letters to the editor from 1999, when the issue first surfaced, to 2003 when it was resolved, was examined, with special attention to the techniques used by these rural residents to first establish their right to speak on behalf of nature and then to redefine the relationship between humans and the environment. The fundamental, underlying question is: how did these residents, who were at first unprepared and only loosely organized, prevail against a well-organized and more powerful opposition?

A BRIEF HISTORICAL BACKGROUND

The controversy examined here centered on whether to construct a one-mile section of road through low-lying, abandoned farmland to the Atlantic Ocean. This project was the final phase of an east-west corridor designed to cross Virginia Beach and end at Sandbridge Beach, a public beach that developed into single-family houses. The area north and west of Sandbridge existed for years as a rural residential or agricultural community, but residential development mushroomed both on the beach and in nearby areas during the 1980s and 1990s.

As the area developed, and as the beach became a popular destination site for tourists and day-trippers, traffic increased on Sandbridge Road, which served as the only access road to Sandbridge Beach. The community of Sigma, which lay along Sandbridge Road and its spur, Lotus Drive, remained as the last remnant of this area's rural past and served as a divide between the city's developed northern section and the agricultural land in the south. The narrow, winding Sandbridge Road became the scene of fatal auto accidents. Sigma residents feared for their safety and thought that the increased noise, traffic, trespassers, and litter threatened their rural lifestyle. This community was loosely organized, and unlike residents of the nearby, more densely developed residential areas, Sigma residents had, up until the time of this controversy, not organized a neighborhood association. The only neighborhood meeting place was Tabernacle United Methodist Church, a small, historic church built in 1830.

The city of Virginia Beach, as early as the late 1960s, recognized that Sandbridge Road was inadequate for the increased traffic, and planned to extend Ferrell Parkway, an east-west corridor that was being constructed in phases, to the beach. During the late 1990s, the U.S. Fish and Wildlife Service, backed by local and national environmental groups and a local ecotour outfitter, decided to oppose the Ferrell Parkway extension into Sandbridge.

John Staskos, manager of Back Bay National Wildlife Refuge during this period of time, and members of some environmental groups claimed that the proposed construction would encroach on property owned by the wildlife refuge, disrupt wildlife and pristine wilderness, and increase the run-off into the Back Bay Watershed. Some locals suggested that these arguments were flawed: the U.S. Fish and Wildlife Service had, in fact, purchased much of the property surrounding the right-of-way during the early 1990s, after the parkway had been proposed. The entire area, including the community of Sigma, was also on the Back Bay watershed, wildlife existed in abundance in Sigma as well as along the right-of-way, and the right-of-way was already mowed and used as an access road by Virginia Power.

In an effort to block the Ferrell Parkway extension, the U.S. Fish and Wildlife Service offered to buy the right-of-way from the city. The federal officials also offered to donate some land that this agency owned along the existing Sandbridge Road in order to upgrade and straighten curves on that road. In a complex land swap, the federal officials also agreed to buy private property that was part of a troubled private development in exchange for the city's agreement to sell the right-of-way to their agency.[4] An upgraded Sandbridge Road was proposed as a means of enhancing tourism by providing cut-outs, scenic views, and signs along the route.

The parkway opponents initially prevailed. City council members voted 8–3 in fall, 2000, to abandon plans to extend Ferrell Parkway to the beach and focused on upgrading Sandbridge Road. This plan would have crossed and destroyed wetlands and required the condemnation and seizure of private land, including four houses and two businesses.[5] The Sigma residents were further marginalized because this decision to abandon the Ferrell Parkway extension and adopt the road-widening proposal was spearheaded by Barbara Henley, the city council representative from their district but an ally of the U.S. Fish and Wildlife Service. Left with no voice on city council, they organized neighborhood associations, and they also combined their resources with the residents of nearby neighborhoods who supported the construction of Ferrell Parkway. This diverse group organized under the name of "Friends of Ferrell Parkway."

This group challenged the city's decision to sell the right-of-way to U.S. Fish and Wildlife, claiming that, under Virginia law, the city council needed the support of three-quarters of its members in order to sell public land. They prevailed in court, but city council then voted to lease the right-of-way to the U.S. Fish and Wildlife Service for forty years. The Friends of Ferrell Parkway again challenged the vote in circuit court and, again, the court ruled in their favor.

The court case prevented the sale or lease of the right-of-way, but it did not resolve the issue of whether or not to construct the roadway. The Friends of Ferrell Parkway set their sights on the May 2002 city council elections in the hopes of unseating council members who were opposed to the Ferrell Parkway extension. Jim Reeve, an engineer and a resident of the affected community, successfully challenged Henley after some Sigma residents helped to spearhead his campaign. The residents also encouraged other city council candidates in that election to support them on this issue. Four new members were elected to city council, and this council voted, in May 2003, to place Ferrell Parkway back on the master transportation plan and abandon plans to radically alter Sandbridge Road or Lotus Drive.

THE LANGUAGE AND THE UNIFORMS: THE TACTICS OF AUTHORITY

Both groups demonstrated perseverance in the battle over Ferrell Parkway, but the federal officials and organized environmentalists were, at first, better organized. The local residents were caught off-guard in June, 1999, when Henley, officials from the U.S. Fish and Wildlife Service, and environmentalists first proposed that the master highway plan be amended to remove the Ferrell Parkway extension. City council did not uphold this proposal at this meeting, but those who supported it succeeded in establishing themselves as environmentalists concerned about preserving an area that they presented as pristine wilderness.

Deluca noted that discourse can include both linguistic and the non-linguistic communication.[6] The U.S. Fish and Wildlife Service and the members of organized groups used non-verbal as well as verbal communication to establish their authority. The federal officials appeared at this and other hearings in uniform and were careful to establish their identity as biologists and federal employees. Those who sided with these officials used other non-verbal gestures to reenforce their authority and perceived superior knowledge. At the June 1999 meeting, they rose from their seats and flanked Staskos as he spoke, taking care to position themselves in front of city council and the television cameras. At subsequent meetings, parkway opponents attempted to humiliate and demoralize parkway proponents by booing, hissing, and snickering at their arguments. Some openly laughed as Sigma residents complained of the threats of land condemnation and increased traffic in their neighborhoods and spoke of their fears for their children's safety. Henley also sought to debase the Sigma residents by denying that the proposed road improvements would require a significant condemnation of private property, although council members conceded at later meetings that it would. These opponents already had the advantage of organization: many were members of local environmental groups, including Friends of Back Bay and the Back Bay Restoration Foundation, and they had ties with national environmental groups. At subsequent meetings, members of national groups who lived outside the community helped to pack the city council chambers to speak in opposition to the Ferrell Parkway extension.

This packaging of nature as a resource was consistent with Merchant's description of the mechanistic metaphor for nature. This metaphor presented the non-human world as a machine made for human use.[7] Metaphors, as scholars have noted, are often imposed by those who hold power.[8] Once accepted, they dominate public discourse and allow members of a society to communicate in concrete terms about abstract notions such as nature.[9] The metaphor of nature as a resource has prevailed in American environmental discourse since the early days of the nineteenth-century conservation movement. It is consistent with the definition of nature as uninhabited wilderness separate from human culture, and it further presents nature as a commodity that must be managed carefully by experts. This metaphor was reflected in comments by the U.S. Fish and Wildlife officials at the June 1999 meeting, when these officials spoke of the Ferrell Parkway right-of-way as a commonly held resource that needed federal protection. Karen Mayne, supervisor of the Virginia Field Office of U.S. Fish and Wildlife, referred to the right-of-way as "a local, regional and national treasure," while Staskos labeled it as "part of our grandchildren's heritage." Staskos also granted himself the authority to speak for non-humans when he confidently told city council members that "I represent 40,000 ducks."

Nature, under this metaphor, was vulnerable and in need of protection by experts. The Ferrell Parkway right-of-way was presented as a part of nature because it was described as "pristine" by speakers arguing for preservation of the right-of-way.[10] The right-of-way, although much of it was abandoned farmland and all of it was mowed, was posited as pristine apparently because it was uninhabited at the time these meetings were held. This term suggested youth, virginity, innocence, and vulnerability: nature was presented as a virgin unspoiled by man. The speakers extended this metaphor by presenting the uninhabited land along the right-of-way as more environmentally valuable than the inhabited terrain along Sandbridge Road, which was spoiled, no longer virgin, and therefore no longer a part of nature. Nature was also mapped and bounded: lines on maps separated the right-of-way, which was posited as nature, with the communities that lay adjacent to it.

Lakoff and Turner noticed the human tendency to rank the non-human world according to its perceived value.[11] Mayne, speaking at the 1999 meeting, ranked the trees along the right-of-way as "old growth" or "rare," although she never defined these terms. She also made references to rare and endangered animals that existed along the right-of-way. The implication was that these animals or plants were isolated on this right-of-way, observed human boundaries, and never strayed into the surrounding areas because only this small strip of land constituted nature. This mapped, bounded nature upheld the nature/culture dichotomy: lines on a map separated the right-of-way, which was labeled as nature, from the surrounding communities. This perspective not only empowered the parkway opponents to assume control of this bounded nature in order to protect it, but it also fueled the impression that the existing communities and wetlands along Sandbridge Road could be desecrated as long as one small area was isolated, labeled as nature, and preserved. No one on city council questioned this perspective at that meeting: no one asked for definitions, numbers and types of endangered species, or information as to why these species had become isolated on this right-of-way.

This metaphor of nature as a resource was particularly effective in Virginia Beach, where tourism is the second largest industry. Lillie Gilbert, owner of a local ecotourism business, argued at a January 23, 2001 hearing that Ferrell Parkway should not be constructed because the area could prove financially lucrative. It provided a "unique habitat"[12] for canoeing and other nature-based activities, and Gilbert indicated that if the road were built her customers would not be as interested in canoeing on the nearby waterways because she would no longer be able to present the view as pristine, unspoiled wilderness. Ferrell Parkway opponents also argued that an upgraded Sandbridge Road, with markers and pull-outs, could also attract tourists, although no one addressed the issues of where these pull-outs would be located, if they would involve the condemnation of private property, and what impact this would have on the traffic situation. Molly Brown, a Sandbridge resident and a member of the Friends of Back Bay, presented the economic metaphor most succinctly when she said "ducks mean bucks." Brown, speaking at a March 11, 2003 meeting, cited a Virginia Department of Tourism advertisement showing pictures of ducks and the words "Flights arriving daily."

This proposal to develop the right-of-way into a revenue-producing tourism destination site was an attempt, on the part of the parkway opponents, to posit themselves as advocates of progress, which Deluca labeled "the grand narrative of industrialized society."[13] An environmentally friendly form of economic development was touted as a progressive approach to land use, with the implicit argument that the rights of urban tourists and ecotourism operators who could benefit from this progress were greater than the rights of rural residents who would suffer from the change.

Hart spoke of "ultimate terms," or "words having special evocative power for a society."[14] Ferrell Parkway opponents framed their arguments in ultimate terms: they were on the side of all that was good because they were advocating both environmental protection and economic development. They also attempted to frame counterarguments as devil terms, or those words that "give us a clear picture of malevolence."[15] The self-proclaimed environmentalists explained, in letters to the editor, that those who supported the Ferrell Parkway construction "failed to understand"[16] the credibility of experts who cited environmental damage. They also charged, in public hearings, that their opponents were residential developers who sought to profit from the increased suburban sprawl the parkway would allegedly encourage.[17] In short, the parkway opponents described those on the other side as either ignorant or greedy.

THE RESPONSE OF LOCALS: NATURE AS
HOME AND MOTHER

The local residents prevailed against the powerful opposition groups by appealing to both emotion and logic and by combining local knowledge with scientific studies to counter the claims made by experts. Perhaps most importantly, they organized, assigned themselves a name, and thereby claimed the legitimacy that they lacked as individual homeowners and church members.

The proponents rejected the definition of nature as uninhabited wilderness and argued in favor of a nature that served as a home and mother. The metaphor of nature as a mother was stated explicitly on at least one occasion. Ruth Wilson, a resident of Sandbridge Road, warned that improving drainage on that road (which would require raising the roadbed several feet above the level of the ground) would take its toll on the quality of human life as well as on the environment because it would increase run-off into wetlands and flood residential property. "You can't fight the tides and Mother Nature," she warned at a January 23, 2001 public hearing. Wilson was not speaking of a vulnerable, passive nature that served as an object to be acted upon by humans. Rather, she referred to the powerful Mother Nature that enveloped human culture. In contrast to the parkway opponents, who spoke of a nature that could be guided and protected by wise humans, Wilson, who was familiar with northeasters, hurricanes, and wind tides, knew a nature that was forceful and rule-governed. She also knew the consequences for violating those rules, but bureaucrats and organized environmentalists granted no credibility to knowledge gained from life experience.

The local residents also challenged the contention that the Ferrell Parkway right-of-way was untouched by humans. The area was cleared, they pointed out, and served as a right-of-way for Virginia Power, which had installed electrical lines in the area.[18] Some also challenged the contention that the Ferrell Parkway construction would displace old growth trees. Marshall Belanga, a waterman and longtime resident of Sandbridge Road, maintained that these trees only dated to 1933, when a fierce hurricane closed an inlet to the ocean and flooded a small area where the trees sprouted.

Sigma residents worried that a wider road would have a generally devastating impact on the community's rural character; culture and nature were intertwined in their arguments. When council members attempted to assure them that their 1830 church building would not be removed by road widening, the church members tried to explain that the church's natural setting, including the broad front lawn, surrounding wetlands, and the creek across the road, was an integral and irreplaceable part of their church, community, and home. They also feared that the road widening would displace graves in the community graveyard across the road from the church, and cited warnings by city staff that this was a very real possibility.[19]

SCIENCE AND LOGIC:
A DIFFERENT PERSPECTIVE

Residents did not confine their discourse to metaphorical appeals, however. They also tailored their arguments to the linear, logical organizations that scholars noted were preferred in western culture.[20] The Sandbridge Road alternative, they said, was more expensive, more damaging environmentally, and less safe than the alternative.

An upgraded Sandbridge Road would cost an estimated $35.7 million, considerably more than the $15 million it would cost to extend Ferrell Parkway.[21] These cost estimates were well-documented and difficult to refute, but the local residents had a more difficult time persuading the members of city council to recognize their environmental arguments. Organized environmentalists at first snickered and booed at local residents, including Wilson and Bill Sinclair, who expressed concern at public hearings about the increased run-off and the impact on air quality that the Sandbridge Road alternative, which was several miles longer, would have. The local residents, however, were not alone in their arguments about air pollution: the city had been denied state funds for the upgraded Sandbridge Road in part because of concerns about the impact on air quality.

Most of the local residents who offered environmental arguments spoke from local knowledge, but Reeve, as an engineer, was trained in science and technology. However, his environmental arguments were ignored by Ferrell Parkway opponents, and these arguments were never quoted in the articles on this subject that appeared in *The Virginian-Pilot*, the Norfolk-based daily newspaper that served the community. Observers have noted that scientific arguments that conflict with the established viewpoint are often granted little credibility by the media, other scientists, and those who hold political power.[22] After his election to city council, however, Reeve commissioned a study that pointed to the environmental damage, including the loss of cypress trees and the increased run-off, that would be caused by upgrading Sandbridge Road. This study confirmed the arguments of local residents, and, coupled with Reeve's status as a member of city council, granted him the credibility to effectively argue against representatives from the U.S. Fish and Wildlife Service and members of organized environmental groups. The Friends of Ferrell Parkway also appealed to common sense when they argued for human safety, and these arguments won them the support of uninvolved persons, including firefighters, who argued that the parkway was needed to decrease the response time of emergency vehicles traveling to and from Sandbridge.[23]

The local residents' struggle to make their voices heard was also an attempt to arrive at truth, which Foucault labeled the primary aim of discourse.[24] Reeve cited studies to support his position that Ferrell Parkway was less disruptive and described himself as "confused by opponents who stand behind their environmental claim."[25] Thomas Blanton, a lifelong Sigma resident and a Sandbridge Road restaurant owner, was more blunt. Blanton refuted claims made by parkway opponents that the business community supported the Sandbridge Road widening, and that business owners had signed a petition requesting this road widening. Speaking at a March 11, 2003 city council meeting, Blanton said "I didn't sign that piece of paper, and I want you to know that everything those people are saying isn't true."

ASSESSMENT: LOGIC, METAPHORS, AND LOCAL WISDOM

Scholars who have studied environmental debates noted that only those groups that hold power can normally assume the right to speak on behalf of nature in a modernist culture.[26] When Staskos posited himself as the representative of wild ducks, he assumed that his role as a federal official assured his authority over the natural world. No one on city council questioned that assumption at the June, 1999 meeting, nor did they question Brown's assertion that she had the right to speak on behalf of the environment because she represented the mainstream, modernist perspective. Local residents, however, had to earn that right through a hard-fought political struggle. Although Wilson described herself as an environmentalist, she did not speak within the dominant metaphor of nature as a resource, so her position was ignored by the media and those organized groups who posited the conflict as one between the rights of humans and non-humans.

The parkway proponents gained credibility through their ability to organize because they could then claim membership in a recognized organization. Then, their ability to seize the power of discourse and to use old and new technology to communicate helped them to prevail. Their methods of communication included group e-mails, community meetings at the historic church, and knocking on front doors to alert neighbors to upcoming hearings or to get signatures on petitions. They also worked with others to elect Reeve, who campaigned on citywide issues, including public education and tax relief for the elderly, to win the support of voters in other areas of the city.

The residents appealed to both emotion and common sense and constructed arguments of both a metaphorical nature and a linear construction.

Johnson spoke of cultural distancing mechanisms, or those techniques used by mainstream groups to dehumanize, humiliate, and debase those groups who hold less power.[27] The bureaucrats and organized environmentalists, through their use of abstract language and their non-verbal behavior, sought to posit local residents as ignorant and illogical, and they presented humans and the environment as separate and opposing forces. In order to explain their construction of nature as home and mother to an urban audience, the rural residents had to first establish their credibility to speak on behalf of the environment, then explain the relationship between humans and non-humans and demonstrate that human and environmental well-being were intertwined.

These rural residents, faced with the disruption of home and community, redefined the rules of discourse that only grant credibility to those who speak within the dominant metaphors of nature as a resource to be managed by experts. They were able to appeal to both moral values and scientific truth. Through the careful use of rhetoric, the residents were finally able to undermine the implicit argument that only members of mainstream groups can assume the right to speak for non-humans. They also demonstrated that emotion and logic were not necessarily opposing forces by linking their desire to save their homes and communities to the common human ideals of safety, conservation of natural and economic resources, and respect for the rights of both humans and the natural world.

NOTES

1. Michael Mayerfield Bell, *Childerley: Nature and Morality in a Country Village* (Chicago: University of Chicago Press, 1994), 85–116.

2. Mary Richardson, Joan Sherman, and Michael Gismondi, *Winning Back the Words: Confronting Experts in an Environmental Public Hearing* (Toronto: Garamond Press, 1993), 17.

3. Michael Foucault, "The Order of Discourse," *The Rhetorical Tradition: Readings from Classical Times to the Present,* ed. Patricia Bizzell and Bruce Herzberg (Boston: St Martin's Press, 1990), 1155.

4. Jon Glass, "Judge Blocks Lease of Parkway Land," *The Virginian-Pilot,* 15 December 2001, sec. B, p. 1.

5. Glass, "Nimmo Parkway Alive," *The Virginian-Pilot,* 9 October, 2002 sec. B, p. 3.

6. Kevin Deluca, *Image Politics: The New Rhetoric of Environmental Activism* (New York: The Guilford Press, 1969).

7. Carolyn Merchant, *Women, Ecology and the Scientific Revolution* (New York: Harper and Row, 1980), 1–41.

8. George Lakoff and Mark Johnson, *Metaphors We Live By* (Chicago: University of Chicago Press, 1980), 159–60.

9. Richard Weaver, *The Ethics of Rhetoric* (South Bend: Gateway, 1953), 203.

10. Herb Jones, Public Hearing (Virginia Beach City Council, Virginia Beach, Virg., 14 August 2001).

11. George Lakoff and Mark Turner, *More Than Cool Reason: A Field Guide to Poetic Metaphor* (Chicago: University of Chicago Press, 1999).

12. Lillie Gilbert, Public Hearing, (Virginia Beach City Council, Virginia Beach, Virg., 23 January 2001).

13. Deluca, *Image Politics*, 241–60.

14. Roderick P. Hart, *Modern Rhetorical Criticism*, 2nd ed. (Boston: Allyn and Bacon, 1997), 159.

15. Ibid.

16. Fred Greene, "Letter to the Editor," *The Virginian-Pilot*, 28 January 2001, sec. O, p. 10.

17. Craig Rentz, Public Hearing, (Virginia Beach City Council, Virginia Beach, Virg., 27 May 2003).

18. Jim Reeve, "Letter to the Editor," *The Virginian-Pilot*, 7 January 2001, sec. O, p. 8.

19. Ann Henley, Public Hearing, (Virginia Beach City Council, Virginia Beach, VA, 23 January 2001).

20. Foucault, "The Order of Discourse," 1155–56.

21. Glass, "Residents Look at Sandbridge Road Options," *The Virginian-Pilot*, 6 September 2002, sec. B, p. 3.

22. Rae Goodell, "How to Kill a Controversy: The Case of Recombinant DNA," *Scientists and Journalists: Reporting Science as News*, ed. Sharon M. Friedman, Sharon Dunwoody, and Carol L. Rogers (New York: The Free Press 1986), 170–81.

23. Jason Skogg, "Beach Council Resurrects Proposal to Build Road Through Back Bay," *The Virginian-Pilot*, 11 March 2003, sec. B.

24. Foucault, "The Order of Discourse," 1155–56.

25. Reeve, "Letter to the Editor," *The Virginian-Pilot*, 7 Janurary 2001.

26. Richardson, Sherman, and Gismondi, *Winning Back the Words*.

27. Barbara Rose Johnson, "Human Rights and the Environment," *Human Ecology: An Interdisciplinary Journal* 23 (1995), no. 2: 11–24.

13

"We Come This Far By Faith"
Memories of Race, Religion, and Environmental Disparity

Sylvia Hood Washington

> Don't be discouraged when troubles in your life. He'll bear your burden
> and move all misery and strife.
>
> —We Come This Far By Faith
> African American Gospel

The title of this chapter, taken from a very popular African American gospel, was selected because it captures the importance that religious faith has played in African Americans' struggles for justice in the United States.[1] The critical role of spirituality and religious faith in the African American community has been recognized and affirmed by both scholars and African Americans themselves as one of their most dominant and enduring means of dealing with all forms of disenfranchisement (social, political, as well as environmental) which they have encountered throughout American history. Religious faith was the foundation of the modern civil rights movement of the 1950s and 1960s. This non-violent movement, based heavily on Christian doctrine, was primarily led, nurtured, and directed by black Protestant religious leaders and organizations like the Reverend Dr. Martin Luther King, Reverend Ralph Abernathy, Reverend Jesse Jackson Jr., Reverend Andrew Young, and the Southern Christian Leadership Conference (SCLC). Similarly, the modern environmental justice movement in the United States was launched into the national and eventually international political arenas because of the involvement and support of black Protestant religious leaders who were also former civil rights activists like the Reverend Benjamin

Chavis. At the beginning of the environmental justice movement in the early 1980s, Benjamin Chavis was a member of the United Church of Christ and his pioneering involvement in the environmental justice movement was instrumental in the church's sponsorship of one of the first environmental justice studies in the United States.[2]

Today when environmental justice scholars, activists, and the media discuss or document the "faith base" that has under girded the environmental justice movement there is an implied and sometimes explicit assumption that there has been a monolithic "religious faith" which has brought African Americans "this far" in demanding and achieving all forms of justice (social, economic, and cultural) including environmental justice. There is also an explicit assumption that this monolithic faith is and has always been Protestant. This widely held and factually false belief of a monolithic Protestant faith among all African Americans has had a disparate impact on efforts to obtain environmental justice for religious subgroups within the larger African American community in the United States. Well intentioned and well meaning agencies and organizations (regardless of racial or ethnic composition) that are involved in ameliorating or addressing environmental justice issues in African American communities have typically gone to only black "Protestant" churches to communicate and inform African American constituencies about their services and their mission. Their environmental practices and emphasis on a singular constituency among African Americans is just a reflection and consequence of an inaccurate memory, held by many including scholars, environmental activists, and environmental organizations, that there is and has only been one type of religious faith held by African Americans. Consequently other religious faith communities in the African American community like, Catholics, Jews, and Muslims, have been left out of the environmental justice communication loop.

Environmental activists developed a blind spot with respect to recognizing and dealing with the existence of the "Black Catholic" community; and the role of their "faith" in understanding, addressing, or responding to environmental inequalities and injustice.[3] This is an incredible irony, since the "Mother of the Environmental Justice Movement," Hazel Johnson, is a confirmed black Catholic from Louisiana who has been at the forefront of the environmental justice movement from its inception. Furthermore since black Catholics have always occupied the same geographical spaces as that of the larger black community they have been equally impacted by the environmental injustices which have occurred in these places like Cancer Alley (in the Mississippi corridor) and the Toxic Doughnut (in Chicago).

Cyprian Davis's path-breaking monograph, *The History of Black Catholics in the United States*, provides two clues about today's current prevalent pattern of excluding black Catholics on an organizational level in the environmental justice dialogue by black Protestants and environmental organizations in the United States. Davis points out that "By and large Catholics, either black or white, were not in the forefront of the civil rights movement or among the leadership of the protest organizations."[4] Since the environmental justice movement was supported for the most part by black Protestant civil rights leaders, religious groups, or organizations of "different faiths" (who were remembered as being non-participants or marginal participants in the civil rights movement) may have been excluded in the initial organization of the environmental justice movement as a natural oversight. Davis however also makes the point that "The story of African American Catholicism is the story of a people who obstinately clung to a faith that gave them sustenance, even when it did not always make them welcome. Black Catholics had to fight for their faith; but their fight was often with members of their own household."[5] The rejection or non-acceptance of black Catholics by a largely black Protestant community for decades is a reality in the United States. A reality which has contributed to them becoming virtually "anonymous" in the United States.[6] To be black and Catholic is an oxymoron for many people in this country regardless of their ethnicity or race. My own experiences as an African American "cradle" Catholic from childhood to today resonate with Cyprian Davis' conclusion that African American Catholics are the postmodern "invisible" people in black communities across the United States. This is not an atypical experience but one which has been recurring for decades among most black Catholics in the United States.

As a result of their "invisibility" and oversight (whether intentional or unintentional) by others regardless of race, black Catholics have become more environmentally disenfranchised than other African Americans despite the emergence of the environmental justice movement. Their disenfranchisement has arisen because they have not been included in efforts to create and promote environmental literacy in African American communities. This environmental illiteracy has also arisen because black Catholic leaders have not been typically included in the ongoing environmental justice dialogues to achieve environmental equity by either African American leaders in the environmental justice movement or by "white" secular agencies that are trying to achieve environmental parity for environmentally disenfranchised communities.[7] A primary objective of this chapter is to elucidate how and why black Catholics in the United States today and in light of this historical exclusion have responded to this dilemma by using their own environmental memories and faith as a means to achieve environmental justice for their communities.

On November 25, 2002 the United States Conference of Catholic Bishops' (USCCB) Environmental Justice Program made its first and largest environmental justice grant ($40,000) ever to a black Catholic organization, in the United States, the Knights of Peter Claver, Inc (KPC).[8] The grant was made to the organization because it was a national and international lay organization that could be effective in reaching a large population that historically suffered from environmental inequalities in the United States. The Clavers at the time of the grant were present in 39 states with 300 Court and Councils (adult membership) and over 100 junior branches (young men and women between the ages of 8 and 18 years old). The decision to proceed with this effort was supported by the organization's chief executive officer, Arthur McFarland, JD, the late Charles W. Keyes, chief financial officer and Mary L. Briers, Supreme Lady (national leader of KPC's women's auxiliary). McFarland a judge in North Carolina was familiar with the national environmental justice struggles that had begun in his own home state of North Carolina in the early 1980s. Charles W. Keyes, a native and lifelong resident of New Orleans, was also familiar with the infamous environmental justice struggles taking place in the Gulf Coast. Mary Briers, a lifelong resident of Birmingham, Alabama was also keenly aware of the environmental justices battles in her own state which was home to one of the largest PCB settlements in the United States. These national officers understood the potential good that would emerge from this project for the benefit of their members and parishes.

The primary objective of the grant was to promote environmental justice and environmental health literacy initially in black Catholic urban communities in northeastern urban communities in the United States beginning with the city of Chicago.

A chief argument of the grant was that despite the launching of the modern environmental justice movement in the United States in 1982, black communities in the United States still carried a disproportionate burden of the environmental costs from pollution sources. Equally as important to this claim was the assertion that a great number of blacks in this country are still unaware of environmental inequalities in their communities and the health impacts associated with this phenomenon.[9] Another critical fact for this project was that in Chicago and across the country the vast majority of environmental justice efforts have been led by and directed toward black Protestant communities. Black Catholics are a minority within a minority representing less than ten percent of the black community in the United States. Consequently many of them have been left out of the environmental justice communication loop over the last twenty years of the environmental justice movement.[10]

Over the last ten years the USCCB's Environmental Justice Program has awarded small grants to dioceses and national Catholic organizations to create an authentically Catholic voice in the environmental debate that is homocentric and focused on the human person's place in nature. This program focused on putting the needs of the poor and vulnerable front and center. Past USCCB grants were given to parishes involved in environmental justice issues in low-income minority communities, however, the Clavers' grant was by far the largest grant targeted to help a community that is particularly vulnerable to environmental health problems.[11]

The USCCB grant to the Clavers emerged after a number of conversations between myself as grant creator (and author) Walt Grazer, director of the USCCB's Environmental Justice Office and Roxanna Barillas, director of the USCCB's Catholic Coalition for Children and Safe Environment (CASE) office between April 2002 and October 2002. Admittedly this grant was the intellectual offspring of seven years of historical research which has attempted to elucidate the environmental cognition and environmental justice activism of racially and socially marginalized groups in the United States. It was also motivated by my own field experiences as an environmental engineer, environmental justice activist and an environmental illness that was diagnosed in 2002 after spending more than 20 years as an environmental scientist and engineer in the field. Both Grazer and Barillas were instrumental in discussing and laying out the initial objectives of the grant efforts which were to be directed at promoting environmental (justice) literacy among African Americans especially youths (between the ages of 15 to 21). The ultimate end goal of the grant was to promote environmental activism to influence future environmental policies that would mitigate environmental health problems directly related to environmental injustices.

In the beginning the grant intended to obtain an environmental history of impacted communities through the completion of a written medium designed by the grant administrator; a 55 multiple choice and fill-in-the-blank questionnaire. This questionnaire was distributed and completed at the Clavers April Kick-Off meeting in Newark, New Jersey to 350 members at their 2003 Northern District Regional meeting. The questionnaire's questions were designed to elicit historical environmental information about respondents' current and previous geographical space and their environmental health status. The questionnaire was also designed to elicit information about their basic understanding of environmental pollution and its relationship to environmental health problems (like asthma and lead poisoning). When the questionnaire, however, was being completed by the Claver membership during the kick-off meeting the conference room became tense as the membership tried to understand the purpose and meaning of the questions. When I as the appointed project administrator began to address the concerns and questions posed by the Claver audience, the room immediately became filled with rich oral environmental memories of members' encounters with environmental pollution and environmental justice battles. They were more comfortable communicating the environmental information orally than in writing. In the typical African American griot tradition environmental memories and histories filled the room. These oral histories contained detailed and pertinent environmental information that would never have been captured by the questionnaire. What was also disturbing at this meeting was the almost constant espousal by many that they "knew something was wrong" because "our families never had asthma until they left the South." What was most alarming however was the repeated claim, by many over several conferences, that they had "never heard of the environmental justice movement." One senior and highly respected Claver member stated that he had been a welder for more than a decade and had subsequently developed a number of environmentally related health problems after taking the job. He said that he didn't know until the presentation that the improper handling of chemicals or chemical containing substances could impact his health.

It was at this moment that it became apparent that gathering environmental information for this project would best be achieved using an oral history methodology rather than by a more quantitative tool like a questionnaire. It was decided at this meeting by the national Claver leadership that the organization would proceed with the suggestion to undertake an Environmental Justice/Health Oral History project that would facilitate a better grasp of the community's history of environmental problems and environmental illnesses. This information would then be used to promote environmental literacy by developing an oral history based environmental justice informational booklet and a documentary videotape project as part of the grant efforts.

Obtaining knowledge of environmental conditions through oral history has proven much more effective than having people fill out questionnaire especially from older Claver members who are completely unaware of the postmodern notion of "environmental justice" and environmental inequalities. The average senior Claver member is close to retirement and approximately 50 to 55 years old. To achieve the original grant objective of developing environmental literacy among African American youth it was decided that the oral history interviews would be conducted by the organization's junior members (between the ages of 14 to 18 years old). This multigenerational collaboration draws upon the African American griot tradition and the long-term practice of elders educating and assimilating the younger generation. The idea was now to have Claver youth learn and understand the environmental history of their geography through the environmental memories of senior Claver members.

The next step was to begin the actual oral history project in Chicago. This was done providing a detailed overview of the grant before the Claver's Chicago Intercouncil in early May 2003. The Claver's Chicago Intercouncil consists of approximately 150 Claver leaders from approximately thirty African American parishes in Chicago's Metropolitan Region. The grant administrator announced the formation of an Environmental Justice Implementation Team (ENJIT) that would support three to four pilot parishes as they implemented the grant based upon the recommendation of Dr. Andrew Hurley, a senior environmental historian who wrote the first environmental inequality history monograph in the United States. The team and pilot parishes were selected at the first meeting of the KPC Environmental Justice Executive Board (that had been hand picked the by KPC's national officers) held at Depaul University in late May. The pilot parishes selected were St. Simeon parish of Bellwood, Illinois whose members were suffering from an incineration plant's operation and a poorly managed landfill; Ascension/St. Susanna's parish in Markham/Harvey Illinois, whose residents were suffering from asthma and incinerator issues; and Holy Angels parish of Chicago, whose parishioners are in one of the highest asthma mortality zones in Chicago. The Clavers also selected St. Monica Parish in Gary, Indiana as one of their pilot parishes because of their close proximity to Chicago and the city's well-documented history of environmental problems elucidated by Andrew Hurley's monograph, *Environmental Inequalities : Class, Race, and Industrial Pollution in Gary, Indiana, 1945–1980.*

On July 26, 2003, a three hour kickoff meeting for the pilot parishes and ENJIT was held at Depaul University on July 26, 2003 to go over in more explicit details the objectives and goals of the grant for 2003. Twelve KPC members representing the various parishes and the Archdiocese of Chicago attended this meeting. It was agreed at this meeting to develop not only a brochure but now two environmental justice videotapes (one informational and one documentary) based upon the collected oral histories and an "Environmental Justice/Health" Website.

An overview and status of the project was then made before 2000 black Catholics at the national KPC meeting in Atlanta, Georgia on July 30 2003 by the National Lay Board member, Dr. Robert Miller. Miller was a member of the KPC Environmental Justice Executive Board that was responsible for overseeing the project.

In August 2003 an environmental justice oral history workshop was conducted by senior environmental historian, Dr. Andrew Hurley for senior Claver members participating in the pilot parishes and ENJIT members at the Chicago Historical Society. Approximately thirty KPC members attended this event. The objective of this meeting was to train the trainers in how to conduct oral history for the oral history portion of this project so that they could facilitate the participation of Claver youths in their parishes. These youths became responsible for taking the "environmental" oral histories of senior members at their respective or designated parishes. Once again the environmental justice memories and reflections filled the room when Hurley asked Claver members to participate in mock "interviews." One of the most poignant points made at this meeting by one of the founding editors of *Deliverance*, the only black Catholic newspaper in Illinois, was that black "folks were too afraid back then [in the 1940s and 1950s] to push too hard" for what is now referred to as environmental justice. Many of the older Clavers at this meeting supported his assessment that they understood that the environmental conditions of their community became dismal and allowed to deteriorate in a way that no white community was subjected to in Chicago. They also remembered participating in letter writing campaigns to inform city officials about the problem but they understood that they could face retaliation if they complained too much.

By September 2003 the Chicago Historical Society (CHS) with the support and endorsement of its president, Dr. Lonnie Bunch, made arrangements to provide a two month oral history training program for the Claver teens by its own Teen Chicago Project members. The Claver youths began their training in November 2003 at a meeting led by Russell Lewis, CHS director of research, Rosemary Adams, CHS director of the Catholic Chicago Project and Marie Scatena, CHS director of Teen Chicago.[12] This oral history training program was initially arranged by Rosemary Adams who was also responsible for providing the project with transcribers and oral history equipment recommendations. It was also decided during this time that an environmental justice tour of the Chicago region would be planned for all KPC project members (adults and youths) in the area by 2004. The objective of this tour was to provide a sense of the state of environmental justice, both past and current in Chicago, as a background for the oral history participants.

On November 8, 2003 the Chicago Historical Society began training eight Claver teens in oral history methodologies. The Claver teens (between the ages of 14 and 18 from the pilot parishes) conducted four initial interviews of senior Claver members from these same parishes ranging in age from 93 to 50 years old as part of their training that day.

The transcripts from these oral history interviews were then used by the Clavers to write the Environmental Justice and Health booklet; its first environmental literacy device. The interviewed Clavers were required to sign release forms so that the material could be used not only in the booklet but also in the future videotape projects and on the Website.

The information gathered by the teens revealed a long-term struggle with environmental inequalities by older members of the organization which had existed since their childhood in the Depression. In the interview conducted by Martin Kaufman , a teen from St. Simeon's parish in Bellwood, Dr. Robert Miller (KPC national lay board member) informed him :[13]

> when I was coming up . . . one of the big things you had was the stench that you would get from the stockyards, the Chicago stockyards . . . and some cities [didn't] have alleys. . . . Right after the Depression when we threw our garbage out . . . it would come to the point many times of overflowing because they didn't have adequate garbage pickup. And so it was a breeding place for . . . maggots and rats.

An interview with Mr. Ron Nightengale during this same session revealed the contemporary problem of environmental illiteracy in African American communities. Mr. Nightengale is a resident of the black suburb, Bellwood, Illinois which is adjacent to a community battling an illegally operated incinerator and a dump. Nightengale informed his interviewer that:

> I really never gave the dump any other thought other than you could always smell the smell. And to me that was just . . . part of you know its being a dump. You live near it, you're going to smell the dump. As the community was protesting about the dump and everything, then I became aware of all the side effects and what actually was happening. Fumes coming into the air, noxious fumes, poisonous fumes. Then I became aware [that] we were not only smelling but breathing and taking [it] in. And also I became aware of the side effects from all this. And then looking around and from conversations with [other] people I learned about the other environmental hazards that we were affected by.

By the second week of December 2003 an Afrocentric environmental justice history essay of Chicago and an accompanying environmental ethics essay (from a Catholic perspective) was completed by myself and Dr. Dawn Nothwehr, OSF, an eco-theologist at Catholic Theological Union. Our essays along with the oral history interviews were the foundations of KPC's first environmental justice booklet which was eventually produced and published by Depaul University's Egan Urban Center.

By January 2004 the eight black Catholic teenagers representing the KPC project and the pilot parishes had met and received training in oral history four times at the Chicago Historical Society. The teens met from December 6 through January 10 to continue their training in oral history (approximately six hours per day) under the direction of the Teen Chicago Project Director, Marie Scatena. The interviews taken during this process continued to reveal the rich history of environmental cognition, activism, and strategies used by African Americans in Chicago.

By the second week of January 2004 a draft of the environmental justice booklet had been completed which employed the transcribed oral history interviews conducted by the teens in 2003.

On January 24 2004, Claver teens met with Depaul University students from my *Race, Place and Space: Environmental Justice in the Twentieth Century* course at the Chicago Historical Society to develop and synthesize an environmental justice history of the pilot parishes using the USEPA and Scorecard websites. The Depaul students discussed information from community fact sheets and neighborhood statistical information with the Claver teens that they had gathered from the archives of the Chicago Historical Society. The objective of this meeting was to provide each group with a sense of the historical environmental justice issues faced by African Americans in Chicago. During this meeting the Depaul students also provided an initial

EJ community report (based on the Scorecard website and their historical research) on each of the participating pilot parishes. This was also the day that the Claver teens conducted their first group interview (as trained oral historians) of a senior Claver, Mrs. Dorothy Thomas, prior to meeting with the Depaul students. The Depaul students were then allowed that same day to discuss with Ms. Thomas her environmental experiences in Chicago.[14]

This initial meeting between the Claver teens and the Depaul students was videotaped by a professional videographer, Ines Sommers, who had been hired by KPC (upon the recommendation of the CHS' Teen Chicago Project Director) to develop a 10-minute informational videotape. The objective was to have the videotape be shown at adult and junior Claver conferences, meetings and conventions across the country to give them a more concrete idea of the organization's environmental justice and health project. The tape was also designed to show audiences examples of environmental justice oral histories as well as to reveal examples of inequitable environmental geographies revealed by the environmental justice (EJ) tour conducted on Chicago's Southside on February 7. This first environmental justice (EJ) tour of Chicago by the Clavers, conducted on Saturday, February 7, 2004, was coordinated with the help of geographers, Michael F. Siola and Dr. Marc Bouman, from Chicago State University's (CSU) geography department and CSU's Calumet Environmental Resource Center. Senior and junior Clavers invited to the EJ tour heard two presentations on environmental justice issues faced by African Americans in Chicago prior to taking the bus tour. The keynote speakers for the presentations was Cheryl Johnson of the People for Community Recovery (Altgeld Gardens).

Cheryl Johnson is the daughter of Hazel Johnson, the internationally recognized environmental justice activist who is considered the "mother of the EJ movement." Both women are African American Catholics. The kick-off speaker for the EJ tour was Chicago State University's African American geographer and EJ activist, Johnny Owens. The tour and presentation also included the Depaul University students the environmental justice history course. These students were allowed to discuss and debate the environmental justice history of Chicago with the presenters and Clavers. They also prepared and delivered written environmental justice histories of the pilot areas covered in the grant.

The KPC environmental justice booklet, *Struggles for Environmental Justice and Health in Chicago, An African American and Catholic Perspective* was finally published by Depaul University on February 13 2004. The booklet contained my own abbreviated environmental justice history of Chicago; theological and social reflections by Dr. Dawn Nothwehr of Catholic Theological Union; and the oral history transcriptions of the environmental memories of senior Clavers obtained in the interviews conducted by the Claver students at the Chicago Historical Society on November 8, 2003. The full-colored booklet, approximately thirty pages in length, also contained maps of the black parishes in Chicago and their environmental relationship to high asthma and lead zones in the city. Of the 3000 copies of the booklet that were produced by Depaul University, two hundred and fifty were distributed to environmental NGOs and environmental agencies in Chicago and in the state of Illinois.

Twenty seven hundred booklets were distributed to senior Claver leaders in the thirty-nine states at the regional Northern District meeting in Springfield (March 2004) and at the national convention in Louisville, Kentucky (July 2004). The EJ videotape was shown several times during the Clavers national convention with an overwhelming positive response. Once again the reaction by many were dismay at the fact that no one had communicated this information to them prior to the convention; especially since the EJ movement had been in existence for over 20 years. There were however other reactions by members like a junior high school teacher who expressed sincere appreciation for the project. She stated that although "I had seen fast glimpses of the problem on TV, I never understood the problem until today." The information and concerns shared in the videotaped oral history interviews from familiar faces resonated with the Claver body. Many of the Clavers present during the national convention were leaders of parish-based KPC groups and it was clear that a significant number of these leaders wanted to not only continue the EJ dialogue at the national but also at the local level. As a result of the national convention some local parishes have held environmental health fairs to discuss the relationship of environmental justice and environmental health.

The Clavers were awarded a second grant of $50,000 for 2004 from the USCCB to continue the project as well as $10,000 from the Illinois Humanities Council and the National Endowment for the Humanities; and $3000 from DePaul University's Vincentian Endowment Fund. The money was used for the development of a Catholic-centered EJ documentary videotape of Chicago specifically designed to facilitate communication about environmental justice issues in black communities that have a black Catholic presence; and that was also sensitive to their religious beliefs.

NOTES

1. This essay will utilize the terms black and African American interchangeably. The term black however embraces people of African descent across the world: Africans, African Americans, Afro Cuban, Afro Brazilian, etc.

2. For a more explicit and recent history of the environmental justice movement in the United States read Luke W. Cole and Sheila R. Foster, *Environmental Racism and the Rise of the Environmental Justice Movement* (New York: New York Univer-

sity Press, , 2001); David Naguib Pellow, *Garbage Wars: The Struggle for Environmental Justice in Chicago* (Cambridge: MIT Press, 2002); J. Timmons Roberts and Melissa M. Tofflon-Weiss, *Chronicles from the Environmental Justice Frontline,* (Cambridge: Cambridge University Press, 2001); Sylvia Hood Washington, *Packing Them In: An Archaeology of Environmental Racism in Chicago, 1865–1954* (Lanham, Md.: Lexington Books, 2004); and Sylvia Hood Washington's "Environmental Justice" in George R. Goethals, Georgia J. Sorenson, and James McGregror Burns, eds., *Encyclopedia of Leadership, Vol.1* (Thousand Oaks, Calif.: Sage Publications, 2004), 449–55.

3. There has never been a singular faith among African Americans in the United States; and in many parts of this country Catholicism has been the dominant faith among African Americans for generations. The failure to recognize the existence of other religious faith communities in the African American community like Muslims, Jews, or Buddhists is critical to achieving environmental parity for all African Americans.

4. Cyprian Davis, OSB, *The History of Black Catholics in the United States* (New York: Crossroad Publishing Company, 1998), 256.

5. Ibid., 259.

6. Ibid.

7. This practice of excluding black Catholics from the discussions of environmental justice dialogues seems to be more prevalent among Northern, Midwestern, and Western states than in the South. The involvement of black Catholics in Louisiana, as Dr. Beverly Wright of Xavier University's Deep South Environmental Justice Center has recently pointed out, in environmental justice struggles in that state is the rule since a large percentage of the African Americans in this state have been practicing Catholics for over two centuries.

8. The Clavers were formed in 1909 in Mobile, Alabama by Josephite priests and black lay Catholics after they were denied admission into the all white Knights of Columbus. The term black is used because it embraces the ethnic diversity of the membership: African Americans, West Indian, Creole, and Africans.

9. This latter claim was based upon the initial audience responses from environmental presentations made by the grant director at Claver conventions and conferences. The audiences totaled over 3000 people across the country.

10. This is not an intentional oversight but one which is undoubtedly tied to the fact that the EJ movement was launched by civil rights leaders and politicians who are rooted in the black Protestant tradition. See Dianne Glave's work on black Protestants, liberation theology, and environmental justice movement, *Public Historian,* 2003.

11. Walt Grazer, *An Emerging Catholic Voice,* http://www.chausa.org/PUBS/PUBSART.ASP?ISSUE=HP0311&ARTICLE=M

12. My affiliation with the CHS was suggested and initiated by Dr. Jeffrey Stine, senior environmental and public historian at the Smithsonian and past president of ASEH.

13. Approximately ten black Catholic teens were involved in the original project. The other teen interviewers for the project were Jessica Scott and Sarah Washington.

14. A total of eight oral history interviews were conducted by the Claver teens between November 2003 and February 2004.

III

INDIGENOUS MEMORIES OF ENVIRONMENTAL INJUSTICE

14

Suttesája

From a Sacred Sami Site and Natural Spring to a Water Bottling Plant? The Effects of Colonization in Northern Europe

Rauna Kuokkanen with Marja K. Bulmer[1]

In northern Finland, homeland of the Sami people, the municipality of Ohcejohka/Utsjoki has started a project that involves a plan to bottle and sell drinking water on a substantial scale from Suttesája, a natural spring and an ancient Sami sacred site. There are several issues and concerns at play in this venture, started in 2001 by the municipality in collaboration with representatives from the Regional Environmental Centre of Lapland without prior informing of, or consultation with, local Sami people or other interest groups who might be affected by the project.

First, the water prospecting plan reflects one of the fastest growing trends of economic, corporate globalization, the commodification and privatization of the world's fresh water resources. As Maude Barlow and Tony Clarke point out in *Blue Gold: The Battle Against Corporate Theft of the World's Water* (2002), fresh water is quickly becoming a big global business. While water, the world's most fundamental and indispensable resource is quickly disappearing, transnational corporations are already claiming monopolies over the world's fresh water resources. As the authors suggest, a global shortage of water presents one of the most threatening ecological, economic, and political crises of the twenty-first century.

Second, Suttesája is about cultural rights of indigenous peoples which also are increasingly threatened by the global market forces and the predominant profit ideology. Protecting cultural, spiritual, and intellectual heritage is among the most urgent concerns for indigenous peoples for whom globalization is not merely a question of marginalization but a multifaceted attack on the very foundation of their existence (Guissé 2003; Hall 2003; WGIP 2003; Indigenous Peoples and Globalization Program 2003; Smith and Ward 2000). Third, the proposed venture poses considerable ecological concerns. It involves a daily extraction of 1300 cubic meters of water from the spring, bottling it on site and transporting the bottles to the world market of drinking water. Besides the boreholes, the onsite construction would include a 300-meter-long water pipe, industrial building, and roads for bottling and transportation (Hautala 2002: 5). The spring feeds the Deatnu (Tana) watershed, one of Europe's finest Atlantic salmon rivers.

Fourth, Suttesája is a precedence-setting case in Finland where immaterial cultural rights of the Sami have so far not been adequately addressed. As Marja K. Bulmer notes in her section below, the Sami cultural rights have not received much attention amongst the Finnish judiciary. Further, the official Sami representative bodies such as the Sami Parliament in Finland and the Sami Council (NGO) have also largely failed in demanding the recognition and protection of these rights. In fact, it was not until some local Sami called for the attention of these organizations with regard to the protection of the sacred site that these bodies considered the water prospecting plans of the Ohcejohka/Utsjoki municipality a concern involving several Sami rights. In their statements, however, they hesitate to take a unanimous stand for the protection of the sacred site. Considering the central role the Sami organizations play in the international indigenous movement, it is striking that these statements also fail to refer to and draw upon the internationally recognized documents and declarations of indigenous peoples' rights which include specific references pertaining to cultural and spiritual practices and sacred sites.

This chapter intends to focus on two main questions. First, it analyzes the planned commodification of Suttesája from a legal perspective, particularly in the light of Sami cultural rights. This section, written by Marja K. Bulmer, gives an overview of the currently pending legal case pertaining to Suttesája and how the Sami cultural rights are recognized in Finland. She discusses the vagueness of the existing Finnish system in taking into account in decision-making the cultural rights of the Sami people particularly when they are not tied to a certain material aspect of culture, such as traditional livelihoods. This makes it even more necessary for government representatives and others to adopt a rigorous approach that ensures profound and meaningful consultation and assessment, both of which are missing in the Suttesája case.

Secondly, the chapter considers the planned exploitation of the sacred site of Suttesája through an analysis of colonization of the Sami people. Colonialism and its effects on indigenous peoples are sometimes discussed in either too limited or too generalized terms. This may result in a hasty conclusion that the Sami people have not been colonized because the colonization process has been much longer and subtler than the colonization of indigenous peoples in the Americas, Australia, and New Zealand where the colonizers came from another continent. A narrow understanding of colonial processes and practices has led not only to false claims according to which the Sami have not been colonized (e.g., Vahtola 1991; see also Harle and Moisio 2000: 131ff) but also to the absence of critical analyses and assessments on the part of the Sami themselves.

In this chapter, I suggest that the various effects of the colonial processes that remain, by and large, unanalyzed with regard to the Sami, enable the municipality to proceed in an arrogant and ignorant fashion with regard to the Suttesája case, that is, without taking the concerns of local Sami or their rights as an indigenous people seriously, not to mention into consideration in their plans and decision making. I also contend that the general lack of analysis of colonialism by both Sami and others for its own part feeds to the prevailing circumstances of arrogance in public discourse and municipal decision making. First, however, it is necessary to give a brief overview of the Sami people and a look at some aspects of their historical colonization.

THE SAMI PEOPLE

The Sami are the indigenous people of Sápmi (Samiland),[2] an area which spans from central Norway and Sweden through northern Finland to the Kola Peninsula of Russia. A rough estimate of the Sami population is between 75,000 to 100,000, the majority of which are in Norway. In Finland, the Sami population is approximately 7,000. There are several Sami languages of which the most widely spoken is the Northern Sami, the language also spoken in the region in question.

The Sami have experienced a long history of colonization that in some regards reflects the colonial processes elsewhere, but in other regards, is quite different from colonization of many other indigenous peoples. During the early Middle Ages, the surrounding kingdoms of Sweden-Finland, Denmark-Norway, and Novgorod became interested in the land and natural resources of Samiland. There was also strong competition between the kingdoms over the Sami territories. The kingdoms imposed taxation on the Sami and encouraged the settlement of the north by outsiders in order to claim rights to the land. This was also a way to make the Sami subjects of the surrounding kingdoms.

As in many other places in the world, Christianization was one of the central means of the early colonization of the Sami. The first churches in Samiland were built as early as the twelfth century but it was not until the 1700s when Christianity started to seriously erode the nature-based Sami world-view or "religion" by outlawing shamanistic ceremonies, executing the *noaidis* (Sami shamans), burning and destroying the Sami drums and also banning yoiking, the Sami way of chanting and expressing oneself.

Moreover, the imposition of Christianity played an important role in the early educational attempts by the government and church representatives. The education of Sami children was organized through an ambulatory school system that was inaugurated in Norway in the seventeenth century and in Sweden-Finland in 1739. During the eighteenth century, the ambulatory school system covered all Sami villages in Scandinavia. The teachers were often local young Sami who were taught to read, write, and count by the church. The language of instruction was in some cases Sami but gradually it was prohibited. This system functioned until World War II (Lehtola 1996: 167–71).

In the nineteenth century, the influence of various governments increased in Samiland. All three Nordic states justified their assimilation policies in the name of education: the only way for the Sami to become equal with the other citizens of the state was to know the official language of the country. Laws that prohibited the use of Sami language both in schools and at home were passed, particularly in Norway and Sweden.

In Finland, which had become an autonomous region under the Russian Empire in 1809, the policies were not as harsh as in Norway or Sweden. At the end of the nineteenth century, the church was quite supportive of using Sami as the language of instruction in schools (Aikio 1992: 209–213). The active use and support of the Sami language by the church, however, was also an attempt to implement the principle of Protestantism by preaching gospel in the language of the people. While the churchmen indicated support of the Sami language, they were very clear on their intentions of overthrowing the Sami worldview or "religion." After the Second World War, the Finnish school system relinquished the policies that were intended to take the special situation of the North into account. Moreover, in 1946, changes in the education law made attending school compulsory even for children of the most remote regions, which led to the creation of boarding schools (Lehtola 1994: 217–218).

SAMI CULTURAL RIGHTS AND CONSULTATION IN THE DECISION-MAKING PROCESS[3]

In November 2002, the municipality of Ohcejohka/Utsjoki passed a resolution whereby it committed itself to a land lease with the Finnish government, which claims ownership to lands traditionally used and occupied by Sami in northern Finland. In January 2003, four local Sami women filed an application for a judicial review of the municipality's decision. After a summary dismissal on a procedural point at the Administrative Court of Rovaniemi, the applicants gained a victory at the Supreme Administrative Court of Finland, which overturned the Administrative Court's decision and sent the application back to the Administrative Court to be determined on merits.

The application, presently pending at the Administrative Court, is based on procedural omissions in the municipality's decision-making process. Specifically, the applicants claim that the municipality failed to properly consult with the local Sami and that the environmental and cultural assessments carried out by the municipality were biased and inadequate.[4] Due to these deficiencies, the municipality did not have sufficient information to make an adequately informed decision, particularly with respect to the decision's potential impact on the constitutionally protected Sami cultural rights.

The Sami cultural rights are based on the Finnish Constitution Act, which provides that the Sami, as an indigenous people, have a right to maintain and develop their own culture (Section 17:3 of the Constitution Act). The Constitution further provides that in Samiland, the Sami enjoy self-government with respect to their culture (Section 121:4 of the Constitution Act). The right to self-government is further defined in the Sami Parliament Act, which provides, among other things, that the government has an obligation to negotiate with the Sami Parliament on all significant and extensive actions that may directly and specifically impact the position of the Sami as an indigenous people in certain specifically listed matters that include leasing of state land. The act states that it is sufficient to provide the Sami Parliament an opportunity to be heard and negotiate, and that failure by the Sami Parliament to do so does not prevent the decision maker from proceeding.[5]

As stated in the applicants' submissions, the central question of the application is the meaning of the Sami culture and how and to what extent a government decision maker has to consider and incorporate the Sami rights into its decision-making process. Legal rights serve to protect certain interests from unjustifiable interference (e.g., Pound 1928: 60). Property rights, for example, protect the owner's interest in the use and enjoyment of his or her property. Property rights (which are constitutionally protected in Finland), and the interests they serve, are often measurable in economic or other tangible terms. For example, it may be a matter of a relatively simple calculation to assess the infringement caused by a proposed power line to a landowner, whose timber has to be removed. The value of the timber can be compared to the proposed expropriation compensation to determine whether the compensation is adequate, thereby justifying the infringement.

Such simple calculations are not available in the Suttesája case. The case is further complicated by the fact that none of the "more tangible" aspects of the Sami culture—reindeer herding, hunting, or fishing, all of which have been recognized and affirmed as integral elements of section 17:3 cultural rights—are at issue. Instead, the applicants' case is based on the impact of the proposed water bottling project on Sami spirituality, heritage, and identity. Specifically, the applicants argue that the municipality failed to consider the cumulative impact of the proposed project and the already existing activities and projects on the Suttesája area on Sami spirituality, heritage, and identity, thereby posing a risk of "death by thousand cuts" on the Sami culture.

Similar to many other social and cultural rights, section 17:3 of the Constitution Act is vague about the meaning of the cultural rights and obligations it mandates on the government decision makers. The law preparation documents do not shed much light on the meaning of the "Sami culture" and due to the novelty of the section, legal precedent is sparse.[6] However, lack of clarity and precision regarding the dimensions of these rights must not be held as a reason for their non-enforcement. The novelty of an interest at issue or lack of legislative or judicial precedent and guidance must not be used as an excuse for thinking that rights simply do not exist if precedent or legislation is silent on the matter. Lack of clarity and precision is a function of repeated application and enforcement. It also puts a particular burden on the decision maker to inform and educate him- or herself of those rights. The fact that the right is not "standard" or "tangible" requires the decision maker to go to further lengths to ensure that he or she has all the necessary facts to make a well-informed decision.

It is specifically because of the intangible and unique nature of the rights at issue that the courts need to adopt a stringent approach to the procedural requirements for consultation and assessment. The procedural requirements are, after all, in place to ensure that certain fundamental principles of fairness and justice are followed in the decision-making process. These principles, which are deeply entrenched in the Finnish administrative law, require, for example, that the parties whose rights may be affected by the purported decision be properly notified and provided with an adequate opportunity to be heard. A further significant principle is the decision-maker's obligation to properly inform himself or herself of all relevant matters so that he or she can make an informed decision that adequately addresses all relevant concerns.[7] These administrative law principles of fairness and justice are further heightened where the rights at issue enjoy constitutional protection. The Constitution Act itself obligates the government to ensure that constitutional and human rights are recognized and affirmed in the decision-making process (Section 22 of the Constitution Act).

While the notion of "culture" and even the interests of spirituality, heritage and identity provide a certain degree of common intelligibility, it is simply not possible for a person with a different set of cultural perspectives and interests to comprehend the many variances of another culture without a careful scrutiny and review of the rights in question. Determining the existence of an interest and the extent of possible infringement are extremely complex tasks, and require thorough consultation with the right holders to ensure that the decision maker is aware of all necessary facts to make a well-informed decision. At the minimum, meaningful consultation requires Sami participation and perspective at various stages of cultural assessment. Firstly, input from the local Sami is critical for ensuring that the factual foundation for the assessment is accurate and complete. In this case, this requires determining which existing projects and activities on the Suttesája area are considered by the Sami to constitute a violation to their culture and interests. Secondly, Sami expertise is required in assessing the cumulative impact of these various projects and activities and the proposed water bottling project on the Sami culture. Thirdly, the assessment must be distributed and made available to a wide Sami audience to ensure that the assessment encompasses all relevant aspects and concerns.

THE SIGNIFICANCE OF SUTTESÁJA FOR SAMI CULTURE AND IDENTITY

The natural spring of Suttesája belongs to a larger area considered sacred by generations of Sami. Suttesája is in the vicinity of the Áilegas Mountain, one of the three major sacred mountains in the region. The sacredness of the area is reflected, for instance, in Sami place names, many of which begin with the word "sacred." The Suttesája area is also marked as a heritage site of cultural and historical significance in the registry of the Finnish National Board of Antiquities.

It has been noted that it is difficult to give a universal definition to the concept of sacred since its meaning varies from a religion, culture, and language to another. It can be said, however, that as a generalization, sacredness implies certain regulations and rules on human behavior. It has been noted that "if something is sacred then certain rules must be observed in relation to it, and this generally means that something is said to be sacred, whether it can be an object or site (or person), must be placed apart from everyday things or places, so that its special significance can be recognized, and rules regarding it obeyed" (Hubert 1994: 11).

Suttesája continues to be a site of spiritual, historical, and cultural significance for many local Sami. As the result of the imposition of Christianity, however, knowledge of the usage of the area has become more invisible. Many Sami today are reluctant to reveal oral tradition pertaining to the spiritual dimensions of Suttesája for fear of being stigmatized or ridiculed. Moreover, it is not uncommon to keep information about traditional sacred sites "secret" from outsiders for fear of exploiting or using the site for inappropriate purposes.

In general, sacred sites are of great significance in Sami culture and society.

They have a central role in the traditional Sami worldview which perceives the world as a living, interconnected entity in which human beings are one part of many. As for other indigenous peoples, the worldview and thereby also the identity of the Sami are inseparably linked to their intimate relationship and interaction with the surrounding environment, which differs from the worldview of modernity in which human beings are considered separate from and above the rest of the world. Therefore, there is a need for governments and their representatives in their decision making to pay special attention to this relationship which differs from dominant society, as pointed out by the UN Special Rapporteur Erika-Irene Daes (2002: 6–7).

Sami scholar of religion and folklore Jelena Porsanger points out: "On an individual and collective level, the relationship to the internal and external world is maintained through rituals. This also keeps the order of life in balance, and this is very important in terms of the survival of the community" (2004: 151). Another central characteristic of this worldview is the understanding that ancestors and other living creatures are present in certain locations which therefore are considered sacred. These places, which particularly traditionally have been the focal points of various ceremonies, can be found all across Samiland, especially in locations that are important for traditional Sami livelihoods such as in the vicinity of migrating routes, settlements, hunting grounds and fishing sites. One of the features of Sami sacred sites "is their location on outstanding formations in the landscape," thus being "naturally demarcated from the surrounding landscape" (Mulk 1994: 125).

One of the many reasons that make Suttesája a special place is that it is a natural spring which, unlike other waterways, does not freeze even in the coldest winter (hence the name which would translate as 'unfrozen stream'). It is located along the old migrating route traditionally used by reindeer herding families but also by other local people for purposes of getting drinking water and also healing (Pentikäinen 1995: 145).[8] At one end of the spring, there is an old sieidi site. In the Sami land-based worldview, sieidi is a sacred place usually consisting of a stone or wood of a special shape to which various gifts are given to thank certain spirits for the abundance of the land but also to ensure fishing, hunting, and reindeer luck in the future. The common location for sieidis are in the vicinity of sacred places, camp grounds, or fishing and hunting sites. Although Christianity has severely eroded the Sami sieidi practices of thanking and sharing with the land by banning it as a pagan form of devil worshipping, there is a relatively large body of evidence that the practice of sieidi gifting is still practiced (Kjellström 1987; see also Juuso 1998: 137).[9]

The conversion to Christianity resulted in outlawing the Sami worldview and its expressions even at the cost of a death penalty. The Christian religion was made the official religion of the Sami, which does not mean, however, that the traditional Sami worldview would have disappeared completely.

Many of its elements still exist and are reflected in thinking and certain practices. As Inga-Maria Mulk emphasizes, Sami sacred sites continue to have a strong emotional significance for many Sami both individually and collectively. This knowledge is transmitted from one generation to another through oral tradition and thus many Sami are aware of the sacred sites of their ancestors (Mulk 1994: 130).

RAMIFICATIONS OF COLONIALISM IN THE SUTTESÁJA CASE

The centuries-long colonial process in Samiland has resulted in the erasure of the Sami land-based value system and worldview which Suttesája is also part of. This kind of cultural displacement of the Sami is evident in the commonplace lack of knowledge about sacred sites and their significance, or the traditional Sami land-based worldview and the accompanying system of values. In the case of older Sami, many of whom are strongly Christian, the cultural displacement is reflected in their reluctance to discuss and share the knowledge that they still may have. For them, the traditional Sami worldview or "religion" is considered a "sin" and thus a taboo. The long-term erasure of the cultural memory of the Sami by the imposition of Christianity and other assimilative, coercive measures has also led to circumstances where internal divisions and tensions in the municipality do not always follow the Sami/non-Sami divide. For example, while Ohcejohka/Utsjoki is the only municipality in Finland where the Sami form the numerical majority (69.9%), some of the municipality representatives actively involved in the water prospecting project are Sami themselves. Also, some other local Sami have indicated their support for the project either directly or by expressing dismissive comments of those who have raised concerns about the venture (e.g., Kojo 2002).

One of the several problems of cultural displacement relates to the question of consultation, a central issue and point of tension in the Suttesája water prospecting project. As discussed above, there are certain general principles that illuminate what consists of appropriate consultation. It could be, however, challenging to implement them in a situation where people in general do not know much about their cultural practices, considering that consultation requires that people recognize and are familiar with their cultural and social practices, values, and beliefs. If the colonization process has already reached a point where a large part of the cultural foundation has been eradicated by various official and more subtle, covert, and ad-hoc measures of the state institutions but also the general attitudes and views of dominant society, how is it possible—and is it even appropriate—to expect individuals and groups of people to participate in a meaningful consultation process? The Suttesája case painfully illustrates the obscene nature of colonialism: after all the eradication attempts of a culture and identity over several generations, it is now required that in order to have finally protected what is left from the prolonged and still continuing attack, one must have knowledge and a viable connection to that culture and identity. In short, the problem is how to counter the effects of the colonialism and even more so, implement the principles aiming at protecting the rights of indigenous peoples when some Sami might be already so assimilated and manipulated into the mainstream society and its values that they do not appreciate and see the importance of intangible aspects of their own heritage such as values and a worldview?

The cultural displacement results in the internalization of colonialism (or some aspects of it). This internalization explains the tendency of some Sami to turn their backs to their cultural and spiritual heritage and side with mainstream views and perspectives that only see the commercial value of the spring.

The concept of hegemony is helpful in analyzing and understanding the internalized colonization of the Sami. Hegemony or domination by consent exercises power not by force or even laws and policies, but by far more subtle and clandestine mechanisms. These mechanisms, such as the education system, media, and public discourse ensure that the interests of dominant society (or the dominant group) appear as the interest of everybody and ultimately, is taken for granted also by those who remain marginalized or colonized. Consent is usually achieved by the imposition of colonial discourse "so that Euro-centric values, assumptions, beliefs, and attitudes are accepted as a matter course as the most natural or valuable" (Ashcroft, Griffiths and Tiffin 2000: 117). The hegemonic control is further enabled "through control of the dominant modes of public and private representation" (ibid.: 78). These representations become manifested, for example, in internalized views about indigenous peoples and their cultures as inherently inferior.

The internalization of inferior status is a process of conditioning through national legislation, education, religion, and socialization. Particularly in the postwar period, the Finnish educational system has played a crucial role in the assimilation and appropriation of the Sami consciousness. Sami children were taught rules and customs of Finnish society which applied not only to behavior and clothing but also values and worldviews. Some children internalized the dominant society's way of thinking and worldview and thus started to despise their own culture (Lehtola 1994: 219–20). Many Sami have described their boarding school experiences and the way by which the internalization of dominant society's foreign values destroyed their self-esteem to the extent that some Sami wanted "to be more Finnish than the Finnish themselves" (Sara 1984: 43). The reason for such behavior was that the formerly direct, open colonialism had become more insidious and invisible. It had settled down in the Sami society and thus the danger of assimilation did not come from outside any longer as the Sami themselves had acquired the views of colonialism which lived within the society (Lehtola 1995: 44). Combined with the strong Christian influence in many Sami regions, including the Deatnu Valley of which the Suttesája area is part, this has resulted in some Sami arguing dominant views according to which Sami spirituality, linked with living in a respectful and reciprocal relationship with the land, is insignificant and even shameful.

In other words, the psychological force of the construction of the modern worldview and its values has been so forceful yet insidious and concealed that without recognizing, some Sami have adopted the notion of the other of themselves. This process could be called "self-othering" by which "the Sami other" is produced by Sami themselves.[10] Ultimately, "self-othering" leads to a situation where the Sami may become their own colonizers by inscribing colonial discourse upon themselves without necessarily being aware of it. This can take place in subtle ways such as adopting assumptions about culture, history, progress, and tradition characterized by modernity and initially generated by the colonizers.[11] In other words, many Sami—at least so it seems with regard to Suttesája case—have come to see themselves and their culture through the eyes of the modern, western worldview, and therefore, participate in mechanisms of control inscribed and employed by dominant, colonial discourses. The Sami participation in the dominant discourse by ridiculing their own culture and calls for its protection can be also understood through theories of power, where the dominant system and its representatives 'reward' more readily those Sami who side with the views of the mainstream society than those who do not (cf. Kailo 2002).

Trivializing and ridiculing are effective mechanisms of control which suppress other perspectives and make opposing arguments invisible (cf. Ås n.d.). These techniques have been commonly employed by those supporting the commodification of Suttesája. At an event organized by the municipality and intended to inform the local people about the water prospecting venture, some local Sami attempted to initiate an indepth discussion on the collective cultural significance of the sacred site. Some others, however, turned the discussion into jokes about what they considered a "sacred" or a proper object of worship, such as a good-looking woman or the television (Kangas 2001: 15). A comment that equates a manifestation of the Sami worldview with worshipping women is not only trivializing and defamatory but also blatantly sexist and it demonstrates how colonialism and patriarchy intersect: the remark, which is intended as a joke, amalgamates the oppression of women and the denigration of Sami culture. Trivializing one's culture in this way also reflects the loss of cultural memory and displacement caused by various insidious colonial processes now linked with pressures of economic globalization. What is more, it assists and reinforces the arrogance and ignorance of the authorities and representatives of dominant society, including the municipality.

For the project coordinators, the venture represents a goldmine that will remedy the dire economics of the northernmost municipality of Finland (e.g., Vakkuri 2002, Ohcejohka/Utsjoki municipality 2002a). Pitting the economy of the municipality against the cultural and spiritual Sami values is inherently a questionable strategy that shows the unwillingness of the municipality to adequately address or deal with issues related to the rights of the Sami as an indigenous people. Instead, the municipality has repeatedly sought to cast any criticism of the project in a negative light as unheeded obstruction of selfish, irresponsiblse individuals who do not understand or care about the well-being or employment of local people (e.g., Väänänen 2001, Ohcejohka/Utsjoki municipality 2002b). The same attitude is reflected in the environmental and cultural impact surveys and assessments of the project, all conducted by individuals who either are involved in the project or who have in public expressed their support for water prospecting. Besides being partial, these surveys are also very limited and deficient (Kuokkanen 2002, Sergejeva 2002).

The blatant, sanctioned ignorance (cf. Spivak 1988, 1999) about cultural, historical, and political issues pertaining to Suttesája is also poignantly illustrated by the chair of the municipal council who is also a member of the coordinating committee of the project. A Finnish man, he is quoted as telling the audience of the briefing session that although he also has a personal sacred site in the Deatnu river, it would never cross his mind to demand that nobody is allowed to fish in the vicinity of his 'site' (Kangas 2001: 14). Comparing the concern of a collective heritage of an indigenous people to his own individual preference represents arrogance at its worst. It also demonstrates the prevailing lack of knowledge and understanding of the collective dimensions of indigenous issues and rights by representatives of dominant society, including those who are expected to be better informed in their roles as government authorities and decision makers. It is alarming to bear witness that the future of Suttesája, a sacred site for the Sami people and one of the largest natural springs in Europe, is in the hands of individuals who are not able to discern between somebody's individual ownership or access to a certain area and the collective rights of a people to culture that defines them and on which their survival is directly dependent.

The sanctioned ignorance of the decision makers, government authorities, and the general public is a result of the continuing colonial processes and practices. Colonialism or the critique of colonial discourses is and cannot, therefore, be an issue pertaining to only those who remain colonized. Particularly in the current situation, where the colonial processes and practices pave the way for economic globalization—which in the Suttesája case takes the form of commodification of fresh water—they are a concern that affects everybody and everything and to what we cannot really afford to close our eyes.

NOTES

1. Marja K. Bulmer is the author of the section "Sami Cultural Rights and Consultation in the Decision-Making Process."

2. "Samiland" or the so-called Sami home region has been defined in the Sami Parliament Act as including the three northernmost municipalities in Finland: Anár/Inari, Eanodat/Enontekiö, and Ohcejohka/Utsjoki as well as the northernmost reindeer herding district of Soaegilli/Sodankylä municipality.

3. This section is by Marja K. Bulmer.

4. The environmental impact assessment does not investigate the long-term effects of extracting water to the surrounding ecosystems, watersheds, or marshlands in spite of the fact that the Suttesája belongs to the marsh protection area. Similarly, the validity of the cultural and social impact assessment has been called into question as it does not consider the cultural significance of Suttesája in a balanced fashion but only presents information that supports the commercial exploitation of the sacred site. The complete lack of inclusion of oral tradition and history of the local Sami also comes as a surprise to many (e.g., Sergejeva [Porsanger] 2002).

5. Apart from the Constitution, the applicants rely on various international conventions ratified by Finland, including article 27 of the International Covenant on Civil and Political Rights, which provides that persons belonging to ethnic or other minorities shall not be denied the right, in community with other members of their group, to enjoy their own culture, December 19, 1966, 99 U.N.T.S. 171. It should be noted that the applicants were not able to directly rely on the International Labour Organization's (ILO) Convention No. 169 Concerning Indigenous and Tribal Peoples in Independent Countries (June 27, 1990) as Finland has so far refused to ratify the Convention.

6. The Sami cultural rights have not received much attention amongst the Finnish judiciary. The few cases that have addressed section 17:3 or article 27 have focused on the impact of logging and mining projects on reindeer herding, which has been determined to constitute an integral aspect of the Sami culture.

7. These principles of "good governance" are now codified in a new Administration Act that came into force after the municipality's decision was made.

8. Due to the border closures, reindeer pastoralism characterized by reindeer herding families migrating between their designated summer and winter grazing lands is no longer possible in Finland.

9. The Sami "religion" has drawn the attention of outsiders for centuries and it has been the subject of innumerable ethnographic, anthropological, and religious studies around the world. See, for instance, Ahlbäck (1987), Louise Bäckman and Åke Hultkrantz (1978), Holmberg (1987), Karsten (1952), Manker (1938, 1950), Pentikäinen (1995), Scheffer (1751), Sommarström (1991), and Vorren (1962).

10. Coined by Spivak (1985), othering refers to the various processes whereby imperial discourse produces its others. It is a dialectical process in which the coloniz-

ing Other is established simultaneously with its colonized others. Of all considerations of the concept of "race," Frantz Fanon (1961) was the first to analyze the objective psychological fact of "race" as a central part of the process of constructing individuals' perceptions of self.

11. This is also reflected in the Sami movement of the 1960s and 1970s which did not emphasize the significance of Sami values and worldview as a foundation in reclaiming and decolonizing Sami society and culture as many other indigenous peoples have done. Rather, the Sami political and cultural elite have focused on creating modern symbols of nation-building such as the flag and national anthem as well as establishment of institutions that are direct copies of their Nordic counterparts, demonstrating the thoroughness of the adoption of the values of dominant societies and their modern emblems of selfhood and identity.

REFERENCES

Ahlbäck, Tore, ed. *Saami Religion*. Stockholm: Almqvist & Wiksell, 1987.

Aikio, Samuli. *Olbmot ovdal min. Sámiid historjá 1700-logu rádjái*. Sámi Instituhtta/ Girjegiisá Oy, Ohcejohka, 1992.

Ashcroft, Bill, Gareth Griffiths, and Helen Tiffin. *Post-Colonial Studies. The Key Concepts*. London & New York: Routledge, 2000.

Barlow, Maude, and Tony Clarke. *Blue Gold: The Battle Against Corporate Theft of the World's Water*. Toronto: M & S, 2002.

Bäckman, Louise, and Åke Hultkrantz, ed. *Studies in Lapp Shamanism*. Acta Universitatis Stockholmiensis. Stockholm Studies in Comparative Religion 16. Stockholm: Almqvist & Wiksell, 1978.

Daes, Erika-Irene. "Indigenous Peoples and Their Relationship with Land." Final Working Paper. United Nations Economic and Social Council, Commission on Human Rights Sub-Commission on the Promotion and Protection of Human Rights, 52nd session, June 30, 2002.

Fanon, Frantz. *The Wretched of the Earth*. Harmondsworth: Penguin, 1961.

Guissé, El Hadji. "Working Paper on Globalization and the Economic, Social and Cultural Rights of Indigenous Populations." Working Group on Indigenous Populations, United Nations Commission on Human Rights, 2003. E/CN.4/Sub.2/ AC.4/2003/14.

Hall, Anthony J. *American Empire and the Fourth World: The Bowl with One Spoon. Part One*. Toronto: McGill-Queen's U P, 2003.

Harle, Vilho, and Sami Moisio. *Missä on Suomi? Kansallisen identiteettipolitiikan historia ja geopolitiikka*. Tampere: Vastapaino, 2000.

Holmberg, Uno. Lapparnas Religion. Uppsala: Multiethnic Papers 10, 1987.

Hubert, Jane. *Sacred Beliefs and Beliefs of Sacredness. Sacred Sites, Sacred Places*. Ed. David L. Carmichael, Jane Hubert, Brian Reeves, and Audhild Schanche. London & New York: Routledge, 1994.

Indigenous Peoples and Globalization Program. International Forum of Globalization, San Francisco, 2003. <http://www.ifg.org/programs/indig.htm>

Juuso, Inga. "Yoiking Acts as Medicine for Me." *No Beginning, No End. The Sami*

Speak Up. Ed. Elina Helander and Kaarina Kailo. Edmonton: Canadian Circumpolar Institute/ Nordic Sami Institute, 1998. 132–46.

Kailo, Kaarina. 2002. "Sukupuoli, Teknologia ja Valta. Nais-ja miesrepresentaatiot Kalevalasta Ööpiseen." *Tieto ja Tekniikka*. *Missä on Nainen*. Ed. Riitta Smeds, Kaisa Kauppinen, and Kati Yrjänheikki ja Anitta Valtonen. Helsinki: Tek, Esaprint.

Kangas, Kirsi. "Pyhästä Vedestä Paha Riita Utsjoella." [A Terrible Quarrel over Sacred Water in Utsjoki]. *Apu* 4 April 2002: 12–17.

Karsten, Rafael. *Samefolkets Religion: De Nordiska Lapparnas Hedniska Tro och Kult i Religionshistorisk Belysning*. Helsingfors: Söderström, 1952.

Kjellström, Rolf. "On the Continuity of Old Saami Religion." *Saami Religion: Based on Papers at the Symposium on Saami Religion Held in Turku, Finland 16–18 August 1984*. Ed. Tore Ahlbäck. Åbo: The Donner Institute for Research in Religious and Cultural History, 1987, 24–33.

Kojo, Raimo O. "Pyhän Lähteen Pullotus." [Bottling the Sacred Spring.] *Lapin Kansa*, 6 September 2002.

Kuokkanen, Rauna. Analysis of the Cultural Study of Suttesája by Pieski and Halinen submitted to the Municipality of Ohcejohka/Utsjoki, 2002.

Lehtola, Veli-Pekka. 1994. *Saamelainen evakko. Rauhan kansa sodan jaloissa*. Vaasa: City Sámit.

———. "Saamelainen kirjallisuus vanhan ja uuden risteyksessä." *Marginalia ja kirjallisuus. Ääniä suomalaisen kirjallisuuden reunoilta*. Ed. Matti Savolainen. Helsinki: SKS, 1995. 36–89.

Lehtola, Teuvo. 1996. *Lapinmaan vuosituhannet. Saamelaisten ja Lapin historia kivikaudelta 1930-luvulle*. Inari: Kustannus Puntsi.

Manker, Ernst. *Die Lappische Zaubertrommel 1. Acta Lapponica I*. Stockholm, 1938.

———. *Die Lappische Zaubertrommel 2. Acta Lapponica VI*. Uppsala, 1950.

Mulk, Inga-Maria. "Sacrificial Places and Their Meaning in Saami Society." *Sacred Sites, Sacred Places*. Ed. David L. Carmichael, Jane Hubert, Brian Reeves, and Audchild Schanche. London and New York: Routledge, 1994, 121–31.

Pentikäinen, Juha. *Saamelaiset—Pohjoisen Kansan Mytologia*. Helsinki: SKS, 1995.

Porsanger, Jelena. "A Close Relationship to Nature—the Basis of Religion." *Siiddastallan. From Lapp Communities to Modern Sámi Life*. Ed. Jukka Pennanen and Klemetti Näkkäläjärvi. Trans. Kaija Anttonen and Linna Weber Müller-Wille. Inari: Siida Inari Sámi Museum, 2004, 151–54.

Pound, Roscoe. *Outline on Lectures on Jurisprudence*. 4th ed. Cambridge: Harvard University Press, 1928.

Sara, Iisko. "Muukalainen omalla maallaan." *Bálggis. Polku. Sámi cuvgehussearvi 1932–1982 Lapin Sivistysseura*. Jyväskylä: Gummerus, 1984, 41–44.

Scheffer, Johannes. *The History of Lapland: Shewing the Original, Manner, Habits, Religion and Trade of that People: with a Particular Account of Their Gods and Sacrifices, Marriage Ceremonies, Conjurations, Diabolical Rites, &c. &c. 1673*. London: R. Griffiths, 1751.

Sergejeva [Porsanger], Jelena. "Pentti Pieski rapporta Suttesádjaga birra." [Pentti Pieski's Report on Suttesája.] *Min Áigi*, 30 April 2002.

Sommarström, Bo. *The Saami Shaman's Drum and the Star Horizon*. Stockholm: Scripta Instituti Donneriani XVI, 1991.

Smith, Claire, and Graeme K. Ward, ed. *Indigenous Cultures in an Interconnected World*. Vancouver: UBC Press, 2000.

Spivak, Chakravorty Gayatri. "The Rani of Simur." *Europe and Its Others*. Vol. 1 Proceedings of the Essex Conference on the Sociology of Literature. Ed. Francis Baker, et al. Colchester: University of Essex, 1985.

———. *In Other Worlds. Essays in Cultural Politics*. New York: Routledge, 1988.

———. *A Critique of Postcolonial Reason. Toward a History of the Vanishing Present*. Cambridge: Harvard UP, 1999.

Ohcejohka/Utsjoki municipality 2002a. "Utsjoen kunnan Natura-arviointi Sulaojan lähdevesialueesta." [The Ohcejohka/Utsjoki Natura Assessment of the Natural Spring of Suttesája.] Statement Delivered to the Ministry of Environment in Finland. June 25.

Ohcejohka/Utsjoki municipality 2002b. The Board of Utsjoki Municipality. Minutes of the Meeting, Agenda Item No. 267. October 29.

Vahtola, Jouko. "Lapin valtaus historiallisessa katsannossa." *Faravid* 15 (1991): 335–55.

Vakkuri, Marjukka. "Utsjoki aikoo tehdä vedestä veturin." [Utsjoki is planning to make water into a driving force.] *Lapin Kansa*, 3 February 2002.

Vorren, Ørnulf. *Lapp Life and Customs*. London & New York, Oxford UP, 1962.

Väänänen, Veikko. "Toimeentulo Säilyttää Saamelaisuuden."[Income preserves Saminess.] *Lapin Kansa*, 31 October 2001.

Ås, Berit. *The Five Master Suppression Techniques. Study Booklet Accompany* [sic] *the Video*. Ed. Eva Lundberg. Växjö Municipality Equal Opportunities Committee. n.d.

WGIP 2003. "Report of the Working Group on Indigenous Populations on Its 21st Session." United Nations Commission on Human Rights. E/CN.4/Sub.2/2003/22.

15

What Lies Beneath? Cultural Excavation in Neocolonial Martinique

Renée Gosson

> The politics of ecology has implications for populations that are deci-
> mated or threatened with disappearance as a people.[1]

INTRODUCTION

In more ways than one, the official departmentalization in 1946 of the island
of Martinique *cemented* an already oppressive relationship between this former colony and France. Not only did it solidify the centuries-old dynamic
of economic exploitation, it also initiated a whole new set of assimilationist
practices on environmental and cultural levels. The French politics of assimilation introduced onto Martinican soil a series of standardizing effects that
would attempt to reconfigure the Martinican political, economic, and cultural landscape in its own image:

> The assimilationist ideology operates within a negation of space. Martinicans
> are so fascinated by France, and they so desperately want to be French, that
> they take all their models of social and urban development and *graft* them onto
> the French West Indian landscape, without any consideration for the geographi-
> cal and ecological realities of the French Caribbean. And this creates an incredi-
> ble devastation to nature.[2]

This study examines the various ways in which one culture grafts itself upon
another. Those most concerned with resisting the *francisation*[3] of the Creole
landscape and founding a Martinican national identity independent of

France insist that identity must begin with a psychic rootedness in the land. This is especially important, of course, for a people that has been disinherited geographically, historically, and culturally. Such is the case in the French West Indies, where the majority of the population is of African descent: "The French West Indian is a descendant of slaves: Dispossessed of both time and space, s/he is uprooted. . . . Geographically alienated, s/he is also excluded from History (with a capital H): that of the Center, of France."[4]

According to Édouard Glissant in an interview with Priska Degras and Bernard Magnier, all cultural zones formerly organized by plantation systems have in common a preoccupation with cultural amnesia and the loss of origins. These societies experience a need to establish a connectedness with their surroundings which lends meaning to their presence in that land: "It is necessary to establish the legitimacy of the inhabitant on his/her land in anchoring him/her in a sense of permanence, of recovered time."[5] Regaining a sense of community with place is a necessary step toward founding an identity.

This process is hindered, however, by French *bétonisation*,[6] which is quite literally coating the Martinican countryside with roads, parking lots, and other cement markers of modernization. This *bétonisation* symbolically continues a tradition of separating a subjugated people from its land, albeit on an entirely different level. For Glissant, the polluted countryside is itself evidence of cultural alienation. He writes:

> Martinique is becoming increasingly sterilized (what a joke to sing Madinina *Island of flowers* when one can travel several kilometers without seeing a flower—except for those cultivated for exportation—or, in the middle of the country, not see or hear a bird)—no need to refer to *rousseauisme* to know that this relationship between man and nature (a nature that he doesn't change by his work since the modifications that occur through construction, homes, crops, [and] enterprise are initiated *elsewhere*) is symbolic of his alienation: The Martinican has been separated from his land, from his environment.[7]

Attempts to take root in the new land are continuously denied. Not only is the natural landscape being physically covered with concrete, but the link to a cultural past embedded in that land is metaphorically severed.

The central metaphor which links the themes of landscape and identity in this article is one of *covering over*: Covering over the landscape with symbols of development and progress (buildings, roads, marinas, airports, etc.); covering over history as so much of Caribbean history has been silenced, obliterated, and forgotten; and covering over the culture, identity, and imagination of a people who have been taught that the only valuable part of their identity and history is that part which is French.

Posed then as a series of questions, this discussion raises the following: What is the relationship between landscape and cultural identity? To what extent is the environmental devastation on the island of Martinique an extension of French colonialism and France's continued sense of ownership, proprietorship, and entitlement on this island? What are the less obvious, cultural effects of over three centuries of French presence on this island?

In an attempt to answer these questions, I will examine several responses from French West Indian cultural representatives. All self-proclaimed ecologists, these writers and musicians adhere to the motto of Martinique's most prominent ecological association, ASSAUPAMAR,[8] which "opposes the destruction of Martinique's natural beauty and her archeological and historical sites, and . . . takes a firm stand against any further upsetting of an already fragile ecological balance in what remains of the country's mangroves and forests by money-hungry developers, urban planners, and highway builders."[9] Through their writing and song, these cultural ecologists voice their reaction against the dependency of Martinique on the French and the effects this continued occupation is having on the land and psyche of their people.

AN ECOCRITICAL APPROACH

There is an undeniable intersection between ecological concerns in the French West Indies and cultural production from Martinique. Land is necessarily central to any discussion of post-colonialism and even more so when we engage in conversation about those geographical areas, like the French West Indies and specifically the island of Martinique which, in many ways (politically, economically, culturally and ecologically), continues to be occupied and dominated by France today.

It can be argued that the island of Martinique deserves special attention in speaking about the cultural and ecological impact of development. First of all, as a former colony of France, Martinique has suffered a legacy of exploitation. From the very moment the French came into brutal contact with the island's indigenous Carib and Arawak populations, to the capture, transport, and enslavement of African peoples, to a continued sense of economic entitlement, the French presence in Martinique has been a harmful one. Second, the small geographical character of Martinique leaves it especially vulnerable to accelerated effects of pollution: "(a) islands are discrete and finite in extent, with a fixed endowment of resources; and (b) they are ecologically fragile and concomitantly vulnerable to the destructive effects of modern-day development technology."[10] Third, the ecological content of the island of Martinique is what distinguishes it from France. When overdevelopment and the French politics of assimilation threaten to politically, culturally, and topologically transform Martinique into a miniature France, it becomes extremely urgent to assert and protect those areas which distinguish Martinique from the *mainland*.

A CERTAIN PREOCCUPATION
WITH THE LANDSCAPE

It is by no coincidence that the literature and theory to emerge out of Martinique, especially in the past ten years, have taken an ecological turn. Martinican novelists, such as Édouard Glissant, Patrick Chamoiseau, and Raphaël
Confiant routinely situate their fiction in ecologically menaced natural
spaces in order to dramatize the cultural face-off at stake between Creole
and French cultures. Likewise, these French West Indian post-colonial theoreticians make extensive use of the mangrove swamp as a metaphor for the
racially—and culturally—diverse nature of French West Indian society
which has seen the arrival, and eventual hybridization, of different branches
of European colonizers, African slaves, and indentured laborers from East
India, Syria, Lebanon, and China. What does it mean then when oftentimes
the same writers, who use the mangrove swamp as a metaphor for Creole
identity in their fiction and theory, are also deeply entrenched in an environmental battle to protect Martinique's mangroves from becoming landfill
sites? What *is* the relationship between landscape and cultural identity?
Between environmental devastation and neocolonialism?

FALSE CHRONOLOGY

In order to situate Martinique within its geographical and historical context,
it is useful to examine a chronology of Martinican history as drawn up by
the prominent French West Indian novelist, poet, and theoretician, Édouard
Glissant. In his first chapter of *Caribbean Discourse*, Glissant calls our attention to certain dates and events that define what has come to be known as
Martinican history, namely the discovery of Martinique by Christopher
Columbus in 1502; the arrival of the French in 1635 (which also marked the
beginning of the extermination of Martinique's indigenous population and
its replacement by African slaves); the abolition of slavery in 1848; and the
Departmentalization of the island in 1946.[11]
 Upon closer examination, the reader observes that what is before her/him
is more than a simple list of significant dates, but a critique of its over-simpli-
fication, one-sidedness, and ultimate falsification of the real history of this
island. This irony is discerned in (1) the heading of "DISPOSSESSION" in
all capital letters; (2) the calling into question of the validity of such a view of
history in such phrases as "the chronological illusion;" and (3) the quotation
marking of "facts," "Discovery," and "economic" assimilation. As if these
signs of resistance are not enough, Glissant closes this chronological table
by stating that "The whole Caribbean history of Martinique remains to be
discovered." Glissant is obviously calling into question the imposition of

colonial History, with a capital "H." He is exposing the legacy of historical cover-up, which has buried collective memory and welded an "official" one in its place.

WHAT LIES BENEATH

About eight years after the publication of Édouard Glissant's *Caribbean Discourse*, three other Martinican theoreticians and, like Glissant, intellectual descendants of Aimé Césaire, continue this diatribe against the persistence of French colonial presence on their island in their manifesto entitled *In Praise of Creoleness*:[12]

> Our history (or more precisely our histories) is shipwrecked in colonial history. . . . What we believe to be Caribbean history is just the history of the colonization of the Caribbeans. Between the currents of the history of France, between the great dates of the governors' arrivals and departures, between the beautiful white pages of the chronicle (where the surges of our rebellions appear only as small spots), there was the obstinate progress of ourselves. . . . This happened with no witnesses, or rather with no testimonies. . . . And the history of colonization which we took as ours aggravated our loss, our self-defamation; it favored exteriority and fed the estrangement of the present. Within this false memory we had but a pile of obscurities as our memory. . . . [O]ur history (or our histories) is not totally accessible to historians. Their methodology restricts them to the sole colonial chronicle. Our chronicle is *beneath* the dates, *beneath* the known facts.[13]

It is this very idea of real Caribbean history as existing beneath the earth's surface that concerns us here. Glissant has repeatedly spoken of the Martinican landscape as the only thing to convey, in its nonanthropomorphic way, some of the tragedy of colonization. The Creolists also speak to this idea of true Martinican history—and by extension, true Martinican identity—as existing not just beneath the rhetoric of Western history, but quite literally *under a layer of Frenchness*. They say that in order to retrieve that part of themselves that has been lost, they must, "Somewhat like with the process of archeological excavations: when the field was covered . . . proceed with light strokes of the brush so as not to alter or lose any part of ourselves *hidden beneath French ways*."[14]

According to the proponents of the most recent identity theories to emerge out of the French-speaking Caribbean, part of why Martinique's landscape is so sacred is because it is the country's only witness and recorder of over three centuries of continuous colonial entitlement, proprietorship, and exploitation. Beginning with the "discovery" of Martinique by Christopher Columbus, its possession by French colonizers, the over 200 years of slave trade and dehumanizing labor in the sugarcane fields, and today, the destruction of the ecosystem, the land itself is a powerful, but endangered, repository for the collective memory and consciousness which is not represented in the history books Martinicans study at school. Physically cementing over the natural landscape, then, can only have disastrous consequences for the preservation of a memory already occulted beneath the rhetoric of Western history.

FROM *BETONISATION* TO *FRANCISATION*

The transformation of the French West Indies into actual overseas departments of France gave rise to a number of devastating trends on economic, ecological and cultural levels: the economic destruction of the traditional productive economy and its replacement by one based on the passive consumption of imported goods; the loss of local political control, since essentially all decisions are handed down from the *métropole*, which often fails to take into account the particularities of the island departments when making decisions appropriate for the *hexagone*; the outward migration of French West Indians to France, where they escape the unemployment of their homeland, all the while participating in the system which occasioned it in the first place. To these, we must add the non-critical adoption of French values and culture, including patterns of consumption and lifestyle; and the consequent dilution and even exoticization of Creole culture.[15]

Patrick Chamoiseau describes the literally and figuratively transformed French West Indian landscape at the moment of Departmentalization as follows:

> Following the law of 1946, the country began to change rapidly: Constructions in king-cement, windows, electricity, traffic lights, television, automobile craze, triumphant low-income housing, sewage, Social Security, welfare, planes, roads and highways, schools, clothing stores, hotels, supermarkets, advertising.[16]

Clearly, Departmentalization affected Martinique on several different levels.

For Raphaël Confiant, *bétonisation* results from the disappearance of an economic system: "Why cultivate the land when you can put a gas station on it, or a hotel, or a supermarket that will earn much more?!"[17] Ecologically speaking, the physical landscape of Martinique is suffering symptoms of overdevelopment. The remorseless spread of concrete used to build condominiums, marinas, and supermarkets is irreparably transforming the island's natural space. Consider, for example, the land filling of the mangrove swamp to make room for the Lamentin airport, and the "colonization" of the hills by secondary residences and access roads.[18] As harbingers of modernization clear and replace the agriculturally rich terrain, a deeper, more insidious process of displacement is taking place on a cultural level.

The massive importation of French manufactured goods, "clothes, shoes, furniture, household implements,"[19] and the consequential transformation of a traditional agriculturally based economy into a consumer-oriented one has had far-reaching effects for French West Indians, who consume much more than tangible objects, but another lifestyle which is threatening their existing one. After Departmentalization, in addition to the importation of French cars and food items, Martinique and Guadeloupe experienced the introduction of mass media—French television, radio, cinema, and news—which contributed to the direct transmission of the more abstract and less detectable metropolitan values to the islands. The establishment of French educational and social security systems also solidified dependency and exteriorization.

According to Burton, the islands of Martinique and Guadeloupe have slowly become detached from those elements which define Creole culture: traditional skills, lore, customs, and language. French West Indians have lost their connectedness to their past, and to their land, as a result of economic and political occupation by France and the imposition of French cultural values. This cultural displacement is a major concern for Édouard Glissant, who sees a parallel between the consumption of imported goods and cultural alienation. In his *Caribbean Discourse* he speaks out against this process of economic and cultural displacement:

> The passive consumption or the non-critical adoption of exterior products (newspapers, literature of alienation, theatre, TV and radio programs, and even moral traits—without even mentioning the common products of consumption: We literally import everything, refined sugar, yogurt, eggs, lettuce, milk, and so on) does not however signify an openness to the outside world.[20]

Glissant indicts his own people for their complicity ("passive consumption," "non-critical adoption") in this culturally devastating process.

French West Indians have grown accustomed to a rapidly elevated lifestyle. Their economic and political association with France invites them to compare their standard of living with that of the *hexagone* and not that of their neighboring islands. Their *embourgeoisment* and complacency are linked as their comfortable social status anesthetizes them to the ill effects such a dependency is having on their culture: "The country is becoming increasingly impoverished, but the standard of living masks its inescapable economic decline."[21] Inherently less perceptible, such intangible forms of assimilation (schools, movies, social security) are easily introduced into an increasingly less resilient Creole environment. As indicated here, Martinicans willingly adopt a new comfortable lifestyle because they don't recognize the potential for indigenous economic decay.

UNDER A DIFFERENT GUISE . . .

Indeed, the most dangerous feature of this new form of colonialism is found in its insidiousness often characterized as "silent" or "invisible." Not only, as Chamoiseau suggests below, does modernization invalidate the accusations against any form of cultural imperialism, it also acts as an opiate in sugarcoating the reality of continued cultural subjugation: "Under welfare, we were no longer hungry. We no longer swooned in this shell of dependency. The surface wealth embalmed our soul."[22] In his *Écrire en pays dominé*, Chamoiseau records his reaction to this maliciously subtle process of brainwashing. Beneath the painted rhetoric of economic development and political promises, he discerns the actuality of exploitation:

> Underneath this varnish, my questions attacked, in vain, the invisible lines of disaster. Why this almost entire disappearance of real production? Why this exponential curve of massive importations? Why this bustling of producers on subsidies? Why this extreme alienation at school and in the media? Why this weakening of Creole values, this mimetic consumption of Western norms, this hyperbolic assistantship? From where was this exclusive desire to obtain the same advantages of French citizens coming? Losing all intensity, the fight for Creole language and culture folklorized. What we used to oppose to the former colonialists hitherto floated in a formalin of seductive values that anesthetized us. No more obvious enemies. Only an auto-decomposition.[23]

Like other French West Indian writers, Chamoiseau dares to call into question what goes otherwise unnoticed by a society content with its newly acquired wealth, a society which doesn't recognize its own indoctrination into the assimilationist system. As Chamoiseau himself clearly suggests, one dangerous characteristic about this system is that it is nearly impossible to detect ("invisible lines," "No more obvious enemies"). In addition, the repetition of the word "Why" in this litany of questions reveals the author's exasperation in fighting, "in vain," what has become an invisible enemy. As colorless and toxic as *formalin*, European values anesthetize French West Indian consumers to their cultural loss.

The insidiousness of continued colonial exploitation is a major preoccupation for contemporary Martinican writers. In their novels, they expose the persistence of the master-slave dynamic of pre-Abolition. For them, colonialism, and the cultural imperialism it encapsulates, resurfaces in a myriad of much less perceptible forms. Édouard Glissant states, "It is no longer a matter of nineteenth century colonization with its pure and simple exploitation of the country, but of something more."[24] Likewise, Chamoiseau detects the colonial lip service underneath the dissimulating guise of "progress": "The silent domination cloaks itself with progressive modernity, democratic access and unstoppable economic virtues."[25] Indeed, it is the task of the French West Indian writer to *dig beneath these surface privileges* in order to expose a continued presence of subjugation.

Because this domination is both "silent" and "invisible," we must learn alternative ways of reading the signs of a "fight without witnesses."[26] French West Indian writers, such as Glissant and Chamoiseau, suggest that one way to identify traces of this imperialism is in the landscape. According to these authors, the land harbors, at the same time, the most obvious symptoms of oppression and the most latent traces of the French West Indian past, if we learn to read it.

MARTINIQUE THEME PARK

At the beginning of his *Caribbean Discourse*, Édouard Glissant compares the rapid mutation of his homeland's natural landscape to an amusement park where cultural subjugation is themed: "A Martinican political figure imagined as a bitter joke that in the year 2100, tourists would be invited by satellite advertisement to visit this island and gain firsthand knowledge of 'what a colony was like in past centuries.' "[27] Here Glissant invites his readers to consider the persistence of colonial elements that have permeated French West Indian history. Under what circumstances would the island of Martinique be transformed into a sort of colonial theme park where certain elements of its enslaved past are preserved?

In more ways than one, the former Plantation Leyritz in Basse-Pointe is a vestige of Martinique's colonial past. Now a bed and breakfast with manicured lawns, flower gardens, and a rum tasting room, tourists pay the equivalent of $125 per night to sleep in former slave huts and experience *what it was like to live on a plantation in pre-Abolition Martinique*. The tourist experience is arguably closer to what it may have been like to live on a plantation as a plantation- and slaveowner. However, before 1848, even the richest of *békés* did not have drywall, plumbing, or air conditioning, not to mention telephones or television. The point is that there is an unmistakable link between physically tampering with the remaining vestiges of Martinique's past and the dissimulation, and some would say, violation, of the history embedded in that space.

According to Glissant, the landscape of Martinique is so sacred because it is a witness to the years of otherwise unrecorded subjugation of the French West Indian people: "Martinican history is a long succession of what we call a fight without witnesses."[28] The landscape functions as a repository for a misrepresented past: "Landscape retains the memory of time past."[29] Consequently, any gesture of destruction against that land is portrayed as an act of violence against the collective memory of the past. The land, states Beverly Ormerod, is the past's "only true guardian ... history waits, latent, in Caribbean nature, which is filled with sorrowful reminders of slavery and regression."[30]

Oruno Lara compares the slave system of forced labor to that of the Holocaust: "Before the Nazi extermination camps (Chelmno, Belzec, Sobibor, Treblinka), the concentration camps on the plantations of the slave system (sixteenth–nineteenth centuries) were also death camps."[31] Unlike Auschwitz and Dachau, however, Martinicans have not preserved these spaces of oppression as *lieux de mémoire*. Instead, as illustrated by the former plantation turned bed and breakfast, these historical loci of oppression are being symbolically, and irreparably, transformed into spaces of commercialization and consumption.

POLITICS OF COMMEMORATION

Another powerful example of the process of covering up is found in the commemorative naming of geographical places on the island and in the numerous statues, monuments, plaques and other commemorative sites covering the island that celebrate the colonial conquest of Martinique. Take, for example, the very commemorative naming of various landmarks and streets on the island:

> In Fort-de-France, Schoelcher street, Schoelcher high school, Schoelcher library and, a few kilometers further, the town of Schoelcher where, by the way, the university is situated, are all there to sustain memory. In the town center, the streets named after Arago, Lamartine, Garnier-Pagès, etc., reinforce the mnemonic device.[32]

The naming of the capital's primary streets after various French historical and literary figures is a concrete example of how Martinique's landscape has been topologically and culturally welded in celebration of another nation's history. Statues, plaques and monuments also serve to embellish a certain version of Martinique's historical past. Made of marble, cement, bronze, and other equally durable materials, statues immortalize more than examples of French "heroism." They also serve to coat minds with what the colonizers want Martinicans to believe about their past. In his article entitled "Trois statues: Le Conquistador, l'Impératrice et le Libérateur: Pour une sémiotique de l'histoire coloniale de la Martinique," Richard D.E. Burton conducts a semiotic reading of three of Martinique's most recognized and visited statues erected in celebration of the following: (1) Pierre Belain Desnambuc, first French colonizer in Martinique; (2) Victor Schoelcher, the French abolitionist; and (3) Joséphine de Beauharnais, the Creole wife of Napoléon I.

According to Burton, these statues can be read as a "marbled summary" of colonial history in Martinique.[33] Each statue, in its own way, represents a different mythic concretization of the France-Martinique relationship that continues to reflect and inform the Martinican imagination today. Erected in 1935 in celebration of the 300th year of French colonization in Martinique,[34] the towering statue of Desnambuc greets Martinicans and visitors alike at the bay of Fort-de-France. This statue immortalizes Martinique's first colonizer in a striking pose: triumphantly waving to incoming French ships. Today this same statue greets hordes of tourists aboard cruise liners. During a recent interview, I asked Patrick Chamoiseau about this statue. He commented:

> Desnambuc? He's the one who eliminated all the Amerindians. . . . Dedicating the place of honor to a statue that represents slavery is the equivalent of erecting a statue to Hitler in Israel, or to any other human torturer. This is an aberration that continues today and people are offended.[35]

Chamoiseau reminds the observer of this statue that acts of "discovery" and "colonization" were not without bloodshed and death. According to him, we must interrogate those spaces on the island that go too easily unnoticed or unquestioned and which are ultimately revealing of a colonial agenda.

A second important site of commemoration is the statue of Victor Schoelcher who is officially accredited with liberating the Martinicans from slavery, even though there exists an unofficial version of liberation which involves, on the eve of Abolition (May 22, 1848), an uprising of Martinican slaves *who freed themselves* before the official word (pronounced in France on April 27, 1848) reached them by boat from France.[36] Here, the practice of embracing and commemorating one version of this history over another is very revealing of an attempt to promote an *indebtedness-to-France* sentiment in Martinique, which is best summarized as follows: It is the benevolent "mother" France who gave freedom to her Martinican "children" who owe her eternal gratefulness. This mentality of indebtedness has come to be known as *schoelchérism* which, according to Marie-José Jolivet, is "the popularity of Schoelcher linked with his abolitionist acts, the memory of which inscribes itself in collective memory in the construction of the instrument of a new credo: that of the grand and generous Mother Country."[37] This myth is embodied in the very posture of the Schoelcher statue in Fort-de-France: a tall, white Schoelcher gently bends over a small, black slave girl whose chains have been broken by her paternal benefactor. One immediately notices the softness of his expression and the protectiveness of his posture, gratefully received by the recently liberated slave girl who lovingly and upwardly blows a kiss of gratitude up to Schoelcher.[38] This monument, and the one of Desnambuc, replace the memory of colonialism and slavery with images of brave exploration and the gracious bestowing of universal liberties. Likewise, at the moment of her inauguration, the statue of Joséphine served more than to embellish the capital with another work of public art. Like the other statues, this monument and the myth that surrounds it, serve to naturalize a certain historical relationship between France and Martinique.[39]

It is especially interesting to consider the timeliness of this statue, that is to say that the discussion of its creation took place right at that moment when there was intense debate in the colony and in France about the possibility of abolition. The decision to create a marbled tribute to Joséphine carried with it an attempt to naturalize the colonial couple Napoléon-Joséphine / France-Martinique. If Napoléon I is colonial France, with all its imperial masculine power, then it follows that Martinique, naturally, is Joséphine: "Joséphine is Martinique, Martinique is Joséphine . . . both are supple, natural, soft."[40] What better way, then, to remind the *békés*[41] and slaves alike of the glorious and divine union of France and Martinique than to erect a statue to Joséphine, herself born and raised on the island?

> One can see that Joséphine is a feminine presence fashioned to replace, soften and disguise under her chiffon, lace and gauze and under the softness of her maternal gaze, an essentially masculine and patriarchal power: that of the white plantation owner and slave holder, that of Imperial France.[42]

In addition to effeminizing Martinique, this statue serves to mask the colonial relationship maintained by France. Fortunately, Richard D.E. Burton is not alone in his criticism of the irony behind this statue. From its very inception, the Martinican public also expressed displeasure at the commemoration of what, for them, was a dubious historical figure. Alfred Parépou's novel *Atipa: Roman guyanais* includes a description of the Joséphine statue just moments after her inauguration:

> "Did you ever hear of Napoleon," asked Atipa, "who used to be a general over there in France? . . . He married a woman from Martinique and cancelled emancipation so that the blacks wouldn't stop working in the canefields of his father-in-law. And the day they raised a statue to his wife in Martinique, a black man covered it all over with shit. It was the only thing he could think of doing. They sentenced him to three months."[43]

This literary description of an unmistakable act of resistance is interesting to this discussion for two reasons. First, given the operating metaphor in this paper of "covering over," I find it absolutely fascinating that a Martinican would cover the statue with his own feces. Second, in a more recent gesture of resistance, the "beheading" of the Joséphine statue, a group of university students also allegedly spray painted, in red paint and in Creole, "Respect for Martinique" on one side and "Respect for May 22" on the other. This Revolutionary act of beheading is rendered even more symbolic by this layer of paint that recalls a significant, although unofficial date in the history of Martinican resistance. In this way, this gesture, and the fecal one, become acts of re-covering Martinican history, in both meanings of the term. Vandalized, desacralized and *graffitied*, these sites of historical and mnemonic manipulation are rendered sites of resistance. It is into this same lineage of resistance that Martinican cultural representatives inscribe themselves.

ISLAND FOR SALE

Brenda Berrian's recent publication, *Awakening Spaces: French Caribbean Popular Songs, Music, and Culture* (2002) is an important contribution to the study of French West Indian music and culture. Her book "focuses on how vocalists, songwriters, and musicians from Martinique (and sometimes Guadeloupe) have treated the themes of empowerment and identity in their song lyrics from 1970 until 1996."[44] Berrian prefaces her work by stating that music is more accessible than literature (which she calls "high-culture") to the Martinican public because it "crosses class lines, [and] is played and heard everywhere: the homes, the supermarkets, the streets, the beaches, the restaurants, and the market places."[45] Music then is potentially a more effective medium for social protest than literature because it penetrates some of those spaces where the role of language and culture is the most menaced.

Chapter 4 of this book, "Cultural Politics and Black Resistance as Sites of Struggle," examines songs that voice their resistance against injustice and cultural denigration and emphasize the "importance of knowing one's history, roots, categories of identity, and the ecological preservation of Martinique."[46] These select songs verge from the most common theme in French-Caribbean music, which is, according to Berrian, "heterosexual love." Instead, these songs are a reaction against the increased dependency of the French Caribbean islands on France.

Berrian discusses one songwriter who is of particular interest to my study here. The Martinican born Kali is known for his social justice consciousness: "Affectionately called 'the banjo man,' Kali reevaluates Martinican culture, and he is praised for constructing an archeological image of it through his music with up-to-date changes."[47] Kali inscribes himself into a cultural political space that echoes the environmental preoccupations of his theoretical counterparts discussed earlier. Like them, Kali is aware of what is happening to his country. Like them, he is culturally engaged in an attempt to protect his "island's natural landscape, language, and agricultural products against homogenization."[48] An ecologist, "Kali draws attention to how detrimental this development has been to the green spaces rather than to the oft-touted 'progress' that bétonisation is made out to be."[49]

The very cover of his 1991 album, which pictures a Martinique literally covered by skyscrapers, roads, residences, cars and a big sign that reads, in French, "Island for sale," is a good indication of what the title track is about.[50] Although a catchy tune, this song has a very sarcastic undertone, which is ultimately very appropriate for the subject at hand. Kali paints at first a pleasant picture of the island, with typical tourist attractions: "a very beautiful tropical terrain"[51] where "the sun shines all year round," this "coconut paradise" at first glance is an ideal vacation destination. However, there is much more lurking just beneath the glistening surface of this tropical paradise.

One soon discovers that the unflinching beauty and comfort of the island are artificial: The trade winds are programmed and the beaches *guaranteed* to have coconut trees on them. Words such as "programmées" and "garanties" suggest that there is an invisible manipulation at play behind a seemingly natural beauty. Indeed, there is something very *unnatural* about all this nature, which is manipulated to cater to the consumer's pleasure. In addition, the visitor is protected from any discomfort or danger on both physical and social levels. Natural disasters are *controlled*, including the eruptions of Mt. Pelé, thanks to reinforced *cemented* cliff walls. In addition, the island's feared snakes have been *anesthetized* and cyclones *rerouted* away from the island.

In Kali's song, Martinique has been fully "proofed" from danger for the pleasure and safe consumption of the tourist and potential buyer of this island paradise. And it is not only the unbridled and savage nature of this island's landscape that has been tamed. The narrator assures us that the "indigenous peoples" are inoffensive and would never even dream of revolution: "Revolution? Oh non! Here, the revolutionaries are state employees." It is here that Kali strikes his most stinging blow for he accuses the island inhabitants of being co-opted, themselves consumers of a commodified culture.

Berrian suggests that one of the possible goals in Kali's song is to awaken Martinicans from their unconsciousness. Like the anesthetized snakes, "lethargic Martinicans had to be awakened from their slumber."[52] This goal is similar to Édouard Glissant's project of making "Martiniquans aware of the potential for the *pays natal* to become little more than an amusement park for metropolitan visitors."[53] The transformation of Martinique into a sort of *ersatz* or *virtual* island is precisely what Kali describes in "Island for sale." All the controlled conditions give the impression that Martinique is a fake, theme park version of Martinique, with its artificial wind, planted coconut trees, and cement volcano.[54]

CONCLUSION

According to Édouard Glissant, land is absolutely central to any discussion of French West Indian identity today. He writes:

> The relationship with the land, one that is even more threatened because the community is alienated from that land, becomes so fundamental in this discourse that landscape in the work stops being merely decorative or supportive and emerges as a full character. Describing the landscape is not enough. The individual, the community, the land are inextricable in the process of creating history. Landscape is a character in this process. Its deepest meanings need to be understood.[55]

As Glissant suggests above, there exists an indissociability between the individual, the community, and the countryside in the forging of French West Indian history and identity. An ecocritical approach is therefore essential for interpreting the numerous descriptions of ecological distress in French West Indian cultural production. In their literature, theory and song, those most concerned with preserving their island's cultural identity express their resistance to tampering with the Martinican landscape. According to them, this affects more than the flora and fauna of the island. It also bears upon Martinican cultural memory because (1) it physically conceals traces of an enslaved past; (2) it replaces the reality of exploitation with a more pleasant narrative of the France-Martinique historical relationship; and (3) it coats the Martinican imagination with dreams of French modernity. In their work, Martinican writers and songwriters alike challenge their audiences to dig beneath the pleasant façade of a colonial past, and present.

NOTES

1. Édouard Glissant, *Poetics of Relation*, trans. Betsy Wing (Ann Arbor: The University of Michigan Press, 1997), 146.
2. Patrick Chamoiseau, interview by author. Fort-de-France. 15 March 2001, (translation mine). I am indebted to Solenne Langelez who dedicated many hours to transcribing this interview and the one with Raphaël Confiant. These interviews serve as the narration to my film, co-directed with Eric Faden: *Landscape and Memory: Martinican Land-People-History*, VHS, (2001; New York: Third World Newsreel, 2003).
3. "Frenchification."

4. Kathleen Gyssels, "Du titre au roman: *Texaco* de Patrick Chamoiseau," *Romans 50/90* 20 (1995): 125, 127–28 (translation mine).

5. Priska Degras and Bernard Magnier, "Édouard Glissant, préfacier d'une littérature future: Entretien avec Edouard Glissant." *Notre Librairie* 74 (1984): 15 (translation mine).

6. "Cementing over."

7. Édouard Glissant, *Discours antillais*, (1981; Paris: Gallimard, 1997), 117–18 (translation mine). For the majority of my citations of Glissant's *Discours antillais*, I have used Michael Dash's translation. However, as his work is a partial translation of the entire and lengthy collection of essays, I have translated certain passages from the original French version.

8. Association pour la Sauvegarde du Patrimoine Martiniquais.

9. Brenda Berrian, *Awakening Spaces: French Caribbean Popular Songs, Music, and Culture*, (Chicago: University of Chicago Press, 2000), 136.

10. Charles Frankenhoff, *Environmental Planning and Development in the Caribbean*, (Puerto Rico: University of Puerto Rico, 1977), 13.

11. Édouard Glissant, *Caribbean Discourse: Selected Essays*, trans. J. Michael Dash (Charlottesville: University Press of Virginia, 1989), 13.

12. Jean Bernabé, Patrick Chamoiseau and Raphaël Confiant, *In Praise of Creoleness*, trans. M.B. Taleb-Khyar (Paris: Gallimard, 1993).

13. Ibid., 98–99 (translation of words in italics mine). I have taken some liberty in retranslating the word "dessous" in M.B. Taleb-Khyar's English translation of *Éloge de la Créolité*. To me, "beneath" is a more accurate translation of the word "dessous" in the original.

14. Bernabé et al., *In Praise*, 84 (italics and translation of "beneath" mine).

15. See Richard D.E. Burton's chapter on this subject: "The French West Indies à l'heure de l'Europe" in *French and West Indian: Martinique, Guadeloupe and French Guiana Today*, ed. Richard D.E. Burton and Fred Reno (Charlottesville: University Press of Virginia, 1995), 1–19.

16. Patrick Chamoiseau, *Écrire en pays dominé* (Paris: Gallimard, 1997), 69–70 (translation mine).

17. *Landscape and Memory*. The entire interview with Raphaël Confiant, "Cultural and Environmental Assimilation in Martinique: An Interview with Raphaël Confiant," will appear in a forthcoming edited volume entitled *Caribbean Literature and the Environment: Between Nature and Culture* (Elizabeth DeLoughrey, Renée Gosson and George Handley, eds.) under contract with the University of Virginia Press.

18. Richard D.E. Burton, "The idea of difference in contemporary French West Indian thought: Négritude, Antillanité, Créolité," in *French and West Indian: Martinique, Guadeloupe and French Guiana Today*, ed. Richard D.E. Burton and Fred Reno (Charlottesville: University Press of Virginia, 1995), 18.

19. Richard D.E. Burton, "French West Indies à l'heure de l'Europe: an overview," in *French and West Indian: Martinique, Guadeloupe and French Guiana Today*, ed. Richard D.E. Burton and Fred Reno (Charlottesville: University Press of Virginia, 1995), 3–4.

20. Glissant, *Discours Antillais*, 167 (translation mine).

21. Alain Anselin, "Consommation et consumérisme en Martinique," *Archipelago* 2 (1982): 69.

22. Chamoiseau, *Écrire*, 70 (translation mine).

23. Ibid., 70–71 (translation mine).

24. Glissant, *Caribbean Discourse*, 49.

25. Chamoiseau, *Écrire*, 21 (translation mine).

26. Glissant, *Discours Antillais*, 177 (translation mine).

27. Glissant, *Caribbean Discourse*, 1.

28. Glissant, *Discours Antillais*, 177 (translation mine).

29. Glissant, *Caribbean Discourse*, 150.

30. Beverley Ormerod, "French West Indian writing since 1970," in *French and West Indian: Martinique, Guadeloupe and French Guiana Today*, ed. Richard D.E. Burton and Fred Reno (Charlottesville: University Press of Virginia, 1995), 170.

31. Oruno D. Lara, *De l'oubli à l'histoire: Espaces et identités caraïbes* (Paris: Maisonneuve et Larose, 1998), 36 (translation mine).

32. Marie-José Jolivet, "La Construction d'une mémoire historique à la Martinique: du schoelchérisme au marronnisme," *Cahiers d'études africaines* 107–108 (1987): 295–96 (translation mine).

33. Richard D.E. Burton, "Trois statues: Le Conquistador, l'Impératrice et le Libérateur: Pour une sémiotique de l'histoire coloniale de la Martinique," *Carbet* 11 (1991): 147.

34. Ibid., 148.

35. *Landscape and Memory.*

36. Marie-José N'Zengou-Tayo, "Exorcising Painful Memories: Raphaël Confiant and Patrick Chamoiseau" in *Slavery in the Caribbean Francophone World*, ed. Doris Y. Kadish (Athens: University of Georgia Press, 2000), 176.

37. Jolivet, "Construction," 293 (translation mine).

38. See Burton's "Trois statues" p. 160.

39. Ibid., 154.

40. Ibid., 156 (translation mine).

41. White plantation and slave owners who resided in colonial Martinique.

42. Burton, "Trois statues," 150 (translation mine).

43. Richard Price, *The Convict and the Colonel* (Boston: Beacon Press, 1998), 218.

44. Brenda Berrian, *Awakening Spaces: French Caribbean Popular Songs, Music, and Culture* (Chicago: University of Chicago Press, 2000), 1.

45. Ibid., ix.

46. Ibid., 8.

47. Ibid., 135.

48. Ibid., 145.

49. Ibid., 136.

50. Kali, *Ile à vendre*, Hibiscus, compact disc 92013–2.

51. Translation of song lyrics mine.

52. Berrian, *Awakening Spaces*, 141.

53. Dash, 93.

54. This physical tampering with nature has disastrous results for more than environmental reasons. According to Glissant, Martinican nature is a locus of cultural

resistance because its natural events, including disasters, are an alternative to European means of measuring time and marking history: "Glissant sees the Antillean tendency to think chronology primarily in terms of natural disasters as resistance to French historical time" Jeannie Suk, *Postcolonial Paradoxes in French Caribbean Writing: Césaire, Glissant, Condé* (Oxford: Clarendon Press, 2001), 73.

    55. Glissant, *Caribbean Discourse*, 105–106.

BIBLIOGRAPHY

Anselin, Alain. "Consommation et consumérisme en Martinique." *Archipelago* 2 (1982): 64–75.

Bernabé, Jean, Patrick Chamoiseau and Raphaël Confiant. *In Praise of Creoleness.* Translated by M.B. Taleb-Khyar. Paris: Gallimard, 1993.

———. 1989. *Éloge de la Créolité.* Paris: Gallimard, 1993.

Berrian, Brenda. *Awakening Spaces: French Caribbean Popular Songs, Music, and Culture.* Chicago: University of Chicago Press, 2000.

Burton, Richard D.E. "French West Indies à l'heure de l'Europe: an overview." In *French and West Indian: Martinique, Guadeloupe and French Guiana Today,* edited by Richard D.E. Burton and Fred Reno, 1–19. Charlottesville: University Press of Virginia, 1995.

———. "The idea of difference in contemporary French West Indian Thought: Négritude, Antillanité, Créolité." In *French and West Indian: Martinique, Guadeloupe and French Guiana Today,* edited by Richard D.E. Burton and Fred Reno, 137–166. Charlottesville: University Press of Virginia, 1995.

———. "Trois statues: Le Conquistador, l'Impératrice et le Libérateur: Pour une sémiotique de l'histoire coloniale de la Martinique." *Carbet* 11 (1991): 147–64.

Burton, Richard D.E., and Fred Reno, eds. *French and West Indian: Martinique, Guadeloupe, and French Guiana Today.* Charlottesville: University Press of Virginia, 1995.

Chamoiseau, Patrick. *Écrire en pays dominé.* Paris: Gallimard, 1997.

———. Interview with Renée Gosson. Fort-de-France. 15 March 2001.

Dash, J. Michael. *Édouard Glissant.* Cambridge: University Press, 1995.

Degras, Priska, and Bernard Magnier. "Édouard Glissant, préfacier d'une littérature future: Entretien avec Édouard Glissant." *Notre Librairie* 74 (1984): 14–20.

DeLoughrey, Elizabeth, Renée Gosson, and George Handley, eds. *Caribbean Literature and the Environment: Between Nature and Culture,* eds. Charlottesville: University of Virginia Press, forthcoming.

Frankenhoff, Charles. *Environmental Planning and Development in the Caribbean.* Puerto Rico: University of Puerto Rico, 1977.

Glissant, Édouard. *Caribbean Discourse: Selected Essays.* Translated by J. Michael Dash. Charlottesville: University Press of Virginia, 1989.

———. 1981 *Discours Antillais.* Paris: Gallimard, 1997.

———. *Poetics of Relation.* Translated by Betsy Wing. Ann Arbor: The University of Michigan Press, 1997.

———. *Le Quatrième siècle.* Paris: Seuil, 1964.

Gosson, Renée. "Cultural and Environmental Assimilation in Martinique: An Interview with Raphaël Confiant." In *Caribbean Literature and the Environment: Between Nature and Culture*, eds. Elizabeth DeLoughrey, Renée Gosson and George Handley. Charlottesville: University of Virginia Press, forthcoming.

Gyssels, Kathleen. "Du titre au roman: *Texaco* de Patrick Chamoiseau." *Romans 50/ 90* 20 (1995): 121–32.

Jolivet, Marie-José. "La Construction d'une mémoire historique à la Martinique: du schoelchérisme au marronnisme." *Cahiers d'études africaines* 107–108 (1987): 287–309.

Kali. *Ile à vendre*. Hibiscus. Compact disc 92013–2.

Landscape and Memory: Martinican Land-People-History. VHS. Directed by Renée Gosson and Eric Faden. 2001; New York, NY: Third World Newsreel, 2003.

Lara, Oruno D. *De l'oubli à l'histoire: Espaces et identités caraïbes*. Paris: Maisonneuve et Larose, 1998.

N'Zengou-Tayo, Marie-José. "Exorcising Painful Memories: Raphaël Confiant and Patrick Chamoiseau." In *Slavery in the Caribbean Francophone World*, edited by Doris Y. Kadish, 176–87. Athens: University of Georgia Press, 2000.

Ormerod, Beverly. "French West Indian writing since 1970." In *French and West Indian: Martinique, Guadeloupe and French Guiana Today*, edited by Richard D.E. Burton and Fred Reno, 167–87. Charlottesville: University Press of Virginia, 1995.

Price, Richard. *The Convict and the Colonel*. Boston: Beacon Press, 1998.

Suk, Jeannie. *Postcolonial Paradoxes in French Caribbean Writing: Césaire, Glissant, Condé*. Oxford: Clarendon Press, 2001.

16

Plight of the Rara'muri
Crises in Our Backyard

Four Arrows
(aka Don Trent Jacobs)

The little girl sat with her father overlooking the vast barrancas of Barranca de Sinforosa, the largest and deepest chasm of the Copper Canyon system in central Mexico. The Rio Urique, thousands of feet below, was winding its way to the Sea of Cortez like a silvery snake. The two people were shelling maize onto a blanket to make beer for a forthcoming ceremony. The girl's mother was close by, grinding parched maize kernels with water on a stone metate, scraping the mush into a wooden bowl with a piece of a broken gourd.

The little girl's joyful countenance dismissed her runny nose, tattered dress, and calloused feet. Laughter and conversation dotted periods of quiet concentration. Then the man looked out at the horizon and sighed. The little girl's face grew tense. The wife immediately stopped grinding the maize. "Chu shika o'mona muhe'?" she asked her husband. "Why are you sad?"

The Tarahumara Indians of central Mexico, who refer to themselves as Rara'muri, are very sensitive to expressions of sadness. Sighing might mean that someone's soul is about to leave the body for some reason. Souls can become injured when they are sad and the body can become ill when a soul departs it. Souls also are responsible for thinking, according to Rara'muri philosophy, in ways that assure that one's behavior is in harmony with the greatest good for the community.[1]

The young man had reason to be sad. He was thinking of how his father had been murdered several years earlier for protesting against the illegal logging of their oak savannas. Since then, the drug cartel leader Artemio Fontes, had managed to lay claim "legally" to his father's homelands, lands that had been given to the Tarahumara community, lands where his father and his father's father had hunted and farmed. Now the lands were being logged by Fontes and his cronies under a plan that was subsidized by a World Bank Forestry Program. Roads, trucks, and machines were raping the landscape and destroying hundreds of plants the Tarahumara used for food and medicine.

Human rights violations and the socio-ecological injustices that are being perpetrated against the "Rara'muri" should awaken conscience and consciousness in the international community, especially in the country that is Mexico's neighbor to the north. Related to the injustices that impact the lives of these indigenous people are deforestation, air and water pollution, water depletion, loss of diverse plants and animals, and increasing consequences of narcotics trafficking and illegal border crossings, all issues that affect health of citizens in the United States also.

I first visited the gentle Rara'muri people in 1984 when I tried to kayak the Rio Urique River deep in the heart of rugged mountains of Chihuahua surrounding Copper Canyon (Barranca del Cobre). When rains raised the river to dangerous proportions, I was sucked into an underground drainage and nearly killed. Some Rara'muri people saved my life. Thirteen years later, I learned about the plight of the Rara'muri and returned to a remote part of Copper Canyon to live and learn with Augustine Ramos, a Rara'muri medicine man and activist. While in the area of Pino Gordo and other villages, I either heard of or saw how members of the Fontes drug cartel and of the Mexican government steal land, log trees without permits, force families to grow opium plants, and imprison or beat Rara'muri men who resist. (My adventures with the Raramuri are chronicled in my book, *Primal Awareness: A True Story of Survival, Transformation and Awakening with the Raramuri Shamans of Mexico*.)[2]

My main contact with the Rara'muri was Augustin Ramos. Augustin was a legendary shaman who had devoted his life to his people both as a healer and as an activist. He had thick gray hair, cropped in the traditional pageboy style, and a glowing face that belied his 102 years of life. Instead of the usual headband or western cowboy hat that many Rara'muri wear, he wore a St. Louis Cardinal's baseball cap. He wore two shirts, the outer one being a gray wool shirt-jacket. Below the waist, he wore the traditional Rara'muri loin cloth, with a shaman's sash hanging down to his knees. On his leathery feet, he wore the common sandals made from automobile tires, secured with a leather thong that passed through the toes and tied around the ankle.

Augustin spent each day walking tens of miles to various homes, helping families shuck corn, helping men plow fields with log plows connected to two oxen, healing ill or injured people, playing with children or leading ceremonies. If this was not enough, he also regularly met with men to organize protests that would require long journeys through the mountains on foot, then by train to Chihuahua. More often than not, the protests ended tragically. Sometimes, the men were arrested or even beaten by police.

Living in such a remote land, where canyons in some places are deeper than the Grand Canyon of Arizona, the Rara'muri have managed to preserve their traditional culture more than most other indigenous nations of North America. They were not conquered by the Spanish Conquistadores nor overwhelmed by Christian missionaries. Smallpox and other European diseases, when introduced to the continent in the early 1600s, had negligible impact on them. Around 1631, the Spaniards captured a number of Rara'muri and forced them to work in their silver mines. However, by the end of the century the Rara'muri revolted. This led to brutal reprisals by the Spanish. The Rara'muri, unaccustomed to warfare, escaped by going deeper into the rugged barrancas. They lived by hunting and by managing to farm the shallow, rocky soil of small plateaus to grow corn and beans.[3]

Loggers started arriving in the Sierra Madre in the late 1800s and conscripted the Rara'muri for cheap labor.[4] Once again, the peaceful people fled even deeper into the labyrinthine maze of canyons. However, in 1962, Rara'muri isolation ended when the last section of the Chihuahua el Pacifico Railroad was finally completed to traverse the Sierra Madre.[5] With the railroad came more loggers, many of whom were merely fronts for large drug cartels who not only destroyed Rara'muri habitat, but also forced them to grow opium and marijuana. The environmental degradation of the area began to accelerate in the early 1990s, as have the gross injustices.

On August 21, 1996, the Commission of Solidarity and Defense of Human Rights received a document signed by thirteen members of the Ejido of San Alonso, a Rara'muri community in the heart of the Sierra Madre Mountains, experiencing large scale logging, that claimed the operations to be a violation of their rights to their natural resources. Although much logging is occurring illegally, a significant portion is being done via legal contracts with the International Paper Company. With annual sales of over 18.5 billion dollars, I.P.C. is the largest private land owner in the United States with operations in twenty-two countries.[6] As a result of this and other formal complaints, much of the logging was finally stopped in March 2003. However, through legal channels, the Fontes family was given permission in February 2004 to start logging again. This time, Boise-Cascade, another U.S. company is also heavily involved.[7]

Multi-agency international study of satellite images found that Mexico lost an average of 2.72 million acres of pine and fir forests each year between 1993 and 2000. Mexico lost an average of 2.72 million acres of pine and fir forests—equivalent to the area of Ireland and nearly twice as fast as what government officials had previously estimated. Mexico has the second-highest deforestation rate in the world.[8] This is especially devastating since the Sierra Madre boasts some of the richest biodiversity anywhere in North America and contains about two thirds of the standing timber in Mexico. Twenty-three different species of pine and many species of oak reside within the Sierra Madre Occidental. So far, deforestation has contributed to the extinction of the imperial woodpecker, the Mexican wolf, and the Mexican grizzly. According to Andrew Martin, an NAU (Northern Arizona University) colleague who has worked in the field near Pino Gordo, there are thirty-two species which receive protected status in 2001 and; "endangered" species include the thick-billed parrot, military macaw, ocelot, jaguar; "threatened" species include Mexican golden trout, Cahita sucker, Ornate shiner, northern goshawk, prairie falcon, Mexican parrotlet, lilac-crowned parrot, Mexican spotted owl, eared trogon, golden eagle, southern river otter, jaguarundi; and others under "special protection" are the Yaqui catfish, roundtailed chub, Yaqui sucker, Sharp-shinned Hawk, Cooper's hawk, Gould's wild turkey, Montezuma's quail, stygian owl, American dipper, Sinaloa martin, brown-backed solitaire, Townsend's solitaire, zone-tailed hawk, common black hawk, and the peregrine falcon.

During the first few days of my relationship with Augustin, he all but ignored me. His willingness to allow me to accompany him on his travels, however, revealed a great generosity, considering his required distrust of outsiders. Other outsiders were now coming to this remote area, one of the last that had not yet been pillaged by the Fontes drug cartel or the loggers affiliated with it. To know which people were there to help and which were there in behalf of Fontes was difficult. I am sure his profound intuitive insight guided Augustin's decisions. After several days, he began smiling at me with a wonderful twinkle in his eye that told me he knew I was a friend. By the end of the week he even waited for me to arrive at his home before he set off for his day's duties. Once he laughed long and wonderfully at my misuse of his language. *Chumana* is the Rara'muri word for "How do you say?" but I confused it with *chimideeway*, which means, "What is your name?" I walked all day with him pointing to objects and saying, "Chimi-deeway." For the rest of our time together, he would share this amusing mistake with others, who would join him in good-hearted laughter.

One day a Rara'muri from another community perhaps one hundred kilometers distant arrived to talk with Augustin. From what I could gather, he was reporting that Fontes was trying to use the names of dead men and women from Pino Gordo to establish legal ownership of this heavily wooded place. Whatever the message, Augustin's eyes revealed a pain I had not seen previously and he immediately called for a meeting of the key members of his community. The next morning, a gathering of more than twenty men had a tone of seriousness that was unusual for these people. Augustin seemed to be telling them that he was too old to continue being the leader of the protests and that other younger men would have to take more responsibility.

Several factors are directly responsible for the deforestation of the Rara'-muri homelands and the attack on their sustainability. NAFTA-related government policies subsidize the expansion of farmlands in an effort to compete with the U.S. and Canada's farming subsidies. The Mexican government legally, though unethically, authorizes the taking of millions of acres of board feet from the forest to export abroad to earn hard cash and to help solve their horrific foreign debt crisis. Nearly 20 percent of the timber logged in the Sierra Madre is sold to the United States as plywood, paper, or pulp. Legal logging in Mexico is largely motivated by efforts to repay its international debts. In 1989, the World Bank loaned Mexico nearly fifty million dollars for a logging project.[9] The plan was to log more than 4 billion board feet of lumber from 20 million acres of forest over six and one-half years. The bank (and ostensibly its 51 percent owner, the U.S. Treasury) accommodated the loan to help Mexico correct its trade deficit by reducing its dependence on imported paper pulp (20 percent of which is sold to the United States, recall.) The loss of the oak and pine covered watersheds have contributed to depleting underground aquifers all the way to Texas.

Erosion from the logging has slowed the headwaters of local rivers. With few trees to protect the exposed slopes, the water does not have time to go underground. This has made traditional springs the Rara'muri depend upon go dry. Without them, they have turned to drinking river water that is increasingly becoming polluted by the herbicide, paraquat, used by the Mexican government to kill opium fields, when some of its authorities are not furnishing seeds to the drug cartel, which I once witnessed.

Of course, in addition to polluting the drinking water, paraquat and other herbicides destroy indigenous plant life. This is especially a problem for the Rara'muri, who use hundreds of different species of plants for food and medicine. Of course, the World Bank repeats such folly against indigenous people the world over. Its managers tend to see forests only as a marketable commodity, not as a home to people, or as a source of livelihood, or as a place where gods dwell and ancestors are buried.

In addition to the Mexican government's "legal" logging, one of the major exploiters of the Mexican forests is the Boise Cascade logging company of the United States. The Boise company started out in the Pacific Northwest in 1994 logging the pine forests. By 1996 the company had already run out of forest in the northwest territory and moved down to the southeast portion of the country. Heavy logging is being done in both the pine forests of the Sierra Madre and the tropical rain forests of Mexico by the Boise company today. One of the more significant but less mentioned causes of deforestation relates to the thousands of acres being logged illegally or burned by Mexican and Columbian drug cartels so they can plant acres of marijuana and opium plants that will ultimately be worth hundreds of millions of dollars in U.S. markets annually. Sometimes lumbering is done merely as a way to transport drugs grown in a region. The lumber companies are paid more for their collusion than they are for the trees, which sometimes are just dumped and left to rot.

Although a drug culture has emerged whereby some Rara'muri choose the drug business over subsistence farming in a worsening environment, others have been forced by threat of violence to grow the drug crops rather than the traditional corn and beans. Rara'muri men who try to resist in some way or who worked with legal groups to make things better have been assassinated by people like Ramiro Arguelles, a honcho for Artemio Fontes Lugo's drug cartel.

One of the men at the meeting with Augustin was Gumercindo Torres. Torres worked for Edwin Bustillos, a man who won the Goldman Environmental Prize for his efforts to neutralize the harm being done to the Rara'muri by both the violent drug cartel and the corrupt Mexican government and who had survived four assassination attempts. (Sadly, Edwin passed on early this year.) Gumercindo was, on December 12, 1993, participating in a ceremony in a church located in Coloradas de la Virgen. Many men and women were enjoying the festivities, when Augustin Fontes, the nephew of Artemio, and another man burst into the church and barred the door so no one could escape. These two narcotraficantes then started shooting into the air with AK-47 machine guns. Fontes shot Gumercino's brother, Louis, eight times in the chest at point blank range. The other man shot Gumercindo, hitting him in both shoulders and the hip. After Gumercio fell, the man fired one last shot at his head.

Gumercindo survived only because of the healing powers of Augustin Ramos. One day when I was visiting Gumercindo and his wife Paola, Gumercindo indicated that he had some pain near his ribs. Apparently he had suffered broken ribs during his last journey away from the village, perhaps because he got drunk and involved in a fight. She asked me to get Augustin. I ran several miles to where he was helping several young men build sheep fencing. I told him he was needed and we began a fast walk back to Gumercindo.

When we arrived back, Augustin asked him to remove his shirt. Augustin took out his peyote button and applied it to several places on and around the wounded area and blew on the places he touched. After several passes, he took a small wooden cross out of his pocket. Holding it between Gumercino and himself, Augustin exhaled so that his breath passed over the cross and onto his patient. He pressed the cross into Gumercindo's ribs and chanted. I later learned that his song was intended to attract the attention of the wandering soul responsible for Gumercindo's pain and that the cross was a pre-Christian symbol used for centuries by the Rara'muri. He then said something to Gumercindo and departed. Gumercindo, no longer wincing in pain, smiled at me and said, "matet'eraba," Rara'muri for "thank you."

There are many others who worked for Edwin Bustillos or for his partner, American activist Randall Gingrich, to help the Rara'muri survive and to expose the corrupt logging practices and the World Bank financing of roads in regions dominated by the drug gangs. Independent Rara'muri, without the support of the organizations founded by these men, such as Edwin's CASMAC (Consejo Asesor Sierra Madre: Advisory Council of the Sierra Madre) and Randall's Sierra Madre Alliance, have gathered to protest in cities only to be beaten by state police. [10] Sometimes, to demonstrate the success of the U.S./Mexican "War on Drugs," Mexican authorities, who too often look the other way when violence is levied against the Natives, will occasionally arrest a Rara'muri man who has been forced to grow the crops and put him in jail for life just to show that the war on drugs is working.

One day Edwin Bustillos paid Augustin and I a surprise visit. He arrived with his uncle, Moises. Moises was a warm-hearted fellow without the intensity of his nephew. He went out of his way to engage in conversation with me, even though most of our communication was sign-language. With a combination of English, Spanish, Rara'muri, and hand signals, and with the aid of Edwin's English translations, I learned of his remarkable story.

Moises, because of his efforts to assist Edwin, had suffered an assassination attempt on his life. Members of the Fontes organization grabbed him and took him far into the wilderness area outside of Aqua Azul, at the bottom of the mountain that cradled Pino Gordo. The men stabbed him with screw drivers in his back, stomach, legs, and arms. Then they buried him alive. Hours later, when Moises came back to consciousness, he managed to dig his way out of the hole. He crawled for three days and nights though the wilds in search of assistance. On the third day, just before he managed to come upon some boys playing romaya, a complicated gambling game that involves passing a rock through a maze of holes, a panther faced him on his path. As he described this part of his amazing story, his eyes glowed like a child's as though seeing this rare animal almost made the ordeal worth it for him.

For two days Edwin attempted to share with me what Augustin and his more youthful activist were trying to do. He confirmed that Fontes was making inroads with fraudulent strategies to obtain ownership of the Pine Forests. Another community, Coloradas de la Virgen, had already experience such agrarian fraud when a number of dead Raramuri souls were added to the title in the place of legitimate community members, and then the fraudulently composed assembly proceeded to elect officials allied with the Fontes drug cartel. The "community" then signed logging contracts advantageous to the cartel.

Edwin also told me good news. He said that international groups were working hard to make an international preserve of the area to preserve it from such efforts. Augustin, respected by Indians and Mexicans alike, had been a major force in keeping the area pristine. However, at 102, Augustin knew that others in his village would have to assume a leadership role and he was upset that the young people were not sufficiently motivated. Many in fact were now participating in the drug trade and their behaviors were reflecting the morals of such an affiliation. Augustin was not happy with the situation Edwin told me. Nonetheless, he understood the frustration of having the Mexican government actually arrest Rara'muri who protested because many of its officials were on the Fontes payroll.

Amnesty International has recorded many such cases in which the legal system was misused in order to persecute, punish and ultimately stop human rights activists from continuing their legitimate activities. For example, Isidro Baldenegro Lopez, a Rara'muri leader and Hermenegildo Rivas Carrillo were arbitrarily detained by the police in March of 2003 and were charged with illegal possession of weapons and with possession of marijuana. Eyewitness accounts show that the evidence was fabricated but the two men were put into prison for a twelve-year term. Fortunately, this is one case where international pressure, stimulated by the work of Gingrich's Sierra Madre Alliance, caused the Mexican Attorney General to release him in July, 2004. Of course, now his life is at great risk of an assassination at the hands of Fontes and his hired guns.[11]

Isidro was singled out because he had participated in a month-long blockade of logging trucks which had been entering his community and cutting timber long after their logging permit had been suspended by a court order. Isidro's case is similar to that of many others who are trying to stop the "drug-logging." For example, Rodolfo Montiel, an environmental activist from Guerrero, was arrested on falsified charges after leading similar protests. For people who wish to join the international work to help these people, contact the Sierra Madre Alliance or inquire at State Human Rights Commission Calle Décima y Mina No. 1000, Colonia Centro Apartado Postal 1354, Chihuahua, Chihuahua C.P. 31000. Tel and Fax: 410-08-28 with five lines. Toll-free number 01-800-201-1. Also contact and complain to President Vincente Fox and to the U.S. president.

During my time with the Rara'muri, I saw men cry as they told their stories about what is happening to their homeland and their relatives. Women also weep when the see their great loss as well. These gentle people, who Antonin Artaud described a philosophers for whom "there is no sin: evil is loss of consciousness"[12] struggle with the shame of being so vulnerable and powerless against civilizations that have lost their consciousness. The children are dying of disease and poverty. Half die before the age of five. Violence increases daily, with more and more Rara'muri children joining the drug cartels, which, according to many, if made legal would end the violence.

And while all this is happening, travel agencies continue to run ads for Copper Canyon that tell people to "Visit the cave homes & ranchos of the Tarahumara Indians who have made the Copper Canyon country their home for three centuries. Our tours work hard to ensure your visits with the Tarahumaras are sensitive, appropriate & positive for all concerned." They do not say that many of the hotels that display the Rara'muri art were built with drug money and drug operations that are decimating the land and the people. They do not talk about the history or the future of these wonderful people, except to say that they weave good baskets that they will sell cheap if you bargain hard.

I just learned from a friend that Augustin Ramos has died. Before leaving us, he asked my colleague, Andrew Martin, to video tape his last words, a long speech for his Rara'muri children so that they might know how to live in this world and stand against the intrusions of disharmony that are destroying the beauty.

It is time for us all to spread the word about what is happening to these people and the diverse resources that keep our planet alive.

NOTES

1. Merrill, William L. *Rara'muri Souls*, Washington, D.C.: Smithsonian Institute Press, 1988.

2. Jacobs, Don Trent, *Primal Awareness: A True Story of Survival, Transformation and Awakening with the Rara'muri Shamans of Mexico*, Rochester, VT: Inner Traditions International, 1998.

3. Deforestation, An International Analysis, Research Paper X21, Kevin L. Hagan, http://www.american.edu/ted/projects/tedcross/xdefor21.htm (Trade Environment Data Base 287 TED Case Studies, Volume 5, Number 2, June, 1996.

4. Shoumatoff, Alex. "Hero of the Sierra Madre." *Utne Reader 70* (July/August 1995): 90–99.

5. Weisman, Alan. "The Drug Lords Versus The Tarahumara." *The Los Angeles Times Magazine*, 9 January 1994, 10.

6. B. Diamond, FOREST Listserve, http://www.metla.fi/archive/forest/1996/11/msg00010.html, July 4, 2004.

7. Common Dreams Progressive Newswire, www.commondreams.org/news2004/0402–01.htm, April 2, 2004, July 28, 2004.

8. ECES, http://eces.org/archive/ec/ecosystems/deforestation.shtml, 2001, May 4, 2004.

9. Mardon, Mark, and Susan Borowitz. "Banking on Mexico's Forests." *Sierra* 75 November/December): 98–100.

10. Jacobs, Don Trent, "The Shaman's Message," a video documentary, 2000, available at www.teachingvirtues.net

11. Sierra Madre Alliance Bulletin, http://www.web.amnesty.org/mavp/av.nsf/pages/HRD), July 7, 2004, July 28, 2004.

12. Artaud, Antonin, *The Peyote Dance*. Trans. Helen Weaver. New York: Farrar, Straus and Giroux, 12.

17

Main Streets and Riverbanks
The Politics of Place in an Australian River Town

Heather Goodall

Brewarrina is a small country town on the banks of the Barwon river, which meanders through curving bends and billabongs as it moves slowly across the wide floodplain of western New South Wales until it joins the mighty Darling. The river runs steadily in this winding course most of the time, but when floods come down from the east, the waters rise to a torrent that cuts a line across the bends, straightening the course of the river, at least until the flood subsides.

The whole Darling system forms one of the longest rivers in the world, a fact often quoted to emphasise its iconic "natural" status. Just as iconic is the Darling's landscape with its beautiful old river gums, slow tranquil flows and the broad grasslands beyond. White settlers from 1830s believed these open, sunlit floodplains were there in the form that their God had created them. Instead the grasslands were the result of centuries of Indigenous people's management with strategies like regular burning. Yet even when its human creation is acknowledged, the calm of these riverbank scenes seems very far from the intrusive tin and concrete structures built by European setters from the mid nineteenth century to stake their claim on the land.

BUILT ENVIRONMENT, RACISM AND MODERNITY

Brewarrina is in most respects typical of Australian town social and racial structures, settled by the British in the 1840s and still surrounded by grazing country which has recently been penetrated by irrigated cotton farming. It has a population of around 1500 of whom half are Indigenous people with the rest being largely of Anglo or western European settler descent.[1] Like most far western towns, this proportion of Aboriginal people is higher than in the larger cities closer to the coast. Recent historical research has explored the way colonizing settlers in such places worldwide created racialized environments around them, segregating, controlling, and creating hierarchies between colonized and colonizer as they built their towns.[2]

Places of leisure are striking, recent examples of this continuing process. Economic changes in western countries by the mid twentieth century meant there was more leisure time available at the same time as the new popular media of radio and cinema carried promises of a "modern" future which was more democratic and egalitarian. Yet in Australia, as in the United States and Canada, the new technologies of modernity led ironically to sharply intensified spatial expressions of racism in the 1940s and 1950s. Take the picture shows which sprang up when silent movies, previously shown in open-air theaters, were replaced by the Talkies. Movies with sound required enclosed buildings so they could be shown and heard effectively, which then allowed much stricter controls over entry and seating.

Public bathing was another situation where modernity dramatically changed the built environment and at the same time the social relations of access. River swimming holes near the townships in the 1920s contained surprisingly large numbers of wooden structures—fences, netting, and slides—built by local government to allow safe swimming, races, diving, and other sports. Such facilities may have had racially segregated operation during some times of the day or week, but being on the open river they could never really keep people out at other times. But the new reinforced concrete technology allowed town pools to be built and chlorinated filters kept them clean, so the shift from river pool to public town baths occurred all across the hot rural interior of Australia from the 1940s to the 1960s. The relatively accessible public river swimming shifted into an imposing and fortress-style of pool enclosure. The scale of the structure differed according to a town's affluence, but each town aimed for the same effect. Pool entrances were built to impress those approaching with civic pride and its conquest over nature. And, just as importantly, they acted as checkpoints to sort people into those allowed in [the "healthy" and "acceptable" citizens of the new democracy] and the "others" [all those judged too poor, too dirty, too unhealthy, or just too black to be allowed in].

Ann Curthoys' recent book, *Freedom Ride*, gives an important account of how these segregations of new swimming pools in rural Australia were a major target of the 1965 student Freedom Riders in their exposure of rural segregation, just as they were one of the most infuriating of the local color bars for Aboriginal people because they were so new and had promised such a change in democratic pleasure for all.[3]

A BREWARRINA HISTORY TOUR

I am arguing, however, that interracial relations were expressed in and conducted through the *natural* environment as much as the buildings and streets of Australian country towns. Colonial relationships and racial discrimination have generated very different geographies of the overall landscape depending on the speaker's position in the racialised social conflicts of these rural areas. This was revealed for me in an incident in 1989 which demonstrated the very different place of the river in the memories of white and Black residents at Brewarrina, and indeed in their very understanding of what the town was and is.

The occasion was an annual history walk, run by a local civic organization, the Lion's Club, early on a Sunday morning during the Festival of the Fisheries. This was an annual promotional event, initiated by the local government council as a tourism strategy in the 1960s. Timed for the pleasant temperate weather of early autumn, it was intended to attract fishermen and other tourists to see the township and to fish in the river there, where good catches are always to be had along the remainder of a set of ancient Aboriginal stone fish traps.

So at 7am in 1989 I arrived with camera and found a tall white townswoman who was the Lion's history guide, chatting to a young lawyer whom I recognised as recently arrived to work in the Western Aboriginal Legal Service. Around them stood a cluster of elderly tourists, of the age and look of many Anglo-Australian retirees taking their leisurely time to tour their own country. We were taken by the guide on a tour of the "main street," to see the sights which marked out settler history: the first police station, the first church, the first bank, the first pub, the first jail. . . . We paraded up and down that main street, hearing about and experiencing the public space where settler social and political life had been shaped for more than a century. Our faces were firmly turned away from the river which had little relevance to this narrative.

But then we stopped for breakfast at the park on the water's edge, and once we'd poured our tea, we slowly turned towards the river, sparkling in the morning sun, and for the first time the older tourists began to talk to each other, gathering in knots to look across the river. They began to point out places and to tell stories about the side of the river which had been invisible in our Lion's guide's story.

"I remember our old house down there in the bend." . . . "Do you remember when we caught all those yabbies after the flood?" . . . "What about the time we got caught trying to go across the bridge into town!" . . . "I wouldn't go across the bridge . . . remember how they used to stop us."

And on they went, more and more animated as they became absorbed in sharing memories.

It became clear as they spoke that they were not newcomers. They had all originally come from Brewarrina, but the greater part of the town in which they had grown up was on *the other side* of the river. The guide was left speechless, because THIS had also made it clear that all the audience, except for myself and the lawyer, were in fact Aboriginal. They had not tried to hide their Aboriginality, but their coloring was fair, as it is with many rural Aborigines of mixed ancestry, and the guide had just assumed, as I had done, that they were white. As they talked they explained that they were all from old Brewarrina Aboriginal families: they had moved away to the city to work but came back when they could for visits. Interestingly, of all the tourists in town that weekend, it was these older Aborigines for whom the history of Brewarrina was important enough to be up early.

They had a different story about the town. In fact, what they remembered was virtually a different town. They had memories of collective community life but also of confrontations at the bridge and exclusion from the main street. It had not ever been THEIR main street! Instead, they recalled a town cut in half, with guarded gates at the bridge, 6pm curfews and color bars. The river in their town was not peripheral but instead was a central part of the story.

THE RIVER AS A BOUNDARY

Reflecting on the town's settler history and combing the municipal and state government archives, as I have done, shows how the settlers consistently tried to use the river as a boundary between the racial groups, and indeed as a way to construct and police racial borders.[4] They used both the river's banks and its flow to do so. In many of the Brewarrina setter records of their own histories, such as the local historical resource books *Bric a Brac* edited by a dedicated local historian, nature is conceived as an expression of a Christian God's permanent works.[5] Despite widening public recognition in the later nineteenth century about geological change and biological evolution, the tendency has persisted to perceive nature as a stable and enduring antithesis of the restless, dynamic colonizing cultures of western societies. Even in Australia, where so much was learnt and lamented by settlers about its unpredictable environment, the idea of "nature" as unchanging and fundamentally permanent has persisted.[6]

In rural towns, the river was a prime example of the way these qualities of nature were drawn upon to express and reinforce social relations. The river's "naturalness" was seen as authorizing and justifying racial segregation. It was particularly used to create a clear and permanent demarcation, in which the river was established as a boundary.

The locations in Brewarrina in which Aboriginal housing was allowed to be built show the process. The section of bank opposite the town park is known as Billy Goat Bend, and it was established as an Aboriginal reserve in 1851, in an early recognition of the importance of the rock fisheries. It was significantly on the "other" side of the river from the town and it is as well the low side of the bank, so it floods earlier than does the higher, town side.[7] The border was marked both by the barrier of the river water and by the disadvantage of its flow across the land in early flood.

The settlers had created a causeway across the shallowest part of the fisheries from their earliest days there, but in the 1870s they were able to build a bridge, to the northeast of the town, which most of the time thereafter provided the only reliable entry point to the town from Billy Goat Bend and other Aboriginal residences.[8] This bridge was able to act as a gateway, and from its earliest construction and certainly into the 1930s when the instructions to police were recorded in the town minutes, an unofficial curfew operated whereby Aborigines had to be away out of town and across the bridge by 6pm and were not permitted to cross the bridge into the town in the evenings after that time.

In the 1880s, a group of missionaries set up a church mission on a small property out of the town, which was later taken over by the state government's Aborigines Protection Board. Still called the "Mission," it was thereafter a secular segregated settlement, run under a white government manager with strict controls over behavior and entry. It was 10 miles away from the town, again on the "other" side of the river, and again was largely flood-prone, another use of the river as border and of its flow to reinforce disadvantage.

Finally, in the 1960s, the social and spatial isolation imposed on the 400 or so Aboriginal residents of this "Mission" was no longer publicly acceptable. The state government acquired the area of the Town Common to the west of the town, which is on very high ground on the same side of the river as the township. Surrounded on three sides by a bend of the river, it was separated from the town by a deep dry gully. The site was officially named "West Brewarrina" when the Aborigines were dumped there in hastily and shoddily constructed huts in 1966. It became known instantly by all, black and white, as Dodge City. The high landform and gully make Dodge very separate from the town even in normal conditions, but as soon as the river floods, the Barwon begins to flow directly from east of the town, through the gully, cutting off the bend and separating Dodge from the town side. Even in dry times, "West Brewarrina" was marked off by the imagined water of the gully just as effectively as if it were on the "other" side of the more permanent river.

NGUNNHU OF THE NGIYAMPAA

So white settlers wanted the river to act as a boundary between the races, as the edge and outer margin of legitimate civil society and social life. The river had not always been seen in this way. Traditional Aboriginal societies of the area had long regarded what was IN the river as crucially important in both their culture and economy. The form, bends, and holes of the river each had their own story, celebrated in song and performance and recording the big, epic struggles to create land, water, and all their life forms which is the fundamental basis of oral tradition. And the variable flow of water here was important too. As the water fell and rose again in small "freshes" and the much bigger floods it revealed different meanings of rock formations as it flowed over the rocks in different ways, with some stories only revealed once in a lifetime.

Tex Skuthorpe, a Yuwalaraay man whose country is just a few miles to the north of Brewarrina, on the smaller rivers which flow into the Barwon, has described what he learnt about his country and its rivers from his grandmothers in the 1940s[9]:

Of course, if you tell a story, then the country tells more of the story for you. When you're out there in the country, you walk *through* your story. One of the ways that I try to explain to white people about how our Aboriginal stories and country come together, is if you were to walk through your Bible, if you could lay the Bible down and walk through all these stories, and all the different colours could come up and tell you all the things that the stories meant. That's how it is for me to walk through my country.

When I look at a Galah,[10] I know that the top of the Galah was hit by a young boy playing with a Boomerang and the red on his chest is the blood off this old man's head. And the small boy who did that was turned into the Bearded Dragon. So those two animals come together.

And when you look at Murray Cod, when we used to catch Codfish or the Yellowbelly, we used to take the skin off the back of the fish. Dry that skin out, and you'd see the map of the river and the tree that this Codfish used to live under was imprinted in the skin that you get out of the back of the thing.

When there's floods come down this river here, there's a stone in the middle of the river. It marks the place where women were first created. And when the flood water first comes over the rock, you have to look there and then you see the story come alive in the rock. It's the water [rising and flowing across it] that makes the story show up. As it goes across the rock here, it tells you the story of how the first woman was created. It shows you Baiami[11] . . . it shows you Baluu, it shows you Wan—the Crow. And the rest of it becomes a pattern of all the creation of the woman. The water shows you how it's all come about [as it flows across the depressions in the rock] . . . that's done by the water.

But at Brewarrina, in what is its unique feature, there is also an extensive example of indigenous fish harvesting. The long fish traps from which the Festival took its name were constructed along a steeply falling section of bed. A 1906 map by Crown Land Surveyor Mullen shows the careful planning and knowledge of the river evident in their design, while photographs taken of the fisheries in use around 1900 reveal their beauty and their scale.[12] Unlike so much of indigenous oral tradition and practice, which remained mysterious to the settlers, these fisheries were instantly recognizable as engineering, so much so that at first they were denied to be of Aboriginal construction. Later they were piecemeal dismantled, with the causeway built across the shallows and stones removed for building.

Tex Skuthorpe has described the fisheries of these rivers and their combination of economic and cultural richness:

These fisheries show you how they used to farm fish. Because the Aboriginal people dug out the river and made it into a keeping pond, where they would take the fish. Because it's wrong for you to kill fish that you're not going to eat. You have to kill and eat it, you know. So they had to have a pen where they kept all the fish and crayfish. So when the floods went down and the fish tried to swim back up, they get caught in the maze of this fish-traps. So it was another way of farming for Aboriginal people—not only just farming the land, but farming the rivers. But it's all about knowing how it works. Learning the knowledge about your country.

Traditionally, this stretch of the river, because of its high productivity, was a meeting place of three bordering peoples. The country belonged to the Ngiyampaa-speaking peoples of the south and river bank, but its resources were ritually shared by Yuwalaraay and Muruwari peoples to the immediate northeast and northwest. These three peoples continue to form the major proportions of the Brewarrina Aboriginal population to this day.

Modern building and growing white populations took their toll on the fisheries too, with a low weir being built across the river in the 1940s. Modernity was again involved in generating a racialised landscape as the weir covered and obscured a large proportion of the rock fish traps. Then, when the impossibility of fish passage upstream across the weir was recognized some years after it had been built, the shire dynamited a big section of the fisheries' rock pens to allow for a "fish-ramp" over the weir in the 1950s. The device never worked, some saying it was put in backwards, and in the end it did little but further damage the fisheries.[13]

RIVERBANKS: NOT BORDERS
BUT SAFE SPACES

The local indigenous oral traditions about the river's creation, and that of
the fisheries themselves, as well as their rich economic role, meant that the
river had very different meanings in the minds of Indigenous people than
those which were motivating European settlers. But beyond its meaning for
its traditional owners, the river and particularly its banks did not function as
the hard and permanent boundary which settlers wanted them to be. Even
without the extreme variability of Australian rivers, unlike those of the
United States of America and Canada, which meant that the Barwon bank
seldom looked the same from one week to the next, the banks were simply
not physically accessible to the penetration of western forms of order and
control. The Barwon characteristically had steep banks, deep gullies, laby-
rinths of twisted gum tree roots and fallen branches, and endless stretches of
black soil which becomes sticky, sucking mud with the slightest moisture.

These inescapable, material qualities of the riverbanks had many social and
cultural implications, which all related to the fact that they made the deep
and secluded gullies into safe places into which settlers had enormous difficulty penetrating. This meant that Aborigines were safe here from the police,
from the earliest days of horses to the very recent times when a four wheel
drive might travel some way farther onto the bank but soon enough becomes
bogged, defeated by its own weight in the steep-sided, muddy gullies.

This has meant that over a century and a half, Aborigines have had a place
to which they could retreat and be protected from pursuit by police trying
to stop drinking or camping. They were safe too from official intervention
to remove children from families and other deeply unwelcome intrusions.
The river banks have been secure places too for teaching children not only
the skills of fishing and the life forms of the river, but the big stories of their
culture, in which all creative activity is somehow related to water and rivers.
So these banks have been places to sustain traditional knowledge as well as
to subvert and escape the intervention of the colonial regimes.[14]

The river banks have been protective not only for Blacks. They have also
been places for whites, where young people could escape the censorious eyes
of the older members of their families for some social or sexual experimenta-
tion and for unrestrained parties with the alcohol which might not be so
readily permitted in town. Many white women I interviewed remembered
the excitement of such forbidden thrills in their youth, when the riverbanks
were about the only places they could indulge themselves without the rumor
mills of local town gossip catching up with them. And just as importantly,
the secluded recesses of the river bank were also places for Blacks and whites
to meet, to drink or have illicit sexual contact, but also simply to fish and
spend time away from those prying town eyes.[15]

Far from being impervious borders, the river banks were actually uncontrollable spaces which invited transgressive social relations. They were liminal zones which fostered just those cultural and social interactions which the town and state policies were aimed at preventing.

THE RIVER INVADES THE MAIN STREET

The troubling ambiguities posed for neat settler hierarchies by the river banks were exacerbated in times of environmental crisis, of which floods were the worst. There had been a twenty-year dry spell in the west until rains over the summer of 1973–1974, and by February it was clear that a massive flood was heading down the tributaries of the Darling.

The danger was far worse for Brewarrina than for other towns which had planned more wisely. Brewarrina had no permanent levee bank protecting the town, and as the size of the flood became apparent higher up river, it began to look like the town would suffer an enormous impact. The State Emergency Services unit [SES] came to assist by offering some staff to direct operations, but it was realized that the town could only be protected by an emergency levee built with every available hand in the town. The route of the levee bank became public and it began to raise concerns among blacks. It was going to protect the Returned Servicemen's League [RSL] Club but to leave unprotected some Aboriginal homes in the outer blocks of the town, just across the road from the RSL. But in this crisis situation, the town council made a formal request to the Aboriginal population to assist the levee construction work. The townspeople, already with some Aboriginal assistance, were working all day and under floodlights at night to try to beat the flood. Their doubts set aside, the people of Dodge enthusiastically threw their organized weight behind the levee work. Their lawyer Peter Tobin observed that many Blacks felt for the first time that they had been really recognized as fellow citizens of the town. They joined in tirelessly, gratified that they were part of the fierce struggle against the clock to save the town. And then the flood waters began to rise.

FLOOD DAMAGE

The desperate flood preparations were closely observed by Tobin who had just arrived to take up the first rural position with the Aboriginal-controlled Legal Service. He wrote about it at the time[16] and talked to friends like me the next time he came to Sydney. The other witnesses who have recalled these events were the key figures in the local Black leadership: Tombo Winters, a Yuwalaraay man and shearer, Steven Gordon, an Ngiyampaa man and a shearer too, and Essie Coffey, a Murawari woman. Their memories have all contributed to this chapter but Tombo Winters' recorded interview forms the basis of the following account.[17]

Soon it became clear that Dodge City was going to be cut off and the Black workers expected that an effort would be made to protect their families there and ensure they were supplied with food and emergency transport once the waters isolated the Black enclave. But there was no emergency plan and no boat was offered. As they worked under the floodlights, the Black workers were asking themselves just whose homes were actually considered worth saving. As Tombo recalls it:

> That was in 1974. We were there, me and Phil Eyre [a non-indigenous employ-ment officer with the NSW Department of Labour and Industrial Relations, married to local indigenous woman Lizzie Williams. Their house was one of those on the wrong side of the levee bank near the RSL].

> We was transporting the people back and forth from Dodge City to the town. I had the Legal Service car, he had a little four wheel drive. When the flood got up and started to get into the town, the council went of course and got all the people from Dodge to come up and get on the sandbags. I went down and went to the SES to ask them if we could get a boat off them, but they wouldn't give us a boat.

The Aboriginal leaders began seeking outside support, and hit on a strategy to gain wide attention, as Tombo continues:

> So I went and rang the Chinese embassy in Canberra, seein' if they wanted to buy us a boat. So I talked to this fellow at the Chinese embassy. They rang the mayor of the town. The mayor of the town, the police and the president of the shire. They all said to us: "We've got no need to get all the Chinamen! We'll give you a boat."
>
> I said, "Oh don't worry about it. Keep your boat. We don't want the boat, we're getting all these Chinamen here now!"

Relations between Australia and China had only just been normalized and the diplomatic atmosphere remained tense. To have rural Aboriginal leaders calling on the Chinese government for aid was a shock not only to the locals but to the whole white population:

> And next thing we know, the media was there. *Sydney Morning Herald*.[18] Mon-ica Attard.[19] There were that many boats in Dodge City, you'd have thought it was Sydney Harbour. There were boats going everywhere. Everyone getting boats, they were joy riding around. As soon as Monica Attard left, so did all the boats! They took all the boats out when Monica Attard left town.
>
> They wouldn't get us a boat and then we got old Mrs. —, she was a welfare

officer. We said, "Why don't you see if you can get us a boat for the people over at west Brewarrina? We've got about seven women over there's that pregnant and what's going to happen to them?" She said, "right ho. And in the meantime," she said, "the SES has got a boat here in town. You can get the people over there to get a flashlight and if anyone gets crook, they should flash the light." That would be a great idea wouldn't it. You're only going to come over once and all the kids over there at Dodge will be putting their money to get a couple of torches and they'll be expecting to go on it all the time. It'd be going back and forwards there all night!

Anyway, she got us this boat come up on a plane. And when it landed, me and Steve Gordon went down to have a look. The SES picked it up! They took it out to X station, to transport the shearers. So, we went looking for it. That's where we found it, out there. So, we gone back into town and met with the Blacks buildin' the levee. They all said "when we get flooded out who'll be there to assist our families?"

Then the cops pull me up: "What do you think you're doing?"

I said, "I'm taking these people home! What happens if water gets into Dodge City. They've got to be there to protect their families."

"Oh," he said, "what about the town?"

I said, "We'll see the town when it floats past!"

He said, "You're a nice sort of a bloke to be in a community aren't you?"

We ended up getting on to the Aboriginal Lands Trust [a NSW state agency] and then me and Steve and Richard Sullivan went to Canberra to where the National Aboriginal Congress was meeting. And we put it to the NAC, why the boat was urgent for the community there at Dodge City and they ended up buying that big yellow boat we got.

While the immediate danger for the Aboriginal community was resolved by securing a boat, the tensions in the town led to different dangers for Tombo and other leaders:

Now I was filling up the car at a service station then back in Bre and this white bloke from the town walked up to me and said, "what do you think you're doing?"

I said, "what do you mean?"

And he said, "Going on the way you are?"

I said, "going on what way? . . . who?"

He said, "You blackfellas!"

Anyhow, he punched me then and the cops come along and they were going to take me but the old bloke at the service station said, "No, he wasn't doing anything except filling the car. That other bloke was the one who come along here and started this." Anyhow, they let me go.

But that night I left me car down near the water's edge because I used to stay at Phil's, on the town side with the car just in case someone wanted to come to the hospital. When I went back down in the morning, all the four tyres had been let down and there was a crowbar hole straight through the front of the window

and somebody had put a crowbar through the bonnet. I went and got Phil and
we got inner tubing in and pumped it up and just kept on going.

This challenge to the town's control over management of the environment
marked the beginning of a new assertiveness in Aboriginal demands for justice. The decades which have followed have seen an increasingly successful
set of campaigns in which Aboriginal people linked calls for civil rights to
have flood safety and decent environmental health conditions with calls for
the recognition of traditional Aboriginal ownership of the river's waters and
its cultural meanings.

TAKING BACK THE FESTIVAL
OF THE FISHERIES 1979

Essie Coffey, a Murawarri leader in Brewarrina, has described[20] the way the
local Aboriginal people's ambivalent relationship to the "Festival of the
Fisheries" was finally resolved by direct confrontation later in the decade:

When the Festival of the Fisheries started, it was a procession through the main
street, and they saw it as a festival for whites of course, for tourists to this town
. . . a way of bringing money into the town.

We was livin' on the Mission then, with my husband and our baby daughter
Sharon, and a group of us from the Mission come in . . . Harry McHughes,
myself, Eric Sullivan playing the guitar for us and we was doin' the hula on the
back of the truck. And we won that first talent quest in the procession, won the
floats, that year. And we were goin' in it every year since.

But that one year, we never put no floats in that year. . . . See it should have
been our privilege to lead the festival and lead the float procession down the
street but we couldn't. . . . Because this is our fisheries, the fish traps . . . and we
couldn't get to lead the rest of the floats into the main street. The council
wanted it to be European-led, by white people, by business people.

So just to prove a point that we are Aboriginals and this is our country . . .
to prove to the white people of the town that we own the fisheries. . . We just
marched in and we led the march with an Aboriginal flag.

We put it down in front of Pippos' café. We put the flag down there, and
everybody just sat down, it was a sit down protest. We stopped the procession
coming through for about a couple of hours, then they called the fire brigades
and the police from all over the country here. Course they were all here for the
parade.

When the police couldn't pull us off the flag, they started to use the fire
hoses. The firemens was using the hose on us. Then all the Kuris[21] rushed in and
grabbed the hose and put it on them. And I was in one paddy wagon after
another. . . . I was in a Cobar one first, and then Kevin Williams pulled me out.
As he pulled me out the one door another fella grabbed me and then chucked

me in another wagon. I was in the Goodooga wagon then, and they pulled me out then, and they put me in the Bourke wagon and they jerked me out of there and put me into the Brewarrina wagon then. That's when everybody protested then, right up to the police station.

And its made a difference, yes, definitely. We got first place now in the processions . . . I just got a loan of one of the railway trucks to lead the procession again with it this year too. It was mainly through the Kuris themselves. They wanted to do something because they own the fisheries and its all ours. We wanted to prove to the white people here that we can control it and look after it and have a festival every year . . . because there is so much racism here and prejudice in this town and its still here, right now, as I'm being recorded—that we got to fight to get what we own and fight for what we want

The community went on to make a formal land claim in 1982 under the impending NSW Land Rights legislation and then they launched a campaign to raise funds to build a cultural center on the banks of the Barwon, on the town side, but overlooking the Fisheries. These two campaigns were in very different terms to the campaigns for civil rights which had been the basis for the local Aboriginal community's securing of the Legal Service office in the early 1970s, for example, or the Black workers support for the shearers' union in its struggles against wage discrimination in the 1960s. The new campaigns, grounded in the local people's relationship to the country and the river, were expressed in the language of culture, tradition, and identity. This continued in the design of the cultural centre once the funding was won, in which the circular museum is built around a beautiful, sculptural, and working water model of the full fisheries. Then in the community's next project, which is continuing with painstaking consultations, the Yuwalaraay, Murawari, and the Ngiyampaa of Brewarrina are rebuilding the fisheries themselves, or at least as much of it as the weir allows. Perhaps the dismantling of the weir itself will be the next project in their sights.

CONCLUSIONS

Settlers have used the "naturalness" of the environment both to mark out and to authorize racial segregation: the natural environment was a means to demarcate settler control and dominance. Not only the material presence of nature, but the British ideas about "nature" as permanent and as external to society, were deployed to form a border which was a short hand way of defining who was and who was not a citizen, who was an insider and who an outsider to the town. Its apparent "naturalness" was seen as some transcendent authorization and in any event a stable and lasting boundary to keep control of citizenship.

This use of the "natural" by European settlers exposed fundamental philosophical differences between the settler and the Indigenous cultures, which instead of seeing the "natural" as the outer border of "society" as Europeans did, saw the "natural" as an expression of and platform for "the social." The river was, for local Aborigines, an integral part of indigenous cultures of the region, and not in a "stable" and "permanent" form either. The variability of the river is well explored in a variety of traditional song cycles and bodies of knowledge, such as that which allowed people to read the stories of creation, for example, from the different imagined forms made visible as the river waters rose in floods and flowed in different ways over the large rock formations of the fisheries stretch.

This fundamental philosophical difference was complicated in Brewarrina by the presence of the fisheries, which were such obviously productive engineering works that the settler society was itself sustained economically by them in its early years. This exposed both differences and similarities between the two cultures. On one hand, Indigenous societies valued very differently the rich life forms within the river itself. But on the other hand, indigenous societies had a very utilitarian value for the fisheries, in a manner comparable to western grazing or agriculture, which is far removed from the mystical and distanced appreciation of "nature" by the romantic poets of western literature in the nineteenth century or by the "wilderness" advocates among environmentalists of the present.[22] This offered some shared appreciation of the river, but otherwise, in two quite different ways, the western settler concepts of the river as border and as external to society were in constant conflict with indigenous understandings of the river.

In any event, the "natural" river did not ever fulfil the settler desire to confine "nature" to an inert and impermeable border. In fact the very essence of "the natural" in Australia is extreme variability and unpredictability. It is this variability to which the river's ecosystems are adapted and in which they are healthy and productive. Then the inaccessible nature of the deeply gullied and unstable black soil banks of these rivers meant that they allowed many places to retreat from the controls over behavior and cohabitation of the "main street" where conformity and dominance were performed regularly by the town's elites. The river banks were then never so easily guarded as the new "modern" pool entrances. They always allowed Aborigines to slip away from white police, to fish, teach, and dance in protected safe and known space. And they allowed transgressions: Aborigines could drink, "trespass," camp, and cohabit with whomever they liked in the riverbank's hidden and cloistered gullies. And so could whites. The river banks formed crucial liminal zones where white people too could hold private and secluded parties for transgressive drinking and sexual activity, where young people could experiment out of sight and reach of elders and family, and where interracial contact could and did occur.

So the "natural" border was an illusion: the river bank was in fact unstable and ever changing. Its ruggedness and literal slipperiness worked in a metaphorical sense as well as a very material one. These were safe spaces where all sorts of sabotaging of settler control could and did go on. So "nature" did not shore up the permanence of spatial racism but actually betrayed and undermined it.

Inevitably then, the "natural" has become a site of conflict and contestation, just as the built environment of modernity and segregation had become before it. This conflict has been played out not only in the language of "civil rights" as the conflict over the segregation of the built environment has been enacted, but in the language of cultural reassertion. Indigenous people have been able to claim their rights ever more effectively as a wider audience, beyond rural Australia, responds to the challenge Indigenous owners pose to Western concepts of nature as well as the rising concerns over environmental degradation. In the specific situation of Brewarrina, the "economic" or productive dimensions of the fisheries are less often highlighted now because they are less attractive to the wider, and indeed global, potential allies. So the Indigenous owners are reclaiming their country and their rivers, washing away in the process the settler illusions that the land bears a witness to the permanence of segregation or to a colonial, racialized hierarchy.

NOTES

1. Population figures based on 1996 Census, Australian Bureau of Statistics. Indigenous people in this area refer to themselves in English as either Aboriginal or Black, or, in local languages, with words which mean "our people," like Mari [pronounced like Murray] or Kuri [pronounced with a short "u" as in the English "put"]. All these terms are used in this chapter, depending on speaker being quoted.

2. Barbara Ching and Gerald Creed. (eds): *Knowing Your Place: Rural Identity and Cultural Hierarchy*, (London: Routledge,1997); Henk Van Houtum, and Ton van Naerssen: "Bordering, Ordering and Othering" *Royal Dutch Geographical Society*, 2001; Donald S Moore: "Clear Waters and muddied Histories: Environmental History and the Politics of Community in Zimbabwe's Eastern Highlands," *Journal of Southern African Studies*, 24(2) 1998: 377–403; Owen Dwyer: "Interpreting the Civil Rights Movement: Place, Memory and Conflict," *Professional Geographer*, 52 (4) (2000): 660–71; David Glassberg, "Interpreting Landscapes" in Martin V. Melosi and Philip V. Scarpino [eds.] *Public History and the Environment*, (Malabar, Florida: Krieger Publishing Company, 2004, 23–36); Denis Byrne, Helen Brayshaw, H and Tracy Ireland: *Social Significance: A Discussion Paper*, (Research Unit, Cultural Heritage Division, NSW NPWS, 2001); Denis Byrne and Maria Nugent: *Mapping Attachment:* (Sydney: University of New South Wales Press, 2004); Francesca Merlan: *Caging the Rainbow: Places, Politics and Aborigines in a North Australian Town*, (Honolulu: University of Hawaii Press, 1998).

3. Ann Curthoys *Freedom Ride: Memories of a Freedom Rider*, (Sydney: Allen

and Unwin, 2003); Heather Goodall: "Gender, Race and Rivers: Women and Water in Northwestern NSW," in Lahiri-Dutt, K. [ed.] *Fluid Bonds*, (Calcutta: Stree 2004).

4. For the active work required in the continual construction of "whiteness" along with other ethnicities in conflictual situations, see Hsu-Ming Teo: "Multiculturalism and the Problem of Multicultural Histories: An Overview of Ethnic Historiography," in Teo, H and White, R., [eds.] *Cultural History in Australia* (Sydney: Allen and Unwin. 2003).

5. Elaine Thompson [ed.] *Bric a Brac*, series of locally published resource books, (Dubbo: Brewarrina Local History Society, 1980s).

6. For contested views of "nature" in settler societies, see Veronica Strang: *Uncommon Ground: Cultural Landscapes and Environmental Values*, Oxford & New York: Berg, 1997, and for a reflective essays on the role of nature in settler narratives see William Cronon: "A Place for Stories: Nature, History and Narrative," *Journal of American History*, 78(4) 1992; and others in William Cronon (ed.): *Uncommon Ground: Rethinking the Human Place in Nature*, New York and London: W.W. Norton and Co, 1995.

7. Heather Goodall: *Invasion to Embassy: Land in Aboriginal Politics, 1770–1970*, Sydney: Allen and Unwin, 1996.

8. Peter Dargin: *Aboriginal Fisheries of the Darling-Barwon Rivers*, Dubbo: Brewarrina Historical Society, 1976

9. Interview with author, Tranby College, Sydney, 1997.

10. A small native parrot.

11. These are major figures of oral tradition: Baiame for example is the overall creator. Baluu is associated with the moon and Wan, the Crow. All are significant actors in the region's narratives.

12. Dargin, 1976.

13. Les Darcy [Ngiyampaa] Interview with author, Brewarrina, 1989

14. Isabel Flick and Heather Goodall: *Isabel Flick: The Many Lives of an Extraordinary Aboriginal Woman*, Sydney: Allen and Unwin, 2004.

15. Barbara Loughnan, Sue Hall and others, non-indigenous residents, Brewarrina, 1996.

16. Peter Tobin: *Report on Brewarrina*, typescript, author's possession, 1974.

17. Tombo Winters, interview with author, Sydney, 2002.

18. The major NSW daily newspaper.

19. An Australian journalist, who would then have been very young, but who eventually became well known for her international reporting for the Australian public broadcaster.

20. Essie Coffee interviews with author, in Brewarrina 1989 and Sydney, 2000.

21. An Indigenous language word used widely among Aboriginal people in NSW to mean "our people." [Pronounced Kuri with the "u" as in the English word "put."]

22. A valuable parallel discussion of this issue in the United States context is that by Richard White: "Are You an Environmentalist or Do You Work for a Living? Work and Nature" in Cronon [ed.] *Uncommon Ground*, 1995, 171–85.

18

"Taking Us for Village Idiots"
Two Stories of Ethnicity, Class, and Toxic Waste from Sydney, Australia[1]

Peggy James

INTRODUCTION

A common story in Australia's history of environmental activism is about a Government initiative to establish a facility to destroy the nation's toxic waste, and the mainstream environment movement's response. Given that the mainstream groups mostly supported the government initiative throughout an unremarkable series of meetings and documents, and the initiative ultimately failed, the story seems an odd inclusion in a narrative about the significance of environmentalism in the nation's history. The story of Australia's high temperature incinerator (HTI) is examined here using discourse analysis to help understand why it has become a part of environmental history, while other potentially illuminating stories of environmental activism have been excluded.

The theory underpinning the analysis holds that history is a socially constructed discourse, and that social institutions both constrain and can be changed by historical narratives, including narratives that explain how an influential environment movement developed.[2] The method involves analysing a number of texts that provide the basic story of the proposed HTI, and identifying *foregrounded issues*, *key players*, and *colorful descriptors*.[3] This sets the scene for the identification of *backgrounded issues and players*, and two new stories about toxic waste destruction facilities that provide alternatives to the standard story. The conclusion briefly considers how main-

271

stream Australian environmentalism may have constrained the story of the HTI, and might be invigorated in the future by the inclusion of new stories in its history, such as those here which take place in diverse, working-class communities.[4]

The key reference for the standard story of the HTI is Hutton and Connors, who set the story in the relevant context of Australia's history of environmental activism.[5] Hutton and Connors are academics who identify themselves as participants in the Australian environment movement. They suggest that urban and anti-pollution campaigns formed part of the wave of environmental activism that continued into the 1980s. In introductory comments to their stories of anti-pollution activism, Hutton and Connors note the importance of local environment groups at this time, but communicate ambivalence about the contribution of local groups to the environment movement. They state that local groups often had a weak knowledge of the environmental impacts of different technologies, were sometimes narrowly self-interested, often were incapable of campaigning effectively, and frequently disappeared from view after having failed. Perplexingly, they suggest that some local campaigners "went on to become activists themselves," presumably in the mainstream groups.[6]

The basic story Hutton and Connors recount about the proposed HTI is nonetheless common in Australia's environmental literature, and versions of the story by Beder and McDonell are also analyzed here, and demonstrate the persistence and consistency of the story across different sources.[7] Beder and McDonell are also academics, and Beder has a history of environmental activism while McDonell was a member of the body that proposed the HTI. The standard story recounted here conforms to the version I picked up during several years work in the mainstream environment movement during the nineties.

THE STANDARD STORY: AUSTRALIA'S TOXIC WASTE INCINERATOR

The standard story of Australia's toxic waste incinerator starts in 1987, when the Commonwealth, New South Wales (NSW), and Victorian Governments established a Joint Task Force on Intractable Waste (JTF). Prior to this time, the story goes, there had been several attempts to site HTI in Australia to deal with hazardous organochlorine wastes, but these had all failed because of local opposition. In the late eighties, these 'intractable' wastes were being stockpiled or taken offshore for destruction. Since the commonwealth government had responsibility for import and export licenses for the wastes, and NSW and Victoria had the largest quantities, these three governments established the JTF to conduct a public inquiry.

The JTF had strong support from most of the mainstream Australian environment groups, and one of its members was closely connected to the Australian Conservation Foundation (ACF). These groups agreed on the need for a waste minimization approach, but were concerned about fires in warehouses storing chemical wastes. An advisory committee, that included representatives of industry, trade unions, government, and mainstream environment groups such as the Total Environment Centre (TEC), provided ongoing input to the JTF, and a phased, public consultation program was undertaken.

In 1988, the taskforce issued a report proposing a government-owned national HTI, and community consultation to identify an appropriate site. It recommended that the HTI form part of a broader waste minimization approach, and be operated in a manner that would avoid environmental problems encountered overseas. At some overseas facilities, operators ran incinerators at temperatures too low to destroy certain chemical compounds, resulting in air emissions of pollutants. In response, the mainstream environment groups on the advisory committee generally approved the JTF's approach.

The public consultations continued, and some twelve sites were investigated for the incinerator. In 1990, the JTF published its final report, recommending the establishment of the HTI in Corowa, in rural NSW. The HTI was strongly opposed by Greenpeace and Friends of the Earth, as well as by the residents of Corowa who organized a campaign against the proposal. Greenpeace was the most prominent critic of the HTI, and campaigned against it because it believed that incineration was unsafe because of air emissions, it represented an end-of-pipe solution that facilitated waste generation, and hazardous waste should remain at its source until development of new treatment technologies.

The campaign was successful and the incinerator proposal was withdrawn. Most versions of the story end here, in 1990, with the issue of hazardous waste management unresolved. McDonell however extends the story up until around 1993.[8] He notes that in 1991, the governments established a new advisory group, the Independent Panel on Intractable Waste (IPIW). The IPIW reported in 1992 that it had made a conceptual shift away from the HTI and now thought the solution was to identify small facilities to deal with particular types of intractable waste near their source. The IPIW recommended the preparation of a scheduled list of wastes to be used to identify solutions for separate waste streams.

Despite the differences in the perspectives of the authors, analysing this story across the different texts reveals interesting similarities. The *foregrounded issues* in the Hutton and Connors, Beder and McDonell accounts include high-temperature incinerator technology, the amount, type, and storage of waste at the time, waste management policy, and the public consultation process. The *key players* are the JTF and mainstream environment groups including Greenpeace, the Corowa community to a lesser extent, and government policy makers and consultation advisers.

The most obvious use of *colorful descriptors* or loaded terms in each account is to describe key players and their activities. Hutton and Connors describe mainstream environmentalists as giving *"cautious approval"* to the HTI and having a *"serious concern"* about fires in chemical waste stores, whereas Corowa residents were simply *"incensed."*[9] McDonell tells us that the JTF relied on *"the best available scientific and technical advice"* and *"enjoyed wide expressions of confidence"* from various groups. He says that *"hostile"* criticism was made by Greenpeace and *"radical"* groups, and even though the JTF conducted an extensive information program in Corowa prior to site selection *"the Corowa community exploded with cries of 'no consultation'."*[10] Even Beder, who argues that public relations campaigns, exemplified by the JTF consultation program, are *"manipulative and cynically conducted,"* says that Greenpeace *"emphasised the things that can go awry"* with HTI's and *"stressed departures from the ideal,"* whereas the Corowa residents were *"particularly incensed"* and had *"a massive angry reaction"* to the HTI proposal.[11] When Hutton and Connors instruct us that the problem with intractable wastes was *"not so much their toxicity"* but their potential to bioaccumulate, readers could be forgiven for concluding that the residents of Corowa were more toxic and intractable than the waste itself.[12]

Looking for *backgrounded issues and players*, or who and what have been left of these accounts, gives rise to numerous possibilities. An obvious omission would seem to be all of the campaigns against the HTI prior to the establishment of the JTF. After all, if any of these campaigns had failed, no Task Force would have been established in the first place. The story provides no information on when and where HTI's were proposed or why the developments were opposed. The story also places in the background the local impacts, both positive and negative, of the HTI. The reader is told that if the incinerator is poorly run there will be pollution, but is not told quantities or types of pollutants, nor what types and quantities of pollution would be produced if the plant were properly run, or if there would have been any benefit for a community that agreed to host the HTI. Finally, apart from a few acknowledgements of the Corowa community, what is left out of this story are the voices of all of the people who might actually have been affected by the HTI had it been established. In the end, the standard story in Australia's history of environmentalism is about the views of a handful of mainstream environmentalists and environmental bureaucrats, who participated in a public inquiry, that produced some recommendations that were not implemented.

A FORGOTTEN STORY: THE PROPOSED
WETHERILL PARK TOXIC WASTE INCINERATOR

One of the episodes left out of the standard story is the campaign against the HTI in Wetherill Park in 1982. Wetherill Park is in the outer suburbs of Sydney, in the Fairfield municipality around 30 kilometers from the city center. Industry and housing, and a resident population of considerable ethnic diversity, developed in Fairfield after World War II. At this time, commonwealth and state governments implemented a Keynesian economic growth strategy involving industry and housing development, town planning to ensure efficient and equitable cities, and immigration to provide labor for industry. Sydney's first comprehensive planning scheme zoned land in Fairfield for residential development, industrial development, and included Wetherill Park in the city's green belt.[13] The commonwealth provided migrant workers hostels at Cabramatta, one of the residential areas, and across the municipal boundary at Villawood, to accommodate displaced persons from Europe. The commonwealth deliberately located the migrant hostels close to industrial workplaces to minimize the journey to work. As displaced person Eastern Europeans moved out of the hostels, many settled in inexpensive housing on the city's fringe in the Fairfield area. An Italian-born community that worked in market gardens in the green belt, and expanded through chain migration, also grew there in the 1950s and 1960s.[14]

When Sydney's second planning scheme was prepared in 1968, most of Wetherill Park was shown zoned for future industry, with nearby land zoned for housing.[15] Like the hostel planners, Sydney's land-use planners placed residential areas close to industrial land to minimize the journey to work. The zoned areas at Wetherill Park developed in the 1970s, at the same time as the hostels accommodated new foreign-born groups including Indo-Chinese refugees. By the 1980s, Fairfield was one of the centers of multicultural Sydney, with nearly half its residents foreign-born, including people from Vietnam, Cambodia, Italy, Poland, and the former Yugoslavia. It was also a working-class municipality, with high levels of unemployment as the economy restructured, and a high percentage of low-income earners.[16]

In 1981, the Metropolitan Waste Disposal Authority (MWDA) developed a proposal for the HTI and a liquid waste plant (LWP) at Wetherill Park. The LWP had been recommended in a 1970 report on Sydney's waste, and the HTI had become part of the LWP design to deal with the chlorinated hydrocarbon waste stream. An earlier LWP/HTI proposal had fallen through, and the MWDA redesigned its plant and identified a site in the industrial estate at Wetherill Park. A key issue in site selection was proximity to liquid waste generators, who were moving out of inner suburbs to large sites in new industrial zones in outer Sydney. The Wetherill Park site was located only 300 meters from the nearest house, close to market gardens that still existed on rezoned land, and about a kilometer from a water supply storage for Sydney at the time, Prospect Reservoir. It was only 700 meters from the local primary school, scheduled for future use as a special school for disadvantaged and disabled children.[17]

The LWP would treat aqueous wastes, such as oil-water-sludge mixtures, using physical-chemical and biological treatment, and the HTI would burn wastes such as granular pesticides, pathogenic wastes and chlorinated hydrocarbons including hexachlorobenzene (HCB), in a rotary kiln. The Environment Impact Statement (EIS) for the project indicated that air emissions would include sulphur dioxide, hydrochloric acid, nitrogen dioxide, and particles, but generally did not specify pollutant loads or concentrations because design of the plant was incomplete. An assurance was provided that pollution control equipment would be selected to ensure compliance with NSW Clean Air Act regulations, however the regulations only covered a limited range of substances. Odors might occur but were *"not expected to be a problem,"* and in relation to hazards, it was considered *"highly unlikely that a major fatal accident would statistically occur."* The EIS conceded that there could be rare explosions at the plant *"which could throw burning materials over small distances,"* but could not assess the risk because there was inadequate design detail to undertake a hazard analysis.[18]

The EIS was apparently completed in June 1981, however with a state election only a few months away, the MWDA's proposal was not immediately brought forward. One member of the MWDA board (until December 1981), was standing as an Australian Labor Party (ALP) candidate for the seat of Fairfield, and the Environment and Planning Minister was standing in the nearby seat of Cabramatta. In the September election, the two were elected in landslide votes.[19] Then in 1982, the MWDA submitted its development application for the HTI to Fairfield Council.

Following newspaper reports about the plant, residents protested to local parliamentarians, sent letters to the paper and attended the next council meeting to express their concerns. A public meeting was organized to fight the proposal, and some 700 attendees elected independent Alderman Sam Barone and Mike Zborowski, a civil engineer, to lead the Action Committee for a Toxic-Free Sydney. The meeting resolved to hold a march through the streets of Cabramatta to protest against the LWP and HTI. A TEC representative reportedly addressed attendees, calling for consideration of alternatives such as incineration at sea. At that stage, the toxics committee of the TEC had only been established for a few years, and Greenpeace did not have a strong campaign presence in Sydney.[20]

Over the following weeks, around 1000 submissions were lodged with council and 1500 letters sent to the member for Fairfield opposing the development. Many residents argued that pollutants from the plant would create a health threat, the plant was too close to the reservoir at Prospect and a toxic waste incinerator should not be located near housing. The local paper reported that Mike Zborowski *"was concerned about the lack of technical data and contradictions contained in the EIS for the scheme,"* and he said dioxins would be emitted to the atmosphere if chlorinated hydrocarbons were not burned at the right temperature.[21] A letter writer from nearby Smithfield said that the *"government is taking us for village idiots"* by putting the waste plant in an electorate where voters had given them a huge majority at the election.[22] Some residents were concerned about property values, hardly surprising given that many people had moved to the lower cost housing to establish a better life for their families.[23]

When the protest march was held, in the middle of the week prior to a council meeting, some 650 people packed the streets of Cabramatta. Reflecting the multicultural nature of the Fairfield community, protesters wearing gas masks, rubber gloves, and protective clothing carried a banner proclaiming their outfits as the new *"Wetherill Park National Costume."*[24] The protest march had its share of colorful and alarmist banners, including a skull and crossbones titled *"Poison Kills,"* and Sydney's broadsheet newspaper described the residents as *"angry"* and *"placard-waving."*[25]

At the council meeting that followed, the chairman of the ALP caucus, the majority group on council, announced that labor councillors had decided against the incinerator because it should not be near residential development. With Fairfield Council now poised to reject the development, the Minister announced a Commission of Inquiry into the proposal and that the state government would make the final decision. However a week later, a commonwealth parliamentary committee that was independently examining hazardous chemicals, tabled a report in Parliament recommending the NSW government be approached to accept intractable waste from all states at its proposed HTI. The report's recommendation featured on the front page of the local paper, and not long after, the MWDA withdrew its development application, apparently to avoid further protest about an expanded facility.[26]

As a key participant in *"the biggest protest movement in Fairfield's history,"* Sam Barone issued a victory statement on behalf of the Action Committee. He said credit for the successful campaign should go to the people of Fairfield, who had refused to be dismissed as *"donkeys"* and shown the government *"that the people of Wetherill Park can read and write."* The statement said *"we appreciate the massive problems entailed in finding a satisfactory solution to what is in fact an Australia-wide problem,"* and added that there was an urgent need for state and federal governments to work together to find acceptable ways of dealing with toxic waste.[27] The Minister indicated that the government now intended to pursue the LWP and HTI proposals separately, and by 1987, toxic waste was on Australia's national policy agenda and the JTF had been established.

The Wetherill Park campaign did not have a perfect outcome, because the LWP was subsequently built in another ethnically diverse, low-income suburb of Sydney. However as a result of the protest, the plant no longer incorporated an HTI to deal with the chlorinated hydrocarbon waste stream, thereby reducing the plant's pollutant emissions and risk. The public now knows, from Australia's National Pollutant Inventory (NPI), that the LWP alone emits a range of toxic pollutants, including dioxins, mercury and benzene, and Friends of the Earth and Greenpeace now work with local residents seeking its closure. Residents have frequently complained about odors from the LWP, and it has been successfully prosecuted on this account. The Wetherill Park industrial area now has more than its fair share of polluting facilities, including several on Australia's NPI. The Wetherill Park campaign did not solve Sydney's waste problems, but it stopped a poor project from proceeding and its environmental and policy outcomes were more significant than those of the failed JTF.

A CURRENT STORY: THE PROPOSED BOTANY HCB DESTRUCTION PLANT

Twenty years after the Wetherill Park protest, a chemical company called Orica Australia Pty Ltd proposed a facility to destroy HCB waste at its Botany site. Orica's site is about 10 kilometers south of central Sydney, located in an industrial zone that stretches into the Randwick area and joins the Port of Botany Bay. Prior to the war, some noxious industries located in Botany to access water resources and avoid pollution complaints from more densely populated inner suburbs. Orica (formerly Imperial Chemical Industries of Australia and New Zealand) established its plant during World War II as part of Australia's war effort. When governments subsequently implemented their Keynesian strategies, the Botany/Randwick area was zoned for industrial and residential growth. Living areas adjoined the industrial areas to minimize the journey to work for future factory workers, even though Botany's industrial land was zoned for noxious and offensive industries. The commonwealth sited two of its migrant workers hostels not far from the Orica site, to ensure a labor supply for the industrial area. The migrant hostels facilitated the development of an ethnically diverse local community, as did small prewar ethnic communities in the Botany/Randwick area, including a Greek-born community that grew mostly through chain migration.

The residents who lived there prior to the war had already experienced pollution problems. However the postwar industrial growth increased the pollution, and the residential zoning allowed more people to move into the area and suffer pollution exposure. By the time Sydney's second strategic plan was prepared in 1968, land in Botany/Randwick was already developed, but Sydney's planners made provision for new industrial land to be reclaimed from Botany Bay for a major port and industrial complex. Hazardous installations such as bulk chemical stores were subsequently established as part of the port development. Around this time, the commonwealth facilitated the settlement of new foreign-born groups in the Randwick area with a replacement migrant center, because of a perceived need for additional labor. However, manufacturing employment wound down in Botany/Randwick as the economy restructured, with job losses offset to an extent by the growth in port-related uses. By 2000, longer-term residents of the diverse Botany/Randwick community could remember worse air pollution and chemical accidents in the past, but were still faced with several hazardous and polluting facilities, contaminated land and groundwater, and a proposed port expansion.

At the Orica site in the 1960s, the manufacture of chlorinated chemicals such as carbon tetrachloride and ethylene dichloride produced HCB wastes, and the HCB waste was stored in drums awaiting disposal. By the late 1980s it became apparent, partly due to campaigning by Greenpeace, that soil and groundwater at the site were contaminated with numerous compounds from a range of previous activities. A subsequent groundwater study mapped a large plume of groundwater contaminated with chemicals such as 1,2 dichloroethane, thought to extend just short of the boundary separating industry from the residential area to the west, and down to the Bay foreshore in the south.[28] As work proceeded on how to address the groundwater contamination, Orica developed its proposal to destroy approximately 10,500 tonnes of stored HCB waste.

Orica's proposal was broadly consistent with the policies developed after the failure of the JTF. Australian governments had agreed on a *National Strategy for the Management of Scheduled Waste*, centered on the identification and treatment of separate types of toxic waste. The national HCB waste management plan focused on Orica's HCB stockpile because it was the only significant source of the waste in Australia, and said that given the perceived hazards of transporting the waste, Orica's waste at Botany should preferably be destroyed on-site.[29] In 2001, Orica proposed a process plant for Botany that would operate for four years, using technology that would melt a mix of HCB waste and soil, producing a vitrified glassy rock. Contaminated off-gases would be treated through several processes including thermal oxidation prior to release, but stack emissions would include low levels of HCB, dioxins, mercury, benzene, and criteria pollutants like nitrogen dioxide. Orica argued that its emissions would comply with limits established by regulators, and said that with modifications, the plant posed less than a ten-in-a-million risk to nearby Hillsdale residents of serious injury.[30]

Many residents however had already experienced pollution incidents caused by various industries in Botany, and were sceptical of what they considered the same old claims that accidents were unlikely and would be limited in impact. Local residents and groups wrote letters and prepared submissions opposing the project when the state government directed a Commission of Inquiry, and many of these referred to pollution accidents experienced first hand. A couple from Hillsdale wrote to the Inquiry *"Although [a local factory] claims it is a safe facility the local people are very aware of the many explosions and odiferous emissions of the plant over the years and we all have grave fears about this new proposal."*[31] One of their neighbours confirmed *"I have lived in Hillsdale . . . for 32 years. We have been subject to emissions of poisonous gases released to the atmosphere from [a local plant] over many years . . . No amount of control and stringent standards can prevent operator or human error."*[32] A woman who worked further away wrote *"I am an ex-School Principal from the Botany area. During the ten years of time there we were constantly inundated with smells of one sort or the other from many and varied places. . . . Indeed on one occasion, as the result of a fire from an industrial site, most of the students and many of the staff were rushed to hospital."*[33]

As at Wetherill Park and during the JTF consultation process, there was no information available in community languages about the HCB destruction proposal, despite the large foreign-born population. Fortunately, this didn't prevent all residents of non-English speaking background from pointing out problems in the expert testimony. One woman, on being told that the wind would blow pollution away from her home in an accident, wrote in her submission to the Commissioner *"Che cosa credona, perche' siamo persone semplici non arriviamo a capire, che il vento non lo comanda nessuno?"* or *"What do they think, that because we are simple people we do not understand that the wind obeys no one?"*[34]

Memories of polluting accidents were provided not only as evidence that expert assumptions and conclusions about risk were questionable, but also as evidence that Botany residents had suffered their fair share of pollution and it was wrong to subject them to more. Nancy Hillier was one resident who had fought numerous campaigns, often successfully, to stop new polluting developments coming into an already polluted area in Botany. Many residents had had enough, and did not think it fair that, in order to eliminate the HCB storage risk inflicted on them for the last thirty-five years, they were the ones asked to sacrifice some of their air quality and peace of mind during the plant's operation. Nancy wrote to the Commission of Inquiry that *"Botany has made many sacrifices for NSW, Sea Port, Air Port, fuel storage; no other area contributes more to provide the necessary resources to keep a country functioning. We are no longer to be seen as a City where you dump your offensive industries."*[35]

Mainstream environment groups such as Greenpeace and TEC were not particularly opposed to selection of the Botany site. In the case of Greenpeace, site selection was consistent with the *"return to sender"* policy it advocated when the JTF was deliberating, that toxic waste should be located where it was generated to avoid transferring risk onto communities hosting waste facilities.[36] The flaw in the Greenpeace policy, of relevance to the Botany HCB dispute, was that toxic waste generators already inflicted pollution and risk on nearby communities, and storing and destroying toxic waste at the site of generation inflicted more risk on the same community. Greenpeace nonetheless opposed the proposed HCB-destruction technology, describing it as *"bucket chemistry with incineration and pollution control equipment bolted on the back end."*[37]

The commissioner recommended approval of the project, but the government ordered an independent review of the proposal prior to its decision. While residents of Botany waited, the state's environmental regulator announced that new tests indicated the contaminated groundwater plume may have shifted under residential areas, and Orica stepped up its work on groundwater remediation. Then in 2004, the government announced that the review panel had found that Botany was an inappropriate location for the HCB destruction facility, and Orica would work with the panel to identify a better site. The government and Orica also promised a reassessment of the risks of interim HCB storage at Botany and improvements to the storage facilities. Greenpeace responded by attacking the decision and independent report, because they did not reject the proposed waste destruction technology.[38]

CONCLUSION

The history of the Australian environment movement includes a story line about increased pollution concern in the 1980s, and activism associated with the JTF and proposed HTI. However, the standard story largely omits environmental campaigns against toxic waste destruction facilities organised by the people who would have been most affected by them. The campaign of the people of Corowa is the only one recognized in the standard story of the HTI, and it is largely sidelined through the use of the same stereotypical terms used against mainstream environmentalists in the past. If the discourse of Australian environmentalism generates a story that silences the voices of the people on the receiving end of polluting toxic waste facilities, then we should ask why.

Discourse theory suggests that discourses influence what can be said and done through their unspoken rules. It seems from the discourse analysis of the standard story that there may be rules of Australian environmentalism that make it difficult to acknowledge environmental campaigns organised by people affected by toxic waste facilities. One rule may be that the Australian environment movement advocates for ecocentric concerns and intergenerational equity, rather than anthropocentric concerns such as equity within the existing generation, because the latter should be undertaken by a separate social movement. Another rule may be that environmentalism rejects the displacement approach to pollution control, because some toxic pollutants bioaccumulate, and place based campaigns that might shift pollution to another location do not qualify as environmentalism.[39]

Rather than identify rules governing such an exclusive discourse of environmentalism, historians may exercise their agency to construct a history of the environment movement that is more plausible and inclusive. If indeed the environment movement is a reasonably influential movement of people actively concerned about the environment, then surely it is made up of activists in diverse, local communities who successfully challenge pollution in their neighbourhoods and achieve environmental improvements, rather than just the advisory group participants and mainstream groups whose recommendations and advice are so readily overturned by angry local residents.

The stories of anti-pollution activism at Wetherill Park and Botany suggest that there may be an insightful narrative of Australian environmentalism that includes environmentalism in diverse, working-class communities. They show that there are policy mechanisms from the past that could underlie some Australian environmental justice activism—the deliberate location of migrant worker hostels and residential zones close to industrial zones, to ensure adequate labor for industry and shorter journeys to work. It remains to be seen whether these policies can be linked to a larger pattern of environmental inequality and anti-pollution protest in Australian cities. Nonetheless, historians who recover the stories of diverse, working-class environmentalists and construct better histories may encourage environmental activism and policy that is based on an understanding that environmental and social concerns are connected, and prevent the growth of an antisocial movement that regards environmental and equity concerns as potentially irreconcilable.

NOTES

1. Carl and Beryl Beauchamp, "Letter to the Editor," *Fairfield Advance*, 28 April 1982, 8.

2. This version of discourse theory draws on Maarten Hajer, *The Politics of Environmental Discourse* (Oxford: Oxford University Press, 1996), who acknowledges his debt to Michel Foucault, *The Archaeology of Knowledge* (London: Tavistock Publications, 1972) and Anthony Giddens, *The Constitution of Society* (Berkeley: University of California Press, 1984).

3. The method used for the discourse analysis is influenced by John Dryzek, *The Politics of the Earth* (Oxford: Oxford University Press, 1997) and Crispin Butteriss, John Wolfenden and Alistair Goodridge, "Discourse Analysis: A Technique to Assist Conflict Management in Environmental Policy Development," *Australian Journal of Environmental Management* 8 no. 1 (2001), 48–58.

4. A similar point about the history and future of the U.S. environment movement is made by Robert Gottlieb, *Forcing the Spring* (Washington D.C.: Island Press, 1993).

5. Drew Hutton and Libby Connors, *A History of the Australian Environment Movement* (Cambridge: Cambridge University Press, 1999).

6. Hutton and Connors, *A History of the Australian Environment Movement*, 198.

7. Sharon Beder, "Public Participation or Public Relations?" *Technology and Public Participation*, ed. Brian Martin (Wollongong: University of Wollongong, 1999), via University of Wollongong, http://www.uow.edu.au/arts/sts/TPP/beder.htm (accessed July 26, 2001); Gavan McDonell, "Toxic Waste Management in Australia," *Environment* 33 no. 6 (1991); Gavan McDonell, "Scientific and Everyday Knowledge: Trust and the Politics of Environmental Initiatives," *Social Studies of Science* 27 no. 6 (1997), 819–63.

8. McDonell, "Scientific and Everyday Knowledge."

9. Hutton and Connors, *A History of the Australian Environment Movement*, 210–11.

10. McDonell, "Toxic Waste Management in Australia," 11–12.

11. Beder, "Public Participation or Public Relations?," 3–8.

12. Hutton and Connors, *A History of the Australian Environment Movement*, 210.

13. Cumberland County Council, *The Planning Scheme for the County of Cumberland, New South Wales* (Sydney: CCC, 1948).

14. Ian Burnley, *The Impact of Immigration on Australia* (South Melbourne: Oxford University Press, 2001).

15. State Planning Authority, *Sydney Region Outline Plan* (Sydney: SPA, 1968).

16. Australian Bureau of Statistics, *Census 86: Profile of Legal Local Government Areas, Usual Residents Counts—NSW* (Canberra: ABS, 1988); Australian Bureau of Statistics, *Sydney: A Social Atlas* (Canberra: ABS, 1989).

17. Gutteridge, Haskins, and Davey Pty Ltd, *Environmental Impact Statement: Regional Liquid Waste Treatment Plant, Sydney NSW* (Chatswood: MWDA, 1981).

18. Gutteridge, Haskins, and Davey, *Environmental Impact Statement*, 40–42.

19. "Janice in Land Slide Poll Win," *Fairfield Advance*, 23 September 1981, 1.

20. "Protesters Plan March in Cabra," *Fairfield Advance*, 7 April 1982, 1; "Demonstrators Pack Street in Cabra Rally," *Fairfield Advance*, 21 April 1982, 2.

21. "Protesters to Slam Bedford," *Fairfield Advance*, 21 April 1982, 8.

22. Carl and Beryl Beauchamp, "Letter to the Editor," 8.

23. R. Lamberton, "Letter to the Editor," *Fairfield Advance*, 7 April 1982, 9.

24. "Waste Plant Axed: Rebuff to Wran," *Fairfield Advance*, 12 May 1982, 36.

25. "ALP Aldermen Oppose Toxic Waste Plant," *Sydney Morning Herald*, 15 April 1982, 10.

26. Amanda Buckley, "Inquiry into Proposed Toxic Waste Plant," *Sydney Morning Herald*, 24 April 1982, 7; "Waste Report Urges National Dump," *Fairfield Advance*, 5 May 1982, 1.

27. "Waste Plant Axed: Rebuff to Wran," 36.

28. Woodward-Clyde, *ICI Botany Groundwater Stage 2 Survey: Overview Report* (Matraville: ICI Australia, 1996).

29. Australian and New Zealand Environment and Conservation Council, *Hexachlorobenzene Waste Management Plan* (Canberra: Environment Australia, 1996).

30. Orica Engineering, Preliminary Hazard Analysis for HCB Waste Destruction Facility, Orica Australia Botany Site NSW, Revision C (Melbourne: Orica Engineering, 2002); Kevin Cleland, Hexachlorobenzene Waste Destruction Facility, Botany Industrial Park (Sydney: Commissioners of Inquiry for Environment and Planning, 2002).

31. Jan and Gustav Düttmer, "Submission to Commission of Inquiry on Proposed HCB Facility, Botany" (Sydney: Unpublished, 2002).

32. Olivera Erturk, "Proposed HCB Facility Environmental Impact Statement Submission" (Sydney: Unpublished, 2002).

33. Juliana Gennison, "Submission on Proposed HCB Facility, Botany" (Sydney: Unpublished, 2002).

34. Giovanna Fuoti, "Submission to Kevin Cleland Re: Proposal for Hexachlorobenzene Waste Destruction Facility by Orica Australia Pty Ltd," Translation Paollo Nocella (Sydney: Unpublished, 2002).

35. Nancy Hillier, "Botany Environment Watch Submission to Commission of Inquiry, Orica Proposed Destruction of HCB Waste at Orica Botany Site" (Sydney: Unpublished, 2002).

36. Greenpeace Australia, *Say No to the Toxic Oven* (Balmain: Greenpeace Australia, 1990).

37. Matt Ruchel, "Greenpeace Commission of Inquiry Submission: Proposed Hexachlorobenzene Waste Destruction Facility by Orica Australia Pty Ltd" (Sydney: Unpublished, 2002).

38. James Woodford, "A Thousand Homes at Risk of Toxic Bore Water," *Sydney Morning Herald*, 12 August 2003, 1; Department of Infrastructure, Planning and Natural Resources, "Media Release Ministers Office 9 September 2004: HCB Waste Destruction," http://dipnr.nsw.gov.au/mediarel/mo20040909_2815.html (accessed September 10, 2004); "Orica Shelves Botany Toxic Waste Plan," *Sydney Morning Herald*, 10 September 2004, 13.

39. Hutton and Connors could argue they have spelt out the rules that generated their narrative, but these rules are open to interpretation and challenge.

19

The Mirrar Fight for Jabiluka
Uranium Mining and Indigenous Australians to 2004[1]

Jacqui Katona[2]

If you have not been to our country, you would have only an image in your mind of what Kakadu looks and feels like, 250 miles east of Darwin in tropical northern Australia. Maybe this image would contain bright sunlight, birds, and animals, paperbark swamps with flowers that smell like a baked potato. *Marrawutii,* the sea eagle, swooping low over Mohla billabong. Cool green grasses on hot days, glorious fires where embers burn low in cool night temperatures. Maybe you can imagine what it's like to see tens of thousands of magpie geese feeding on lush floodplains.

These lands give to us our identity, our history, and our future as Mirrar people. We are obligated to take care of this country not only because of what the country provides for us, but because our law requires it. It has been a sustainable economy for thousands of years.

The Australian government passed an Aboriginal Land Rights law in 1976 which was supposed to protect our people and help to rebuild our communities, but in north Kakadu land rights never arrived. Instead, our people's lives have been dominated by uranium mining companies which since the 1970s have forced the opening of one uranium mine on our land, at Ranger, and have campaigned to open a second, at Jabiluka. These companies have been driven by narrow financial imperatives and have shown little regard for the future of the Aboriginal community.[3] Traditional elder and senior custodian Yvonne Margarula has said:

The Mirrar People have fought against uranium mining in Kakadu for two generations. My father fought against the Ranger mine and today, with my sisters and other Mirrar, we are fighting against the Jabiluka mine. Jabiluka threatens to destroy our sacred sites, our connection to country, our life. Rio Tinto has promised that it will not mine Jabiluka unless the Mirrar say yes; we want Rio Tinto and ERA[4] to put that promise in writing. Rio Tinto has promised that it will clean up Jabiluka; we want Rio Tinto and ERA to get the uranium they took from Jabiluka and put it back down the hole, we want them to do this during this dry season. Until Rio Tinto and ERA do these things the Mirrar will not believe the company's words. We will continue to fight to protect our country and our culture.[5]

URANIUM MINING IN THE TOP END

Aboriginal land in northern Australia had been threatened by uranium miners from the 1954, when uranium began to be mined at Rum Jungle to the south of Darwin. But the pressure on the northern areas, around Mirrar land in Kakadu, increased in the 1960s, as more and more uranium was being used around the world for both power generation and weapons manufacture. In 1969 uranium was discovered at the Ranger site, and with the Rum Jungle mine running low on ore, the pressure on Kakadu intensified. It was clear that Aboriginal people in the area were going to be heavily affected and that the fragile tropical wetlands could be severely damaged by the mining of such a potentially dangerous mineral.

Power in the Australian government was held, from 1972, by the Labor Party, which had been sympathetic to the long-standing call by northern Australian Aboriginal people for recognition of their rights to land and also wanted to be seen to protect the environment. But the government also wanted the funds from taxes and other financial benefits which would come from mining. So it set up an inquiry, led by Judge Fox, to gather facts on which to base a decision. Justice Fox heard from Aboriginal people about their fears, but it also heard from mining companies who argued that this mine was going to be safe and to make all Australians economically better off.[6] The Fox inquiry reported in 1975 that there were serious dangers both to Aboriginal people and to the environment, but that the mining would be of such great national benefit that these dangers were not enough to stop the mine going ahead. However, the Fox inquiry said the mine and its impacts would need to be strongly controlled and carefully monitored, and the Australian government agreed to do this. In the other major recommendation, Fox argued that the whole area should be made a national park, named Kakadu, and that the Aboriginal people, the Mirrar, should be recognized as Traditional Owners and given title to the land, which would ensure that the mining which did go ahead would be done with the approval of those Traditional Owners.[7]

These recommendations gave the government the green light to approve the mining at one site, Ranger, but the Mirrar people had never agreed to the mine. Our elders campaigned strongly against the mine ever starting, but after a bitter and often dishonest campaign by the mining companies, the government passed laws to override our veto. In an attempt to look environmentally responsible, the government did set aside the Kakadu area as a national park, but with the new legal powers to mine in the park, the only real protection for the environment was to be in the hands of the government authority which was to regulate the safe operation of the mine. Almost before the first trucks of ore had pulled out of Ranger, the pressure began to open a second mine at nearby Jabiluka.

MIRRAR RESPONSIBILITIES FOR COUNTRY AND PEOPLE

To understand how important the environment is to Mirrar, it is necessary to understand we see our country. We Mirrar have rights and interests that arise from country and flow from Mirrar law and custom. These rights are recognised under the 1976 Aboriginal Land Rights Act, which acknowledged that in exercising their rights to their land, Mirrar are guided by their obligations and responsibilities to other *Bininj*[8] affected by Mirrar decisions about Mirrar country.

The living tradition of the Mirrar is integral to the cultural values of the Kakadu World Heritage Area and is directly affected by mining activities in the Jabiluka Mineral Lease enclave. It is important to note that those accustomed to European *(Balanda)* notions of heritage, tradition, cultural landscape, and land ownership need to adjust to very different Aboriginal *(Bininj)* understandings of such concepts when examining living tradition in the Kakadu World Heritage Area.[9]

There are two main approaches to the way Mirrar view their responsibilities: one is looking after country *(gunred)* and the other is looking after people *(guhpleddi)*. *Gunred* encompasses control of country including the prevention of both destruction of country and desecration of sites.

It is also the recognition, assertion, and promotion of cultural rights and the carrying out of living tradition on country. *Guhpleddi* is intrinsically tied to *gunred* because *Bininj* and country are as one. It encompasses an extremely complex set of relationships between Mirrar, other *Bininj* and country.

The Mirrar and other *Bininj* have dreaming tracks that traverse country. These dreaming tracks cross both the Jabiluka and Ranger Mineral Leases and the World Heritage Area. The Mirrar and other *Bininj* have many sacred sites within the Jabiluka and Ranger Mineral Leases. Customary Aboriginal law is inextricably linked to country and ceremony and these sites are interconnected with the spiritual and cultural significance of the entire Mirrar estate and to other *Bininj* country, including the World Heritage Area. These spiritual connections to country should only be described by particular Traditional Owners and Custodians, that is, by particular people at particular times.

Some of the sacred sites on the Jabiluka Mineral Lease, including rock art and ancestral living areas, are recognized under *Balanda* law inside the large areas of the lease registered by the Australian Heritage Commission (AHC). There are no current plans to mine in these AHC areas, but the Mirrar believe these areas are nevertheless affected by mining activity. The entire Jabiluka Mineral Lease was covered by AHC listing until objections by mining companies saw the AHC areas reduced.

There are also sacred sites that are not afforded the "protection" of the AHC areas. One that has been publicly identified by the Traditional Owners and Custodians is the Boywek-Almudj site that is very close to the proposed Jabiluka uranium mine. There are many other sites on the Jabiluka excision that have not been identified by *Bininj* for a range of cultural reasons. Some of these sites are at present being directly and severely impacted upon by the proposed Jabiluka uranium mine.

The importance of sites of significance to the cultural values of Kakadu National Park was confirmed by the Australian government in its 1991 World Heritage renomination document, stating:

> a major aspect of the past that affects the present and future is the creative behaviour of beings said to have travelled across the landscape when it was flat, featureless and lacking the presence of ordinary men and women. These beings are said to have moulded the landscape into its present form and to have established people's languages and social institutions. Aboriginal people hold as significant features of the landscape that mark the temporary or permanent abodes of these beings. This system of beliefs gives Aboriginal people vital links with the land; the links continue through membership of a clan or local descent group.[10]

The Mirrar and other *Bininj* have traditionally hunted, gathered, held ceremonies, lived and died at places all over the Mirrar estate, including the Jabiluka Mineral Lease. *Balanda* scientists have "proved" this by discovering ancient remains and rock art all over Mirrar country, including the Jabiluka Mineral Lease. The Australian government believed one of the archaeological sites inside the Jabiluka Mineral Lease (Malakananja II) to be so important that it specifically referred to it when seeking inscription of Kakadu National Park on the World Heritage List. Following the World Heritage Committee

Mission visit to Kakadu in October 1998, the Mission recommended that Kakadu be declared as 'World Heritage in Danger', and that uranium mining at Jabiluka not proceed. Kakadu is one of less than twenty-five sites world-wide listed by UNESCO's World Heritage Center for both natural and cultural values. These values are intrinsically linked to the living tradition of the Mirrar and are currently under direct threat from existing and proposed uranium mining operations. Although the Mirrar are legally recognised as the traditional owners of the area, the European economic imperative of mining has meant they cannot enjoy their rights as traditional owners.

One of Australia's most respected heritage experts, Professor D. J. Mulvaney, has provided some important guidelines for *Balanda* when considering *Bininj* concepts of living tradition. He states, "expressed succinctly, their traditional world is a humanised landscape which is indivisible and immutable, and every natural feature has a name and meaningful mythological association. Place and person are inseparable, while past and present form a unity of ongoing creation."[11]

IMPACTS OF THE RANGER MINE

So, as everyone had predicted, the impact of the Ranger mine on Mirrar people was severe. Once the demands to begin a second mine at Jabiluka began, we have had to document the damage done by the Ranger mine to help us argue against the even greater impact of a second mine.

The Mirrar believe that their living tradition has sustained an extreme attack as a result of the process by which industrial development has taken place. This attack lies in the refusal by the Australian government to recognize fundamental Mirrar rights to land and the exercise of those rights by the Mirrar. This attack is most clearly manifested in the extinguishment of the Mirrar's right to say "no" to the development of the existing Ranger uranium mine and the duress applied to the Mirrar to gain their consent for development at Jabiluka. The consequences of this attack have exacerbated the poor social and economic conditions experienced by the Aboriginal community. Unemployment, social discord, health, housing, and education problems plague the Kakadu Aboriginal community.

Against the backdrop of national controversy about legislating land rights for Aboriginal communities in the Northern Territory, the mining industry and governments were well aware of the potential for social destabilisztion in the Aboriginal community as a result of uranium mining at Ranger. In the 1970s the federal government Fox Report highlighted the poor social and economic conditions of the Aboriginal people of Kakadu at the time. It said:

personal incomes depend . . . largely on social service payments such as age pensions and family allowance payment, contributions from relatives who are earning wages and the sale of artefacts.[12]

This is still the case.

The Fox Report went on to say that:

> Excessive consumption of alcohol by a large proportion of the Aboriginal peo-
> ple in the Region will have a deleterious effect on their general welfare; their
> future will depend in a large part on removing or substantially reducing the
> causes of this problem.[13]

These causes have never been identified. Alcohol is still an inescapable
problem.

The Fox Report concluded:

> the Aboriginal people of the Region are a depressed group whose standards of
> living are far below those acceptable to the wider Australian society. They are a
> community whose lives have been, and are still being, disrupted by the intru-
> sions of an alien people. They feel the pressures of the white man's activities in
> relation to their land. In the face of mining exploration, and the threat of much
> further development, they feel helpless and lost.[14]

This continues to be the case. Mirrar believe that since the Fox Inquiry in
1977, a continuing cycle of cultural genocide has taken place.

Damage or restricted access to spiritual sites caused by *Balanda* mining
projects contributes to disempowerment and a general pessimism amongst
Bininj that complete loss of culture is imminent. This historical, psychologi-
ca,l and sociological impact is one of the key reasons for abandonment of
traditional living culture by many *Bininj,* and is recognized in symptoms
such as alcoholism and other socioeconomic indicators of cultural decline.

This loss of cultural significance extends to all aspects of Mirrar living tradition, including food collection, ceremony, customary law, spiritual connection, and sociopolitical systems.

MINING INTERFERES WITH TRADITIONAL
MANAGEMENT PRACTICES

Contemporary patterns of living tradition include decision making about
the management and use of the landscape in accordance with Aboriginal traditions. A sense of hopelessness is created if Traditional Owners believe that
fundamental decisions about management of their land are ignored or violated.

This fosters abandonment of traditional management practices that are
integral to living tradition, to continuing cultural practice, and to the World
Heritage values of the Kakadu National Park.

Balanda political systems and notions of jurisdiction are usurping traditional political systems based on the living tradition of *Bininj*. The systems of committees, action groups, and other bodies designed by *Balanda* industry and governments to replace traditional political systems have nearly always failed due to exhaustion and/or disinterest resulting from cultural inappropriateness. The Mirrar believe that the continued presence of mining in the region will complete this domination.

The traditional cultural system of relations between clans in the region is based on cooperation, mutual obligation and respect for Traditional Owner decision making. The development of the Jabiluka uranium mine, and the associated promises of financial benefit for people other than the Traditional Owners, has created social fragmentation that is destroying the traditional methods of maintaining harmony and equality.

The Jabiluka uranium mine project cannot be viewed in isolation from other social impacts on *Bininj* in the region, including the cumulative impact of the operating Ranger uranium mine. The Mirrar do not argue that mining is the only threat to living tradition, but do maintain that mining and its associated social, economic, and political impacts poses the single greatest threat. An additional mine would push *Bininj* culture beyond the point of cultural exhaustion to genocidal decay.

So important is the issue of *Bininj* control over country and so dire is the position of the Mirrar living tradition that the senior Traditional Owner of the Mirrar, Yvonne Margarula, has indicated that she would have no choice but to enter into self-imposed exile from her country if the Jabiluka uranium mine proceeds, and her clan's authority is usurped by government and the mine proponent ERA. The Senior Traditional Owner is the main repository of knowledge that allows for Mirrar living tradition to continue and exercise jurisdictional power. Ms. Margarula's exile from country would deliver a fatal blow to the survival of Mirrar culture.

Our ongoing campaign had alerted many Australians to the real problems with Ranger and the dangers of Jabiluka. This campaign had been effective in persuading the Labor government to keep the number of uranium mines in the country at a limit of three, which meant that Jabiluka would not be developed. But in 1996 a conservative government came to power again and declared an "open slather" uranium mining policy.

THE BLOCKADE AND AFTER

The Mirrar had achieved a great deal of success in their public campaign against Jabiluka. So the new government's accelerated plans for mining brought together a wide coalition of Australians to confront the policy. Peace activists united with environmentalists and with some unionists to fall in behind the leadership of the Mirrar and challenge government policy. In

1998, a major nonviolent direct action blockade near the Jabiluka mine site was conducted in conjunction with these anti-uranium and environmental organisations.

The eight-month blockade directly involved over 5,000 people and saw more than 500 arrests as people from across Australia and around the world undertook nonviolent action to highlight the human and environmental impacts of the mine plan. Along with speaking tours, legal action, and national and international lobbying, the blockade helped make Jabiluka a household word in Australia and created attention throughout the world.

Apart from significant public and political attention, the campaign was also recognised in 1998 when Yvonne Margarula received the Friends of the Earth International Environment Award. In 1999 Ms. Margarula and myself, Jacqui Katona, were jointly awarded the U.S. Goldman Environment Prize.

The Blockade was successful in mobilizing public opinion to recognize Mirrar rights. Despite some tensions between the many *Balanda* organizations involved, there had been a new global awareness of the importance of Kakadu and the strength of Mirrar determination not to allow mining to go ahead on our land. Obstruction of development of Jabiluka had been helped as well since September 1999 due to the weak international uranium market and ongoing Aboriginal and community opposition. However, in August 2000, Rio Tinto, one of the world's largest mining companies, acquired its majority shareholding in Energy Resources of Australia (ERA), the operator of Ranger and Jabiluka, as part of a broader corporate takeover. Since then Rio Tinto has stated that it does not support the development of Jabiluka in the "short term." But Rio Tinto has not committed either to selling or developing the Jabiluka project.[15] Since then calls for greater world output of uranium are increasing. More and more countries are planning to build nuclear power generators as the world shortage of fossil fuels is leading to projected higher commodity prices in the near future. The international tension since September 11, 2001 has as well worsened the arms race and the demand for both legal and illegal components for nuclear weapons.

These trends made it more likely that Jabiluka would still go ahead despite the Mirrar refusal to agree and despite the massive opposition to the mines shown in the blockade. However, there have been two recent major events which have intervened.

THE FAILURE OF THE REGULATOR EXPOSED

The Mirrar feared that the Ranger mine would be dangerous when it was forced on us in 1977. Our main fears were the damage to our land which the massive mining operation cause, and so the desecration of our sacred sites. But we also feared the effects on our health of exposing to the air the mineral uranium which is only safe when it is buried deeply in the ground. The Fox inquiry also feared the danger of this exposure and the damage which a spill of contaminated water could produce if it were released into the surrounding extensive wetlands. For this reason, Fox demanded and the Australian government agreed to very strict regulatory guidelines which were to be monitored and enforced by the government.

But from the beginning of the Ranger mine, we have been suspicious that the mining company was not living up to its obligations to protect the environment, the workers or the Mirrar people. There have been a series of breeches of safety requirements over the years and rumours have circulated widely that there had been many more. But only recently in April 2002 has a whistleblower from within the mining organization, Mr. Geoffrey Kyle, had the courage to speak up about the serious risks which the company has allowed to happen and which the government has ignored or failed to report. Mr. Kyle reported that he had recorded unacceptably high levels of uranium within the surrounding Kakadu National Park and that in a subsequent cover-up, the company records had been altered and that overall there were substandard laboratory practices at Ranger. If the level of contamination which Kyle had found in the park had been registered inside the Ranger Project Area, it would have shut the mine down. These allegations led to a Senate Inquiry, set up June 2002, which demonstrated that the government monitoring body, the Office of the Supervising Scientist [OSS] had ignored or minimised the recordings and the subsequent actions of the mining company in altering records. Despite a severe recommendation against the government regulating body by the Senate Inquiry, the Australian government was disinterested in the findings and took no action.[16]

Yet since then, further contaminated water releases have occurred, spreading dangerous substances into the park area as well as exposing mining workers and Mirrar residents in the surrounding areas to the polluted water sources. In March 2004, the Ranger mine site had to be shut down as contaminated water spillages were discovered. Mine workers had been exposed to water contaminated with 8,000 parts per billion uranium (400 times the drinking water standard) in their drinking water supply. It is believed the contamination occurred after mine process water was allowed to mix with the potable water supply due to an incorrect connection of pipes. Then, 48 hours later, the mine had to be closed again following the discovery overnight that some 150,000 litres of water contaminated with uranium levels estimated at 108 parts per billion (five times the Australian drinking water standard) spilled from the Jabiru East water supply off the mine site. This incident has exposed the surrounding environment, the drinking water of businesses based at Jabiru East and downstream Aboriginal communities to an unprecedented threat. Jabiru East lies some 3 kilometers from the Ranger mine site and is the location of the Jabiru Airport and related facilities, and the offices of the Environmental Research Institute of the Supervising Scientist. So the contamination had been allowed to occur right in the office area of the regulating body itself! Mr. Andy Ralph, executive officer of the Mirrar's organization, the Gundjehmi Aboriginal Corporation, said that at a minimum these events have breached the environmental requirements that the mining company is obliged to meet and that the regulator was set up to discover and prevent. He stressed that the Mirrar people are, however, more concerned for people and country.

> This incident has potentially put at risk not only the ecosystems of Kakadu's waterways, but also the health of the Aboriginal people who live and hunt nearby, as well as employees based at Jabiru East and tourists passing through the airport. It appears that this incident is not simply a matter of human error but that there is an endemic problem with the management of process and potable water at Ranger. At present no one can rule out that the events which led to this contamination have not taken place before.[17]

Still further leaks and exposures were discovered over the next few days, but the mining company focussed on cleaning up the actual mining site and delayed testing and cleaning up the residential sites at Jabiru East and surrounding areas. Mrs. Yvonne Margarula said that she was increasingly worried for Aboriginal and non-Aboriginal people living and working in Kakadu and called on the mining company and government to better protect people.

> I felt bad about the staff and our members working there who drank the water and I'm worried myself. I'm worried about me and my organisation getting blamed. All we need is for the staff at ERISS and the mine itself to look after our members working there because otherwise we'll have problems with our own people and people from other clans.

Andy Ralph commented: "With what's happened over the past few weeks you wouldn't put the miners and the government regulators in charge of a sandpit in your local playground."

FORCING RIO TINTO TO LIVE
UP TO ITS PROMISE

The other important recent event has happened because of the growing international awareness of the Mirrar opposition to the Jabiluka mine. The Rio Tinto company began to face heavy questioning in international forums like the Johannesburg World Summit on Sustainable Development about its failure to recognize Traditional Owner opposition to the mine. The Rio

Tinto chairman, Sir Robert Wilson, finally stated on BBC radio in September 2002 that his company would not develop the mine at Jabiluka without Mirrar consent.[18] Yet when the Mirrar called on Rio Tinto and Wilson to put this promise into writing, the company at first delayed and avoided the issue. Sustained Mirrar pressure, backed by the Northern Aboriginal Land Council, the peak northern Australian body representing Aboriginal land-owning communities, eventually drew Rio Tinto to the negotiating table. After 18 months, the NLC, with the full support of the Mirrar people, was able to ratify an agreement in which the Rio Tinto company finally committed itself to the Jabiluka Long-Term Care and Maintenance Agreement with the Mirrar, in which it agreed not to undertake any mining activity without the full written consent of the Mirrar Traditional Owners. The Gundjehmi Aboriginal Corporation, speaking on behalf of the Mirrar, said: "This agreement will see the Mirrar People in the driving seat for the first time in thirty years of mining activity on their country."[19]

THE MIRRAR PERSPECTIVE: LESSONS FROM JABILUKA[20]

Looking back now on the course of our history of struggle [so far] to protect our land from the Jabiluka mine, we believe there are some lessons to be learnt from the involvement of the mining companies in Kakadu. It is the responsibility of each and every member of any community to make their views known, and to teach the lessons, because we all have to live with the consequences.

1. *Mining companies should never proceed without informed Aboriginal consent.* There is a problem when no doesn't mean no. This is a violation of Aboriginal consent at the most basic level. It might take place because of "legal reasons" or it might take place in the "national interest" but it will always be a violation. Added to this there is the continuing insult of ignoring the consequences. Rewriting history or attempting to sanitize the reality of environmental, cultural and human rights abuses, and present them as "negative social impacts" is an exercise in gross deception.

The Mirrar have been repeatedly told that the removal of the right of veto over the Ranger project is an unpleasantness best forgotten and that it is the future that is all-important. The reality is that the problems suffered by our people in the past are what we must take responsibility for now. Why should Aboriginal people be expected to put the interests of a private company before the interests of their children and grandchildren? A dramatic change is required in the terms on which Aboriginal people are expected to negotiate around mining issues. There is a demand currently being made on government and industry that Aboriginal people in Kakadu be assisted to manage and control their own affairs. So far this fundamental aspiration has been consistently ignored.

2. *Mining projects should facilitate economic and political independence and not merely transfer welfare provision and political control from the white public sector to the white private sector.* A major social impact study completed in the early 1980s clearly documented the absence of government action to assist the Mirrar community in dealing with the effects of a series of major industrial developments. The most recent social impact study, completed in 1997, has simply recommended an increase in welfare programs. In effect this approach is little more than turning up a kind of a drip feed. The study failed to recognize the most fundamental traditional owner rights, it marginalized traditional owners as "stakeholders," and again denied indigenous people the right to exercise control over their future.

Studies, reports, inquiries, assessments and the like are increasingly industry-driven processes that have become an end in themselves. They are touted as the solution, conveniently crafted and promoted as justification for further abuse of indigenous and environmental rights. Too often, such mechanisms exist to entrench the dominance of government and industry, and facilitate the ambitions of a privately owned company.

Rio Tinto and its subsidiary ERA's answer to the existing social problems created by the mining operation at Ranger was for the Traditional Owners to condone more mining by saying "yes" to Jabiluka. The company believed that if this happened all the problems would be solved and mine money would be there to right the wrongs of the past. For the Mirrar this was like taking a gunshot wound to the chest, leaving the wound open, while increasing the amount of blood supply to the patient, through a drip. This was not an acceptable solution. Wounds must be allowed to heal and the mistakes of the past must not be replicated.

3. *There must be recognition that mining projects have irreversible impacts that destroy aspects of culture forever.* There is a point when a community can take no more. Jabiluka cannot go ahead for this reason. One enormous uranium mine, combined with little concern for social impacts over 20 years, is surely enough in anyone's language. There is a point at which the development of the community by the community at the community's own pace must take priority over external pressures and imperatives. In the case of the Mirrar and Jabiluka that point is now.

Our senior Traditional Owner, Mrs. Yvonne Margarula, said this in 2002[21] and it still stands today:

> It doesn't matter how many times they ask, I'm not going to agree to the Jabiluka mine, for whatever reason they want from it, money or whatever else. Mining ruins the land. Just like the way the Ranger mine has destroyed the land. My

mind is firmly set. I'm not going to allow them to destroy any more of my land. . . .

The Mirrar People still say no to Jabiluka mine! All the Mirrar are together; we are united against any more uranium mining on Mirrar country. No amount of money, no amount of political pressure, no backroom deals, no bribery or blackmail will make us change our mind. We cannot change the law and the law is that we protect our sacred sites.

Since 1996, the Mirrar have fought against Jabiluka across Australia and overseas. We have won many friends and our supporters are strong and stand with us. We have travelled a long road. We have been to many meetings in many different places. We will continue to resist more mining on Mirrar country. We have no choice—this is our land and our life, we can never leave, we must protect it.

NOTES

1. This paper is a revised and updated version of an earlier chapter published as : "Mining Uranium and Indigenous Australians: The Fight for Jabiluka" in Geoff Evans, James Goodman and Nina Lansbury [eds.]: *Moving Mountains: Communities Confront Mining and Globalisation*, Contemporary Oxford Series, Sydney: Oxford Press, 2001.

2. Jaqui Katona is a Mirrar woman who is a Traditional Owner of the lands on which the Ranger and Jabiluka mines are located.

3. Katona, J. (1999), *Address by Gundjehmi Aboriginal Corporation to Public Health Association of Australia Conference*, September, Darwin.

4. Rio Tinto, one of the world's largest mining companies, is an English-based multinational. In 2000 it secured a 68 percent controlling interest in ERA [Energy Resources Australia], a previously Australian-owned company formed with the privatization of government holdings in uranium fields in 1979.

5. Statement by Yvonne Margarula to the London Board of Rio Tinto, 17th April, 2003, quoted in Mirrar people's Media Release, 29th April, 2003, "Kakadu Traditional Owners call for Rio action on Jabiluka" on Mirrar Website, http://www.mirrar.net.

6. The Environment Centre, Northern Territory: http://www.ecnt.org/uranium/

7. Summary of Fox Report Recommendations, Reports 28th October 1976 and 17th May 1977, *The Agreements, Treaties and Negotiated Settlements Database*, University of Melbourne, 2003, http://www.atns.net.au/biogs/A001270b.htm.

8. Indigenous people.

9. Mirrar Submission to the World Heritage Committee Mission to Kakadu (October 1998), "Mirrar Living Tradition In Danger: World Heritage In Danger," http://www.mirrar.net.

10. Australian government (1991), World Heritage Re-nomination document, 88.

11. D. J. Mulvaney "The Landscape of the Aboriginal Imagination and Its Heritage Significance," Unpublished Paper, September, 1998.

12. *Report* 1, "Ranger Uranium Environmental Inquiry ("the Fox Inquiry")," 28

October. 1976; *Report* 2, "Ranger Uranium Environmental Inquiry ("the Fox Inquiry")," 17 May 1977.

13. Ibid.

14. Ibid.

15. For further information visit the Mirrar peoples' Website at www.mirrar.net.

16. Gundjehmi Aboriginal Corporation, 26th September, 2002, media release: "Government Lets ERA Off the Hook," www.mirrar.net.

17. Gundjehmi Aboriginal Corporation, 26th March 2004, media release: "Uranium Contamination Spreads," www.mirrar.net.

18. Gundjehmi Aboriginal Corporation, 4th September media release: "Troubled Rio Tinto Must Rehabilitate Jabiluka," www.mirrar.net.

19. Gundjehmi Aboriginal Corporation, 22nd April 2004, media release: "Mirrar Welcome NLC Endorsement of Jabiluka Agreement," www.mirrar.net.

20. Katona, J. (1999), *Address by Gundjehmi Aboriginal Corporation to Public Health Association of Australia Conference,* September, Darwin.

21. Gundjehmi Aboriginal Corporation, 11th April 2002: Statement by Senior Traditional Owner Mrs. Yvonne Margarula and, 4th September 2002, media release "Troubled Rio Tinto Must Rehabilitate Jabiluka," www.mirrar.net.

20

Guardians of the Land
A Maori Community's Environmental Battles

Rachael Selby and Pataka Moore

In New Zealand and throughout many parts of the world, people dream of having a house by the sea. The sight of rolling ocean waves in winter, expanses of blue and green in the summer, seaspray, changing colors as clouds move by, millponds on still clear days, footprints in the sand, rocky shores, sunsets and sunrises, crashing waves breaking on rocks or sand, all capture the imagination.

Mountain folk might dream of a cabin by the lake. White capped mountains framing lakes, fresh water trout, the peace and solitude in the evening, are seductive. River folk bond just the same with wide expansive rivers sheltering salmon or steady flowing streams which conjure up memories of paddling, boating, and warm summer days. For many indigenous communities, bodies of water invoke sadness at the loss of access to traditional fishing grounds and in New Zealand, bodies of water have become sites of pollution and effluent disposal.

This chapter examines a brief history of one indigenous community in Aotearoa New Zealand, a community which in the nineteenth and twentieth centuries lived beside a clear sparkling stream, fed by a clear sparkling lake half a mile away.

New Zealand is located in the south Pacific Ocean, 1600 kilometers east of Australia. It is made up of two main islands, Te Ika a Maui, the fish of Maui, and Te Waipounamu, the greenstone land. They were unimaginatively renamed North Island and South Island by the British colonizers. New Zealand is about the same size as California, but with a population of four million people, of whom the indigenous Maori make up 15 percent. Maori are the descendants of the Polynesian settlers who arrived in Aotearoa— New Zealand in the tenth century.

As with many indigenous communities, settlements were established beside bodies of water. Water is valued not only for its spiritual, healing, and cleansing qualities, but as a source of food, for human hygiene, animal use, and as a means of transport. It was also used as a place to store food, as is a refrigerator in the modern world.

The tribal group discussed here, are called Ngati Raukawa. We are the descendants of Raukawa, who lived in the seventeenth century. One of his descendants was a woman called, Pareraukawa, an ancestress who lived in the eighteenth century. Her descendants are collectively known Ngati Pareraukawa, the descendants of Pareraukawa. We identify ourselves as such, to this day. The tribal group, numbering several thousand people living throughout the world, is associated with land and bound by familial ties.

The land base from which the extended family or tribal group draws its strength and which it identifies as "home" is the land and marae, called Ngatokowaru, also named after an ancestor. The marae is the Maori word for the land on which the community lives. A marae typically includes a large carved house, with a pitched roof. It is built as one large meeting room, where families discuss issues of importance, where church services may be held, and it is also used for sleeping on mattresses on the floor at night. Other buildings include a kitchen and communal dining room which seats from 100–200 or more people. There is an ablution block, with showers, toilets and a laundry and other buildings for storage of equipment. Marae vary is size. Some are surrounded by family homes. Others such as Ngatokowaru, had families living and farming in the immediate environs until the early 1950s. Most marae communities also have a designated family cemetery. The dead are brought to the marae for three days mourning following death, then farewelled and buried in a family cemetery. The families associated with Ngatokowaru have a family cemetery east of the marae closer to the shores of the lake. It is wistfully referred to as: the warms sands of Raumatangi. Family members anticipate that they will return from wherever they are around New Zealand and the globe to the warm sands of Raumatangi when they die.

This ancestral marae is nestled on the south bank of the Hokio Stream. It is five kilometers from the Tasman Sea to the west, and enjoys a view across the lake to the east of the mountain range, known as the Tararua Ranges. The marae community has been located at Hokio since the early nineteenth century and faces the sun rising over the Tararua ranges. The area from the sea to the lake is known as Hokio.

The community was located itself beside the Hokio Stream because it provided food: shellfish, flounder, an abundance of eel, and freshwater crayfish.

The stream was also used as a place in which to store food. Each year when the eels migrated from the lake to the sea in the late summer and early autumn, between February and April, the family trapped the eels and stored them in large wooden boxes in the stream to be used over the winter as a source of protein. The boxes were about a meter in length and about half a meter by half a meter in height and width. Small holes at both ends ensured that the water continued to flow through the box and the eels were prevented from escaping as a lid was secured to the top. Eels were, for centuries, a staple food consumed by Maori communities several times a week. As families moved to town or to other blocks of land to live away from the immediate vicinity of the stream, they maintained their eel boxes in the stream and returned to collect their eels for dinner, using the stream as a place to store food. Eels varied in length from half a meter to two meters in length.

Across the lake, the town of Levin grew in size in the late 1800s, as thousands of immigrants arrived in New Zealand from Europe and the new colonial provincial government bought land from people who did not own it. This was of no consequence to the land-hungry settlers. They wanted to build a railway from the capital city, Wellington, sixty miles to the south, linking it to the largest city, Auckland, five hundred miles to the north. It was believed a railway through the North Island would open up the country for development. The settler population increased from 2,000 in 1840 to 772,719 in 1901 while the Maori population decreased from 100,000 in 1840 to 43,143 in 1901 (Durie 1994: 37).

The settlers introduced a majority-rules system of democracy which took away any political influence from indigenous Maori. The treaty which had been signed in 1840 between the English Queen and the Maori Chiefs, was disregarded by the settler government and indeed the politicians anticipated that within time the Maori population would die out. A government official, Dr. Isaac Featherston "echoed liberal European sentiment in the late nineteenth century when he spoke of the responsibility to 'smooth the pillow of the dying race'" (King 1997: 38). This was the benign patronizing attitude which abounded.

The Maori families which built houses at the marae in the late 1800s worked the land, milked cows and found multiple uses for the stream as a source of food and water for the community. Children who were born and raised there in the latter part of the century were taken to the local school by horse and trap or walked the dusty road to the town until a school bus service began. The community was self-sufficient, providing for its members and bringing in cash by selling surplus crops to the market and by selling milk to the local dairy factory. The matriarch, Ema, who bore fourteen children in the mid and late 1800s, warned them never to sell any of their land to the white settlers. Despite her father having been an Englishman who lived in New Zealand within a Maori community, and despite her having had a boarding school education in Wellington, she foresaw the disasters which would befall the community if they sold their land to the hungry Pakeha (white foreigner) who would become a neighbor and potentially cause problems for the community.

Ema's children and grandchildren, who grew up at the marae and lived through to the mid-twentieth century, used the stream as a place to gather food and for recreation: for swimming, diving from the trees and banks, and to learn from parents the techniques of catching and cleaning fish. They learned about caring for the stream: clearing weeds, planting the banks, disposing of parts of fish not used for food. They learned about how to construct traps for different species of fish in each of the seasons, how to preserve the food, store it and present it to visitors. They learned the most appropriate methods of preserving food taken by travelers on a journey. When relatives came from a distance with food from other regions, the family used the stream as a storehouse for the food they brought with them.

In the autumn, when the corn was harvested, some was placed in bags and lowered into the stream where, over the next few weeks, it was left immersed in the water to ferment as the cool clear water washed over and through it. It was for many years a delicacy, eaten with cream or milk from the dairy cows on the farm. The family grew their own vegetables, churned the butter, collected eggs from the ducks and chickens, and fished in the stream. They were self-sufficient.

Those who lived beside the stream had a responsibility and an obligation to it: to maintain its health and well-being. Maori believe that the relationship with the environment is one of interdependence. We are guardians of the environment and reap the benefits. The land, the stream and the lake provide sustenance for us and in turn we do not misuse that which provides for us. For many generations Maori communities lived in harmony with the environment and in turn the environment provided.

In 1952, the town council across the lake made the decision to discharge its sewage into the lake. The western side of the lake is located less than a kilometer east of the community and is the lake from which the stream flows. Within a short time, the raw sewage floated in the lake and down the stream beside the marae. It was a filthy statement about the price of progress and a warning about the power of the council. Children were gathered up and forbidden to go near the stream. A fence at the top of the slope was designated the boundary and the community stayed on one side, the stream on the other.

The families moved away, abandoning the marae as a place to live. "Civilization" and urbanization were the new realities and the children born after the Second World War were frequently brought up believing that the most advantageous stance to take was to abandon their indigenous heritage and to become "European." Their parents often thought the best approach was to ensure they were literate in English and that they fitted snugly into the white man's world. Those who were literate in Maori deliberately spoke only English to their children. Many never admitted to their children that they knew the Maori language. It was an effective means of forcing the children to be literate in English and provided opportunity for the children to live more effectively in the European world.

Durie (1994: 37) claims, "The separation of Maori from their land had social as well as economic consequences. Land was part of the internalized identity." For the descendants of Pareraukawa, it forced many to focus on surviving in the Pakeha world leaving the Maori world behind them. For those who struggled, it was a double blow as they also lost the knowledge and skills associated with the Maori world based at the marae. When they returned to the marae to Maori functions, they were like fish out of water. Many fitted uneasily in both worlds, the European and the Maori.

In 1953, one of the few families which remained living full-time at the marae sold seven acres on the western boundary to Joe Knight. The land bordered the stream and while he did not live there, he built a pig sty. Each day he arrived with drums of food scraps to feed and fatten the seven sows and their thirty piglets. Ema's words about never selling to the Pakeha were not heeded.

The community had experienced dramatic change in a very short period. At the conclusion of the Second World War, several families had been self-sufficient living off the land and the stream. Within a decade they had a growing community's sewage poisoning the stream on the north and the lake to the east. As the piggery on the west also grew, the elders who had inherited the marae from their ancestors grieved that they would be the last generation to use the marae, the last to practice their culture and promote the values of their ancestors. As each one died, their families returned them to the marae where the extended family returned to farewell them in the traditional manner over three days prior to burial. They were then buried in the family cemetery beside the lake.

Over the next twenty years, the marae was used almost exclusively for ceremonial occasions, not as a place of permanent residence. The dead were farewelled before being carried across the fields to the cemetery on the hill located between the marae and the lake. The cemetery had been chosen for its prime location overlooking the lake and beside the stream, and for its site near to the marae. The generations buried there had never anticipated the environmental disasters which were created by the town growing in size in the distance across the lake.

The new settlers who had migrated to New Zealand over the previous seventy years had little sympathy for the indigenous community or for their customs and values. The settlers saw themselves as "transforming the Maori from barbarism to civilized life" (Walker 1985: 73). There had been little thought given to the impact that a growing community would have on the lake and stream, and the consequent disposal of waste in the area. Values and beliefs which were different from those espoused around the town council's table were disregarded. Appeals against the decision that the lake was the best place for sewage were regarded as attempts to be obstructive. The brand of democracy and "civilized life" which had been imported to New Zealand from Britain was that the majority ruled and minority opinion was irrelevant. The Maori custom of debating openly with all issues on the table until a consensus was reached, was seen as time wasting and long winded. That Maori people were left feeling disenfranchised was of no consequence.

A further blow which has had long term consequences occurred in the 1960s. The council made a decision to relocate the town's rubbish dump to Hokio. A landfill was created a quarter of a mile south of the marae community. The decision effectively meant that the marae was surrounded by the rubbish and effluent from the town. Such was the price of progress.

The effect on the tribal community was they came to believe the marae was doomed. The policy of assimilation was promoted by government. The last members of the generation which had been born in the ancestral home made sentimental trips back to the land and marae. Ema's youngest daughter maintained the lawns and grounds with help from nieces and nephews for many years, though some wondered why they bothered as months would pass by without anyone using the buildings. When a death would occur, those who heard the news would travel to the marae to assist with the hosting of visitors and mourners, cooking for them, feeding them, and making beds in the old meeting house.

Many of the family lost the use of the Maori language during this postwar period, and the values and beliefs of the people became subsumed within the majority culture. Maori became relegated to the position of being a minority culture in their own land without a voice in political or decision-making circles.

In 1975, a group of trustees of the tribe noted the deteriorating condition of many marae in the region which in some locations, were all but abandoned. They talked long into the night about whether the Maori culture and traditions would die out completely or whether this generation should revive and rejuvenate the Maori traditions before they were lost. They made a decision that was to change the future of the people.

They reviewed the status of the tribal group as a whole and noted that the language was seriously endangered, that few people under thirty-five could speak the Maori language, that the educational attainment of the tribal group was poor, that if a program of revival was not undertaken, Maori would no longer exist. (Winiata 1979). They noted that most of the marae where the sub-tribal groups were located, throughout the lower North Island, were in a state of disrepair, neglected and reflected the suffering of the people. Ngatokowaru Marae, on the southern bank of the Hokio Stream, stood lonely and seldom used.

A group of the descendants of Pareraukawa met in the mid 1970s and decided to begin by building a new meeting house. It would be larger than the small house in which they were sitting, which had been completed in 1900. The new house would face the Tararua ranges and the lake, be fully carved and adorned in traditional style. This decision brought dozens of families back to the marae every weekend as the new house was planned, and grew up from the ground from 1976. It became a labor of love as the men gathered every Saturday morning to build and the women plaited the wall panels and helped with painting rafters. After years of work, the house was finally opened in March 1978, a statement to the nation and the town across the lake that Maori language and culture would be revived, that we regarded the marae as our home and our traditions were worth maintaining and should be cherished. The dawn opening was attended by over two thousand people.

On the western boundary, the pig sty had grown into a piggery. The smell was always present when families arrived for a meeting, a wedding, a church service, a family reunion or other celebration or cultural activity. It was to take another twenty years to rid ourselves of an activity which became a source of considerable embarrassment to us and to our pride in our ancestral home.

After the meeting house had been formally opened in 1978, the sub-tribe undertook to learn more about ourselves as a people. Many of our family committed to reviving and promoting our language, learning about our history and many committed to increasing their educational attainment and that of their children. With increased confidence in ourselves and in our abilities, the community took on the local council and voiced opposition to the continued discharge of sewage into the lake and the stream.

A series of public hearings were conducted in 1979 and 1980 in which the families of the sub-tribe opposed the council, the town, and the continued pollution of the lake. They were joined by local people who supported the restoration of the lake. The battle to persuade the board sitting at the decision-making table was intense. The council employed "experts" to assure the board that the effluent was treated to such a high standard that it was almost "drinkable" by human beings. The tribal families urged the board to decline the council's application for consent to continue pouring effluent into the lake.

The outcome was that in the early 1980s, the board hearing the submissions granted consent to the council to divert the effluent from the lake and pipe it directly into the stream. Initially the community was devastated; however, when the conditions were reviewed it was found that the conditions were so stringent in terms of the quality of the effluent treatment required, that the council was unable to meet them. They were forced to build a pipeline from the treatment plant located east of the lake, westward to a land-based collection point. The negative impact was that the site chosen to build the land-based holding place, was again at Hokio, in the locality of the marae on its south side. Hokio was confirmed as the region's effluent disposal area.

During the 1970s and 1980s, the small piggery on the western boundary of the marae had grown in size and operation. By the 1990s it was a large operation with 1200 breeding sows and thousands of piglets being fattened for the market. The piggery generated gallons of effluent and the offensive odors drifted from the piggery across the marae, wafted into the dining room and meeting house as families sat down for breakfast, lunch, or the evening meal. The next battle began: to rid ourselves of the flies and odious stench surrounding the marae, particularly in summer evenings when we gathered to learn about our history, traditions, and customs—those precious gifts handed down from our ancestors and which we wanted to pass on to our children. The marae community had, over the last twenty years of the twentieth century, grown, revived, reenergized, and recommitted to ensuring that we leave the marae stronger than it was in 1975.

The owners of the piggery argued that in order to operate a viable business they needed a thousand breeding pigs. The marae community argued that the land had been gifted to us by our ancestors, and that we would never sell it. We had a responsibility to care for it and for the stream. It appeared by the end of the twentieth century we had reached an impasse.

In 1998, the piggery owners were required to apply for resource consent under the Resource Management Act 1991, to continue their farming operation, but under stricter conditions. The marae committee wrote submissions asking that the offensive odors be eliminated. The owners of the piggery suggested that planting a belt of trees between the piggery and the marae would reduce the terrible offensive odors. The marae committee stood its ground and demanded elimination of the odors. In the middle of 1999, the Commissioners granted the piggery owners a further six month consent to operate the business. The time was a period during which they were required to build an effective system to more effectively deal with effluent on the property, the main cause of the offensive odors. In December 1999, the piggery owners closed down their operation and sold the remaining pigs. They decided they would not comply with the consent requirements.

In January 2000, the family representatives gathered for the first meeting of the new year. The Marae Committee Minute Book records, "It was noted that the Bierstekers no longer have a resource consent to operate the piggery on the western boundary and that it is unlikely that they would get one again without having to comply with strict standards in terms of effluent disposal, control of odor and cleanliness. A year ago they had over 1200 breeding pigs on the property—which produced waves of offensive odors at the marae.

The property is now pig-free and the land and buildings are for sale. The marae is odorless and relatively free of flies."

The sixteen family members who had traveled to the marae for the first meeting in the new millennium were silent and reflective. For the younger people present, they could not remember a time when the air at the marae did not stink. The smell from the piggery had worsened over the previous twenty-five years, but for those under twenty-five it had always had an offensive smell in the air. People gently sniffed the warm midsummer evening air, hardly believing what their noses confirmed.

We had come to believe that the place would always have an offensive smell, that we would not be able to change that. No one spoke. Then, an elderly aunt was reminded of a saying from her past when someone proposes something quite preposterous and quietly she said, "Well, pigs might really fly!" Her voice broke the silence and began a quiet rumbling of laughter, a semi-hysterical laughter. We had begun the new millennium with a win, an important win. We might really have clean air, a sweet-smelling place to leave to our grandchildren and our great grandchildren. In 1950, our great grandmother had left us a clean, sweet-smelling marae, a clean, clear stream full of fish-life and a source of clean water. In fifty years, we had seen more damage done to the environment around us than all the generations on the earth before us.

Our ancestors had not mismanaged and mistreated the land, the stream, the lake, or the seashore. The Maori people of New Zealand claim special responsibility for the environment and claim guardianship of the earth mother and all the gifts of the land. The price of progress has been that becoming a minority in our own land, results in injustice. Ridding our environment of a piggery was a significant move forward.

In 2004, the town council announced that the waste management plan for the next thirty-five years included the expansion of the landfill site south of the marae. They had commenced the building of massive pits which would be lined and filled with rubbish from neighboring counties. This would provide an income for the local council as they now proposed bringing refuse from other districts. In a letter to the Marae Committee in April 2004, they assured the marae community that the liner would be "effective in stopping all or almost all leachate from entering the ground water. . . . Whether refuse comes into the landfill from within our district or from outside of it is not considered by council to be a matter of significance." It is a matter of significance for the landowners at Hokio.

In 2000, the Marae Committee acting on behalf of a community now numbering several thousand people, thought that we had begun to make progress. The effluent had been removed from the lake in the 1980s. It had not been discharged into the stream for nearly twenty years. The piggery, so offensive for nearly thirty years, was gone. We now face the prospect of a super landfill site to the south and again it appears that the council is driven by economic gain, not by environmental concerns.

There are other environmental issues. On the south there are many acres of market gardens. The farmers use chemicals on the land in large quantities. The run-off into the streams is considerable. It washes into streams which feed into the lake. In the summer the nutrients cause algal blooms. In the winter, the growth settles on the bottom of the lake and decomposes on the lakebed. The decomposition uses oxygen, depriving the fish of the oxygen they need to survive. The effluent is not directly discharged into the lake, but there are other poisons in its place.

The past twenty-five years has seen a new generation take pride in being Maori, in claiming the marae as their ancestral home and in claiming their indigenous ancestry. They have learned the Maori language and committed to the revival of Maori as a living language. There is a commitment to maintain the marae and its environment. The stream banks beside the marae have been cleared of willows and other species. The family has committed to planting native species of trees on the banks. In the distance, closer to the lake, the wetlands are drained and perhaps gone forever.

Each year when the eels migrate to the sea in the autumn, a group of young men gathers to catch the eels and teach the boys how to trap, clean, and prepare the eels, just as their ancestors did a century and more ago. They clean and prepare them, cook them, and take them to the homes of the elders who remember the days when their grandfather took them to the stream. The knowledge has been gathered from the elders who are overjoyed that the stream is clean again, that the knowledge is not lost, that there are young men interested in the way they did things when they were young. The smell of eels cooking brings back joyous memories for them. These young people have reconnected to the land and the stream. They do not need any reminder of the special qualities and significance of the stream for the tribe. The fence is still standing at the top of the bank, but when one looks down to the stream, it is no longer a thick sludge, the water is clear and there is life in it again.

BIBLIOGRAPHY

Durie, Mason (1994) *Whaiora: Maori Health Development*. Auckland: Oxford University Press.

King, Michael (1997) *1000 Years of Maori History: Nga iwi o te motu*. Auckland: Reed Publishing.

Ngatokowaru Marae Committee Minute Books (unpublished).

Walker, R.J. (1985) "Cultural Dominance of Taha Maori: The Potential for Radical

Transformation," in J. Codd, R. Harker, and R. Nash (eds.), *Political Issues in New Zealand Education.* Palmerston North: Dunmore Press.

Winiata, W. (1979) "Generation 2000: An Experiment in Tribal Development," in *He Mätäpuna: Some Mäori Perspectives*, 69–73. Wellington: New Zealand Planning Council.

21

Parameters of Legitimation and the Environmental Future of a Taipei Neighborhood

Anya Bernstein

THE COLLECTIVE CONSTRUCTION OF PERSONALIZED HISTORY

On a warm March evening in 2003, a group of residents of the Juluo neighborhood in southwestern Taipei gathered in a basement to plan a line of attack.[1] They were preparing for a public meeting with representatives of the city government, and they knew from experience that it paid to get their stories straight. The meeting would allow members of the public to express their views on the historical status—and therefore on the preservation—of several neighborhood buildings that had been part of the sugar refinery that, until the late 1940s, had dominated local industry. The refinery, which had not been active in over fifty years, belonged to the Taiwan Sugar Corporation, which opposed any decision that would limit its right to modify or tear down the buildings, as a "heritage site" or "historical site" label would. The group of residents gathered here were all members of the Juluo neighborhood's Cultural Association, a government-recognized civic group that had grown out of several ad-hoc neighborhood-wide protests about the disposition of local land.[2] They had come to the basement to rehearse the speeches they would give in favor of preserving the old buildings.[3]

This chapter will actually go on to focus on another battle going on in the same neighborhood: an ongoing conflict with the Taiwan Electric Company about whether it can expand an electric substation located at one end of the neighborhood. Unlike some other papers in this volume, I deal here less with memories of environmental disaster than with the way that a personalized history of the local environment is mobilized to avert future environmental degradation. In this section, I present one instance of the construction of a personalized history that is vital to political processes in this neighborhood, and introduce some of the cultural and political concerns important to the chapter's protagonists. Section 2 examines the notion of *collective memory* as an object of analysis. I suggest that the part of social life usually covered by that term would be better served by an emphasis on the process and context in which a general past is made relevant to an individual's present, which I refer to by the shorthand of *personalized history*. In Section 3, I situate the neighborhood in the context of Taipei City development. The connection between the neighborhood's land-use past and its environmental future does not necessarily seem direct or obvious to an outside observer. But it becomes direct and obvious within the discursive context of contemporary Taiwanese political culture. Section 4 provides an introduction to the relevant political history, explaining the *parameters of legitimation* within which Juluo neighborhood residents operate and showing how the neighborhood's history has been personalized, or taken up by residents as a point of self-definition and identification. In Section 5, I examine how this personalized past can provide a seamless connection between history and demand.

To set the scene, though, I'd like to pause on the basement meeting. An electric substation in a poor neighborhood raises questions of environmental safety and justice, and may at first appear unrelated to a bunch of old buildings, which bring up questions of cultural preservation. In local terms, however, these issues are of the same kind: in the Taiwanese ontology of socio-political problems, both of these are issues having to do with *community* (*shèqū*社區), and specifically with community *environment* (*huánjìng* 環境).

The notion of *community* in Taiwan is usually defined explicitly with reference to social cohesion, with an underlying assumption of geographic proximity. This *geo-social* relation—placement in physical space interacting with situation in social networks and institutions—has become a key arena in which to strengthen bonds of group-belonging. The community has become an important political unit in contemporary Taiwanese political discourse. Group-based political action on Taiwan is vibrant and varied, and it is clearly an overstatement to claim that it actually originates primarily from geographically connected and broadly inclusive social groups. But it is largely presented as doing so in official discourses, mass media, and everyday conversations, and people interested in effecting political change—people who need to justify their version of justice—tend often to present themselves as located in this way.

The notion of environment, in turn, covers a broad spectrum of issues including everything from ecology and pollution; to physical infrastructure and locations for social activities; to sites for the production, preservation, and dissemination of objects and practices recognized as cultural.[4] Community and environment are both components of the larger category of the *local* (地方 *dìfāng*), which has taken on central importance in Taiwan through the political changes of the last two decades. *Dìfāng* means *local* in the context of a contrast with *zhōngyāng*, *central*, in Taiwanese political discourse; the unmarked, everyday translation of *dìfāng* is simply *place*, or *locality*. It is on the importance of the local, and the characteristics of the locality, that neighborhood residents lean in their attempts to sway city administrators both to preserve the old sugar refinery buildings, and to prevent a new electric substation.

In other words, the methods of persuasion that neighborhood residents employ reveal important aspects of Taiwan's political culture. At the basement meeting, several Cultural Association members spoke of the historical value the buildings held not only by virtue of their old and unusual architectural styles, but also through their connection with sugar production. Sugar production was Taiwan's chief industry under Japanese colonialism (which lasted from 1895 to 1945). Although increasingly marginalized economically in the decades following, cane growing and refining remained an important part of the economy. The nationalized Taiwan Sugar Corporation, which diversified its enterprises considerably in the 1960s and 1970s, was still the country's largest company in 1980 (Williams 1980). Most sugar production had been located in the south; this refinery had been the only one at its latitude, and one of only two ever operating in the northern third of the island. It was thus a *unique* site that *contributed* to the economic and cultural development of Taiwan, and which was therefore *representative* of a wider Taiwanese history and culture. I return to this set of parameters below.

The other main tactic in the attempt to sway city government administrators was to *move* them (*gǎndòng* 感動) through oral history. Sugar-related activities in this area had largely stopped by the late 1940s, and most of the neighborhood's residents have lived there only since the late 1970s, when the Taiwan Sugar Corporation sold off most of its land here to private developers and the Taipei city government's public housing office. However, a few elderly residents who were born in the small private dwellings dotting what were by then fallow sugarcane fields did recall some cane-related activities, as well as the stories their own elders had told them about the heyday of sugar production in Taipei decades earlier. In my fieldwork I encountered only two residents with this firsthand knowledge (although I heard of a couple of others), and both of them had volunteered to speak at the upcoming meeting. The first speaker, who used a highly modulated oratorical style appropriate for telling exciting stories to a young child, described how he had watched cane-laden trains roll in to the refinery as a child, and how he had stolen sugarcane to chew (an experience shared by a great many adult Taiwanese). A highly skilled storyteller (with, I couldn't help thinking, very lucky grandchildren), he was received with cheers and applause.

Unlike the initial speakers, who spoke in clear, formal Mandarin—the official language on Taiwan and the state-enforced medium for education and official business under martial law (roughly 1947–1987)—both of the less educated, older residents who presented oral histories used Taiwanese, the island's majority language.[5] In one sense Taiwanese was their only really viable choice. Having come to Mandarin only later in life and not having received much education, they had only limited competence in it. At the same time, one effect of the political movements and changes of the last two decades has been to shift the relative valuation of local languages. Previously devalued in public discourse and forbidden in some official settings, Taiwanese has increasingly been valorized as presenting the authentic voice of the authentic Taiwanese people (cf. Gal and Woolard 1995). At this point it is pretty much de rigueur for even ethnically mainlander politicians who grew up speaking only Mandarin to learn some Taiwanese to toss into their speeches. Though they are often laughed at for their unconvincing accents, a total absence of Taiwanese can elicit accusations of a regressive martial-law era mentality. This kind of cultural authenticity also figures in the uniqueness-contribution-representation nexus I refer to above.

The second older resident to speak at the meeting was not so adept as the first: using a flat, low voice, he skipped about from topic to topic, not bothering to package his memories into a coherent story line, not exhibiting the earnest enthusiasm of the first speaker, and relying largely on what others had told him rather than his own lived experience. Impatiently, people broke in to give advice. Don't hem and haw so much, he was told, figure out what you want to say and stick to it. "Okay," he restarted uncertainly, "my uncle told me—" Once more he was interrupted as a woman called out *"Say* 'my grandpa,' 'my grandpa' is better."[6]

Being both a generation higher and in a direct agnatic line, a grandfather's word would, in patrilineal terms, hold more authority than an uncle's. The speaker started once more, substituting grandpa for uncle. In the following months, as the preservation effort gathered steam (and ultimately succeeded), I would hear this bit of memory retold with the uncle decisively replaced by the grandfather. The historical fact voiced and overridden at the basement meeting would be replaced by a slightly altered story, which would become part of the store of personalized history on which residents could draw to describe their neighborhood and to place themselves in geo-social terms.

Scholars of collective memory, to which I turn in the next section, have described how historical stories held in common and made relevant to present situations can strengthen group-belonging and inform people's attitudes toward themselves, their groups, and the world around them. This type of scholarship often focuses on how people use or interpret the facts of the past. Sitting in the basement, I had had the privilege to observe a moment typical of the behind-the-scenes production of what I call personalized history, which precedes its use. I begin with this scene because it seems useful to keep in mind that the recognition of historical facts as relevant to some situation—and, as in this case, the production of those facts *as* facts to begin with—is itself irreducibly a collective project.

COLLECTIVIZED MEMORY AND PERSONALIZED HISTORY

The notion of *memory* in the social sciences is so diffuse as to be almost undefinable, sometimes covering a domain so large that it might substitute for *culture*. Even leaving aside studies of memory as neural process, the term can signal everything from personal autobiography to an amorphous ideational substance shared among members of a nation, society, or identity group.[7] While it can be praised for bridging the gap between these two extremes, it can also be criticized for obscuring it. Most social science writing on the topic refers back to Maurice Halbwachs' (1980[1950]) work on collective memory.[8] The difficulty of defining the term and delineating its object of analysis can be traced back to this seminal work as well. Below, I summarize Halbwachs' famous treatise and point out its moments of greatest vagueness in an effort to understand why the notion of memory in the social sciences is so slippery, and to suggest why the label of memory, individual or collective, may be less useful than a focus on the ways that the past is made relevant to the present in particular contexts.

Halbwachs introduces the notion of collective memory by explaining that individual memories are based in and supported by the groups to which the individual belongs. In the first component of memory—the strictly autobiographical—other people corroborate and correct one's memories of one's own experiences. Group norms determine the typical ways in which memories are presented (what might be called genres, or narrative forms), and the typical objects a person is likely to remember to begin with. In the words of a later idiom, this initial explanation of "collective memory" simply means that the memories of an individual person are intersubjectively produced and perpetuated.

Autobiographical memory joins with a "historical memory" of events one learns about from sources other than one's own experience, like mass media, schoolbooks, or the accounts of others (1980[1950]: 52). In another idiom, "historical memory" could also be called "knowledge:" whether a historical event or period happened in one's lifetime or not is irrelevant. What is remembered is not the event itself but the fact of knowing about it.

The third component of intersubjectively created individual memory involves one's impressions of the "currents" (1980[1950]:65) or tenor of a time period, garnered from an unspecifiable variety of repetitive, noncontradictory sources (such as clothing styles, bodily behavior, and utterances) evinced by some group which is acknowledged as being set apart in some way—for instance by generation (one's grandparents) or by biographical background (colonial expatriates). Again, in another idiom, this type of memory could be termed something like "understanding:" the child does not experience his grandparents' youth himself, but can understand some of its characteristics through their words and habitual behavior. In other words, much of what Halbwachs calls memory is not memory at all in the common use of the word. This use of the term, while it has the advantage of pointing out the intersubjective production of the person, has the drawback of conflating experience, knowledge, and understanding.

Having explained the collective nature of individual memory, Halbwachs then uses the term "collective memory" in a new way, to refer to memory held in common by a group of people. He does not mark this transition or redefine the term, but simply contrasts it to "history" as another type of knowledge or understanding held in common by a group.[9] The result is an implicit equation between the intersubjectively constructed memories of the experiences of an individual person and a common knowledge of the history of a group—a history that exceeds the experiences of any of its individual members but which they nonetheless take up as personally relevant. This equation is bound to be confusing because it models processes and organizational modes pertaining to groups on those of the individual. Claims to a shared memory of unexperienced events modeled on individual remembering of experienced events, crystallized in phrases like "Never forget," extrapolate metaphorically from the concept of memory as a property of an individual to that of memory as a property of a group. They presuppose (that is, they implicitly posit) a unity among the members of a group that is analogous to (that is, of the same type as) the unity within an individual over time.

This person-like unity of the group, of course, is an ideological claim common to many modern groups (especially ethno-national ones), and is therefore of limited utility in the analysis of groupness itself. Rather, as I suggested in my description of the basement meeting, the decisive thing is not experience but relevance. To become what I call *personalized history*—in which a swatch of the past is taken up by group members as a descriptor of the qualities or origins of their group—that swatch must be, or become, or be made, relevant to the present. Few writers have captured the striving for relevance better than Nietzsche (1980[1874]: 22), who writes of the "battle

... [to] implant a new habit, a new instinct, a second nature so that the first nature withers away," adding that "this first nature also was, at some time or other, a second nature and that every victorious second nature becomes a first."[10] An analysis of how a piece of the past becomes relevant looks at the sociopolitical and rhetorical parameters of relevance in a particular context.[11] In this chapter I examine a small portion of these parameters by asking how neighborhood residents' demands about their environment are publicly justified; that is, I ask about the parameters of legitimation for this kind of local action in Taipei.

The ways in which the past becomes relevant in personalized history presents a spectrum of incorporation.[12] People might simply notice some aspect of the past. This in itself is a certain slight significance. Or they can figure themselves as *addressees of the past* by responding to or taking up this knowledge—for instance, by acting or speaking on the presupposition of some understanding of the past.[13] At the furthest extreme, they can act like this swatch of the past is *about* them: it describes them, it enjoins them to action, it is a way to present themselves to others. In contrast to the assumption of being addressed that signals participation in a *public*, such explicit self-ascription might be thought of as participation in an *identity*. Members of the Juluo neighborhood Cultural Association often demonstrate this furthest extreme of incorporation by taking up one part of local land-use history—the unexperienced past of sugarcane growing and refining—as the most important descriptor of the present neighborhood, vitally relevant to the character of the area and the people who inhabit it now.

GEOSOCIAL SITUATION

When you ask Cultural Association members why they want to prevent the expansion of the electric substation, they typically respond in terms of environmental health hazards. Talking about a woman living near the current substation whose husband had died of cancer, one of my interviewees commented: *"Look at ... the people living there—if it's not cancer it's something else. Everyone is so—scared to death, do you know, everyone's so afraid."*[14] The Juluo neighborhood is made up of lower-income subsidized rented apartments, lower-middle income subsidized apartments mostly owned by their inhabitants, and a number of small, privately built, inhabitant-owned apartment buildings.[15] Although the buildings in this neighborhood are mostly of relatively recent provenance, the area in which they stand, which lies in the southwestern part of the city and used to serve as its main river port, is the oldest settled section of Taipei.[16] It is also among the poorest and most crowded.

The last 20 years have seen the speedy development of Taipei's eastern sections: 1980s photographs of what are now some of the city's most bustling neighborhoods and most traveled avenues show nothing but forests and farms. Juluo residents are painfully conscious of their lower geo-social status: the eastward push to develop spaces to serve the needs of financial markets and upscale shopping left the older western regions of Taipei, sites for manufacture and the sale of cheaper goods, underserved and largely ignored in government policy for the better part of two decades.[17] Only recently—and spurred largely by protests from this neighborhood—has the city government turned its attention to the older, neglected city districts.[18]

The area is relatively economically underprivileged even in Taiwan's remarkably even wealth distribution; it is largely ethnically Taiwanese (traditionally, though not currently, politically disempowered);[19] and it is one of the most densely populated areas of Taipei, which is one of the most densely populated cities in the world.[20] So residents' perception and fear of environmental injustice is situated in a broader understanding of neglect by the state: discussing the electric company's plans, residents sometimes ask rhetorically why the substation must be placed in their densely populated neighborhood rather than someplace with fewer people.[21]

Residents' understanding of the undesirability of enlarging the substation is phrased in terms of environmental danger, but *how* the Cultural Association maneuvers in the world of politics and protest has more to do with a personalized history of land use that serves to describe and unite residents, and gives them a legitimating basis on which to engage in political action. In other words, the actual objections that this group has to enlarging its local substation probably resemble that of many groups in similar situations. But the ways in which the group presents the neighborhood as a coherent whole, justifies its own right to make demands on the behalf of the neighborhood, and legitimates those demands by reference to neighborhood characteristics, all instantiate a particular aspect of Taiwanese society, which is increasingly concerned with grounding politics in locality in a new way. Environmentalism was probably the first major activist movement to emerge after Taiwan's political liberalization. But as I will explain in the next section, environment, in the broad sense discussed above, also plays an important discursive role in Taiwan today: political demands and calls for justice are not only often *about* the environment, they are also often justified by being rooted in the land itself.

THE PARAMETERS OF LEGITIMATION AND THE IMPORTANCE OF THE LAND

The Cultural Association has taken the area's land-use history as its defining *local particularity* (*dìfāng tèsè*), ascribing to neighborhood residents, and especially to the Cultural Association itself, the duty and honor of preserving the area's sugarcane culture. While the contents of this culture are not spelled out, its preservation is carried out in a variety of ways ranging from the ritualized to the everyday: periodic rituals (the annual Sugarcane Festival and other parties); symbolic naming (the neighborhood's Sugarcane Park); pilgrimage-type trips to sugar refining sites around Taiwan; the accrual of possessions associated with sugar processing (sugar refining tools, several cars from an old Taiwan Sugar Corporation train that once carried sugarcane); and repeated references to the area's sugarcane-related past.

Why the Cultural Association can—and in some sense must—utilize this history to such an effect has to do with the terms on which political legitimacy is established in Taiwan today. With the end of Japanese colonialism on Taiwan and the island's retrocession to the mainland Chinese government under the KMT in 1945,[22] political power was concentrated in the hands of recent immigrants from the mainland (外省人 *wàishěngrén*, outside-province-people, usually called "mainlanders" in English). The majority of the population, whose ancestors had migrated to the island in the seventeenth and eighteenth centuries (*běnshěngrén*, this-province-people, which I render as "ethnic Taiwanese"), was left politically disenfranchised, at least at the higher levels of government. About 2 percent of Taiwan's total population is comprised of indigenous people, originally speakers of Austronesian languages whose ancestors arrived on the island hundreds of years before the first migrants from the Chinese mainland (the exact date of first indigenous population is not known).[23]

Although the indigenous population has become more politically vocal and empowered over the last two decades, Taiwan's main ethnicized division is between the ethnic Taiwanese (whose ancestors had migrated to the island centuries earlier) and the mainlanders (those who came in the mid-to-late 1940s and their children).[24] This distinction had a long development, including a violent uprising and subsequent massacre of ethnic Taiwanese elites in 1947 (in what is known as the February 28th Incident, or 2-2-8), and the resettlement of around two million KMT officials and soldiers fleeing the victorious Communist Party on the mainland in 1949 (at which point Taiwan had around six million inhabitants). The state of emergency that suspended the constitution and the martial law that replaced it effectively lasted from 1947 to around 1987, but the regime was increasingly less severe as time went on, and the KMT started to actively localize in the late 1970s and early 1980s.[25]

One of the conditions of possibility for the Juluo Cultural Association's community activism was the repeal of martial law and democratization, an ongoing process since roughly 1986. Democratization itself happened in tandem with, and to some extent grew out of, a cultural and political localization (*běntǔhuà*, literally 'this-land-ization,' also known as 'Taiwanization' and 'indigenization' in English), which began in the late 1970s, under martial law, within both the ruling party and its opposition. At the administrative level, localization meant increasing the number of ethnic Taiwanese in positions of formal political power, "localizing the state apparatus" (Chun 2000: 15). Culturally, it involved a shift, in both official and non-official discourses, in the *object* of nationalism. Cultural localization promoted the island of Taiwan itself—as opposed to a rhetorical China primordially centered on the mainland and only temporarily exiled on Taiwan—as the appropriate concern of nationalist sentiments (cf. Chun 1996).

Localization, then, was part of an ethno-nationalist democratization movement that brought the focus of public attention and legitimation away from the Chinese mainland and onto the island of Taiwan itself.[26] A central component of this movement was the changing valence of the *local*. Where previously the history of Taiwan was denigrated and ignored in favor of the Chinese mainland, in the last twenty years Taiwanese history has become a central concern for state agencies as well as local organizations. The mid-1980s saw the emergence of Taiwanese ethnic identity as a unified and valorized protagonist in island politics, a change implicitly recognized in many people's biographic periodization. As one informant put it, commenting on something that had happened in the 1970s, "At that time I didn't yet know I was Taiwanese."[27]

While ethnicized Taiwaneseness originally emerged through a (politically and militarily enacted) contrast with mainlanderness, in the process of localization and valorization it increasingly rooted itself in the land—"this piece of earth," *zhèikuài tǔdì*, is a typical way for people to refer to the island in the context of affect-laden expressions of concern for the country. For instance, a personal awakening narrative that I have heard in similar form from a number of people uses geographic and environmental terms to describe their emerging recognition of themselves as Taiwanese rather than Chinese. One interlocutor presented her story in a wonderfully dramatic way: one day while hiking she looked around and realized that she did not even know the name of the mountain before her or the river below her. Having learned all about mainland Chinese history and geography in school, she even knew the term for the kind of straw that people in northern China stuff their shoes with in the winter to stay warm—an experience that she, a resident of a semi-tropical island who had never seen snow in her life, could not even imagine. But she did not know what the wavy, wheat-like plant that covers Taiwanese mountainsides in the winter was called. As these images, and the term *běntǔhuà* 'this-land-ization' itself, suggest, Taiwanese ethno-nationalism is often phrased in geographic and environmental terms.[28] This discourse easily translates into a concern with community and environment—issues that fit the overarching rubric of the local.

Local here has a double meaning: on the one hand, it indicates the island of Taiwan (as opposed to the Chinese mainland). At the same time, the promotion of the local encourages the discursive division of Taiwan into nodes of ever more local culture and history. In state publications, unofficial discourses, and even everyday conversation, every area of Taiwan, from county to neighborhood, is figured as ideally having its own *local particularities* (地方特色, *dìfāng tèsè*)—aspects of local culture and history that are unique to that place, contribute to Taiwanese society, and represent a part of Taiwanese (rather than Chinese) history or culture.[29] City government officials, NGO administrators, and community activists alike emphasize the importance of the local particularity as a prerequisite to getting a demand heard (and, by extension, to getting it funded).

In other words, the parameters of legitimation for a wide spectrum of demands in contemporary Taiwan involve the discursive transformation of landscape history into personalized history, presented by a community in order to further an ethno-national narrative of historico-cultural development. In the Juluo neighborhood, the area's sugarcane growing and processing past has been made relevant to residents' fight against an enlarged power substation. This piece of the past, which has become a personalized history that suggests a unified historical development and a coherent culture, undergirds a claim to cultural authenticity that has been mobilized to combat what most residents agree is impending environmental injustice.

GEOSOCIAL COHERENCE AND
LEGITIMATING STRATEGIES

Invoking this unwitnessed history brings the entire geographical area of the neighborhood and its environmental development into one coherent narrative line that implicitly includes not only the land itself and its uses, but also the people using and living on it. The presupposed historical coherence of the geographic area, which allows it to be described as a unit with continuity over time, makes it easier to posit the neighborhood's *social* coherence and continuity as well.[30] For instance, Cultural Association members address unaffiliated neighborhood residents as members of a group that currently, because of their particular situation, has interests in common; but at the same time they can address people as members of a group that already, simply by virtue of physical location, shares a common culture. If this mode of address seems to resonate with Gramsci's (1971) advice to treat people as though they were already part of a party even when the party does not exist yet, it is because the continuity and coherence of geography and environment allow activists to treat their neighbors as always-already part of a geosocial network. And it works: drawing non-members into events organized around sugarcane commemoration has proved an effective recruitment technique for the Cultural Association.

With the discursive conflation of *here-then* and *here-now* that is typical of ethno-nationalist rhetoric, the existence of a common culture is predicated on the existence of a common history that almost nobody concerned actually experienced: the land use that predated the building of this neighborhood. The fact that the relevant history here should be a geographic and environmental one is no accident, but reflects a larger, societywide concern with locality and environment that permeates Taiwanese public discourse. At the same time, this historical narrative of coherence allows the Cultural Association to claim a cultural authenticity—a unique, contributory, and representative place in Taiwanese history—that bolsters its right to make demands about the neighborhood's spatial management in the first place.

After the first Juluo neighborhood protests against the Taiwan Electric Company's plan to expand the neighborhood's electric substation in the late 1990s, the company signed an agreement with the activist group (which later grew into the Cultural Association) promising to proceed only with the approval of a majority of neighborhood residents. In 2003, the company once again put forward its plans to enlarge the electric substation. When I ask about the status of the contractual agreement between the electric company and the residents, Cultural Association members tend to respond with a dismissive hand wave and a resigned assessment: "The Taiwan Electric Company has never lost."[31] Why contractual agreements can be so easily dismissed by both parties—by the electric company as not having binding force, and by Cultural Association members as unenforceable—has to do with what Jane Winn (1994) has called the "marginalization" of the law in Taiwan: "The development of a modern formal legal system may belie the social realities in Taiwan, obscuring the propensity of legal institutions to foster relational practices rather than displace them" (195).

"Relational practices"—private, behind-the-scenes brokering based on long term personal associations of mutual aid and mutual obligation—are indeed a central component of getting things done in Taiwan. But there is a public side to the process as well, practices of representation and legitimation that many groups must negotiate in order to gain the support and sympathy they need to succeed. It is in this sense that the tactic of moving people (*gǎn-dòng*) that I discuss in section 1 is integral to political activity. In general, my fieldwork with activist groups and the Taipei city government indicates that claims or demands based on rights or contractual obligations tend to carry less weight—both with state agencies and in public discourse—than those grounded in a unity of purpose arising out of a sentimental connection to a unique, contributory, representative local history and local culture.

Ethnographically, this essay has no conclusion: the debate over the substation's expansion continues to this day and may not be settled for years to come. What seems clear, however, are the terms on which the debate is held.[32] Personalized history of the type described here—presenting a unique contribution to the represented whole of Taiwan, and often oriented around the environment, land use, or other geographic factors—has become indispensable to political projects on the island. Here I have sketched out how Taiwan's recent sociopolitical changes have given rise to a discursive field whose parameters of legitimation for political action encourage, and sometimes require, the construction and presentation of such an environmentally situated memory.

I said in section one that the connection between the neighborhood's land-use past and its environmental future may be neither direct nor obvious to the outside observer. I hope that the rest of the chapter has demonstrated the ways in which the connection *is* direct and obvious to the people involved. Nobody to my knowledge has ever questioned the connection that the Cultural Association draws between the area's unexperienced environmental past and its socio-political present. In its discursive context, this connection, via personalized history, between an unexperienced land-use history and the current culture and viability of the neighborhood looks quite direct. Similarly, the relevance of this cultural and historical connection to larger political projects like protesting the expansion of the electric substation looks so obvious as to become obligatory. The parameters of legitimation corral political actors into the language of personalized history, whose tropes are drawn from personal memory, and in whose terms they must wage their battles.

NOTES

1. A pseudonym.

2. The group has protested several land-use plans in the neighborhood, including a proposed overpass on the edge of the neighborhood (the overpass was finally built further down the street, past the neighborhood); the sale of a large chunk of land to a hospital that would to build a large-scale retirement home on it (city government approval of the sale was finally reversed and the land was converted to a park); and the enlarging of the neighborhood's electric substation, on which this chapter will focus. Cultural Associations are registered civic organizations with a thematic or geographic focus, and with membership drawn potentially from anywhere in the city. They are registered with the Department of Civil Affairs of the Taipei City Government, and can receive financial assistance from the government for various activities. Under martial law, civic organizations of most sorts were effectively outlawed by strict restrictions on association. With the end of martial law in 1987, Cultural Associations took off as a popular way to formalize networks that were originally private, and give them some standing with regard to the state.

3. The refinery was built under Japanese colonial rule (1895–1945) and was therefore of too recent provenance to be automatically protected under Taiwan's heritage preservation laws, in which age is the determining factor.

4. That is, it's environment in the broad sense—living environment, surroundings, context—rather than in the narrow ecology-pollution sense typically found in contemporary American political usage.

5. Taiwanese, also called Hokien or Hoklo, is a variant of the Southern Min dialect spoken in southern Fujian province on mainland China. Although the choice between Mandarin and Taiwanese in public settings, as well as the romanization of both languages, have become fraught political issues explicitly linked to stands on Taiwanese independence and Taiwan-PRC unification, the question of whether Taiwanese is a 'dialect' or a 'language' does not, surprisingly, seem to be a big deal in Taiwan. While it is commonly referred to as *dialect* or *regional speech* (*fāngyán* 方言), it is usually named *Tai(wanese) language* (*táiyǔ* 台語), directly contrasting the KMT's name for Mandarin, *national language* (*guóyǔ* 國語). The PRC term for Mandarin is *common language* (*pǔtōng huà* 普通話). Due to diacritical limitations, in this essay I use standard symbols to render the four tones of Mandarin but numbers to represent the seven tones of Taiwanese (second and sixth tone are equivalent in Taiwanese, so there are eight numbers but only seven differentiated tones). In quotations with code-switching, I italicize Mandarin but not Taiwanese.

6. "Ho2, gun2 ah-be3 kah8 gua2 kong2—", "*Shuō* gun2 ah-gong2, gun2 ah-gong2 khah8 ho2." *Ah-be3* means father's older brother. *Ah-gong2* is father's father.

7. Memory has been seen to play an integral role in group-construction, particularly its ethnic and national versions, throughout the twentieth century. In terms of its role in the academy, it makes sense that memory would become popular as an object of study as these kinds of groups took center stage in social analysis. There may also be broader historical reasons, however, for our current fascination with memory. Hacking (1995) traces changes in the meaning of autobiographical memory over the nineteenth and twentieth centuries. Memory started out as a skill—the ability to memorize or recall facts—but gradually came to be seen as the scientific entry-point to the soul. Rather than a neutral repository of knowledge—something to know things *with*—memory became something to know things *about*: a topic of investigation rather than a storage room for the results of investigation. Having been turned into an object of analysis, Hacking continues, memory gradually came to define the soul and, later, the twentieth century version of the soul, the self. Thus in twentieth-century theories, for instance, the basis of group identity is in what we remember (e.g., Halbwachs); and the root of the individual personality is in what we forget (e.g., Freud). Hacking's study illuminates how our current fascination with shared memory is itself part of a broader analytic trend that sees memory as *the* clue to the constitution of the self.

8. A number of useful works summarize the role of the notion of memory in the social sciences at the same time as they demonstrate to incoherent and undefined quality of the term in most of the scholarship, see, e.g., Climo and Cattell (2002), Misztal (2003), Olick and Robbins (1998), and Radstone (2000).

9. This contrast involves continuity versus change, perspectivalism versus relativism, and living matter versus dead. Memory arises from "a current of continuous thought" (1980[1950]: 80) and describes how a group stays the same, while history describes how groups change, presenting "a break in continuity between the society reading this history" and the society it describes (1980[1950]: 79). Memory narrates

the past from the viewpoint of the group, while history tries to weigh all facts and participants equally. Memory is "a living history that perpetuates and renews itself through time" (1980[1950]: 65), as opposed to the "written history" that comes into being when memories are dead and all that remain are traces, archival or otherwise, from which the historian deduces, but does not recreate, the past. The problem with these contrasts is not that the two sides of each binary is not different. Rather, any term used to cover all of them simply becomes overloaded, so abstracted from any actual instance of the use or description of the past that it does not have much analytic utility.

10. In other words, Nietzsche gets out of the natural vs. constructed and authentic vs. utilitarian dilemmas described above by recognizing that relevance is *never* totally obvious or natural, but is always interpreted as being so.

11. There are two typical problems with literature that talks about the importance of the past to group identity, both of which I hope to avoid here. On the one hand, it sometimes seems obvious to scholars that some part of the past should be meaningful in some way, which allows them to elide the processes by which the record of the past can turn into a personally significant narrative, and take for granted the creation of that which is the object of the analysis. The basement vignette that introduces this essay is an attempt to focus on that part of the process in which something is picked out as fact and constructed as shared personalized history. The discussion of *parameters of legitimation* later on in the essay focuses on the part of the process that involves setting up the conditions for the determination of relevance. On the other hand, many scholars looking to debunk 'invented traditions' deny the relevance of some piece of history to the people invoking it. In doing so, however, they actually buy into the naturalizing ideology of collective memory, assuming that there is a universal standard for natural, authentic connection between history and group to which the group they are investigating does not conform (cf. Sahlins' [1999] critique of the invented traditions approach). For both of these types of scholarship, the emotional pull of collective memory and the *kinds* of significance it can take on are often assumed rather than examined. Here, I want as much as possible to avoid the issues of natural vs. constructed and authentic vs. utilitarian, and focus instead on the process by which people can perceive something as personalized history, how this attitude is conditioned by the sociopolitical realm in which they are situated, and how it comes to have pragmatic effects.

12. Here I draw on a variety of works that address or relate to the study of *publics*: Althusser (1971[1970]), Bakhtin (1986), Errington (1995), Goffman (1981), Gramsci (1971), Warner (2002), and Woolard (1989).

13. Warner (2002) discusses how a person can be incorporated into a public by feeling addressed by some set of messages. Warner is focused on the contact between the medium of address and the (somewhat self-selecting) addressee; the question of how addressivity is manifested, or how an analyst could claim the addressivity of his subject, is secondary. My hope in this essay and in general is to continue the exploration of pragmatic manifestations of public-belonging or addressivity.

14. "*Nǐ kàn . . . zhù zài zhèbiān de rén, bùrán, bùshì dé áizhèng jiùshì zěnmeyàng hah, dàjiā duōme* kiaN5 si2 ah li2 chai2 bo5 *dàjiā duōme pà.*" As often happens with bilingual informants, there is a code switch (from Mandarin to Taiwanese) at the

affective high point of the sentence ("kiaN5 si2 ah li2 chai2 bo5," "scared to death do you know").

15. Most Taipei residents own their apartments. The private, non-subsidized residences fall into two groups. Small one- or two-story houses lining the alleys on the edges of the neighborhood house many of the neighborhood's most long-term residents, who are among its poorest. Along the bigger streets, small apartment buildings (with owned, not rented, units) house primarily migrants who have moved to the area in the last twenty years or so. Many of these people are in the watch or clothing business (the two industries that dominate the area).

16. In Taiwan twenty-year-old buildings are considered very old, and people both in and outside of this neighborhood refer to the area as such. This has something to do, I suspect, with the age of the district in which the neighborhood lies, and something to do with people's generally low expectations of building quality, especially for post-retrocession (1945), pre-economic miracle consolidation (late 1980s) structures.

17. While practically all of Taipei is a shopping district of some sort, the eastern part of the city houses many more upscale shops and transnational chain stores, in addition to the small-scale, locally run retail establishments and restaurants that fill up much of the city's buildings, sidewalks, and alleys. But the retail environment for even cheaper goods has changed in the last twenty years, its center of gravity increasingly moving east. For instance, the Juluo area used to be the city's main wholesale clothing district ("wholesale" is a term used loosely here, indicating both shops that really do sell to other shops and shops that sell at such low prices that they may as well be). But as the city's public transportation systems (especially the subway and elevated line systems built in the 1990s and the improved train tracks with new train schedules) increasingly focused on the center and eastern sections of the city, the business in the west dried up. While the western neighborhood retains a wholesale clothing area, it has been eclipsed by a new wholesale clothing district centered around the train station on the city's east side.

18. In the wake of one prolonged Juluo protest, the new mayor—who owed his victory in part to the unexpected support of this neighborhood—announced a new policy that refocused urban development and renewal onto the city's older, western sections.

19. This district houses a few outposts of demobilized KMT soldiers who came over in the late 1940s—enough to render its average age the highest in Taipei—but city administrators and the public seem to agree that the majority of the rest of its population is primarily ethnically Taiwanese. Ethnicity faded out as a category of census studies in the late 1980s, and the reliability of census information on Taiwan is somewhat questionable to begin with. For me, such opinions are mostly valuable as a reflection of popular images of the area rather than as accurate depictions of its actual population.

20. 9,720 persons per square kilometer in Taipei City proper in 2002. The population density of Taiwan itself is second only to that of Bangladesh (622 persons per square kilometer, for a total population of around 22.51 million, in 2002). Taiwanese census statistics are somewhat questionable partly because many rural-to-urban migrants keep their household registration in their place of birth. In other words,

insofar as this data is unreliable, it's at least possible that it *under*represents the population of Taipei City. See Government Information Office (2003).

21. They do not, in general, ask why the substation must be enlarged in their *lower class* neighborhood rather than in the backyards of people with more money. Class terminology is very rare among this group of people (and, in my experience, in Taiwan generally), and phenomena that an American might attribute to low economic status are usually presented as caused by age, government neglect, or a lack of personal connections with the relevant people—that is, as infrastructural, political, or relational clout problems. It seems reasonable to think that this aversion to the language of class is at least partly due to forty years of vehemently (and sometimes violently) anti-communist rhetoric and activity by the KMT. But scholars of Chinese society have also suggested that, until the advent of Communism on the mainland, Chinese social life was largely not organized by class (Fei 1939 is the classic exposition of this view, cf. Fei 1992).

22. The party name, *guómíndǎng*, is usually rendered in English as Chinese Nationalist Party (the literal translation might be National People's Party or Citizens' Party). To avoid confusion between this party and Taiwanese nationalists—not capitalized, not a party but people holding a political position that advocates Taiwanese independence rather than unification with the mainland, I use only the standard romanized abbreviation used in Taiwan, KMT, in this essay. (The name is sometimes abbreviated GMD as well, depending on romanization system, audience, and writer's background.)

23. Indigenous people are known as *yuánzhùmín*, original inhabitants, or in less politically correct terms *shāndìrén*, mountain-land people, or *gāoshānrén*, high-mountain people—so named for the areas that they were known to inhabit, having been pushed there through successive waves of Chinese, followed by Japanese, colonization. They are never called *běnshěngrén*, this-province-people.

24. There are also subethnic divisions: ethnic Taiwanese are divided into the majority *mǐnnánrén*, Hokien or Hoklo people whose ancestors came from the southern coast of Fujian province and who speak a variant of Southern Min, the southern Fujian dialect, and the minority *kèjiārén*, Hakka people, who speak a Cantonese dialect. Their ancestors are considered to have been wanderers all over China (hence their name in Chinese, which means 'guest people'), and to have come to Taiwan from northern Guangdong (Canton) province. Mainlanders came from all over the mainland, originally spoke a variety of dialects, and only came to be seen as a unified ethnic group by distinction with the ethnic Taiwanese.

25. Since martial law was not actually a single law but an elaboration on the state of emergency that enacted a series of provisions and restrictions to keep political power within a limited sphere, its repeal is best seen as a gradual process that in some sense is still being worked out, rather than a stroke-of-the-pen revocation. I've seen 1986, 1987, and 1988 cited as dates for the end of martial law in American scholarly literature. The non-linear quality of developments might be demonstrated by the legalization of opposition political parties in 1987, shortly *after* the undisturbed public, formal founding of the first opposition party in 1986 (the Democratic Progressive Party). The state of emergency that had been the official justification for martial law was lifted in 1991. As opposed to the scholarship, which provides a variety of decisive

dates for the end of martial law, not one of my Taiwanese interlocutors ever pin-pointed a particular date, even when specifically asked. Rather, people tended to rec-ognize two periods: martial law (*jièyán*) and its 'relaxation' or 'loosening' (*jiěyán*), felicitously named to sound completely the same except for the tone of the initial syllable.

26. Taiwan's democratization movement in some ways resembles anti-colonial ethno-nationalism, although it has several very different features. While in one view the KMT dictatorship might be seen as a foreign occupying power (and is described as such by Taiwanese nationalists) it can also be seen as simply an everyday dictator-ship whose rulers are of the same race or culture as the governed population. As I indicate in this paper, one of the reasons that local culture and local history have become so important in Taiwan is that the status of Taiwanese culture—as Chinese or as something else—has become a linchpin in arguments about the relation between Taiwan and the PRC. Another twist to the anti-colonial form is that having given up its dictatorial power on Taiwan, the KMT couldn't go back where it came from because it no longer controlled that territory. Instead, the party has successfully made the transition into the new politics of post-martial law Taiwan. In a way remi-niscent of the Communist Parties of post-socialist Eastern European states, but with rather less strong-arming, it has retained much of its prestige and importance.

27. "*Nèige shíhòu wǒ hái bù zhīdào wǒ shì Táiwān rén.*"

28. A recent newspaper photograph (*The Taipei Times* 3/14/04:1) of the KMT presidential candidate, his wife, and another KMT official prostrating themselves and kissing the ground to show their love for Taiwan might serve as a snapshot of more than an electioneering gambit. The discourse of localization now permeates the pub-lic realm—even, as here, in the case of a party that is technically still in favor of unifi-cation with mainland China. Thanks to Jeff Martin for bringing this photograph to my attention.

29. Local particularities are often special geographic or architectural sites, as well as sites for specific activities. Very often they have something to do with the produc-tion, distribution, or invention of some kind of food.

30. This use of objects and sites from the past to unite and represent a group of people in the present is, of course, well known from all sorts of nationalist move-ments, see, e.g., Abu El-Haj (1998), Dominguez (1986), and Handler (1985).

31. "*Táidiàn cónglái méi shūguò.*"

32. And even these are not as clear as they may seem. There is an emerging ten-dency among younger, more educated activists—college graduates who came of age during democratization—to utilize legal or contractual relations, along with claims to local culture and local history, as methods of persuasion and legitimation. So far, however, these new techniques, based on an emerging relation to the state, have had little influence on the relatively older, relatively less educated people described in this paper.

REFERENCES

Abu El-Haj, Nadia. "Translating Truths: Nationalism, the Practice of Archaeology, and the Remaking of Past and Present in Contemporary Jerusalem." *American Ethnologist* 25, no. 2 (1998): 166–88.

Althusser, Louis. "Ideology and Ideological State Apparatuses." In *Lenin and Philosophy and Other Essays*. New York: Monthly Review Press, 1971[1970].

Bakhtin, Mikhail M. "The Problem of Speech Genres." In *Speech Genres and Other Late Essays*. Austin: University of Texas Press, 1986.

Chun, Allen. "Democracy as Hegemony, Globalization as Indigenization, or the 'Culture' in Taiwanese National Politics." In *Taiwan in Perspective*, edited by Wei-Chin Lee. Leiden: Brill, 2000.

———. "From Nationalism to Nationalizing: Cultural Imagination and State Formation in Post-war Taiwan." In *Chinese Nationalism*, edited by Jonathan Unger. Armonk, N.Y.: M. E. Sharpe, 1996.

Climo, Jacob J. and Maria G. Cattell. "Introduction: Meaning in Social Memory and History: Anthropological Perspectives." In *Social History and Memory: Anthropological Perspectives*, edited by Jacob J. Climo and Maria G. Cattell. Walnut Creek Calif.: AltaMira Press, 2002.

Dominguez, Virginia R. "The Marketing of Heritage." *American Ethnologist* 13, no. 3 (1986).

Errington, Joseph. "State Speech for Peripheral Publics in Java." *Pragmatics* 5, no. 2 (1995): 213–24.

Fei Xiaotong. *Peasant Life in China: A Field Study of Country Life in the Yangtze Valley*. London: Routledge, 1939.

———. *From the Soil: The Foundations of Chinese Society. A Translation of Fei Xiaotong's Xiangtu Zhongguo*. Translated by Gary G. Hamilton and Wang Zheng. Berkeley: University of California Press, 1992.

Gal, Susan and Kathryn A. Woolard. "Constructing Languages and Publics: Authority and Representation." *Pragmatics* 5, no. 2 (1995): 129–38.

Goffman, Erving. "Footing." In *Forms of Talk*. Philadelphia: University of Pennsylvania Press, 1981.

Government Information Office. *Taiwan Yearbook 2003*, http://www.gio.gov.tw/taiwan-website/5-gp/yearbook/chpt02.htm, 2003.

Gramsci, Antonio. "The modern prince." In *Selections from the Prison Notebooks*, edited and translated by Quintin Hoare and Geoffrey Nowell Smith. New York: International Publishers, 1971.

Hacking, Ian. *Rewriting the Soul: Multiple Personality and the Sciences of Memory*. Princeton N.J.: Princeton University Press, 1995.

Halbwachs, Maurice. *The Collective Memory*, translated by Francis J. Ditter, Jr. and Vita Yazdi Ditter. N.Y.: Harper & Row, 1980[1968].

Handler, Richard. "On Having a Culture." In *Objects and Others: Essays on Museums and Material Culture*, edited by George W. Stocking, Jr. Madison, Wisc.: University of Madison Press, 1985.

Misztal, Barbara A. *Theories of Social Remembering*. Maidenhead, Philadelphia: Open University Press, 2003.

Nietzsche, Friedrich. *On the Advantage and Disadvantage of History for Life*, translated by Peter Preuss. Indianapolis Ind.: Hackett, 1980[1874].

Olick, Jeffrey and Joyce Robbins. "Social Memory Studies: From 'Collective Memory' to the Historical Sociology of Mnemonic Practices." *Annual Rev of Sociology* 24(1998): 105–140.

Radstone, Susannah. "Working with Memory: An Introduction." In *Memory and Methodology*, edited by Susannah Radstone. Oxford, N.Y.: Berg, 2000.

Sahlins, Marshall. "Two or Three Things That I Know About Culture." *Journal of the Royal Anthropological Institute* 5, no. 3 (1999): 399–422.

The Taipei Times http://www.taipeitimes.com/News/front/archives/2004/03/14/2003102366, 3/14/04.

Warner, Michael. *Publics and Counterpublics*. New York: Zone Books, 2002.

Williams, Jack F. "Sugar: The Sweetener in Taiwan's Development." In *China's Island Frontier: Studies in the Historical Geography of Taiwan*, edited by R. G. Knapp. Honolulu: University Press of Hawaii, 1980

Winn, Jane Kaufman. "Relational Practices and the Marginalization of Law: Informal Financial Practices of Small Businesses in Taiwan." *Law and Society Review* 28, no. 2 (1994): 193–232.

22

Remembering the Mother River
The Impact of Environmental Injustice on National Identity in Contemporary China

Jane Sayers

The Yellow River is considered the "cradle of Chinese civilisation," the mother river that gave birth to the nation. It flows west to east across the north of China, from the mountains in the far west, through the arid loess plateau, and out to the sea in Shandong province. But the Yellow River is more than a geographical feature to the Chinese. It is along this river that the Han people, the ethnic majority of China, originated. Throughout the long history of the river, people have braved the harsh climatic elements and the threat of both drought and flood in order to eke out an existence. In conjunction with these harsh survival conditions, they have developed mythological and cosmological narratives to make sense of this life. This forms a cultural legacy that in still resonates in Chinese identity today.

This legacy, with its roots in mythology and cosmology, is vast. The river dragon, He Bo, is one of the oldest relics of the river; offerings made to him can be dated back to the Zhou dynasty (1030–221 BC).[1] Later on, in imperial times, the control of the waters of the Yellow River was held as a gauge of political power; drought and flood both indicated to the people that the mandate of heaven had been removed from the emperor of the day, and were read as signs of dynastic decline.[2] In the 1930s and 1940s, it was in this same region that the Chinese Communist Party made their base, and it was here that they developed the "moral template" for the new China they would try to establish under the leadership of Mao Zedong.[3] This cultural tradition lies deep in the Chinese collective memory, informing their view of the landscape of the Yellow River and their relationship to the land and the nation. This is indeed a region that is inscribed with the cultural identity of the Chinese people.

However, this is not a cultural legacy that has always been celebrated. For much of the twentieth century, the urban, intellectual elite of China worked to break the bounds of traditional identity formation in a bid to make China a modern, cosmopolitan force on the international stage. In a groundbreaking and controversial documentary made in 1988,[4] filmmakers Su Xiaokang and Wang Luxiang argued that it was the tendency of Chinese to look backward, to their roots in the Yellow River and to their historical triumphs that impeded them from looking forward, to the much less insular future that was possible. Su and Wang described the Chinese people's link to the Yellow River thus:

> This is truly a rather unique river in the world. Arising from the snow-covered peaks on the north slope of the Bayan Kara Mountains, after passing the yellow soil plateau on its way eastward, it becomes a river of yellow mud. It just so happened that this yellow river bred a yellow-skinned people; and this people just happened to call their first ancestor the Yellow Emperor. On the earth today one out of every five people is a descendent of the Yellow Emperor. Yellow water, yellow soil, yellow people: what a mysterious yet natural connection this is. It would appear as if the skin of this yellow people were dyed by the Yellow River.[5]

It is in the context of these well-established yet diverse cultural understandings of the Chinese people's relationship with the Yellow River that the China Youth Development Foundation (*Zhongguo qing shao nian fazhan jijinhui*) campaign of 2000 to rehabilitate this region can be read. The rapid modernisation of the post-Mao era has brought with it a slew of environmental issues that have hit this region hard. Water pollution and shortage, desertification, soil erosion and air pollution have all become severe. The riverbed of the Yellow River is dry for longer and longer each year,[6] and sandstorms rise from the ever-expanding Gobi Desert and move east each spring, affecting Beijing and even Japan. In 2002 they started in March; one of the earliest lasted 51 hours and carried 30 000 tons on sand into Beijing in that time.[7] For those who live in apartment buildings in cities along the Yellow River, it is not considered exceptional for apartments above the second floor of a building to have unreliable water supplies, as there simply is not enough water to reach the upper floors.[8]

For those who live outside the cities, these new environmental conditions have made farming even harder in a region where it has always been hard. Overgrazing and overexploitation of the land has caused rapid desertification in the regions surrounding the Yellow River. Over use of the land has become more and more necessary as the earth yields less and less.[9] This has created a spiral of decline from which rehabilitation of the earth becomes less and less likely: the earth yields less so the farmers have to work the land harder in order to meet their production requirements, so the earth yields less, and so on. Rural incomes decline[10] while urban consumers demand ever-higher levels of produce. Farmers are forced to head to the cities in search of work, for the land cannot sustain them any longer, and cannot help them boost their incomes. Those on the move see their migration into the cities as the answer to their problems in rural China, for the cities have been the centres of the modernising reforms of recent history. It is in the cities that construction is flourishing and incomes are rising steadily. It is in the cities that people have increasing opportunities and improving quality of life.

This movement of farmers into the cities is a major contributing factor in the dramatic development of the "floating population" (*liudong renkou*).[11] The institutional and economic reforms of the post-Mao era are generally regarded as the catalysts to this population movement, which began in the mid-1980s. As agricultural techniques have become more technologically sophisticated, the required labor force in rural areas has shrunk, leaving a large surplus labor force. These surplus workers have been heading to the cities in search of an income they can send home to their families. This movement has been further facilitated by the changes to the household registration system that used to tie people to their hometowns, as this was the only location in which they could buy grain.[12] People can now buy food anywhere, and the opportunities of the city beckon.

But changing environmental conditions that are due to the accelerated rates of degradation that modernization has brought with it have also contributed to the movement of people into the cities. As reliable sources of water become harder to find and the earth yields less, as the soil erodes and the desert expands across the countryside, peasants are forced to seek alternative ways of supporting their families. These are environmental factors that are contributing to the size of the movement of people into the cities; this movement can be partially understood as a response to environmental injustices.

For urban residents, the floating population has been a source of considerable concern.[13] There are prevalent discourses on the "backward" nature of the rural immigrants, who are considered by many to be people of "low quality" (*suzhi cha*).[14] They are often understood as a threat to social stability for their move to the cities has weakened their ties to a community and thus left their behavior unrestrained.[15] In the popular imagination of urban Chinese, people from the countryside belong to that landscape: they are a part of the rural hinterland that serves as the repository of the essential understanding of "Chineseness." They are not a part of the modern, urban, international face of China. They embody the landscape of the nation, and their presence in the cities destabilizes this construction of place, and consequently destabilizes the construction of national identity.[16]

CAMPAIGNING FOR CHANGE

It is in this context of rural to urban migration and severe environmental deterioration of a national landscape of great cultural significance that I will to examine the campaign launched by the China Youth Development Foundation. This campaign aims to raise money for reforestation along the Yellow River and taps into the cultural legacy of that river, arguing that if the river and its surrounds are not protected, it will not only be an environmental loss: it is also the landscape that houses the essential and traditional construction of Chinese identity that will be lost. It argues that to allow the Yellow River and its environs to become any further degraded will be to erode the current construction of national identity.

This is not the only campaign that has sought to address environmental injustices in rural China. Most sustained efforts in this vein have been initiated from urban centers and include education programs that aim to teach rural inhabitants of their effect on the land and ways in which they can try to minimise this impact. The oldest environment non-government organization in China, Friends of Nature (*Ziran zhi you*), has an 'Antelope Car' (*ling yang che*) that is designed to visit schools both in Beijing and in the surrounding countryside to provide environmental education.[17] Similarly, in 2000, a group of students from Beijing's Forestry University dedicated their summer vacation to travelling to rural areas of Gansu province in the country's northwest to provide environmental education to students and their families.[18] These efforts seek to empower rural inhabitants on environmental justice issues and give them some tools to understand the principles that underlie environmental conditions. Rural residents themselves have organized protests against environmental injustices, such as local factories polluting village waterways, but these protests tend to be issue specific and generally disband once the immediate problem has been addressed.[19]

The China Youth Development Foundation campaign seeks not to engage local people in the fate of their own region, but rather aims to raise money in China's large cities in order to change the rural landscape without local input. It is firmly focused on raising awareness within urban areas, and in channelling funds from the urban elite back into the impoverished rural hinterland. The foundation was established in 1989 and is a semi-autonomous government agency, which means it has strong institutional links to the structures of the state, but is responsible for its own income generation.[20] Its activities are largely concerned with poverty alleviation; its best know project is the Hope Project (*xiwang gongcheng*), which seeks to help children in remote and impoverished areas continue with their education and to improve the standard of education children in these regions receive. The Green Hope Project (*lüse xiwang gongcheng*), of which the campaign herein under discussion is a part, seeks to reforest similarly remote and impoverished areas in order to address the issues of poverty and environmental injustice the people living in these areas face.[21]

The campaign that is the focus of this chapter aims to raise funds for the reforestation of the banks of the Yellow River, and is run in conjunction with a popular literary magazine *Reader* (*Duzhe*). It is through this magazine that the reforestation campaign is promoted under the slogan "Save the Mother River by Planting a *Reader*'s Forest" ('*baohu muqin he, gong jian Duzhe lin*'). This chapter will discuss the cultural resonances of three of the images used in the promotion of this campaign. This discussion is not intended as a thorough analysis of the cultural narratives and discourses that will be highlighted as operational in the images to be examined; it is rather intended as a first step in understanding the kinds of cultural constructions that inform current expressions of the newly emerging field of environmental justice in China. The first image to be discussed is a map of China with the Yellow River drawn as a dragon facing the sea.[22] The second is a picture of the river cutting a path through a misty valley with steep lush banks on each side.[23] The third is a picture of an old, weathered peasant woman gazing into the distance next to a vista of the river winding through the loess plateau.[24]

It is on the back of the historical associations that can be so readily made with these images portraying the landscape of the Yellow River that the case for saving that landscape is made. The message is: if we don't protect the river's environs, then we lose not only those natural features (and indeed natural resources), but we also lose all the cultural connections we have to that landscape. And people have responded to this message. Thousands of people have made donations to the campaign, ranging from pocket money donations from primary school children through to large donations from the corporate sector.[25]

REMEMBERING THE RIVER DRAGON

The first image is of the Yellow River drawn as a dragon on the map of northern China. His tail is in the mountainous west, his mouth forms the river's delta, and his claws reach into the surrounding countryside. This image resonates with the legend of He Bo. In ancient times, it was believed that He Bo, a male deity who took the dragon form, lived in the Yellow River and controlled its waters. He was understood as a fierce and wild guardian of the river, who had to be appeased. This is a legend specific to the Yellow River, for most rivers in China were believed to have female guardians who were alluring and enticing, unpredictable, but kind of spirit.[26] He Bo was not like these other river deities. Every traveler who crossed the river made an offering to him in the hope of receiving safe passage, and each year a young woman was sacrificed to him in the hope that such an act would bring rains but not floods to local areas. In the documentary *Heshang (The River Elegy)*, Su Xiaokang speculated as to why such a terrific deity was believed to inhabit the Yellow River when other Chinese rivers held such charming and feminine deities:

> In short, the reason why dragon worship could originate in the Yellow River basin was exactly due to the fear and respect of this river people for its river of life. For without doubt, the Yellow River is the most brutal and most unrestrained river in the world.[27]

He Bo embodies this brutal and fearful attitude toward the river.[28]

The legend of the annual sacrifice tells that each spring a bride was chosen for He Bo and was placed on a marriage bed that was launched into the river. In this way, the sacrificial bride drowned in order to meet and marry the river dragon deity.[29] Legend tells us that this religious tradition was ended by a Confucian official who was disdainful of the sacrificial ceremony, and so one year he asked to see the chosen girl before she was sacrificed. He declared that she was not beautiful enough for He Bo, and he told the head sorceress to go tell He Bo he would have to wait until a more beautiful bride could be found for him. When the head sorceress did not return from the river, Pao had her three assistant sorceresses thrown into the river, one after the other, to see what was taking so long. When they did not return, he had the top male official of the town thrown into the river to see what was taking the women so long. When this man did not return the next most senior male official was thrown in. When three officials had been thrown in, it became clear to the people that Pao would throw them all in one at a time, and they begged him to spare them. Legend has it that no further mention was ever made of the sacrificial ceremony.

This is a tale that tells of the rise of Confucian political power in China, but it also suggests the ways in which people made sense of the environmental conditions they lived within; it accounts for environmental injustices. Floods and droughts were understood to be the decisions of the dragon and sacrifices made to him sought his support, particularly in issues of water access. If the sacrifice was not good enough, the dragon's vengeance would be visited upon the people, and only an immediate threat to their own lives (here made by the Confucian official who would throw them all into the river to drown on the one afternoon) outweighed this risk.

In representing the river as a dragon, the China Youth Development Foundation draws on this cultural heritage. What can be seen in this modern representation is a rewriting of the ancient legend. In times gone by, the river and its dragon were to be feared for their unpredictability. The Yellow River was understood as both life-granting and life-threatening, and appeasing the dragon was the way in which people tried to negotiate their dependence on the river's forces. In contemporary China, however, the predominant fear is that the river itself will be lost, and the dragon with it. The dragon is now understood amongst urban Chinese as a threatened cultural artifact rather than as a threatening deity.[30] In recalling the dragon in this conservation effort, an emotional response concerning the cultural history of the region is drawn upon. The dragon mythology of the Yellow River is a part of a traditional sense of Chinese identity. To lose the river is to lose this site of cultural memory, to lose touch with ancient constructions of environmental justice.

REMEMBERING THE MISTY RIVER

The second image shows a river weaving through steep, almost cliff-like banks that are covered in lush green growth and disappear into the low hanging clouds. It is an image that resembles a traditional Chinese landscape painting; it is not hard to imagine this portrayal of the river done in brush and ink, on a scroll. It contains all the elements of a landscape painting—the banks are like mountains that symbolise permanence and stability, the flowing river represents change, and the clouds and mist suggest the cosmic and spiritual realm.[31] In the terms of this symbolic order, the only thing missing from this picture is some sign of human settlement in this landscape. The purpose of this picture however, to encourage participation in a conservation campaign, speaks to the human place in and impact upon this scene.

What is striking about this depiction of the river is that it appears to draw on the representational history of the Yangtze River, which flows through the south of China, rather than that of the Yellow River.[32] It is the Yangtze that flows through a lush, wet misty landscape and it is the Yangtze that is renowned for its gorges, with their steep banks. In contrast, the Yellow River is a raised river for many miles of its length, and is set in a barren, dry landscape. There are stretches of the Yellow River along its uppermost reaches in the far northwest of China that more closely resemble this picture, but for most Han Chinese who live along the eastern seaboard, this is not an image that reflects their concept of the physical reality of the Yellow River.

So how does this image, used in the reforestation campaign, speak to the reality of the Yellow River? What this image reflects, it can be argued, is a generalised, national imagining of what rivers in China look like. The poetic and painting traditions of the nation were largely located in the south of China from the late Tang dynasty, when the Yellow River region was not under Chinese control at all, that area having been conquered by the Jurchen. Thus, the cultural construction of river landscapes in China from the late Tang dynasty on was predominately influenced by the landscape of the Yangtze River with its mist and lush banks. This was the river at hand and the reality of this river landscape influenced the portrayal of all rivers by these Tang artists and poets. This is particularly clear in the Tang dynasty tradition of river poetry as appears in the *Songs of the South*.[33] The Yangtze is a far more feminised river than the Yellow River, as is evident from a comparison between He Bo and the female guardians of the southern river, and poets and painters have taken these more feminine elements of wetness and lush growth that are derived from the yin-yang breakdown of masculine and feminine properties, and have romanticised the national imagining of rivers. Over time, this predominance of the Yangtze River in the cultural traditions of poetry and painting has come to colour the ways in which the Yellow River is portrayed. In the China Youth Development Foundation campaign this image of the northern river, the Yellow River, portrayed in the tropes of the southern river, the Yangtze, speaks to Chinese peoples' sense of what a river *should* look like. It is the physical reality of the Yangtze that people are drawn to, and it is this image that has been transcribed onto the landscape of the Yellow River in this campaign image. This flattens out important historical differences between the two landscapes, but it speaks to the cultural understandings Chinese people have of what rivers ought to look like and, importantly, what kind of river they are prepared to save.

As in the case of the reinterpretation of the dragon, discussed above, this representation of the river landscape speaks to a reconstruction of the national memory. Both these representations draw on an aesthetic and emotional realm of art and mythology rather than on an experienced reality of the river in question. It is arguable that most urban Chinese don't have a sense of what else the Yellow River might look like other than a polluted waterway, heavy with silt, running through a barren landscape; it is arguable they don't have a sense of what kind of a landscape the reforestation campaign is attempting to create or re-create. This knowledge is a lost memory for most urban Chinese, who live at a distant remove from the non-human world, and from the national landscapes that express a timeless quality of "Chineseness." This reforestation campaign has chosen a river image that is appealing to people because they still have a sense of the romance associated with the Yangtze River; a emotional response to the river that they have largely lost in relation to the Yellow River, which is generally seen in terms of its polluted lower course. It reconstructs the way in which people feel about the Yellow River by bringing new tropes to bear on its representation.

The campaign organizers have had to find ways of making the landscape and space of the Yellow River important to the people they are trying to solicit funds from. They have tackled this by trying to create a role for tradition in the modern world. Environmental restoration, protection and conservation are granted importance through this campaign because of their value in the construction and maintenance of national identity. In this image, the landscape of the Yellow River is given a generalised value that minimises regional specificity in an effort to tap into a national construction of identity and memory.

REMEMBERING THE PEASANTRY

The third image is the only one to be printed in color. It shows a hand drawn picture of a weathered peasant woman gazing quietly off into the distance off the left side of the page and behind her, a river that does look stark and barren wends its way through the plateau, into the sunset that serves as a backdrop. The sunset colors that dominate the image give the river a yellow hue and suggest the loess plateau in a romanticised light. While such romance can be read as a link back to the portrayals of the Yangtze River, it is perhaps more productive to read this image as conveying a sense of a nostalgic yearning for the timeless nature of the Yellow River. The image of the peasant woman also speaks to such a nostalgic construction of the landscape. It is arguable that she is intended to represent the "mother" in the call to "Protect the Mother River" (*baohu muqin he*), but she can also be understood to carry with her resonances of the longstanding cultural tension between the rural and the urban.

Throughout the twentieth century, urban Chinese have struggled to reconcile their desire to be modern with their desire to retain traditional and what are considered to be inherently Chinese values in their sense of themselves. They have done this by using the countryside as a repository for traditional values, a strategy that allows them to embrace modernity in the urban centres because they know that their understanding of their own "Chineseness" is safely stored away in the countryside. The arrival of the floating population in urban centres in the post-Mao era has disrupted this construction. These rural migrants in the city destabilise the dualistic construct in which the city is the modern centre and the countryside the site of traditional culture and values. These migrants bring the association of traditional cultural values with them, into the urban centre, but they also bring the problems of the countryside with them. No longer can urban residents pretend the rural hinterland is an idyllic site in which cultural memory is played out; the presence of rural migrants in the cities forces urban Chinese to acknowledge the hardships of rural life in a way they have never had to before.

There is nothing uniquely Chinese in this construct[34] and, as is common in cultures across the world, the Chinese countryside is often used as a symbolic marker of the nation precisely because it is understood as a repository of traditional cultural values. The specificities of non-urban areas, the features of the landscape, and the agricultural conditions found there, are often used as indicators of what is unique about the nation state. In a fast-paced, modern, urban present, the traditional values of the nation are safely stored in the countryside. In so doing, the countryside comes to be seen as the past of the city.[35] It is this construction of the countryside as the past of the city that the floating population disrupts. The rural migrants are very much migrants of the present, and they are moving into the cities in an attempt to address their great need. These people suffer very real economic, institutional, political, and environmental disadvantage, and these injustices cannot be relegated to the past.

The peasant woman in this image represents the construction of the countryside and the national past that is preferred by urban Chinese. She looks old and wise, weathered and also timeless; she looks as peasant women have looked for hundreds of years. She is closely associated with the land and the river of the rural hinterland in this picture, and this association is expressed in nostalgic, romantic colors. In calling on urbanites to save the mother river and in giving the mother river this woman's face, the saving of the river is associated with the redeeming of the nation's past. In saving the landscape of the river, the homeland of this woman, the repository of traditional values is also saved, and this marker of Chinese identity is preserved. In reforesting the river the environmental injustices this peasant woman is likely to have suffered will be addressed.

Again we can see here a return to the cultural values that were set aside in the quest for modernisation. Just as the dragon was lost in the race to leave behind the traditions that impeded the process of modernization, so too the traditional values represented by the peasant woman, the new guardian of the river, were lost in the process of modernization. No acknowledgement is made in this image of the new history that informs this reading of it; no acknowledgement of the peasants' migration into the city is associated with the environmental degradation the river is facing. This is an acknowledgement that urban Chinese, who do not suffer the same injustices their rural counterparts do, are not yet ready to make. The inequities between these two regions are profound, and organizations like the China Youth Development Foundation are still trying to find ways of engaging the urban elite in the issues facing the poor, rural majority.

IDENTITY AND ENVIRONMENTAL JUSTICE

The China Youth Development Foundation campaign seeks to address issues of environmental injustice by channelling funds into a reforestation project for poor and remote areas along the Yellow River. They aim to improve the quality of life for the people who live in these regions by rehabilitating the environment. This can be understood as an attempt to address issues of environmental justice that affect rural China, and rural Chinese. In order to raise funds for this purpose, the China Youth Development Foundation has had to combat the negative associations many urban Chinese have with their rural compatriots; they have had to frame the campaign in terms that speak to issues that are seen as relevant to the urban population.

The images they have used to make this link between rural environmental degradation and urban residents target issues of urban Chinese identity construction; the landscape of the Yellow River needs to be reforested not so much for the benefit of those who live in that landscape, or for environment reasons, but rather so as to retain its significance as a symbol of what it means to be Chinese. The plight of rural inhabitants and the environment they rely on is left unspoken in this construction. The only image that includes a representation of a rural inhabitant is the final picture which depicts the old peasant woman. This woman is an imagined construction of the ideal peasant—weathered, wise, and silent. She is firmly associated with the land of the countryside rather than with the city, both by the picture of the river behind her and by the direction of her gaze; she looks to the west, to the interior of China rather than to the east and the world beyond China. By extension, she gazes to China's history, which is figuratively located in the countryside for urban inhabitants, rather than to the future of the nation, which is associated with the cities of the eastern seaboard.

The second picture discussed, in which the portrayal of the river recalls the Yangtze rather than the Yellow, also speaks to the urbanites' idealized construction of the Chinese landscape. People are not prepared to face the realities of the social and environmental issues that plague their nation, in the current campaign the river of the north in particular. They are more prepared to donate funds that are seen to be channelled into the maintenance of their national identity. The dragon in the first image is an iconic example of the cultural memory that this landscape houses, and the historic foundations of contemporary identity formation. As a consequence, this campaign inscribes the landscape with cultural history and then argues for saving that landscape because of its cultural connotations, rather than for an environmental or quality-of-life reason. It addresses environmental degradation and injustice obliquely, by targeting issues urban Chinese understand as relevant to themselves, and to which they are more likely to respond. This has proven an effective fund raising strategy, but it highlights a considerable obstacle for the still young environmental movement in contemporary China. Whether this is a problem of a lack of education and an associated ignorance of environmental significance that will be addressed as the burgeoning movement grows and gains more widespread public recognition than it currently has, or whether it is a more consciously held lack of interest or concern for environmental and rural issues is yet to be determined. It is understandable that people who have only recently experienced the material benefits of modernization should want to revel in them for a while. But will a broad-based concern for the state of the environment and environmental justice emerge in China? This remains to be seen.

NOTES

1. Edward H. Schafer, *The Divine Woman: Dragon Ladies and Rain Maidens in T'ang Literature* (Berkeley: University of California Press, 1973) 25. Oracle bone inscriptions show that offerings were made to the spirit of the Yellow River earlier than this, but to date no records have been found that describe He Bo as the river god until the late Zhou.

2. Randall A. Dodgen, *Controlling the Dragon: Confucian Engineers and the Yellow River in Late Imperial China* (Honolulu: University of Hawai'i Press, 2001).

3. Mark Selden, *China in Revolution: The Yenan Way Revisited* (Armonk: M.E. Sharpe, 1995); James R. Townsend, *Political Participation in Communist China* (Berkeley: University of California Press, 1969) 51–64.

4. *Heshang (The River Elegy)* Written and produced by Su Xiaokang and Wang Luxiang (Beijing: China Central Television, 1988).

5. Su Xiaokang and Wang Luxiang 'The Reader's Guide', in Su Xiaokang and Wang Luxiang, *Deathsong of the River: A Reader's Guide to the Chinese TV Series Heshang*, translated by Richard W. Bodman and Pin P. Wan (Ithaca: East Asia Program, Cornell University,1991) 104.

6. Li Pingri, "China's Natural Disasters and Global Climate Change in 1998" in *China Environment 1998* (Hong Kong: Greenpeace China, 1999).

7. "Sandstorm Leaves 30 000 Tons of Dust in Beijing" *China News Digest*, March 24, 2002, http://www.cnd.org/Global/02/03/24/020324-2.html.

8. Anecdotal data collected during field work in Beijing, February 2001.

9. Cheng Xiaonong describes China's agricultural land as of "poor quality," stating "79 percent of the farmland is of medium to low output. Only 40 percent of the land has proper water sources and irrigation facilities, of which a lot is on 25-degree slopes and of poor quality." He Qinglian and Cheng Xiaonong, "Rural Economy at a Dead End: A Dialogue on Rural China, Peasants and Agriculture" *Modern China Studies* 3 (2001) 30. Also available at http://www.uscc.gov/rural.pdf.

10. According to He Qinglian: "A report in 2000 by the rural survey team of the State Statistics Bureau indicates that while per capita salary incomes reached 16 641 yuan and 14 054 yuan for residents of Shanghai and Beijing, respectively, the annual net income per capita for rural residents in 1999 was merely 2 210 yuan." He Qinglian and Cheng Xiaonong "Rural Economy at a Dead End" 13. (1USD ≈ 8 yuan)

11. The floating population is a term that refers to population movement more generally than just to rural to urban migration, but this is generally understood as the largest component. For definitions and discussion of the floating population see, for example, Laurence J.C. Ma and Biao Xiang, "Native Place, Migration and the

Emergence of Peasant Enclaves in Beijing" *China Quarterly*, 155 (September 1998): 546–81; Dorothy J. Solinger, *Contesting Citizenship in Urban China: Peasant Migrants, the State, and the Logic of the Market* (Berkeley: University of California Press, 1999).

12. For a discussion of the reform era changes to the household registration system, see, for example, Tiejun Cheng and Mark Selden, "The Origin and Social Consequences of China's *hukou* System," *China Quarterly*, 139 (1994): 644–668.

13. For more on urban attitudes toward the floating population see, for example, Tamara Jacka, "Working Sisters Answer Back: The Representation and Self-Representation of Women in China's Floating Population" *China Information* 13, 1 (1998): 43–75; Tamara Jacka, "Other China's/China's Others: A Report on the First National Forum on the Protection of Rights of Migrant Women Workers, June 16–18, 1999, Beijing" *New Formations* 40 (1999): 128–37; Ma and Biao, "Native Place"; Wang Shan, *Di San Zhi Yanjing Kan Zhongguo (The Third Eye on China)* (Shanxi: Shanxi Renmin Chubanshe, 1994), an excerpt of this book is translated in Michael Dutton, *Streetlife China* (Cambridge: Cambridge University Press, 1998).

14. For discussions of 'backward' and 'low quality' peasants, see, for example, Ann Anagnost, *National Past-Times: Narrative, Representation, and Power in Modern China* (Durham: Duke University Press, 1997); Jacka, "Working Sisters"; Jacka, "Other Chinas"; Wang, *Di San Zhi*.

15. Wang, *Di San Zhi*, Dutton translation in *Streetlife*, 89.

16. For more on this idea see Jane Sayers, "China's Mother River Scolds Her Young: Modernization and the National Landscape" *Transformations*, 5 (December 2002) http://www.ahs.cqu.edu.au/transformations/.

17. For more on the Antelope Car, see Noah Bessoff, "Teacher's Pet: Antelope Car Drives Home Environmental Lessons" *China Online News*, 19 June 2000. http://www.chinaonline.com/topstories/000619/1/C00061930.asp; Hao Bing, "Lingyang che, meng kaishide difang" ("The Antelope Car: A Place Where Dreams Begin") *Zhongguo huanjing bao (China Environment Times)*, 1 August 2000; Jane Sayers, "Start with the Little Things: Environmental Education as Political Participation in Contemporary China" (PhD, diss, University of Melbourne, 2004).

18. For more on this student initiative, see Liu Bing and Peng Meiying, "Wei xibu bosong lüse xiwang: Gansu shan qu ertong de huanjing jiaoyu" ("Sewing the Seeds of Green Hope in the West: Environmental Education of the Children of Gansu's Mountainous Areas") *Shan Nuo Hui Kan (The SENOL Magazine)* 4 (2000): 5–11; and Sayers, "Start with the Little Things."

19. See Jun Jing, "Environmental Protests in Rural China" in *Chinese Society: Change, Conflict and Resistance*, ed. Elizabeth J. Perry and Mark Selden (London: Routledge, 2000): 143–60.

20. For more on this kind of organization, see Elizabeth Knup, "Environmental NGO's in China: An Overview" *China Environment Series* (1997): 9–15, http://ecsp.si.edu/pdf/China1b.pdf.

21. For more information on the Foundation and its activities, visit their Web site at www.cydf.org.cn.

22. *Zhongguo Qing Jihui Tongji (China Youth Development Foundation News)*, "Baohu muqin he, gong jian Duzhe lin" ("Save the Mother River by Planting a Reader's Forest"), 9, 12 (2000) 1.

23. *Zhongguo Qing Jihui Tongji* (*China Youth Development Foundation News*), "Baohu muqin he xingdong" ("The Save the Mother River Activity"), 2, 66 (1999) 3.

24. *Duzhe* (*Reader*), 'Baohu muqin he, gong jian Duzhe lin' ('Save the Mother River by Planting a Reader's Forest'), 4, 7 (2001) 32.

25. *Zhongguo Qing Jihui Tongji* (*China Youth Development Foundation News*), "Baohu muqin he, gong jian Duzhe lin" ("Save the Mother River by Planting a Reader's Forest"), 9, 12 (2000) 1–4.

26. See Schafer, *The Divine Woman*.

27. Su and Wang, 'A Reader's Guide' 106.

28. Whalen Lai reminds us that He Bo did have a softer side as well, as can be seen in his portrayal as a lover in *The Songs of the South*. This fits with the view of the Yellow River as dual in nature, being both life-giving and life-threatening. So too, He Bo was understood as both a lover and a destroyer. See Whalen Lai, "Looking for Mr Ho Po: Unmasking the River God of Ancient China," *History of Religions* 29, 4 (1989): 335–50, 340.

29. This retelling of the myth is based on Lai, "Looking for Mr Ho Po" and Anthony Christie, *Chinese Mythology* (Feltham: Paul Hamlyn, 1968) 79–83.

30. This is not the only understanding of the river dragon however. As recently as August 1975 (which, given the age of this mythological tale, is very recent) the river dragon was recalled in fear and despair when the Banqiao dam on the Huai River, a tributary of the Yellow River, burst. The dam had experienced a rapid increase in the volume of silt it contained, and the water from the sudden storms proved too much for it to bear. As people fled the surging flood waters the broken dam let forth, they cried out 'the river dragon has come!'. See Gørild M. Heggelund, review of *The River Dragon Has Come! The Three Gorges Dam and the Fate of China's Yangtze River and Its People*, ed. Dai Qing, *China Information*, 13 (1998) 155–57; Yi Si, "The World's Most Catastrophic Dam Failures: The August 1975 Collapse of the Banqiao and Shimantan Dams" in *The River Dragon Has Come! The Three Gorges Dam and the Fate of China's Yangtze River and Its People*, ed. Dai Qing (Armonk: M.E. Sharpe, 1998).

31. Sarah Allen, *The Way of Water and Sprouts of Virtue* (Albany: State University of New York Press, 1997) 56.

32. I am indebted to Lewis Mayo for this observation.

33. See David Hawkes, *The Songs of the South: An Ancient Chinese Anthology of Poems by Qu Yuan and Other Poets* (Harmondsworth: Penguin Books, 1985).

34. See, for example, James Ferguson, "The Country and the City on the Copperbelt" in *Culture, Power, Place: Explorations in Critical Anthropology*, ed. Akhil Gupta and James Ferguson (Durham: Duke University Press, 1997) 137–54.

35. Han Shaogong, "Wenxue de gen" ("The Roots of Literature") *Zuojia* (*Writers*) 4, 2 (1985): 2–5.

23

Environmental Justice and Popular Protest in Thailand

John Walsh

INTRODUCTION

Those who live on the plateau away from the Mekong River need reservoirs to conserve water for their use during the dry season. Those who are close to the Mekong need embankments and flood gates to keep the water from rushing in and spoiling young padi during the early part of the season and from rushing out too much later. These improvements can be carried out largely by the farmers themselves if the local officials with the help of engineers will explain the methods and the benefits to the people.[1]

The Isaan region of Northeastern Thailand is the poorest part of the country. The salt fields underlying the plain of Korat render much of the land difficult for agriculture and this is compounded by vulnerability to both flooding and drought. The region houses today some 20 million or so ethnic Lao people with a set of cultures and traditions distinct from the central Thais into whose kingdom they have been progressively integrated since the first period of modernization at the end of the nineteenth century. While it would be wrong to claim that Isaan people want to be part of Laos or even to be fully independent, they do resent the suppression of local languages, customs, and economic systems. Many of the revolts that have taken place in Thailand over the last few hundred years have resulted from resentment at the imposition of taxes or other unwanted forms of integration. Charismatic figures, often credited with having supernatural mystical powers, rose to lead rebellions often aimed at replacing corrupt local officials. Over time, officials became replaced by politicians but the same issues remained.[2]

After the 1932 revolution, absolute monarchy gave way to parliamentary democracy and constitutional monarchy. Yet democratization remained a shallow process and provincial politicians in many cases were offered the votes of electors on the understanding that constituents would be rewarded in one way or another. This process helped give rise to the "Greening Isaan" policy which aimed to increase infrastructure links in the region, both drawing it closer to the rest of the Kingdom and also providing development opportunities for the people of the region. Following the Second World War and later the Vietnam War, substantial grants and loans were available from bodies such as the World Bank to states following just such priorities, especially when this could be presented as helping to hold back the advance of communism. Armed groups and bandits still remain in border forest areas today and this was a significant security issue during periods of turbulence in Cambodia.

From this situation was the concept of the Pak Moon (sometimes spelled "Mun" or "Mool") Dam created. Not only would the dam provide enhanced water security to the people of Isaan, it would also constitute a potential export in the form of hydroelectric energy which would fuel additional development and economic opportunities for those involved in the project. As a matter of course, the opinions of villagers—"little people" as they are routinely thought of as being—were not considered and neither was the possible impact upon them of the development. Remarkably, however, a local, national, and international campaign gathered to protest against the impact of the dam and to highlight the negative consequences for villagers who have had to abandon traditional ways of life. Years after the dam was completed, appeals and protests continue, with hopes reignited that the populist Prime Minister (PM) Thaksin Shinawatra, with his massive personal support across the Kingdom, would take further action in favor of the little people. Those hopes have since foundered as the PM has taken recourse in authoritarian campaigns against illegal drugs and dark influences (corruption), in addition to a hard line against protesters in the south of Thailand seeking autonomy.

CREATION OF THE DAM

General Chatichai Choonhavan (1988–1991) was a principal supporter of the "greening Isaan" policy, in part because that was the location of his constituency. This policy provided fresh stimulus to the creation of a dam at Pak Moon that had been in the planning stages since 1967. Pak Moon is literally the "Mouth of the Moon" river and it is located at the confluence of the

Moon with the Mekong in the province of Ubon Ratchathani. The state-controlled Electricity Generating Authority of Thailand (EGAT) had submitted various plans to build dams in the region, most notably at Nam Choan on the upper Khwai River, which project was forcibly abandoned when local and international protestors joined together to try to prevent the destruction of the Thung Yai nature reserve and the forcible relocation of ethnic Karen people.[3] Nam Choan may have been abandoned in 1988 but its spirit seems to be living on in fresh agreements between PM Thaksin and the vicious autocratic regime of Myanmar (Burma) to create dams on the Salween River, which many believe will lead to other forcible relocations.

The Pak Moon site was chosen as a compromise between maximum power generation and disruption to tourism and local industry. Technical reports were supported by the World Bank and the decision was taken to go ahead with development in 1989. In 1991, the World Bank made a US$54 million loan to support the project. Despite protests, construction commenced and full operations began in 1995. During the period of construction and indeed after, there were many clashes between local people and police. Villagers complained that their traditional lifestyles were ruined since they could no longer fish (which provided both a valuable source of protein and a commodity that could be traded for rice) and, supported by non-governmental organizations (NGOs), some of which were international in nature, sought compensation from EGAT as the representative of the state. Rival research studies were commissioned and, given different terms of reference, came up with different sets of findings. EGAT-supported survey and census data, for example, found that overall levels of income in the affected areas had risen and that claims for compensation, which had been met by generous payments by EGAT of some US$260 million, were mostly opportunistic in nature. By contrast, a Thailand Development Research Institute study to the World Commission on Dams (which had by now been established by the World Bank) in 2000 used cost-benefit analysis to indicate high levels of overspending and discrepancies between claimed and actual production of electricity. All research studies have been used as banners and rejected by opponents.[4] Above all, villagers feel that their issues and concerns have been ignored.

> "We, Isaan, are peace loving people who would rather stay at home than move around," said Mrs Noo, who came to offer some fermented fish and sticky rice to the rally. "These members of the Assembly of the Poor are marching because they are very unhappy about their way for life."[5]

The Pak Moon Dam has directly affected more than 20,000 people, with many others obliged to change their way of life. Fishing has been almost completely ruined and the fisheries ladder promoted by a technical expert found to be inadequate. Inappropriate choice of crops, high price of water charges and inadequate irrigation have combined to render conditions for local farmers to be almost untenable.[6] The low and inconsistent level of electricity generation suggests that the need for the dam has not been demonstrated, although in fairness this has been significantly affected by the 1997 Asian financial crisis. Household incomes in many cases declined significantly. As a result of these problems, some 3,000 villagers peacefully occupied the site of the dam and in an escalation of the protest nearly 500 more conducted a hunger protest outside the parliament grounds in Bangkok. Owing to the nature of the Thai media, many events outside Bangkok do not receive widespread coverage and so moving protests into the capital is a common tactic. This has occurred with respect to a number of other protests focusing on degradation of the environment.

In some cases, violence has been used against protestors and there are allegations of official support for such uses of violence. In December of 2002, for example, some 250 huts used by protestors were burnt to the ground, apparently by around forty hooded men who were seen in the vicinity. A Kamnan (village headman) and about twenty villagers from Sirinthorn district are said to have confessed to the attacks which were conducted because the protestors were asking for too much. EGAT officials denied involvement, although PM Thaksin did describe the incident as "abnormal" since it appears that knowledge of the arson attacks was widespread before they even began. Indeed, protestors moved the site of their demonstration to Thaksin's own home with banners declaring "You burnt our houses, now we're going to destroy your dam."[7]

PROTEST AND OTHER
ENVIRONMENTAL ISSUES

Emergent environmental issues in Thailand have become numerous over the years. These include extensive and often illegal logging of hardwood trees, monocropping and the planting of non-indigenous trees such as eucalyptus, the widespread inland and mangrove swamp prawn farming, noise, air and water pollution in urban areas such as Bangkok and, increasingly in Chiang Mai too. Historically, the land and its resources in Thai law have belonged to the state. As part of the social contract with the people which each monarch is expected to obey to continue to receive the mandate of heaven, the state and its ceremonial representatives must help to provide water for the people and participate in rituals and ceremonies to ensure the regular and adequate provision of rainfall and other necessary agricultural inputs. After the 1932 Revolution, which ended the absolute monarchy, this form of contract has been deemed inadequate for the modern age and the rights of Thais have come to be protected by the Constitution. The most recent version of the Constitution was promulgated in 1997 and it provides in articles 45, 56, 58 and 59 for the rights of people to be involved in decision-making about the allocation of environmental resources and about policies likely to have a significant impact upon the environment.[8] However, the issue taken up by those concerned with environmental degradation has not centred on the law itself so much as the policing of the law and the monitoring of its administration. Away from the center of power, local politicians and officials have had in many cases a free rein in exploiting resources to their own benefit free from restraint. In addition, the scrutiny of the media has fallen away rapidly away from the capital and this has further enabled local power-wielders to follow policies of personal enrichment at their own discretion.

Most protests concerning environmental issues have been small scale in nature and located in specific provinces. The level of political discourse continues at a low level and public awareness of environmental protest, which necessarily is rooted in particular areas, remains low. Public participation is not an embedded concept in much of Southeast Asia. This is unfortunate since, in environmental issues in particular, the application of local knowledge is of considerable importance. The current procedure when people wish to make themselves heard is for the organisation of demonstrations or establishing a "village" outside the appropriate ministry or other organization where people will camp until such time as their grievance is met. This is unproductive and promotes confrontation. Frequently, police or unofficial groups are brought in to break up these camps. Partly as a result, episodes of private resistance to large-scale environmental change continue to be linked with a fatalistic attitude toward the power of external forces and the inability to resist them. At the same time, the desire of the civil service—which is otherwise projected to be an important protector of the people and of the values of the Kingdom—has started to be undermined in just those sectors crucial to resistance to environmental degradation as a result of plans to privatise EGAT and, although this has not yet entered the public domain, the water authority. EGAT workers opposing privatization are being depicted as self-interested individuals who place personal ease above the public interest and who may be both lazy and greedy. The willingness of the media to embrace a pro-privatization policy is quite at odds with a previous anti-IMF stance which obtained in the wake of the 1997 financial crisis when the conditionality that the IMF placed upon its loans included widespread privatization and was widely concluded to be inappropriate and, indeed, unfair.

When protests have achieved a positive outcome, this has generally been the result of a specific policy change by an influential power-wielder with an interest in pleasing or rewarding an important constituency, either temporarily or in the long term. However, policy decisions have not always been consistently supported and implemented in the past and this also applies to decisions that have, perhaps incidentally, contributed to environmental justice. It is no coincidence that policy initiatives occur more commonly through periods of comparatively weak government.[9]

Activists who do make visible protests also place themselves in danger. More than a dozen such individuals have died in unexplained circumstances in recent years and the police have been unable to provide suspects in many of these cases. On August 11th, 2004, Supol Sirichan, village chief of Ban Den Udom was gunned down after leading police to a stockpile of illegally felled logs.[10] He was the sixteenth victim since the election of PM Thaksin and there is little indication that this murderous practice is likely to cease. Harassment at lesser levels is also a common phenomenon. In such circumstances, it is even more urgent that individuals seek protection from organizations and communities able to provide a united front to help resist intimidation.

NGOS AND THE ASSEMBLY OF THE POOR

The Assembly of the Poor is the people, people living in poverty, people facing troubles from government policies, law, the bureaucratic chain of command, and national development that doesn't respect the people, community, culture, or sustainability of resources.[11]

Villagers affected by environmental change and wishing to protest against it have had few skills and little experience in how to structure and organize their demonstrations. To assist them, various NGOs have developed both locally or else been imported from overseas countries to play an active role. The attitude of successive Thai governments toward them has been one of ambivalence, touched by suspicion. Although missionaries have been accepted into the Kingdom and left more or less unmolested for hundreds of years, this has generally been on the basis that they do not overstep certain bounds. These bounds may have changed in nature over the years but they have primarily been based on any real or perceived threat to the state. Any organization that has been constituted on ethnic lines, for example or, else, espoused social or political goals that could be construed as communist in intent has, therefore, been subject to official intervention, often with force involved. As a long-term ally of the United States and a country used to dealing diplomatically with European powers with a view to enhancing trade while avoiding any threat to Thai sovereignty, the Thai state has always reacted forcefully to the possibility that agents might be fomenting communist insurrection or else linking with foreign communists. Since communists acted according to the Maoist strategy that stresses the mobilization of rural peasantry and because many provinces remained comparatively remote from Bangkok's reach, any NGO that has worked in the countryside or with agricultural projects has necessarily come under suspicion. This suspicion has continued.

In the modern age of protest, international networks are swiftly mobilized through internet and mobile technologies. This technology places NGOs further beyond the reach of government action. There have been suggestions that the state has been involved over the years in smear campaigns against NGOs generally, alleging that they are funded by foreign powers bent on destabilizing Thailand, that they are "unusually rich" or that they are only interested in self-aggrandizement to the detriment of the Thai people. Modern technology has helped NGOs to spread information to local people in a context in which involvement of the public in decision making has been traditionally very limited.

One notable indigenous NGO that has aimed to lead public participation in protests against environmental degradation has been the Assembly of the Poor. Created in December 1995 and spearheaded by villagers affected by the Pak Moon Dam, the Assembly has taken the form of a shifting network of members dedicated to raising public consciousness with respect to threats to the environment and organizing demonstrations and protests against those projects. The large number of NGOs that have shown support for the Assembly is claimed to be proof that it represents the whole of Thai society. Such claims are rejected by the state when confrontation is involved.

Activities undertaken by the Assembly have included protests against a possible lignite-fueled power plant in Chiang Mai and against the use of reclaimed land for new government offices. The network also broadened its interests to include calls for a freedom of information act and a progressive property tax for landowners. This broadening of interests, which has been justified by the need to consider environmental concerns as part of a broader social program of changes, has enabled state sources to claim that partisan political interests—possibly with an international component—have subverted the Assembly so that it acts, therefore, against the interests of the people of the Kingdom as a whole. There has been some truth in this in that the Assembly consists of a network of groups with a variety of areas of grievance. By 1997, the groups that had joined included the Network of People Affected by Dams, Isaan Farmers' Assembly for Protection of Land Rights, Slum Organisation for Democracy and others concerned with alternative agriculture, workplace and environmental safety and the issues facing local fisher people.[12] The aims of the Assembly became necessarily broader and may never be satisfied, therefore.

The election of Thai Rak Thai in January 2001 was viewed with considerable enthusiasm by NGOs and protesters alike, since it was believed that his populism and anti-establishment sentiments would favor their cause over that of the state monopoly EGAT. PM Thaksin had consulted with Assembly of the Poor members throughout the election campaign and joined them at the village on the day after his triumph. He promised that suitable committees would be established and the village was dissolved. However, the PM's initiative to resolve outstanding issues depended on his offer of money to affected villagers and he appeared to show genuine surprise that this was considered to be insufficient for the affected people to rebuild their lives. Subsequently, the complainants were dismissed and their camp dismantled.[13] Villagers complained that this was performed with undue force and that their possessions were taken from them while they were being forcibly evicted. The National Human Rights Commission became involved and the governor of Bangkok, Samak Sundaravej, was invited to explain why protestors were provided with no access to power or water supplies and the actions of the 1,000 *thetsakit* (city inspectors) who committed the acts.[14]

Relations between the government and NGOs have since suffered greatly. Indeed, most forms of criticism of the prime minister are likely to be dismissed out of hand. Thaksin said in 2002: "NGOs that use violence will be blacklisted and severely dealt with by law. . . . Some of these people live an easy life, and have no occupation but at times create confusion and trouble."[15]

CONCLUSION

The currently contested issue with Pak Moon Dam is in the opening of the sluice gates for at least part of the year. Opening the gates will at least allow some fish to pass through while migrating and since the dam is not currently required to operate at full capacity there should be no difficulty with a shortfall in power generation. When the gates have been opened, the results have once again been contested, with some noting resurgence in local household incomes and others pointing to continued loss of biodiversity and the non-sustainable nature of such activities. Establishing a consensus and identifying the truth seems to be a low priority. Indeed, any desire for justice appears to be a low priority since a campaign to tackle illegal drugs in the Kingdom in 2003 that led to more than 2,000 deaths was met with apparent indifference by the Thai public, apparently happy to accept the police view that deaths were mostly the result of criminal gang members killing each other to prevent them from informing. Indeed, PM Thaksin's popularity has increased rather than decreased and there is speculation that his party will achieve 400 seats or more in the next parliament, which would be another unprecedented electoral feat. His position seems to be so unassailable that all opposition parties are in complete disarray and many individual members of Parliament are negotiating to join Thai Rak Thai.

This situation has enabled the prime minister to push ahead with his own policies and, in the international field, he has engaged on a round of bilateral free trade agreements (FTAs). It is believed that the forthcoming FTA with the United States will require an agreement to permit access to the Thai market to genetically modified crops and foods originating from America and that this is connected with current policies permitting GM trials in the Kingdom. Since the PM's fallout with NGOs, when his offer of money to Pak Moon villagers was publicly rejected, many of the activists with whom he had been involved and who had made important inputs into policy design, have been replaced with businesspeople. The response to environmental disasters that have recently befallen people in Thailand has also been the same—a handout of money, occasionally from the PM's own pocket. It seems unlikely that any other response will be forthcoming in the immediate future.

NOTES

1. Zimmerman, 1999 [1931], 155–56.
2. Seri and Hewison, 2001, 70–79.
3. Walsh, 2003.
4. Ibid.
5. Supara, 2003.
6. Taweekun, 2002.
7. The Nation, 2002.
8. Suntariya, 2000.
9. Kanokrat, 2003.
10. Wasant, 2004.
11. Assembly of the Poor, 1997.
12. Missingham, 2003, 45.
13. Pasuk and Baker, 2004, 144–46.
14. Kultida, 2003.
15. Pasuk and Baker. Op.cit. 146.

REFERENCES

"Attack Was Suspicious." 2002. *The Nation* (December 17th). Hosted at: http://www.thai.to/aop/news20021217PMDe.htm

Assembly of the Poor. 1997. Samatcha khon chon ekkasan phoei phrae chabap thi 1 [Assembly of the Poor Publicity Leaflet No.1]. Bangkok: Assembly of the Poor. Translated by Bruce D. Missingham.

Kanokrat Lertchoosakul. 2003. "Conceptualising the Roles and Limitations of NGOs in the Anti-Pak Moon Dam Movement," in Ji Giles Ungpakorn, ed., *Radi-*

calising Thailand: New Political Perspectives. Bangkok: Institute of Asian Studies, Chulalongkorn University, 226–52.

Kultida Samabuddhi. 2003. NHRC Wants Samak to Explain Demolition. *The Bangkok Post* (February 4th). http://www.bangkokpost.com/News/04Feb2003_news 10.html

Missingham, Bruce D. 2003. *The Assembly of the Poor in Thailand: From Local Struggles to National Protest Movement*. Chiang Mai: Silkworm Books.

Pasuk Phongpaichit and Chris Baker. 2004. *Thaksin: The Business of Politics in Thailand*. Chiang Mai: Silkworm Books.

Seri Phongphit and Kevin Hewison. 2001. *Village Life: Culture and Transition in Thailand's Northeast*. Bangkok: White Lotus Co. Ltd.

Suntariya Muanpawong. 2000. Public Participation in Thai Environmental Law. *Tai Culture* V.2 (December) 35–45.

Supara Janchitpah. 2003. Weapons of the Poor. *Assembly of the Poor Website*. http://www.thai.to/aop/new20011202pm.htm

Taweekun Sawantranon (main researcher) and Ubon Ratchathani University. 2002. *Project to Study Approaches to Restoration of the Ecology, Livelihood, and Communities Receiving Impacts from Construction of Pak Mun Dam* (executive summary). http://www.irn.org/programs/pakmun/021022.ubonexecsum.pdf.

Walsh, John. 2002. Pak Moon Dam: Displaced Villagers and World Bank Sponsored Researchers Force the Government to Change Its Policy—But for How Long? *Case Study Submitted to the Global Development Network's Bridging Research and Policy Global Research Project*. http://www.gdnet.org/rapnet/research/stud ies/case_studies/Case_Study...31_Full.html.

Wasant Techawongtham. 2004. Protecting Resources Is a Deadly Business. *The Bangkok Post* (August 20th). http://www.bangkokpost.com/News/20Aug2004_news 39.php

Zimmerman, Carle C. 1999 [originally 1931]. *Siam: Rural Economic Survey 1930–1* Bangkok: White Lotus Books.

24

"Aiee, Our Fields Will Be Destroyed"[1]
Dubious Science and Peasant Environmental Practices in Madziwa, Zimbabwe[2]

Guy Thompson

Agriculture has been a key area of political and economic conflict in Zimbabwe since the country was colonized in 1890. The racial division of land in the colonial period and the difficult legacies of this partition after independence are the most publicized dimensions of this confrontation, particularly due to the chaotic land reform efforts of Robert Mugabe's government since 2000. Less well known, however, are the effects of the state's efforts to control land use, individual holdings, and agricultural methods in the designated African farming areas. Legitimated by a veneer of environmental protection and science, these measures played a key role in the segregation plans of Southern Rhodesia's white minority regime. "Improved" agricultural practices also imposed onerous demands on peasants and therefore loom large in Africans' accounts of the inequities and injustices of the colonial period.

This article explores peasants' detailed memories of the imposition of colonial agricultural policies in the Madziwa Communal Area from 1940 to 1965. In interviews that I undertook in the community, elderly people recounted their understandings of, and reactions to, these disruptive state initiatives, which undermined local production methods and threatened important social bonds within their community. They explained how official models of farming imposed a demanding new labor regime to maintain soil fertility, while dismissing indigenous methods of production and environmental management. A few individuals openly questioned the effectiveness of the techniques promoted by officials, but most people were reluctant to

355

go this far, as the postindependence government has continued to draw on these models in their agrarian policies and extension services. Thus, I argue that memories of colonial practices retain their vitality because of rural people's continued efforts to challenge the policies of the contemporary government and assert control over the meaning of their collective past. While this article foregrounds the experiences of people in Madziwa, there are strong commonalities for peasants throughout Zimbabwe, particularly as widespread resistance to restrictions on peasant farming was a key element in the waves of unrest that threatened state control in 1961 and 1962.

"IMPROVED" AGRICULTURE

Today, Madziwa Communal Area is a peasant farming district of roughly 30,000 inhabitants on 130,000 acres of land in northeast Zimbabwe, 90 miles north of the capital city, Harare. Madziwa was demarcated as an African reserve in the early 1900s, as part of the Southern Rhodesian administration's segregation policy that divided the country into African and European areas, reserving the extensive commercial farming districts for whites. As a self-governing European settlement colony, the government prioritized white interests, particularly the concerns of commercial farmers, the symbolic core of the settler community. Contradictory colonial interests, however, meant that African peasant production for the market as well as subsistence was generally tolerated, although there were many discriminatory practices that penalized Africans, including the land policies, limited access to credit, and racially differentiated crop prices.[3] Despite their political value as a liberal, developmental measure, agricultural services for blacks were controversial, particularly during the Depression when many white settlers struggled to survive. White opposition diminished after the Second World War, however, when industrialization, urbanization, rapid immigration, and massive exports of tobacco produced by European farmers generated an economic boom. The accompanying dramatic increases in demand for food led to shortages, particularly of grain; as white farmers concentrated on tobacco production, the black peasant sector acquired a renewed importance for the national economy.[4]

Although limited in scale, state agricultural extension services for Africans were launched in 1926, providing key features of later government conservation and improvement policies. The government's initial efforts were based on models developed by Christian missionaries, who saw agrarian change as a means to convert Africans and undermine indigenous religious practices that promoted the social and productive health of the community through rainmaking, the protection of sacred spaces, and contact with ancestral spirits.[5] Missionaries emphasized European techniques such as permanent landholdings and crop separation, along with crop rotation and manuring to maintain soil fertility. These methods remained central to the approaches promoted by the state, although they were later proclaimed to have been developed scientifically.[6]

As the extension services slowly expanded, they developed new programs that were increasingly justified on environmental grounds. Moving beyond planting practices, the state imposed restrictions on land use in the reserves, introduced a range of soil conservation works, and set limits on cattle holdings. With limited staff and funding, however, the state's initiatives focused on a minority of the reserves, constraining the programs' impact through the 1930s and into the 1940s. The government's focus on watercourse protection and soil conservation was rooted in international debates that developed around the American dustbowl in the 1930s.[7] Official statements emphasized the ecological damage purportedly caused by African peasants:

> As is to be expected, the Native is rarely alive to the importance of conserving the soil; his concern is to get crops, with the consequence that the disease of erosion is spreading at an alarming pace where the primitive methods of agriculture have given place to the plough. . . . In some districts, the Natives' quest for more and more land has transformed once beautifully clad hills into gaunt spectres of ruin. One trustworthy witness instanced a hill, formerly covered with grass and trees, losing every atom of soil after having been attacked by Native cultivation.[8]

This type of environmental alarmism played a key role in justifying the expansion of state agricultural programs in the African areas, where they grew dramatically after 1945.

The postwar economic boom and accompanying food shortages generated a new interest in peasant agriculture, leading to a dramatic enlargement of government extension and conservation programs. This growth can be seen in the expansion of the extension staff complement from 92 in 1936 to 192 in 1944, 484 in 1949, and then 998 in 1955.[9] Moreover, the 1951 Native Land Husbandry Act [NLHA] consolidated earlier conservation and improvement measures into a single scheme that gave the state new coercive powers over peasants. Officials could determine who lived in each reserve, and were empowered to assign standardized arable holdings on the basis of individual tenure, controlled through a permit system. Individual cattle holdings were similarly managed through grazing permits, which set strict limits for individual and community herd size based on the state's calculation of the reserve's carrying capacity, which often meant a dramatic reduction in the number of animals when the act was implemented. Landholders were required to build and maintain prescribed conservation measures in their fields, such as massive contour ridges to direct water flow, and were encouraged to follow government sanctioned agricultural methods. They could also be called upon as labor for public projects and conservation measures within the reserve, at local officials' discretion. Further sections of the law empowered extension officers to "centralize" reserves, dividing the land into discrete permanent arable, grazing, and residential areas, as well as to enact regulations to limit the use of ecologically sensitive areas such as wetlands and riverbanks. Finally, the measure imposed harsh penalties on farmers who refused to follow its provisions, including fines, ploughing crops under, and confiscation of land rights for refusing to maintain the prescribed conservation measures.[10]

Initial implementation of the NLHA went slowly, and was restricted to a handful of reserves. However, in 1955 the government announced a dramatic acceleration of the provisions of the law, declaring that it would be enacted in virtually all of the African areas by 1961. This ambitious scheme was justified in a number of ways by its proponents; their ideas were echoed in state propaganda. The NLHA was presented as a key mechanism to promote the colony's economic development, as officials proclaimed it would dramatically increase peasant production and incomes. It was widely promoted as a means to modernize the peasantry, and was upheld as a model for Africa by international agrarian experts.[11] Environmental protection remained a key rationale, as the Director of Native Agriculture explained: "Basically this Act is a conservation measure, because it gives the individual a stake in the land and fixes the responsibility for conservation squarely on his shoulders."[12]

In private, however, the white minority government also saw rapid implementation of the NLHA as a means to further entrench racial segregation. They argued the scheme would increase the carrying capacity of the reserves through the controls it imposed on individual holdings and land use practices. This would allow the state to forcibly relocate Africans living on designated European land to the reserves, clearing the potential farms for new white owners. Since the end of the war, the government had been trying to move roughly 85,000 black families from white areas, but overcrowding in many reserves meant these plans had been seriously delayed. Moreover, officials felt they needed to relocate a further 50,000 families from densely populated reserves to prevent serious environmental degradation, so that they had to find space for roughly 750,000 people, a third of the colony's population.[13] This was the key factor in the cabinet discussions that approved the rapid implementation plan, although the conservation, developmental, and propaganda benefits were also weighed.[14]

Thus the NLHA, and the earlier agricultural extension efforts in the African reserves, helped to facilitate racial segregation and the implementation of the Rhodesian government's discriminatory land policies, using environmental protection and economic development to disguise these goals. Ironically, very few people in Madziwa drew this connection, or even voiced direct criticism of racist colonial policies; these grievances have retreated in many peasants' memories, becoming part of the assumed background to the mental landscape of the Rhodesian period. Peasant accounts focus, instead, on a different set of grievances, particularly labor demands, the shortcomings of the conservation and production practices promoted by officials, and the conflict between the goals of the state and Africans' social, productive, and environmental priorities.

PEASANT MEMORIES FROM MADZIWA

In my interviews with elderly Madziwans, people did not distinguish between the period of NLHA implementation and the earlier interventions. In part, this is because the first extension efforts in the area began in 1940, with the NLHA following in 1956, but it also reflects the strong continuities in state programs. The commonalities in farmers' comments provide a potent critique of "improved" agriculture, underlining a fundamental clash in agrarian systems and priorities as the rigid prescriptions of officials ran up against the complex and fluid ways that people worked the land.

By the 1940s, farming methods in Madziwa varied widely, but most peasants were drawing on a mix of European and indigenous practices that promoted food security—and environmental protection, contrary to the alarmist statements of officials. Animal drawn ploughs, which offered a huge labor advantage in preparing fields, were rapidly replacing hoe cultivation. Peasants, however, were combining this borrowed implement with a variety of indigenous techniques. These included a local system of shifting cultivation that involved clearing a new field every two or three years, and then leaving it fallow to allow the thin soil to recover; fertility was also promoted by burning vegetation and crop residues. Tree stumps were left in place to help reduce erosion and encourage regrowth when a field was fallowed. Most farmers practiced intercropping, planting a variety of different foodstuffs and crop varieties together to manage the vagaries of Zimbabwe's rainy season, which could bring prolonged dry periods and bursts of intense rain. Intermingling low growing plants helped to keep moisture in the soil, and, combined with careful construction of crop ridges, also limited soil erosion. In addition to their conventional rain-fed fields, many households also grew rice in a wetland area, or raised a variety of vegetables and grains in a riverbank or dry streambed garden, drawing on the accessible groundwater to produce early crops.

A few Madziwa farmers in the 1940s were moving closer to European techniques, and did not intercrop extensively. This group used ploughs and cultivators to work large fields and take advantage of the buoyant agricultural market; weeding with a cultivator required row planting and open space between lines of crops. This meant they were increasingly growing crops in separate areas, but most continued to intermingle pumpkins and beans within rows of maize or other grains to get more produce from their lands, reduce hand weeding, and retain some of the benefits of intercropping.[15]

These peasant practices could not be reconciled with the government agricultural programs that began to be introduced in Madziwa in 1940, particularly the state's land-use regulations, means of maintaining soil fertility, and emphasis on creating permanent arable plots. African farmers were, and continue to be, extremely critical of the alternatives advanced by officials. Peasants readily expressed a number of complaints about colonial interventions in our conversations. Their grievances coalesced around several issues, particularly the loss of property and opportunities for accumulation, the threat to their long term security, labor demands, the productive and ecological shortcomings of official methods, and the intrusion of the state into their lives.

Madziwa, like most of the reserves, was densely populated when the state began implementing the NLHA. As the area was already at its maximum capacity under the government formulas, residents were assigned small arable holdings of 6 to 8 acres, with no possibility of expansion. Returning labor migrants and young people coming to adulthood were effectively declared to be landless, unless they inherited a holding. Farmers were also ordered to reduce the number of cattle they held. These dispossessions loom large in peasants' accounts, such as Levison Chanikira's, who also offered a broader political critique. "When the period of cutting the cattle ended, then came the cutting of the land. People began to see how bad the white man was because of the shortage of land and because they were left with few cattle."[16] The cattle restrictions were seen as particularly onerous, because acquiring animals was one of the few ways peasants could accumulate wealth, as VaShangwe observed: "Cattle were our wallets to maintain our lives. If you had cattle, it meant you had a granary full of crops. If you had cattle, then you had a strong back. That is why we argued with the government when it was cutting our stock."[17] He went on to explain that people were puzzled by the limits placed on stock holdings, as they held there was a lot of forest and grazing land to support the animals. Cattle had additional significance because of their central role in marriage exchanges, so that they were both a symbol and a real manifestation of economic security. Moreover, in an economy in which wages were low and pension benefits for black employees virtually unknown, access to land and the opportunity to raise cattle in the reserves were vital to long term security and family viability. Older peasants also relied on their adult children living nearby to help in their fields, as Amai Chaparira Paiena explained:

> I wanted to stay with my children, I told him [her youngest son] to go and build there [points to adjoining homestead]. So now, we are looked after. I wanted

my children [her son and his wife] to look after me at all times saying "How did you sleep mother?" Today the rain is about to come, a son knows that his mother needs her land ploughed.[18]

Thus, the restrictions imposed on land access and cattle holdings threatened the long term security of people of all ages.

Many Madziwans complained about the soil conservation works introduced by the government, particularly the work involved in building and maintaining them. Some people recalled the compulsory labor on public works that officials required:

Shingaidzo Madeve: Our husbands were taken and made to work for nothing!

Guy Thompson: Was that the time when people were moved into residential lines?

Shingaidzo Madeve: People were forced to work in their area. They worked for nothing! Like that dam down there [points], it was built through *chibaro* [forced labor].[19]

More commonly, grievances focused on the anti-erosion measures farmers had to construct in their fields as a condition of tenure. After experimenting with grass buffer strips between and around fields in the 1940s, the government shifted to contour ridges, which became a powerful symbol of colonial inequities in peasant recollections. On a typical field, agricultural officials not only required owners to build contours along the boundaries, but several additional ridges in the midst of the plot to manage and direct water flows during heavy rains. The contours prescribed during the 1950s were huge, much larger than the ones used in Zimbabwe today. Ridges were supposed to be four feet across, rising 26 inches above the ground level, accompanied by a drainage ditch along one side that was wide enough for a Land Rover to drive through.[20] Building them was a protracted process, which Amai Manyika vividly recalled: "Aaiiee, it took a long time! One week to dig one contour!"[21] Residents said they put in a week to two months of heavy labor preparing the ridges and ditches, which had to be completed before people began preparing and planting their permanent plots. Compliance was rigidly enforced, with agricultural demonstrators cajoling people and reminding them of the penalties for not constructing the ridges, features that loomed large in Cyrus Nyamapfukudza's memories: "Then they came and cut [allocated] these lands. The demonstrators said we had to build contour ridges. If you refused or did not make the ridges, the land was given to someone else."[22]

Building on complaints about the exertions involved in the mandatory conservation works, some people went on to question the utility and very validity of the measures imposed by the government. Handidya Mazaradope contrasted the labor demands imposed on farmers with the limited benefits that the new methods brought when he recalled:

> People felt that the agricultural demonstrators were being very unfair when they made them dig contours. It was just too much hard work for us! We started asking them why contours were needed, we did not use them in the past, but we still got good harvests.[23]

Shingaidzo Madeve made a similar argument. "Those agricultural demonstrators, people did not hate them. It was just that the work they gave us was too much, it was *chibaro*! It did not pay or help us in any way."[24] VaMusonza, like Joseph Musikiwa whose comments opened this essay, went further, challenging the assumptions behind "improved" agriculture.

> Yes, you were told that this is your field, the one where you had to dig contours. So now it was hard to move. It was laborious, although some of us were used to it as we used to work on the [white] farms. Those who thought that they prevented soil erosion were the ones who dug wholeheartedly. But I tell you, contours are what cause erosion, and they are the cause of silt building up in the river.[25]

Further, he held that repeatedly cultivating the same land encouraged soil to wash away, aggravating erosion and fertility problems.

Deeper questions about the ecological value of state sanctioned farming methods run through peasants' recollections, along with complaints about the onerous work regime they required. Maintaining the viability of small, permanent fields was a challenge, particularly as most of Madziwa had fragile sandy soil of limited fertility. Given the size of the holdings, farmers could not leave part of their field fallow and produce a reasonable crop, while shifting cultivation was closed off by centralization. The government held out three possible solutions to this challenge. The first was to dig in manure from the household cattle pen; officials said that a ton of manure worked into each acre every four years as part of the prescribed crop rotation cycle would maintain the soil's fertility. For a typical Madziwan, this meant moving 1.25 to 2 tons of manure every year to fertilize one quarter of their field. This was an unpleasant, backbreaking task, made more difficult as very few people had access to a cart to move the manure.[26] Moreover, most households did not have the 5 to 8 cattle necessary to produce the required amount of dung. It is very hard to reconstruct cattle holding patterns, but it appears that roughly one-third of the population did not own any cattle, and the majority of owners had only a few animals. Stock limits and reductions imposed by officials compounded this challenge. The second solution offered by officials was to make compost and collect rotting leaves to plough into the fields, but this option also required a lot of labor and some means of moving the organic matter.[27] The final option was chemical fertilizers, which some peasants began using in the 1950s. However, they were far too expensive for the majority of farmers. They also needed to be transported, and required training and experience to use effectively.

By permanently dividing and assigning land, the government forced people to follow its agricultural system, cutting off many of the indigenous practices that peasants had used and modified as they adopted new crops and tools. The allocations made in the 1950s remain a key factor in landholding in Madziwa today, and agricultural extension officers continue to promote many of the same farming methods as their colonial predecessors, including manuring and a modified version of contour ridges. So when people recall their grievances with the land restrictions and onerous agricultural practices imposed by the white minority regime, they are also indirectly complaining about the challenges they face today, so that memories not only represent the past, they also reflect the present.[28] This kind of veiled critique is common in Zimbabwe's increasingly repressive political order, where few people are willing to take the risk of direct complaint, particularly in a recorded conversation. It is certainly evident in peasants' grievances about environmental change, such as Amai Bowas Matumba's comments about the declining quality of the soil, which I suspect also serve as a metaphor for the health of the community.

> When I was young, the soils were very good and rich, so our crops grew well without anything being added to it. But today, if one grows crops without fertilizers the harvest will be a disaster, a complete disaster. This shows that the soils we have now are not fertile and strong.[29]

Veiled complaints about current conditions are certainly embedded in Madziwans' accounts of colonial agricultural policies, but I don't think that means we simply dismiss their historical meaning. Rather, people are using their detailed memories of the past to reflect on the present; this dynamic runs through peasants' explanations of the labor demands of "improved" agriculture and the ecological and productive shortcomings of the rigid land use and farming methods imposed by colonial officials. Intriguingly, agronomists have also questioned the value of these "scientific" techniques, looking to indigenous methods to develop farming systems that are better adapted to Zimbabwe's thin soils, tropical sun, and capricious rains. In the early 1960s, J.D. Jordan, a state agricultural official, argued that shifting cultivation was the best farming system for most of the African areas in the colony, given their ecology and vulnerable soils. He also held that a modified system of shifting cultivation that allowed long fallow periods would not only protect the environment and provide better yields, but would also allow the reserves to support a higher population density than was possible with permanent allocations.[30] Recent work in Zimbabwe has also questioned the restrictions on wetland farming that were introduced in the colonial period and remain state policy, albeit a widely evaded one. With careful cultivation and ridging, researchers argue it is possible to grow crops in wetlands without causing soil erosion or damage to waterways.[31] Indigenous techniques such as intercropping, ridging, and burning are also being reconsidered by the country's permaculture movement, and by some extension workers. More basically, peasants in Madziwa and other communal areas continue to draw on these methods in their fields, questioning official knowledge through their actions.[32]

On a very different level, one of the key objections to colonial agricultural interventions recalled by many Madziwans was their sheer intrusiveness. Peasants were frustrated by the social tensions created by centralization, as they were forced to move from scattered homesteads to new closely settled residential areas. Mazivaramwe Kanyerere remembered the discomforts of adjusting to the new living patterns:

> It was not that bad, but people said "now that we have been brought together, we study each other." . . . Most people prefer not to be known, we like to do our work privately. . . . It was very difficult to come back after hunting, bringing meat for your family. One of the neighbors might come and say "May I have some meat?" If you refused to give it to them, then you could be bewitched.[33]

Many people also complained about intensified official supervision and direction, echoing VaKapfunde, who explained "Some of us, we did not want to be ordered to do this, do that. We preferred to work on our own without the demonstrators coming to give advice."[34] Initially people tried to evade and question orders, but in the late 1950s, implementation of the NLHA in Madziwa intensified state pressures on peasants, triggering growing anger with officials. Mai Matumba recalled this shift, arguing that "They [officials] distressed us by changing where we could live. People ended up saying "We don't want these demonstrators! We want to stay living the way we are!'"[35] As anger grew, residents turned to open protest and angry confrontations with agricultural officers. VaHore presented government restrictions as an attack on African culture, drawing connections between this assault and the growth of the nationalist movement:

> The whites wanted us to follow their culture and disregard our own culture. The Europeans wanted us to stop burning grass, and hunting was forbidden. The digging of contour ridges was also an idea that was forced on us. The things that were done by the government at that time troubled us. . . . The action of the demonstrators made people support the liberation struggle.[36]

Public anger and protest in Madziwa grew as NLHA implementation accelerated, leading the Native Commissioner [NC] for the area to report that 1960 and 1961 had been marked by "vicious political agitation that seeks to breed any sort of opposition to Government as a means to achieve its end."[37]

This type of discontent spread throughout the colony as meetings with agricultural officers and other officials failed to address Africans' grievances. The state's efforts to enact and enforce the NLHA became a flashpoint for rural protests, which were also inspired by the growing, but predominantly urban, nationalist movement. Land allocation in Mhondoro reserve, just south of Harare, had to be suspended three times in 1959 because people refused to move to new fields and residential sites. Tensions came to a head in October of that year when there was a near riot after an angry confrontation between the Native Commissioner and a group of women who were pulling up the pegs used to mark out the new individual arable plots.[38] Two hundred people at a March 1961 meeting to distribute land rights in Buhera reserve prevented the first grantee from accepting his allocation. The enraged NC then hit several people, fired his gun into the air and threatened to shoot people until the white Land Development Officer took the gun away from him. The crowd ran off in the midst of this melee, but some of them blocked the wheels of the Commissioner's Land Rover with piles of stones.[39]

By 1961, virtually every district in the colony reported open opposition, defiance, and acts of sabotage directed against state property in the reserves, frequently triggered by agricultural programs and the NLHA.[40] The government was clearly concerned that it was losing control of the countryside by March; they deployed the police and army in the reserves, slowed NLHA implementation, and ordered a series of sweeping policy reviews to find ways to contain opposition. In February 1962, the cabinet suspended NLHA implementation and dramatically slashed funding for African agricultural services, although these decisions were never publicly announced to avoid any appearance of weakness. The government returned the power to distribute land in the reserves to the chiefs, and gave them the right to override the restrictions on land use that had been created by centralization.[41] The wave of protests, defiance, and challenges to government authority slowed, partly because the state was no longer antagonizing people by trying to enforce the NLHA and improved farming methods. Rural discontent continued, however, openly resurfacing in support for the guerilla movements during the liberation war of the 1970s.

Although the government abandoned NLHA implementation, this decision did not undo the individual allocations that had been made in Madziwa and other reserves. Intense land pressures, the result of a rapidly growing population and the unwillingness of the white minority regime to increase the size of the area designated for Africans, meant that the chiefs could do little to change conditions in the reserves, beyond offering holdings to returning labor migrants and young people coming of age in the 1960s. In many areas, the allocations made by the state remain, having been passed on, and in many cases, subdivided. Peasants today continue to face the environmental and productive challenges that they were presented with by the NLHA and earlier improvement schemes, given the limited amount of formerly white land opened up to peasants by the resettlement programs of the early 1980s, and the recent, chaotic, fast track land reform. Although there are some signs of change, extension workers offer many of the same solutions to these difficulties as their colonial predecessors. Peasants' memories of Rhodesian initiatives therefore retain their vitality and meaning, providing a mechanism to understand and critique the challenges that rural Zimbabweans continue to face.

NOTES

1. Joseph Musikiwa, interview by author, tape recording, Madziwa, Zimbabwe, October 9, 1997.

2. I would like to gratefully acknowledge financial support for this project from the Social Sciences and Humanities Research Council of Canada, the University of Alberta, as well as the Graduate School, History Department and the MacArthur Interdisciplinary Program on Global Change, Sustainability and Justice of the University of Minnesota. I would also like to thank the members of the Department of Economic History at the University of Zimbabwe for their input and support. Finally I would like to acknowledge the vital assistance of my research assistants in Madziwa, Rangarirai Gurure, Obert Kufinya, and Solomon Mahdi, who not only helped with introductions and translation when my Shona failed me, but provided important insights into my work.

3. This is a very compressed account of land and agrarian polices in colonial Zimbabwe. The best general accounts, particularly for the period before the Second World War remain: G. Arrighi, *The Political Economy of Rhodesia* (The Hague: Mouton and Co., 1967), Robin Palmer, *Land and Racial Domination in Rhodesia* (Berkeley and Los Angeles: University of California Press, 1977), Ian Phimister, *An Economic and Social History of Zimbabwe, 1890–1948* (London and New York: Longman, 1988), Terence Ranger, *Peasant Consciousness and Guerilla War in Zimbabwe: A Comparative Study* (Berkeley: University of California Press, 1985).

4. For a full discussion of post-war economic and political dynamics, see my doctoral dissertation: Guy Thompson, "Cultivating Conflict: Modernism and 'Improved' Agriculture in colonial Zimbabwe, 1920–1965" (PhD Dissertation, University of Minnesota, 2000).

5. The first Agriculturalist for Natives, E. D. Alvord, was a Methodist missionary from the United States, who ran the extension services until 1949. A prime example of his concerns is E. D. Alvord, "The Great Hunger." *NADA*, 6 (1928), 36–37. For early missionary activity in South Africa that influenced developments in Zimbabwe, see Jean Comaroff and John Comaroff, *Of Revelation and Revolution* (Chicago: University of Chicago Press, volume 1, 1991, volume 2, 1997).

6. Southern Rhodesia, *What the Native Land Husbandry Act Means to the Rural African and to Southern Rhodesia* (Salisbury: Government Printer, 1955) ii.

7. For a detailed discussion of the development of state agricultural extension polices and conservation discourse in southern Africa, see William Beinart, "Soil Erosion, Conservationism and Ideas about Development: a Southern African Exploration, 1900–1960." *Journal of Southern African Studies*, 11 (1984), 52–83, Michael Drinkwater, *The State and Agrarian Change in Zimbabwe's Communal Areas* (New York: St Martin's Press, 1991), Ian Phimister, "Discourse and the Discipline of Historical Context: Conservationism and Ideas about Development in Southern Rhodesia 1930–1950." *Journal of Southern African Studies* 12 (1986): 263–75.

8. Southern Rhodesia, *Report of the Native Production and Trade Commission, 1944*, (Salisbury: np, 1944) 12, 19.

9. Southern Rhodesia, *Report of the Chief Native Commissioner, 1939* (Salisbury, Government Printer, 1940), 27, Southern Rhodesia, *Report of the Chief Native Commissioner, 1949* (Salisbury, Government Printer, 1950), 66, *What the NLHA Means*, 28.

10. "The Native Land Husbandry Act" in Southern Rhodesia, *The Statute Law of Southern Rhodesia, 1951*, (Salisbury, Government Printer, 1952), 893–916, A. Pendered and W. von Memerty, "The Native Land Husbandry Act of Southern Rhodesia," *Journal of African Administration*, v. 7, no. 3 (1955), 99–109, J.E.S. Bradford, "Survey and Registration of African Land Units in Southern Rhodesia" *Journal of African Administration*, v. 7, no. 4 (1955): 165–70, Mary Elizabeth Bulman, "The Native Land Husbandry Act of Southern Rhodesia: A Failure in Land Reform," (MSc Thesis, University of London, 1970), 5–10.

11. See in particular, the glossy *What the Native Land Husbandry Act Means*, as well as Pendered and von Memerty, and Bradford. These justifications also run through state propaganda directed at Africans and two films about the NLHA produced by the Central African Film Unit, *The New Acres* and *Changing the Land*. For international approval, L. see Braney, "Towards the Systematic Individualization of African Land Tenure: The Background to the Report of the Working Party on African Land Tenure in Kenya" *Journal of African Administration*, 11 (1959): 208–214, G. Kingsley Garbett, "The Land Husbandry Act of Southern Rhodesia" in Daniel Biebuyck (ed) *African Agrarian Systems* (London: Oxford University Press for the International African Institute, 1963), Montague Yudelman, *Africans on the Land: Economic Problems of African Agricultural Development in Southern, Central, and East Africa, with Special Reference to Southern Rhodesia* (Cambridge, Mass.: Harvard University Press, 1964).

12. D. A. Robinson, "Soil Conservation and the Implications of the Land Husbandry Act" *NADA*, 37 (1960): 27–35.

13. Phimister, *Economic and Social History*, 281, National Archives of Zimbabwe [NAZ] S2807/7, Director of Native Agriculture, "Carrying Capacity of the Reserves and Special Native Areas," October 20, 1950, 3.

14. NAZ S 3240/5, Cabinet Conclusions January to June 1955, SRC (55) 21st Meeting, May 6, 1955, 1–5.

15. For a full discussion of indigenous farming methods in Madziwa, and how they were being modified, see my doctoral dissertation. For farming practices in

other parts of Zimbabwe see Drinkwater, K. W. Nyamapfene, "Adaption to Marginal Land Use amongst the Peasant Farmers of Zimbabwe" *Journal of Southern African Studies*, 15 (1989): 384–89, Ian Scoones, "Landscapes, Fields and Soils: Understanding the History of Soil Fertility Management in Southern Zimbabwe." *Journal of Southern African Studies*, 23 (1997): 615–34, K. B. Wilson, "Trees in Fields in Southern Zimbabwe" *Journal of Southern African Studies*, 15 (1989): 369–83.

16. Levison Chanikira, interview by author, tape recording, Madziwa, Zimbabwe, May 30, 1998.

17. VaShongwe, interview by author, tape recording, Madziwa, Zimbabwe, October 30, 1997. The idea of having a strong back is a very potent metaphor, one that implies physical, social, and sexual health in Shona.

18. Amai Chaparira Paiena, interview by author, tape recording, Madziwa, Zimbabwe May 7, 1998.

19. Shingaidzo Madeve, interview by author, tape recording, Madziwa, Zimbabwe, May 24,1998.

20. VaMusonza, interview by author, tape recording, Mount Darwin Resettlement Area, Zimbabwe June 14, 1998.

21. Amai Manyika, interview by author, tape recording, Madziwa, Zimbabwe, May 31, 1998.

22. Amai Chaparira Paiena, Mandizva Mandizva, interview by author, tape recording, Madziwa, Zimbabwe, May 9, 1998, Levison Chanikira, interview by author, tape recording, Madziwa, Zimbabwe, May 30, 1998, Cyrus Nyamapfukudza, interview by author, tape recording, Madziwa, Zimbabwe, May 28, 1998.

23. Handidya Mazaradope interview by author, tape recording, Madziwa, Zimbabwe, 6 May 1998.

24. Shingaidzo Madeve, interview by author, tape recording, Madziwa, Zimbabwe 24 May 1998.

25. VaMusonza.

26. NAZ S2827/2/2/3, volume 1, Report of the Native Commissioner, Mount Darwin, for the Year Ended 31/12/55, 6, NAZ S2797/4539, Meeting of the Madziwa Reserve Native Council, 28/9/48, 2.

27. VaMusonza, Dahwa Gono, interview by author, tape recording, Madziwa, Zimbabwe, May 22, 1998.

28. For a full discussion of the interaction of memory and present day concerns in oral history, see, Luisa Passerini, "Introduction" in Luisa Passerini (ed.) *Memory and Totalitarianism (International Yearbook of Oral History and Life Stories volume 1)* (Oxford: Oxford University Press, 1992), Popular Memory Group, "Popular memory: Theory, politics, method," in Richard Johnson, Gregor McLennan, Bill Schwarz, and David Sutton (ed.), *Making Histories: Studies in History-Writing and Politics*, (London: Hutchinson, 1982), Alessandro Portelli, *The Battle of Valle Giulia. Oral History and the Art of Dialogue*, (Madison: University of Wisconsin Press, 1997), Alistair Thomson, *ANZAC Memories: Living with the Legend*, (Melbourne: Oxford University Press, 1994).

29. Amai Bowas Matumba, interview by author, tape recording, Madziwa, Zimbabwe, November 8, 1997.

30. J. D. Jordan, "Zimutu Reserve: A Land Use Appreciation." *Rhodes-Livingstone Institute Journal*, no. 35 (1965): 59–77.

31. R. Owen, K. Verbeek, J. Jackson, T. Steenhuis (ed), *Dambo Farming in Zimbabwe: Water Management, Cropping and Soil Potentials for Smallholder Farming in the Wetlands* (Harare: University of Zimbabwe Publications, 1995).

32. See Ian Scoones, William Wolmer (eds.), *Pathways of Change in Africa: Crops, Livestock and Livelihood in Mali, Ethiopia, and Zimbabwe* (Westport: Heinemann, 2002).

33. Mazivaramwe Kanyerere, interview by author, tape recording, Madziwa, Zimbabwe, June 2,1998.

34. VaKapfunde and VaNyamapfene, interview by author, tape recording, Madziwa, Zimbabwe, October 23, 1997.

35. Mai Matumba, interview by author, tape recording, Madziwa, Zimbabwe, October 17, 1997.

36. VaHore, interview by author, tape recording, Madziwa, Zimbabwe, May 31, 1998.

37. NAZ S2827/2/2/8, volume 3, Report of the Native Commissioner, Shamva, for the Year Ending 31/12/61, 16–17.

38. NAZ S2825/4 "Near Riot in Mhondoro," *African Daily News*, 21/10/59, "Mhondoro Reserve," *African Daily News*, 27/10/59.

39. Ngwabi Bhebe, "The National Struggle, 1957–1962" in Canaan S. Banana (ed.) *Turmoil and Tenacity: Zimbabwe 1890–1980* (Harare: The College Press, 1989) 97.

40. See the district reports for 1961 in NAZ S2827/2/2/8, all 3 volumes.

41. NAZ S3240/21 SRC (61) 55th Meeting of the Cabinet, October 3, 1961, 6–11, NAZ S3240/21 SRC (62) 7th Meeting of the Cabinet, February 2, 1962, 6–8, NAZ S3240/22, SRC (62), 16th Meeting of the Cabinet, March 22, 1962, 3, NAZ Records Centre Box 84526 DSD 38/1, 'Special NAAB Meeting, 20–22 March 1961, 1–3, Southern Rhodesia, *Financial Statements, 1961–1962*, 7, Southern Rhodesia, *Financial Statements, 1962–1963*, 7, NAZ Records Centre Box 98229 1195/DSD.39/10/2 Working Party D Paper 8.

25

Shell International, the Ogoni People, and Environmental Injustice in the Niger Delta, Nigeria

The Challenge of Securing Environmental Justice in an Oil-based Economy

Phia Steyn

INTRODUCTION

We have woken up to find our lands devastated by agents of death called oil companies. Our atmosphere is has been totally polluted, our lands degraded, our waters contaminated, our trees poisoned, so much so that our flora and fauna have virtually disappeared. We are asking for the restoration of our environment, we are asking for the basic necessities of life—water, electricity, education; but above all we are asking for the right to self determination so that we can be responsible for our resources and our environment.

—Dr Gary Leton[1]

What Shell and Chevron have done to Ogoni people, land, streams, creeks and the atmosphere amount to genocide. The soul of the Ogoni people is dying and I am witness to the fact.

—Ken Saro-Wiwa[2]

Back in 1958 when oil of commercial quantity and quality was first discovered in Ogoniland by the Shell-BP Petroleum Development Company of Nigeria, Ltd (hereafter Shell-BP until 1979, and Shell Nigeria from 1979

371

onwards),[3] the Ogoni did not envision that they would one day wake up to find their lands, water, fauna, and flora degraded. Like too many other oil-producing communities in the developing world, the Ogoni was tricked into believing that the oil wealth would transform their own communities and enable this ethnic minority group in Nigeria to realize their developmental aspirations. Instead, the oil wealth was transported to areas with no oil and dominated by the three majority ethnic groups, especially the Hausa-Fulani in the north, and the Ogoni, along with the other oil-producing ethnic minority groups in the Niger Delta were neglected and marginalized in the name of national development.[4]

Decades of neglect spilled over in the early 1990s and resulted in the founding of the Movement for the Survival of the Ogoni People (MOSOP) in 1990 to address the environmental, political, economic, and social margin-alization of the Ogoni people at the hands of the Nigerian federal govern-ment and Shell Nigeria. Their well-known oil-related struggle in the first half of the 1990s, succeeded in focusing global attention on the human and envi-ronmental rights abuses associated with the Nigerian oil industry. But, their struggle also eventually robbed this ethnic minority group of their political and charismatic leader, Ken Saro-Wiwa, who, along with eight other Ogoni, were executed by the Gen. Sani Abacha regime on 11 November 1995 under strong international protest and on dubious legal grounds. While the shock of Saro-Wiwa's death impacted negatively on MOSOP's activities and the Ogoni struggle as a whole (it took a few years for MOSOP to organise prop-erly again), their struggle succeeded in triggering popular discontent amongst most of the other oil-producing ethnic minority groups residing in the Niger Delta. This discontent gradually plunged the whole region into political instability and chaos in recent years, thereby threatening the very basis of the Nigerian economy.[5]

In addition, Saro-Wiwa's death impacted greatly on Shell International and its subsidiary in Nigeria and forced this company to redefine its role and responsibilities to the people and the environment in the countries in which they operate.[6] However, the oil industry is in essence a dirty industry that pollutes and degrades the immediate and distant environments in which pro-duction, transportation, and refining takes place. Especially if no provision had been made for proper environmental safeguards and pollution control mechanisms, as is the case in the Niger Delta. Consequently, the Ogoni's claims of suffering environmental injustice at the hands of Shell Nigeria is as valid today as it was back in 1993 when Shell Nigeria withdrew from this region. This chapter aims at exploring the Ogoni's claims of environmental injustice perpetrated by Shell Nigeria and will therefore focus on the envi-ronmental impact of Shell-Nigeria's oil production in Ogoniland, and will conclude with a discussion of the challenges in promoting and securing environmental justice in this region.

BACKGROUND TO THE OGONI PEOPLE
AND THEIR STRUGGLE

Ogoni people are one of approximately 240 ethnic minority groups in Nigeria and number about 500,000 people out of a total Nigerian population of about 132 million people (2003 estimate). Historically the Ogoni inhabited the region in the Niger Delta situated between latitude 4°05' and 4°20' north, and longitudes 7°10' and 7°30' east, which is bounded in the west by the territory of the Ikwerre of Rumukrushe, in the north and east by the Imo river, and in the south by the traditional territory of the Andoni. Their traditional territory, called Ogoniland, spans about 1,030 km² and forms part of the coastal plain terrace characterised by a sloping plateau, numerous deep valleys, marshland and higher lying dry agricultural land. The highest point in Ogoniland is situated a mere 33 m above sea level.[7]

Historically the Ogoni consisted of four clans, namely the Khana, Gokana, Tai, and Eleme. During the course of colonial rule the Khana clan gradually split, firstly into the Northern Khana and the Southern Khana, and by the 1960s consisted of three clans, namely the Nyo-Khana, Ken-Khana, and Babbe, with the Babbe clan established as a separate clan as late as 1959.[8] The Ogoni people have no mythological progenitor that serves as a unifying force amongst the six clans, and, according to Osaghae, are grouped together as an ethnic group on the basis of a common language,[9] tradition, cultural practices, farming methods, and similar attitudes.[10] However, these factors have not always provided enough common ground for all six clans with a lack of unity in general characterizing inter-clan relationships in the post-colonial era.[11]

In pre-colonial Ogoni society the village chief, who normally descended from the original founder of the village along patrilineal lines, constituted the main political and social authority. On village level, the chief was aided by the village council which consisted of the most powerful elders, and on clan level a *Gbenemene Barasin* (or clan chief) generally exercised nominal control over the clan villages. The onset of British colonial rule changed the relatively weak position of the *Gbenemene Barasin* by entrusting these men with the powers to collect taxes, and consequently the position of clan chief not only became attractive, but also highly sought after.[12] Clan and village chiefs continued to exercise political, economic and social control over their people in the post-colonial era. However, in most cases traditional chiefs did not participate in national and regional politics, which spheres were left to their sons and a new breed of professional and educated men who represented the Ogoni in state and federal political structures. It was from these ranks that MOSOP emerged in 1990 and who have remained in control of the organization since its inception.[13]

Traditional Ogoni society subsisted on swidden agriculture, hunting, and fishing. Their major agricultural crops included cassava, yam, pepper, corn, melon, beans, okra, and gourds. Their farming plots were either house gardens or outlying farming plots. House gardens were situated adjacent to their homesteads and were used to cultivate household crops such as gourds, pepper, coco-yam and a few yams to serve as emergency supplies. Their outlying farming plots were situated up to 8 km from the village and were characterized by high-diversity intercropping which constituted both the main food supply for the family and their main source of income, since surplus crops formed the basis of the Ogoni's contribution to the active inter-Niger Delta and intra-Ogoniland trade networks. Traditionally, outlying farming plots were only cultivated for one year and were then left to lie fallow for four to five years before being utilized again. This practice was gradually abandoned in the course of colonial rule due to land scarcity in the Niger Delta, which scarcity increased in the post-colonial era to pressing levels. Hunting constitutes an important source of protein for those Ogoni communities living inland and is mostly done via trapping. Fishing, on the other hand, is a full-time occupation for those communities living on the creeks and in the Imo river basin and also provides these communities with their main source of income.[14]

Despite the implementation of British colonial rule over Ogoniland and the rest of Eastern Nigerian by 1900, the Ogoni culture and economy remained rooted in traditional practices well into the second half of the twentieth century. The reason being that the Ogoni, as an ethnic minority group within both colonial and independent Nigeria, were not regarded as a priority development zone.[15] The biggest single impact on the Ogoni's traditional modes of production stemmed from the exploration for and development of oil resources in their traditional territory from the late 1950s onwards. Over time, these oil developments had a tremendous impact on the Ogoni and their ability to practice their traditional culture, and resulted in the political, economic, social, and environmental marginalization of this oil-producing ethnic minority group. This long process of marginalization, in turn, prompted the founding of MOSOP in 1990 and the launch of the Ogoni struggle against the Nigerian federal government and Shell Nigeria. Though the Ogoni struggle amounted to more than just a struggle for environmental justice and rights, the rest of this chapter will confine its focus to the Ogoni's struggle against the adverse environmental and social impacts of Shell Nigeria's oil production in their traditional territory.

SHELL NIGERIA, OIL PRODUCTION, AND ENVIRONMENTAL INJUSTICE IN OGONILAND.

The flames of Shell are flames of Hell,
We bask below their light,
Naught for us to serve the blight,
Of cursed neglect and cursed Shell.

—Ogoni song[16]

As mentioned earlier, oil of commercial quantity was first discovered in Ogoniland at Dere in 1958, and Shell-BP started with oil production in that area (the Bomu oil field) in the same year. In 1964 Nigeria's first oil refinery was built at Alesa Eleme which falls within Ogoni territory. As elsewhere in the Niger Delta, oil production also expanded in Ogoniland, and by the 1990s Shell Nigeria was producing oil in this area at ninety-six oil wells situated in five oil-fields (Bomu, Korokoro, Ebubu, Bodo, and Yorla). The maximum daily capacity of Shell Nigeria's oil production in Ogoniland by 1993 was 28,000 barrels per day, which accounted for 3 per cent of Shell Nigeria's daily oil production at that stage. Chevron Nigeria Limited, a subsidiary of the multinational oil company, also became involved in oil production in Ogoniland in 1980 when it bought an interest in two oil wells in the region in which Shell Nigeria operated. However, Shell Nigeria acted as sole operator for all the joint oil ventures in Ogoniland until its withdrawal from the region in January 1993.[17]

The exploration for and the production of oil in Ogoniland have, since 1958, led to radical changes in the economic activities of this ethnic group. The polluting of their agricultural land and water networks by the oil industry gradually denied the Ogoni access to their traditional economic modes of production while at the same time denying them the right to live in a safe and healthy environment. By 1990 Ogoniland's natural and human environments had deteriorated to such an extent that MOSOP was founded with the initial objective of pressuring the federal government and Shell Nigeria to address the adverse environmental impacts of oil production and development in Ogoni territory. Since 1990, this pressure has developed into an international campaign against Shell International, that blames the multinational oil company and its subsidiary in Nigeria for all Ogoniland's environmental problems.[18]

The founding of MOSOP in 1990 to address oil-related environmental problems in Ogoniland was but the latest strategy employed by the Ogoni to seek redress for the detrimental environmental impacts of oil production in their territory. Their struggle against Shell Nigeria dates back to 1970, when the Ogoni sent a letter to Shell-BP expressing their grievances against this joint venture for the first time. In this letter the Ogoni Divisional Union accused Shell-BP of polluting the Ogoni's agricultural land and water resources, neglecting to compensate them for damaged land, inadequate rents paid to local communities, the destruction of roads in this region by Shell-BP's trucks, inadequate employment of Ogoni by Shell-BP in this region, and a lack of development in Ogoniland by the joint venture.[19]

Shortly after the letter was sent, an oil spill occurred in June 1970 at Dere in Shell-BP's Bomu oil field, which the joint venture neglected to repair for three weeks and which caused large-scale damage to the surrounding natural environment. Sam Badilo Bako, spokesperson for the Dere community, summed up the spill and its impact as follows:

> We in Dere today [1970] are facing a situation which can only be compared with our experiences during the civil war. This village of no less than 20,000 inhabitants produces the greatest oilfield this country has—BOMU, SHELL-BP chooses to call it for reasons best known to that Shylock of a company. It is nearly two weeks now when suddenly we were told that there was an explosion on this oilfield and that people should be on their alert. This 'revelation' came casually, perhaps secretly, from some friends who are employees of the company. Since then an ocean of crude oil had emerged, moving swiftly like a great river in flood, successfully swallowing up anything that comes on its way. These include cassava farms, yams, palms, streams, animals etc etc for miles on end. There is no pipeborne water and yet the streams, the only source of drinking water is coated with oil. You cannot collect a bucket of rain water for the roofs, trees and grass are all covered with oil. Anything spread outside in the neighbourhood is soaked with oil as the wind carries the oil miles away from the scene of the incident. Nor can you enter a bush without being soaked to the skin. . . . But men and women forced by hunger 'steal' occasionally into the 'ocean', some have to dive deep in oil to uproot already rotten yams and cassava. . . . We are thus faced with a situation where we have no food to eat, no water to drink, no homes to live in and worst of it all, no air to breathe.[20]

An investigation launched by the Rivers state government followed, and Shell-BP was eventually found guilty of negligence and ordered to pay damages to the Dere community. These damages increased greatly after the Dere community successfully sued Shell-BP, demanding £250,000 in compensation for the loss of land and water resources owing to the oil spill. The Rivers State High Court subsequently found Shell-BP guilty and imposed a penalty of £168,468 on the company.[21]

Numerous smaller oil spills continued to occur in Ogoniland at Shell-BP and later Shell Nigeria oil infrastructure throughout the 1970s which resulted in a number of law suits being filed against this joint venture. In the early 1980s the largest oil spill in the territory was discovered near Ejamah in the Ebubu oil field, where approximately ten hectares of land had been totally submerged in a few metres of oil. An investigation launched into this oil spill revealed that the original spill had actually taken place several years earlier in 1968 during the federal invasion of Ogoniland in the Biafran civil war. During this period Shell-BP was not active in oil production in the territory and it was assumed that the oil infrastructure had been damaged by military hardware and bombings. However, the damage at the Ebubu oil field was overlooked in the hasty repairs carried out by Shell-BP during 1968 in an attempt to get oil production back online as quickly as possible.[22] Shell Nigeria did initiate an environmental rehabilitation program in the early 1980s in the affected areas and compensated the local inhabitants for their damages. Following further complaints by the Ejamah community in 1985 and 1986, Shell Nigeria bought the polluted ten hectares of land from the community at market price, and undertook to rehabilitate the area. By 2001, however, this specific piece of land was still heavily polluted with oil and seemingly beyond rehabilitation.[23]

By 1990 the Ogoni objected to Shell Nigeria's oil-related activities in their traditional territory mainly on four grounds, namely that their land and water resources had been polluted by numerous oil spills over the course of thirty-eight years; that these oil spills resulted from outdated equipment which broke down during the production processes on a regular basis; that gas flaring polluted the air, posed a major health risk and was an inconvenience to oil-producing communities, and that Shell Nigeria did not initiate enough development projects in Ogoniland, which region remained underdeveloped and poor when compared with non-oil-producing communities in other parts of Nigeria.[24]

By 1990 oil spills and the corresponding environmental pollution had been a constant factor in the lives of the ethnic minority oil-producing communities residing in the Niger Delta. They had been exposed to the detrimental impacts of more than 4,000 oil spills since production started in 1958. Between 1976 and 1996, for example, a total of 2,768 reported oil spills occurred in which an estimated 3.8 million barrels of oil were spilled directly into the sensitive Niger Delta ecosystem. These included major oil spills such as the Faniwa oil well blowout (January 1980, 146,000–200,000 barrels of oil spilled) and the Fantua oil spill (1984, about 200,000 barrels of oil spilled).[25]

In Ogoniland, eighty-seven separate incidents of oil spills involving an estimated 5,352 barrels of oil were registered at Shell Nigeria's oil facilities in this region between 1985 and 1993 alone. Opinions regarding the causes of these oil spills differ considerably, with Shell Nigeria claiming that 60 percent were caused by sabotage, while international environmental non-governmental organizations, in particular Greenpeace, and MOSOP strongly opposed this position. According to Greenpeace, which conducted a study in 1994 into the environmental and human impact of Shell Nigeria's oil production in Ogoniland, it was not possible for Shell Nigeria to be responsible for only 40 percent of all oil spills in this area given the fact that between 1982 and 1992, 40 percent of Shell International's total global oil spills occurred in Nigeria. For Greenpeace, this was proof in itself that Shell International did not take the necessary precautions in Nigeria to ensure that their oil-related activities were environmentally sound, and that it was therefore possible that most of the oil spills in Ogoniland resulted from outdated and faulty equipment. After Shell Nigeria's withdrawal from Ogoniland, a further 24 oil spills occurred up to October 1994, and in all these cases the company was quick to attribute the spills to sabotage. However, Shell Nigeria's own data eventually proved it wrong and by May 1996 the company had to admit that at least 75 percent of all oil spills in Ogoniland resulted from pipe corrosion, which could have been prevented if the company had replaced outdated equipment and corroded pipelines on a regular basis.[26]

Oil-producing Ogoni communities remained vulnerable to oil spills beyond October 1994 of which the Yorla oil well blow-out in May 2001 bears witness. This oil well blow-out in the Yorla oil-field in Ogoniland renewed the direct confrontation between the Ogoni and Shell Nigeria and the company was again quick to attribute the blow-out to sabotage. They took a week to send a team of three specialists from the Houston-based Boots & Coots International Well Control Company to cap the well, along with a team of Shell Nigeria logistics, medical and well service staff. The team were not well received in Ogoniland and were taken hostage by Ogoni youth who released them a few hours later, following negotiations. After careful consideration of their position on the causes of the Yorla oil spill, Shell Nigeria has taken in the position that oil well blow-outs are to be expected in Ogoniland because the company was summarily forced to abandon production in the area in 1993 as a result of the militant campaign of MOSOP, and was not allowed back into Ogoniland to institute the proper procedure to ensure the safety of its oil wells in the territory since 2001. The Yorla oil spill, like too many previous oil spills in Ogoniland, has not been properly cleaned up, to the detriment of the local natural and human environments.[27]

The environmental impact of oil spills is the most visible environmental damage of the oil industry when compared with that of, for example, seismic surveys and gas flaring. Oil spills damage crops, pollute water and soil, and kill marine resources within the immediate vicinity of the spill, while flooding during the rainy season can and does transport the oil to other locations, thereby enlarging the geographical impact of the oil spill. A major problem in assessing the real environmental impact of oil spills is the lack of scientific data and the general lack of independent and timely research into oil spills. In the absence of proper scientific data it has become a standard practice for the Nigerian government and Shell Nigeria to downplay the adverse environmental impact of oil spills in Ogoniland by focusing attention on the ability of tropical zones, through weathering and microbial processes, to rapidly degrade acutely toxic substances in crude oil which therefore limits the impacts and accelerates the recovering period of the affected area. Despite this natural rehabilitation ability of tropical climates, it still takes a long time for the natural environment to recover fully after an oil spill. Soil polluted in a major oil spill, for example, takes about ten years to recover to such a level where peasant farmers can consider cultivation again—and this is with human-assisted rehabilitation.[28]

Not only were the Ogoni's land and water resources polluted by oil spills, but they had been subjected to uninterrupted gas flaring at Shell Nigeria's oil production sites since oil production started at Dere in 1958. Associated gases are natural by-products of oil production which can be utilised as an energy source if the necessary structures are in place. When Shell Nigeria built most of its facilities in Nigeria in general and in Ogoniland in particular, there was no market for these gases, and consequently the company did not develop the necessary infrastructure in Ogoniland to utilize natural gas in a meaningful manner nor did they install the necessary equipment to re-inject the gas. As a result, gas flaring became the standard and cheapest method for Shell Nigeria to deal with associated gas in its Ogoniland production sites. The practice continued initially because the Nigerian government did not enforce its own environmental laws, and later on because the fines levied against gas flaring were insignificant compared to the costs involved in developing the appropriate infrastructure (e.g., a 3 kobo fine was levied per 28.317 m³ gas flared in terms of the Associated Gas Re-injection Amendment Act of 1985). As a result, up to the mid-1990s, Nigeria flared 95 percent of all associated gas during production. Since then the percentage of gas flared has dropped to around 75 percent, while the Nigerian government committed itself in October 2001 to end all gas flaring by 2008.[29]

Because gas flaring was standard practice at Shell Nigeria's oil production sites in Ogoniland the local inhabitants in this densely populated territory were subjected, on a daily basis, to 24 hours of gas flaring prior to Shell Nigeria's withdrawal from the territory in January 1993. This practice exposed both the Ogoni and their natural environment to thermal air, water, and soil pollution, the destruction of vegetation and wildlife, damage to infrastructures by acid rain, and damage to soil, crops, and vegetation by the severe heat and the deposition of contaminants. The oil-producing villages in Ogoniland were further exposed to severe heat, noise, and fumes which constituted serious health risks, and the discomfort of 24 hours of synthetic, bright, orange light.[30]

Claims by the Ogoni that Shell Nigeria did not develop their territory are not completely correct. Development initiatives by Shell Nigeria started in this region in 1965 when the company introduced an agriculture project in Ogoniland which involved the permanent stationing of two agriculture experts in the region to help and advise Ogoni farmers. Between 1986 and 1993, Shell Nigeria built and equipped Ogoniland's only hospital and supplied equipment to two health clinics. Money was also provided for the construction of seven school blocks, each consisting of six classrooms; bursaries were granted to high school pupils and university students, and five water schemes were developed to provide potable water to some Ogoni communities.[31] Despite these developments, Ogoniland was by 1990 an underdeveloped region that had an inadequate infrastructure and there existed a real need for electricity provision, roads, schools, hospitals, and potable water. This region also had only one doctor for every 70,000 people, one hospital for the whole ethnic group of 500,000 people, an unemployment rate of 85 percent, a literacy rate of only 20 percent and life expectancy was only 51 years, which was three years below the national average.[32]

Only after the unexpected consumer backlash against Shell International in the aftermath of the execution of Ken Saro-Wiwa and his eight co-accused Ogoni in November 1995, did Shell Nigeria reconsider its developmental responsibilities in Ogoniland. Consequently, from 1996 onwards, in addition to extending its established and successful agricultural project in this region, the company launched new projects aimed at improving the medical services and vocational training in the territory. In 1996 Shell Nigeria took over the running of the Gokana hospital, became involved in the reopening of three clinics and began to provide clinics in Ogoniland with medicine. In May 1997 it announced plans to launch a ten-month Ogoni Youth Training Scheme which would provide 366 Ogoni youths with vocational training in a variety of skills, including carpentry, welding, and computer studies.[33]

THE CHALLENGE OF SECURING ENVIRONMENTAL JUSTICE IN OGONILAND

Over the past decade the pursuit of environmental justice has found wide acceptance across the world to the extent where it has became an integral part of development planning and an important basis for restitution claims lodged by communities adversely affected by past developments. Within the Nigerian context, however, the promotion of environmental justice has proved to be challenging since successive Nigerian governments showed a general tendency not to support just claims for environmental justice from oil-producing communities, including the Ogoni. Much rather, the federal government has reacted not only negatively but in numerous instances violently and uncompromising when confronted with demands by sections of their national population for better environmental standards, environmental rights and the right to participate in the processes of local oil exploitation.

One of the main reasons for this state of affairs is because environmental struggles in the developing world are almost never solely environment-based, and more often than not form part of a greater struggle for political, economic, social, *and* environmental rights. Consequently, it is almost impossible to remove claims of environmental injustice from claims of political, economic and social marginalization within the developing world in general, and in Nigeria in particular. The Ogoni case is no exception and both the Ogoni Bill of Rights (1990) and its Addendum (1991) underscore this reality and clearly show the interrelatedness of their claims of environmental injustice with that of their perceived and real political, economic, and social marginalization in independent Nigeria.[34]

Due to the publicity created by the Ogoni struggle, especially after the Saro-Wiwa execution in 1995, many international interest groups and academics have offered solutions to the Ogoni's problems and listed conditions that the Nigerian federal government and Shell Nigeria must adhere to in order to secure environmental justice for this ethnic group, the most important of which include the political empowerment of the Ogoni by giving them access to political positions on both federal and state levels; their economic empowerment through back payments for thirty-five years of oil-production in their traditional territory and payment of all associated oil rents and royalties directly to this group; and their environmental empowerment through an environmental rehabilitation program to reverse the detrimental environmental impacts of oil production on their living and natural environments. In addition, it is demanded that Shell Nigeria ensure that oil revenue reach the oil-producing communities, pay proper and full compensation for past environmental injustices, adhere to the same environmental standards in Nigeria as it does in the developed world, and break its relationship with the Nigerian federal government.[35]

While most of these conditions make sense, especially on a theoretical level, the problem with both the Ogoni demands and literature dealing with environmental injustice in Ogoniland and other onshore oil-producing regions in the country is that it ignores the political realities in contemporary Nigeria. It is simply not possible to give the Ogoni the level of political empowerment that they aspire to and neither is it politically feasible for the government to allow one ethnic minority group of only 500,000 people to dictate their terms to the rest of the 132 million people classified as Nigerians. To a large extent, ethnic majority domination and the complex negotiated relationship between the three ethnic majority groups is the glue that keeps Nigeria together and without which the Nigerian state would probably disintegrate. Oil-related ethnic minority struggles have shown that they are capable of disrupting the flow of oil and by implication the fragile relationships between the ruling ethnic majorities and oil-producing ethnic minority groups. Addressing the political aspiration and marginalization of oil-producing ethnic minorities is no easy matter and would involve genuine dialogue and negotiations between the various role-players in which it will be necessary for all sides to compromise in order to arrive at a mutually acceptable negotiated settlement.

Addressing the economic aspects of the Ogoni's environmental justice demands is also no easy task given the fact that these not only directly threaten the very basis of the Nigerian economy and the continuation of the Nigerian state, but further also threatens the tax, lease, and royalty base of resource exploitation across the world. Their demand for US $6 billion for accumulated rents and royalties for thirty-five years of oil production is not only unrealistically high, but also controversial since payment of these monies to oil-producing Ogoni communities would expose Shell Nigeria and other multinational oil companies to similar claims both within and outside Nigeria. The equitable and fair distribution of the material benefits of oil production is a central issue in the Ogoni struggle. And, unfortunately for the Ogoni, it is also a key political issue in independent Nigeria. As a typical petro-state, Nigeria is a rentier and distributive state in which political authority and economic control depend almost exclusively on the ability of the federal government to secure profits from the oil industry and to distribute these profits internally to those sectors of Nigerian society (i.e., the dominant ethnic groups) on whose survival the federal government depends.[36]

Attempts had been made since the 1990s to address the material needs of oil-producing communities through the establishment of the Oil Mineral Producing Areas Development Commission (OMPADC) and the earmarking of 13 per cent of oil revenue to be spent by OMPADC on development in these regions. However, the vast majority of these funds never make it to oil-producing communities with the majority of funds utilized by OMPADC to support this new bureaucratic institution.[37] Reforming the way in which oil-producing communities benefit from oil production in their traditional territory is probably, along with addressing the adverse environmental impacts, the most important aspect the federal government needs to address if it wants to restore order to the Niger Delta region. This, however, is no simple process and would have to be negotiated by the federal government with the majority ethnic groups, as principal beneficiaries of the oil wealth, and the oil-producing communities in the Niger Delta.

Compared to their political and economic demands, realizing the environmental component of the Ogoni demands is seemingly less complicated. Truth is, their struggle and that of other oil-producing ethnic minorities in the Niger Delta have forced Shell International and its subsidiary in Nigeria to start cleaning up their act due to consumer pressures in the developed world.[38] Ogoniland, however, still suffers from the adverse environmental impacts of thirty-five years of oil production in their traditional territory and has demanded US $4 billion compensation from Shell International in this regard since the early 1990s.[39] Tired of political instability in the Niger

Delta oil-producing areas, the Nigerian Senate entered this compensation debate in August 2004 when its members voted overwhelming in favour of a resolution in terms of which a US $1.5 billion payment is demanded from the Shell Petroleum Development Company of Nigeria, Ltd (SPDC) for compensation to oil-producing Niger Delta communities for environmental damages that resulted from oil production since production started in 1958.[40]

The Senate resolution is indicative of the real problem when dealing with the need to rehabilitate oil-polluted areas, namely the joint venture nature of oil developments in the country. As mentioned earlier, the SPDC is a joint venture between Shell International (30 percent), the Nigerian National Petroleum Company (NNPC, 55 percent), Total (10 percent), and Agip (5 per cent). Consequently, the state, through the NNPC is also being held responsible for the devastating environmental impacts of oil production in the country, and as the majority partner will have to make the majority contribution if ever such a resolution became law. However, the NNPC has showed little inclination toward implementing and adhering to minimum environmental standards while the Nigerian federal government continues to fail to enforce environmental legislation in place. In addition, it made no real effort in the past to regulate the industry, and the enormous environmental problems that plague the Nigerian oil industry in part can be attributed to the unwillingness of the NNPC to make infrastructural investments over the years. The prevailing dismal economic conditions since the 1980s also did not help and ensured that the state was and continues to be very reluctant to invest money into environmental safeguards for the oil industry.[41]

Given the massive involvement of the federal government in the country's oil industry, no real progress will be made in ensuring proper environmental stewardship in the oil industry before the federal government and the ethnic majority groups make a lasting commitment toward sustainable environmental management. Without governmental commitment it is uncertain if oil companies active in the country will pay constructive attention to environmental issues beyond the implementation of cosmetic changes to satisfy consumers in the developed world. Truth is, oil is, in essence, a dirty industry and having the first-mover advantage has turned into a major environmental disadvantage for Shell Nigeria due to the constant failure of aging equipment that in turn results in oil spills and associated environmental problems. At the very least Shell Nigeria will have to start with an extensive program to replace aging equipment in order to address the abnormally high number of equipment failure-related oil spills and oil-well blow-outs.

The Senate resolution is the first proper initiative to address the need to rehabilitate the polluted and damaged Niger Delta environment. However, questions regarding who will pay for the rehabilitation, just how much money will be needed and how to ensure that a rehabilitation program does not become yet another avenue to obtain fast money and become "spill-millionaires" (as was the case with the 1989 *Exxon Valdez* oil spill in Alaska) remain highly contested. Without international, national, and regional consumer, political and economic pressures it is doubtful if the Nigerian federal government and oil companies active in the country will be inclined to pay constructive attention to oil-related environmental problems in the Niger Delta.

Finding a lasting solution for the environmental, political, social, and economic injustices in Ogoniland is no simple matter and will involve compromises from all role-players in the struggle. Unfortunately, there is currently no indication that any of the three role-players is willing to negotiate a lasting solution to the Ogoni crisis, and consequently the Ogoni will continue to occupy what M. J. Watts calls the "margin of the margin of Nigerian society."[42]

NOTES

1. Anon, "Drilling Fields," *Multinational Monitor* 17 (1995), http://multinationalmonitor.org/hyper/ issues/1995/01/mm0195_06.html.

2. K. Saro-Wiwa, *Genocide in Nigeria: The Ogoni Tragedy* (Port Harcourt: Saros International Publishers, 1992), 83.

3. The Shell Petroleum Development Company of Nigeria Ltd is a joint venture between Shell International (30 percebt), the Nigerian National Petroleum Company (NNPC, 55 percent), Total (10 percent), and Agip (5 percent). Shell is the operator for this joint venture.

4. The oil-producing regions in the Niger Delta are mostly inhabited by ethnic minority groups such as the Abriba, Andoni, Effiks, Isekiri, Kalabari, and the Ogoni. These and other oil-producing communities have largely been excluded from the benefits of oil production in their traditional territories where poor infrastructure, poor housing and lack of water supply, electricity, and sanitation prevail. A.A. Ikein, *The Impact of Oil on a Developing Country: The Case of Nigeria* (New York: Praeger, 1990), 23, 28–29.

5. M.S. Steyn, "Oil Politics in Ecuador and Nigeria: A Perspective from Environmental History on the Struggles between Ethnic Minority Groups, Multinational Oil Companies and National Governments" (Ph.D. dissertation, University of the Free State, South Africa, 2003), 373–78, 386–87.

6. Richard Sykes (Group Environmental Advisor for Shell International), personal interview with Phia Steyn, London, 15 September 2001.

7. G.N. Loolo, *A History of the Ogoni* (Port Harcourt: n.p., 1981), 1; Saro-Wiwa, 5; E.E. Osaghae, "The Ogoni Uprising: Oil Politics, Minority Agitation and the Future of the Nigerian State," *African Affairs* 94 (1995): 327–29.

8. Nigerian National Archives, Enugu Branch (NNAE), OGONDIST 4/1/12–6402/1: P.E.M. Richards, *Ogoni Tribe: Intelligence Report*, 1931, 8–11.

9. According to Mann and Dalby, it is not possible to refer to Ogoni as a language and at most the term Ogoni language can be used as an umbrella term to refer to three different languages, namely Eleme, Khana (or Kana), and Gokana. Only Khana boasts dialects and is divided into Tai, Northern Khana and Southern Khan. Gokana and Khana are mutually intelligible, while Eleme is unintelligible to all other Ogoni members. M. Mann and D. Dalby, eds. *A Thesaurus of African Languages: A Classified and Annotated Inventory of the Spoken Languages in Africa with an Appendix on Their Written Representation* (London: Zell Publishers), 10.

10. Osaghae, 327–28.

11. NNAE, OGONDIST 4/1/12–6402/1: P.E.M. Richards, *Ogoni Tribe: Intelligence Report*, 1931, 7–11.

12. Loolo, 12–17.

13. M.S. Steyn, 338–42.

14. NNAE, CALPROF 16/2/852-OP1730: J.A.J. Tanguhan, Forestry and Agriculture in the Ogoni Country, 1907; Saro-Wiwa, 12–14; Loolo, 33–36.

15. NNAE, OGONDIST 4/1/12–6402/1: P.E.M. Richards, *Ogoni Tribe: Intelligence Report*, 1931; *Mail & Guardian* (South Africa), January 13–19, 1995, 14.

16. Earthlife Africa, *Factsheet on the Ogoni struggle* (Johannesburg: ELA, 1995), 1.

17. Saro-Wiwa, 24; Human Rights Watch, *The Price of Oil: Corporate Responsibility and Human Rights Violations in Nigeria's Oil Producing Communities* (New York: Human Rights Watch, 1999), http://www.hrw.org/hrw/reports/1999/Nigeria/Nigew991.htm, Chapter 3; Chevron, "RE: Operations in Nigeria," e-mail correspondence between Chevron and Phia Steyn, June, 15 1999.

18. See, for example, Human Rights Watch, *The Price of Oil*; Carte Blanche. "Crude," http://www.mnet. co.za/carteblanche/cbl_story_page.asp?StoryID = 1646, 2001 (Original text to documentary); Catma Films, "The drilling fields," http://www.oneworld.org/owbt/drilling_video.html, 1993–1994 (Original text to documentary).

19. Saro-Wiwa, 44–50, 58–59, 63–80.

20. Sam Badilo Bako as quoted in ibid., 58–59.

21. Ibid., 80.

22. It is perhaps possible, to some extent at least, to attribute the abnormally high number of oil spills recorded by Shell Nigeria in the Niger Delta to these hasty repairs of Shell-BP during the Biafran civil war. The joint venture boasted of the limited time that it took to do these repairs, of the unorthodox methods used and the relatively low costs involved. Combined with the fact that Shell Nigeria failed to reinvest in their oil infrastructure and neglected to replace aging equipment, it could only be expected that the oil infrastructure in Ogoniland and elsewhere in the Niger Delta would fail on numerous occasions. See S. Webb, "Then the War Came," *Shell Magazine*, February 1969, no pagination.

23. Patrick Omuku (Spokesman for the Shell Petroleum Development Company of Nigeria, Ltd), personal interview with Phia Steyn, Lagos, July10, 2001; Phia Steyn, Field notes from research trip to Nigeria, 2001: Notes on the informal conversation with Eric Nworgor, Ebubu oil field, June 19, 2001.

24. I. Inbeau, "Oil, Conflict and Security in Rural Nigeria: Issues in the Ogoni Crisis," *Occasional Paper Series* 1 (1997): 14–16; I. Okonta and O. Douglas, *Where*

Vultures Feast: Shell, Human Rights, and Oil in the Niger Delta (San Francisco: Sierra Club Books, 2001), 190–205; B. Naanen, "Oil-Producing Minorities and the Restructuring of Nigerian Federalism: The Case of the Ogoni People," *Journal of Commonwealth and Comparative Politics* 33 (1995): 64–67.

25. I.M. Aprioku, "Collective Response to Oil Spill Hazards in the Eastern Niger Delta of Nigeria," *Journal of Environmental Planning and Management* 42 (1999): 391–96; E. Okoko, "Women and Environmental Change in the Niger Delta, Nigeria: Evidence from Ibeno," *Gender, Place and Culture* 6 (1999): 375.

26. Catma Films, "The Drilling Fields"; A. Rowell, *Shell-Shocked: The Environmental and Social Costs of Living Next Door to Shell* (Amsterdam: Greenpeace International, 1994), http://archive.greenpeace.org/ comms/ken/enviro.html, Chapter 1; J. Hattingh, "Shell International and the Ogoni People of the Rivers Province in Nigeria: Towards a Better Understanding of Environmental Justice in Africa" (paper presented at conference, Environmental Justice: Global Ethics for the 21st Century, October 1–3, 1997, Melbourne), 13–15. The Nigerian oil industry makes a distinction between three types of oil spills, namely equipment failure, human error and sabotage oil spills. Equipment failure accounts for the majority of oil spills in Nigeria and results from a variety of factors including overflow at loading terminals, valve failure that leads to pressure problems, and ruptured and/or corroded pipes. Oil spills at Shell operations, in particular, result from equipment failure mainly because the company set up its oil infrastructure in the 1960s and 1970s, and has failed to maintain and replace aged equipment and pipelines properly, thereby making it more prone to rupture and corrosion. Human error oil spills, on the other hand, result mainly from negligence and personnel failure to perform tasks properly. By contrast, sabotage oil spills are regarded as deliberate and malicious damage to oil pipelines and equipment by disgruntled people who either regard compensation paid for damage as inadequate or who want to increase compensation for damage already inflicted, or oil-producing communities who want to force oil companies to provide amenities for them. Despite the fact that equipment failure and human error constitute the majority of oil spills, oil companies are quick to attribute oil spills to sabotage since oil companies do not pay for damages caused by sabotage oil spills. On the contrary, the government compensates them for the damages caused in these oil spills to their oil pipelines and equipment. O.R. Ogri, "A Review of the Nigerian Petroleum Industry and the Associated Environmental Problems," *The Environmentalist* 21 (2001): 17–18; N. Ashton-Jones, *The Human Ecosystems of the Niger Delta: An ERA Handbook* (Benin City: ERA, 1998), 151–53, 160; Aprioku, 392–95.

27. Anon, "Shell Says Ogoni Oil Blow-Out Is Now Under Control," *Reuters Business Briefing*, May 9, 2001; Anon, "Nigeria Update: 2-oil Experts Briefly Blocked after Capping Nigeria spill," *Reuters Business Briefing*, May 9, 2001; Anon, "Royal Dutch/Shell Oil workers Detained by Nigerian Youths After Capping Well," *Reuters Business Briefing*, May 9, 2001. The author visited the Yorla oil spill in June 2001. By that time all the oil spill rehabilitation equipment had already been removed despite the fact that the whole affected territory was still covered with oil.

28. J.G. Frynas, *Oil in Nigeria: Conflict and Litigation between Oil Companies and Village Communities* (Hamburg: Lit Verlag, 2000), 165–166; Human Rights Watch, Chapter 5; The World Bank, *Defining an Environmental Development Strategy for the Niger Delta* I (Washington: The World Bank, 1995), 47–48.

29. Frynas, 164–165; The World Bank, Vol. II, 40–44; Energy Information Administration, "Nigeria," http://www.eia.doe.gov/emeu/cabs/ nigeria.html, 2002.

30. Okoko, 375; Ashton-Jones, 144; A.O. Isichei and W.W. Sanford, "The Effects of Waste Gas Flares on the Surrounding Vegetation in South-Eastern Nigeria," *Journal of Applied Ecology* 13 (1976): 17–187; The World Bank, Vol. II, 40–44.

31. Anon, *Nigeria: The Untold Ogoni Story* (Information provided by the Nigerian High Commission in Pretoria, South Africa), 9; Omuku, 2001.

32. Naanen, 64; Osaghae, 332–33; *Mail & Guardian* (South Africa), January 13–19, 1995, 14.

33. Human Rights Watch, Chapter 9; Omuku, 2001; M.S. Steyn, 381–83.

34. M.S. Steyn, 356–59; Osaghae, 331–38; Saro-Wiwa, 84–103.

35. Hattingh, 34–36.

36. T. Karl, *The Paradox of Plenty: Oil Booms and Petro-states* (Berkeley: University of California Press, 1997), 47–49.

37. Frynas, 49–50; I. Oguine, "Nigeria's Oil Revenues and the Oil-producing Areas," *Journal of Energy and Natural Resources Law* 17 (1999): 114–19.

38. P. Steyn, " '(S)hell in Nigeria': The Environmental Impact of Oil Politics in Ogoniland on Shell International" in *African Environment and Development: Rhetoric, Programs, Realities*, ed. W.G. Moseley and B.I. Logan (London: Ashgate, 2004), 222–225.

39. Osaghae, 336; *Weekly Trust* (Nigeria), February 16–22, 2001, 17.

40. Anon, "Shell Face $1.5 bn Nigeria Bill," http://news.bbc.co.uk/1/hi/business/3598148.stm, August 25, 2004.

41. Ikein, 38, 42–43, 62; M.S. Steyn, 152–59, 185–92.

42. M.J. Watts, *Petro-violence: Some Thoughts on Community, Extraction, and Political Ecology* (Berkeley Workshop on Environmental Politics Working Papers no WP 99–1, Berkeley: Institute for International Studies, 1999), 15.

26

The Community, Industry, and the Quest for a Clean Vaal River 1997–2004[1]

Elise and Johann Tempelhoff

An outstanding feature of twentieth century environmental issues in South Africa, was that the voice of the ordinary people was all too seldom heard. Until the *National Environmental Management Act* (No. 107 of 1998) was passed by Parliament,[1] communities had few legal rights in respect of the manner in which their lives were being affected by local industries. They were literally left powerless in the face of industrial activities that were directly related to environmental degradation. The reasons for this state of affairs can be ascribed to a number of factors. In the second half of the century the country's rate of development was high. Industrial activity was at a premium in the face of the country's need to develop in the face of political and economic isolation, as a result of the apartheid policies pursued by the former government. Particularly, after 1976, as the country's border war was stepped up, the defence industry was large. Strategic considerations in respect of security and the need to give priority to the arms production industry made it necessary to keep matters of environmental concern on the backburner, at least up to the end of 1989. Furthermore, South Africa's industrial environment (with the exception of the nuclear industry) was not necessarily subjected to international environmental scrutiny.

There had been indications since the late 1980s that the situation was changing.[2] At the time of the passing of new *Environment Conservation Act* (No. 73 of 1989), as well as the gradual lifting of sanctions, the government and South African society at large, tended to take note of environmental issues. Especially in the period after the Rio Earth Summit (1992) there were numerous plans afoot to start addressing environmental matters.[3] The former government was however not in a position to act. The country was in a state of political transition.

The transition to multi-racial governance in 1994 was noted for its commitment to environmental protection. In the new constitution, passed in 1996, specific attention was given to the right of each individual to a sound environment.[4] Also, there were indications that the government, in a more concerted manner than its predecessor, was committed to taking care of the environment in the interest of South African society at large.

In the discussion to follow the objective is to provide a historical overview of the actions taken by a peri-urban community, in the southern parts of South Africa's Gauteng Province, in order to prevent a major steel manufacturing concern from polluting the local air and the underground as well as surface water supplies.

Attention is given to the National Environmental Management Act, as well as related water legislation, in order determine to the extent environmental protection measures have been effective in doing justice to attempts at conservation.

It is argued that in the process of industry and the community clashing over matters of pollution, the ultimate solution would be for both to find common ground, i.e., the environment, and start with a process of mutual collaboration in the restoration and maintenance of a sound environment.

THE FIRST COURT CASE

In August 1997, a year before the National Environmental Management Act was passed, a group of 150 peri-urban owners of small holdings decided to show their discontent with the local plant of the South African steel giant Iscor,[5] situated outside Vanderbijlpark, in the south of Gauteng. They were arranging a protest march because the company's plant polluted their water and the air they breathed.[6] This was a remarkable development. Since 1974 there had been periodical clashes between Iscor and local residents. But these were isolated and of an almost insignificant nature. Consequently, their attempts at trying to improve the environment, remained a futile experiments.

Iscor, until 1989 a parastatal industrial concern, known as the South African Iron and Steel Corporation, had formed the backbone of the country's iron and steel industry. It was begun in 1928 with the specific objective of promoting macro-industrial development. Currently producing 84 percent of South Africa's flat steel requirements,[7] the plant in the 1940s was responsible for the establishment of the town of Vanderbijlpark (population: about 40,000 residents in 2004).

The discontent came from a community of people, resident on smallhold-ings adjacent to the steel manufacturing plant, to the west of Vanderbijlpark. In the 1940s a number of large farms were subdivided into some 250 small holdings, as urban and peri-urban settlement gained momentum in the wake of the industrial development. These holdings were subsequently grouped into the peri-urban townships of Drakeville, Steel Valley, Louisrust and Lin-kholm to accommodate people who preferred to live outside the urban con-fines of the industrial town of Vanderbijlpark.

Most of the property owners and tenants were employed at the local steel plant. They acquired the properties in order to be close to their places of work. They tended to be have small-scale part-time farming operations, pri-marily for their own benefit. Schools and congregations of a number of churches were established with a smattering of small commercial retail out-lets to serve the community. At its peak the larger community had a popula-tion of about 2500 people in 500 families. They consisted of the property owners, tenants and unskilled farm labourers.

In later years the agricultural activities dwindled, as a result of the pollu-tion of the subterranean water supplies. Once the first disputes were settled out of court in 2000 many of the properties were vacated by the owners and tenants, leaving behind small pockets of unskilled African laborers. Most of them were then literally forced to move to nearby overpopulated squatters' camps. The land now belonged to Iscor. Some of the properties that had not been purchased by the steel concern were sold at prices, well below their value. A number of these properties were then purchased by Africans who were eager to buy land.

The microhistory of the community, currently in a dispute with Iscor, can thus be interpreted against the backdrop of settlement and demographic trends that had taken place in South Africa's industrial areas since the 1940s. It tells the story of the country's industrial development, the process of urbanization, the racial transformation of the society and, particularly for the purposes of this study, the manner in which environmental awareness reshaped the way in which ordinary people in civil society have started thinking about their living conditions.

In the 1970s, when the property owners started taking the first steps against Iscor, it was the direct result of increased production. Greater steel output intensified the rate of environmental pollution. With the onset of South Africa's border war the country's arms industry was expanding at a rapid rate. Iscor's steel production consequently also increased. There was little the community could do. A state of war prevailed and the government was intent on giving preference to sustained job opportunities and industrial production. In an effort partially to take note of the public concern, the management of the Iscor plant had a number of boreholes drilled and also regularly tested the water in the boreholes of the small holdings. The objective was not necessarily intended to come to the rescue of the residents. It was instead seen as a way of securing their water licensing certification from the national department of water affairs and forestry (DWAF) for extracting water from the Vaal River. Once the steel giant had used its water, it was summarily discarded into the Vaal River.

The Vaal River, since the start of the twentieth century, had been the country's hardest working river.[8] Although not the largest, it was responsible for accommodating, in the Vaal Dam the water supplies to the Witwatersrand, South Africa's premier commercial and industrial region. The South African state's responsible department[9] renewed the certification for a period of forty years as a rule. The understanding was that industrial consumers would conform to the minimum requirements for preventing the unnecessary degradation of the local water resources. There had been times ever since the early 1940s when the regional water utility, Rand Water, took steps against iron and steel industries in the Vaal Triangle to prevent industrial contamination of the water supply in the Barrage area of the Vaal River.[10] By the 1970s the water authorities became more stringent and, as a rule granted certification for water usage, for a period of five years.

THE CRISIS OF 1997

Over the years there had been indications that water pollution levels were increasing. The quality of the groundwater in the vicinity of Iscor was beginning to deteriorate. Also the waterways passing through the Rietspruit into the Vaal River were subjected to severe contamination. This state of affairs reached crisis proportions in 1997 when a resident of a small holding, near the factory, found a piece of tar in his borehole. Iscor conceded that it came from its plant at Vanderbijlpark. The property owner was immediately granted R500,000 in compensation. This motivated other residents to assert pressure on the steel giant to buy them out. They claimed their properties had become literally worthless. At the time banking institutions declined from granting bonds against the security of the residents' properties.

One of the major problems was that the residents had no bulk local water service provider. They were self-reliant, extracting water from boreholes on their properties. Like residents in all rural areas of South Africa, it was customary, that no piped water or sanitation service was available beyond urban municipal boundaries.

In an effort to contend with the imminent crisis Iscor announced that it intended constructing a water purification plant to the value of R183 million. This undertaking put paid to the plans of the community to march in protest against Iscor. Behind the scenes they were however hard at work planning legal action against Iscor.

At the time a report was completed in which evidence was produced that the area to the west of Iscor's plant was not suitable for human habitation. Attempts to have the small holdings declared a disaster area were at first thwarted. Government tended to recognize that Iscor was a major industrial concern. The result was that it was hesitant to assert any pressure in favour of civil concerns about environmental degradation. A major consideration was, without a doubt, the fact the Iscor provided employment for 14,000 workers in the Vaal Triangle. In a region where unemployment had skyrocketed since the start of the 1990s, there were obvious reasons to be slow in taking official steps.

The report on the environment's desiccation was issued on 4 December 1997.[11] Two legal experts on environmental issues had spent two years preparing the report. Then, with the backing of the National Environmental Management Act, as well as reports compiled by Iscor's consultants, the residents and their legal team took the steel concern to court. In terms of the act the plaintiffs had the right of access to the reports.[12]

ISCOR TAKEN TO COURT IN 2000

South Africa's first court case in terms of the new legislation started in the Johannesburg High Court in 2000. The department of water affairs and forestry meanwhile also started with an independent investigation and came to the conclusion that Iscor was responsible for the plume pollution of the subsurface water to the west of its Vanderbijlpark plant. The steel concern was forced by these circumstances to buy up more than 100 smallholdings in the Louisrust area, adjacent to Vanderbijlpark. Other residents of neighboring small holdings at Steel Valley and Drakeville at the time asked the High Court for an interdict against Iscor immediately to stop its desiccation of the environment. They wanted the steel concern to be granted three months for the environmental rehabilitation of the area. The parties spent three days in court when Iscor offered the community of small holdings R33 million in an out of court settlement. Iscor reasoned that if the court's judgement had to be in the favour of the community it would cost at least R1 billion to restore the environment. It also meant that some 9 000 people would literally be unemployed. One of the more negative scenarios was that the steel plant might have to close down. The only practical alternative was for the steel concern to settle out of court. The settlement was a groundbreaking event. Environmental experts were of the opinion that the court case marked a new era in the legal history of pollution in South Africa.[13]

It was pointed out that the manner in which the court case had been conducted was proof that the country's constitution was capable of empowering ordinary people against large concerns, such as Iscor. They could take these industries to court on the grounds of the contamination of the environment. Previously ordinary people had been hesitant to dare follow the "legal route." It simply was too expensive.

The settlement out of court between the residents of the small holdings and Iscor also had its down side. The fact that the court had not made a judgement, meant that there would not be a reference framework for previous cases in terms of the environmental management act, to go by, when similar steps were to be taken in future. Meanwhile legal experts were exploring the potential of the act. One, Mr Duard Barnard, pointed out that the directors, managers and other employees of an industry, also in their private capacity, could be taken to task if they refrained from making disclosures in matters relating to instances where pollution threatened the environment. He based his argument on an interpretation of the act dealing with compliance, enforcement, and protection.[14]

Another important development was that since 1994, in line with the general commitment to environmental conservation in the constitution, various government agencies had taken comprehensive measures to prevent specific forms of environmental desecration. The department of water affairs and forestry, as a result of its greater powers of control over water resources, with the passing of the National Water Act, No 36 of 1998, could take firm actions against transgressions.[15] The law now stipulated that applications for water permits would be subjected to public scrutiny. It formed part of an international trend, particularly in Africa, toward community empowerment and government commitment to effective water resource management, following the Rio Earth summit and the subsequent introduction of Agenda 21.[16] The reports industries had to submit with their applications for water permits had to be compiled by independent consultants. Similar reports, submitted by Iscor since 1983, contained references to large scale pollution. In 1998, the residents of the small holdings used these reports in court against Iscor.

Following the court case Iscor let it be known that it chose to settle out of court because it was intent on managing the environment better. Consequently a consultant was appointed immediately and work started on the compilation of a master plan. A consultant, Dr Ockie Fourie, received R2 million for the preliminary plan. He was subsequently contracted to complete the master plan at a fee of R15 million. The plan was to be submitted to the community in December 2002. At first Iscor refrained from making public the complete report. Only copies of an executive summary of the report were circulated in the public realm as from August 2003. Following considerable pressure by the community the complete report of some 9000 pages was made public. Another two factors forced the company to come into the clear on the matter. There were increasingly rumours that Iscor was illegally extracting water from the river. In some circles it was said that the department of water affairs and forestry were not satisfied with the lack of openness on the master plant.[17] This might have forced the company to make public the report and its contents. Secondly, Iscor's management started fearing for internal information leaks.[18]

In 1998 some of the owners of the small holdings, after receiving payouts, started vacating their properties. Within the space of less than a year more than 1 000 residents faced the prospect of starting a new life, either in the Vaal Triangle or in other parts of South Africa. Locally it caused a socio-economic crisis. Small businesses, a school and the local church had either shut down, or faced imminent closure. As hundreds of houses, built over a period of more than fifty years, were demolished, the local church congregation became too small to afford a permanent minister. The local school started taking in larger numbers of deprived black school children who could not be accommodated in township schools closer to Vanderbijlpark.[19] In the greater region of the Vaal Triangle recessionary conditions set in as a result of Iscor's policy of laying off thousands of workers in the aftermath of privatization. The objective was to turn the concern into a profitable undertaking.[20] Circumstantial evidence also suggests that the company's poor environmental record was partially to blame for the state of affairs.

SECOND COURT CASE

In mid-2001 another group of sixteen property owners in the region resorted to legal steps against Iscor. They now claimed that not only did Iscor pollute their water, the steel concern was in fact responsible for the bouts of illness to which members of the community had been frequently subjected over a period of many years.[21]

Shortly before proceedings started, the case was recalled. A senior scientist had leaked documents on water pollution to the legal representatives of the property owners.[22] This marked the start of a lengthy struggle for the right to use the material in the court case. Because the information had been leaked after the case started, and it thus did not form part of the court proceedings, the material was not considered to be *sub judicae*. Members of the editorial staff of *Beeld*, an Afrikaans daily newspaper in Gauteng, were able to locate the the so-called "whistle blower." He was Dr Pieter van Eeden, a senior environmental scientist, who was responsible for the original report. In an interview with *Beeld*, he disclosed that it was in fact he who had conducted many of the tests. He had particularly concentrated on the quality of run-off water.[23] As whistle blower Van Eeden was entitled to protection in terms of the National Environmental Management Act. Over a period of two years he had monitored the run-off water from Iscor. The water was, as a rule, tested to determine whether it conformed to the requirements of the department of water affairs and forestry. It was crucial to determine if consumers conform to the legal requirements for obtaining water permits from the department.

Van Eeden, who had by then openly sided with the local residents, took Iscor to task for polluting the environment with contaminated water for longer than forty years. He claimed that the firm had also chosen to ignore expert proposals to set matters right.[24] Then Iscor suspended Van Eeden as an employee, following his claims to the effect that the polluted run-off water could well be the cause of cancer when people drank it for extended periods of time.[25] Van Eeden seemed to be in a strong position. He had conducted toxicity tests of Iscor's run-off water at the boreholes on some nearby smallholdings. Some of his claims had even more far reaching implications. Van Eeden maintained that the run-off water flowing down the Rietspruit, later ended up in the Vaal River. This was responsible for surplus deposits of inorganic materials that tended to attack living organisms.[26] As a public water stream which served thousands of people farther down the river, this had even greater implications.

What perhaps exacerbated the strong differences between Van Eeden and Iscor was the fact that the company tended to ignore his opinions. He had earlier submitted his findings to management. He expressed serious concerns about the pollution of the environment and the potential health hazard these conditions posed. Iscor's response was: "We make steel." As the available evidence started flowing, informally into the public realm Van Eeden was prohibited from carrying on with his research. He found himself in a dead-end street. This caused considerable frustration. He was eager to make his contribution as a scientist, but was now prevented from doing so.[27] He also admitted that he had illegally taken a report, on the quality of borehole water, from the desk of a colleague. Also this information was "leaked" out.

Interpretations of the reports of interviews with Van Eeden suggest that his actions were possibly motivated by written undertakings by Iscor, dating back to 1981, in which the steel manufacturer promised the department of water affairs that it would put an end to environmental contamination. Van Eeden, in several interviews and private discussions, claimed nothing had come of these promises. He also had problems with the consultants appointed by Iscor to draw up the master plan. He alleged they were constantly interfering with the run-off water. It was thinned in an effort to sooth the conscience of the department of water affairs and forestry in order to secure the essential water permits. Shortly after his suspension, Van Eeden was recalled and offered a severance package. Iscor, after having threatened him with disciplinary steps, let it be known that it no longer intended firing him. Instead his post was declared redundant and he was notified that he could vacate his post with immediate effect.[28]

In the media, Van Eeden who had meanwhile become a celebrity was reported to have said that in the seventeen months he had been in the employment of Iscor he had frequently been concerned about the malpractices at the steel manufacturing plant. There were high rates of water and air pollution. He had made comprehensive proposals for addressing the problems, but they fell on deaf ears.[29] According to him the company was more than aware of the pollution disaster. It had spent "millions of rands" on consultants, but still the issue had not yet been addressed.[30]

Van Eeden was not alone in his allegations. Dr Mike Whitcutt, a scientist of an independent concern, who had helped Van Eeden with his tests, also was of the opinion that the groundwater of the small holdings adjacent to Iscor's factory constituted "poison" water. It was not suitable for human consumption. Tests had proved, he claimed, that consumers suffered from liver, kidney and bladder problems. This was ascribed to the chemical substances and procedures Iscor used in the steel manufacturing process. Whitcutt had exposed human cells for eighteen-hour periods to the borehole water.[31]

"It looked like a battlefield inside the laboratory test-tubes. Practically all the cells were dead," he said in an interview. His findings were that the water had been polluted by tar, salts, sulphur, battery acid and various types of oil.[32]

Both Van Eeden and Whitcutt had used biotoxicity tests. Up to that point the department of water affairs had primarily conducted tests to check the levels of certain metals and chemicals. Van Eeden claimed that the Rietspruit, in which the water of Iscor flowed into the Vaal River, had been so polluted that only barbells, an indigenous resilient member of the catfish family, could survive. The eye of the stream, which was situated close to the Iscor plant, passed through the small holdings area before it flowed into the Vaal River at Loch Vaal. The fact that Van Eeden was fired from his job attracted considerable publicity and it squarely placed the National Environmental Management Act in the foreground. Technically Van Eeden was entitled to protection against dismissal by his employer.[33] In fact, in terms of the law, managers and employers who are aware of the pollution, but refrained from taking steps, could themselves be fined and even finish up in jail.[34]

For the local residents who had taken up cudgels with Iscor, Van Eeden's high public profile and strong stand, was favorable. Arguments of the steel producer to the effect that the polluted borehole water on the small holding were the result of inferior sanitation on the side of the property owners, did not stand up to the flood of criticism that the company now had to face. The residents merely continued with claims that their boreholes stank and were poisonous.[35] In an effort to maintain a socially responsible image the com-

pany let it be known that millions would be invested in turning its Vanderbijlpark plant into an environmentally friendly operation.[36]

WATER AFFAIRS CLAMPS DOWN

Shortly after the debacle the department of water affairs and forestry let it
be known that Iscor would in future have to apply for a water permit every
18 months, instead of every five years. In commenting on the public furore
on the matter, the government department stated that for fifteen years it had
asserted pressure on Iscor to address their pollution problem. It meant that
since 1986 mere lip service had been paid to the problem. In a show of support for the plight of the local residents, the department also instructed Iscor
to transport, at its own cost, water tankers to the small holdings where pollution, presumably affected local subterranean water supplies. Van Eeden
stated in public that he would forthwith act on behalf of the sixteen owners
of smallholdings who were taking Iscor to court.[37]

Iscor tended to denigrate Van Eeden's reports, by stating that the investigations were of a temporary and preliminary nature.[38]

In view of the World Summit on Sustainable Development (WSSD) that
was scheduled to take place in South Africa in August 2002, one of the major
trade unions in South Africa, Solidarity,[39] tabled an environmental manifesto. The union was determined to get all industries that were known to be
responsible for environmental pollution to become signatories to the manifesto. This "green paper" implied that the industries would enter into an
agreement with their local communities to ensure that the environment
would be respected, according to Mr. Dirk Hermann, a spokesperson for the
union. The union clearly had Iscor in mind. It was, after all, the union with
the largest membership at the steel manufacturing concern.[40] What was interesting, at the time was that this particular trade union, which had been well-
known for its rightwing leanings in the previous dispensation, had now
taken up an environmental cause that tended to cross over racial boundaries.
People of all racial orientations were affected by the pollution threat.

It was in particular the outcry of people of colour who shed some light
on the critical proportions that the crisis had taken on. In November 2001
Mr. Captain Ntele of Linkholm, told the media:

Every swig of water we take from our borehole is a step nearer to our death. . . .
The environment is polluted and we are now being left to our own devices to
die. We cannot drink our water. We shout but no one listens to us.[41]

In March 2002 South Africa's legal aid board took the unusual step of providing the community with legal aid to the tune of R2 million to take their

case against Iscor to court. At the time it was described as a groundbreaking case.[42] It is still not completed. The merits of the case have, after two years, not been heard. Technically the legal representatives of the community can not stand up to the highly skilled legal representatives of Iscor. They (Iscor's representatives) apparently went abroad to see how this kind of case is done in the United States. In many respects the case at the time came close to being a blueprint of the movie Erin Brockovich.[43] However, although the Hollywood version of an environmental crisis could well serve as a source inspiration, the real life experiences in South Africa proved to be considerably stranger than fiction.

Despite clampdowns another document had leaked out to the press on 13 August 2003. It was in the form of an email letter to all people concerned with the master plan of Iscor and was marked "Strictly Confidential." In the document members of the management team were asked by Dr Fourie to help centralize all information. Nothing was to be left at Iscor's plant in Vanderbijlpark. All test results had to be shredded after it had been submitted.[44] This was a clear indication that the company's environmental consultant was now trying to mop up all potential traces of potential evidence.

When the contents of the email were made public, there was an outcry. The property owners and local residents argued that Iscor was in the process of closing down potential sources of public information. Moreover, in the factory itself, it appeared as if management had become afraid of employees "leaking out" information. On the surface it appeared as if the company was justified in its attempts at consolidating the information before making an official disclosure before issuing the complete master plan for public scrutiny. However, when the chief executive officer of Iscor's Vanderbijlpark plant resigned three days after the information was leaked to the media, more critical questions were being raised.[45] Also the department of water affairs started asking questions about the contents of the master plan that had apparently been completed but not made public. This led to the document being made available to the public.

MOUNTING PRESSURE ON ISCOR

Ever since 1997 there had been concerns about the apparent unwillingness of Iscor to respond to pollution allegations. When in August 2002 Iscor released its annual report, it coincided with the World Summit on Sustainable Development that was being held in Johannesburg. Many environmental agencies, and in particular some of the leading nongovernmental organizations, considered this to be a good opportunity for taking steps. Consequently representatives of international NGO's, such as Greenpeace,

CorpWatch, and groundWork collaborated and held a protest march at Iscor's Vanderbijlpark plant.[46]

Iscor at the time, together with another nineteen other South African companies, became a signatory to a green paper of the trade union Solidarity and informed the public that it intended, in terms of its master plan, to recycle the run-off water before it entered the Vaal River. At the signing ceremony, Iscor's CEO, Mr. Louis van Niekerk, gave some perspective on the problems the company had faced since 1994. He stressed that subsidies from the state fell away and they had to restructure. Previously it had not been required of them to take precautions in respect of the environment. They were now under mounting pressure to do so. The company was at pains to give an indication that they wanted to set matters right. Van Niekerk told the media:

> What we want to do now, is to go on with our production without causing damage to the environment or the people.[47]

Mr. Phaldi Kalam, spokesperson for the company at the time, said Iscor inherited the pollution:

> What we have at Vanderbijlpark, is the result of bad practice in the past. We now want to turn the ship around. We won't say we are sorry, but we say we want to rectify the situation.[48]

In many respects Iscor, at the time, came out of a severe public image crisis with flying colors. It had the decency to acknowledge that there was a crisis that had to be addressed. The fact that they had come into the open provided them with a favorable platform from which to operate. However, the company was soon again under fire for refusing to release the full contents of the master plan. Iscor argued that it could not do so in view of the litigation in the High Court. The company also maintained that, as a result of its technical nature, the master plan would be incomprehensible for the community. It did however in July 2003 release a summary of the report.[49] In the introduction Dr Fourie of Ockie Fourie Toxicologists, who was the leader of the project, stated that it had taken 30 months to complete the investigation.

In the summary it was pointed out that for evey ton of steel Iscor produced required 7kl of water. The factory on average consumed 4,4 million tonnes of iron ore, 2,5 million tonnes of coal, 0,4 million tonnes of lime, dolomite, binding agents and alloys annually. The factory annually produced three million tonnes of steel.[50]

The consultant pointed out that a massive waste dump situated in the northwestern part of its property, and a so-called Dam 10 where polluted water was stored, posed the greatest problems. An estimated 1,2 million tonnes of potentially dangerous materials and slick were deposited at these sites.

Residents adjacent to the Iscor site complained that conditions deteriorated in rainy weather when their groundwater was saturated with polluted rainwater. The toxic materials in the dump then tended to be compounded when it siphoned into the ground with the rainwater. In the report it was noted:

> The disposal site can not be closed and rehabilitated at this point in time.[51]

Furthermore, it was difficult to locate an alternative site. Over the short term there were attempts at watering the dump to prevent air pollution, but then the groundwater was polluted. Dam 10, the other problem area, was not provided with a lining. It was situated on top of a massive geological fault which extended a distance of two kilometers into a rock formation.

It was pointed out:

> The geological contract . . . represent(s) potential geological flaws in terms of the development of waste management facilities.[52]

The report stressed that Iscor's plant was situated in close proximity to wetlands. The Iscor plant itself had been built on top of a dolomite area. This caused water pollution, as a result of the industrial activities, which had a vast impact on the environment.[53]

In private discussions local residents of the nearby small holdings maintained that their major point of criticism against the summary of the master plan was that nowhere was it admitted that the industry had been responsible for polluting the groundwater. There were mere references to the "potential" pollution of groundwater.

The report summary also explained that the water that Iscor used came primarily from the Vaal dam. It was released on the western side into the Rietspruit and later flowed into the Vaal River. To the east of Iscor the water was released into the Leeuspruit, flowing into the Vaal River at Vanderbijlpark. Water was extracted directly from the Vaal River. The report summary also pointed out:

> The Vaaldam water qualities are relatively good, while water obtained from the Vaal River varies in quality, but is generally poor.[54]

Iscor claimed responsibility for only 30 percent of the pollution of the Rietspruit. The remaining 70 percent was ascribed to local farming activities, informal housing, and mining activities. The industry admitted that the tar deposits in the notorious Dam 10 posed a major problem. It was reported in the summary that:

> Inorganic contamination plumes exist beyond the works perimeter in sections to the west and east of the works. . . . "The distance of impact beyond the works

perimeter in the impacted section varies between 300 meters and 700 meters on the western boundary. Secondly inorganic plumes exist in the ares between the canal (Rietkuil) and the La Mont Park and Louisrus Small Holdings. All these plumes have reached a steady state. . . . This is because irrigation practices . . . have been stopped. The main contaminants of concern are Cl (chloride), SO4 (sulphate), Ca (Calcium), Mg (magnesium). . . . For the eastern catchment, the analyses indicated that a number of elements exceed the water qualities as stated in the IVS (Iscor Vanderbijlpark Works) water licence. Specific reference is made to iron, sulphates, calcium and magnesium . . . The situation is being addressed and will change significantly after zero effluent discharge (ZED) is implemented in 2005."[55]

Furthermore:

Generally, it can be stated that the degree of groundwater contamination is such that it poses an unacceptable risk to the environment within the IVS perimeter (if available for consumption).The risk in this regard is a result of inorganic, and to a much lesser extent organic contamination.[56]

The consultant proposed that the rehabilitation programme for the area had to be conducted in twenty steps. One of the first steps towards giving substance to the plans was when work started on the coke furnaces. Later phases in the proposed rehabilitation made provision for a "groundwater abstraction system" that was necessary. It implies sucking out the plume of polluted water. At the time the consultants were of the opinion that the work could cost in excess of R1,3 billion.

In August 2004 the community seemed, for a short while, to be in the process of reviving their contest with the steel concern. Prof. Jacklyn Cock of the University of the Witwatersrand told a meeting of local residents of Steel Valley, Louis Rust, Rosashof, Boipatong, that she was prepared to do research and take up their cause. Plans had also been put in place to get some support from the United States of America to try and get some international legal standing for the case.[57]

The meeting that had been attended by almost 100 residents was noted for the fact that South Africans of all racial orientations showed solidarity in an environmental matter that directly affected their lives. Representatives of European environmental groups were also at the meeting. They indicated that their attention had been given to the issue and it would be investigated further.[58] Adv. Margaret Victor, the legal representative of the group, who was behind moves to get the case into an American court of justice, told the meeting that tests had been conducted on 100 of the 700 remaining residents of the area. Preliminary findings suggested that almost 40 percent of the people tested had traces of the heavy metal, cadmium, in their blood. There were also various strains of cancer and serious kidney problems that had been traced in the health conditions of local children.[59]

On the surface it appeared, by the end of 2004, as if there was still some life in the initiative aimed at securing an outcome for the local residents. However there were indications that many of the local residents had been left devastated and helpless in the face of a crisis that only periodically was brought to the attention of the world outside the immediate vicinity of the small holdings close to the steel factory. Their plight seemed futile. The company had given the undertaking, in the media, that it intended spending R1 billion on the conservation of the local environment.[60]

CONCLUSION

The saga of Iscor, the community and the issue of the polluted water continues. It is difficult, at this point in time to predict what will be the outcome. What does appear to be a distinct issue is the fact that the steel concern, no matter how it tries to respond by setting things right, will finish up being criticised. This could, in future, lead to further legal claims by the community of residents on the small holdings near the Vanderbijlpark plant. In the process the environment is suffering and continuously subjected to further degradation. At a regular public forum of the department of water affairs, where members of the community and Iscor were present, meetings tended to finish up with arguments and sustained acrimony. This led to the collapse of constructive lines of communications. Consequently little was done to find a common ground for constructive collaboration to start setting matters right.

The mutual distrust between the parties, fed persistent fears and uncertainties. It affected the performance of the steel concern. It also affected the lives of the local residents.

By the end of 2004 there was an intense sense of distrust amongst some members of the community. Several persons in private discussions, said they doubted if it would be possible to work toward a favorable outcome after the Indian billionaire, Mr Lakshmi Mittal, operating from London, stepped in to secure control of Iscor for his company, LNM, in June 2004.[61] The fact that Ispat Iscor,[62] as the transformed firm is presently still called, was no longer in South African hands, left them with a sense of uncertainty. It was argued that Mittal, who has built up the world's second largest steel manufacturing conglomerate, would not hesitate to press for higher profits.[63] This could come at a cost for the environment. For a considerable time the demand for steel in all parts of the world had increased considerably. Old steel plants were once again being brought into operation to meet the demand.[64] This was considered to be detrimental to environmental restorative initiatives in Vanderbijlpark.

A further consideration that frequently crops up in discussions on Mittal's stryle of management, is that he is known for having bought up underperforming steel plants in all parts of the world. In order to bring about a recovery, purchasing costs are cut and workers are laid off. The plants are then operated at maximum capacity for profit.[65] In some cases plants were summarily closed down, following community pressure on Mittal's company. Some local residents feared that Mittal might follow the same strategy at Vanderbijlpark. Others argued that it would at least level the playing field for a more clean environmental future.

When, toward the end of 2004, some of the senior management staff and non-executive figureheads resigned, to seek greener pastures in South Africa's boisterous business sector, further gossip was rife. Local residents took note of speculation in the media that there were indications of a "brain drain" at Iscor.[66] It was argued that the company would not keep its promise to restore the environment. A new management team would not be sufficiently sensitive to undertakings, given in a previous dispensation.

Meanwhile the river, situated in a picturesque region of South Africa's Gauteng Province, has been relegated to a source of pollution. It is disconcerting to think that matters could have been so different had there only been willingness for constructive engagement in the interest of a healthy environment. Perhaps one solution would be for the parties to concede that the National Environmental Management Act is currently not effective. It could well become more useful, if for example, Iscor is given an opportunity, without being constantly harassed by the local residents, to start with the cleaning up process. It would then be necessary for the residents, in conjunction with the steel concern's environmentalists, to start with an independent monitoring process. Then, when pollution has been reduced to the minimum, the law can be acknowledged for the authority it deserves. It would mean that the residents of the small holdings and Iscor would have to start a process of constant communications in which both parties undertake to work together for the benefit of the society. Whether the parties to the environmental dispute would be prepared to agree to this type of arrangement remains to be seen.

NOTES

1. For the full text of the law see, SA Government, *National Environmental Management Act,* No 107 of 1998 at http://www.polity.org.za/html/govdocs/legislation/1998/act98–107.html

2. P. Devereaux and own correspondent, "Environment Now a Budding Political Issue in SA" in *The Star,* 1989.10.14.

3. P. Steyn, "Environmental Management in South Africa, 1972–1992" in *Historia*, 46(1), May 2001: 45–49.

4. See *Constitution of Republic of South Africa 1996, Act No. 108 of 1996*, Section 24, in which it is stipulated that everyone has the right to an environment that is not harmful to their health or well-being. See http://www.polity.org.za/html/govdocs/constitution/ saconst.html?rebookmark = 1 and http://www.icon.co.za/~embo/008/00801027.htm

5. For the purposes of this study the name Iscor is used for the iron and steel company responsible for the steel plant in Vanderbijlpark. Subsequent to its privatisation the firm underwent a number of name changes. The most recent has been Ispat Iscor. In 2004, it was announced that in future it be known as Mittal Steel South Africa. A spokesperson for the company informed the authors on 12 January 2005 that the new name was still subject to the approval of shareholders. See C. Lourens, "Ispat Iscor to change name to Mittal Steel SA" in *Business Day*, 2004.12.22 at

6. E. Tempelhoff, "Eienaars van hoewes wil Iscor hof toe vat oor water" in *Beeld*, 1997.08.09.

7. See Iscor Limited at South African Iron and Steel Institute, http://www.inter-data.co.za/saisi/portal/index.asp?inc = iscor

8. JWN Tempelhoff, "Time and the River: Observations on the Vaal River as Source of Water to the Witwatersrand 1903–24" in *Historia*, 46(1), May 2001: 248–49.

9. Until 1956, the government department responsible for water, was the department of irrigation. With the passing of a new water act in that year, it became the department of water affairs. In 1994 it became known as the department of water affairs and forestry (DWAF).

10. JWN Tempelhoff, *The Substance of Ubiquity: Rand Water 1903–2003* (Report on the centenary history of Rand Water, Kleio Publishers, Vanderbijlpark, 2003), 184–87.

11. E. Tempelhoff, "Iscor voor stok oor waterbesoedeling" in *Beeld*, 1997.12.05.

12. *National Environmental Management Act*, No 107 of 1998, Section 7(2).SA Government, *National Environmental Management Act*, No 107 of 1998 at http://www.polity.org.za/html/govdocs/legislation/1998/act98-107.html, Act

13. E. Tempelhoff, "Besoedelwet maan individue: Maatskappydirekteurs,-werkers kan aan die pen ry" in *Beeld*, 2001.12.04.

14. SA Government, *National Environmental Management Act*, No 107 of 1998, Section 7(1), at http://www.polity.org.za/html/govdocs/legislation/1998/act98-107.html; E.Tempelhoff, "Besoedelwet maan individue; Maatskappydirekteurs,-werkers kan aan die pen ry" in *Beeld*, 2001.12.04.

15. J. Glazewski, *Environmental Law in South Africa* (Butterowrths, Durban, 2000), 523–31, 764–68.

16. S. Zondi, "Taking Its Head Out of the Water: An Appraisal of Africa's Water Challenges" in *AISA Electronic monograph*, 2003.07.27 at http://www.ai.org.za/electronic_ monograph.asp?ID = 7

17. Personal disclosure Mr. Marius Keet, deputy director for water affairs and forestry, 2003.10.21.

18. This aspect is discussed in greater detail below.

19. E. Tempelhoff, "'Gees van agteruitgang' heers in Louisrus" in *Beeld*, 2002.11.30.

20. J. Tempelhoff, "Armes in 'n maalstroom: Vanderbijl se sorge belig 'n groter problem" in *Beeld*, 2002.08.15; E. Tempelhoff, "Verpletterde droom: Vanderbijl 'n vuisvoos dorp weens globalisering" in *Beeld*, 2001.12.14.

21. E. Tempelhoff, "Iscor verras in hoewe-saak" in *Beeld*, 2001.11.21.

22. Ibid.

23. E. Tempelhoff, "Geskorste Iscor-ekoloog sê hy veg terug teen onbillikheid" in *Beeld*, 2001.11.30.

24. Ibid.

25. E. Tempelhoff, "Kanker water, Iscor besoedel al 40 jaar sonder om reg te maak" in *Beeld*, 2001.11.30.

26. E.Tempelhoff, "Kanker water, Iscor besoedel al 40 jaar sonder om reg te maak," Beeld, 2001/11/30

27. Ibid.

28. E. Tempelhoff, "Iscor bied Van Eeden 'n pakket; nou's ek aan hoewemense se kant" in *Beeld*, 2001.12.04.

29. Van Eeden had been interviewed by representatives of the printed media. He was also given special prominence in the investigative television program "Carte Blanche" of the Mnet broadcasting channel in Africa.

30. E. Tempelhoff, "Kanker water, Iscor besoedel al 40 jaar sonder om reg te maak" in *Beeld*, 2001.11.30; E.Tempelhoff, "Geskorste Iscor-ekoloog sê hy veg terug teen onbillikheid" in Beeld, 2001.11.30.

31. E. Tempelhoff, "Iscor 'vergif' grondwater: Proefbuise in toetse 'lyk soos slag-veld'" in *Beeld*, 2001.11.30.

32. Ibid.

33. SA Government, *National Environmental Management Act*, No 107 of 1998, Section 7(4) at http://www.polity.org.za/html/govdocs/legislation/1998/act98–107.html.

34. E. Tempelhoff, "Besoedelwet maan individue: maatskappydirekteurs, werkers kan aan die pen ry" in *Beeld*, 2001.12.04.

35. E. Tempelhoff, "Vuil water nie Iscor se skuld' swak infratruktuur, riolering geblameer vir problem,e by hoewes" in *Beeld*, 2001.08.30.

36. Ibid.

37. E. Tempelhoff, "Iscor bied Van Eeden 'n pakket: nou's ek aan hoewemense se kant" in *Beeld*, 2001.12.04.

38. This was extensively argued during the court proceedings of 2002; E. Tempelhoff, "Iscor sê verslae kan nie teen hom gebruik word nie" in *Beeld*, 2003.02.19.

39. Previously known as the Mynwerkersunie.

40. E. Tempelhoff, "MWU-Solidariteit teken omgewingsmanifes" in *Beeld*, 2002.01.22.

41. Translated from a quote in a news report. See E Tempelhoff, "'Elke sluk 'n tree nader aan dood': nóg hoewebewoners takel Iscor in hof oor besoedeling" in *Beeld*, 2001.11.22.

42. E. Tempelhoff, "R2m. vir regstryd teen Iscor: raad help kleinhoewe-gemeenskap in keerpuntsaak. 2002/ 3/28 Beeld

43. See Universal Studios 2000, *Erin Brockovich* at http://www.erinbrockovich .com/flasher.html

44. E. Tempelhoff, "Iscor feite vernietig" in *Beeld*, 2003.08.15.

45. E. Tempelhoff, "Ondersoek geëis oor Iscor-hoe skielik waai" in *Beeld*, 2003.08.23.

46. E. Tempelhoff "Groepe betoog saam teen Iscor-besoedeling" in *Beeld*, 2002.08.23.

47. E. Tempelhoff, "Iscor teken belofte om omgewing te verbeter" in *Beeld*, 2002.08.29.

48. Ibid.

49. The rest of the report was made public later in the year.

50. Iscor, Vanderbijlpark Steel, Environmental master plan: executive report, July 2003, 10.

51. Ibid., 20.

52. Ibid., 11.

53. Ibid. 11.

54. Ibid., p.13.

55. Ibid., 16.

56. Ibid., 18.

57. E. Tempelhoff, "Groep wat gegrief is, gaan Iscor in VSA pak: Vanderbijlparkers, 'het geen vertroue in SA howe'" in *Beeld*, 2004.08.02.

58. Both authors of this chapter attended the meeting and spoke informally with the people attending the meeting.

59. E. Tempelhoff, "Groep wat gegrief is, gaan Iscor in VSA pak: Vanderbijlparkers, 'het geen vertroue in SA howe'" in *Beeld*, 2004.08.02.

60. Ibid.

61. L. Claasen, "Mittal's LNM edges up to a controlling stake in Iscor" in *Business Day*, 2004.06.11; A. Visser, "Iscor is nou amptelik LNM s'n" in *Beeld*, 2004.06.09, 19 at http://152.111.1.251/argief/berigte/beeld/2004/06/09/B1/19/ 03.html; Also see Anon., "Lakshmi N. Mittal" in *Steeleye* at http://www.steelprofiles.com/ceo/pro files/mittal1.htm

62. Ispat means steel in Sanskrit.

63. P. Marsh, "LNM's Mittal Is a Reluctant Global Mogul," in *Business Day*, 2004.04.22 at http://www.bday.co.za/bday/content/direct/1,3523,1598968–6078– 0,00.html

64. J. de Lange, "Iscor laat sak afdankbyl" in *Beel*, 2004.08.18, 1 at http:// 152.111.1.251/argief/berigte/beeld/2004/08/18/F1/01/02.html

65. Anon., "Lakshmi N. Mittal" in *Steeleye* at http://www.steelprofiles.com/ceo/ profiles/mittal1.htm

66. L. Claasen, "Governance Cloud Hovers as Mittal Fails to Stem Brain Drain," in *Business Day*, 2004.12.31 at http://www.bday.co.za/bday/content/direct/1,3523, 1780623–6078–0,00.html; Anon., "Groot uittog van senior mense by Ispat Iscor" in *SakleBeeld*, 2004.12.31, 17; Anon., "Louis van Niekerk bedank by Iscor" in *Sake-Beeld*, 2004.12.24, 22.

Epilogue

Jeffrey K. Stine

Ensuring or restoring environmental quality represents one of the greatest challenges confronting humanity in the twenty-first century. The implications of human-induced environmental degradations are wide-ranging. Some directly endanger human health. Others threaten to undermine basic ecological systems over the course of decades or generations.

But what is the meaning of environmental quality without equity? As the chapters in this volume so vividly discuss, matters of social justice are essential to the debate over the environment. Understanding how to achieve equity requires also understanding failures of equity, and that is a task to which environmental history can contribute. The essays assembled by Sylvia Hood Washington, Paul C. Rosier and Heather Goodall, point both to universalities among environmental injustices and to important differences among how nations, cultures, social organizations, and activists have responded in the past. The essays emphasize the complexity of environmental injustices and the close association each case has with its physical setting, community history, and political economy. Variables and contingencies matter. Yet, the essays also point to certain unifying themes: the corrosive impact of racism and indifference; the progressive contributions of women and community action; and the growing unification of the pursuits for civil rights and environmental quality.

To examine this perplexing social problem, the contributors use the lens of individual and community memory. They demonstrate how perceptions range from the highly personal to the communal and national level. They highlight the fact that the currents run far back into human history, even if the environmental justice *movement* is but a generation old.

In their examinations of the origins of environmental injustices, authors explore the plight of groups such as Native Americans, African Americans, and indigenous populations in Africa and Asia Pacific. The 500-year history of Native Americans' encounters with Europeans, for example, points to the diverse and complex range of environmental injustices imposed by settlers. Often separated from their traditional lands and resources, or forced to deal with degraded lands and resources, Native American women, we now recognize, played an instrumental role in the fight for environmental justice. A world away, in the New South Wales town of Brewarrina, other types of "racialized landscapes" were shaped by forced segregation, as a river was used as a racial divide, with Aborigines relegated to the lower lying, flood-prone areas.

Many of the essays invite readers to focus new attention on the central role that women have played in these fights for environmental equity. Historians have often neglected gender biases and gender-based abuses, as well as the contributions of women in advancing the cause of environmental justice. Women have served disproportionately as leaders, organizers, researchers, and strategists in these struggles, just as they have often shouldered a disproportionate share of risks. As in many areas of life, however, a combination of forces—a tendency of men to promote themselves; a tendency of women to be less self-aggrandizing; a gender bias that prompts the media to highlight, and the public to seek, male leadership roles—have led those not closely involved with the movement to miss this element.

Another textual theme in these essays is the role that memory, and especially community history, plays in framing the political debates. Many of the authors tackle specific case studies: the Lee-Seville community in Cleveland, Ohio, where middle-class African Americans waged a decades-long struggle "for sustainable space" and city and regional planning for "urban renewal" in New York. There is also attention to the environmental injustices suffered by the "unsheltered homeless," using evidence provided by the people themselves. Such personal accounts help to raise our consciousness about the issues affecting particular groups, as well as the cross-cutting aspects of these far-flung struggles.

The temporal and geographic expanse of this book deepens our understanding of the origins and consequences of environmental injustices, just as its concrete examples and theoretical insights suggest new areas for study. Although it ventures no solution to this global problem, its authors make an invaluable contribution by heightening our awareness of the looming confrontation between two powerful moral imperatives—preserving and protecting the natural environment and ensuring the survival, health, and dignity of human populations—and the need for an inclusive strategy to address it.

Maps

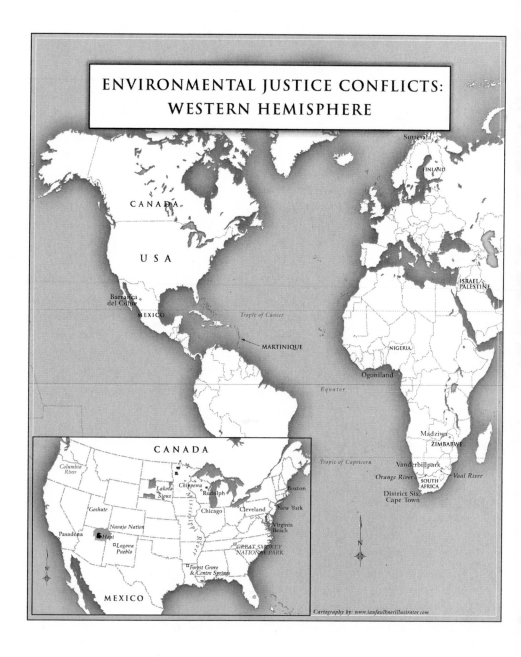

ENVIRONMENTAL JUSTICE CONFLICTS:
WESTERN HEMISPHERE

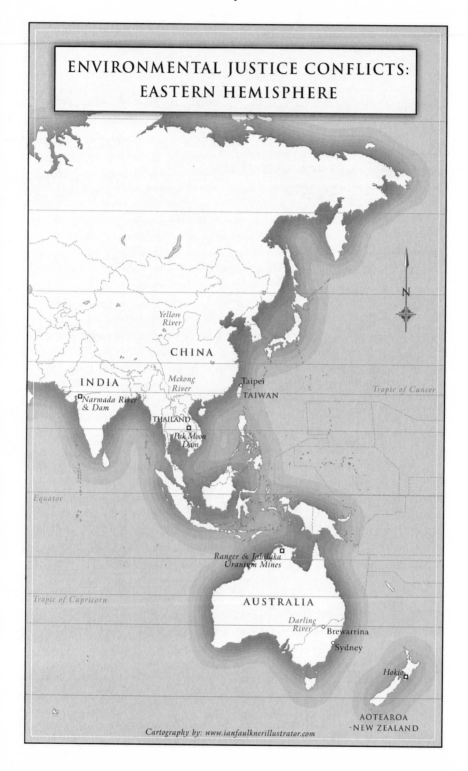

ENVIRONMENTAL JUSTICE CONFLICTS:
EASTERN HEMISPHERE

Yellow River

CHINA

INDIA   *Mekong River*   Taipei
                                       TAIWAN
Narmada River
& Dam

THAILAND

Pak Moon
Dam

Tropic of Cancer

Equator

Ranger & Jabiluka
Uranium Mines

Tropic of Capricorn   AUSTRALIA

Darling River   Brewarrina
                         Sydney

Hokio

AOTEAROA
-NEW ZEALAND

Cartography by: www.ianfaulknerillustrator.com

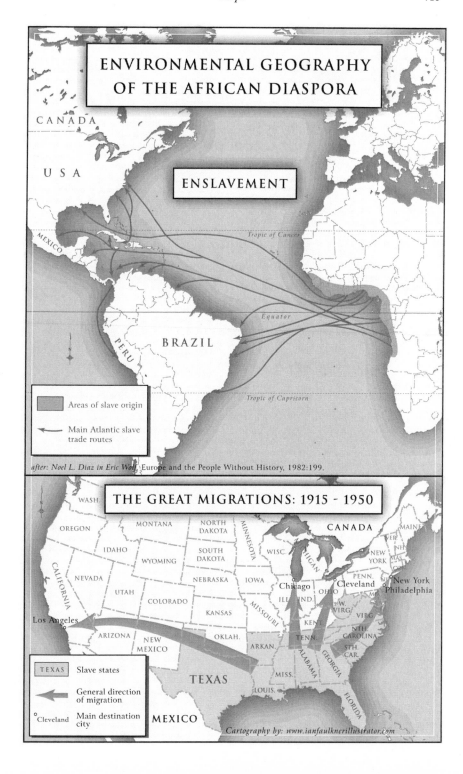

ENVIRONMENTAL GEOGRAPHY
OF THE AFRICAN DIASPORA

ENSLAVEMENT

CANADA

USA

MEXICO

Tropic of Cancer

PERU

BRAZIL

Equator

Tropic of Capricorn

Areas of slave origin

Main Atlantic slave trade routes

after: Noel L. Diaz in Eric Wolf, Europe and the People Without History, 1982:199.

THE GREAT MIGRATIONS: 1915 - 1950

WASH
OREGON
MONTANA
NORTH DAKOTA
MINNESOTA
CANADA
MAINE
IDAHO
SOUTH DAKOTA
WISC.
NEW YORK
CALIFORNIA
NEVADA
WYOMING
NEBRASKA
IOWA
Chicago
PENN.
Cleveland
New York
Philadelphia
UTAH
COLORADO
ILL.
IND
OHIO
W. VIRG.
VIRG.
Los Angeles
ARIZONA
NEW MEXICO
KANSAS
MISSOURI
KENT.
NTH CAROLINA
OKLAH.
TENN.
STH. CAR.
ARKAN.
GEORGIA
ALABAMA
TEXAS
Slave states
MISS.
General direction of migration
TEXAS
LOUIS.
Cleveland
Main destination city
MEXICO
FLORIDA

Cartography by: www.ianfaulknerillustrator.com

Index

1968 Fair Housing Act (see housing)

abolition, 228, 232–233, 235–236
Aboriginal (Australian), 256–269
Aboriginal Land Rights Act, 285, 287
abortion, 19
Action Committee for a Toxic Free Sydney, 276
Adams-William, Lydia, 23, 24, 25
African Americans, 20–21, 31, 39, 43, 55–68, 97–107, 112–115, 118–119, 127–129, 132–134, 136, 139, 140, 195–205
  Africa (or Africans), 56–60
  Civil War, 63
  Great Depression, 62, 65
  Reconstruction, 57, 64
  slavery (see Slaves and Slavery)
Agent Orange, 15
agricultural methods, 355, 357
Agricultural Street landfill, 118–119
anti-drugs campaign, 346, 352
anti-uranium activist, 292 (see also Native Americans)
Apartheid, 80, 84, 88
Artaud, Antonin, 252
Asian financial crisis, 348
Asian Pacific Environmental Network, 12
Asmus, Peter, 47

ASSAUPAMAR, 227
Assembly of the Poor, 347, 350–352
assimilation, 225–228, 231–232, 304
asthma, 173–175, 177–178
Atlantic Ocean, 184
Audobon Society, 24
Australian Conservation Foundation (ACF), 273

Back Bay National Wildlife Refuge, 184–186, 188
Bangkok, 348, 351–352
Bantustans, 82, 84
Barlow, Rebecca, 36
Barwon River, 255
Bayview Hunters Point, 118–119
Beder and McDonell, 272–274
Bennett, Kelly, 163
Berry, Wendell, 146
Bertell, Rosalie, 29
Bétonisation, 226, 230, 238
biography of place, 152
birds, 24–25
Black Catholics, 196–201, 204
Black Mesa, 41–42
Black Protestants, 197
Bloomberg, Michael, 6,
Boise Cascade Co., 247, 249
Boldt Decision, 39
Boldt, George, 39

borders, 75, 81, 82, 86, 87, 90, 91, 258, 262–263
Boston, Massachusetts, 144–154
Boxill, Bernard, 106
Boy Scouts of America, 42
breastfeeding, 19
Brewarrina, 258–261, 263, 265–269
Bronx Lebanon Medical Waste Incincerator, 171, 177
Bryson City, North Carolina, 158, 160–163
Bullcreek, Margene, 46
Bunch, Lonnie, 202
Burdette, Mrs. Robert, 23
Bustillos, Edwin, 250–251

California Federation of Women's Clubs, 25
Cancer Alley, 119
carceral archipelago, 116
Carney, Judith, 21
Caribbean Discourse, 228–229, 231, 233
Carson, Rachel, 26
causality, 109, 119–120
Cheney, Jan, 28
Cerrell Associates report, 5
Chamoiseau, Patrick, 228, 230, 232–233, 235
Chatham County report, 5
Chem-Nuclear Systems, Inc., 5
Chevron Nigeria Limited, 371, 375
Chiang Mai, 348, 351
Chicago, Illinois, 56, 57, 68, 101, 104
Chicago Historical Society, 201–204
China, 331–341
China Youth Development Foundation, 332, 334–336, 338, 340–341
Chippewa, 39–40
Choonhavan, General Chatichai, 346
Citizens Against Nuclear Trash (CANT), 118
Citizens Against Wilderness (CAW), 163–164
Civil Rights (Movement), 66–67
class, 275, 282
clean air, 173–175, 177

Cleveland, Ohio, 127–140
    City Council, 134, 136–139
    Cleveland Metropolitan Housing Authority (CMHA), 131–137, 139–140
    Zerubbabel Evans, 139, 140
    Arthur R Johnson, 129
    Carl B. Stokes, 128, 133, 134, 135, 136, 138, 140
    Cleveland Plain Dealer, 133, 138
    Cleveland Press, 134
    [*Cleveland*] *Call and Post*, 134
    Lee-Seville, 135–140
    Lee-Seville View, 137
    Miles Heights (The Village), 128–130, 135, 137–138
    Clarence Thompson, 135–136, 138
Cleveland, Ohio, environment, 129–131, 133–140
    Upton Sinclair, 138
    The Jungle, 138
    Ward 30, 135–137
    sewers, 135–136, 138
    sewage, 127, 129–131, 133, 138–140
    slums, 134, 135
Clinton, President William J., 12, 14
Cold War, 26, 42
collective memory, 331
collective rights, 220
Columbia River Inter-tribal Fisheries Commission, 40
commodification of water and sacred sites (Finland), 209–210, 219–220
Communities for a Better Environment, 31
community, 189, 190
Community-Based Planning, 177–178
community environment, 312–313
Community Right to Know law, 12
Confiant, Raphaël, 228, 230
confrontations, 258
conservation, 356–359, 361–362
constitutional rights, 213–214
consultation, 209–210, 212, 214–215, 217
containment, 112, 114–116, 118

contamination (of land and water), 42–43, 279–281, 293–294
contour ridges, 357, 361, 363–364
Copper Canyon, 245–246, 253
CorpWatch, 400
Council of Energy Resource Tribes (CERT), 47
Creole, 225–226, 228–232, 235, 237
Crocker, Marion, 24, 25
Cronon, William, 18
cultural and environmental assessment, 210–211, 213, 215, 220
cultural authenticity, 314, 321–322
cultural heritage, 336–337
cultural identity, 332, 334
cultural memory, 337, 339, 341
cultural reassertion, 269
cultural rights, 209–210, 212–214
cultural/spiritual heritage, 210, 214, 218, 220
cultural tension, 339
culture, 183, 187, 189–191
curfew, 258–259
Cypress trees, 190

dams, 75, 87, 88
Darling River, 255, 263
Davis, Cyprian, 196–197
Days, Angela, 10
Department of Water Affairs and Forestry (DWAF), 392
Departmentalization, 225, 228, 230–231
development, 372, 374–377, 379–380, 382–383
Dine Citizens Against Ruining Our Environment (Dine Care), 43, 44, 47
dioxin, 13–15
discourse, 183, 186, 187, 190–192, 281–282
  discourse analysis, 281
  discourse theory, 281
displacement, 75, 79–83, 88, 91
dispossession, 75–79, 82, 91
Douglas, Frederick, 7
Drakeville, 391, 393
Dubois, W. E. B., 57, 64–65

Dusk of Dawn, An Essay Toward an Autobiography of a Race Concept, 64
ducks, 187, 188, 191

Eastern Navajo Dine Against Uranium Mining, 46
ecocritical, 227, 239
ecofeminism, 26, 27
ecotourism, 188
eel boxes, 301
eels, 301, 308
effluent, 299, 304–308
Electricity Generating Authority of Thailand (EGAT), 347–349, 352
Energy Resources of Australia Ltd [ERA], 286, 291–292
entrapment, 75, 82–83
environmental activism, 271–272, 282
environmental alarmism, 357
environmental coalitions, 97–107
environmental movement, 271–272, 281–282
environmental justice movement, 4–5, 17–18, 31, 42–44, 56, 67–68, 105–106, 111, 128, 141, 195–201
environmental justice research, 109–110, 120
environmental nationalism, 75, 85, 88
environmental racism, 43–45, 47, 57, 101, 109, 111, 117, 119–120, 127, 133, 171
environmentalism, 157, 271–274, 281–282
Eply Associates report, 5
equity, 282
  procedural equity, 110
ethnic diversity, 275, 278
ethnic minority politics, 372–375, 377, 381–383
ethnic Taiwanese, 319–320
ethno-national, 316, 320–322
exclusionary zoning, 101
Exxon Corp., 41

fallow, 359, 362–363
fermented corn, 302

Fernando, Andy, 40
Festival of the Fisheries, 257, 266
Finnish Constitution, 213
First Amendment (U.S. Constitution), 165
First People of Color Environmental Leadership Summit, 12, 43
fish harvesting, 261
fish traps, 257, 261, 266
fisheries, 257–259, 261–262, 266–269
floating population, 333–334, 339–340
flood, 261–266, 268
flooding, 136–138
Fontana Dam, 159, 161, 166
Fontes cartel, 247, 248, 250, 251, 252
Fontes, Artemio, 246, 247, 248, 250
Foucault, Michel, 116
Fox Report, 289–290, 293
Francisation, 225, 230–231
French West Indies, 226–227, 230
Friends of the Earth, 273, 278

Gary, Indiana, 201
gas flaring, 377–379
Gauteng (Province), 390, 395, 404
geographic isolation, 112, 117, 121
geo-social relations, 312, 318
ghetto, 57
Gingrich, Randall, 251–252
Glissant, Édouard, 226, 228–229, 231–233, 238–239
Goodman, Laurie, 44, 47
Graham County, North Carolina, 160, 161
Grand Central Winter, 149
Great Smoky Mountains National Park, 158–159
Greenpeace, 43, 117, 273–274, 276, 278–279, 281, 399
groundWork, 400
guardianship, 307
Gumercindo, 250–251
Gundjehmi Aboriginal Corporation, 294–295

Hansberry, Lorraine,103–104
Han Chinese, 337

Harney, Corbin, 37
hazardous waste (see waste)
Health Care Without Harm, 14–15
HEAT (Homeless Emergency Action Taskforce), 154
Heider, Karl, 151
Helms, (U.S. Sen.) Jesse, 164
Henley, Barbara, 185–186
heritage site, 311
High Temperature Incinerator (HTI), 271–281
highways, 171, 172, 178
Hockings, Nick, 40
homelessness, 144–154
Hopi, 41, 47, 48
Hogue, Linda, 164
Hokio Stream, 300–302, 305
Homer (Louisiana), 118
housing, 128–129, 131–140, 275, 277
    Fair Housing Act (1968), 100, 133, 139
    war housing, 128, 131, 133
    U.S. Housing and Urban Development (HUD), 139
Hughes, Lance, 36
Humans Against Nuclear Waste Dumps, 46
human rights, 214
Hurley, Andrew, 201
Hutton and Connors, 272–274
hypersegregation, 115 (see also racial segregation)

identity, ecological, 144, 151
identity, place-based, 38, 146, 148–149
illegal logging, 348 (see also logging)
'Improved' agriculture, 355–359, 362–363
Indigenous Environmental Network (IEN), 12, 43, 45, 90, 117
indigenous methods, 355, 363
indigenous people, 255–256, 262, 269, 319
indigenous practices, 359, 363
indigenous rights, 218, 220
indigenous spirituality, 214, 219
infanticide, 19
insurance redlining (racial zoning), 103

intangible culture, 214, 218
intercropping, 359–360, 364
International Monetary Fund (IMF), 39
International Paper Company, 247
intractable waste (see waste)
invisibility, 75, 85–87, 90, 117–118
Isaan Farmers' Assembly for Protection of Land Rights, 351
Iscor, 390–404
island, 225–231, 234–239
Ispat, 403

Jabiluka mine, 285–297
Japanese colonialism, 313, 319
Johnson, Cheryl, 204
Johnson, Hazel, 196, 204
joint management, 78
joint oil ventures, 375
Joint Task Force on Intractable Waste (JTF), 272–274, 278–281 (see also 'waste')
judicial review, 213
Juluo Neighbourhood Cultural Association, 311, 313, 317–323

Kaiser Permanente, 14–15,
Kakadu National Park, 288–290, 293
Kephart, Horace, 157–158, 166
Khwai River, 347
Kindness, Kla, 37
King, Martin Luther Jr., 195
KMT (Kuomintang), 319
Knights of Peter Claver, Inc., 197–205
    Supreme Lady, 198
    Arthur McFarland, 198
    Mary Briers, 198
    Charles Keyes, 198
    National Convention, 205
    Regional Conference, 199, 205
labor, 355, 358–363, 366
LaDuke, Winona, 44
Laguna Pueblo, 42–43, 44
Lake, Bobby, 37
Lakewood Plan, 113
land claim, rights, 267
land condemnation, 186
land lease, 212–213

land reform, 355, 366
land rights, native title, 89
land use practices, 358
landfill, 304, 307–308
landscape, 333–345, 337–341
    history, 151–152
Latina, 31, 43
Laws, Rufina Marie, 46
League Against Nuclear Disaster (LAND), 29–30
Leal, Teresa, 37
Lee, Charles, 45
legitimacy, political, 319
legitimation, parameters of, 312, 317–323
Lehto, Darelynn, 45
Lester, A. David, 47
Lewis, Gloria, 44
liberal democracy, 105
lieux de mémoire, 234
life-writing, environmental, 144, 146, 149, 153
Linkholm, 391, 398
Little Tennessee River, 157, 159
local, the; locality; 312–313, 317–322
localization, 319–320
Loeffler, Jack, 41
logging, 247, 249, 251–252, 348
logic, 189–192
Lopez, Isidro Baldenegro, 252
Louisrust, 391, 393, 402
Love Canal, 3, 13, 15, 46

Madziwa, Zimbabwe, 355–366
mainlander, 314, 319–320
Mangrove (swamp), 227–228, 230
Maori, 299–308
    burial, 303
    language, 303–305, 308
    revival of, 304, 308
    population, 299–301
Margarula, Yvonne, 285–286, 291–292, 294, 296
marginalization, 381
martial law, 314, 319–320
Martinique, 225–239
massacre, 76, 85
McDonalds, 12

McGary, Howard, 105, 106
mechanisms of control, 219
Mekong River, 345–347
memories, 104, 106, 107
memory, collective, 312–316
memory, environmentally-situated, 323
Merchant, Carolyn, 25, 45, 46
metaphor (of nature), 186–189, 190, 191–192
migrant workers hostels, 275, 278, 282
migration, 57, 129, 333–334, 339–340
Mills, Sidney, 39
mining, 36, 37, 41, 42, 44, 46, 47, 285–297
mining workers, 36, 42, 293
Mirrar clan, 285–297
Mittal, Lakshmi, 403–404
modernity, 255–256, 261, 269, 339
Monitored Retrievable Storage (MRS) program, 45
monuments, 234
Moses, Robert, 171–172, 174–177
MOSOP (Movement for the Survival of the Ogoni People), 372, 374–378
Mother Earth, 27, 41, 44, 46
moving, 322
multinational oil companies, 375, 382
mythology, 88, 331, 337–338

narrative, 144, 147–149, 152, 153
nation state, 81, 86, 89, 90, 91
National Association for the Advancement of Colored People (NAACP), 28
National Congress of American Indians, 43
National Environmental Coalition of Native Americans, 36
National Environmental Management Act, 389–390, 393, 395, 397
national identity, 331, 334, 339, 341
national interest, 89
national landscape, 334, 338
National Low Income Housing Coalition, 145
National Tribal Environmental Council (NTEC), 43, 45

Native Americans, 18–19, 30, 35–48, 78, 82, 83, 85, 88, 117
Native Land Husbandry Act (NLHA), 357–360, 364–366
natural environment, 257, 267
natural spring, 215–216, 220
Navajo Nation Dependents of Uranium Workers Committee, 43
Navajo Uranium Radiation Victims Committee, 43
Navajo, 36, 37, 41–42, 43, 46–47
Network of People Affected by Dams, 351
New York City, New York, 171–173, 175–177, 179
New Zealand, 299–308
Ngati Raukawa, 299–308
Niger Delta, 371–384
Nigeria, 371–384
non-verbal, 186, 192
North River Sewage Treatment Plant, 171, 173–174
North Shore Cemetery Association (NSCA), 163–165
nostalgia, 339–340
nuclear waste (see waste)

Occidental Petroleum, 3
Ogoni People, 371–384
Ogoniland, 371–384
Ohcejohka/Utsjoki (municipality), 209–210, 212–213, 217, 220
oil production, 371–384
oil spills, 376–379, 383,
opium, 246, 247, 249–250
oral history, 146, 148, 200–205
oral traditions, 262

Pak Moon Dam, 346–348, 351–352
panopticon, 116
paraquate, 249
parks, 171, 172, 174–175
parkway (Ferrell), 184–188
Passaro, Joanne, 144–145
patriarchy, 22, 26
Peabody Coal Co., 42, 46, 48
peasantry, 333, 335, 339–341

Pena, Devon, 38
personalized history, 312–318, 321
pesticides, 26
picture show (cinema), 256
piggery, 303, 305–308
pig sty, 303, 305
Pino Gordo, 246, 248, 251
planning, 275
pollution, 272, 274, 276, 278–282, 299,
    305, 372, 377, 379, 392, 395–397,
    400–401(also see waste)
preservation, cultural, 311–314, 319
Primal Awareness, 246
progressive era (United States), 22–23
pristine, 184, 186, 187, 188
property rights, 98–100, 102
Protecting Mother Earth conference, 43
protests, 276–278, 346–351, 364–365
Protest Villages, 352
public housing, 172, 176
public participation, 173–175

racial intimidation, 104
racial segregation, 112–117, 120, 259,
    267, 355–356, 358
racialized space, 109–121
racist property holdings, 97–107
Ramos, Augustin, 246, 250, 253
Rand Water, 392
Ranger mine, 285–297
Rara'muri, 245–253
Rawls, John, 97–98
Reader, 335
Red Hook, 172, 173, 175–178
redlining (racial zoning), 101–104
Reeve, Jim, 185, 190
reforestation, 334–335, 337–338,
    340–341
reservations, 79, 82, 83, 117 (see also
    Native Americans)
Reserves, 357–358, 360
resistance, 38, 40, 44–46, 48, 78, 82
"resistance identity," 38
resource, 185–188, 191–192
resource consent, 306
Resource Management Act (of 1991), 306
restrictive covenants, 101–104, 112–114

Rietspruit, 396–397, 401
Rio Tinto Ltd, 286, 292, 294–296
Rio Urique River, 245, 246
risk, 276, 278–281
rivers, China, 335–338
roads, 183, 184, 185, 186, 189
    construction, 159–165
"Road to Nowhere," 162
rubbish dump, 304
rural, 183–184, 188, 189, 192
rural/urban, 333–334, 339–341

sacred sites, 209–210, 215–217, 219–220,
    286–290, 292, 297
Sami people, 209–221
    women, 212–213, 219,
    worldview, 212, 216–219
Sandbridge, 184–191
Sasser, U.S. Sen. James, 164
Saro-Wiwa, Ken, 371–372, 380–381
segregation (see racial segregation)
self-government, 213
settler colonies, 75–77, 80, 83–86, 88–89
sewage, 56, 65, 66, 127, 129–131, 133,
    138–140, 302–305
sewers, 135–136, 138
Shell International (Royal Dutch/Shell),
    371–372, 375, 378, 380, 382–383
Shell Nigeria (Shell Petroleum Develop-
    ment Company of Nigeria),
    371–383
shifting cultivation, 359, 362–363
Sierra Madre Alliance, 252
Sierra Madre, 247–249, 251
Sigma (community), 184–186, 189, 191
Silent Spring, 26
siting history, 171, 173, 174, 177, 178
siting politics, 171, 174, 177, 178
slaves (and slavery), 20–21, 57–63
    Atlantic Slave Trade, 58–60
    Butler Island, 63
    Richard Carruthers, 62
    Fanny Kemble, 63
    Harriet Beecher Stowe, 61
    Jacob Stroyer, 61
    Middle Passage, 56–59
    plantations, 60–63

Theodore Dwight Weld, 61–62
Peggy Shepard, 67
Booker T. Washington, 57, 64
　Up from Slavery, 64
slums, 134, 135
Slum Organisation for Democracy, 351
social control, 112, 116
socio-spatial relations, 114
South Bronx, 171, 172, 177–178
South Bronx Clean Air Coalition, 177
Southern Organizing Committee, 12
Southwest Network for Economic and
　Environmental Justice, 12
spatial power, 74, 85, 90
spatial racism, 45
Squires, Gregory, 103
Staskos, John, 184, 186–187, 191
statues, 234–236
steel, 390–393, 395–398, 400, 402–404
Steel Valley, 391, 393, 402
Stop Dioxin Exposure, 13
Stringer, Lee, 149
Suagee, Dean, 36
sugar refinery, 311, 313
Superfund (EPA), 11
surveillance, 112, 116
Suttesája (Sulaoja), 209–220
Swain County, North Carolina, 159–165
swimming pool, 256

Tabernacle United Methodist Church,
　184, 189–190
Taipei, 311–323
Taiwan, 311–323
Taiwan Sugar Corporation, 311, 313, 319
Tarahumara, 245–253
Tennessee Valley Authority (TVA), 159–
　160, 164–165
Thai Rak Thai, 351–352
Thaksin, Shinawatra, 346–348, 350, 352
The New York Times, distrust of, 104
The Virginian-Pilot, 190
Third Citizens Conference on Dioxin,
　14
Thorpe, Grace, 36, 45, 48
Tinker, George, 37, 48

Total Environment Centre (TEC), 273,
　276, 281
toxic waste (see waste)
tourists and tourism, 159–164
tradition, 331, 336–340
traditional culture, 290–291
traditional owner, 286, 289, 294–296
traffic, 184, 186, 188
transnational mining corporations, 89

U.S. Bureau of Indian Affairs, 41
U.S. Environmental Protection Agency
　(EPA), 13
U.S. Fish and Wildlife Service, 184–187,
　190
U.S. National Park Service (USA), 159,
　164
ultimate terms, 188
United Church of Christ, 12
United Farm Workers (UFW), 31
United Nations, 86, 90
United States Conference of Catholic
　Bishops (USCCB), 197–199, 205
　Walt Grazer, 199
　Roxanna Barillas, 199
　Catholic Coalition for Children and a
　　Safe Environment (CASE), 199
　Environmental Justice Office, 199
uranium, 35–37, 42–44, 46–47, 285–289,
　291–293, 296–297
Urban Redevelopment Policy, 178
urban renewal, 171–173, 175, 176, 178

Vaal Dam, 392, 401
Vaal River, 389–404
　Barrage area, 392
Van Eeden, Pieter, 395–398
Vance, Helen Cable, 164–166
Vanderbijlpark, 390–393, 395, 398–404
Vietnam War, 15, 27, 28, 39
Virginia Beach City Council, 185–188,
　190–191
Virginia Beach, Virginia, 183–184, 188

Wallin, Luke, 151
Warren County, North Carolina, 7, 41
Washington, Sylvia, 101

waste,
   hazardous waste, 272–273, 277–279
   intractable waste, 272–274, 277
   medical waste, 171, 177–178
   nuclear waste, 29, 37, 42–46, 87, 88, 89
   toxic waste, 271–281
Waste Management Plan, 307
water, 209–210, 214–217, 219–220, 293–294
water ownership, 266
water pollution, 392, 395–397, 400–401
waterfront, as site of leisure, 172, 175, 177–178
waterfront, industrial, 172, 175, 177
Weaver, Jace, 36, 46
West Harlem Environmental Action (We ACT), 173–175
West Harlem, 171–175, 177–178
Western North Carolina Associated Communities (WNCAC), 160
wetlands, 185, 187, 189, 286, 293, 358, 364
whistle blower, 395–397

White minority, 355, 358, 363, 365
White Plague, 56
wilderness, 183, 184, 186–189
   land use designation, 162–164
   preservation, 77
Witwatersrand, 392, 402
Women for a Peaceful Christmas (WPC), 27–29
Women of All Red Nations (WARN), 30, 46
Women's Boycott for Peace, 27
World Bank, 246, 249, 251, 346–347
World Heritage, 287–290, 297
World Uranium Hearing, 47

Yucca Mountain, 117
Yellow River, 331–341
Yazzi, Jane, 46
Yazzi, Ted, 42

Zile, Frances Van, 41
Zimbabwe, 355–366
zoning, 112–113, 173, 275, 278
   expulsive zoning, 113

About the Contributors

K. Animashaun Ducre has completed her dissertation, "Racialized Spaces: Exploring Space as an Explanatory and Independent Variable in Environmental Justice Analysis" at the University of Michigan. She graduated in Summer 2005 from the Environmental Justice Program within Michigan's School of Natural Resources and Environment. She is currently a faculty member in the Department of African American Studies at Syracuse University. Ducre has been a committed advocate for environmental justice for over a decade. Her first foray in environmental activism was as a Toxics Campaigner for Greenpeace from 1994–1997. She also served a brief stint with Ralph Nader's, Essential Action. Under her coordination, her team at Greenpeace assisted in the victories of the nation's key environmental justice battles: defeating an AES power plant in San Francisco, halting the licenses of a uranium enrichment facility in rural Louisiana and the nation's largest proposed plastic manufacturing complex by Shintech in Convent, Louisiana. She combines her experiences on the frontlines of the environmental justice movement and academic training in geographic information systems and demography for a unique perspective on economic and environmental inequality in the United States. Her next projects include a manuscript profiling female environmental activists of color and a case study on communities of color devastated by federal highway construction projects. She can be reached at kanimash@umich.edu.

Four Arrows (Wahinkpe Topa), aka Don Trent Jacobs, Ph.D., Ed.D. serves as a professor in the College of Educational Leadership and Change at Fielding Graduate University and in the College of Educational Leadership at Northern Arizona University. Previous to these positions he was Dean of Education at Oglala Lakota College on the Pine Ridge Indian Reservation.

He is the author of thirteen books and numerous chapters and articles relating to critical education, wellness, and Indigenous worldview, including Teaching Virtues, Primal Awareness, and his forthcoming book from the University of Texas Press, *Unlearning the Language of Conquest*. He can be contacted via his Website at www.teachingvirtues.net.

Marja K. Bulmer has LL.B and LL.M. both from the University of Helsinki, Finland, and the University of British Columbia, Canada where she specialized in environmental law. She is presently a litigation counsel with the Department of Justice, Canada, where she primarily works in large environmental cases, including contaminated sites. She is also presently providing pro bono legal assistance to the four Sami women, including Rauna Kuokkanen, in their judicial review application discussed in her and Kuokkanen's article in this volume.

Lois Gibbs is the founder and executive director of the Center for Health, Environment and Justice (CHEJ), an organization that has assisted over 12,000 Grassroots groups nationwide. Lois has been recognized extensively for her critical role in the grassroots environmental justice movement. Her vision has guided CHEJ's efforts to provide critical organizing and technical assistance to communities engaged in their own environmental struggles. She has spoken at numerous conferences and has been featured on many television and radio shows including *60 Minutes, 20/20, Oprah Winfrey, Good Morning America*, and the *Today Show*. Lois is the recipient of an honorary Doctorate from SUNY at Cortland, New York, the 1990 Goldman Environmental Prize, the 1998 Heinz Award, and the 1999 John Gardner Leadership Award from the Independent Sector.

Heather Goodall is a historian who teaches in Social Inquiry in the Faculty of Humanities and Social Science at the University of Technology Sydney as Associate Professor. Her doctorate was a social and political history of Aboriginal people in NSW and was published in 1996 as *Invasion to Embassy: Land in Aboriginal Politics in NSW*. Her work has involved collaborative investigations with Indigenous people in public inquiries like the Royal Commission into British Nuclear Testing in central Australia, 1984–1985. She is currently researching the conflicting perceptions of environmental change and rivers in two projects, one, the Black Soil Country project, on the northern floodplain of the Darling River and the other, the Georges River project, in south western suburban Sydney. Each of these projects explores cultural diversity in relationship to environment and rivers and investigates the way perceptions and claims over rivers are mobilized in political and social conflicts. She has recently completed a collaborative life

story co-authored with Isabel Flick, an Indigenous activist from north western NSW, published in April 2004 by Allen and Unwin, titled *Isabel Flick:
The Many Lives of an Extraordinary Aboriginal Women*.

Renée Gosson is an assistant professor of French and Francophone Studies
at Bucknell University where she teaches courses on the literature and culture of the French Caribbean. She has co-produced a film entitled *Landscape
and Memory: Martinican Land-People-History*, which juxtaposes Martinique's Creolists' ecological and ideological concerns with actual footage of
symptoms of environmental and cultural distress on the island. She is co-
editor, with Elizabeth DeLoughrey and George Handley, of a forthcoming
collection of essays: *Caribbean Literature and the Environment: Between
Nature and Culture* (University of Virginia Press, fall 2005).

Peggy James has worked as a Ministerial adviser, in government environment agencies, and for numerous environmental non-government organisations, including the group that coordinated the input of Australian-based
environmental groups to the Sydney 2000 Olympic Games. Dr James' articles on the environmental aspects of the Sydney Olympics have been published in *Australian Planner, Specifier*, and the *Valuer and Land Economist*,
and in an edited collection by R. Cashman and A. Hughes (1998), *The Green
Games: A Golden Opportunity*. Peggy James was awarded the prestigious
2005 NSW Premier History Fellowship to write the biographies of a series
of key Sydney environmental activists. She is currently lecturing in environmental policy at the University of Adelaide.

Jacqui Katona is an Australian Indigenous environmental activist and community advocate. She is a Djork woman whose clan is a neighbour of the
Mirrar clan, who are the traditional owners of the lands in the Kakadu
National Park on which the Ranger and Jabiluka uranium mines are located
in the far north of Australia. In the period of the disputes about which she
writes in this volume, she was the executive officer of the Gundjehmi
Aboriginal Association representing the Mirrar clan and was the campaign
leader in those people's national and international actions against Jabiluka.
She is currently the chief executive officer of the Lumbu Foundation, Indigenous Development and Research organization and continues her work as an
editor, development worker, campaigner, researcher, and writer.

Rauna Kuokkanen is a post-doctoral fellow with a collaborative research
project on Globalization and Autonomy at McMaster University (Hamilton,
Ont.). She is one of the four Sami women who have filed an application for a
judicial review of the municipality's decision discussed in her and Riihijärvi's
article in this volume. She holds a M.A. on Sami Language and Literature

(University of Oulu, Finland) and Comparative Literature (University of British Columbia) and PhD on Education and Indigenous Studies (UBC). She has edited an anthology on contemporary Sami literature (Juoga mii gea-suha, 2001) and published articles on Sami and other indigenous literature, research and higher education, oral tradition, and women. She has long been involved in the public life of Sami society. She was the founding chair of the Sami Youth Organization in Finland, established in 1991, and has served as the vice-president of the Sami Council.

Bill E. Lawson is currently professor of philosophy at Michigan State University. He received his Ph.D. from the University of North Carolina at Chapel Hill. His research interests include African American Social and Political Philosophy, Political Obligation Theory, and Urban Environmental Philosophy. He has published articles on the underclass, John Locke's theory of political obligation, social contract theory and African Americans, Jazz, and Urban Environmental Philosophy. His books include *The Underclass Question* (Editor) (Temple University Press), *Between Slavery and Freedom* (with Howard McGary) (Indiana University Press), *Frederick Douglass: A Critical Reader* (edited with Frank Kirkland) (Blackwell Publishers); *Faces of Environmental Racism* (edited with Laura Westra) (Rowman &Littlefield), and *Pragmatism and the Problem of Race* (edited with Donald Koch) (Indiana University Press).

Martin V. Melosi is Distinguished University Professor of History and Director of the Center for Public History at the University of Houston. In 2000–01, he held the Fulbright Chair in American Studies at the University of Southern Denmark. He is the author of eleven books, including the award-winning *The Sanitary City*. He is past president of the American Society for Environmental History, the National Council on Public History, and the Public Works Historical Society.

Cynthia J. Miller is a cultural anthropologist, specializing in community development, social activism, and popular culture. She is a faculty member at Emerson College, in Boston, MA, where she teaches courses on urban studies, community-building, and social justice. Her writing and photography has appeared in *Women's Studies Quarterly*, *Human Organization*, *ISLE*, *Contexts*, and *Anthropologica*, as well as in several edited volumes. She also recently produced two visual exhibitions linked to her essay presented here: "Underground Talent: Art and Poetry by Boston's Homeless" and "Images from the Streets: Boston's Homeless Photograph Their Worlds." Her research has included studies of the social impacts of mass media on rural communities in the Yucatan and South India, immigrants' social and spatial recreations of homelands, and her current project on homelessness and cultural identity.

Paul C. Rosier received his Ph.D. in American History from the University of Rochester in 1998. Dr. Rosier currently serves as assistant professor of history at Villanova University, where he teaches The Environmental History of America, Native American History, and World History; he also serves as chairperson of the University's Earth Day committee and advises the Villanova Environmental Group. In 2001, The University of Nebraska Press published *Rebirth of the Blackfeet Nation, 1912–1954;* in 2003, Greenwood Press published *Native American Issues* as part of its Contemporary Ethnic American Issues series. His next book will be published by Harvard University Press in 2008. Dr. Rosier has also published in various journals, including the *American Indian Culture and Research Journal* and the *Journal of American Ethnic History.*

Jane Bloodworth Rowe, a Virginia native, has a Ph.D. in communication from Regent University in Virginia Beach, Virginia, and a Master of Art in Communication from Norfolk State University in Norfolk, Virginia. Her dissertation, entitled *The Virginian-Pilot and the Metaphors of Nature*, analyzed the media coverage of three local environmental issues. She has continued her research in environmental issues, and is particularly interested in the intersection of nature, culture and the community. She is currently preparing a paper entitled "The Mattaponi and the Shad: The Use of Synecdoche in Environmental Disputes," that focuses on a water rights issue involving a local Native American tribe for presentation at fall 2005 conference of American Association of Culture in the South. An adjunct at Old Dominion University, she has also had a paper entitled "The Rhetoric of the Columbia: Conflicting Metaphors of Earth and Space" accepted for publication in *The Environmental Communication Yearbook.*

Jane Sayers completed her PhD "Start with the Little Things: Environmental Education as Political Participation in Contemporary China" in 2004 at the University of Melbourne. This work examined the structures and discourses of environmentalism in Beijing, using six environmental non-government organizations as case studies. Jane is currently engaged in research examining the rise and efficacy of community-based environmental education in Australia in recent years.

Rachael Selby and **Pataka Moore** are New Zealand Maori researchers who combine an interest in oral history with a passion for environmental issues. Rachael is a senior lecturer in social policy and Maori Development at Massey University in Palmerston North, N.Z. Pataka is an environmental researcher at an indigenous Centre of Higher Learning, Te Wananga-o-Rau-kawa, based in Otaki, N.Z. They are a mother and son team working to promote the restoration of streams and rivers in their tribal area. This restoration includes planting of stream banks, promoting restoration in the wider community and influencing local government to take responsibility for past damage. They have been involved in several oral history projects collecting the stories of elders about the ways in which streams and rivers were managed by their ancestors.

Phia Steyn is a native South African who lectures African environmental history in the Department of History at the University of Stirling in Scotland. She holds a Ph.D. from the University of the Free State in Bloemfontein, South Africa and her academic career started at this university where she taught in the history department for just over seven years until July 2003. Her publications deal with the history of South African environmentalism, global environmental management, water and drought policy, and multinational oil production in the Niger Delta. She is currently revising her Ph.D. dissertation on oil politics in Ecuador and Nigeria for publication, and doing research for an environmental history of apartheid South Africa.

Jeffrey K. Stine is curator of Engineering and Environmental History at the Smithsonian Institution's National Museum of American History. He received his B.A. and Ph.D. in history from the University of California, Santa Barbara. Prior to joining the Smithsonian in 1989, he served as an American Historical Association Congressional Fellow with the House Committee on Science and Technology, where he assisted the special Task Force on Science Policy by writing *A History of Science Policy in the United States, 1940–1985* (1986). He then worked as an independent consultant, writing policy histories for the U.S. Army Corps of Engineers's Office of History, the National Science Foundation's Office of Policy Research and Analysis, the American Association for the Advancement of Science's Directorate for Science and Policy Programs, the Library of Congress's Office of Scholarly Programs, and the Carnegie Commission on Science, Technology, and Government. He co-edited the University of Akron Press book series on *Technology and the Environment* from 1993–2001 and has been an Editorial Advisor with RFF Press since 2003. He has served as president of the American Society for Environmental History (1999–2001) and the Public Works Historical Society (2002–2003).

Julie Sze is an assistant professor of American Studies at the University of California at Davis. Her research focuses on the culture and politics of the environmental justice movement, urban environmentalism and environmental health. Her forthcoming book from MIT Press examines environmental justice activism in New York City, asthma politics, garbage and energy policy in the age of privatization and deregulation.

Stephen Wallace Taylor is the author of *The New South's New Frontier: A Social History of Economic Development in Southwestern North Carolina.* He received the Ph.D from the University of Tennessee and serves as Assistant Professor of History at Macon State College in Macon, Georgia. A member of the executive committee of the Southern Industrialization Project, he has presented his research at meetings of the Organization of American Historians, the American Society for Environmental History, the American Studies Association, the Appalachian Studies Association, and the Southern Historical Association. His other works emphasize the relationship between technology, industrialization, and tourism in the American South.

Elise Tempelhoff is a senior member of the editorial staff of the Afrikaans newspaper, Beeld, in the Gauteng region of South Africa. She specializes in environmental reporting and has won a national award (Media24) for her investigative reporting on the Iscor pollution saga. She was nominated for the Nat Nakasa Award for Media Integrity & Courageous Journalism in 2002 for her exposé of steel giant Iscor's pollution in the Vaal Triangle. A total of 109 reports on the issue were published. She was also in 2002 a finalist for the Mondi award for print journalism.

Johann Tempelhoff is a historian and director of the School of Basic Sciences in the Faculty Vaal Triangle at Potchefstroom [North-West] University. He specializes in the methodology of history and environmental history. His most recent publications are: a monograph on the water utility, Rand Water, *The Substance of Ubiquity: Rand Water 1903–2003* (July 2003) and *African Water Histories: Transdisciplinary Discourses* (2005), of which he is the editor.

Guy Thompson completed his PhD in history at the University of Alberta and is now an assistant professor in the Department of History and Classics at the University of Alberta. He specializes in the history of colonial Zimbabwe, and is particularly interested in rural social dynamics, agrarian change, indigenous knowledge, and rural protest. In his current research, he is exploring how Zimbabweans understood and debated historical and cultural change in the colonial period, and how these debates have continued into the present; ideas about race, morality, gender, and the meaning of modernity figure prominently in these disputes. He spent three years working as a teacher at a large rural high school in Madziwa, Zimbabwe, and returned to the area for fieldwork and interviewing, inspired by the stories he heard from local women and men.

Nancy C. Unger is assistant professor of history, women and gender studies, and environmental studies at Santa Clara University. Her work on the La Follette family, a progressive political dynasty that began in Wisconsin at the turn of the twentieth century, includes the prize-winning biography *Fighting Bob La Follette: The Righteous Reformer* (North Carolina University Press, 2000). Some of her recent research has been in collaboration with French scholar Marie Bolton, and centers on the potential of direct democracy to solve California's environmental crises. Their jointly-authored work includes the essay "Pollution, Refineries, and People: Environmental Justice in Contra Costa County, California, 1980," in *The Modern Demon: Pollution in Urban and Industrial Societies* (France: University of Clermont Press, 2002), and "The Case for Cautious Optimism: California Environmental Propositions in the Late Twentieth Century," in *La Californie: Périphérie ou laboratoire?*, edited by Annick Foucrier and Antoine Coppolani (Paris: L'Harmattan, 2004). Her current book project is "Beyond 'Nature's Housekeepers': American Women and Gender in Environmental History." This study investigates the impact of prescribed gender roles on men and women's frequently differing responses to the environment and to environmental issues. A preliminary publication is "Women, Sexuality, and Environmental Justice in American History," in *New Perspectives on Environmental Justice: Gender, Sexuality, and Activism,* edited by Rachel Stein (Rutgers University Press, 2004). She lives in Mountain View, California with her husband and two children.

John Walsh is assistant professor at Shinawatra University in Bangkok. His doctorate research concerned market entry strategy in East Asia and was awarded by Oxford University. His research now mainly focuses on social and economic development in the Greater Mekong Sub-Region.

Sylvia Hood Washington is an interdisciplinary trained environmental scholar. She received her MS in Systems Engineering and her Ph.D. in the history of science, technology, and the environment from Case Western Reserve University. She has been involved in the environmental field for over twenty-five years and her research has been deeply influenced by her experiences as a corporate and government environmental engineer, environmental activist, and as a professor developing and teaching environmentally focused science technology and society courses for non-science students. Washington, a former full professor of physical sciences and chemistry and former dean of engineering is the originator and the director for the joint United States Conference of Catholic Bishops (USCCB) and the Knights of Peter

Claver, Inc. Environmental Justice and Health Project. She is currently managing and directing the development of an environmental justice and health video documentary of Chicago which has been funded by grants from the Illinois Humanities Council/National Endowment for the Humanities, the USCCB, the Knights of Peter Claver, Inc. and DePaul University. A charter member of the University of Illinois at Chicago's Environmental Justice Board, she also teaches environmental ethics and environmental justice courses at DePaul University and African American history at the University of Maryland, University College. Her first monograph, *Packing Them In: An Archaeology of Environmental Racism in Chicago, 1865–1954* (Lexington Books) was published in 2005 and she is now completing her second monograph, *The Color of Trees: African American Struggles for Sustainable Communities, 1915–1975* (Lexington Books, 2006).